THE NEW CAMBRIDGE SHAKESPEARE

GENERAL EDITOR
Brian Gibbons

ASSOCIATE GENERAL EDITOR
A. R. Braunmuller

From the publication of the first volumes in 1984 the General Editor of the New Cambridge Shakespeare was Philip Brockbank and the Associate General Editors were Brian Gibbons and Robin Hood. From 1990 to 1994 the General Editor was Brian Gibbons and the Associate General Editors were A. R. Braunmuller and Robin Hood.

THE SONNETS

In his own time, Shakespeare was best known to the reading public as a poet, and even today copies of his Sonnets regularly outsell everything else he wrote. For this new edition, Stephen Orgel offers a warmly personal and original introduction to Shakespeare's best-loved and most widely read poems. Careful readings emphasise their sexual and temperamental ambiguity, their textual history and the special perils an editor faces when modernising the original quarto's spelling, punctuation and even layout.

The edition retains the text of the Sonnets prepared by Gwynne Evans, together with his detailed notes on each, and a line-by-line commentary. Throughout, the 'voices' of the Sonnets appear in all their intricacy and dramatic power.

THE NEW CAMBRIDGE SHAKESPEARE

All's Well That Ends Well, edited by Russell Fraser
Antony and Cleopatra, edited by David Bevington
As You Like It, edited by Michael Hattaway
The Comedy of Errors, edited by T. S. Dorsch
Coriolanus, edited by Lee Bliss
Hamlet, edited by Philip Edwards
Julius Caesar, edited by Marvin Spevack
King Edward III, edited by Giorgio Melchiori
The First Part of King Henry IV, edited by Herbert Weil and Judith Weil
The Second Part of King Henry IV, edited by Giorgio Melchiori
King Henry V, edited by Andrew Gurr
The First Part of King Henry VI, edited by Michael Hattaway
The Second Part of King Henry VI, edited by Michael Hattaway
The Third Part of King Henry VI, edited by Michael Hattaway
King Henry VIII, edited by John Margeson
King John, edited by L. A. Beaurline
King Lear, edited by Jay L. Halio
King Richard II, edited by Andrew Gurr
King Richard III, edited by Janis Lull
Macbeth, edited by A. R. Braunmuller
Measure for Measure, edited by Brian Gibbons
The Merchant of Venice, edited by M. M. Mahood
The Merry Wives of Windsor, edited by David Crane
A Midsummer Night's Dream, edited by R. A. Foakes
Much Ado About Nothing, edited by F. H. Mares
Othello, edited by Norman Sanders
Pericles, edited by Doreen DelVecchio and Antony Hammond
The Poems, edited by John Roe
Romeo and Juliet, edited by G. Blakemore Evans
The Sonnets, edited by G. Blakemore Evans
The Taming of the Shrew, edited by Ann Thompson
The Tempest, edited by David Lindley
Titus Andronicus, edited by Alan Hughes
Troilus and Cressida, edited by Anthony B. Dawson
Twelfth Night, edited by Elizabeth Story Donno
The Two Gentlemen of Verona, edited by Kurt Schlueter

THE EARLY QUARTOS

The First Quarto of Hamlet, edited by Kathleen O. Irace
The First Quarto of King Henry V, edited by Andrew Gurr
The First Quarto of King Lear, edited by Jay L. Halio
The First Quarto of Othello, edited by Scott McMillin
The First Quarto of King Richard III, edited by Peter Davison
The Taming of a Shrew, edited by Stephen Roy Miller

THE SONNETS

Updated edition

Edited by
G. BLAKEMORE EVANS

With a new Introduction by
STEPHEN ORGEL
Jackson Eli Reynolds Professor of Humanities, Stanford University

CAMBRIDGE
UNIVERSITY PRESS

CAMBRIDGE UNIVERSITY PRESS
Cambridge, New York, Melbourne, Madrid, Cape Town, Singapore, São Paulo

Cambridge University Press
The Edinburgh Building, Cambridge CB2 2RU, UK

Published in the United States of America by Cambridge University Press, New York

www.cambridge.org
Information on this title: www.cambridge.org/9780521678377

First published 1996
Reprinted 1998, 1999, 2003, 2004
Updated edition 2006

Printed in the United Kingdom at the University Press, Cambridge

ISBN-13 978-0-521-86118-2 hardback
ISBN-10 0-521-86118-7 hardback
ISBN-13 978-0-521-67837-7 paperback
ISBN-10 0-521-67837-4 paperback

CONTENTS

ILLUSTRATIONS

Illustrations are reproduced by permission of the Houghton Library, Harvard University.

PREFACE

An editor of Shakespeare's Sonnets incurs perhaps even larger debts than an editor of one of Shakespeare's plays, except possibly *Hamlet*. Like all more recent scholars, I am most substantially indebted to the New Variorum Sonnets (2 vols., 1944) edited by the late Professor Hyder Edward Rollins, who, with the kind rigour for which he was so affectionately known, guided, by precept and example, my graduate studies many years ago. Scarcely less important, of course, is my debt to the scholarship of the last thirty years, particularly to the editions by W. G. Ingram and Theodore Redpath (1964), Stephen Booth (rev. edn, 1978), and John Kerrigan (1986).

Considerations of space have forced me to treat the work of earlier editors and critics – those included in the New Variorum – as, in a sense, public property; hence, their work has generally been cited without individual acknowledgement. However, I have tried, wherever possible, to acknowledge the many new critical insights offered by Ingram and Redpath, Booth, and Kerrigan, whose approach to the Sonnets takes fresh and somewhat more analytical directions.

I have been, as usual, particularly fortunate in the generous help I received from old friends and colleagues. special thanks are due to Professor Helen Vendler, who took time out from her own study of the Sonnets to read through my Commentary, correcting my missteps and suggesting incisive and critically sensitive glosses, and to Professors Heather Dubrow, John Klause, and J. J. M. Tobin, who also read several parts of the Commentary and offered sound advice and many helpful suggestions. I am further indebted to the General and Associate Editors of the New Cambridge Shakespeare, Professors Brian Gibbons and A. R. Braunmuller and Mr R. C. Hood, each of whom not only gave me unstinting and valuable criticism but contributed new and perceptive notes of their own, and to Ms Sarah Stanton, Mr Paul Chipchase, and Miss Judith Harte of the Cambridge University Press, who were responsible for seeing the edition through the press, and who (as before) exercised an oft-tried patience in the face of mighty odds. What shortcomings and errors remain – all too many, I fear – are my responsibility alone.

I am also most grateful to Professors Douglas Bruster and Scott Gordon. Between them, while finishing their graduate work, they transformed a messy and frequently illegible manuscript into a model of sightly tidiness – all with the wave of a computer mouse.

As always, I have received ready aid from the staffs of the Widener and Houghton Libraries, with specially notable help from Miss Carolyn Fawcett and Mrs Marion Schoon.

My greatest debt, as ever, is to my wife – for her more than fifty years of loving care and unshakable support.

G. B. E.

ABBREVIATIONS AND CONVENTIONS

Shakespeare's plays, when cited in this edition, are abbreviated in a style modified slightly from that used in the *Harvard Concordance to Shakespeare*. Other editions of Shakespeare are abbreviated under the editor's surname (Malone, Ingram and Redpath) unless they are the work of several editors. In such cases, an abbreviated series title is used (Cam.). When more than one edition by the same editor is cited, later editions are discriminated with a raised figure (Gildon [2]). All quotations from Shakespeare, except those from the Sonnets, use the text and lineation of *The Riverside Shakespeare*, textual editor, G. Blakemore Evans.

I. Shakespeare's plays

Ado	*Much Ado About Nothing*
Ant.	*Antony and Cleopatra*
AWW	*All's Well That Ends Well*
AYLI	*As You Like It*
Cor.	*Coriolanus*
Cym.	*Cymbeline*
Err.	*The Comedy of Errors*
Ham.	*Hamlet*
1H4	*The First Part of King Henry the Fourth*
2H4	*The Second Part of King Henry the Fourth*
H5	*King Henry the Fifth*
1H6	*The First Part of King Henry the Sixth*
2H6	*The Second Part of King Henry the Sixth*
3H6	*The Third Part of King Henry the Sixth*
H8	*King Henry the Eighth*
JC	*Julius Caesar*
John	*King John*
LLL	*Love's Labour's Lost*
Lear	*King Lear*
Mac.	*Macbeth*
MM	*Measure for Measure*
MND	*A Midsummer Night's Dream*
MV	*The Merchant of Venice*
Oth.	*Othello*
Per.	*Pericles*
R2	*King Richard the Second*
R3	*King Richard the Third*
Rom.	*Romeo and Juliet*
Shr.	*The Taming of the Shrew*
STM	*Sir Thomas More*
Temp.	*The Tempest*
TGV	*The Two Gentlemen of Verona*
Tim.	*Timon of Athens*

Tit.	*Titus Andronicus*
TN	*Twelfth Night*
TNK	*The Two Noble Kinsmen*
Tro.	*Troilus and Cressida*
Wiv.	*The Merry Wives of Windsor*
WT	*The Winter's Tale*

2. Other works cited and general references

Abbott	E. A. Abbott, *A Shakespearian Grammar*, 3rd edn, 1872 (references are to numbered paragraphs)
Adams	J. Q. Adams (in Rollins)
Alden	*Sonnets*, ed. R. M. Alden, 1916
Alexander	*Works*, ed. Peter Alexander, 1951
AV	The Authorised Version of the Bible, 1611 (also known as the King James Bible)
Baldwin	T. W. Baldwin, *Literary Genetics of Shakspere's Poems and Sonnets*, 1950
Barnes	Barnabe Barnes, *Parthenophil and Parthenophe* (1593), ed. V. A. Doyno, 1971
Barnfield	Richard Barnfield, *Poems*, ed. Montague Summers, n.d.
Beaumont	Francis Beaumont, *Salmacis and Hermaphroditus* (1602) in *Elizabethan Narrative Verse*, ed. Nigel Alexander, 1968
Beeching	*Sonnets*, ed. H. C. Beeching, 1904
Bell	*Poems*, ed. Robert Bell, 1855 (English Poets)
Benson	*Poems: Written by Wil. Shake-speare. Gent.*, published by John Benson, 1640
Bevington	*Works*, ed. David Bevington, 4th edn, 1992
Bishops' Bible	Translation of the Bible revised by the English and Welsh bishops, 1568, based on the Great Bible of 1539
Book of Common Prayer	Cited in the 1st edition (1549), unless otherwise noted; 2nd edn, 1552; 3rd edn, 1559
Booth	*Shakespeare's Sonnets*, ed. Stephen Booth, 1977 (rev. edn, 1978, here cited)
Booth, *Essay*	Stephen Booth, *Essay on Shakespeare's Sonnets*, 1969
Boswell	*Works*, ed. James Boswell, vol. xx, 1821
Brandon	Samuel Brandon, *The Virtuous Octavia* (1598), ed. R. B. McKerrow, MSR, 1909
Braunmuller	A. R. Braunmuller (privately)
Breton	Nicholas Breton, *Works*, ed. A. B. Grosart, 2 vols., 1875–9
Brooke	*Shakespeare's Sonnets*, ed. Tucker Brooke, 1936
Burto	*Sonnets*, ed. William Burto, 1964 (Signet)
Bush	*Sonnets*, ed. Douglas Bush and Alfred Harbage, 1961 (Pelican)
Butler	*Shakespeare's Sonnets*, ed. Samuel Butler, 1899
Cam.	*Works*, ed. W. G. Clark, John Glover, and W. A. Wright, vol. ix, 1866 (Cambridge)
Cam. ^{2}	*Works*, ed. W. A. Wright, vol. ix, 1893 (Cambridge)

Campion	Thomas Campion, *Works*, ed. Percival Vivian, 1909
Capell	Unpublished edn prepared by Edward Capell in a copy of Lintott's reprint (1711) of Q (1609)
Castiglione	Baldassare Castiglione, *The Courtier* (trans. Sir Thomas Hoby (1561), Everyman edn, n.d.)
Catullus	*Poems*, ed. and trans. F. W. Cornish, 2nd edn rev. by G. P. Goold, 1988 (Loeb)
Cellini	*Sonnets*, ed. Benvenuto Cellini, in *Vita e Arte nei Sonetti di Shakespeare*, 1943
Cercignani	Fausto Cercignani, *Shakespeare's Works and Elizabethan Pronunciation*, 1981
Chapman, *Plays*	George Chapman, *Plays*, General Editor, Allan Holaday, 2 vols., 1970, 1987
Chapman, *Poems*	George Chapman, *Poems*, ed. P. B. Bartlett, 1941
Chapman's Homer	*Chapman's Homer*, ed. Allardyce Nicoll, 2 vols., 1956
Chaucer	Geoffrey Chaucer, *The Riverside Chaucer*, General Editor, L. D. Benson, 1987
Collier	*Works*, ed. J. P. Collier, vol. VIII, 1843
Collier²	*Works*, ed. J. P. Collier, vol. VI, 1858
conj.	conjecture
Constable	Henry Constable, *Poems*, ed. Joan Grundy, 1960
corr.	corrected state of Q (1609)
Cotgrave	Randle Cotgrave, *A Dictionarie of the French and English Tongues*, 1611
Craig	*Works*, ed. W. J. Craig, 1891 (Oxford)
Daniel	Samuel Daniel, *Works*, ed. A. B. Grosart, 5 vols., 1885–96
Davies	Sir John Davies, *Poems*, ed. Robert Krueger, 1975
Davies of Hereford	John Davies, *Works*, ed. A. B. Grosart, 2 vols., 1878
Dekker	Thomas Dekker, *Works* [non-dramatic], ed. A. B. Grosart, 5 vols., 1864–86
Delius	*Werke*, ed. Nicolaus Delius, vol. VII, 1860
Donne	John Donne, *The Elegies and the Songs and Sonnets*, ed. Helen Gardner, 1965
	John Donne, *The Divine Poems*, ed. Helen Gardner, 1952
	John Donne, *Ignatius His Conclave*, ed. T. S. Healy, 1969
Dowden	*Sonnets*, ed. Edward Dowden, 1881
Drayton	Michael Drayton, *Works*, ed. J. W. Hebel, 5 vols., 1931–41
Duncan-Jones	Katherine Duncan-Jones, 'Was the 1609 *Shake-speares Sonnets* really unauthorized?', *RES*, new series, 34 (1983), 151–71
Dyce (1832)	*Poems*, ed. Alexander Dyce, 1832 (Aldine Poets)
Dyce	*Works*, ed. Alexander Dyce, vol. VI, 1857
Dyce²	*Works*, ed. Alexander Dyce, vol. VIII, 1866
Edward III	*The Raigne of King Edward the Third* (1596), ed. C. F. Tucker Brooke, in *The Shakespeare Apocrypha*, 1908
ELN	*English Languages Notes*
Empson, *Ambiguity*	William Empson, *Seven Types of Ambiguity*, 1931
Empson, *Complex*	William Empson, *The Structure of Complex Words*, [1951]
Empson, *Pastoral*	William Empson, *Some Versions of Pastoral*, rev. edn, 1968
Evans	*Poems*, printed for Thomas Evans, 1775

Ewing   *Poems*, printed for Thomas Ewing, 1771
Fletcher the Elder   Giles Fletcher (the Elder), *English Works*, ed. L. E. Berry,
                              1964
Fletcher the Younger   Giles (the Younger) and Phineas Fletcher, *Poetical Works*, ed.
                              F. S. Boas, 2 vols., 1908–9
Franz   Wilhelm Franz, *Die Sprache Shakespeares*, 1939 (4th edn of
                              Shakespeare-Grammatik) (references are to numbered
                              paragraphs)
Geneva   Translation of the Bible by scholars of Calvinist sympathy,
                              1560
Gentleman   *Poems*, ed. Francis Gentleman, 1774
Gibbons   Brian Gibbons (privately)
Gildon   *Poems*, ed. Charles Gildon, 1710 (vol. VII of *Works*, ed.
                              Nicholas Rowe, 1709)
Gildon [2]   *Poems*, ed. Charles Gildon, 1714 (vol. IX of *Works*, ed.
                              Nicholas Rowe, 1714)
Globe   *Works*, ed. W. G. Clark and W. A. Wright, 1864
Golding   Arthur Golding, trans., *The. xv. Bookes of P. Ovidius Naso,
                              entytuled Metamorphosis* (1576), ed. W. H. D. Rouse, 1904
Greene   Robert Greene, *Works*, ed. A. B. Grosart, 15 vols., 1881–6
Greville   Fulke Greville (Lord Brooke), *Poems and Dramas*, ed
                              Geoffrey Bullough, 2 vols., 1945
Guilpin   Everard Guilpin, *Skialetheia* (1598/9), ed. D. A. Carroll,
                              1974
Hall   Joseph Hall, *Collected Poems*, ed. A. Davenport, 1949
Halliwell   *Works*, ed. J. O. Halliwell[-Phillipps], vol. XVI, 1865
Harrison   *Sonnets*, ed. G. B. Harrison, 1938 (Penguin)
Hazlitt   *Supplementary Works*, ed. William Hazlitt, 1852
Herbert   George Herbert, *Works*, ed. F. E. Hutchinson, 1941
Herford   *Works*, ed. C. H. Herford, vol. X, 1899
Hoby   Sir Thomas Hoby, see Castiglione
Hood   R. C. Hood (privately)
Horace   *Odes and Epodes*, ed. and trans. C. E. Bennett, 1914 (Loeb)
                              Satires, ed. and trans. H. R. Fairclough, 1929
Hotson   Leslie Hotson, *Shakespeare's Sonnets Dated and Other Essays*,
                              1949
Hubler   *Songs and Poems*, ed. Edward Hubler, 1959
Hudson   *Works*, ed. H. N. Hudson, vol. XI, 1856
Hudson [2]   *Works*, ed. H. N. Hudson, vol. XX, 1881
Ingram and Redpath   *Sonnets*, ed. W. G. Ingram and Theodore Redpath, 1964
Jackson   MacD. P. Jackson, 'Punctuation and the compositors of
                              Shakespeare's *Sonnets*, 1609', *The Library*, fifth series, 30
                              (1975), 1–24
Jonson   *Ben Jonson*, ed. C. H. Herford and Percy Simpson, 11 vols.,
                              1925–52
Joseph   Sister Miriam Joseph, *Shakespeare and the Arts of Language*,
                              1947
Keightley   *Plays and Poems*, ed. Thomas Keightley, 1865
Kerrigan   *Sonnets* and *A Lover's Complaint*, ed. John Kerrigan, 1986
                              (New Penguin)

Kittredge	*Works*, ed. G. L. Kittredge, 1936
Knight	*Works*, ed. Charles Knight, 'Tragedies', vol. II, 1841
Kökeritz	Helge Kökeritz, *Shakespeare's Pronunciation*, 1953
Landry	H. J. Landry, *Interpretations in Shakespeare's Sonnets*, 1963
Leishman	J. B. Leishman, *Themes and Variations in Shakespeare's Sonnets*, 2nd edn, 1963
Lever	Christopher Lever, *Queene Elizabeths Tears* (1607), ed. A. B. Grosart, 1872
Lintott	*A Collection of Poems*, printed for Bernard Lintott, vol. II, [1711] (a semi-diplomatic reprint of Q)
Lodge	Thomas Lodge, *Rosalynde* (1590), ed. Geoffrey Bullough, in *Narrative and Dramatic Sources of Shakespeare*, vol. II, 1958
Lyly	John Lyly, *Works*, ed. R. W. Bond, 3 vols., 1902
Mahood	M. M. Mahood, *Shakespeare's Wordplay*, 1957
Malone	*Supplement to the Edition of Shakespeare's Plays Published in 1778*, ed. Edmond Malone, vol. I, 1780
Malone ²	*Works*, ed. Edmond Malone, vol. X, 1790
Marlowe	Christopher Marlowe, *Works*, ed. Fredson Bowers, 2 vols., 1973
Martial	*Epigrams*, ed. and trans. N. C. Ker, 2 vols., 1919–20 (Loeb)
Martin	P. J. Martin, *Shakespeare's Sonnets: Self, Love, and Art*, 1972
Massey	*Shakespeare's Sonnets Never Before Interpreted*, ed. Gerald Massey, 1866
Massey ²	*Secret Drama of Shakespeare's Sonnets*, ed. Gerald Massey, 1888
Melchiori	Giorgio Melchiori, *Shakespeare's Dramatic Meditations: An Experiment in Criticism*, 1976
Meres	Francis Meres, *Treatise 'Poetrie'* (from *Palladis Tamia*, 1598), ed. D. C. Allen, 1933
MP	*Modern Philology*
MSR	Malone Society Reprints
Munro	*Works* (London), ed. John Munro, vol. IV, 1958
Murden	*Poems*, printed for A. Murden etc., [1741?]
N&Q	*Notes and Queries*
Nashe	Thomas Nashe, *Works*, ed. R. B. McKerrow, 5 vols., 1904–10 (rev. F. P. Wilson, 1958)
Neilson	*Works*, ed. W. A. Neilson, 1906
Neilson ²	*Works*, ed. W. A. Neilson and C. J. Hill, 1942
ODEP	*Oxford Dictionary of English Proverbs*, 3rd edn, 1970
OED	*Oxford English Dictionary*
Oulton	*Poems* (vol. II), ed. W. C. Oulton, 1804
Ovid	*Metamorphoses*, ed. and trans. F. J. Miller, 2 vols., 1916 (Loeb; see also Golding)
	Amores, ed. and trans. Grant Showerman, 2nd edn, rev. by G. P. Goold, 1986 (Loeb) *Ars Amatoria* and *Remedia Amoris*, ed. and trans. J. H. Mozley, 2nd edn, rev. by G. P. Goold, 1979 (Loeb)
Palgrave	*Songs and Sonnets*, ed. F. T. Palgrave, 1865
Partridge	Eric Partridge, *Shakespeare's Bawdy*, rev. edn, 1968

Pequigney	Joseph Pequigney, *Such Is My Love: A Study of Shakespeare's Sonnets*, 1985
Petrarch	Francesco Petrarca, *Lyric Poems (Rime sparse)*, trans. R. M. Durling, 1976
Plato	*Lysis, Symposium, Gorgias*, ed. and trans. W. R. M. Lamb, 1925 (Loeb)
PMLA	*Publications of the Modern Language Association of America*
Pooler	*Sonnets*, ed. C. Knox Pooler, 1918 (rev. edn, 1931, here cited) (Arden)
Porter	*Sonnets and Minor Poems*, ed. Charlotte Porter, 1912
PQ	*Philological Quarterly*
Puttenham	George Puttenham, *The Arte of English Poesie* (1589), ed. G. D. Willcock and Alice Walker, 1936
Q	*Shake-speares Sonnets. Neuer before Imprinted*, published by Thomas Thorpe, 1609 (facsimiles by Sidney Lee (Oxford), 1905; J. M. Osborn (Yale), 1964)
Raleigh	Sir Walter Raleigh, *Poems*, ed. A. M. C. Latham, 1951
RES	*Review of English Studies*
Ridley	*Sonnets*, ed. M. R. Ridley, 1934 (New Temple)
Riverside	*The Riverside Shakespeare*, textual editor, G. Blakemore Evans, 1974
Rolfe	*Poems*, ed. W. J. Rolfe, 1890
Rollins	*Sonnets*, ed. H. E. Rollins, 2 vols., 1944 (New Variorum)
Rollins (1951)	*Sonnets*, ed. H. E. Rollins, 1951 (Crofts Classics)
Rowse	*Sonnets*, ed. A. L. Rowse, 1984 (3rd edn)
SB	*Studies in Bibliography*
Schmidt	Alexander Schmidt, *Shakespeare Lexicon*, rev. Gregor Sarrazin, 1902
Sewell	*Poems*, ed. George Sewell, 1725 (vol. VII of *Works*, ed. Alexander Pope, 1723–5)
Sewell ²	*Poems*, ed. George Sewell, 1728 (vol. X of *Works*, ed. Alexander Pope, 1728)
Seymour-Smith	*Sonnets*, ed. Martin Seymour-Smith, 1963
Sidney	Sir Philip Sidney, *Arcadia* (1590), *Arcadia* (1593), *Old Arcadia* (from MS.), in *Prose Works*, ed. Albert Feuillerat, 3 vols., 1922, 1926
	Sir Philip Sidney, *Poems*, ed. W. A. Ringler, 1962
	Sir Philip Sidney, *An Apology for Poetry*, ed. F. G. Robinson, 1970
Simpson	Percy Simpson, *Shakespearian Punctuation*, 1911
Sisson	*Works*, ed. C. J. Sisson, 1954
Sisson, *New Readings*	C. J. Sisson, *New Readings in Shakespeare*, 2 vols., 1956
SP	*Studies in Philology*
Spenser	Edmund Spenser, *Works* (Variorum), ed. Edwin Greenlaw *et al.*, 8 vols., 1932–49
SQ	*Shakespeare Quarterly*
S.Sur.	*Shakespeare Survey*
Staunton	*Works*, ed. Howard Staunton, vol. III, 1860
Steevens	George Steevens, see Malone
subst.	substantively

Taylor   Gary Taylor, 'Some manuscripts of Shakespeare's Sonnets',
                                     Bulletin of the John Rylands University Library of Manchester,
                                     68 (1985), 210–46
Theobald   Lewis Theobald, see Rollins (New Variorum)
Tilley   M. P. Tilley, *A Dictionary of the Proverbs in England in the
                                     Sixteenth and Seventeenth Centuries*, 1950 (references are to
                                     numbered proverbs)
Tobin   J. J. M. Tobin (privately)
Tottel   *Tottel's Miscellany (1557–1587)*, ed. H. E. Rollins, 2 vols.,
                                     1928 (rev. edn, 1965)
Tucker   *Sonnets*, ed. T. G. Tucker, 1924
Tyler   *Sonnets*, ed. Thomas Tyler, 1890
Tyrwhitt   Thomas Tyrwhitt, *Observations and Conjectures upon Some
                                     Passages of Shakespeare*, 1766
uncorr.   uncorrected state of Q (1609)
Vendler   Helen Vendler (privately)
Verity   *Works*, ed. A. W. Verity, vol. VIII, 1890 (Henry Irving
                                     Shakespeare)
Walsh   *Sonnets*, ed. C. M. Walsh, 1908
Watson   Thomas Watson, *Poems*, ed. Edward Arber, 1870
Wells   *Works*, ed. Stanley Wells and Gary Taylor, 1986 (New
                                     Oxford)
White   *Works*, ed. R. G. White, vol. I, 1865
White [2]   *Works*, ed. R. G. White, vol. IV, 1883
Willen and Reed   *Sonnets (A Case Book on)*, ed. Gerald Willen and V. B. Reed,
                                     1964
Wilson   Thomas Wilson, *The Arte of Rhetorique* (1553), ed. T. J.
                                     Derrick, 1982
Dover Wilson   *Sonnets*, ed. J. Dover Wilson, 1966 (New Shakespeare)
K. M. Wilson   Katherine M. Wilson, *Shakespeare's Sugared Sonnets*, 1974
Wyatt   Sir Thomas Wyatt, *Collected Poems*, ed. K. Muir and
                                     P. Thomson, 1969
Wyndham   *Poems*, ed. George Wyndham, 1898
Yale   *Sonnets*, ed. E. B. Reed, 1923 (Yale)

INTRODUCTION

Shakespeare the poet

In his own time, Shakespeare was much better known to the reading public as a poet than as a playwright. Indeed, during his life, his best seller by a wide margin, far outstripping the modern blockbusters *Romeo and Juliet* and *Hamlet*, was *Venus and Adonis*. This went through ten editions before his death in 1616, and another six before 1640. His other long narrative poem *The Rape of Lucrece* was less popular, but it too circulated far more widely than any of the plays, appearing in six editions during his life, and in two more by 1640. The most popular of the plays for Elizabethan and Jacobean readers were *Richard III* and *Richard II*, each of which went through five editions before 1616. *Romeo and Juliet* went through four; *Hamlet* appeared in three.

For readers since the eighteenth century, however, the narrative poems have been at best marginal to the Shakespeare canon. The Sonnets, on the other hand, which were the least known of his non-dramatic poems until the end of the eighteenth century, had by the twentieth century become essential to the construction of the canonical Shakespeare. They have seemed increasingly enlightening, fragments of life, or perhaps of a fantasy life; but in either case offering tantalising clues to the sources of the poet's dramatic imagination. The biography, which is ample by the standards of the time – we have more hard information about Shakespeare's life than about that of any of his contemporary playwrights with the possible exception of Jonson – offers nothing so richly passionate and emotionally ambiguous.

This transformation, to be sure, involved a good deal of revision, emendation, and especially elucidation, for which the eighteenth-century editor Edmond Malone, who did more to define what we mean by Shakespeare than anyone since the editors of the First Folio, is chiefly responsible. Malone's versions of the most problematic of these poems vary significantly from the original texts, but they have essentially replaced the originals in the modern Shakespeare.

The canonical Shakespeare, however, has, since the publication of the First Folio in 1623, been Shakespeare the playwright; and it is interesting to consider how Shakespeare would appear to us had his poems been included in the Folio – had the Folio been a volume of Complete Works, rather than Complete Plays. We are always told that the model for the First Folio was the first folio of Ben Jonson's *Works*, published in 1616. But this is, in a crucial way, incorrect: Jonson's folio comprised not only plays but poems, masques, entertainments, and even some prose commentary. Indeed, it was his epigrams that Jonson designated 'the ripest of my studies', and he endured a certain amount of scorn for presuming to include the plays at all, for claiming the status of Works for scripts from the popular theatre. The Shakespeare Folio is evidence enough that by 1623 Jonson had made his point, and in that sense Jonson's *Works* were indeed an enabling precedent. Still, Jonson is for literary history as much a poet as a playwright, and his involvement in the world of aristocratic patronage and connoisseurship, amply revealed in his poems and masques, is an essential element in our sense of his career. Had Shakespeare's poems been, from the outset, part of the canon, we might at the very least take seriously his involvement in that same social world of patronage, erudite readers, and aristocratic admirers. Certainly the dedications to his two long narrative poems, and the care with which they were prepared for and seen through the press, make clear that his ambitions extended beyond the stage.

Why were they not included in the First Folio? Probably for simple, practical reasons. The volume was put together by the King's Men, the acting company of which Shakespeare had been a principal shareholder, playwright, and performer, as a memorial to their most admired colleague. What they owned the rights to – and what chiefly concerned them – was the plays. Since the narrative poems were still selling well in 1623, to have acquired the rights to reprint them would have been difficult, if not impossible. As for the Sonnets, who knows? The quarto volume published in 1609 was the only edition in Shakespeare's lifetime, and it seems to have generated little interest – so little, in fact, that a second edition, published in 1640, could imply that the poems had never been printed before. Perhaps the Sonnets were simply not considered worth including.

Editorial history

The editorial history of Shakespeare's poems is an index to how complex and conflicted our sense of Shakespeare the poet has been. The first quartos of *Venus and Adonis* (1593) and *Lucrece* (1594) are well-printed, elegant little books. They addressed an audience of readers who knew the classics, both Latin and English; they recall, in both their physical presentation and versification, recent editions of Ovid, Spenser, Sidney. Both poems include fulsome dedications to the Earl of Southampton, a glamorous young aristocrat (he was nineteen when *Venus and Adonis* appeared) who was, moreover, the ward of William Cecil, Lord Burghley. This is how ambitious Elizabethan poets got on in the world: by finding a generous aristocratic patron, whose taste, praised in a lavish dedication, in turn constituted a marketable endorsement. That it worked for Shakespeare, at least initially, is indicated by the fact that the *Lucrece* dedication is significantly warmer than that for *Venus and Adonis*; conversely, the fact that there are no further dedications to Southampton implies that it ultimately failed to pay off. For though Southampton was liberally endowed with taste and charm, when at the age of twenty-one he finally came into his inheritance, it turned out to be nothing: what he inherited was debts, and artistic patronage does not live by taste alone.

The aura of aristocratic patronage was not, however, the only attraction of Shakespeare's first published poetry. *Venus and Adonis* was witty, inventive, and stylish; it was also daring, erotically explicit, even amoral. Though it seems to us sexually more comic than pornographic, its immense popularity is cited frequently in Shakespeare's own time as an index to the decline of morals among the young, or the literate classes, or – in an extraordinary example – the Roman Catholic Church. Thomas Robinson, a lapsed friar, in a pamphlet published in 1622 called *The Anatomy of the English Nunnery at Lisbon*, described the comfortable life of a father confessor to the nuns there: 'Then after supper it is usual for him to read a little of *Venus and Adonis*, the jests of George Peele, or some such scurrilous book: for there are few idle pamphlets printed in England which he hath not in the house.' *Lucrece* is less obviously licentious (and certainly much less fun), but for all its moralising, it lingers provocatively over the way Tarquin's rising lust is heightened by the chaste Lucrece's fears and pleas – there is a good deal here to feed the Renaissance erotic and sadistic imagination. Moreover, the elements that we find tiresome in these two poems, their formality, dilation, extensive description, and digression – in short, the sheer undramatic quality of these narratives by our greatest dramatist – would have been a good part of what contemporary readers admired: these qualities were what put Shakespeare, as a poet, in the league of Spenser and Marlowe.

The Sonnets are, editorially and bibliographically, another matter entirely. They were, to begin with, not a book. At least some of them circulated initially in manuscript, and the fact that these poems were first conceived as coterie literature is essential to our understanding of the nature of the book that finally materialised as *Shake-speares Sonnets*. Our evidence for their circulation in manuscript – it should be emphasised that it is our only evidence – comes from the miscellaneous writer Francis Meres, who in 1598, in *Palladis Tamia* (Athena's Thames), a volume comparing London's literary scene with that of ancient Athens, praises Shakespeare's 'sugred Sonnets among his private friends'; and while it is difficult to imagine 'sugred' applying to poems like 'They that have pow'r to hurt and will do none' (94) or 'Th'expense of spirit in a waste of shame' (129), the adjective certainly describes many of the sonnets written to the beloved young man. There was nothing secretive about this mode of publication; manuscript circulation was a normal mode of transmission for much lyric poetry in the period. Even such monuments of Elizabethan verse as Sidney's *Astrophil and Stella*, Marlowe's *Hero and Leander*, and Donne's *Songs and Sonnets* were initially conceived as coterie literature, and presumed a relatively small readership of uniform tastes: the poet was writing for an audience he knew. In fact, Donne refused to allow his lyric poetry to be published in his lifetime because he said he would then have no control over who read it. The Shakespeare of the 'sugred sonnets' is very much the Shakespeare of the social and cultural world implied by the dedications to *Venus and Adonis* and *Lucrece*; but, as Meres's reference to an audience of 'private friends' suggests, precisely because the Sonnets circulated only in manuscript, their poet is far more deeply embedded in that world than Shakespeare the narrative poet is. The subtext of *Venus and Adonis* and *Lucrece* may be the search for a noble patron; but the Sonnets imply a literary circle of taste and wit in which Shakespeare moves with ease. Patronage is still an issue in these poems, with the poet promising immortality to the aristocratic youth, and another poet competing for his attention; but the patronage relationship is no longer simply a matter of dedications: it is here the subject of the poems, and is intense, intimate, and even at times explicitly erotic. That sense of intimacy was shared, too, by the 'private friends'; the social world in which the Sonnets circulated was correspondingly complex and sophisticated.

SHAKE-SPEARES

SONNETS.

Neuer before Imprinted.

AT LONDON

By *G. Eld* for *T. T.* and are
to be folde by *William Afpley.*
1609.

1   The title page of the 1609 quarto

It is disappointing, therefore, that none of the 'sugred Sonnets' have been found in commonplace books of the 1590s – a small number of the poems appear in manuscript compilations, but all date from after the publication of Thorpe's 1609 quarto. Manuscript circulation typically involved a reciprocity between author and recipient, in the sense that the reception of manuscript poems was not passive. The gift of a poem really was a gift, its text often specifically reworked to appeal to a particular recipient; and the recipient treated it as a valued possession, copying it out – or more often having it copied by a professional scribe – into personal collections of favourite poems, bits of wisdom, and selections from his or her reading. Often the transcribed versions of the poems would include the recipient's own revisions, so that the poem became even more definitively the owner's, not the author's; and often as not the author's name would be indicated only by initials, or not at all. Such compilations give us a striking sense of how ambiguous the notion of literary property was in the period (whose poems are these, the author's or the recipient's?), and – especially important to emphasise – how little the circulation of literature, as opposed to its preservation, depended on the printing press.

What does it mean, then, that Shakespeare's 'private friends' survive only in Meres's report? Probably very little – certainly not that Meres was misinformed, or that none of them thought Shakespeare's poetic gifts worth preserving. The survival rate of private papers from the age is low, and Meres's claim is not in doubt. The fact that some of the poems were in fact in circulation is demonstrable from the appearance of two of the sonnets, in versions different from those of Thorpe's 1609 quarto, in a miscellaneous collection of twenty poems called *The Passionate Pilgrim* published by William Jaggard in 1599. The whole volume is ascribed to Shakespeare on its title page,[1] though only five of the poems included, the two sonnets and three more excerpted from *Love's Labour's Lost*, are Shakespearean – the play had been published in 1598 with Shakespeare's name on the title page. Four other sonnets, on the subject of Venus and Adonis but obviously not by Shakespeare, nevertheless enabled Jaggard to trade on the poet's name by evoking his best-known poem. Shakespeare clearly had nothing to do with the book's publication, though there is no reason to consider it piratical: Jaggard was publishing a manuscript that he had acquired, or more probably assembled, perfectly legally; though the ascription of the whole volume to Shakespeare is undoubtedly a misrepresentation.

The two sonnets, versions of Thorpe's 138 and 144, have generally been treated as earlier states of the texts, and have therefore been used as evidence – once again, the only evidence we have – of Shakespeare the lyric poet in the process of revision. This is a reasonable but not inevitable assumption: Thorpe's copies certainly did not come from Shakespeare, any more than Jaggard's did, and there is no way of knowing how many intermediate versions lay between the holographs and the printer's copy. Some of the differences between Jaggard's and Thorpe's versions may instead reveal the tastes of one or two of the 'private friends', revising to suit their own sense of prosody and poetic language, or even to simplify poems they found too complex.

[1] The title page to the first edition, published probably in 1599 but possibly as early as September 1598, does not survive, but the book was quickly reprinted, and a small number of complete copies of the second edition of 1599 are extant.

How Thomas Thorpe's edition of the Sonnets got into print is unclear, but there is no reason to believe that the 1609 quarto was surreptitious. Thorpe had published play quartos, including Ben Jonson's *Volpone* and *Sejanus*, and Shakespeare certainly might have given him a manuscript of sonnets to publish. The volume is, however, provided with a dedication by the publisher, not by the author, which suggests that Shakespeare was not involved in the matter. The dedication, 'to the only begetter of these ensuing Sonnets Mr. W. H.', has been the source of endless dispute and speculation, which is summarised in the Commentary to this edition. Suffice it to say here that if one thing is clear about the dedication, it is that Thorpe intended it to be teasingly obscure, and that if there is in fact a name behind the initials W. H., it is not one that any amount of close reading will extract. It is perhaps best to read W. H. as standing for 'Whoever He (may be)' – and therefore as an acknowledgement that Thorpe knew no more about the 'begetter' of the sonnets than we do. The manuscript, moreover, was not prepared with the sort of care evident in the texts of *Venus and Adonis* and *Lucrece*. It seems likely that Thorpe had some source other than the author for his copy, which also would not necessarily have been in Shakespeare's hand. Whether Shakespeare approved of the publication or not is unknowable, but the issue would not have been a significant one: intellectual property is largely a modern concept, and the rights to the poems would have belonged to whoever owned the manuscript. Though there are occasional muddles in the book, Thorpe's copy must have been clear enough, because the text is on the whole a satisfactory one. Its editorial problems are undeniable, but they are not, for the most part, the fault of the printer.

The volume concludes with a long Spenserian lament called *A Lover's Complaint*, not included in this edition (see *The Poems*, edited by John Roe, 2006). Its text has fewer muddles, and its presence in the volume remains a puzzle. Thorpe obviously considered it an appropriate way of concluding the book, but whether Shakespeare did, or whether it was part of the same manuscript, or whether Shakespeare wrote it at all, are impossible to say with any certainty. Thorpe believed that he had done so, explicitly including Shakespeare's name after the title – there is no reason to suspect any misrepresentation in this; Thorpe was a perfectly reputable publisher. But in cases where the author is not involved in a book's publication, the ascription of even a reputable publisher in the period has only limited value.

To conclude a volume of Sonnets with a long poem was not unusual: Spenser's *Amoretti* concludes with the *Epithalamion*, Drayton's *Delia* with *The Complaint of Rosamond*. As for the question of authorship, critics remained dubious about the matter until the 1960s. The poem is in the same stanza form as *Lucrece*, but includes a number of archaisms uncharacteristic of Shakespeare, and forty-nine words or forms found nowhere else in his works. This vocabulary evidence against Shakespeare's authorship has been countered by the argument that plays that are unquestionably Shakespearean often employ new vocabulary, and include new verbs made from nouns and newly invented compound adjectives, and that therefore the unusual and unique usages indicate, on the contrary, that the poem is in fact by Shakespeare. This argument may, of course, primarily constitute evidence of how manipulable stylometric analysis can be. In the past two decades, several impressive critical readings of the poem have insisted

TO.THE.ONLIE.BEGETTER.OF.
THESE.INSVING.SONNETS.
M^r.W.H. ALL.HAPPINESSE.
AND.THAT.ETERNITIE.
PROMISED.

BY.

OVR.EVER-LIVING.POET.

WISHETH.

THE.WELL-WISHING.
ADVENTVRER.IN.
SETTING.
FORTH.

T. T.

2   Thomas Thorpe's so-called 'Dedication' prefaced to the 1609 quarto

that it is both authentically Shakespearean and has an integral place among the Sonnets.[1] Colin Burrow, in the most authoritative recent essay on Shakespeare's poems, declares discussion about the poem's attribution 'definitively ended'.[2] But consensus remains elusive: Brian Vickers, shortly after the declaration of the definitive end of discussion, ascribed the poem to John Davies of Hereford.[3] All one can say with absolute confidence is that to read the Sonnets as the readers of Thorpe's quarto did – which is to say, as Shakespeare's contemporaries did – one must take take *A Lover's Complaint* into account.

Why, given the continuing success of *Venus and Adonis* and *Lucrece*, the Sonnets were not popular in 1609 is difficult to say, but it should make us take with a grain of salt the claim that Shakespeare's name on a title page was enough to guarantee a publisher's profit. The tantalising evidence of emotional turmoil and non-vanilla sex that makes them irresistible to us apparently was not a big selling point for Shakespeare's contemporaries: it was in Sidney's sonnets (which strike us as relentlessly literary) that early readers found the satisfactions of autobiography and erotic revelation. The usual explanation for the Shakespeare Sonnets' neglect is that the vogue for sonnets was past; but in 1609 the vogue for Shakespeare certainly was not. The Sonnets in print remained what they had originally been: coterie literature, experimental and daring both linguistically and erotically, and seriously playful. The fact that their attractiveness to a coterie audience did continue is clear from the number of these sonnets that reappear in Jacobean and Caroline commonplace books: even after publication, people continued to copy the ones they liked, circulate them, make them their own. The number is admittedly small – there are twenty-five manuscript versions of only twelve sonnets out of the hundred and fifty-four – and this may suggest that the coterie had diminished significantly as well.[4]

Refashioning the Sonnets

There was no second edition of the Sonnets until 1640, twenty-four years after Shakespeare's death. That edition, however, involved wholesale revision. The publisher John Benson, capitalising on the undiminished sales of *Venus and Adonis*, produced a volume of what looked to be not old-fashioned sonnets but new Shakespeare love poems. The transformation involved both format and erotics: many of the sonnets are run together, making them 28-line poems, and all are given titles, such as 'True Admiration', 'Self-Flattery of her Beauty', 'An Entreaty for Her Acceptance' – as the latter two indicate, most of the love poems addressed to the young man are now addressed to a woman. To

---

[1] See especially John Kerrigan's Introduction to the New Penguin *Sonnets and A Lover's Complaint* (revised edn, 1995), pp. 15–18.

[2] Introduction, William Shakespeare, *Complete Sonnets and Poems* (Oxford, 2002), p. 139.

[3] 'A rum "do". The likely authorship of "A Lover's Complaint"', *TLS*, 5 December 2003, pp. 13–15.

[4] It has been argued, most persuasively by Gary Taylor and Jeremy Maule, that two of the manuscript versions, late as they are, nevertheless preserve earlier readings than those of Thorpe's quarto. See Gary Taylor, 'Some manuscripts of Shakespeare's Sonnets", *Bulletin of the John Rylands Library* 68 (1985), 210–46, and the excellent summary by John Kerrigan in the New Penguin *Sonnets and A Lover's Complaint* (revised edn, 1995), 428, 441–53.

This Shadowe is renowned Shakespear's Soul, of th' age
The applause? delight! the wonder of the Stage.
Nature her selfe, was proud of his designes
And joy'd to weare the dressing of his lines;
The learned will Confess, his works are such,
As neither man, nor Muse, can prayse to much.
For ever live thy fame, the world to tell,
Thy like, no age, shall ever paralell.
                                    W. M. sculpsit

POEMS:
VVRITTEN
BY
WIL. SHAKE-SPEARE.
Gent.

Printed at *London* by *Tho. Cotes*, and are
to be fold by *Iohn Benfon*, dwelling in
Sᵗ. *Dunftans* Church-yard. 1640.

3   The title page and facing portrait of the 1640 *Poems*

effect this, it was necessary only to change three masculine pronouns within the poems
to feminine ones and supply a few gendered titles, but since the sonnets to the young
man, as they are arranged in the volume, imply a fairly consistent narrative, the pronoun
changes were sufficient to change the story. Benson's motive for these revisions was
probably less any nervousness about Shakespeare's sexuality than a publisher's desire
to bring the poems up to date, and transform the book from an Elizabethan sonnet
sequence to a volume of Cavalier love lyrics. As a marketing strategy, this was an
old one: almost a century earlier, the publisher Richard Tottel had effected a similar
transformation in Thomas Wyatt's sonnets and lyrics, regularising the manuscript
versions that came to his hand, and giving them sentimental titles when he published
them in *Songs and Sonnets* ("Tottel's Miscellany") in 1559.

   Benson's volume was not a great success, and there was no subsequent edition
until 1710, when a supplementary volume to Nicholas Rowe's Shakespeare, edited
by Charles Gildon and published by Jacob Tonson, reprinted Benson's text. In the
next year Bernard Lintot produced a competing edition that returned to the 1609

quarto, probably not through any devotion to authenticity, but merely as a way of circumventing Tonson's copyright. Nevertheless, Benson's revision remained the text of the Shakespeare Sonnets until late in the eighteenth century; and indeed, these versions of the poems were still being reprinted in the nineteenth century. The definitive return to the 1609 quarto was the work of Edmond Malone, who in 1780 produced an edition that finally brought the editing of the poems in line with the editing of the plays by taking the first published texts into account. It rationalised Thorpe's text, certainly, but its clarifications have on the whole stood the test of time. In a few critical instances, however, Malone undertook wholesale rewriting to produce the kind of sense the eighteenth-century Shakespeare seemed to demand. The most famous of these involves a crux in Sonnet 129, 'Th'expense of spirit in a waste of shame'. Here 'lust in action' is described, in the 1609 quarto, as 'A blisse in proofe and proud and very wo'. The line continued to read this way, with minor adjustments to modernise spelling and punctuation, throughout the next century – through John Benson's 1640 edition, Charles Gildon's in 1710, and the numerous popular editions throughout the eighteenth century, until Malone's, in which the line became 'A bliss in proof, and prov'd, a very woe'. Thereafter, with very few demurrals, this became the line: Malone was acknowledged to have restored Shakespeare's original.

Orthographically, the quarto's 'proud' could in 1609 be read as either 'proud' or 'provd' – though for the latter, considering the compositor's practice in the rest of the volume, 'prou'd' would have been the expected form – but, as with 'travaill' meaning both travail and travel in Shakespeare's English, the reader of 1609 who saw 'proved' in the word would not have seen only that, and would have read it as both: *provd* retained the sense of *proud*. It is a sense, in fact, that we should certainly not edit out of the poem: 'pride', says the Bible, is what 'goeth before . . . a fall' (Proverbs 16:18) – before the sonnet's 'very woe', before 'this hell', in which the poem ends. *Proud* also means erect, or tumescent (as in Sonnet 151, line 10), a usage still current today in the medical term 'proud flesh'. Therefore, whatever Shakespeare intended, the most we may reasonably argue is that both readings are possible; or to put it more strongly, that the two readings are not separable. It should be emphasised, however, that there is no published evidence that anyone before 1780 ever read the word as anything but 'proud'.[1] Simply to eliminate one of the word's senses, as Malone's emendation does, is both to falsify the text and abolish its history.

But the transformation of 'proud' to 'proved' required Malone to make another revision in the line, less noticeable, though arguably even more radical: the change of the second 'and' to 'a', so that the clause reads not 'and proud and very wo' but 'and prov'd, a very woe.' This emendation transforms the view of sex from a tripartite act – a bliss both during action and when completed, and also true woe – to a simple before and after contrast, bliss in action, woe afterwards. There is no room for 'proud' in this neatly balanced pair. If the 1609 quarto (or, for that matter, Benson's 1640 volume) was the

---

[1] Edward Capell's unpublished draft edition of the Sonnets, now in the library of Trinity College, Cambridge, and probably seen by Malone, first proposed this reading; see, e.g., W. G. Ingram and Theodore Redpath, eds., *Shakespeare's Sonnets* (1964), pp. xxi–xxii.

form in which Donne, Jonson, Herbert, Milton, Marvell, Dryden read Shakespeare's Sonnets, Malone's poem is not the poem they read. But of course Malone's poem has its history too. It is now not only our poem, but the poem of Keats, Wordsworth, Browning, Yeats, Eliot, Auden. Only Robert Graves and Laura Riding saw through it;[1] but to return with them to the Shakespeare of Donne and Marvell is to abolish the Shakespeare of Keats and Yeats.

Malone's Sonnets, of course, had a more problematic consequence for Shakespeare: it had him pining once more, in the first 126 of the poems, not for a woman but for a man; and when in 1793 the editor George Steevens explained his refusal to include the poems in his Shakespeare edition by asserting that 'the strongest act of Parliament that could be framed, would fail to compel readers into their service', adding that Malone's 'implements of criticism . . . are on this occasion disgraced by the objects of their culture', it is unlikely that syntactic and metaphoric complexity were what bothered him.[2] Everyone remembers that Wordsworth said of the Sonnets that 'with this key / Shakespeare unlocked his heart,'[3] but he also declared them 'abominably harsh, obscure, and worthless".[4] For the nineteenth and a good part of the twentieth centuries it was usual to deal with what looks, from the perspective of the past thirty years, like an overtly homoerotic narrative by arguing, when it was acknowledged at all, that the homoeroticism was purely conventional, or that the Sonnets were not autobiographical – the lovestruck poet was a persona, and the sonnets to the young man no more implied that Shakespeare was gay than *Macbeth* implies that he was a murderer. Of course, in an age when it is being argued that internet pornography featuring virtual sex with computer-generated minors should be a prosecutable offence, claiming that Shakespeare was gay only in his imagination does not help much. But in fact, recent editors have accepted the Sonnets' homoeroticism without worrying much about Shakespeare's, and contemporary commentary on these poems has tended to be sexually much more open than it is in similar editions of the plays.

Homoeroticism

It will be useful, therefore, to begin a discussion of the poems with the issue of homo-eroticism in the age, and in the Sonnets. Sodomy was a capital crime, and fulminations against the act were a staple of polemical literature of all kinds. Antitheatrical tracts assumed that the boys who played the women's roles on stage played them in life as well; anti-Catholic invective declared ecclesiastical celibacy to be a cover for institu-tionalised buggery; judicial indictments for political or religious crimes often included additional charges of sodomy – indeed, sodomy tended to serve as a gloss on whatever

---

[1] Laura Riding and Robert Graves, 'William Shakespeare and E. E. cummings: a study in original punctuation and spelling', in *A Survey of Modernist Poetry* (1927). For further discussion of this sonnet and the others mentioned here, see the appropriate commentary below.

[2] *The Plays of William Shakespeare*, ed. Samuel Johnson and George Steevens, fourth edn (1793), Intro-duction.

[3] In 'Scorn not the sonnet' (1827), lines 2–3.

[4] Quoted in Peter Jones, ed., *Shakespeare: The Sonnets* (1977), p. 41.

the culture considered worst or most threatening: those accused of atheism or sedition were almost invariably declared also to be sodomites. The corollary, however, is that the charge is almost never found in isolation; and in fact, the legal definition of sodomy was exceedingly narrow. According to the Lord Chief Justice Sir Edward Coke, the sex had to be nonconsensual, a rape; the prosecution had to be able to prove that there had been both anal penetration and an ejaculation ('*emissio seminis*' alone, Coke observes, 'maketh it not buggery'); the courts also required a witness, and there were strict rules about who could serve as a witness in such cases. The law as elucidated by the Lord Chief Justice said nothing about sex between consenting male partners, about sex between men other than anal sex, about homosexual activity of any sort performed in private: none of these legally constituted sodomy. In the popular mind the term covered a multitude of horrendous sins, not all of them by any means involving homosexuality; but precisely for that reason it is significant that sodomy was legally construed in such a way that it could hardly ever be prosecuted. Bruce Smith's study of the Assize courts in the home counties reveals a total of only six sodomy trials in the entire reign of Elizabeth; all but one involved the rape of a minor, and five of the six resulted in aquittals.[1] Sex with animals was prosecuted much more energetically.

How can Shakespeare's Sonnets, with their open declarations of the poet's love for the beautiful young man, 'the master–mistress of my passion' (Sonnet 20), be part of this cultural scene? The most direct answer is that sodomy was not equivalent to homoeroticism, and English Renaissance culture did not, in fact, display a morbid fear of homoeroticism as such. On the contrary, the love of men for other men was both a fact of life and an essential element in the operation of the patronage system. The love of men for other men tended to be idealised, whereas the love of men for women was often presented as dangerous and destructive – as it is in the Shakespeare Sonnets. The rhetoric of male friendship in the period is precisely that of passionate love – the line between the homosocial and the sodomitical was a firm but exceedingly fine one, and could, of course, lie dangerously in the eye of the beholder.[2]

One's point of view was everything. The association of the stage's transvestite boys with homosexual prostitution is found not only in Puritan polemicists but in the playwrights themselves; in the latter cases, however, the attitude implied tends to be neither anxious nor outraged, but liberal and permissive. In Thomas Middleton's *Father Hubburd's Tales*, a budding London rake is advised 'to call in at the Blackfriars, where he should see a nest of boys able to ravish a man'.[3] – this is not a warning, but a recommendation. At the opening of Ben Jonson's *Epicoene*, the fashionable Clerimont appears with a page boy who is described as 'his ingle' – his catamite, or boy lover – but the fact is offered merely as one of a number of indications of the pleasant life of a London playboy.[4] In *The Alchemist*, the case is cited of a bankrupt captain who has, through the magician's art, been able to

---

[1] *Homosexual Desire in Shakespeare's England* (1991), p. 47
[2] The essential works on homosexuality in England in the age of Shakespeare are Bruce Smith, *Homosexual Desire*, and Alan Bray, *Homosexuality in Renaissance England* (1982).
[3] *Works of Thomas Middleton*, ed. A. H. Bullen (1886), VIII.77.
[4] I.1.23

> Arrive at competent means, to keep himself,
> His punk, and naked boy, in excellent fashion,
> And be admired for't.   (3.4.80–2)

The 'punk' and 'naked boy' are female and male prostitutes respectively. None of these good-natured invocations of homosexual activity displays any animus whatever against sodomy.

For the readers of Shakespeare's age, the locus classicus for the idealisation of homosexual feeling was Christopher Marlowe's *Hero and Leander*, published (twice) in 1598, but circulating in manuscript for at least five years before that. Indeed, one of the most striking aspects of the poem is its overt sexuality. There are Italian poems like this, but almost none in English until the next century; it is emotionally very daring. It is also very open about its sexual interests – the tradition that says that Marlowe was gay gets a good deal of support from *Hero and Leander*. Nevertheless (or perhaps therefore), it became an instant classic, cited by Shakespeare in *As You Like It*, only a year after its publication, as a source of eternal wisdom about love. Phebe, instantly smitten by Rosalind disguised as the youth Ganymede, invokes Marlowe as the archetypal pastoral poet, and quotes the poem's already famous aphorism:

> Dead shepherd, now I feel thy saw of might,
> 'Who ever loved that loved not at first sight?'
>   (3.6.80–1)[1]

Marlowe describes both Hero and Leander as infinitely desirable; but the praise of Leander is much more frankly sexual than that of Hero, and specifically homosexual. Gods and men pine away for Hero, but the measure of Leander's beauty is not that women desire him, but that men do: 'Jove might have sipped out nectar from his hand' (1.62)[2] – he is as desirable as Ganymede; had Hippolytus seen him he would have abandoned his chastity; 'The barbarous Thracian soldier, moved with naught, / Was moved with him, and for his favour sought' (1.81–2) – rough trade solicits him. None of this comes from Marlowe's source, Musaeus, where Leander is not described – in the Greek original, Hero is beautiful, and Leander is all desire, the validation of her beauty.

Marlowe is certainly daring, though less so in a Renaissance context than he seems now – for adult men to be attracted to good-looking youths was quite conventional. Still, there is no way of arguing that Marlowe is being *merely* conventional, that he does not really mean it, or does not mean it the way it sounds. The first sestiad includes a teasing description of how beautiful Leander's body is:

> I could tell ye
> How smooth his breast was, and how white his belly,
> And whose immortal fingers did imprint

---

[1] *As You Like It*, ed. Michael Hattaway, New Cambridge Shakespeare (2000).
[2] Line references are to the text of *Hero and Leander* in my own edition, *Marlowe: The Complete Poems and Translations* (1971).

> That heavenly path, with many a curious dint,
> That runs along his back   (1.65–69)

and the second sestiad has an extraordinary passage about Neptune making passes at Leander as he swims the Hellespont.

> He clapped his plump cheeks, with his tresses played,
> And smiling wantonly, his love bewrayed.
> He watched his arms, and as they opened wide
> At every stroke, betwixt them would he slide
> And steal a kiss, and then run out and dance,
> And as he turned, cast many a lustful glance,
> And threw him gaudy toys to please his eye,
> And dive into the water, and there pry
> Upon his breast, his thighs, and every limb,
> And up again, and close beside him swim,
> And talk of love.   (II.181–91)

Nothing here suggests that Marlowe feels, or expects his readers to feel, any anxiety over the enthusiastic depiction of a man making love to another man. The scene is not moralistic, but appreciative and comic.

The closest analogue to Shakespeare's sonnets to the young man is Richard Barnfield's overtly homoerotic series of sonnets to a beloved youth, published in *Cynthia, With Certaine Sonnets* in 1595. These poems, in their directness and sexual openness, provide an important context for Shakespeare's Sonnets. Shakespeare was not writing in a vacuum; love poetry in the 1590s included celebrations of the love of men for men:

> Sometimes I wish that I his pillow were,
> So might I steale a kisse, and yet not seene,
> So might I gaze upon his sleeping eine,
> Although I did it with a panting feare:
> But when I well consider how vaine my wish is,
> Ah foolish bees (thinke I) that doe not sucke
> His lips for hony; but poore flowers doe plucke
> Which have no sweet in them: when his sole kisses,
> Are able to reuiue a dying soule . . .   (viii, 1–8)[1]

Most striking, the revelation of the speaker's homosexuality is part of the drama of the sequence – the sonnet is worth quoting in full:

> Sighing, and sadly sitting by my Love,
> He ask't the cause of my hearts sorrowing,
> Coniuring me by heauens eternall King,
> To tell the cause which me so much did move.
> Compell'd: (quoth I) to thee will I confesse,
> Love is the cause; and only love it is

---

[1] Richard Barnfield, *The Complete Poems*, ed. George Klawitter (1990), p. 126.

That doth deprive me of my heavenly blisse.
Love is the paine that doth my heart oppresse.
And what is she (quoth he) whom thou do'st love?
Looke in this glasse (quoth I) there shalt thou see
The perfect forme of my faelicitie.
When, thinking that it would strange Magique proue,
He open'd it: and taking off the cover
He straight perceav'd himselfe to be my Lover.   (xi)[1]

The Sonnets include no record of the effect of this revelation on the beautiful young man, but it changes nothing in the progress of the love: the beloved remains perfectly narcissistic, the poet hopelessly infatuated. Ingles and kept boys – and, for the most part, sexual satisfaction, whatever the gender of the beloved – belong to the world of comedy, not to the world of love Sonnets. Barnfield's long poem *The Affectionate Shepherd* (1594), celebrating the poet's love for a youth inevitably called Ganymede, confronts the cultural ambivalence implicit in idealised homoeroticism:

If it be sinne to love a sweet-fac'd Boy,
              . . .
If it be sinne to love a lovely Lad;
Oh then sinne I, for whom my soule is sad.
              (7, 11–12)[2]

A letter written by King James to his favourite the Duke of Buckingham gives a good sense of how much the homoerotic was part of the currency of social relationships in Shakespeare's age:

I cannot content myself without sending you this present, praying God that I may have a joyful and comfortable meeting with you and that we may make at this Christmas a new marriage ever to be kept hereafter; for, God so love me, as I desire only to live in the world for your sake, and that I had rather live banished in any part of the earth with you than live a sorrowful widow's life without you. And so God bless you, my sweet child and wife, and grant that ye may ever be a comfort to your dear dad and husband. James R.[3]

The metamorphic quality of the King's sexuality in this rhetoric is notable: he proposes marriage to Buckingham, and then imagines himself in succession as widow, father and husband, and Buckingham as his child and wife. Gender here is entirely permeable; the King's erotic imagination expands Shakespeare's 'master–mistress' conceit into an image of an endlessly mutating family.

The rhetoric of patronage, and of male friendship generally, was precisely the language of love, and it rendered all such relationships literally ambiguous. Such language does not necessarily imply a sexual relationship; but it is important to add that, by the same token, nothing in the language precludes it either – James *was* accused of making his favourites his lovers. The language of love in the age implies everything but tells

---

[1] Ibid., p. 127.
[2] Ibid., pp. 79–80.
[3] *Letters of King James VI and I*, ed. G. P. V. Akrigg (1984), p. 431.

nothing. It is to the point that Shakespeare's Sonnet 20 explicitly denies that the poet is sleeping with the young man. Nothing can be taken for granted.

The Sonnets as a collection

We have customarily referred to the Sonnets as a sequence (a term not in use for a collection of sonnets until the nineteenth century), and take the sequence to imply a narrative, or a series of related narratives. A narcissistic young man is urged to marry and produce heirs; the poet is captivated by a beautiful, aristocratic youth – perhaps the same young man, perhaps not – who reciprocates his love for a time, but then treats him with coldness, prefers another writer, has an affair with the poet's mistress; the poet falls in love with a beautiful, dark, married woman – perhaps the mistress of the previous narrative, perhaps not – who betrays him with his dearest friend – perhaps the friend of the previous narrative, perhaps not. Tantalising bits of specificity appear: Sonnet 135 plays on the fact that the poet's own name, Will, is also that of both the friend in the 'Dark Lady' narrative and of the Dark Lady's husband; 107 refers to a datable event; 111 seems to allude obliquely to the poet's career as a playwright; 145 puns on the name of Shakespeare's wife Anne Hathaway. But these moments punctuate a relentlessly unspecific texture. Even the repeated claim that the poems will immortalise the beloved's name frustrates us by simultaneously concealing that name. None of this would matter if we did not want to read the Sonnets autobiographically. Attempts to do so began only in the late eighteenth century, and no remotely satisfactory identification of the beloved youth, the rival poet or the Dark Lady has ever been proposed. Though the Sonnets must be, in some respect, autobiographical, we simply know too little about Shakespeare's personal life, and more important, about the imaginative relation between his life and his art, to treat these poems as biographical evidence.

Reading the Sonnets

How, then, should we we read this book? To begin with, by abandoning any assumption that the implied narrative corresponds with a sequence of events in Shakespeare's life, or – more importantly – that the process of composition bears any relation to the order of the poems in Thorpe's quarto. The poems range from the style of the earliest Shakespeare to that of the great middle-period work; the period of composition seems to have been from the early 1590s to about 1604. But the groupings do not move from early to late – some of the poems that are stylistically earliest are in the final group of sonnets, 127–54. Some of the poems were obviously written to be read together: 15, 'When I consider every thing that grows', with its assurance of the poet's successful war against Time on behalf of the beloved young man, is answered by 16, 'But wherefore do not you a mightier way / Make war upon this bloody tyrant Time . . . ?' Sonnet 44 contemplates the slow and heavy elements of earth and water that keep the poet from the beloved and materialise from within as tears; 45 completes the thought: 'The other two, slight air and purging fire. . . ' Sonnets 40 to 42 allude to a sexual betrayal; 50 and 51 meditate on a journey that takes him from the friend. Some groups have larger structures of concern – the ambiguous power of poetry; the far less ambiguous power of mutability. But for the most part, the collection seems to have been arranged in its present order long after most of the individual poems were written, and into groups that are associated by theme, imagery, or on occasion by an underlying narrative only glancingly alluded to. Thus the sonnets to the beautiful young man may not have been written together, or to only one young man; just as the mistress and friend of 40 to 42 may not be those of 127 to 154. Whatever continuous narratives we derive from the volume are a function of its ultimate arrangement, not of its composition. That the arrangement is powerful, and persuasive, is undeniable; it is an authoritative arrangement, and it seems inconceivable that anyone but Shakespeare could have been responsible for it.

The 'sugred Sonnets among his private friends', then, would have given scarcely a hint of the richness and complexity of the final collection. The poems read, in fact, quite differently in the context of Thorpe's volume and out of it. Many of the love poems to the young man can be seen to have a gendered subject only because of their placement in the sequence, and the most famous ones, such as 18, 'Shall I compare thee to a summer's day?', regularly appear in modern anthologies with no indication that the addressee is not a woman. There are often elements in the poems themselves that preclude such a reading, but to recognise them depends, again, on a knowledge of the book as a whole. The Shakespeare of the Sonnets does not talk about women in this way:

> Shall I compare thee to a summer's day?
> Thou art more lovely and more temperate.

The lovely and temperate are, throughout the volume, masculine attributes. As for the poem's confident declaration of the immortalising power of verse, in context it is preceded by a sonnet that asks 'Who will believe my verse in time to come /If it were filled with your most high deserts?', and goes on to compare the poem to 'a tomb / Which hides your life, and shows not half your parts'. It is followed by 'Devouring Time, blunt thou the lion's paws', which vainly pleads for an ageless – and unambiguously male – beloved:

> O carve not with thy hours my love's fair brow,
> Nor draw no lines there with thine ˉàntique pen;
> Him in thy course untainted do allow
> For beauty's pattern to succeeding men.   (19)

Even out of context, however, 18 is a very unorthodox love poem, to which the gender of the beloved is ultimately irrelevant:

> But thy eternal summer shall not fade,
> Nor lose possession of that fair thou ow'st,
> Nor shall Death brag thou wand'rest in his shade,
> When in immortal lines to time thou grow'st.
>> So long as men can breathe or eyes can see,
>> So long lives this, and this gives life to thee.

The beloved is unchanging and eternal only because the poem is claimed to be; the object of love and celebration is the poet's own craft – the beloved is the poem.

The most famous of these Sonnets have been relentlessly sentimentalised – their accessibility to such treatment doubtless explains their celebrity. Often, however, poems that begin with the grandest declarations of love proceed to an account of the passion that is anything but ideal:

> Let me not to the marriage of true minds
> Admit impediments; love is not love
> Which alters when it alteration finds,
> Or bends with the remover to remove.
> O no, it is an ever-fixèd mark . . .   (116)

This poem is often read at weddings. But by the third line the marriage of true minds includes 'alteration', and one of the partners is a 'remover'. By the second quatrain, the 'ever-fixèd mark' is definitively alone, by the end of the third, 'even to the edge of doom'. The couplet emphasises the poet's isolation:

> If this be error and upon me proved,
> I never writ, nor no man ever loved.

Whether the final line is taken to mean 'no man ever loved' or 'I never loved any man', surely the most striking thing about it, as about the poem as a whole, is the briefness imagined for any reciprocal love – the poet in this marriage has remained faithful to a lover who has left him at the altar.

The lover's gender in this case is unspecified, though since the poem comes among the Sonnets to the young man, the gender is presumably male. When the beloved is a woman, the tone changes radically; the final section from 127 to 154, includes poems that are the most erotically intense in the volume, but are also characteristically frustrated, sarcastic, and disillusioned. The difference between the poems to the youth and those to the woman has often been viewed in Petrarchan terms, with the contrast between spiritual and sensual love being dramatised through the ideal male lover and the passionate and deceitful mistress; but this reading ignores how much sexuality is involved in the love for the young man, 'the master–mistress of my passion', and how much deception and betrayal the idealised love struggles to accept and accommodate:

> That thou hast her, it is not all my grief,
> And yet it may be said I loved her dearly;
> That she hath thee is of my wailing chief,
> A loss in love that touches me more nearly.
> Loving offenders, thus I will excuse ye:
> Thou dost love her because thou know'st I love her,
> And for my sake even so doth she abuse me,
> Suff'ring my friend for my sake to approve her.
>   . . .
> But here's the joy, my friend and I are one.
> Sweet flattery! then she loves but me alone.
>   (42)

The witty speciousness of the reasoning depends on the co-ordinates that increasingly define the love these poems address: the friend and he are one; the mistress is the Other. It is the loss of the friend that chiefly matters, because it is a loss of self. The touch is light in this poem, but the tone is one that can scarcely be maintained – Sonnet 40 has a much more precarious sense of balance about the betrayal:

> Take all my loves, my love, yea, take them all;
> What hast thou then more than thou hadst before?
>   . . .
> I do forgive thy robb'ry, gentle thief,
> Although thou steal thee all my poverty;
> And yet love knows it is a greater grief
> To bear love's wrong than hate's known injury.
>   Lascivious grace, in whom all ill well shows,
>   Kill me with spites, yet we must not be foes.

   The conclusion of this is almost wistful, a testimony to the ultimate powerlessness of the art that has been so hyperbolically praised. The mistress and the friend are finally both the Other. The difference is that Shakespeare keeps finding excuses for the young man's behaviour, 'in whom all ill well shows', whereas there are none for the woman's; but in both cases the poet is in the grip of a profoundly unsettling and disorienting passion that can only partly and intermittently be contained by the power of his mind and his verse.

Loving women

The poems addressed to the 'Dark Lady' begin with a justification of her complexion – it is assumed from the outset that her variance from the traditional ideal requires a justification.

> In the old age black was not counted fair,
> Or if it were it bore not beauty's name;
> But now is black beauty's successive heir,
> And beauty slandered with a bastard shame . . .
>   (127)

The second quatrain ascribes the bastardisation of beauty to the use of cosmetics, whereby anyone can be blonde; and the mistress's dark hair is then a sign of mourning for the disgrace of beauty. The ambivalence of this praise becomes increasingly apparent as we read further – it is ultimately not cosmetics, but the dark beauty herself, 'beauty's successive heir', that, through her actions, slanders beauty 'with a bastard shame'. She is an emblem of the depravity of the modern world, a complete inversion of the ideal represented by the beloved young man, who outdoes the glories of antiquity and sets a standard for future ages.
   This poem is followed by an easygoing sonnet about the mistress playing music on a keyboard instrument, concluding 'Since saucy jacks [the keys of the instrument] so

happy are in this, / Give them thy fingers, me thy lips to kiss.' But what follows this lighthearted compliment is Sonnet 129, the most violent and frustrated poem in the collection, 'Th'expense of spirit in a waste of shame . . .', in which the desire for a kiss is now rampant lust, fierce, destructive, and – most striking – solitary, eventuating in an 'action' that involves no reciprocal passion, and has no object but the satisfaction of lust itself. The poet, 'Had, having, and in quest', declares himself, and all men, in hell.

In such a context, the poem that follows, Sonnet 130, the famous 'My mistress' eyes are nothing like the sun', looks much less playful, not a riff on Petrarchan tropes but a rejection of poetic idealisation of all kinds, and a radical assertion of the centrality of the poet's consciousness – even here, the poet is alone with his desire. In the couplet,

> And yet, by heaven, I think my love as rare
> As any she belied with false compare,

the key words are clearly 'I think', from which derive all the ways in which love and the lovers are constructed throughout the volume – it is 'I think' that creates 'the heaven that leads men to this hell'.

Shakespeare's handling of the traditional Petrarchan tension between physical and spiritual love is worth pausing over. The love for the young man is initially both idealised and unproblematic; this changes radically during the course of the relationship, but the young man remains an ideal, even as he falls short of it. It is the love of women that turns out to be the disruptive force in the sequence. In the first group of sonnets, when the young man is urged to marry and have children, the process is described in terms of planting gardens and growing flowers, not in terms of men and women making love. The painful and frustrating aspects of sexuality are ultimately projected onto the false and seductive mistress, who is dark-haired when she ought to be blonde, and lies when she claims to be faithful – these are the corollaries of physical love: to love women is to love the wrong one. But the identification with the friend remains complete – even the great betrayal, when the mistress and the friend start sleeping together, can be ironically accommodated because 'my friend and I are one'.

The drama of the Sonnets

If there is a single overriding subject in Shakespeare's Sonnets, it is the transforming power of the mind, the imagination's attempt to re-form the realities of human relationships. And though it is a commonplace to praise the overwhelming force of Shakespeare's imagination, the theme as expressed in the Sonnets is of relentless failure; the poems, over and over, are about self-deception and betrayal, and about the inadequacy of the mind, or the imagination, or poetry, to have any effect, even on the poet's own feelings. Where poetry for Donne and Carew could serve as a celebration of their erotic conquests, Shakespeare's volume of love poems stands as a monument to frustration and loss, anatomising the inadequacies and the radical loneliness of the self, and the ultimate elusiveness of the Other. Sonnet 87 bids farewell to the lover he is not good enough for, 'too dear for my possessing':

> Thus have I had thee as a dream doth flatter,
> In sleep a king, but waking no such matter.

These poems look forward to Prospero's world, to the discovery that even when the imagination is conceived as magic power, it can do little to abate your passions or satisfy your needs, to bring about reconciliations or changes of heart – even changes of your own heart. Prospero is a megalomaniac of the imagination, but even he finally renounces his magic, acknowledging at last that it does not really get you what you want. The poet of the Sonnets is, in his way, equally megalomaniacal about the power of his verse, but given all the boasting about the defeat of Time and the conferral of immortality, it is the abjectness of this poet that is striking, the repeated insistence that the beloved, even as he betrays the poet with a mistress or prefers a rival poet, is too good for him, that the poet–lover deserves the neglect he suffers, and that the love, however compelling, however much the source of a poetry more lasting than monuments, is nothing but a flattering dream. Prospero's megalomania is in the Sonnets recognised as a fantasy about mental power, about the absolute control the poet can only dream of exercising over his subject through his poetry. The beloved youth, the object of the passion, all but disappears in the most assertive of these poems. 'Shall I compare thee to a summer's day?' turns almost at once from praise of the young man to vaunting instead the power of the poet, power even over death – the theme is often repeated:

> 'Gainst death and all oblivious enmity
> Shall you pace forth
>
>   . . .
>
> So, till the Judgement that yourself arise,
> You live in this. . .   (55)

Prospero, at a similar moment of equally dubious imaginative triumph, claims he can raise the dead: 'Graves at my command / Have waked their sleepers, oped, and let 'em forth / By my so potent art' (5.1.48–50) The poet of the Sonnets veers back and forth from the dream of omnipotence to the dread of mortality and impending loss, whereby the very thought of the beloved 'is as a death, which cannot choose / But weep to have that which it fears to lose' (64). For the omnipotent Prospero, too, 'every third thought shall be my grave' (5.1.309). The Sonnets to the 'lovely boy', in fact, end not with celebration, not even with a farewell sonnet, but only with an assurance of transience and inconclusiveness, which are evident even in the metrics and typography. The anomalous 126, twelve lines of couplets, acknowledges that all-powerful Nature herself will have to relinquish the peerless youth to Time:

> Yet fear her, O thou minion of her pleasure,
> She may detain, but not still keep, her treasure!
> Her audit (though delayed) answered must be,
> And her quietus is to render thee.

The couplet up to this point had served, for 125 poems, as a peculiarly Shakespearean way of concluding the sonnet, but these six couplets conclude nothing; they only warn of the debt remaining to be paid, and the impending loss that will have no ending. Emphasising the inconclusiveness of this conclusion, the typography inserts two final lines of empty brackets, as if yet another couplet might do the trick, really produce the quietus.

What is it that typographer, editor – or perhaps author – believed had been left unsaid? Implicit in the sonnets to the young man is an alternative scenario, already suggested in the poems about the intruding mistress and the rival poet, and fully articulated in the subsequent sonnets to the deceitful Dark Lady, in which the protagonist's abjection turns resentful, sarcastic, cynical, and witty:

> In nothing art thou black save in thy deeds,
> And thence this slander as I think proceeds.
> (131)
>
> Him have I lost, thou hast both him and me;
> He pays the whole, and yet I am not free.
> (134)
>
> Why should my heart think that a several plot [private property],
> Which my heart knows the wide world's common place?
> Or mine eyes seeing this, say this is not,
> To put fair truth upon so foul a face?
> In things right true my heart and eyes have erred,
> And to this false plague are they now transferred.   (137)
>
> When my love swears that she is made of truth,
> I do believe her, though I know she lies,
>   . . .
> Therefore I lie with her, and she with me,
> And in our faults by lies we flattered be.
> (138)

Such sonnets look ahead to a poetry in which lyric concessiveness is reconceived as dramatic vindictiveness; in which the wit of the lyric sequence is refigured into a drama in which the poet, the witty deviser of conceits, schemes, and devices, really is in control. *Shake-speares Sonnets* does in fact conclude in this way; *A Lover's Complaint* is spoken by a forsaken woman, seduced and abandoned by an eloquent charmer, as if the betrayed poet–lover has finally turned the tables, not only on his mistress, but also on all women, on all lovers. This plot begins where the Sonnets end, with betrayal and frustration, and as Shakespeare pursues and develops it in his drama, it shows the master of language and argument getting his own back, the dramatic poet avenging himself on the lyric subject. This poet says, if I can't make you love me I can make you hate me; if I can't give you life I can take it away. Dramatically, the Sonnets culminate as much in Iago as in Prospero. The Sonnets' claim that 'my friend and I are one' achieves a dangerous dramatic reality as Iago declares to Othello that 'I am your own forever" (3.3.480), and asserts that 'In following him I follow but myself' (1.1.59).

NOTE ON THE TEXT

The copy-text for the Sonnets is the quarto published by Thomas Thorpe in 1609 (= Q); the second edition (in the volume entitled *Poems*), published by John Benson in 1640, is without any independent textual authority (see Textual Analysis, pp. 265–7 below). All substantive and semi-substantive emendations of the Q copy-text are recorded in the textual collation at the foot of each page; the authority for the emendation is given after the square bracket following the lemma, which, except for the manuscript copies collated in the Appendix (pp. 268–71 below), is taken from the present text. Changes in Q accidentals (i.e. punctuation and spelling) which neither affect meaning nor represent distinctive Elizabethan variant forms are not recorded. When more than one edition by the same editor has been consulted (e.g. Gildon, Gildon²), the siglum *Gildon* means that both editions agree on a reading; if the editions differ, they are cited as *Gildon*¹ or *Gildon*². The collations also record: (1) conjectural emendations proposed for the most debated readings in Q (a few of which have been adopted in the present text); (2) Q syllabic or stressed preterite and participial *-ed* forms not here accepted but reduced, for metrical reasons, to non-syllabic or unstressed forms (e.g. Q 'recured' (45.9) is recorded in the collation as '9 recured] *Boswell* (recur'd); recured Q'); (3) distinctive Q variant Elizabethan forms (see Textual Analysis, p. 267) here given in the form commonly in use today; (4) the source for the use of personified forms (i.e. Death, Time, etc.) not personified in Q (the readings of Gildon and Sewell, who regularly capitalised nouns, are excluded).

The Sonnets

TO.THE.ONLIE.BEGETTER.OF.
THESE.INSVING.SONNETS.
M^r.W.H. ALL.HAPPINESSE.
AND.THAT.ETERNITIE.
PROMISED.   [5]
BY.
OVR.EVER-LIVING.POET.
WISHETH.
THE.WELL-WISHING.
ADVENTVRER.IN.   [10]
SETTING.
FORTH.

      T. T.

SHAKESPEARE'S SONNETS

1

From fairest creatures we desire increase,
That thereby beauty's rose might never die,
But as the riper should by time decease,
His tender heir might bear his memory: 4
But thou, contracted to thine own bright eyes,
Feed'st thy light's flame with self-substantial fuel,
Making a famine where abundance lies,
Thyself thy foe, to thy sweet self too cruel.   8
Thou that art now the world's fresh ornament,
And only herald to the gaudy spring,
Within thine own bud buriest thy content,
And, tender churl, mak'st waste in niggarding: 12
    Pity the world, or else this glutton be,
    To eat the world's due, by the grave and thee.

2

When forty winters shall besiege thy brow,
And dig deep trenches in thy beauty's field,
Thy youth's proud livery so gazed on now
Will be a tottered weed of small worth held: 4
Then being asked, where all thy beauty lies,
Where all the treasure of thy lusty days,
To say within thine own deep-sunken eyes
Were an all-eating shame, and thriftless praise.   8
How much more praise deserved thy beauty's use,
If thou couldst answer, 'This fair child of mine
Shall sum my count, and make my old excuse',
Proving his beauty by succession thine.   12
    This were to be new made when thou art old,
    And see thy blood warm when thou feel'st it cold.

Sonnet 1

Drop-title: SHAKESPEARE'S SONNETS] SHAKE-SPEARES, / *SONNETS.* Q   **Number:** 1] *Malone; not in* Q
2 rose] *Murden (after Gildon² Rose); Rose* Q   6 self-substantial] *Gildon²;* selfe substantiall Q   12 And, . . .
churl,] *Chapell (after Gildon Churl);* And . . . chorle Q

Sonnet 2

4 tottered] Q *(totter'd);* tatter'd *Gildon (variant form)*   6 days,] *Collier;* daies; Q   7 deep-sunken] *Gildon²;*
deepe sunken Q   10 answer,] *Lintott, Gildon²;* answere Q   10–11 'This . . . excuse',] *Quoted, Malone (after
Capell);* this . . . excuse Q   14 cold.] *Benson;* could, Q *For MS. versions of Sonnet 2, see Appendix, pp. 268–70 below.*

3

Look in thy glass and tell the face thou viewest,
Now is the time that face should form another,
Whose fresh repair if now thou not renewest,
Thou dost beguile the world, unbless some mother.   4
For where is she so fair whose uneared womb
Disdains the tillage of thy husbandry?
Or who is he so fond will be the tomb
Of his self-love to stop posterity?   8
Thou art thy mother's glass, and she in thee
Calls back the lovely April of her prime;
So thou through windows of thine age shalt see,
Despite of wrinkles, this thy golden time.   12
    But if thou live rememb'red not to be,
    Die single, and thine image dies with thee.

4

Unthrifty loveliness, why dost thou spend
Upon thyself thy beauty's legacy?
Nature's bequest gives nothing, but doth lend,
And being frank she lends to those are free: 4
Then, beauteous niggard, why dost thou abuse
The bounteous largess given thee to give?
Profitless usurer, why dost thou use
So great a sum of sums, yet canst not live?   8
For having traffic with thyself alone,
Thou of thyself thy sweet self dost deceive:
Then how when Nature calls thee to be gone,
What àcceptable audit canst thou leave?   12
    Thy unused beauty must be tombed with thee,
    Which usèd lives th'executor to be.

Sonnet 3
2 another] *Gildon;* an other Q *(usually; not hereafter noted)*   4 dost] *Gildon* (do'st); doo'st Q *(not hereafter noted)*
7 tomb] *Gildon;* tombe, Q   8 self-love] *Lintott, Gildon²;* selfe love Q   13 rememb'red] Q; remember'd *Capell*

Sonnet 4
11 Nature] *Bell;* nature Q   12 audit] *Murden;* Audit Q

28

5

Those hours that with gentle work did frame
The lovely gaze where every eye doth dwell
Will play the tyrants to the very same,
And that unfair which fairly doth excel;   4
For never-resting time leads summer on
To hideous winter and confounds him there,
Sap checked with frost and lusty leaves quite gone,
Beauty o'ersnowed and bareness every where: 8
Then were not summer's distillation left
A liquid prisoner pent in walls of glass,
Beauty's effect with beauty were bereft,
Nor it nor no remembrance what it was.   12
    But flowers distilled, though they with winter meet,
    Leese but their show; their substance still lives sweet.

6

Then let not winter's ragged hand deface
In thee thy summer ere thou be distilled:
Make sweet some vial; treasure thou some place
With beauty's treasure ere it be self-killed: 4
That use is not forbidden usury
Which happies those that pay the willing loan;
That's for thyself to breed another thee,
Or ten times happier be it ten for one;   8
Ten times thyself were happier than thou art,
If ten of thine ten times refigured thee:
Then what could death do if thou shouldst depart,
Leaving thee living in posterity?   12
    Be not self-willed, for thou art much too fair
    To be death's conquest and make worms thine heir.

Sonnet 5

5 never-resting] *Gildon²;* never resting Q   7 leaves] *Gildon;* leau's Q   7 gone,] *Sewell;* gon. Q   8 bareness]
Sewell; barenes Q; barenesse *Benson;* Barenness *Gildon¹;* Barrenness *Gildon²*   8 every where] Q; everywhere *Knight*
14 Leese] Q; Lose *Gildon (variant form)*

Sonnet 6

1 ragged] *Gildon;* wragged Q; rugged *Capell*   4 beauty's] *Gildon² (after Benson* beauties*);* beautits Q   4 self-
killed] *Gildon;* selfe kil'de Q   13 self-willed] *Gildon (self-will'd);* selfe-wild Q

7

Lo in the orient when the gracious light
Lifts up his burning head, each under eye
Doth homage to his new-appearing sight,
Serving with looks his sacred majesty;   4
And having climbed the steep-up heavenly hill,
Resembling strong youth in his middle age,
Yet mortal looks adore his beauty still,
Attending on his golden pilgrimage: 8
But when from highmost pitch, with weary car,
Like feeble age he reeleth from the day,
The eyes (fore duteous) now converted are
From his low tract and look another way: 12
    So thou, thyself outgoing in thy noon,
    Unlooked on diest unless thou get a son.

8

Music to hear, why hear'st thou music sadly?
Sweets with sweets war not, joy delights in joy:
Why lov'st thou that which thou receiv'st not gladly,
Or else receiv'st with pleasure thine annoy?   4
If the true concord of well-tunèd sounds,
By unions married, do offend thine ear,
They do but sweetly chide thee, who confounds
In singleness the parts that thou shouldst bear;   8
Mark how one string, sweet husband to another,
Strikes each in each by mutual ordering;
Resembling sire, and child, and happy mother,
Who all in one, one pleasing note do sing;   12
    Whose speechless song being many, seeming one,
    Sings this to thee, 'Thou single wilt prove none.'

Sonnet 7

3 new-appearing] *Murden;* new appearing Q   5 steep-up heavenly] *Gildon;* steepe vp heauenly Q; steep up-heavenly
or steep-up-heavenly *conj. Craig (in Rollins)*   9 pitch] *Benson;* pich Q   9 car] Q; care *Benson*   12 tract] Q;
Track *Gildon² (variant form)*

Sonnet 8

1 sadly?] *Gildon;* sadly, Q   5 well-tunèd] *Gildon²;* well tuned Q   8 the parts] Q; a part *conj. Pooler*   14 thee,]
Gildon; thee Q   14 'Thou . . . none.'] *Quoted Malone;* thou . . . none. Q *For a MS. version of Sonnet 8, see Appendix,
p. 270 below.*

9

Is it for fear to wet a widow's eye
That thou consum'st thyself in single life?
Ah! if thou issueless shalt hap to die,
The world will wail thee like a makeless wife;   4
The world will be thy widow and still weep,
That thou no form of thee hast left behind,
When every private widow well may keep,
By children's eyes, her husband's shape in mind: 8
Look what an unthrift in the world doth spend
Shifts but his place, for still the world enjoys it,
But beauty's waste hath in the world an end,
And kept unused the user so destroys it: 12
      No love toward others in that bosom sits
      That on himself such murd'rous shame commits.

10

For shame deny that thou bear'st love to any,
Who for thyself art so unprovident.
Grant, if thou wilt, thou art beloved of many,
But that thou none lov'st is most evident;   4
For thou art so possessed with murd'rous hate,
That 'gainst thyself thou stick'st not to conspire,
Seeking that beauteous roof to ruinate
Which to repair should be thy chief desire: 8
O change thy thought, that I may change my mind!
Shall hate be fairer lodged than gentle love?
Be as thy presence is, gracious and kind,
Or to thyself at least kind-hearted prove: 12
      Make thee another self for love of me,
      That beauty still may live in thine or thee.

Sonnet 9
1 Is it] Q; It is *Benson*   3 Ah!] *Gildon*; Ah; Q   9 Look what] Q; Look, what *Capell*   10 it,] *Riverside*; it Q; it; *Sewell (after Gildon)*

Sonnet 10
1 shame] Q; shame: *Gildon²*; shame, *Staunton*   2 unprovident.] *Malone (after Gildon)*; vnprouident Q   9 mind!] *Gildon²*; minde, Q   11 is,] *Gildon*; is Q   12 kind-hearted] *Gildon²*; kind harted Q

11

As fast as thou shalt wane, so fast thou grow'st
In one of thine, from that which thou departest,
And that fresh blood which youngly thou bestow'st
Thou mayst call thine, when thou from youth convertest: 4
Herein lives wisdom, beauty, and increase,
Without this, folly, age, and cold decay:
If all were minded so, the times should cease,
And threescore year would make the world away.   8
Let those whom Nature hath not made for store,
Harsh, featureless, and rude, barrenly perish:
Look whom she best endowed she gave the more;
Which bounteous gift thou shouldst in bounty cherish: 12
    She carved thee for her seal, and meant thereby,
    Thou shouldst print more, not let that copy die.

12

When I do count the clock that tells the time,
And see the brave day sunk in hideous night,
When I behold the violet past prime,
And sable curls all silvered o'er with white,   4
When lofty trees I see barren of leaves,
Which erst from heat did canopy the herd,
And summer's green all girded up in sheaves
Borne on the bier with white and bristly beard: 8
Then of thy beauty do I question make
That thou among the wastes of time must go,
Since sweets and beauties do themselves forsake,
And die as fast as they see others grow,   12
    And nothing 'gainst Time's scythe can make defence
    Save breed to brave him when he takes thee hence.

Sonnet 11

1–3 grow'st . . . bestow'st] *Collier;* grow'st, . . . bestow'st, Q   6 this,] *Gildon²;* this Q   8 year] Q; yeares *Benson*   9 Nature] *Knight;* nature Q   11 Look] Q; Look, *Capell*   11 endowed] *Gildon²* (endow'd); indow'd, Q *(variant form)*   11 the] Q; thee *Sewell¹*, *Capell*   14 not] Q; nor *Murden*

Sonnet 12

4 all silvered o'er] *Malone;* or siluer'd ore Q; are silver'd o'er *J. Poole, 'English Parnassus' (1677), p. 473, Gildon²;* o'er-silverèd *conj. Anon (in Rollins);* o'er-silver'd all *conj. Verity;* ensilvered o'er *Wells;* o'er-silvered are *conj., this edn*   4 white,] *Rollins (1951);* white: Q   14 breed . . . him] *Ingram and Redpath;* breed . . . him, Q; Breed, . . . him *Gildon²*

13

O that you were your self! but, love, you are
No longer yours than you yourself here live;
Against this coming end you should prepare,
And your sweet semblance to some other give: 4
So should that beauty which you hold in lease
Find no determination; then you were
Your self again after yourself's decease,
When your sweet issue your sweet form should bear.   8
Who lets so fair a house fall to decay,
Which husbandry in honour might uphold
Against the stormy gusts of winter's day
And barren rage of death's eternal cold?   12
  O none but unthrifts: dear my love, you know
  You had a father, let your son say so.

14

Not from the stars do I my judgement pluck,
And yet methinks I have astronomy,
But not to tell of good or evil luck,
Of plagues, of dearths, or seasons' quality;   4
Nor can I fortune to brief minutes tell,
Pointing to each his thunder, rain, and wind,
Or say with princes if it shall go well
By oft predict that I in heaven find: 8
But from thine eyes my knowledge I derive,
And, constant stars, in them I read such art
As truth and beauty shall together thrive
If from thy self to store thou wouldst convert: 12
  Or else of thee this I prognosticate,
  Thy end is truth's and beauty's doom and date.

Sonnet 13
1 your self!] *Gildon*[2]*; your selfe,* Q*; yourself* Capell   1 but, love,] *Gildon;* but loue Q   6 determination;] *Gildon;* determination, Q   7 Your self] *Benson;* You selfe Q   13 unthrifts:] *Gildon*[2]*;* vnthrifts, Q   13 know] *Gildon*[2]*;* know, Q*;* know. *Boswell*

Sonnet 14
4 seasons'] *Capell;* seasons Q*;* season's *Dyce (1832)*   5 minutes] *Gildon;* mynuits Q *(variant form)*

33

15

When I consider every thing that grows
Holds in perfection but a little moment,
That this huge stage presenteth nought but shows
Whereon the stars in secret influence comment;   4
When I perceive that men as plants increase,
Cheerèd and checked even by the selfsame sky,
Vaunt in their youthful sap, at height decrease,
And wear their brave state out of memory: 8
Then the conceit of this inconstant stay
Sets you most rich in youth before my sight,
Where wasteful Time debateth with Decay
To change your day of youth to sullied night,   12
    And all in war with Time for love of you,
    As he takes from you, I ingraft you new.

16

But wherefore do not you a mightier way
Make war upon this bloody tyrant Time,
And fortify yourself in your decay
With means more blessèd than my barren rhyme?   4
Now stand you on the top of happy hours,
And many maiden gardens, yet unset,
With virtuous wish would bear your living flowers,
Much liker than your painted counterfeit: 8
So should the lines of life that life repair
Which this time's pencil or my pupil pen
Neither in inward worth nor outward fair
Can make you live yourself in eyes of men: 12
    To give away yourself keeps yourself still,
    And you must live drawn by your own sweet skill.

Sonnet 15

1 every thing] Q; everything *Hazlitt*   2 moment,] *Malone*[1]; moment. Q; Moment; *Gildon*   6 selfsame] *Knight;* selfe-same Q   6 sky,] *Gildon*[1]; skie: Q   8 wear] *Gildon;* were Q   11 Time] *Dyce;* time Q   11 Decay] *Dyce;* decay Q   14 ingraft] Q; engraft *Capell (variant form)*

Sonnet 16

2 Time] *Malone;* time Q   6 gardens,] *Capell;* gardens Q   10 this time's . . . pen] *Rolfe (subst.);* this (Times pensel or my pupill pen) Q; this (Time's pencil) or . . . Pen *Sewell*[2]; this, – time's pencil, or . . . pen, – *Capell;* this, Time's pencil, or . . . pen, *Malone*   11 fair] *Gildon*[2]; faire Q   14 skill.] *Benson;* skill, Q

17

Who will believe my verse in time to come
If it were filled with your most high deserts?
Though yet, heaven knows, it is but as a tomb
Which hides your life, and shows not half your parts. 4
If I could write the beauty of your eyes,
And in fresh numbers number all your graces,
The age to come would say, 'This poet lies;
Such heavenly touches ne'er touched earthly faces.' 8
So should my papers (yellowed with their age)
Be scorned, like old men of less truth than tongue,
And your true rights be termed a poet's rage
And stretchèd metre of an àntique song: 12
    But were some child of yours alive that time,
    You should live twice, in it and in my rhyme.

18

Shall I compare thee to a summer's day?
Thou art more lovely and more temperate:
Rough winds do shake the darling buds of May,
And summer's lease hath all too short a date; 4
Sometime too hot the eye of heaven shines,
And often is his gold complexion dimmed;
And every fair from fair sometime declines,
By chance or nature's changing course untrimmed: 8
But thy eternal summer shall not fade,
Nor lose possession of that fair thou ow'st,
Nor shall Death brag thou wand'rest in his shade,
When in eternal lines to time thou grow'st. 12
    So long as men can breathe or eyes can see,
    So long lives this, and this gives life to thee.

Sonnet 17

2 filled] *Gildon* (fill'd*); fild Q 2–4 deserts? . . . parts.] *Gildon;* deserts? . . . parts: Q; deserts − . . . parts − *Tucker*
3 yet, . . . knows,] *Gildon*[2]; yet . . . knows Q 7–8 'This . . . lies; . . . faces.'] *As pointed and quoted, Collier;*
this . . . lies, . . . faces. Q 9 yellowed] *Gildon* (yellow'd*); yellowed Q 12 metre] *Gildon;* miter Q *(variant
form)* 14 twice, in it] *Cam.;* Twice in it, Q; twice, − in it *Capell;* twice; in it *Globe*

Sonnet 18

18] *This sonnet omitted by Benson through Evans (except Lintott)* 7 sometime] *Lintott;* some-time Q; sometimes
Hudson 10 lose] *Capell;* loose Q *(variant form)* 10, 12 ow'st . . . grow'st] Q; owest . . . growest *Malone;*
owest . . . grow'st *Cam.* 11 Death] *Knight;* death Q 11 wand'rest] *Wyndham;* wandr'st Q; wander'st *Capell*
13 breathe] *Malone;* breath Q *(variant form)* 14 thee.] *Benson;* thee, Q

19

Devouring Time, blunt thou the lion's paws,
And make the earth devour her own sweet brood;
Pluck the keen teeth from the fierce tiger's jaws,
And burn the long-lived phoenix in her blood;   4
Make glad and sorry seasons as thou fleet'st,
And do whate'er thou wilt, swift-footed Time,
To the wide world and all her fading sweets;
But I forbid thee one most heinous crime: 8
O carve not with thy hours my love's fair brow,
Nor draw no lines there with thine àntique pen;
Him in thy course untainted do allow
For beauty's pattern to succeeding men.   12
      Yet do thy worst, old Time: despite thy wrong,
      My love shall in my verse ever live young.

20

A woman's face with Nature's own hand painted
Hast thou, the master–mistress of my passion;
A woman's gentle heart, but not acquainted
With shifting change, as is false women's fashion;   4
An eye more bright than theirs, less false in rolling,
Gilding the object whereupon it gazeth;
A man in hue, all hues in his controlling,
Which steals men's eyes and women's souls amazeth.   8
And for a woman wert thou first created,
Till Nature as she wrought thee fell a-doting,
And by addition me of thee defeated,
By adding one thing to my purpose nothing.   12
      But since she pricked thee out for women's pleasure,
      Mine be thy love, and thy love's use their treasure.

Sonnet 19

19] *This sonnet omitted by Benson through Evans (except Lintott)*   1   Time] *Malone;* time Q   3   jaws] *Capell;* yawes Q
4   long-lived] *Capell;* long liu'd Q   5   fleet'st] Q; fleets *Dyce (1832)*   6   Time] *Malone;* time Q   13   Time:]
Malone (after Capell time;*);* Time Q

Sonnet 20

1   Nature's] *Dyce;* natures Q   2   Hast] *Benson;* Haste Q   2   master-mistress] *Capell;* Master Mistris Q; Master,
Mistress *Gildon*   5   rolling,] *Sewell¹;* rowling: Q   7   man in] Q; maiden *conj. Beeching;* native *conj. Mackail
(in Beeching);* woman's *conj. Pooler;* maid in *conj. Tannenbaum (in Rollins)*   7   hue,] *Capell;* hew Q   7   hues]
Malone; Hews Q; 'hues' *Globe;* hearts *conj. Pooler*   10   Nature] *Knight;* nature Q   10   a-doting] *Malone;* a dotinge
Q   12   nothing] Q; no thing *conj. Tucker*

21

So is it not with me as with that Muse,
Stirred by a painted beauty to his verse,
Who heaven itself for ornament doth use,
And every fair with his fair doth rehearse,   4
Making a couplement of proud compare
With sun and moon, with earth and sea's rich gems,
With April's first-born flowers, and all things rare
That heaven's air in this huge rondure hems.   8
O let me, true in love, but truly write,
And then believe me, my love is as fair
As any mother's child, though not so bright
As those gold candles fixed in heaven's air: 12
    Let them say more that like of hearsay well,
    I will not praise that purpose not to sell.

22

My glass shall not persuade me I am old,
So long as youth and thou are of one date,
But when in thee time's furrows I behold,
Then look I death my days should expiate: 4
For all that beauty that doth cover thee
Is but the seemly raiment of my heart,
Which in thy breast doth live, as thine in me.
How can I then be elder than thou art?   8
O therefore, love, be of thyself so wary
As I not for myself but for thee will,
Bearing thy heart, which I will keep so chary
As tender nurse her babe from faring ill: 12
    Presume not on thy heart when mine is slain;
    Thou gav'st me thine, not to give back again.

Sonnet 21

3 itself] *Capell;* it selfe Q *(so throughout; not hereafter recorded)*   6 sea's] *Gildon²;* seas Q*;* seas' *conj., this edn*
6 gems,] *Sewell¹;* gems: Q   7 first-born] *Gildon;* first borne Q   9 me, . . . love,] *Gildon²;* me . . . loue Q

Sonnet 22

3 furrows] *Benson* (forrowes), *Lintott;* forrwes Q *(variant form);* Sorrows *Gildon*   4 expiate:] *Ingram and Redpath;*
expiate, Q*;* expirate. *conj. Steevens* (in *Malone*)   9 therefore, love,] *Sewell¹;* therefore loue Q*;* therefore, Love!
Gildon²

23

As an unperfect actor on the stage,
Who with his fear is put besides his part,
Or some fierce thing replete with too much rage,
Whose strength's abundance weakens his own heart;   4
So I, for fear of trust, forget to say
The perfect ceremony of love's rite,
And in mine own love's strength seem to decay,
O'ercharged with burthen of mine own love's might: 8
O let my looks be then the eloquence
And dumb presagers of my speaking breast,
Who plead for love, and look for recompense,
More than that tongue that more hath more expressed.   12
   O learn to read what silent love hath writ:
   To hear with eyes belongs to love's fine wit.

24

Mine eye hath played the painter and hath stelled
Thy beauty's form in table of my heart;
My body is the frame wherein 'tis held,
And pèrspective it is best painter's art,   4
For through the painter must you see his skill
To find where your true image pictured lies,
Which in my bosom's shop is hanging still,
That hath his windows glazèd with thine eyes.   8
Now see what good turns eyes for eyes have done:
Mine eyes have drawn thy shape, and thine for me
Are windows to my breast, wherethrough the sun
Delights to peep, to gaze therein on thee.   12
   Yet eyes this cunning want to grace their art,
   They draw but what they see, know not the heart.

Sonnet 23
6 rite] *Malone;* right Q 8 burthen] Q*; burden Gildon² (variant form)* 9 looks] *Sewell;* books Q 14 with . . . wit] *Benson;* wit . . . wiht Q

Sonnet 24
1 stelled] *Capell (*stell'd*);* steeld Q 3 'tis] *Lintott;* ti's Q 4 painter's] *Gildon;* Painters Q; painters' *conj., this edn*
4 art,] *Dowden;* art. Q 9 good turns] *Gildon;* good-turnes Q 11 wherethrough] *Gildon²;* where-through Q
12 thee.] *Gildon;* thee Q 13 art,] *Gildon;* art Q; art; – *Capell*

38

25

Let those who are in favour with their stars
Of public honour and proud titles boast,
Whilst I, whom fortune of such triumph bars,
Unlooked for joy in that I honour most.   4
Great princes' favourites their fair leaves spread
But as the marigold at the sun's eye,
And in themselves their pride lies burièd,
For at a frown they in their glory die.   8
The painful warrior famousèd for fight,
After a thousand victories once foiled,
Is from the book of honour rasèd quite,
And all the rest forgot for which he toiled: 12
      Then happy I that love and am belovèd
      Where I may not remove, nor be removèd.

26

Lord of my love, to whom in vassalage
Thy merit hath my duty strongly knit,
To thee I send this written ambassage
To witness duty, not to show my wit;   4
Duty so great, which wit so poor as mine
May make seem bare, in wanting words to show it,
But that I hope some good conceit of thine
In thy soul's thought (all naked) will bestow it,   8
Till whatsoever star that guides my moving
Points on me graciously with fair aspèct,
And puts apparel on my tottered loving,
To show me worthy of thy sweet respect: 12
      Then may I dare to boast how I do love thee,
      Till then, not show my head where thou mayst prove me.

Sonnet 25
9 famousèd for fight] *Conj. Theobald, Malone;* famosed for worth Q; famoused for might *Capell;* for worth famoused *conj. Steevens (in Malone)*   11 rasèd quite] Q; razed quite *Benson;* raised forth *conj. Theobald (if* worth *is retained in 9);* quite rased *conj. Steevens (in Malone);* razed forth *Collier*   13–14 belovèd . . . removèd] Q; belov'd . . . remov'd *Malone²*

Sonnet 26
2 knit,] *Capell;* knit; Q   3 ambassage] Q; Embassage *Gildon² (variant form)*   6 it,] *Collier;* it; Q   8 it,] *Ingram and Redpath;* it: Q   11 tottered] *Gildon² (totter'd);* tottered Q; tattered *Sewell¹;* tatter'd *Sewell² (variant forms)*   12 thy] *Capell;* their Q   14 me.] *Benson;* me Q

39

27

Weary with toil, I haste me to my bed,
The dear repose for limbs with travel tired,
But then begins a journey in my head
To work my mind, when body's work's expired;   4
For then my thoughts (from far where I abide)
Intend a zealous pilgrimage to thee,
And keep my drooping eyelids open wide,
Looking on darkness which the blind do see;   8
Save that my soul's imaginary sight
Presents thy shadow to my sightless view,
Which like a jewel (hung in ghastly night)
Makes black night beauteous, and her old face new.   12
 Lo thus by day my limbs, by night my mind,
 For thee, and for myself, no quiet find.

28

How can I then return in happy plight
That am debarred the benefit of rest?
When day's oppression is not eased by night,
But day by night and night by day oppressed;   4
And each (though enemies to either's reign)
Do in consent shake hands to torture me,
The one by toil, the other to complain
How far I toil, still farther off from thee.   8
I tell the day to please him thou art bright,
And dost him grace when clouds do blot the heaven;
So flatter I the swart-complexioned night,
When sparkling stars twire not thou gild'st the even: 12
 But day doth daily draw my sorrows longer,
 And night doth nightly make griefs' length seem stronger.

Sonnet 27

2 travel] *Gildon²;* trauaill Q 2 tired] *Malone²* (tir'd*)*; tired Q 4 expired;] *Malone²* (expir'd:*)*; expired. Q
6 thee,] Q *corr.;* thee; Q *uncorr.* 10 thy] *Capell;* their Q 11 Which . . . jewel (hung . . . night)] Q; Which, . . . jewel hung . . . night, *Capell*

Sonnet 28

5 either's] *Malone;* ethers Q; others *Benson;* other's *Gildon²* 9 day . . . him] Q (Day); day . . . him *Capell;* day, . . . him, *Malone* 11 swart-complexioned] *Gildon;* swart complexiond Q 12 gild'st] *Gildon²* (guild'st*)*; guil'st Q; gildest *conj. Pooler (preserving* Q th'*)* 12 the] *Sewell (after Lintott* the'*)*; th' Q 13–14 longer, . . . length . . . stronger] Q; longer . . . strength . . . stronger *Capell;* stronger . . . length . . . longer *conj. Capell (in Malone)*
14 griefs'] *This edn;* greefes Q; Grief's *Gildon* 14 stronger.] *Lintott;* stronger Q

29

When in disgrace with Fortune and men's eyes,
I all alone beweep my outcast state,
And trouble deaf heaven with my bootless cries,
And look upon myself and curse my fate,   4
Wishing me like to one more rich in hope,
Featured like him, like him with friends possessed,
Desiring this man's art, and that man's scope,
With what I most enjoy contented least;   8
Yet in these thoughts myself almost despising,
Haply I think on thee, and then my state
(Like to the lark at break of day arising
From sullen earth) sings hymns at heaven's gate;   12
    For thy sweet love rememb'red such wealth brings
    That then I scorn to change my state with kings.

30

When to the sessions of sweet silent thought
I summon up remembrance of things past,
I sigh the lack of many a thing I sought,
And with old woes new wail my dear time's waste;   4
Then can I drown an eye (unused to flow)
For precious friends hid in death's dateless night,
And weep afresh love's long since cancelled woe,
And moan th'expense of many a vanished sight;   8
Then can I grieve at grievances foregone,
And heavily from woe to woe tell o'er
The sad account of fore-bemoanèd moan,
Which I new pay as if not paid before: 12
    But if the while I think on thee (dear friend)
    All losses are restored, and sorrows end.

Sonnet 29
4 fate,] *Malone;* fate. Q   **10–12** state . . . earth*)*] *Malone (after Capell);* state, *(*Like . . . arising*)* . . . earth Q*;*
State, Like . . . Lark, . . . arising From . . . Earth, *Gildon²;* state, Like . . . day, arising From . . . earth, *Tucker*
13 rememb'red] Q*;* remember'd *Capell*   **14** kings] Q*;* kings' *Wells*

Sonnet 30
4 time's] *Gildon²;* times Q*;* times' *Dyce (1832)*   **7** afresh] *Gildon²;* a fresh Q   **8** sight] Q*;* sigh *conj. Malone¹*

31

Thy bosom is endearèd with all hearts,
Which I by lacking have supposèd dead,
And there reigns love and all love's loving parts,
And all those friends which I thought burièd. 4
How many a holy and obsequious tear
Hath dear religious love stol'n from mine eye,
As interest of the dead, which now appear
But things removed that hidden in thee lie! 8
Thou art the grave where buried love doth live,
Hung with the trophies of my lovers gone,
Who all their parts of me to thee did give;
That due of many now is thine alone. 12
    Their images I loved I view in thee,
    And thou (all they) hast all the all of me.

32

If thou survive my well-contented day,
When that churl Death my bones with dust shall cover,
And shalt by fortune once more re-survey
These poor rude lines of thy deceasèd lover, 4
Compare them with the bett'ring of the time,
And though they be outstripped by every pen,
Reserve them for my love, not for their rhyme,
Exceeded by the height of happier men. 8
O then vouchsafe me but this loving thought:
'Had my friend's Muse grown with this growing age,
A dearer birth than this his love had brought
To march in ranks of better equipage: 12
    But since he died, and poets better prove,
    Theirs for their style I'll read, his for his love.'

Sonnet 31
1 endearèd] *Capell;* indeared Q *(variant form)* 3 love . . . love's] *Murden;* Loue . . . Loues Q 8 thee lie!] *Gildon;* there lie. Q 9 Thou] Q *(but Q catchword is* To*)* 11 give;] *Sewell¹, Malone;* giue, Q

Sonnet 32
1 well-contented] *Gildon²;* well contented Q 2 Death] *Ewing;* death Q 3 re-survey] *Lintott, Gildon;* resuruay: Q 4 lover,] *Malone;* Louer: Q 9 vouchsafe] *Benson;* voutsafe Q *(variant form)* 10–14 'Had . . . love.'] *Quoted, Malone;* Had . . . loue. Q

33

Full many a glorious morning have I seen
Flatter the mountain tops with sovereign eye,
Kissing with golden face the meadows green,
Gilding pale streams with heavenly alcumy,   4
Anon permit the basest clouds to ride
With ugly rack on his celestial face,
And from the fòrlorn world his visage hide,
Stealing unseen to west with this disgrace: 8
Even so my sun one early morn did shine
With all triumphant splendour on my brow;
But out alack, he was but one hour mine,
The region cloud hath masked him from me now.   12
　　Yet him for this my love no whit disdaineth:
　　Suns of the world may stain, when heaven's sun staineth.

34

Why didst thou promise such a beauteous day,
And make me travel forth without my cloak,
To let base clouds o'ertake me in my way,
Hiding thy brav'ry in their rotten smoke?   4
'Tis not enough that through the cloud thou break,
To dry the rain on my storm-beaten face,
For no man well of such a salve can speak,
That heals the wound, and cures not the disgrace: 8
Nor can thy shame give physic to my grief;
Though thou repent, yet I have still the loss:
Th'offender's sorrow lends but weak relief
To him that bears the strong offence's cross.   12
　　Ah, but those tears are pearl which thy love sheeds,
　　And they are rich, and ransom all ill deeds.

Sonnet 33
3 green,] *Sewell*[1]*;* greene; Q　4 alcumy,] *Conj. Lowell (*alchemy,*) (in Rollins)*; alcumy: Q; alchymy: *Capell (variant forms)*　7 fòrlorn] *Gildon;* for-lorne Q　10 all triumphant] Q; all-triumphant *conj. Walker (in Rollins)*　11 But out alack,] Q; But out, alack! *Gildon*[2]*;* But out! alack! *Knight;* But, out, alack! *Dowden*　14 staineth] *Benson;* stainteh Q

Sonnet 34
2 travel] *Gildon*[2]*;* trauaile Q　4 smoke?] *Gildon*[2]*;* smoke. Q　9 grief;] *Ewing;* griefe, Q　10, 12 loss . . . cross] *Capell;* losse . . . losse Q; Cross . . . Cross *Sewell*[2]　13 sheeds] Q; sheds *Gildon (variant form)*

35

No more be grieved at that which thou hast done:
Roses have thorns, and silver fountains mud,
Clouds and eclipses stain both moon and sun,
And loathsome canker lives in sweetest bud.   4
All men make faults, and even I in this,
Authòrising thy trespass with compare,
Myself corrupting salving thy amiss,
Excusing thy sins more than their sins are;   8
For to thy sensual fault I bring in sense –
Thy adverse party is thy advocate –
And 'gainst myself a lawful plea commence:
Such civil war is in my love and hate   12
    That I an àccessary needs must be
    To that sweet thief which sourly robs from me.

36

Let me confess that we two must be twain,
Although our undivided loves are one:
So shall those blots that do with me remain,
Without thy help, by me be borne alone.   4
In our two loves there is but one respect,
Though in our lives a separable spite,
Which though it alter not love's sole effect,
Yet doth it steal sweet hours from love's delight.   8
I may not evermore acknowledge thee,
Lest my bewailèd guilt should do thee shame,
Nor thou with public kindness honour me,
Unless thou take that honour from thy name: 12
    But do not so; I love thee in such sort,
    As thou being mine, mine is thy good report.

Sonnet 35
8 Excusing] Q; Accusing *conj., this edn*   8 thy . . . their] *Wyndham;* their . . . their Q; thy . . . thy *Capell;* their . . . thy *Bullen;* thee . . . thy *conj. Beeching*   9–10 sense– . . . advocate–] *Malone (subst.);* sence, . . . Aduocate, Q   14 me.] *Benson;* me, Q

Sonnet 36
9 evermore] *Gildon;* ever-more Q; ever more *conj. Walker (in Rollins)*   13 so;] *Capell;* so, Q

37

As a decrepit father takes delight
To see his active child do deeds of youth,
So I, made lame by Fortune's dearest spite,
Take all my comfort of thy worth and truth;   4
For whether beauty, birth, or wealth, or wit,
Or any of these all, or all, or more,
Intitled in thy parts, do crownèd sit,
I make my love ingrafted to this store: 8
So then I am not lame, poor, nor despised,
Whilst that this shadow doth such substance give,
That I in thy abundance am sufficed,
And by a part of all thy glory live: 12
    Look what is best, that best I wish in thee;
    This wish I have, then ten times happy me.

38

How can my Muse want subject to invent
While thou dost breathe, that pour'st into my verse
Thine own sweet argument, too excellent
For every vulgar paper to rehearse?   4
O give thyself the thanks if aught in me
Worthy perusal stand against thy sight,
For who's so dumb that cannot write to thee,
When thou thyself dost give invention light?   8
Be thou the tenth Muse, ten times more in worth
Than those old nine which rhymers invocate,
And he that calls on thee, let him bring forth
Eternal numbers to outlive long date.   12
    If my slight Muse do please these curious days,
    The pain be mine, but thine shall be the praise.

Sonnet 37
6 more,] *Gildon*²*; more Q   7 Intitled] Q*; Entitled *Malone (variant form)*   7 thy] *Capell;* their Q   7 parts,] Q*; parts *Malone*   8 ingrafted] Q*; engrafted *Capell (variant form)*

Sonnet 38
2 breathe,] *Gildon*²*; breath Q *(variant form)*   4 rehearse?] *Gildon*²*; rehearse: Q   7 dumb] Q*; dull *Gildon*

39

O how thy worth with manners may I sing,
When thou art all the better part of me?
What can mine own praise to mine own self bring?
And what is't but mine own when I praise thee?   4
Even for this, let us divided live,
And our dear love lose name of single one,
That by this separation I may give
That due to thee which thou deserv'st alone.   8
O absence, what a torment wouldst thou prove,
Were it not thy sour leisure gave sweet leave
To entertain the time with thoughts of love,
Which time and thoughts so sweetly dost deceive,   12
    And that thou teachest how to make one twain,
    By praising him here who doth hence remain.

40

Take all my loves, my love, yea, take them all;
What hast thou then more than thou hadst before?
No love, my love, that thou mayst true love call;
All mine was thine, before thou hadst this more.   4
Then if for my love thou my love receivest,
I cannot blame thee for my love thou usest;
But yet be blamed, if thou this self deceivest
By wilful taste of what thy self refusest.   8
I do forgive thy robb'ry, gentle thief,
Although thou steal thee all my poverty;
And yet love knows it is a greater grief
To bear love's wrong than hate's known injury.   12
    Lascivious grace, in whom all ill well shows,
    Kill me with spites, yet we must not be foes.

Sonnet 39
3 bring?] *Gildon;* bring; Q   4 thee?] *Lintott;* thee, Q   6 lose] *Gildon;* loose Q *(variant form)*   7 give] *Lintott, Gildon²;* giue: Q   12 dost] Q; doth *Malone;* do *conj. Boswell*   12 deceive,] *Malone (subst.);* deceiue. Q

Sonnet 40
6 thee] *Knight;* thee, Q   7 this self] Q; thy self *Gildon*   8 thy self] Q; thy sense *conj. Ingram and Redpath*
11 yet . . . knows] Q; yet . . . knows, *Capell;* yet, . . . knows, *Knight;* yet, . . . knows *Craig*

41

Those pretty wrongs that liberty commits,
When I am sometime absent from thy heart,
Thy beauty and thy years full well befits,
For still temptation follows where thou art.   4
Gentle thou art, and therefore to be won,
Beauteous thou art, therefore to be assailed;
And when a woman woos, what woman's son
Will sourly leave her till he have prevailed?   8
Ay me, but yet thou mightst my seat forbear,
And chide thy beauty and thy straying youth,
Who lead thee in their riot even there
Where thou art forced to break a twofold truth: 12
    Hers, by thy beauty tempting her to thee,
    Thine, by thy beauty being false to me.

42

That thou hast her, it is not all my grief,
And yet it may be said I loved her dearly;
That she hath thee is of my wailing chief,
A loss in love that touches me more nearly.   4
Loving offenders, thus I will excuse ye:
Thou dost love her because thou know'st I love her,
And for my sake even so doth she abuse me,
Suff'ring my friend for my sake to approve her.   8
If I lose thee, my loss is my love's gain,
And losing her, my friend hath found that loss;
Both find each other, and I lose both twain,
And both for my sake lay on me this cross.   12
    But here's the joy, my friend and I are one.
    Sweet flattery! then she loves but me alone.

Sonnet 41

2 sometime] Q *(some-time);* sometimes *Benson*   6   assailed;] *Malone (*assail'd*; after Sewell'* assailed;*); *assailed. Q
8   he] Q*; she conj. Tyrwhitt, Malone*   8   prevailed?] *Malone (*prevail'd? *after Gildon* prevailed?*);* preuailed. Q
9   Ay] *Gildon;* Aye Q*;* Ah *Murden*   9   mightst] *Benson;* mighst Q

Sonnet 42

9, 11 lose] *Gildon;* loose Q *(variant form)*   10   losing] *Gildon;* loosing Q *(variant form)*   13   one.] *Capell (subst.);*
one, Q   14   flattery! then] *Ewing;* flattery, then Q*;* flattery then! *Tucker*

43

When most I wink, then do mine eyes best see,
For all the day they view things unrespected;
But when I sleep, in dreams they look on thee,
And darkly bright, are bright in dark directed.   4
Then thou, whose shadow shadows doth make bright,
How would thy shadow's form form happy show
To the clear day with thy much clearer light,
When to unseeing eyes thy shade shines so!   8
How would (I say) mine eyes be blessèd made,
By looking on thee in the living day,
When in dead night thy fair imperfect shade
Through heavy sleep on sightless eyes doth stay!   12
    All days are nights to see till I see thee,
    And nights bright days when dreams do show thee me.

44

If the dull substance of my flesh were thought,
Injurious distance should not stop my way,
For then despite of space I would be brought,
From limits far remote, where thou dost stay.   4
No matter then although my foot did stand
Upon the farthest earth removed from thee,
For nimble thought can jump both sea and land
As soon as think the place where he would be.   8
But ah, thought kills me that I am not thought,
To leap large lengths of miles when thou art gone,
But that, so much of earth and water wrought,
I must attend time's leisure with my moan,   12
    Receiving nought by elements so slow
    But heavy tears, badges of either's woe.

Sonnet 43

43] *This sonnet omitted by Benson through Evans (except Lintott)*   6 form form] *Capell;* forme, forme Q   8 so!]
Knight; so? Q   11 thy] *Capell;* their Q   12 stay!] *Dyce;* stay? Q   14 me.] *Lintott;* me, Q

Sonnet 44

11–12 that, . . . attend] *Capell;* that . . . attend, Q; that . . . attend *Lintott*   12 moan,] *Neilson;* mone. Q
13 nought] *Gildon²* (after *Gildon¹* Naught); naughts Q   14 woe.] Q; woe: *Malone²*

45

The other two, slight air and purging fire,
Are both with thee, wherever I abide;
The first my thought, the other my desire,
These present-absent with swift motion slide,   4
For when these quicker elements are gone
In tender embassy of love to thee,
My life, being made of four, with two alone
Sinks down to death, oppressed with melancholy,   8
Until life's composition be recured
By those swift messengers returned from thee,
Who even but now come back again assured
Of thy fair health, recounting it to me.   12
    This told, I joy, but then no longer glad,
    I send them back again and straight grow sad.

46

Mine eye and heart are at a mortal war,
How to divide the conquest of thy sight:
Mine eye my heart thy picture's sight would bar,
My heart mine eye the freedom of that right.   4
My heart doth plead that thou in him dost lie
(A closet never pierced with crystal eyes),
But the defendant doth that plea deny,
And says in him thy fair appearance lies.   8
To 'cide this title is impanellèd
A quest of thoughts, all tenants to the heart,
And by their verdict is determinèd
The clear eye's moiety and the dear heart's part,   12
    As thus: mine eye's due is thy outward part,
    And my heart's right thy inward love of heart.

Sonnet 45

4   present-absent] *Malone;* present absent Q   5   For] Q; Forth *conj. Tucker;* So *Ingram and Redpath*
8   melancholy,] *Wells;* melancholic. Q; Melancholy; *Gildon²*   9   life's] *Gildon² (after Gildon¹* Live's*);* liues Q *(variant form)*   9   recured] *Boswell (*recur'd*);* recured Q   11   assured] *Boswell (*assur'd*);* assured Q   12   thy] *Gildon²,*
Capell; their Q

Sonnet 46

3   thy] *Capell;* their Q   4   freedom] *Benson (*freedome*);* freeedome Q   8   thy] *Capell;* their Q   9   'cide] *Gildon²;*
side Q   12   part,] *Sewell²;* part. Q   13   thus:] *Gildon¹ (subst.);* thus, Q   13   thy] *Capell;* their Q; thine *Malone²*
14   thy] *Capell;* their Q; thine *Malone²*

47

Betwixt mine eye and heart a league is took,
And each doth good turns now unto the other:
When that mine eye is famished for a look,
Or heart in love with sighs himself doth smother,   4
With my love's picture then my eye doth feast,
And to the painted banquet bids my heart;
Another time mine eye is my heart's guest,
And in his thoughts of love doth share a part.   8
So either by thy picture or my love,
Thyself, away, are present still with me,
For thou not farther than my thoughts canst move,
And I am still with them, and they with thee;   12
    Or if they sleep, thy picture in my sight
    Awakes my heart to heart's and eye's delight.

48

How careful was I, when I took my way,
Each trifle under truest bars to thrust,
That to my use it might un-usèd stay
From hands of falsehood, in sure wards of trust!   4
But thou, to whom my jewels trifles are,
Most worthy comfort, now my greatest grief,
Thou best of dearest, and mine only care,
Art left the prey of every vulgar thief.   8
Thee have I not locked up in any chest,
Save where thou art not, though I feel thou art,
Within the gentle closure of my breast,
From whence at pleasure thou mayst come and part;   12
    And even thence thou wilt be stol'n, I fear,
    For truth proves thievish for a prize so dear.

Sonnet 47

2 other:] *Gildon;* other, Q   4 smother,] *Capell;* smother; Q   7 Another] *Benson;* An other Q   10 Thyself,] *Capell;* Thy selfe Q *corr.;* Thy seife Q *uncorr.*   11 not] *Benson;* nor Q; no *Capell;* ne'er *(spelled* ner; *see OED* Ne'er *adv* 1*) conj., this edn*

Sonnet 48

3 un-usèd] Q; unused *Benson*   4 trust!] *Malone;* trust? Q

49

Against that time (if ever that time come)
When I shall see thee frown on my defècts,
Whenas thy love hath cast his utmost sum,
Called to that audit by advised respects;   4
Against that time when thou shalt strangely pass,
And scarcely greet me with that sun, thine eye,
When love converted from the thing it was
Shall reasons find of settled gravity: 8
Against that time do I insconce me here
Within the knowledge of mine own desert,
And this my hand against myself uprear,
To guard the lawful reasons on thy part.   12
    To leave poor me thou hast the strength of laws,
    Since why to love I can allege no cause.

50

How heavy do I journey on the way,
When what I seek (my weary travel's end)
Doth teach that ease and that repose to say,
'Thus far the miles are measured from thy friend.'   4
The beast that bears me, tirèd with my woe,
Plods dully on, to bear that weight in me,
As if by some instinct the wretch did know
His rider loved not speed being made from thee: 8
The bloody spur cannot provoke him on
That sometimes anger thrusts into his hide,
Which heavily he answers with a groan
More sharp to me than spurring to his side;   12
    For that same groan doth put this in my mind:
    My grief lies onward and my joy behind.

Sonnet 49

3 Whenas] *Gildon²;* When as Q   4 Called] *Benson (*Cald*);* Cauld Q   9 insconce] Q*;* ensconce *Malone (variant form)*   10 desert] *Gildon;* desart Q

Sonnet 50

2 travel's] *Gildon²;* trauels Q*;* travels' *Bell*   4 'Thus . . . friend.'] *Quoted, Malone;* Thus . . . friend. Q   6 dully] *Benson;* duly Q

51

Thus can my love excuse the slow offence
Of my dull bearer, when from thee I speed:
From where thou art, why should I haste me thence?
Till I return, of posting is no need.   4
O what excuse will my poor beast then find,
When swift extremity can seem but slow?
Then should I spur though mounted on the wind,
In wingèd speed no motion shall I know: 8
Then can no horse with my desire keep pace;
Therefore desire (of perfect'st love being made)
Shall neigh (no dull flesh) in his fiery race,
But love, for love, thus shall excuse my jade: 12
     Since from thee going he went wilful slow,
     Towards thee I'll run and give him leave to go.

52

So am I as the rich whose blessèd key
Can bring him to his sweet up-lockèd treasure,
The which he will not ev'ry hour survey,
For blunting the fine point of seldom pleasure.   4
Therefore are feasts so solemn and so rare,
Since, seldom coming, in the long year set,
Like stones of worth they thinly placèd are,
Or captain jewels in the carcanet.   8
So is the time that keeps you as my chest,
Or as the wardrobe which the robe doth hide,
To make some special instant special blest,
By new unfolding his imprisoned pride.   12
     Blessèd are you whose worthiness gives scope,
     Being had, to triumph, being lacked, to hope.

Sonnet 51

2 speed:] *Malone (after Gildon);* speed, Q   3 thence?] *Gildon;* thence, Q   6 slow?] *Gildon;* slow, Q
10 perfect'st] *Dyce;* perfects Q; perfect *Gildon*   11 neigh (no dull flesh)] *Malone;* naigh noe dull flesh Q; need no
dull Flesh *Gildon²;* neigh to dull flesh, *conj. Malone;* neigh, no dull flesh *Dowden;* neigh – no dull flesh *Tucker;* wait no dull
flesh *conj. Bulloch (in Rollins);* weigh no dull flesh *conj. G. C. M. Smith (in Rollins);* rein no dull flesh *Wells (conj. Gary
Taylor)*   11 race,] Q; race; *Malone;* race – *Tucker*   12 But love, for love,] Q; But Love for Love *Gildon²;* But,
love for love, *Tucker*   12 jade:] *Gildon²;* iade, Q   13 wilful slow] Q; wilful-slow *Malone²*

Sonnet 52

8 carcanet] *Capell;* carconet Q   10 wardrobe] *Benson;* ward-robe Q   14 had, . . . lacked,] *Capell (lack'd);* had . . .
lackt Q

53

What is your substance, whereof are you made,
That millions of strange shadows on you tend,
Since every one hath, every one, one shade,
And you, but one, can every shadow lend?   4
Describe Adonis, and the counterfeit
Is poorly imitated after you;
On Helen's cheek all art of beauty set,
And you in Grecian tires are painted new;   8
Speak of the spring and foison of the year:
The one doth shadow of your beauty show,
The other as your bounty doth appear,
And you in every blessèd shape we know.   12
    In all external grace you have some part,
    But you like none, none you, for constant heart.

54

O how much more doth beauty beauteous seem
By that sweet ornament which truth doth give!
The rose looks fair, but fairer we it deem
For that sweet odour which doth in it live.   4
The canker blooms have full as deep a dye
As the perfumèd tincture of the roses,
Hang on such thorns, and play as wantonly,
When summer's breath their maskèd buds discloses;   8
But, for their virtue only is their show,
They live unwooed, and unrespected fade,
Die to themselves. Sweet roses do not so,
Of their sweet deaths are sweetest odours made: 12
    And so of you, beauteous and lovely youth,
    When that shall vade, by verse distils your truth.

Sonnet 53

2 tend,] *This edn;* tend? Q*;* tend; *Capell*   3 one hath,] *Malone;* one, hath Q   4 you,] *Capell;* you Q   4 lend?] *Gildon;* lend: Q   5 Adonis, . . . counterfeit] *Lintott; Adonis* . . . counterfet, Q

Sonnet 54

2 give!] *Gildon²;* giue, Q   9 But,] *Capell;* But Q   10 unwooed] Q *(vnwoo'd);* unmoov'd *Benson*   14 vade] Q*;* fade *Gildon (variant form)*   14 by] Q*;* my *Capell*

55

Not marble nor the gilded monuments
Of princes shall outlive this pow'rful rhyme,
But you shall shine more bright in these contènts
Than unswept stone, besmeared with sluttish time.   4
When wasteful war shall statues overturn,
And broils root out the work of masonry,
Nor Mars his sword nor war's quick fire shall burn
The living record of your memory.   8
'Gainst death and all oblivious enmity
Shall you pace forth; your praise shall still find room
Even in the eyes of all posterity
That wear this world out to the ending doom.   12
     So, till the Judgement that yourself arise,
     You live in this, and dwell in lovers' eyes.

56

Sweet love, renew thy force, be it not said
Thy edge should blunter be than appetite,
Which but today by feeding is allayed,
Tomorrow sharp'ned in his former might.   4
So, love, be thou: although today thou fill
Thy hungry eyes even till they wink with fullness,
Tomorrow see again, and do not kill
The spirit of love with a perpetual dullness: 8
Let this sad int'rim like the ocean be
Which parts the shore, where two contracted new
Come daily to the banks, that when they see
Return of love, more blest may be the view;   12
     As call it winter, which being full of care,
     Makes summer's welcome, thrice more wished, more rare.

Sonnet 55

1 monuments] *Malone;* monument, Q   7 Mars his] Q *(Mars);* Mars's *Gildon²*   9 all oblivious] Q; all-oblivious *Malone;* all oblivion's *conj. Ingram and Redpath*   9 enmity] *Gildon²;* emnity Q   10 forth;] *Gildon²;* forth, Q 13 Judgement] *Neilson²;* iudgement Q

Sonnet 56

56] *This sonnet omitted by Benson through Evans (except Lintott)*   4 sharp'ned] Q (sharpned); sharpen'd *Capell* 5 So, love,] *Capell;* So loue Q   5 thou:] *Capell;* thou, Q   9 int'rim] Q *(Intrim);* Interim / *Lintott*   11 see] *Capell;* see: Q   13 As] Q; Or *Capell, Malone;* Else *Palgrave;* Ah *conj. Anon. (in Rollins)*   14 welcome,] Q; welcome *Capell*

57

Being your slave, what should I do but tend
Upon the hours and times of your desire?
I have no precious time at all to spend,
Nor services to do till you require.   4
Nor dare I chide the world-without-end hour
Whilst I (my sovereign) watch the clock for you,
Nor think the bitterness of absence sour
When you have bid your servant once adieu.   8
Nor dare I question with my jealous thought
Where you may be, or your affairs suppose,
But like a sad slave stay and think of nought
Save where you are how happy you make those.   12
    So true a fool is love that in your will
    (Though you do any thing) he thinks no ill.

58

That god forbid, that made me first your slave,
I should in thought control your times of pleasure,
Or at your hand th'account of hours to crave,
Being your vassal bound to stay your leisure.   4
O let me suffer (being at your beck)
Th'imprisoned absence of your liberty,
And patience, tame to sufferance, bide each check,
Without accusing you of injury.   8
Be where you list, your charter is so strong
That you yourself may privilege your time
To what you will; to you it doth belong
Yourself to pardon of self-doing crime.   12
    I am to wait, though waiting so be hell,
    Not blame your pleasure, be it ill or well.

Sonnet 57

3   spend,] *Benson;* spend; Q   5   world-without-end] *Gildon²;* world without end Q   9   jealous] *Benson;* jealious Q *(variant form)*   12   are how] *Yale;* are, how Q; are: how *Gildon²*   13   will] *Murden;* Will Q

Sonnet 58

7   patience, tame to sufferance,] *Gildon²;* patience tame, to sufferance Q; patience tame to sufferance; *Capell;* patience-tame, to sufferance *Ingram and Redpath;* patience-tame to sufferance, *F. L. Lucas (in Ingram and Redpath)*   10–11 time / To] Q; time: / Do *Malone*   11   will;] *Gildon²;* will, Q

59

If there be nothing new, but that which is
Hath been before, how are our brains beguiled,
Which, labouring for invention, bear amiss
The second burthen of a former child!   4
O that recòrd could with a backward look,
Even of five hundred courses of the sun,
Show me your image in some àntique book,
Since mind at first in character was done,   8
That I might see what the old world could say
To this composèd wonder of your frame:
Whether we are mended, or whe'er better they,
Or whether revolution be the same.   12
    O sure I am the wits of former days
    To subjects worse have given admiring praise.

60

Like as the waves make towards the pebbled shore,
So do our minutes hasten to their end,
Each changing place with that which goes before,
In sequent toil all forwards do contend.   4
Nativity, once in the main of light,
Crawls to maturity, wherewith being crowned,
Crookèd eclipses 'gainst his glory fight,
And Time that gave doth now his gift confound.   8
Time doth transfix the flourish set on youth,
And delves the parallels in beauty's brow,
Feeds on the rarities of nature's truth,
And nothing stands but for his scythe to mow.   12
    And yet to times in hope my verse shall stand,
    Praising thy worth, despite his cruel hand.

Sonnet 59

1–2 is / Hath] *Gildon;* is, / Hath Q   4 burthen] Q; Burden *Gildon²* *(variant form)*   4 child!] *Knight;* child? Q
6 hundred] *Gildon;* hundreth Q *(variant form)*   8 mind] Q; mine *Benson*   8 done,] *Cellini;* done. Q; done!
Gildon²   10 frame:] *This edn;* frame, Q; Frame; *Gildon²*   11 Whether] Q; Whe'r *Craig*   11 whe'er] *Capell*
*(*whe'r*);* where Q; whether *Globe*

Sonnet 60

1 pebbled] *Murden;* pibled Q *(variant form)*   2 minutes] *Gildon;* minuites Q *(variant form)*   2 end,] Q; end;
Capell (after Gildon)   5 Nativity,] *Capell;* Natiuity Q   5 light,] *Lintott;* light. Q   8 Time] *Knight;* time Q
13 times in hope] *Capell;* times in hope, Q; Times, in hope, *Gildon²*

61

Is it thy will thy image should keep open
My heavy eyelids to the weary night?
Dost thou desire my slumbers should be broken,
While shadows like to thee do mock my sight?   4
Is it thy spirit that thou send'st from thee
So far from home into my deeds to pry,
To find out shames and idle hours in me,
The scope and tenure of thy jealousy?   8
O no, thy love, though much, is not so great;
It is my love that keeps mine eye awake,
Mine own true love that doth my rest defeat,
To play the watchman ever for thy sake.   12
    For thee watch I, whilst thou dost wake elsewhere,
    From me far off, with others all too near.

62

Sin of self-love possesseth all mine eye,
And all my soul, and all my every part;
And for this sin there is no remedy,
It is so grounded inward in my heart.   4
Methinks no face so gracious is as mine,
No shape so true, no truth of such account,
And for myself mine own worth do define,
As I all other in all worths surmount.   8
But when my glass shows me myself indeed,
Beated and chopped with tanned antiquity,
Mine own self-love quite contrary I read;
Self so self-loving were iniquity.   12
    'Tis thee (my self) that for myself I praise,
    Painting my age with beauty of thy days.

Sonnet 61

8   tenure] Q; tenour *Capell (variant form)*   14   off] *Gildon;* of Q   14   all too near] *Benson;* all to neere Q; all-too-near *Malone*

Sonnet 62

7   for . . . do] Q; for . . . so *conj. Walker (in Rollins), Delius;* so . . . do *conj. Lettsom (in Rollins);* for . . . to *Keightley;* I . . . so *conj. Beeching*   9   indeed,] *Gildon;* indeed Q   10   Beated] Q; 'Bated *Malone¹;* Batter'd *conj. Malone¹ (dropped in Malone²);* Blasted *conj. Steevens (in Malone);* Beaten *conj. Collier;* Bated *conj. Collier²*   10   chopped] Q (chopt); chapp'd *Dyce (variant form)*   11   own self-love] *Lintott;* owne selfe loue Q; ownself-love *conj. Tucker*   11   read;] *Capell;* read Q; read, *Gildon²*   12   self-loving] *Gildon;* selfe louing Q   13   'Tis] *Benson;* T'is Q   14   days.] *Benson;* daies, Q

57

63

Against my love shall be as I am now,
With Time's injurious hand crushed and o'erworn;
When hours have drained his blood and filled his brow
With lines and wrinkles; when his youthful morn   4
Hath travelled on to age's steepy night,
And all those beauties whereof now he's king
Are vanishing, or vanished out of sight,
Stealing away the treasure of his spring: 8
For such a time do I now fortify
Against confounding age's cruel knife,
That he shall never cut from memory
My sweet love's beauty, thought my lover's life.   12
       His beauty shall in these black lines be seen,
       And they shall live, and he in them still green.

64

When I have seen by Time's fell hand defaced
The rich proud cost of outworn buried age;
When sometime lofty towers I see down rased,
And brass eternal slave to mortal rage;   4
When I have seen the hungry ocean gain
Advantage on the kingdom of the shore,
And the firm soil win of the wat'ry main,
Increasing store with loss, and loss with store;   8
When I have seen such interchange of state,
Or state itself confounded to decay,
Ruin hath taught me thus to ruminate:
That Time will come and take my love away.   12
       This thought is as a death, which cannot choose
       But weep to have that which it fears to lose.

Sonnet 63

1 now,] *Gildon²;* now Q   2 Time's] *Knight;* times Q   2 o'erworn;] *Gildon²* (o'er-worn); ore-worne, Q
3 filled] *Lintott* (fill'd), *Gildon;* fild Q; filed *conj. Kerrigan*   4 wrinkles;] *Gildon²;* wrincles, Q   5 travelled]
Gildon² (travel'd); travaild Q *(variant form)*

Sonnet 64

1 Time's] *Malone;* times Q   1 defaced] *Gildon* (defac'd); defaced Q   3 down rased] *Gildon²* (down raz'd);
downe rased Q; down-ras'd *Malone*   11 ruminate:] *Capell* (ruminate, –); ruminate Q   14 lose] *Gildon²;* loose Q
(variant form)

65

Since brass, nor stone, nor earth, nor boundless sea,
But sad mortality o'ersways their power,
How with this rage shall beauty hold a plea,
Whose action is no stronger than a flower?   4
O how shall summer's honey breath hold out
Against the wrackful siege of batt'ring days,
When rocks impregnable are not so stout,
Nor gates of steel so strong, but Time decays?   8
O fearful meditation! Where, alack,
Shall Time's best jewel from Time's chest lie hid?
Or what strong hand can hold his swift foot back,
Or who his spoil of beauty can forbid?   12
     O none, unless this miracle have might,
     That in black ink my love may still shine bright.

66

Tired with all these, for restful death I cry:
As to behold desert a beggar born,
And needy nothing trimmed in jollity,
And purest faith unhappily forsworn,   4
And gilded honour shamefully misplaced,
And maiden virtue rudely strumpeted,
And right perfection wrongfully disgraced,
And strength by limping sway disablèd,   8
And art made tongue-tied by authority,
And folly (doctor-like) controlling skill,
And simple truth miscalled simplicity,
And captive good attending captain ill: 12
     Tired with all these, from these would I be gone,
     Save that to die, I leave my love alone.

Sonnet 65

5 honey] Q *(hunny)*; hungry *Benson*   6 wrackful] Q; wreckful *Gildon²* *(variant form)*   8 Time] *Dyce;* time Q
9 meditation!] *Gildon²;* meditation, Q   10 Time's . . . Time's] *Knight;* times . . . times Q   12 of] *Malone;* or
Q; on *Gildon;* o'er *Capell*

Sonnet 66

11 simple truth] *Gildon* (simple Truth*); simple-Truth Q   12 captive good] *Gildon²* (Captive Good*); captiue-good Q
12 captain ill] Q (Captaine ill*); captain-ill *or* Captian-Ill *conj. this edn (matching* Q captiue-good*)*

67

Ah wherefore with infection should he live,
And with his presence grace impiety,
That sin by him advantage should achieve,
And lace itself with his society?   4
Why should false painting imitate his cheek,
And steal dead seeming of his living hue?
Why should poor beauty indirectly seek
Roses of shadow, since his rose is true?   8
Why should he live, now Nature bankrout is,
Beggared of blood to blush through lively veins,
For she hath no exchequer now but his,
And proud of many, lives upon his gains? 12   12
    O him she stores, to show what wealth she had,
    In days long since, before these last so bad.

68

Thus is his cheek the map of days outworn,
When beauty lived and died as flowers do now,
Before these bastard signs of fair were borne,
Or durst inhabit on a living brow;   4
Before the golden tresses of the dead,
The right of sepulchres, were shorn away,
To live a second life on second head;
Ere beauty's dead fleece made another gay: 8
In him those holy àntique hours are seen,
Without all ornament, itself and true,
Making no summer of another's green,
Robbing no old to dress his beauty new;   12
    And him as for a map doth Nature store,
    To show false Art what beauty was of yore.

Sonnet 67

1 Ah] Q; Ah, *Capell*; Ah! *Malone*   6 steal dead seeming] *Capell*; steale dead seeing Q; steal, dead-seeing, *conj. Verity*   9 Nature] *Knight*; nature Q   9 bankrout] Q; bankrupt *Gildon (variant form)*   10–12 veins, . . . gains?] Q; Veins? . . . Gains. *Gildon*; veins; . . . gains? *Capell*   12 proud] Q; prov'd *Capell*; 'priv'd *or* poor *conj. Ridley*

Sonnet 68

2 died] *Benson* (dy'd); dy'ed Q   3 borne] Q; born *Gildon*   7 a second] *Benson*; a scond Q   7 head;] *Capell*; head, Q

69

Those parts of thee that the world's eye doth view
Want nothing that the thought of hearts can mend;
All tongues (the voice of souls) give thee that due,
Utt'ring bare truth, even so as foes commend.   4
Thy outward thus with outward praise is crowned,
But those same tongues that give thee so thine own,
In other accents do this praise confound
By seeing farther than the eye hath shown.   8
They look into the beauty of thy mind,
And that in guess they measure by thy deeds;
Then, churls, their thoughts (although their eyes were kind)
To thy fair flower add the rank smell of weeds: 12
    But why thy odour matcheth not thy show,
    The soil is this, that thou dost common grow.

70

That thou are blamed shall not be thy defect,
For slander's mark was ever yet the fair;
The ornament of beauty is suspèct,
A crow that flies in heaven's sweetest air.   4
So thou be good, slander doth but approve
Thy worth the greater, being wooed of time,
For canker vice the sweetest buds doth love,
And thou present'st a pure unstainèd prime.   8
Thou hast passèd by the ambush of young days,
Either not assailed, or victor being charged,
Yet this thy praise cannot be so thy praise
To tie up envy, evermore enlarged: 12   12
    If some suspèct of ill masked not thy show,
    Then thou alone kingdoms of hearts shouldst owe.

Sonnet 69

3 that due] *Capell;* that end Q; thy due *Gildon²*   5 Thy] *Gildon²;* Their Q; Thine *Malone²*   11 Then, churls, their] *Capell (subst.);* Then churls their Q; Then their churl *Gildon²;* Then churls, their *Pooler (with comma after thoughts)*   14 soil] *Benson* (soyle); soyle Q; Toil *Gildon;* solve *Malone;* sole *conj. Steevens (in Malone);* assoil *conj. Anon. (in Rollins), reading* The *as* Th'; sully *conj. Dover Wilson, reading* is *as* 's   14 dost] *Gildon;* doest Q

Sonnet 70

1 are] Q; art *Benson*   6 Thy] *Capell;* Their Q   6 wooed of time] Q (woo'd); woo'd oftime *MS. conj. (see Rollins);* wood oftime [*or* of time] *conj. Capell;* void of crime *conj. Malone¹;* weigh'd of time *conj. Delius;* woo'd of crime *conj. Staunton;* woo'd o' th' time *conj. Ingram and Redpath*   8 unstainèd] *Benson;* vnstayined Q   12 enlarged:] *Sewell¹* (inlarg'd;); inlarged, Q *(variant form)*

71

No longer mourn for me when I am dead
Than you shall hear the surly sullen bell
Give warning to the world that I am fled
From this vile world with vildest worms to dwell;   4
Nay, if you read this line, remember not
The hand that writ it, for I love you so
That I in your sweet thoughts would be forgot,
If thinking on me then should make you woe.   8
O if (I say) you look upon this verse,
When I (perhaps) compounded am with clay,
Do not so much as my poor name rehearse,
But let your love even with my life decay,   12
> Lest the wise world should look into your moan,
> And mock you with me after I am gone.

72

O lest the world should task you to recite
What merit lived in me that you should love,
After my death (dear love) forget me quite;
For you in me can nothing worthy prove,   4
Unless you would devise some virtuous lie
To do more for me than mine own desert,
And hang more praise upon deceasèd I
Than niggard truth would willingly impart: 8
O lest your true love may seem false in this,
That you for love speak well of me untrue,
My name be buried where my body is,
And live no more to shame nor me nor you: 12
> For I am shamed by that which I bring forth,
> And so should you, to love things nothing worth.

Sonnet 71

2   Than] *Malone;* Then Q; When *Sewell, Capell*   4   vildest] Q; vilest *Gildon (variant form)*   11   rehearse,] *Gildon²;* reherse; Q   12   decay,] *Globe;* decay. Q

Sonnet 72

2   love,] *Capell;* loue Q; love; *Gildon*   3   forget] *Benson;* for get Q   3   quite;] *Staunton;* quite, Q   4   prove,] *Staunton (subst.);* proue. Q; prove; *Malone (after Gildon²)*

73

That time of year thou mayst in me behold
When yellow leaves, or none, or few, do hang
Upon those boughs which shake against the cold,
Bare ruined choirs, where late the sweet birds sang.   4
In me thou seest the twilight of such day
As after sunset fadeth in the west,
Which by and by black night doth take away,
Death's second self, that seals up all in rest.   8
In me thou seest the glowing of such fire
That on the ashes of his youth doth lie,
As the death-bed whereon it must expire,
Consumed with that which it was nourished by.   12
  This thou perceiv'st, which makes thy love more strong,
  To love that well which thou must leave ere long.

74

But be contented when that fell arrest
Without all bail shall carry me away,
My life hath in this line some interest,
Which for memorial still with thee shall stay.   4
When thou reviewest this, thou dost review
The very part was consecrate to thee:
The earth can have but earth, which is his due;
My spirit is thine, the better part of me.   8
So then thou hast but lost the dregs of life,
The prey of worms, my body being dead,
The coward conquest of a wretch's knife,
Too base of thee to be remember'èd: 12
  The worth of that is that which it contains,
  And that is this, and this with thee remains.

Sonnet 73

1 year] *Benson (yeare)*; yeeare Q   2 none, or few,] *Capell*; none, or few Q; none or few, *Tucker*   4 Bare ruined choirs] *Malone (after* Bare ruin'd quires *in Benson)*; Bare rn'wd quiers Q; Barren'wed quiers *Lintott*; Barren'd of quires *Capell*   11 death-bed] *Benson (death bed)*; death bed, Q   14 long.] Q; long: *Malone*

Sonnet 74

1 contented] Q; contented: *Malone (retaining* Q *comma after* away *in* 2)   2 away,] Q; away; *Gildon²*   5 dost] *Benson;* doest Q   5 review] Q *(reuew)*; renew *conj. this edn*   12 remember'èd:] *Gildon² (remembered.)*; remembred, Q

63

75

So are you to my thoughts as food to life,
Or as sweet seasoned showers are to the ground;
And for the peace of you I hold such strife
As 'twixt a miser and his wealth is found: 4
Now proud as an enjoyer, and anon
Doubting the filching age will steal his treasure;
Now counting best to be with you alone,
Then bettered that the world may see my pleasure: 8
Sometime all full with feasting on your sight,
And by and by clean starvèd for a look;
Possessing or pursuing no delight
Save what is had or must from you be took.   12
      Thus do I pine and surfeit day by day,
      Or gluttoning on all, or all away.

76

Why is my verse so barren of new pride?
So far from variation or quick change?
Why with the time do I not glance aside
To new-found methods and to compounds strange?   4
Why write I still all one, ever the same,
And keep invention in a noted weed,
That every word doth almost tell my name,
Showing their birth, and where they did proceed?   8
O know, sweet love, I always write of you,
And you and love are still my argument;
So all my best is dressing old words new,
Spending again what is already spent: 12
      For as the sun is daily new and old,
      So is my love still telling what is told.

Sonnet 75

75] *This sonnet omitted by Benson through Evans (except Lintott)*   3   peace] Q; price *or* sake *conj. Malone;* prize *conj. Staunton;* piece *conj. Tucker*   5   enjoyer] *Capell;* inioyer Q *(variant form)*   10   look;] *Capell;* looke, Q   14   away.] *Lintott;* away, Q

Sonnet 76

76] *This sonnet omitted by Benson through Evans (except Lintott)*   4   new-found] *Capell;* new found Q   4, 8   strange? . . . proceed?] *The question marks fail to print in one copy of* Q *(see Rollins, II, 5)*   7   tell] *Capell;* fel Q; spell *conj. Nicholson (in Rollins)*   9   know, . . . love,] *Capell;* know . . . loue Q   14   told.] *Lintott;* told, Q

77

Thy glass will show thee how thy beauties wear,
Thy dial how thy precious minutes waste,
The vacant leaves thy mind's imprint will bear,
And of this book, this learning mayst thou taste: 4
The wrinkles which thy glass will truly show
Of mouthèd graves will give thee memory;
Thou by thy dial's shady stealth mayst know
Time's thievish progress to eternity;   8
Look what thy memory cannot contain
Commit to these waste blanks, and thou shalt find
Those children nursed, delivered from thy brain,
To take a new acquaintance of thy mind.   12
      These offices, so oft as thou wilt look,
      Shall profit thee, and much enrich thy book.

78

So oft have I invoked thee for my Muse,
And found such fair assistance in my verse,
As every alien pen hath got my use,
And under thee their poesy disperse.   4
Thine eyes, that taught the dumb on high to sing,
And heavy ignorance aloft to fly,
Have added feathers to the learnèd's wing
And given grace a double majesty.   8
Yet be most proud of that which I compile,
Whose influence is thine, and born of thee:
In others' works thou dost but mend the style,
And arts with thy sweet graces gracèd be;   12
      But thou art all my art, and dost advance
      As high as learning my rude ignorance.

Sonnet 77

1, 2 Thy] Q; The *conj. Ingram and Redpath*   1 wear] *Gildon²*; were Q   2 minutes] *Gildon*; mynuits Q *(variant form)*   3 The] Q; These *Capell*   10 blanks] *Conj. Theobald, Capell*; blacks Q   14 enrich] *Gentleman*; inrich Q *(variant form)*

Sonnet 78

3 alien] *Murden; Alien* Q   7 learnèd's] *Gildon;* learneds Q; learnedst *conj. Anon (in Rollins)*   10 born] *Gildon*; borne Q *(variant form)*

79

Whilst I alone did call upon thy aid,
My verse alone had all thy gentle grace,
But now my gracious numbers are decayed,
And my sick Muse doth give another place.   4
I grant (sweet love) thy lovely argument
Deserves the travail of a worthier pen,
Yet what of thee thy poet doth invent
He robs thee of, and pays it thee again: 8
He lends thee virtue, and he stole that word
From thy behaviour; beauty doth he give,
And found it in thy cheek; he can afford
No praise to thee but what in thee doth live.   12
    Then thank him not for that which he doth say,
    Since what he owes thee, thou thyself dost pay.

80

O how I faint when I of you do write,
Knowing a better spirit doth use your name,
And in the praise thereof spends all his might,
To make me tongue-tied speaking of your fame.   4
But since your worth (wide as the ocean is)
The humble as the proudest sail doth bear,
My saucy bark (inferior far to his)
On your broad main doth wilfully appear.   8
Your shallowest help will hold me up afloat,
Whilst he upon your soundless deep doth ride,
Or (being wracked) I am a worthless boat,
He of tall building and of goodly pride.   12
    Then if he thrive and I be cast away,
    The worst was this: my love was my decay.

Sonnet 79

6   travail] Q; travell *Benson*   10   behaviour;] *Gildon²;* behauiour, Q   14   pay.] *Benson;* pay, Q

Sonnet 80

11   wracked] Q *(wrackt);* wreck'd *Gildon² (variant form)*   14   this:] *Malone (subst.);* this, Q

81

Or I shall live your epitaph to make,
Or you survive when I in earth am rotten,
From hence your memory death cannot take,
Although in me each part will be forgotten.   4
Your name from hence immortal life shall have,
Though I (once gone) to all the world must die;
The earth can yield me but a common grave,
When you intombèd in men's eyes shall lie: 8
Your monument shall be my gentle verse,
Which eyes not yet created shall o'er-read,
And tongues to be your being shall rehearse,
When all the breathers of this world are dead;   12
    You still shall live (such virtue hath my pen)
    Where breath most breathes, even in the mouths of men.

82

I grant thou wert not married to my Muse,
And therefore mayst without attaint o'erlook
The dedicated words which writers use
Of their fair subject, blessing every book.   4
Thou art as fair in knowledge as in hue,
Finding thy worth a limit past my praise,
And therefore art inforced to seek anew
Some fresher stamp of the time-bettering days.   8
And do so, love; yet when they have devised
What strainèd touches rhetoric can lend,
Thou, truly fair, wert truly sympathised
In true plain words by thy true-telling friend;   12
    And their gross painting might be better used
    Where cheeks need blood; in thee it is abused.

Sonnet 81

2 rotten,] Q; rotten; *Capell;* rotten? *Gildon*   8 intombèd] Q; entombed *Capell (variant form)*   8 lie;] *Gildon²;*
lye, Q   11–12 rehearse, . . . dead;] *Sewell;* rehearse, . . . dead, Q; rehearse . . . . dead, *Benson;* rehearse: . . . dead,
Gildon²   14 breathes] *Gildon²;* breaths Q *(variant form)*

Sonnet 82

2 mayst] *Benson;* maiest Q   7 inforced] Q *(inforc'd);* enforc'd *Capell (variant form)*   8 the] Q; these *Wells*
8 time-bettering] *Gildon;* time bettering Q; time's bettering *Capell*   9 so,] *Capell;* so Q   9 love;] *Malone (after*
Capell); loue, Q   11 Thou,] *Capell;* Thou Q   12 true-telling] *Gildon²;* true telling Q

83

I never saw that you did painting need,
And therefore to your fair no painting set;
I found (or thought I found) you did exceed
The barren tender of a poet's debt: 4
And therefore have I slept in your report,
That you yourself, being extant, well might show
How far a modern quill doth come too short,
Speaking of worth, what worth in you doth grow.   8
This silence for my sin you did impute,
Which shall be most my glory, being dumb,
For I impair not beauty, being mute,
When others would give life, and bring a tomb.   12
    There lives more life in one of your fair eyes
    Than both your poets can in praise devise.

84

Who is it that says most which can say more
Than this rich praise – that you alone are you,
In whose confine immurèd is the store
Which should example where your equal grew?   4
Lean penury within that pen doth dwell
That to his subject lends not some small glory,
But he that writes of you, if he can tell
That you are you, so dignifies his story: 8
Let him but copy what in you is writ,
Not making worse what nature made so clear,
And such a counterpart shall fame his wit,
Making his style admirèd every where.   12
    You to your beauteous blessings add a curse,
    Being fond on praise, which makes your praises worse.

Sonnet 83

2 set] Q; fet *conj., this edn*   8 grow.] *Gildon;* grow, Q   10   glory,] *Gildon²;* glory Q   11   beauty,] *Gildon²;* beautie Q

Sonnet 84

1   most] *Kittredge (after conj. Pooler);* most, Q; most? *Malone*   1   more] *Gildon²;* more, Q   2   praise –] *Capell;* praise, Q   2 alone] *Gildon;* alone, Q   2   are you,] Q; art you, *Benson;* are you? *Gildon;* are you; *Capell;* are you – *Booth (retaining Q comma after* praise*)*   4   grew?] *Capell;* grew, Q; grew. *Gildon*   11   wit] Q; writ *Benson*   12   every where] Q; everywhere *Hazlitt*

85

My tongue-tied Muse in manners holds her still,
While comments of your praise, richly compiled,
Reserve their character with golden quill
And precious phrase by all the Muses filed.   4
I think good thoughts, whilst other write good words,
And like unlettered clerk still cry 'Amen'
To every hymn that able spirit affords
In polished form of well-refinèd pen.   8
Hearing you praised, I say, ''Tis so, 'tis true',
And to the most of praise add something more;
But that is in my thought, whose love to you
(Though words come hindmost) holds his rank before.   12
    Then others for the breath of words respect,
    Me for my dumb thoughts, speaking in effect.

86

Was it the proud full sail of his great verse,
Bound for the prize of all-too-precious you,
That did my ripe thoughts in my brain inhearse,
Making their tomb the womb wherein they grew?   4
Was it his spirit, by spirits taught to write
Above a mortal pitch, that struck me dead?
No, neither he, nor his compeers by night
Giving him aid, my verse astonishèd.   8
He, nor that affable familiar ghost
Which nightly gulls him with intelligence,
As victors, of my silence cannot boast;
I was not sick of any fear from thence;   12
    But when your countenance filled up his line,
    Then lacked I matter, that infeebled mine.

Sonnet 85

3 Reverse their] Q; Preserve their *Gildon²*; Rehearse thy *conj. Anon. (in Rollins)*; Rehearse your *conj. Anon. (in Rollins)*; Deserve their *conj. Dowden;* Reserve your *conj. Anon. (in Rollins)*; Reserve thy *Butler;* Rehearse their *conj. Herford;* Receive their *conj. Herford;* Rescribe their *conj. Mackail (in Rollins)*; Record thy *conj. Bullen (in Rollins)*; Re-serve thy *conj. E. Hedger (in Rollins)*; Treasure their *conj. Tucker;* Refine their *conj. Brooke* 6 unlettered] *Lintott* (vnletter'd*)*; vnlettered Q 6 'Amen'] *Gildon²* *(subst.)*; Amen Q 8 well-refinèd] *Gildon²*; well refined Q 9 ''Tis . . . true',] *Quoted, Malone;* 'tis . . . true, Q

Sonnet 86

2 all-too-precious] *Capell (after Gildon²)*; (all to precious*)* Q 11 victors,] *Gildon²*; victors Q 13 filled] *Gildon (*fill'd*)*; fild Q; fil'd *Malone (conj. Steevens)* 14 infeebled] Q; enfeebled *Malone (variant form)*

87

Farewell, thou art too dear for my possessing,
And like enough thou know'st thy estimate:
The charter of thy worth gives thee releasing;
My bonds in thee are all determinate.   4
For how do I hold thee but by thy granting,
And for that riches where is my deserving?
The cause of this fair gift in me is wanting,
And so my patent back again is swerving.   8
Thy self thou gav'st, thy own worth then not knowing,
Or me, to whom thou gav'st it, else mistaking;
So thy great gift, upon misprision growing,
Comes home again, on better judgement making.   12
    Thus have I had thee as a dream doth flatter,
    In sleep a king, but waking no such matter.

88

When thou shalt be disposed to set me light,
And place my merit in the eye of scorn,
Upon thy side against myself I'll fight,
And prove thee virtuous, though thou art forsworn: 4
With mine own weakness being best acquainted,
Upon thy part I can set down a story
Of faults concealed wherein I am attainted,
That thou in losing me shall win much glory;   8
And I by this will be a gainer too,
For, bending all my loving thoughts on thee,
The injuries that to myself I do,
Doing thee vantage, double vantage me.   12
    Such is my love, to thee I so belong,
    That for thy right myself will bear all wrong.

Sonnet 87

3 charter] Q *(Charter); Cha ter* Q *(some copies)*   9 Thy self] Q; Thyself *Murden*

Sonnet 88

1 disposed] *Benson* (dispos'd); dispode Q   7 attainted,] *Capell;* attainted: Q   8 losing] *Gildon²;* loosing Q
(variant form)   10 For,] *Capell;* For Q

89

Say that thou didst forsake me for some fault,
And I will comment upon that offence;
Speak of my lameness, and I straight will halt,
Against thy reasons making no defence.   4
Thou canst not (love) disgrace me half so ill,
To set a form upon desirèd change,
As I'll myself disgrace, knowing thy will:
I will acquaintance strangle and look strange,   8
Be absent from thy walks, and in my tongue
Thy sweet belovèd name no more shall dwell,
Lest I (too much profane) should do it wrong,
And haply of our old acquaintance tell.   12
    For thee, against myself I'll vow debate,
    For I must ne'er love him whom thou dost hate.

90

Then hate me when thou wilt, if ever, now,
Now while the world is bent my deeds to cross,
Join with the spite of Fortune, make me bow,
And do not drop in for an after-loss.   4
Ah do not, when my heart hath scaped this sorrow,
Come in the rearward of a conquered woe;
Give not a windy night a rainy morrow,
To linger out a purposed overthrow.   8
If thou wilt leave me, do not leave me last,
When other petty griefs have done their spite,
But in the onset come; so shall I taste
At first the very worst of Fortune's might;   12
    And other strains of woe, which now seem woe,
    Compared with loss of thee, will not seem so.

Sonnet 89

3 Speak] Q *corr. (*Speake*), catchword on sig.* F3; The Q *uncorr.*   3 halt,] *Capell;* halt: Q   7 disgrace,] Q; Disgrace; *Gildon*   7 will:] *Capell;* wil, Q; will *Butler;* will. *Kittredge*   8 strange,] *Neilson;* strange: Q   11 profane] Q *corr. (*prophane*);* proface Q *uncorr.*   11 wrong,] *Gildon²;* wronge: Q

Sonnet 90

1 wilt,] Q; wilt; *Gildon²*   3 Fortune] *Tyler;* fortune Q   4 after-loss] *Capell;* after losse Q   10 spite,] Q; Spight; *Gildon (retaining comma in line 11)*   11 come;] *Capell;* come, Q   11 shall] *Benson;* stall Q   12 Fortune's] *Lintott (*Fortunes*);* fortunes Q

91

Some glory in their birth, some in their skill,
Some in their wealth, some in their body's force,
Some in their garments, though new-fangled ill,
Some in their hawks and hounds, some in their horse;   4
And every humour hath his adjunct pleasure,
Wherein it finds a joy above the rest;
But these particulars are not my measure:
All these I better in one general best.   8
Thy love is better than high birth to me,
Richer than wealth, prouder than garments' cost,
Of more delight than hawks or horses be;
And having thee, of all men's pride I boast: 12
       Wretched in this alone, that thou mayst take
       All this away, and me most wretched make.

92

But do thy worst to steal thyself away,
For term of life thou art assurèd mine,
And life no longer than thy love will stay,
For it depends upon that love of thine.   4
Then need I not to fear the worst of wrongs,
When in the least of them my life hath end;
I see a better state to me belongs
Than that which on thy humour doth depend.   8
Thou canst not vex me with inconstant mind,
Since that my life on thy revolt doth lie.
O what a happy title do I find,
Happy to have thy love, happy to die!   12
       But what's so blessèd-fair that fears no blot?
       Thou mayst be false, and yet I know it not.

Sonnet 91

2   body's] *Capell;* bodies Q; bodies' *1797 edn (in Rollins), Globe*   3   ill,] *Gildon²;* ill: Q   9   better] *Benson;* bitter Q
10   garments'] *Capell;* garments Q

Sonnet 92

6   end;] *Gildon²;* end, Q   7   see] *Lintott;* see, Q   13   blessèd-fair] *Malone;* blessed faire Q   13   fears] Q; bears
conj., this edn   13   blot?] *Gildon;* blot, Q   14   not.] Q; not: *Malone*

93

So shall I live, supposing thou art true,
Like a deceivèd husband; so love's face
May still seem love to me, though altered new;
Thy looks with me, thy heart in other place: 4
For there can live no hatred in thine eye,
Therefore in that I cannot know thy change.
In many's looks, the false heart's history
Is writ in moods and frowns and wrinkles strange,   8
But heaven in thy creation did decree
That in thy face sweet love should ever dwell;
What e'er thy thoughts or thy heart's workings be,
Thy looks should nothing thence but sweetness tell.   12
    How like Eve's apple doth thy beauty grow,
    If thy sweet virtue answer not thy show!

94

They that have pow'r to hurt, and will do none,
That do not do the thing they most do show,
Who, moving others, are themselves as stone,
Unmovèd, cold, and to temptation slow –   4
They rightly do inherit heaven's graces,
And husband nature's riches from expense;
They are the lords and owners of their faces,
Others but stewards of their excellence.   8
The summer's flow'r is to the summer sweet,
Though to itself it only live and die,
But if that flow'r with base infection meet,
The basest weed outbraves his dignity: 12
    For sweetest things turn sourest by their deeds;
    Lilies that fester smell far worse than weeds.

Sonnet 93

2 husband;] *Gildon;* husband, Q   4 place:] *Malone;* place. Q   6 change.] *Gildon;* change, Q   8 strange,] *Malone*[1]; strange. Q   10 dwell;] *Gildon;* dwell, Q   11 What e'er] Q; Whate'er *Gildon*   13 Eve's] *Benson (Eves); Eaues* Q   14 show!] *Gildon*[2]; show. Q

Sonnet 94

2 thing] *Lintott;* thing, Q   4 slow –] *Capell;* slow: Q

95

How sweet and lovely dost thou make the shame
Which, like a canker in the fragrant rose,
Doth spot the beauty of thy budding name!
O in what sweets dost thou thy sins inclose!   4
That tongue that tells the story of thy days
(Making lascivious comments on thy sport)
Cannot dispraise, but in a kind of praise,
Naming thy name, blesses an ill report.   8
O what a mansion have those vices got
Which for their habitation chose out thee,
Where beauty's veil doth cover every blot,
And all things turns to fair that eyes can see!   12
    Take heed (dear heart) of this large privilege:
    The hardest knife ill used doth lose his edge.

96

Some say thy fault is youth, some wantonness,
Some say thy grace is youth and gentle sport;
Both grace and faults are loved of more and less:
Thou mak'st faults graces that to thee resort.   4
As on the finger of a thronèd queen
The basest jewel will be well esteemed,
So are those errors that in thee are seen
To truths translated, and for true things deemed.   8
How many lambs might the stern wolf betray,
If like a lamb he could his looks translate!
How many gazers mightst thou lead away,
If thou wouldst use the strength of all thy state!   12
    But do not so; I love thee in such sort,
    As thou being mine, mine is thy good report.

Sonnet 95

3 name!] *Dyce (1832);* name? Q   4 dost] *Gildon;* doest Q   4 inclose] Q; enclose *Malone (variant form)*
7 dispraise, . . . praise,] Q; dispraise . . . praise; *Capell*   8 name,] Q; name *Malone*   14 lose] *Gildon;* loose
Q *(variant form)*

Sonnet 96

96] *This sonnet omitted by Benson through Evans (except Lintott)*   6 esteemed,] *Collier;* esteem'd: Q   7 seen] *Knight;*
seene, Q   10 translate!] *Malone;* translate. Q   11 mightst] *Lintott;* mighst Q   12 state!] *Malone;* state? Q
13 so;] *Capell;* so, Q

97

How like a winter hath my absence been
From thee, the pleasure of the fleeting year!
What freezings have I felt, what dark days seen!
What old December's bareness every where!   4
And yet this time removed was summer's time,
The teeming autumn big with rich increase,
Bearing the wanton burthen of the prime,
Like widowed wombs after their lords' decease: 8
Yet this abundant issue seem'd to me
But hope of orphans, and unfathered fruit,
For summer and his pleasures wait on thee,
And thou away, the very birds are mute;   12
      Or if they sing, 'tis with so dull a cheer
      That leaves look pale, dreading the winter's near.

98

From you have I been absent in the spring,
When proud-pied April (dressed in all his trim)
Hath put a spirit of youth in every thing,
That heavy Saturn laughed and leapt with him.   4
Yet nor the lays of birds, nor the sweet smell
Of different flowers in odour and in hue,
Could make me any summer's story tell,
Or from their proud lap pluck them where they grew: 8
Nor did I wonder at the lily's white,
Nor praise the deep vermilion in the rose;
They were but sweet, but figures of delight,
Drawn after you, you pattern of all those.   12
      Yet seemed it winter still, and, you away,
      As with your shadow I with these did play.

Sonnet 97

2 year!] *Gildon;* yeare? Q   3 seen!] *Dyce (1832);* seene? Q   4 bareness] Q *(*barenesse*);* Barenness *Gildon¹;*
Barrenness *Gildon²*   4 every where] Q; everywhere *Knight*   4 where!] *Malone;* where? Q   7 burthen] Q; burden *Gildon² (variant form)*   8 widowed] *Gildon* (widow'd*);* widdowed Q   10 unfathered] *Gildon* (un-father'd*);*
vn-fathered Q

Sonnet 98

2 proud-pied] *Ewing;* proud pide Q   3 every thing] Q; everything *Knight*   3 thing,] *Gildon²;* thing: Q
7 tell,] *Capell;* tell: Q   9 lily's] *Capell;* Lillies Q   11 were] *Benson;* weare Q   11 but sweet, but] Q; my
sweet, but *conj. Malone;* but fleeting *conj. Lettsom (in Rollins);* best sweet, but *conj. Lowell (in Rollins);* but suite, but
conj. Bulloch (in Rollins); but cunning *conj. Hudson²;* but, sweet, but *Butler;* but sweet-fraught *or* sweetful *conj. Tucker;* but
sweets, but *conj., this edn*   11 delight,] *Gildon;* delight: Q   13 and,] *Capell;* and Q   14 play.] Q; play: *Malone*

75

99

The forward violet thus did I chide:
'Sweet thief, whence didst thou steal thy sweet that smells,
If not from my love's breath? The purple pride
Which on thy soft cheek for complexion dwells   4
In my love's veins thou hast too grossly dyed.'
The lily I condemnèd for thy hand,
And buds of marjoram had stol'n thy hair;
The roses fearfully on thorns did stand,   8
One blushing shame, another white despair;
A third, nor red nor white, had stol'n of both,
And to his robb'ry had annexed thy breath,
But for his theft in pride of all his growth   12
A vengeful canker eat him up to death.
     More flowers I noted, yet I none could see
     But sweet or colour it had stol'n from thee.

100

Where art thou, Muse, that thou forget'st so long
To speak of that which gives thee all thy might?
Spend'st thou thy fury on some worthless song,
Dark'ning thy pow'r to lend base subjects light?   4
Return, forgetful Muse, and straight redeem
In gentle numbers time so idly spent;
Sing to the ear that doth thy lays esteem,
And gives thy pen both skill and argument.   8
Rise, resty Muse, my love's sweet face survey,
If Time have any wrinkle graven there;
If any, be a satire to decay,
And make Time's spoils despisèd every where.   12
     Give my love fame faster than Time wastes life;
     So thou prevent'st his scythe and crookèd knife.

Sonnet 99

2–5 'Sweet . . . dyed.'] *Quoted, Bell*; Sweet . . . died, Q   2   smells,] *Benson;* smels Q   3–4   breath? The . . . dwells] *Gildon¹;* breath, the . . . dwells? Q   5   dyed.] *Gildon²;* died, Q   7   marjoram] *Gildon²;* marierom Q *(variant form)*   9   One] *Sewell;* Our Q   15   thee.] Q; thee: *Malone*

Sonnet 100

4   light?] *Gildon;* light. Q   10   Time] *Ewing;* time Q   11   satire] *Capell;* Satire Q   12   Time's] *Ewing;* times Q   12   every where] Q; everywhere *Knight*   13   Time] *Ewing;* time Q   14   prevent'st] *Gildon;* preuenst Q; prevene'st *Wells*   14   scythe] Q *(sieth);* scathe *conj. Tucker;* fierce *conj. Tobin*

101

O truant Muse, what shall be thy amends
For thy neglect of truth in beauty dyed?
Both truth and beauty on my love depends;
So dost thou too, and therein dignified.   4
Make answer, Muse, wilt thou not haply say,
'Truth needs no colour with his colour fixed,
Beauty no pencil, beauty's truth to lay;
But best is best, if never intermixed'?   8
Because he needs no praise, wilt thou be dumb?
Excuse not silence so, for't lies in thee
To make him much outlive a gilded tomb,
And to be praised of ages yet to be.   12
  Then do thy office, Muse; I teach thee how
  To make him seem long hence as he shows now.

102

My love is strength'ned, though more weak in seeming;
I love not less, though less the show appear:
That love is merchandised whose rich esteeming
The owner's tongue doth publish every where.   4
Our love was new, and then but in the spring,
When I was wont to greet it with my lays,
As Philomel in summer's front doth sing,
And stops his pipe in growth of riper days: 8
Not that the summer is less pleasant now
Than when her mournful hymns did hush the night,
But that wild music burthens every bough,
And sweets grown common lose their dear delight.   12
  Therefore like her, I sometime hold my tongue,
  Because I would not dull you with my song.

Sonnet 101

5 Muse,] Q; muse; *Capell* 6–8 'Truth . . . intermixed'?] *Quoted, Malone;* Truth . . . intermixt. Q
8 intermixed'?] *Capell (for question mark);* intermixt. Q 11 him] Q; her *Benson* 11 tomb,] *Gildon²;* tombe: Q
13 office, Muse;] *Capell (muse);* office Muse, Q 13 I . . . how] *Lintott;* I . . . how, Q; (I . . . how): – *Ingram and Redpath* 14 him . . . he] Q; her . . . she *Benson*

Sonnet 102

1 strength'ned] Q; strengthen'd *Ewing, Capell* 4 every where] Q; everywhere *Knight* 8 his] Q; her *Housman (1835, in Rollins)* 11 burthens] Q; burdens *Gildon² (variant form)* 12 lose] *Gildon;* loose Q *(variant form)*
13 tongue,] *Gildon;* tongue: Q

103

Alack, what poverty my Muse brings forth,
That, having such a scope to show her pride,
The argument all bare is of more worth
Than when it hath my added praise beside.   4
O blame me not if I no more can write!
Look in your glass, and there appears a face
That overgoes my blunt invention quite,
Dulling my lines, and doing me disgrace.   8
Were it not sinful then, striving to mend,
To mar the subject that before was well?
For to no other pass my verses tend
Than of your graces and your gifts to tell;   12
    And more, much more than in my verse can sit,
    Your own glass shows you, when you look in it.

104

To me, fair friend, you never can be old,
For as you were when first your eye I eyed,
Such seems your beauty still. Three winters cold
Have from the forests shook three summers's pride,   4
Three beauteous springs to yellow autumn turned
In process of the seasons have I seen,
Three April perfumes in three hot Junes burned,
Since first I saw you fresh which yet are green.   8
Ah yet doth beauty, like a dial hand,
Steal from his figure, and no pace perceived;
So your sweet hue, which methinks still doth stand,
Hath motion, and mine eye may be deceived;   12
    For fear of which, hear this, thou age unbred:
    Ere you were born was beauty's summer dead.

Sonnet 103

10 well?] *Lintott;* well, Q   13 much more] Q; much more, *Lintott*

Sonnet 104

1 friend] Q; love *Benson*   3 winters] Q *(Winters);* winters' *Knight*   5 autumn] Q *(Autumne);* autumns *Capell*
8 you fresh] Q; you, fresh, *Gildon;* you fresh, *Sewell¹*   10 pace] Q; place *Benson*   11 stand,] *Lintott;* stand
Q *(the d prints brokenly and may have been followed by a comma which hence failed to print)*   12 deceived] *Gildon¹*
(deceiv'd); deceaued Q

78

105

Let not my love be called idolatry,
Nor my belovèd as an idol show,
Since all alike my songs and praises be
To one, of one, still such, and ever so.   4
Kind is my love today, tomorrow kind,
Still constant in a wondrous excellence;
Therefore my verse, to constancy confined,
One thing expressing, leaves out difference.   8
'Fair, kind, and true' is all my argument,
'Fair, kind, and true', varying to other words,
And in this change is my invention spent,
Three themes in one, which wondrous scope affords.   12
    'Fair', 'kind', and 'true' have often lived alone,
    Which three till now never kept seat in one.

106

When in the chronicle of wasted time
I see descriptions of the fairest wights,
And beauty making beautiful old rhyme
In praise of ladies dead and lovely knights,   4
Then in the blazon of sweet beauty's best,
Of hand, of foot, of lip, of eye, of brow,
I see their àntique pen would have expressed
Even such a beauty as you master now.   8
So all their praises are but prophecies
Of this our time, all you prefiguring,
And for they looked but with divining eyes
They had not skill enough your worth to sing: 12
    For we, which now behold these present days,
    Have eyes to wonder, but lack tongues to praise.

Sonnet 105

9 'Fair . . . true'] *Quoted, Globe;* Faire . . . true, Q   10 'Fair . . . true'] *Quoted, Globe;* Faire . . . true Q; 'Fair,' 'kind,' and 'true' *Brooke*   13 'Fair', . . . 'true'] *Beeching;* Faire, . . . true, Q   13 alone,] *Malone;* alone. Q; alone: *Gildon*[2]

Sonnet 106

5 beauty's] *Gildon*[1]; beauties Q   12 skill] *Capell, conj. Tyrwhitt;* still Q; style *conj. Tucker*   *For MS. versions of this sonnet, see Appendix, pp. 270–1 below.*

107

Not mine own fears, nor the prophetic soul
Of the wide world, dreaming on things to come,
Can yet the lease of my true love control,
Supposed as forfeit to a confined doom.   4
The mortal moon hath her eclipse endured,
And the sad augurs mock their own presàge,
Incertainties now crown themselves assured,
And peace proclaims olives of endless age.   8
Now with the drops of this most balmy time
My love looks fresh, and Death to me subscribes,
Since spite of him I'll live in this poor rhyme,
While he insults o'er dull and speechless tribes.   12
    And thou in this shalt find thy monument,
    When tyrants' crests and tombs of brass are spent.

108

What's in the brain that ink may character
Which hath not figured to thee my true spirit?
What's new to speak, what now to register,
That may express my love, or thy dear merit?   4
Nothing, sweet boy; but yet, like prayers divine,
I must each day say o'er the very same,
Counting no old thing old, thou mine, I thine,
Even as when first I hallowèd thy fair name.   8
So that eternal love in love's fresh case
Weighs not the dust and injury of age,
Nor gives to necessary wrinkles place,
But makes antiquity for aye his page,   12
    Finding the first conceit of love there bred,
    Where time and outward form would show it dead.

Sonnet 107

1–2 fears, . . . soul . . . world, . . . come,] *Gildon;* feares, . . . soule, . . . world, . . . come, Q, *Dover Wilson;* fears, . . . soul . . . world . . . come *Capell;* fears, . . . soul . . . world . . . come, *Malone (after Lintott);* fears . . . soul . . . world . . . come *Booth*   8   age.] *The period (though accepted as such by Rollins without comment) may be a lightly printed comma in Q and is so printed in both Alden and the Oxford old-spelling text (1987); Benson's compositor, however, read it as a period.*   10   Death] *Malone;* death Q

Sonnet 108

2   spirit?] *Gildon;* spirit, Q   3   new . . . now] Q; now . . . now *Gentleman;* new . . . new *Malone*   5   sweet boy;] *Malone (after Capell);* sweet boy, Q; sweet-love *Benson*   8   hallowèd] Q *(accent not in Q);* hallow'd *Gildon*   10   injury] Q; injuries *Benson*   13   bred,] Q; bred *Globe*

109

O never say that I was false of heart,
Though absence seemed my flame to qualify;
As easy might I from my self depart
As from my soul, which in thy breast doth lie· 4
That is my home of love. If I have ranged,
Like him that travels I return again,
Just to the time, not with the time exchanged,
So that myself bring water for my stain. 8
Never believe, though in my nature reigned
All frailties that besiege all kinds of blood,
That it could so preposterously be stained
To leave for nothing all thy sum of good; 12
    For nothing this wide universe I call,
    Save thou, my rose; in it thou art my all.

110

Alas 'tis true, I have gone here and there,
And made myself a motley to the view,
Gored mine own thoughts, sold cheap what is most dear,
Made old offences of affections new. 4
Most true it is that I have looked on truth
Askance and strangely; but, by all above,
These blenches gave my heart another youth,
And worse essays proved thee my best of love. 8
Now all is done, have what shall have no end:
Mine appetite I never more will grind
On newer proof, to try an older friend,
A god in love, to whom I am confined. 12
    Then give me welcome, next my heaven the best,
    Even to thy pure and most most loving breast.

Sonnet 109

3 my self] Q*; myself *Murden*   **5** love. If] *Sewell (subst.)*; loue, if Q   **8** stain.] *Gildon²;* staine, Q   **14** thou, my rose;] *Capell;* thou my Rose, Q

Sonnet 110

1 true,] Q*; true *Dyce*   **6** Askance] *Gildon²;* Asconce Q *(variant form)*   **8** essays] Q*; assaies *Benson* **8-9** love . . . done,] *Gildon²;* loue, . . . done, Q*; love: . . . done; *Capell*   **9** end:] *Malone (after Capell);* end, Q   **12** god] *Murden;* God Q

111

O for my sake do you with Fortune chide,
The guilty goddess of my harmful deeds,
That did not better for my life provide
Than public means which public manners breeds.   4
Thence comes it that my name receives a brand,
And almost thence my nature is subdued
To what it works in, like the dyer's hand.
Pity me then, and wish I were renewed,   8
Whilst like a willing patient I will drink
Potions of eisel 'gainst my strong infection;
No bitterness that I will bitter think,
Nor double penance to correct correction.   12
     Pity me then, dear friend, and I assure ye
     Even that your pity is enough to cure me.

112

Your love and pity doth th'impression fill
Which vulgar scandal stamped upon my brow,
For what care I who calls me well or ill,
So you o'er-green my bad, my good allow?   4
You are my all the world, and I must strive
To know my shames and praises from your tongue;
None else to me, nor I to none alive,
That my steeled sense or changes right or wrong.   8
In so profound abysm I throw all care
Of others' voices, that my adder's sense
To critic and to flatterer stoppèd are.
Mark how with my neglect I do dispense: 12
     You are so strongly in my purpose bred
     That all the world besides methinks th'are dead.

Sonnet 111

1 with] *Gildon;* wish Q   1 Fortune] *Knight;* fortune Q   2 harmful] Q; harmelesse *Benson*   12 to] Q; too *conj. Kenyon (in Rollins)*

Sonnet 112

8 or changes] Q; e'er changes, *conj. Malone*; so changes *conj. Knight*; changes, or *conj. Keightley;* or charges *conj. Anon. (in Rollins)*; o'erchanges *conj. Tucker*   8 wrong.] *Gildon*[2]; wrong, Q   9 abysm] *Murden (subst.); Abisme*Q
14 besides methinks th'are] *This edn;* besides me thinkes y'are Q; besides me, thinks I'm *Sewell*[1]; besides me thinks I'm *Sewell*[2]; besides, me thinks, are *Capell;* besides methinks are *Malone*[1]; besides, methinks, is [*or* are] *conj. Steevens (in Malone);* besides methinks they are *Malone*[2]; besides methinks they're *Dyce;* besides, methinks y'are *Tyler (reading That,);* besides methinks you're *Neilson*[1]

113

Since I left you, mine eye is in my mind,
And that which governs me to go about
Doth part his function, and is partly blind,
Seems seeing, but effectually is out;   4
For it no form delivers to the heart
Of bird, of flow'r, or shape which it doth latch;
Of his quick objects hath the mind no part,
Nor his own vision holds what it doth catch: 8
For if it see the rud'st or gentlest sight,
The most sweet favour or deformèd'st creature,
The mountain, or the sea, the day, or night,
The crow, or dove, it shapes them to your feature.   12
    Incapable of more, replete with you,
    My most true mind thus maketh mine eye untrue.

114

Or whether doth my mind being crowned with you
Drink up the monarch's plague, this flattery?
Or whether shall I say mine eye saith true,
And that your love taught it this alcumy,   4
To make of monsters, and things indigest,
Such cherubins as your sweet self resemble,
Creating every bad a perfect best
As fast as objects to his beams assemble?   8
O 'tis the first, 'tis flatt'ry in my seeing,
And my great mind most kingly drinks it up;
Mine eye well knows what with his gust is greeing,
And to his palate doth prepare the cup.   12
    If it be poisoned, 'tis the lesser sin
    That mine eye loves it and doth first begin.

Sonnet 113

6 bird, of] Q; birds, or *Benson*   6 latch;] *Capell;* lack, Q   10 sweet favour] *Benson;* sweet-fauor Q; sweet-favour'd *conj. Delius*   11 night,] *Gildon²;* night: Q   13 more, replete] *Gildon;* more repleat, Q   14 maketh mine eye] *Keightley;* maketh mine Q; makes mine eye *Capell;* maketh my eyne *conj. Collier;* mak'th mine eye *conj. Lettsom (in Rollins);* maketh m'eye *Cartwright (in Rollins);* maketh m'eyne *conj. Cartwright (in Rollins);* maketh mind *White²;* maketh eyne *conj. Verity*

Sonnet 114

2 plague,] *Gildon;* plague Q   4 alcumy,] *Malone (after Capell); Alcumie?* Q; *Alcumie / Benson; Alchymy? / Sewell (after Gildon / Alchimy?);* alchemy, *Hudson (variant forms)*   6 cherubins] *Capell;* cherubines Q; *Cherubims Gildon² (variant form)*   8 assemble?] *Gildon;* assemble: Q   10 kingly] Q; kindly *Benson*

83

115

Those lines that I before have writ do lie,
Even those that said I could not love you dearer;
Yet then my judgement knew no reason why
My most full flame should afterwards burn clearer.   4
But reckoning Time, whose millioned accidents
Creep in 'twixt vows, and change decrees of kings,
Tan sacred beauty, blunt the sharp'st intents,
Divert strong minds to th'course of alt'ring things –   8
Alas, why, fearing of Time's tyranny,
Might I not then say 'Now I love you best',
When I was certain o'er incertainty,
Crowning the present, doubting of the rest?   12
    Love is a babe: then might I not say so,
    To give full growth to that which still doth grow.

116

Let me not to the marriage of true minds
Admit impediments; love is not love
Which alters when it alteration finds,
Or bends with the remover to remove.   4
O no, it is an ever-fixèd mark
That looks on tempests and is never shaken;
It is the star to every wand'ring bark,
Whose worth's unknown, although his heighth be taken.   8
Love's not Time's fool, though rosy lips and cheeks
Within his bending sickle's compass come;
Love alters not with his brief hours and weeks,
But bears it out even to the edge of doom.   12
    If this be error and upon me proved,
    I never writ, nor no man ever loved.

Sonnet 115

5 Time] *Ewing;* time Q   5–8 Time, . . . intents, / Divert . . . things –] Q *(subst.,* time, . . . things:*);* time, – . . . intents, – Diverts . . . things. *Capell*   5 millioned] *Lintott* (million'd*);* milliond Q   9 Alas, why,] *Capell;* Alas why Q; Alas! why *Gildon;* Alas! why, *Malone*   9 Time's] *Ewing;* times Q   10 'Now . . . best'] *Quoted, Malone;* now . . . best Q   11 incertainty] *Gildon²;* in-certainty Q   12 rest?] *Gildon;* rest: Q   13 babe:] *Capell (subst.);* Babe, Q   13 not] Q; *not / Beeching*   13 so,] *Gildon²;* so Q   14 grow.] Q; grow? *Gildon*

Sonnet 116

Number: 116] Q *corr;* 119 Q *uncorr.*   2 impediments;] *Gildon²;* impediments, Q   5 ever-fixèd] *Gildon²;* euer fixed Q 7 wand'ring] Q; wandering *Malone*   8 worth's] Q (worths*);* north's *conj. Walker (in Rollins)*   8 heighth] *Munro;* hight Q; hight *Benson;* Height *Gildon;* highth *Capell*   13–14 proved . . . loved] *Ewing* (prov'd . . . lov'd*);* proued . . . loued Q *For a text of 116 set to music, see Appendix, p. 271 below.*

117

Accuse me thus: that I have scanted all
Wherein I should your great deserts repay,
Forgot upon your dearest love to call,
Whereto all bonds do tie me day by day;   4
That I have frequent been with unknown minds,
And given to time your own dear-purchased right;
That I have hoisted sail to all the winds
Which should transport me farthest from your sight.   8
Book both my wilfulness and errors down,
And on just proof surmise accumulate;
Bring me within the level of your frown,
But shoot not at me in your wakened hate;   12
    Since my appeal says I did strive to prove
    The constancy and virtue of your love.

118

Like as to make our appetites more keen
With eager compounds we our palate urge,
As to prevent our maladies unseen
We sicken to shun sickness when we purge: 4
Even so, being full of your ne'er-cloying sweetness,
To bitter sauces did I frame my feeding,
And, sick of welfare, found a kind of meetness
To be diseased ere that there was true needing.   8
Thus policy in love, t'anticipate
The ills that were not, grew to faults assured,
And brought to medicine a healthful state
Which, rank of goodness, would by ill be cured.   12
    But thence I learn, and find the lesson true,
    Drugs poison him that so fell sick of you.

Sonnet 117

6 dear-purchased] *Sewell¹*, *Capell;* deare purchas'd Q   9 errors] Q; errour *Benson*   10 proof surmise] *Knight;* proofe surmise, Q; Proof, Surmise, *Sewell¹*, *Capell;* proof, surmise *Malone*   10 accumulate] *Gildon²;* accumilate Q *(variant form)*   12 wakened] *Capell* (waken'd); wakened Q   14 love.] *Benson;* loue Q

Sonnet 118

5 ne'er-cloying] *Conj. Theobald, Capell;* nere cloying Q; neare cloying *Benson*   6 feeding,] *Malone;* feeding; Q   7 welfare] *Gildon;* wel-fare Q   10 were not,] *Gildon;* were, not Q   10 assured] *Malone²* (assur'd); assured Q   12 Which, . . . goodness,] *Capell;* Which . . . goodnesse Q   12 cured] *Malone²* (cur'd); cured Q

119

What potions have I drunk of Siren tears
Distilled from limbecks foul as hell within,
Applying fears to hopes, and hopes to fears,
Still losing when I saw myself to win!   4
What wretched errors hath my heart committed,
Whilst it hath thought itself so blessèd never!
How have mine eyes out of their spheres been fitted
In the distraction of this madding fever!   8
O benefit of ill! now I find true
That better is by evil still made better,
And ruined love when it is built anew
Grows fairer than at first, more strong, far greater.   12
     So I return rebuked to my content,
     And gain by ills thrice more than I have spent.

120

That you were once unkind befriends me now,
And for that sorrow which I then did feel
Needs must I under my transgression bow,
Unless my nerves were brass or hammerèd steel.   4
For if you were by my unkindness shaken
As I by yours, y'have passed a hell of time,
And I, a tyrant, have no leisure taken
To weigh how once I suffered in your crime.   8
O that our night of woe might have rememb'red
My deepest sense, how hard true sorrow hits,
And soon to you, as you to me then, tend'red
The humble salve, which wounded bosoms fits!   12
     But that your trespass now becomes a fee;
     Mine ransoms yours, and yours must ransom me.

Sonnet 119

1 Siren] *Murden; Syren* Q   4 losing] *Gildon;* loosing Q *(variant form)*   4–8 win! . . . never! . . . fever!] *Malone;* win? . . . neuer? . . . feuer? Q   7 been fitted] Q; been flitted *conj. Lettsom (in Dyce);* e'en flitted *conj. Hudson²*
9 ill!] *Gildon;* ill, Q   14 ills] Q; ill *Malone*

Sonnet 120

4 hammerèd] Q *(accent added);* hammer'd *Gildon*   6 time] *Lintott;* Time Q   8 suffered] *Gildon²* (suffer'd); suffered Q   9–11 remember'd . . . tend'red] Q; remember'd . . . tender'd *Murden*   11 you, . . . me then,] *Conj. Walker (in Rollins);* you, . . . me then Q; you, . . . me then, *Capell;* you . . . me then *Ingram and Redpath*

121

'Tis better to be vile than vile esteemed,
When not to be receives reproach of being,
And the just pleasure lost, which is so deemed
Not by our feeling but by others' seeing.   4
For why should others' false adulterate eyes
Give salutation to my sportive blood?
Or on my frailties why are frailer spies,
Which in their wills count bad what I think good?   8
No, I am that I am, and they that level
At my abuses reckon up their own;
I may be straight though they themselves be bevel;
By their rank thoughts my deeds must not be shown,   12
    Unless this general evil they maintain:
    All men are bad and in their badness reign.

122

Thy gift, thy tables, are within my brain
Full charactered with lasting memory,
Which shall above that idle rank remain
Beyond all date, even to eternity;   4
Or, at the least, so long as brain and heart
Have faculty by nature to subsist,
Till each to razed oblivion yield his part
Of thee, thy record never can be missed.   8
That poor retention could not so much hold,
Nor need I tallies thy dear love to score;
Therefore to give them from me was I bold,
To trust those tables that receive thee more: 12
    To keep an adjunct to remember thee
    Were to import forgetfulness in me.

Sonnet 121

1 vile esteemed] *Gildon* (vile esteem'd*)*; vile esteemed Q; vile-esteem'd *conj. Walker (in Rollins)*   3 deemed] *Malone* (deem'd *after Gildon²* deem'd,*)*; deemed, Q   5 For why] Q; Forwhy *conj. Pooler*   7 spies,] *Capell;* spies; Q   11 bevel;] *Gildon²;* beuel Q   12 thoughts . . . shown,] *Gildon;* thoughtes, . . . shown Q

Sonnet 122

1 Thy gift,] *Benson;* TThy guift,, Q   6 subsist,] Q; subsist; *Gildon¹;* subsist – *Booth (with dash after eternity in 4)*

87

123

No! Time, thou shalt not boast that I do change:
Thy pyramids built up with newer might
To me are nothing novel, nothing strange;
They are but dressings of a former sight. 4
Our dates are brief, and therefore we admire
What thou dost foist upon us that is old,
And rather make them born to our desire
Than think that we before have heard them told. 8
Thy registers and thee I both defy,
Not wond'ring at the present, nor the past,
For thy recòrds, and what we see, doth lie,
Made more or less by thy continual haste. 12
    This I do vow and this shall ever be:
    I will be true despite thy scythe and thee.

124

If my dear love were but the child of state,
It might for Fortune's bastard be unfathered,
As subject to Time's love, or to Time's hate,
Weeds among weeds, or flowers with flowers gathered. 4
No, it was builded far from accident;
It suffers not in smiling pomp, nor falls
Under the blow of thrallèd discontent,
Whereto th'inviting time our fashion calls; 8
It fears not Policy, that heretic,
Which works on leases of short-numb'red hours,
But all alone stands hugely politic,
That it nor grows with heat, nor drowns with show'rs. 12
    To this I witness call the fools of Time,
    Which die for goodness, who have lived for crime.

Sonnet 123

1 No! Time,] Q; No Time, *Lintott;* No, Time! *Sewell;* No, time, *Capell*   7 born] *Gildon;* borne Q; borne *Wyndham* (= bourn)   11 see,] *Capell;* see Q   14 thee.] Q; thee; *Malone²*

Sonnet 124

2 Fortune's] *Knight;* fortunes Q   2 unfathered] *Gildon²* (un-father'd); vnfathered Q   3 Time's . . . Time's] *Ewing;* times . . . times Q   9 Policy] *Kittredge;* policy Q   9 heretic,] *Capell;* Heriticke, Q; heretic *Tucker* 10 short-numb'red] *Capell* (short-number'd); short numbred Q   13 fools of Time] *Massey (after Benson* fooles); foles of time Q

88

125

Were't aught to me I bore the canopy,
With my extern the outward honouring,
Or laid great bases for eternity,
Which proves more short than waste or ruining?   4
Have I not seen dwellers on form and favour
Lose all, and more, by paying too much rent,
For compound sweet forgoing simple savour,
Pitiful thrivers, in their gazing spent?   8
No, let me be obsequious in thy heart,
And take thou my oblation, poor but free,
Which is not mixed with seconds, knows no art
But mutual render, only me for thee.   12
    Hence, thou suborned informer! A true soul
    When most impeached stands least in thy control.

126

O thou my lovely boy, who in thy power
Dost hold Time's fickle glass, his sickle, hour;
Who hast by waning grown, and therein show'st
Thy lovers withering, as thy sweet self grow'st;   4
If Nature (sovereign mistress over wrack),
As thou goest onwards still will pluck thee back,
She keeps thee to this purpose, that her skill
May Time disgrace, and wretched minutes kill.   8
Yet fear her, O thou minion of her pleasure,
She may detain, but not still keep, her treasure!
Her audit (though delayed) answered must be,
And her quietus is to render thee.   12

Sonnet 125

1 Were't . . . me] Q *(Wer't ought to me)*; Were it aught to me *Malone*   6–7 rent, . . . sweet] *Malone;* rent . . . sweet; Q; rent . . . sweet, *Lintott;* rent; . . . sweet *Capell;* rent – . . . sweet *Tucker*   8 spent?] *Capell;* spent. Q   11 art] *Capell;* art, Q   13 informer!] *Murden (after Gildon / Informer!)*; *Informer*, Q

Sonnet 126

126] *This sonnet omitted by Benson through Evans (except Lintott)*   2 Dost] *Capell;* Doest Q   2 Time's] *Malone²;* times Q   2 fickle] Q; tickle *conj. Kinnear (in Rollins);* sickle, *Butler;* brittle *conj. W. B. Brown (in Rollins);* brickle *conj. Tucker*   2 sickle, hour] Q *(hower);* fickle hower *Lintott, Capell;* sickle-hour *conj. Walker (in Rollins);* fickle mower *conj. Bulloch (in Rollins);* sickle hour *Tyler;* tickle hour *conj. Anon. (in Rollins);* sickle lower *conj. Anon. (in Rollins)*   3 show'st] *Capell;* shou'st, Q   4 lovers] Q; lover's *conj. Delius;* lovers' *conj. Booth*   5 mistress] *Capell;* misteres Q *(variant form)*   6 onwards still] Q; onwards, still *Malone;* onwards still, *conj., this edn*   7 skill] *Lintott;* skill. Q   8 Time] *Tyler;* time Q   8 minutes] *Capell* (minuits); mynuit Q   11 audit] *Malone (after Capell, who accidentally forgot to cancel the italics);* Audite Q   12 quietus] *Capell;* Quietus Q   12] Q *indicates that there are two missing lines following 12 by two pairs of parentheses, spaced out the full line length and, indented, set one above the other; first omitted by Malone*

89

127

In the old age black was not counted fair,
Or if it were it bore not beauty's name;
But now is black beauty's successive heir,
And beauty slandered with a bastard shame: 4
For since each hand hath put on Nature's power,
Fairing the foul with art's false borrowed face,
Sweet beauty hath no name, no holy bower,
But is profaned, if not lives in disgrace.   8
Therefore my mistress' eyes are raven black,
Her eyes so suited, and they mourners seem
At such who not born fair no beauty lack,
Sland'ring creation with a false esteem: 12
    Yet so they mourn, becoming of their woe,
    That every tongue says beauty should look so.

128

How oft, when thou, my music, music play'st
Upon that blessèd wood whose motion sounds
With thy sweet fingers when thou gently sway'st
The wiry concord that mine ear confounds,   4
Do I envỳ those jacks that nimble leap
To kiss the tender inward of thy hand,
Whilst my poor lips, which should that harvest reap,
At the wood's boldness by thee blushing stand!   8
To be so tickled they would change their state
And situation with those dancing chips
O'er whom thy fingers walk with gentle gait,
Making dead wood more blest than living lips.   12
    Since saucy jacks so happy are in this,
    Give them thy fingers, me thy lips to kiss.

Sonnet 127

2 were] *Benson;* weare Q   6 art's] *Capell (after Lintott* arts*);* Arts Q   7 bower,] *Gildon;* boure, Q; bower *Capell;* hour, *Malone*   9 mistress'] *Gildon²;* Mistersse Q *(variant form);* Mistresse *Benson*   9–10 eyes . . . eyes] Q; eyes . . . hairs *Capell;* hairs . . . eyes *conj. Walker (in Rollins);* brows . . . eyes *conj. Staunton;* eyes . . . brows *conj. Staunton;* hairs . . . brows *conj. Kinnear (in Rollins);* eyes . . . brow *Ingram and Redpath;* eyes . . . hair *conj., this edn*   9 raven black] Q; raven-black *Wells*   10 and] Q; that *Gildon¹;* as *Dyce*   13 mourn,] *Lintott;* mourne Q

Sonnet 128

1 music play'st] *Lintott;* musike playst, Q; Musick-play'st, *Gildon²;* music playest, *Collier*   8 stand!] *Malone;* stand. Q; stand? *Capell*   9 tickled] Q *(*tikled*);* tickl'd *Capell*   11 thy] *Gildon¹, Capell;* their Q   12 lips.] *Benson;* lips, Q   14 thy fingers] *Benson;* their fingers Q *For a slightly different manuscript version, see Appendix, p. 271 below.*

129

Th'expense of spirit in a waste of shame
Is lust in action, and till action, lust
Is perjured, murd'rous, bloody, full of blame,
Savage, extreme, rude, cruel, not to trust,   4
Enjoyed no sooner but despisèd straight,
Past reason hunted, and no sooner had,
Past reason hated as a swallowed bait
On purpose laid to make the taker mad: 8
Mad in pursuit, and in possession so,
Had, having, and in quest to have, extreme,
A bliss in proof, and proved, a very woe,
Before, a joy proposed, behind, a dream.   12
        All this the world well knows, yet none knows well
        To shun the heaven that leads men to this hell.

130

My mistress' eyes are nothing like the sun;
Coral is far more red than her lips' red;
If snow be white, why then her breasts are dun;
If hairs be wires, black wires grow on her head.   4
I have seen roses damasked, red and white,
But no such roses see I in her cheeks,
And in some perfumes is there more delight
Than in the breath that from my mistress reeks.   8
I love to hear her speak, yet well I know
That music hath a far more pleasing sound;
I grant I never saw a goddess go –
My mistress when she walks treads on the ground.   12
        And yet, by heaven, I think my love as rare
        As any she belied with false compare.

Sonnet 129

3 bloody,] *Lintott;* blouddy Q   5 Enjoyed] *Murden;* Inioyd Q *(variant form)*   6 had,] *Lintott;* had Q
7 swallowed] *Gildon*² *(*swallow'd*);* swollowed Q   8 mad:] *Capell;* mad. Q   9 Mad in] *Gildon*¹, *Capell;* Made
In Q   10 quest to have,] *Capell;* quest, to haue Q   11 proved, a] *Capell;* proud and Q; prov'd, and *Gildon*¹;
proud, and *Gildon*²; prov'd a *Sewell*¹

Sonnet 130

2 Coral] *Gildon;* Currall Q *(variant form)*   2 lips'] *Capell;* lips Q; lip's *conj., this edn*   11 go –] *Malone;* goe, Q;
go; *Gildon*²

131

Thou art as tyrannous, so as thou art,
As those whose beauties proudly make them cruel;
For well thou know'st to my dear doting heart
Thou art the fairest and most precious jewel.   4
Yet in good faith some say that thee behold,
Thy face hath not the power to make love groan;
To say they err, I dare not be so bold,
Although I swear it to myself alone.   8
And to be sure that is not false I swear,
A thousand groans but thinking on thy face
One on another's neck do witness bear
Thy black is fairest in my judgement's place.   12
  In nothing art thou black save in thy deeds,
  And thence this slander as I think proceeds.

132

Thine eyes I love, and they, as pitying me,
Knowing thy heart torment me with disdain,
Have put on black, and loving mourners be,
Looking with pretty ruth upon my pain.   4
And truly not the morning sun of heaven
Better becomes the grey cheeks of the east,
Nor that full star that ushers in the even
Doth half that glory to the sober west   8
As those two mourning eyes become thy face.
O let it then as well beseem thy heart
To mourn for me, since mourning doth thee grace,
And suit thy pity like in every part.   12
  Then will I swear beauty herself is black,
  And all they foul that thy complexion lack.

Sonnet 131

5 Yet . . . faith] Q; Yet, . . . faith, *Capell*   9 swear,] *Gildon¹*, *Capell*; sweare Q; swear; *Gildon²*   14 slander . . . think] Q; Slander, . . . think, *Gildon*

Sonnet 132

1 they,] *Gildon¹*; they Q   1 me,] Q; me, – *Ingram and Redpath*   2 heart] Q; heart, *Malone*   2 torment] Q; torments *Benson*   6 the east] *Gildon²*; th'East Q   9 mourning] *Gildon*; morning Q

133

Beshrew that heart that makes my heart to groan
For that deep wound it gives my friend and me!
Is't not enough to torture me alone,
But slave to slavery my sweet'st friend must be?   4
Me from myself thy cruel eye hath taken,
And my next self thou harder hast engrossed:
Of him, myself, and thee I am forsaken,
A torment thrice threefold thus to be crossed.   8
Prison my heart in thy steel bosom's ward,
But then my friend's heart let my poor heart bail;
Whoe'er keeps me, let my heart be his guard,
Thou canst not then use rigour in my jail.   12
     And yet thou wilt, for I, being pent in thee,
     Perforce am thine, and all that is in me.

134

So now I have confessed that he is thine,
And I myself am mortgaged to thy will,
Myself I'll forfeit, so that other mine
Thou wilt restore to be my comfort still: 4
But thou wilt not, nor he will not be free,
For thou art covetous, and he is kind;
He learned but surety-like to write for me
Under that bond that him as fast doth bind.   8
The statute of thy beauty thou wilt take,
Thou usurer, that put'st forth all to use,
And sue a friend came debtor for my sake,
So him I lose through my unkind abuse.   12
     Him have I lost, thou hast both him and me;
     He pays the whole, and yet am I not free.

Sonnet 133

2 me!] *Capell;* me*;* Q   4 be?] *Gildon;* be. Q   6 engrossed:] *Dyce (after Gildon²* engross'd*;);* ingrossed, Q *(variant form)*   8 crossed.] *Gildon²* (cross'd*.);* crossed: Q

Sonnet 134

1 So now] Q*;* So, now *Capell*   1 thine,] Q*;* thine *Neilson*   2–3 myself . . . Myself] *Murden;* my selfe . . . My selfe Q   12 lose] *Gildon;* loose Q *(variant form)*

135

Whoever hath her wish, thou hast thy Will,
And Will to boot, and Will in overplus;
More than enough am I that vex thee still,
To thy sweet will making addition thus.   4
Wilt thou, whose will is large and spacious,
Not once vouchsafe to hide my will in thine?
Shall will in others seem right gracious,
And in my will no fair acceptance shine?   8
The sea, all water, yet receives rain still,
And in abundance addeth to his store;
So thou being rich in Will add to thy Will
One will of mine to make thy large Will more.   12
    Let no unkind, no fair beseechers kill;
    Think all but one, and me in that one Will.

136

If thy soul check thee that I come so near,
Swear to thy blind soul that I was thy Will,
And will thy soul knows is admitted there;
Thus far for love, my love-suit, sweet, fulfil.   4
Will will fulfil the treasure of thy love,
Ay, fill it full with wills, and my will one.
In things of great receipt with ease we prove
Among a number one is reckoned none: 8
Then in the number let me pass untold,
Though in thy store's account I one must be;
For nothing hold me, so it please thee hold
That nothing me, a something sweet to thee.   12
    Make but my name thy love, and love that still,
    And then thou lovest me for my name is Will.

Sonnet 135

1 Will] *Murden; Will* Q *(also italicised in* 2 *(twice),* 11 *(twice),* 12 *('large Will'),* 14*);* will *Malone (except in* 14*)*
6 thine?] *Gildon;* thine, Q   8 shine?] *Lintott;* shine: Q   13 Let no unkind, no] Q; Let no unkind 'No' *conj.*
Dowden; Let no unkind no *Tyler;* Let no unkindness *Butler;* Be not unkind, no *(or* nor*) conj. Pooler;* Let 'No' unkind
no *Tucker;* Let 'No', unkind, no *Ingram and Redpath*

Sonnet 136

2 Will] *Murden; Will* Q *(also italicised in* 5*,* 14*);* will *Malone (capitalised roman in* 5*,* 14*)*   4 love-suit, sweet,] *Malone*
(after Capell); loue-sute sweet Q*;* love-suit, sweet *Butler*   5 Will will] *Lintott (Will* will*); Will,* will Q*;* With *Will* /
conj. Adams (in Rollins)   6 Ay] *Capell;* I Q   7 prove] *Dyce;* prooue, Q *(some copies may possibly read* prooue.*);*
prove; *Malone*   10 store's] *Gildon²;* stores Q; stores' *Malone*   12 nothing me,] Q; Nothing-me, *Gildon¹;* nothing,
me, *Hudson¹;* no thing, me *conj. Tucker;* no-thing me *Ingram and Redpath*   12 something sweet] Q *(some-thing);*
something *(sweet) Capell;* some-thing, sweet, *Ingram and Redpath*   14 lovest] Q; lov'st *Sewell*

137

Thou blind fool, Love, what dost thou to mine eyes,
That they behold, and see not what they see?
They know what beauty is, see where it lies,
Yet what the best is take the worst to be   4
If eyes, corrupt by over-partial looks,
Be anchored in the bay where all men ride,
Why of eyes' falsehood hast thou forgèd hooks,
Whereto the judgement of my heart is tied?   8
Why should my heart think that a several plot,
Which my heart knows the wide world's common place?
Or mine eyes seeing this, say this is not,
To put fair truth upon so foul a face?   12
    In things right true my heart and eyes have erred,
    And to this false plague are they now transferred.

138

When my love swears that she is made of truth,
I do believe her, though I know she lies,
That she might think me some untutored youth,
Unlearnèd in the world's false subtleties.   4
Thus vainly thinking that she thinks me young,
Although she knows my days are past the best,
Simply I credit her false-speaking tongue:
On both sides thus is simple truth suppressed.   8
But wherefore says she not she is unjust?
And wherefore say not I that I am old?
O love's best habit is in seeming trust,
And age in love loves not t'have years told.   12
    Therefore I lie with her, and she with me,
    And in our faults by lies we flattered be.

Sonnet 137

1 fool, Love,] *Malone*; foole loue, Q; fool, love, *Tucker*   2 behold,] *Gildon*²; behold Q   2 see?] *Gildon;* see: Q
5 eyes,] *Gildon*¹, *Capell*; eyes Q   11 this is not,] *Sewell*¹; this is not Q; quoted, *Tucker (after Capell)*   12 face?]
*Gildon*²; face, Q   13 erred] *Gildon* (err'd); erred Q   14 transferred] *Gildon* (transferr'd); transferred Q

Sonnet 138

138] *A variant version of this sonnet was printed in 'The Passionate Pilgrim' (1599), the text of which (from the 1612 edition)
was reprinted by Benson through Evans (except Lintott)*   4 Unlearnèd . . . subtleties] Q (subtilties); Vnskilful . . .
forgeries '*Passionate Pilgrim*'   6 she . . . are] Q; I know my yeares be '*Passionate Pilgrim*'; I know my yeres are *Folger
MS. 2071.7*   7 Simply I] Q; I smiling '*Passionate Pilgrim*'   7 false-speaking] *Sewell*¹, *Capell*; false speaking Q
8 On . . . suppressed] Q; Outfacing faults in loue, with loues ill rest '*Passionate Pilgrim*'   9 she . . . unjust] Q; my
loue that she is young '*Passionate Pilgrim*'   11 habit is in] Q; habit's in a '*Passionate Pilgrim*' (*1st edn, 1599*); habite
is a '*Passionate Pilgrim*' (*2nd edn, 1599*), *Gildon*   11 seeming trust] Q; soothing toung '*Passionate Pilgrim*'; smoothinge
tongue *Folger MS. 2071.7*, *Gildon*   12 t'have] Q; to haue '*Passionate Pilgrim*'   13 I . . . she] Q; I'le lye with Loue,
and loue '*Passionate Pilgrim*'   14 And . . . flattered] Q; Since that our faultes in loue thus smother'd '*Passionate
Pilgrim*'; Since yᵗ oʳ faults in loue thus smothered *Folger MS. 2071.7*   14 flattered] *Capell* (flatter'd); flattered Q

139

O call not me to justify the wrong
That thy unkindness lays upon my heart;
Wound me not with thine eye but with thy tongue;
Use power with power, and slay me not by art.   4
Tell me thou lov'st elsewhere; but in my sight,
Dear heart, forbear to glance thine eye aside;
What need'st thou wound with cunning when thy might
Is more than my o'erpressed defence can bide?   8
Let me excuse thee: 'Ah, my love well knows
Her pretty looks have been mine enemies,
And therefore from my face she turns my foes,
That they elsewhere might dart their injuries.'   12
    Yet do not so, but since I am near slain,
    Kill me outright with looks, and rid my pain.

140

Be wise as thou art cruel, do not press
My tongue-tied patience with too much disdain,
Lest sorrow lend me words, and words express
The manner of my pity-wanting pain.   4
If I might teach thee wit, better it were,
Though not to love, yet, love, to tell me so –
As testy sick men, when their deaths be near,
No news but health from their physicians know.   8
For if I should despair, I should grow mad,
And in my madness might speak ill of thee;
Now this ill-wresting world is grown so bad,
Mad slanderers by mad ears believèd be.   12
    That I may not be so, nor thou belied,
    Bear thine eyes straight, though thy proud heart go wide.

Sonnet 139

1 O] Q; O! *Gildon¹*; O, *Capell*   9–12   'Ah, . . . injuries.'] *Quoted, Tucker*; ah . . . iniuries: Q   10   mine] Q; my *Benson*   13   near] *Gildon*; neere Q

Sonnet 140

2 tongue-tied] *Lintott*; toung tide Q   2   disdain,] *Capell*; disdaine: Q   4   pity-wanting] *Gildon*; pittie wanting Q
5 were] *Gildon*; weare Q   6   yet, love,] *Capell (subst.)*; yet loue Q   6   so –] *Gildon²* (so:); so, Q   7   sick men]
Gildon²; sick-men Q   11   Now] Q; Know *conj., this edn*   11   ill-wresting] *Lintott*; ill wresting Q   13   belied]
Gildon (bely'd); be lyde Q; be-lide *Benson*

141

In faith, I do not love thee with mine eyes,
For they in thee a thousand errors note,
But 'tis my heart that loves what they despise,
Who in despite of view is pleased to dote. 4
Nor are mine ears with thy tongue's tune delighted,
Nor tender feeling to base touches prone,
Nor taste, nor smell, desire to be invited
To any sensual feast with thee alone; 8
But my five wits nor my five senses can
Dissuade one foolish heart from serving thee,
Who leaves unswayed the likeness of a man,
Thy proud heart's slave and vassal wretch to be. 12
    Only my plague thus far I count my gain,
    That she that makes me sin awards me pain.

142

Love is my sin, and thy dear virtue hate,
Hate of my sin, grounded on sinful loving.
O but with mine compare thou thine own state,
And thou shalt find it merits not reproving, 4
Or if it do, not from those lips of thine,
That have profaned their scarlet ornaments,
And sealed false bonds of love as oft as mine,
Robbed others' beds' revènues of their rents. 8
Be it lawful I love thee as thou lov'st those
Whom thine eyes woo as mine impòrtune thee:
Root pity in thy heart, that when it grows
Thy pity may deserve to pitied be. 12
    If thou dost seek to have what thou dost hide,
    By self-example mayst thou be denied.

Sonnet 141

1 faith,] *Capell;* faith Q   6 feeling] Q; feeling, *Malone*

Sonnet 142

1 thy] Q; my *Benson*   7 mine,] Q; mine; *Malone;* mine *Hudson*[1], *Tucker;* mine – *Ingram and Redpath*   8 beds' revènues] *Oulton, Knight;* beds reuenues Q; bed-revenues *Capell*   10 thee:] *Malone;* thee, Q   14 self-example] *Gildon*[2]; selfe example Q

143

Lo, as a careful huswife runs to catch
One of her feathered creatures broke away,
Sets down her babe and makes all swift dispatch
In pùrsuit of the thing she would have stay,   4
Whilst her neglected child holds her in chase,
Cries to catch her whose busy care is bent
To follow that which flies before her face,
Not prizing her poor infant's discontent: 8
So runn'st thou after that which flies from thee,
Whilst I, thy babe, chase thee afar behind;
But if thou catch thy hope, turn back to me,
And play the mother's part, kiss me, be kind.   12
    So will I pray that thou mayst have thy Will,
    If thou turn back and my loud crying still.

144

Two loves I have, of comfort and despair,
Which like two spirits do suggest me still:
The better angel is a man right fair;
The worser spirit a woman coloured ill.   4
To win me soon to hell my female evil
Tempteth my better angel from my side,
And would corrupt my saint to be a devil,
Wooing his purity with her foul pride.   8
And whether that my angel be turned fiend
Suspect I may, yet not directly tell,
But being both from me, both to each friend,
I guess one angel in another's hell.   12
    Yet this shall I ne'er know, but live in doubt,
    Till my bad angel fire my good one out.

Sonnet 143

1 Lo,] *Capell;* Lo Q; Lo! *Gildon*   1 careful] Q *(carefull);* care-full *Wells*   1 huswife] Q; housewife *Gildon²*
(variant form)   2 feathered] *Lintott (*fether'd*);* fethered Q   4 stay,] *Neilson²;* stay: Q; stay; *Capell*   7 face,]
Gildon¹, Capell; face: Q   11 me,] *Gildon;* me: Q   12 part,] *Benson;* part Q   13 Will] *Sewell¹, Murden; Will* Q

Sonnet 144

144] *A slightly variant version of this sonnet was printed in 'The Passionate Pilgrim' (1599), the text of which (from the 1612
edition) was reprinted by Benson through Evans (except Lintott)*   1 have,] *'Passionate Pilgrim';* haue Q   2 Which]
Q; That *'Passionate Pilgrim'*   2 suggest] *'Passionate Pilgrim';* sugiest Q   3, 4 The] Q; My *'Passionate Pilgrim'*
6 side] *'Passionate Pilgrim';* sight Q   7 devil,] *'Passionate Pilgrim';* diuel: Q   8 foul] Q; faire *'Passionate Pilgrim'*
9 fiend] *'Passionate Pilgrim' (*feend*);* finde Q   11 But . . . from] Q; For . . . to *'Passionate Pilgrim'*   13 Yet . . .
ne'er] Q; The truth I shall not *'Passionate Pilgrim'*

145

Those lips that Love's own hand did make
Breathed forth the sound that said 'I hate'
To me that languished for her sake;
But when she saw my woeful state,   4
Straight in her heart did mercy come,
Chiding that tongue that ever sweet
Was used in giving gentle doom,
And taught it thus anew to greet: 8
'I hate' she altered with an end
That followed it as gentle day
Doth follow night, who like a fiend
From heaven to hell is flown away: 12
    'I hate' from hate away she threw,
    And saved my life, saying 'not you'.

146

Poor soul, the centre of my sinful earth,
[. .] these rebel pow'rs that thee array,
Why dost thou pine within and suffer dearth
Painting thy outward walls so costly gay?   4
Why so large cost, having so short a lease,
Dost thou upon thy fading mansion spend?
Shall worms, inheritors of this excess,
Eat up thy charge? Is this thy body's end?   8
Then, soul, live thou upon thy servant's loss,
And let that pine to aggravate thy store;
Buy terms divine in selling hours of dross;
Within be fed, without be rich no more: 12
    So shalt thou feed on Death, that feeds on men,
    And Death once dead, there's no more dying then.

Sonnet 145

2 'I hate'] *Quoted, Knight (after Malone's italics);* I hate Q   7 doom,] *Gildon (after Benson* doome:*);* dome: Q
8 anew] *Gildon* (a-new*);* a new Q   9, 13 'I hate'] *Quoted, Knight (after the italics in Gildon²);* I hate Q   14 'not
you'.] *Quoted, Knight (after the italics in Gildon²);* not you. Q

Sonnet 146

2 [. . .] these] *Globe;* My sinfull earth these Q *(see Commentary);* Fool'd by those *Malone;* Starv'd by the *conj. Steevens
(in Malone);* Fool'd by these *Dyce;* Foil'd by these *Palgrave (in Rollins);* Press'd by these *Dowden;* Feeding these *conj.
Sebastian Evans (in Rollins);* Rebuke these *conj. Pooler;* Bearing these *conj. Harrison;* Fenced by these *Sisson;* Gull'd
by these *Seymour-Smith (more than eighty other possible readings have been suggested; see Rollins, 1, 374, and Ingram and
Redpath, pp. 358–9)*   13, 14 Death] *Ewing;* death Q

147

My love is as a fever, longing still
For that which longer nurseth the disease,
Feeding on that which doth preserve the ill,
Th'uncertain sickly appetite to please.   4
My reason, the physician to my love,
Angry that his prescriptions are not kept,
Hath left me, and I desperate now approve
Desire is death, which physic did except.   8
Past cure I am, now reason is past care,
And, frantic mad with evermore unrest,
My thoughts and my discourse as madmen's are,
At random from the truth vainly expressed: 12
    For I have sworn thee fair, and thought thee bright,
    Who art as black as hell, as dark as night.

148

O me! what eyes hath love put in my head,
Which have no correspondence with true sight?
Or, if they have, where is my judgement fled,
That censures falsely what they see aright?   4
If that be fair whereon my false eyes dote,
What means the world to say it is not so?
If it be not, then love doth well denote
Love's eye is not so true as all men's: no,   8
How can it? O how can love's eye be true,
That is so vexed with watching and with tears?
No marvel then though I mistake my view:
The sun itself sees not till heaven clears.   12
    O cunning love, with tears thou keep'st me blind,
    Lest eyes, well seeing, thy foul faults should find.

Sonnet 147

7 approve] *Knight;* approoue, Q; approve; *Gildon;* approve, – *Capell*   10 evermore] Q *(euer-more);* ever more *conj. Anon. (in Rollins)*   10 unrest,] Q; unrest; *Capell (retaining the comma after* care *in 9)*   11 madmen's] *Gildon²* (Madmens); mad mens Q   12 random] *Benson;* randon Q *(variant form)*

Sonnet 148

2 sight?] *Malone;* sight, Q   8 men's: no,] Q (mens); mens: no *Benson;* mens. No, *Gildon¹;* Mens. No; *Gildon²;* men's no. *conj. Lettsom (in Rollins), Dyce²;* men's: no. *conj. Walker (in Rollins), Craig;* men's: no; *Staunton;* men's: 'No.' *Globe;* men's. No! *Keightley;* men's – no, *Alexander*   9 it? O] Q; it, O, *Wells, Kerrigan*

149

Canst thou, O cruel, say I love thee not,
When I against myself with thee partake?
Do I not think on thee when I forgot
Am of myself, all tyrant for thy sake?   4
Who hateth thee that I do call my friend?
On whom frown'st thou that I do fawn upon?
Nay, if thou lour'st on me, do I not spend
Revenge upon myself with present moan?   8
What merit do I in myself respect
That is so proud thy service to despise,
When all my best doth worship thy defect,
Commanded by the motion of thine eyes?   12
    But, love, hate on, for now I know thy mind:
    Those that can see thou lov'st, and I am blind.

150

O from what pow'r hast thou this pow'rful might
With insufficiency my heart to sway,
To make me give the lie to my true sight,
And swear that brightness doth not grace the day?   4
Whence hast thou this becoming of things ill,
That in the very refuse of thy deeds
There is such strength and warrantise of skill
That in my mind thy worst all best exceeds?   8
Who taught thee how to make me love thee more,
The more I hear and see just cause of hate?
O, though I love what others do abhor,
With others thou shouldst not abhor my state.   12
    If thy unworthiness raised love in me,
    More worthy I to be beloved of thee.

Sonnet 149

2 partake?] *Gildon;* pertake: Q   4 all tyrant] Q; all, Tyrant, *Sewell*[1], *Capell;* all tyrant, *Malone;* all truant
conj. Malone; all-tyrant, *Hazlitt*   5 friend?] *Gildon*[2]; friend, Q   6 upon?] *Gildon*[2]; vpon, Q; upon. *Benson*
9 respect] *Kittredge;* respect, Q   12 eyes?] *Gildon*[2]; eyes. Q

Sonnet 150

6 deeds] *Malone;* deeds, Q *corr.;* deeds; Q *uncorr.*   10 hate?] *Gildon;* hate, Q

151

Love is too young to know what conscience is,
Yet who knows not conscience is born of love?
Then, gentle cheater, urge not my amiss,
Lest guilty of my faults thy sweet self prove.   4
For thou betraying me, I do betray
My nobler part to my gross body's treason:
My soul doth tell my body that he may
Triumph in love; flesh stays no farther reason,   8
But rising at thy name doth point out thee
As his triumphant prize. Proud of this pride,
He is contented thy poor drudge to be,
To stand in thy affairs, fall by thy side.   12
      No want of conscience hold it that I call
      Her 'love' for whose dear love I rise and fall.

152

In loving thee thou know'st I am forsworn,
But thou art twice forsworn to me love swearing:
In act thy bed-vow broke, and new faith torn
In vowing new hate after new love bearing.   4
But why of two oaths' breach do I accuse thee,
When I break twenty? I am perjured most,
For all my vows are oaths but to misuse thee,
And all my honest faith in thee is lost.   8
For I have sworn deep oaths of thy deep kindness,
Oaths of thy love, thy truth, thy constancy,
And to enlighten thee gave eyes to blindness,
Or made them swear against the thing they see: 12
      For I have sworn thee fair: more perjured eye,
      To swear against the truth so foul a lie.

Sonnet 151

2 love?] *Gildon;* loue, Q   10 prize.] *Gildon*² *(*Prize;*)*; prize, Q   13 call] *Gildon;* call, Q   14 Her 'love'] *Dyce;* Her loue, Q; Her – love, *Malone*²

Sonnet 152

2 me love swearing:] *Gildon;* me loue swearing, Q; me, Love-swearing; *Sewell*¹ ; me *(*love*)* swearing; *conj. Fleay (in Rollins)*   3 broke,] *Gildon*²; broake Q; brooke *Benson*   3 torn] *Globe;* torne, Q   6 twenty?] *Gildon;* twenty: Q; twenty! *Butler*   9 kindness,] *Capell;* kindnesse: Q   11 enlighten] *Gildon;* inlighten Q *(variant form)*   13 eye] Q; I *Sewell*   14 so] *Benson;* fo Q

153

Cupid laid by his brand and fell asleep:
A maid of Dian's this advantage found,
And his love-kindling fire did quickly steep
In a cold valley-fountain of that ground;   4
Which borrowed from this holy fire of Love
A dateless lively heat, still to endure,
And grew a seething bath, which yet men prove
Against strange maladies a sovereign cure.   8
But at my mistress' eye Love's brand new fired,
The boy for trial needs would touch my breast;
I, sick withal, the help of bath desired,
And thither hied, a sad distempered guest;   12
    But found no cure: the bath for my help lies
    Where Cupid got new fire – my mistress' eyes.

154

The little Love-god lying once asleep
Laid by his side his heart-inflaming brand,
Whilst many nymphs that vowed chaste life to keep
Came tripping by; but in her maiden hand   4
The fairest votary took up that fire
Which many legions of true hearts had warmed,
And so the general of hot desire
Was sleeping by a virgin hand disarmed.   8
This brand she quenchèd in a cool well by,
Which from Love's fire took heat perpetual,
Growing a bath and healthful remedy
For men diseased; but I, my mistress' thrall,   12
    Came there for cure, and this by that I prove:
    Love's fire heats water, water cools not love.

Sonnet 153

1 asleep] *Benson;* a sleepe Q   5 Love] *Dyce;* loue Q   6 dateless lively] Q*; dateless-lively conj. Walker (in Rollins)*
6 heat,] *Capell;* heat Q   6 endure] *Benson;* indure Q *(variant form)*   8 strange] *Benson;* strang Q*; strong
conj. Tyler*   9 Love's] *Knight;* loues Q   9 new fired] *Malone²* (new-fir'd)*;* new fired Q*;* new-fired *Malone¹*
11 bath] Q*; Bath / Capell, conj. Steevens (in Malone)*   11 desired] *Malone²* (desir'd)*;* desired Q   12 thither]
Gildon; thether Q *(variant form)*   12 hied] *Capell* (hy'd)*;* hied Q   14 eyes] *Benson;* eye Q

Sonnet 154

1 asleep] *Gildon²;* a sleepe Q   2 heart-inflaming] *Capell* (heart-enflaming)*;* heart inflaming Q   4 by,] *Gildon;*
by, Q   10 Love's] *Knight;* loues Q   12 diseased;] *Gildon;* diseasd, Q   14] *Centred, and approximately four lines
below 14,* Q *reads* FINIS.

THE COMMENTARY

Introductory note

> Where matter is so full, and so perplex't,
> The *Comment's* forced to out-swell the *Text*.
> (Eldred Revett, *Poems* (1657), 'To her taxing him for late writing to her')

A short review of what we actually know, and, equally important, how much we do not know about the genesis of the Sonnets and Shakespeare's relation to them may serve to focus some of the challenging questions discussed or touched on in the Introduction and Commentary.

Shakespeare's Sonnets may fairly be said to raise more questions than they answer, and the little we really know about them can 'be bounded in a nutshell'. Some of the Sonnets, perhaps even the majority, were probably written before September of 1598, the year in which Francis Meres, in his *Palladis Tamia* (entered in the Stationers' Register on 7 September 1598), claimed that 'the sweete wittie soule of *Ovid* lives in mellifluous & hony-tongued *Shakespeare*, witnes his *Venus* and *Adonis*, his *Lucrece*, his sugred Sonnets among his private friends, &c.', (281ᵛ–282ʳ). Variant versions of two of the Sonnets (138 and 144), neither of which can be described as 'sugred', escaped into print in *The Passionate Pilgrim* (1599), an unauthorised collection of lyric verse that its publisher, William Jaggard, ascribed to 'W. Shakespeare'. And, finally, the bookseller, Thomas Thorpe, entered 'a Booke called Shakespeares *sonnettes*' in the Stationers' Register on 20 May 1609. Shortly after this (before 19 June of the same year), Thorpe published the first and only substantive text of the Sonnets: 'SHAKESPEARES / SONNETS. / Neuer before Imprinted. / . . ./ 1609' (hereafter referred to as Q; see Textual Analysis, pp. 258–67 below). It was printed by George Eld in quarto format. Such are the bare facts – more, to be sure, than we possess for a number of Shakespeare's plays. Given, however, the seemingly personal nature of most sonnets (the 'I to you' formula) and the potentially autobiographical implications of Shakespeare's two-part sequence – Sonnets 1–126 addressed to a young man ('my lovely boy', 126.1); and 127–52 to a 'Dark Lady' or mistress (see, however, (3) below) – with its somewhat vestigial 'sonnet story' and cast of four, possibly more, interacting 'characters' (the poet-persona, the young man, the mistress, and the 'rival poet(s)'), each of them, except the poet himself (whose name is 'Will', 136.14), cloaked in an intriguing anonymity, it is scarcely surprising that conjecture of all kinds, much of it the wildest of 'wild surmise', has, since the last years of the eighteenth century, flourished so luxuriantly. Thus editors and critics alike have vied with, and outvied, each other in their attempts to plumb the so-called 'mystery' of the Sonnets – question upon question and speculation upon speculation.

In any final reckoning, of course, all such questions and conjectures are irrelevant and intrusive. Like other great poetry, the Sonnets are secure in themselves, beyond 'Time's tyranny' or the critic's 'lion's paws' – not merely 'pretty rooms' (as John Donne punningly described the sonnet form), but 'eternal numbers to outlive long date' (38.12), unchallengeable and hauntingly universal. Nevertheless, even the general reader cannot entirely escape the burden of the 'mystery' that the Sonnets impose. Students of Shakespeare must, therefore, as fairly and objectively as possible, face these questions, most of which are as legitimate as the proposed answers are hypothetical, and make it possible for readers to examine the 'evidence' and arrive at their own conclusions.

Briefly, then, the central and most frequently asked questions are:

(1) Are the Sonnets to some extent autobiographical? Or are they only dramatically conceived fictions? Or a mixture of both? These questions are at the heart of the 'mystery'. Are the Sonnets, indeed, the 'key' with which 'Shakespeare unlocked his heart', as Wordsworth was one of the first to claim? (If so, Browning retorted, 'the less Shakespeare he'.) Or do they project imaginatively conceived characters and situations, playing on, or perhaps parodying, the conventional sonnet themes and postures – a hundred-and-fifty-four little playlets tacked loosely together and featuring a triangular love affair – wittily contrived by Shakespeare to amuse himself and his 'private friends'? Such a view in itself prompts another question: why, then, would a master dramatist like Shakespeare, creating a dramatic fiction, produce a confused, weakly articulated, and sometimes contradictory 'sonnet story'?

To some extent, of course, all significant art is autobiographical, an unconscious projection of the artist's 'self' that individualises, as with an 'informing hand', the creative act. No critic with a conscience (unlike Baconians, Oxfordians, etc.) would now deny that such a Shakespearean signature is writ large in the Sonnets, as it is, of course, in the plays and other poems. While allowing for such personal stamping, some readers have refused to permit Shakespeare to step out of his more usual dramatic mode and will allow him no consciously autobiographical intention. Much of the opposition to an autobiographical approach, particularly among nineteenth- and early-twentieth-century critics, was motivated in great part by an unwillingness to accept the homoerotic implications suggested by Shakespeare's often passionately expressed 'love' for a 'beauteous and lovely youth' (54.13). To avoid such a consideration – at that time nearly unthinkable – most critics were forced either to deny any personal identity between Shakespeare and his poet-persona (even resorting on occasion to treating the Sonnets as a form of allegory) or, if they accepted an autobiographical interpretation, to explain his 'love' for the youth as Platonic and his passionate language as conventionally acceptable in terms of the long-established male friendship tradition; a few even attempted to dodge these issues by seeing Shakespeare as a 'hired hand', who supplied one or more patrons with sonnets written 'to order' and appropriately suited to some particular occasion (see Rollins, II, 133–65; 232–8). Today, in an age more open and understanding where sexual mores are concerned, the possibility that 'our Shakespeare' may have been emotionally, perhaps actively, bisexual no longer shocks us as much as it would have done even fifty years ago.

(2) If the Sonnets are to be read autobiographically, who in real life were the other persons who figure in the 'sonnet story' (the young man, the 'Dark Lady', and the 'rival poet(s)')? And is 'Mr. W. H.' who is addressed as 'THE.ONLIE. BEGETTER.OF. / THESE.INSVING.SONNETS.' (in Thorpe's dedicatory inscription prefacing the Sonnets in Q) to be identified with the 'young man'? For a short list of proposed candidates for the 'young man' and 'Mr. W. H.', see the Commentary notes on Thorpe's dedication (p. 115 below). The most frequently cited are Henry Wriothesley, third Earl of Southampton (1573–1624), to whom Shakespeare dedicated *Venus and Adonis* (1592–3) and *The Rape of Lucrece* (1593–4), and William Herbert, third Earl of Pembroke (1580–1630), one of the dedicatees of the First Folio of Shakespeare's works (1623). The identities of the 'Dark Lady' and the principal 'rival poet' are, if possible, even more 'shadowy' than that of the youth (see the headnote to Sonnet 127 and 86.5–12 n.).

(3) Are all the sonnets in the first series (1–126) addressed to a young man, or even to the same young man? Are all those in the second series (127–52) addressed to the same woman? It is generally assumed, for lack of evidence to the contrary, that all of Sonnets 1–126 are addressed to the same young man, and all Sonnets 127–52 to the same woman. A few critics, however, argue that in the first series those sonnets in which the sex of the person addressed is ambiguous may have been written to a woman (e.g. 21, 27–9, 36), and some protest that such sonnets as 20, 21, 48, 56, 66, 69, 73–5, 118, 119, and 126 could never conceivably have been addressed to a nobleman. None of these assumptions can be either proved or disproved.

(4) During what period (or periods) in Shakespeare's career were the Sonnets composed? That Shakespeare had written some 'sugred sonnets' before June of 1598 and that two (138 and 144) of the 1609 Q collection were published in 1599 has already been noted. Unfortunately, such evidence leaves us with no clue as to a *terminus a quo* and only 1609 as an end. The publication in 1591 of Sir Philip Sidney's sonnet sequence, *Astrophil and Stella*, almost immediately sparked a substantial number of other sequences by, among others, Samuel Daniel (1592), Henry Constable (1592), Thomas Watson (1593), Giles Fletcher the Elder (1593), Thomas Lodge (1593), Barnabe Barnes (1593), Michael Drayton (1594), and Edmund Spenser (1595), and it is generally believed that Shakespeare, under the influence of Sidney, Daniel, and Constable, from each of whom he appears to have borrowed, began writing sonnets in 1592–3, a view given some support by the larger number of verbal and thematic parallels between the Sonnets and *Venus and Adonis* (1592–3), *The Rape of Lucrece* (1593–4), and the earlier plays through *King John* (1594–6) than with the middle or late plays (*Hamlet* and *As You Like It* excepted). On the other hand, Sonnet 107, which shows some remarkable verbal links with *Hamlet*, is now usually accepted as dating from 1603/4 (see Commentary notes), together with some other sonnets – those between Sonnets 104 and 126 – which are also considered, in terms of their freer style and verbal density, probably to have been composed after 1600. Most of the Dark Lady series (127–52) is usually thought of as having been written before and during the situations alluded to in Sonnets 33–5 and 40–2. The dating of the main body of the Sonnets, in good part because of the so-called 'procreation sonnets' (1–17), has often been influenced by which candidate in the role of the young man (Southampton or

Pembroke) a critic happened to espouse: an early date for Southampton, who was nineteen in 1592; a later date (about 1598) for Pembroke, who was only twelve in 1592. Two
recent full-dress attempts to date the Sonnets (neither with a particular Southampton
or Pembroke axe to grind) will illustrate how radically dating-limits can vary. The
first (A. K. Hieatt, C. W. Hieatt, A. L. Prescott, 'When did Shakespeare write *Sonnets*
1609', *SP* 88 (1991), 69–109), based on an analysis of Shakespeare's use of 'early' and
'late' rare words at different times in his career, dates the Sonnets as: Sonnets 1–103
and 127–54, 1591–5; and Sonnets 104–26, 1597–1603; with Sonnets 1–60 undergoing
revision some time before 1609 (*A Lover's Complaint* now being generally thought of as
composed about the same time as this revision, probably after the turn of the century).
The second (D. W. Foster, 'Reconstructing Shakespeare', *Shakespeare Newsletter*, Fall
1991, pp. 26–7), working on the theory that when Shakespeare memorised a role in
one of his own plays, the memorised lines strongly influenced – at least for a period of
time – his use of language in his subsequent work, arrives at the following conclusions:
Sonnets 127–44, 1598/9; Sonnets 18–55, 1599; Sonnets 56–96, 1600; Sonnets 97–115,
1602–4; and Sonnets 1–17, 116–26, and 145–54 (plus *A Lover's Complaint*), 1608.

(5) Is the sonnet order in Q 1609 more or less chronological and the result of Shakespeare's own arrangement? Or is the order, as many critics have insisted, essentially
random, without authority, and chronologically badly confused? Although John Benson in his 1640 *Poems* rearranged and grouped the Sonnets under specific headings,
his reordering was without any chronological or biographical intention (see Textual
Analysis, pp. 265–7 below). Beginning, however, with Charles Knight in 1841, many
attempts to rearrange the Sonnets and in some way to improve the 'sonnet story' have
been perpetrated. The utter futility of such exercises is graphically exposed by Rollins
(II, 113–16) in his tabular arrangement of nineteen such proposed reorderings (e.g. Sonnet 1 becomes variously no. 105, 120, 92, 95, 2, 43, 29, 12, 3, 20, 26, and 15 – in only
five rearrangements retaining its initial position) and a similar chaotic diversity appears
in the proposed rearrangement of the other 153 sonnets. Although the Q order may at
times appear confused and difficult to rationalise (aside from the major divisions, 1–126
(to the youth), 127–52 (to the Dark Lady), the procreation sonnets (1–17; see headnote
to Sonnet 1), and a number of clearly linked groups of two or more sonnets), all recent
editors have retained the Q order, an order which gains some indirect support from
Duncan-Jones's now widely accepted view that the last two anacreontic Cupid sonnets
(153–4) and *A Lover's Complaint* are integral to a kind of tripartite sonnet-sequence
arrangement that can be paralleled in several other contemporary sequences – Daniel's
Delia (1592), Lodge's *Phillis* (1593), Giles Fletcher the Elder's *Licia* (1593), Spenser's
Amoretti (1595), and Barnfield's *Cynthia* (1595). See Duncan-Jones, pp. 165–71, and
Kerrigan, pp. 12–14; for *A Lover's Complaint*, see Roe (ed.), *Poems*, 1992, new edition
2006.

(6) Were the Sonnets published with or without Shakespeare's knowledge or consent?
Since Knight first mooted the question (1841) majority opinion has generally agreed
that Thorpe published Q (1609) surreptitiously, at least so far as Shakespeare's personal involvement was concerned. Recently, however, this view has been challenged by
Duncan-Jones, who argues (a) that Thorpe was a respectable publisher of such leading

writers as Marlowe, Jonson, and Chapman, none of whose texts, so far as Thorpe was concerned, was obtained surreptitiously (pp. 156–65); and (b) that Q shows definite evidence of authorial arrangement (see the conclusion of (5) above). These points are well taken, but the evidence educed from the general probity of Thorpe's other dealings as a publisher, while suggestive, remains necessarily speculative, and, though this may be considered equally speculative, it is possible that at the time Thorpe entered the Sonnets in the Stationers' Register he knew that Shakespeare was visiting (or even residing at) Stratford to escape from the plague, which in 1609 was especially serious in London. Moreover, the lack of any sign of authorial oversight in the printing-house production of Q would be strange if Shakespeare himself did indeed have some direct hand in its publication (see Textual Analysis, p. 279). There also remains the potentially embarrassing question of what seems to be, at least on the surface, the homoerotic nature of the relationship between Shakespeare and the 'young man' to whom the majority of the Sonnets are addressed. Duncan-Jones dismisses any such embarrassment on Shakespeare's part, but is it probable, unless the youth involved were dead by 1609, that Shakespeare would have dared (particularly if the youth were of upper-class or noble position) to have broadcast the suggestion of a relationship that might otherwise have been known only to an inner circle of 'private friends'? The argument that Q shows evidence of some authorial arrangement is, I think, almost certainly correct and marks an important turning-point in our evaluation of the extent to which Shakespeare was responsible for the overall arrangement of the Sonnets in Q, but such evidence does not of itself prove Shakespeare's involvement in the publication of Q. The manuscript copy for Q was, most would now agree, a scribal transcript perhaps at one or more removes from Shakespeare's holograph (see Textual Analysis, pp. 263–5), and such a scribal copy could have fallen into Thorpe's hands in a variety of ways having no immediate connection with Shakespeare.

Perhaps Sir William Alexander's teasing comment on the 'mystery' inherent in so many sonnet sequences may serve as a fittingly ambiguous conclusion:

> Yet Lines (dumbe Orators) ye may be bold,
> Th'ink will not blush, though paper doth looke pale,
> Ye of my state the secrets did containe,
> That then through clouds of darke inventions shin'd:
> Whil'st I disclos'd, yet not disclos'd my mind,
> Obscure to others, but to one ore plaine.

> (*Aurora* (1604), Sonnet 9.3–8)

Thomas Thorpe's dedication

Cast in the form of a lapidary inscription (like those sometimes found on tombs or other monuments), Thomas Thorpe's dedication to 'M‍ʳ. W. H.' 'has caused the spilling of more ink, the utterance of more futile words, than almost any other personage or problem of Q' (Rollins, II, 166). The lapidary form may have been suggested to Thorpe by Ben Jonson's dedication of *Volpone*, which Thorpe had published in 1607. Setting aside for the moment the various subtleties of language and syntax that have been proposed (see notes below), a common-sense paraphrase would seem to be as follows: 'To the sole inspirer of these following sonnets, Master W. H., all happiness and that eternity promised by our ever-living poet [William Shakespeare], wishes the well-wishing adventurer [T. T.] in publishing [these sonnets].' Ingram and Redpath (pp. 3–5) give an excellent summary of the various questions which critics have raised, most of them hingeing, of course, on the supposed identity of the mysterious 'Mʳ. W. H.' Recently, D. W. Foster ('Master W. H. R. I. P.', *PMLA* 102 (1987), 42–54) has once again attacked the problems posed by what he prefers to call Thorpe's 'epigraph'. He shows how conventional and formulaic Thorpe's language is when viewed in terms of many other contemporary dedications and argues (1) that 'W. H.' is a compositor's misreading for 'W. S.' or 'W. SH.' i.e. William Shakespeare (first suggested by A. E. Brae in 1869); (2) that 'begetter' can properly refer only to 'author as parent', not to an 'inspirer', although he acknowledges a single such use by Daniel in *Delia* (1594), who in a dedicatory sonnet to the Countess of Pembroke (perhaps, known to Shakespeare; see 38.13–14) describes her as the true author of his verses ('begotten by thy hand and my desire'); and (3) that 'our.ever-living.poet' refers not to Shakespeare, as almost universally agreed, but to God metaphorically described as 'poet', an attribution necessary to his argument that 'W. H.' is a misprint for 'W. S.' But Foster's argument founders on what I feel is a forced interpretation of God as 'our.ever-living.poet'. The pointing of the dedication offers no guide to syntax since a full stop follows each word.

1 ONLIE.BEGETTER. Sole or incomparable (1) inspirer, (2) procurer (of the manuscript). *OED* records 'begetter' in only two senses: (1) 'One who begets; a procreator'; (2) 'The agent that originates, produces, or occasions' (citing the present passage under (2)), and offers no support (after 1393) for the verb 'beget' in the sense of 'acquire' or 'procure' (even in earlier cases, as Ingram and Redpath note, it is always used with the implication of 'acquiring something for oneself'). Moreover, it is surely fair to ask why Thorpe would have wasted all his 'flowers of rhetoric' on some individual who had merely helped him to acquire the manuscript – one from whose suggested identity he could expect to receive no favourable publicity for his publishing venture.

3 Mʳ.W.H. The candidates proposed for the role of 'Mʳ. [i.e. Master] W. H.' are legion (see Rollins, II, 177–232), most of them having been returned by more recent scholars to the oblivion from which they had been dragged. Among the suggested 'inspirers' only two candidates are still seriously considered: (1) William Herbert, third Earl of Pembroke (1580–1630); (2) Henry Wriothesley, third Earl of Southampton (1573–1624), his initials being reversed as initials sometimes were in prefatory matter. Among 'procurers': (1) Sir William Hervey, stepfather of the Earl of Southampton; (2) William

Hathaway, Shakespeare's brother-in-law; (3) William Hall – several people of this name have been suggested. See Rollins, II, 171–232.

4–5 THAT.ETERNITIE. / PROMISED. i.e. that (kind of) eternity promised in some of 'these.insuing.sonnets' (e.g. in 18, 19, 60, 63, 101). 'promised' may also perhaps carry the sense of 'augured by the quality of the poet's work' (Ingram and Redpath). 'that' implies, I think, 'that kind of'; whereas, if, as Foster argues (see headnote), 'our.ever-living.poet' is intended as a reference to God, we would expect 'the', not 'that'.

7 OVR.EVER-LIVING.POET. i.e. William Shakespeare. See, however, Foster (p. 46), who points out that 'ever-living' elsewhere is used only of the dead or of God, though, with his usual fairness, he suggests the possibility that Thorpe 'may nevertheless have intended "ever-living" for Shakespeare, since hyperboles were heaped on poets of far less talent or reputation'.

9–10 THE.WELL-WISHING. / ADVENTVRER. i.e. Thomas Thorpe, who 'wishes well' to 'Mʳ. W. H.' Like many a 'Merchant Adventurer' at this time, Thorpe was laying out and risking capital on a commercial 'venture'. Does Thorpe's metaphor suggest, perhaps, that he was conscious of the somewhat risky (or risqué) nature of his publication?

10–12 IN. / SETTING. / FORTH. To 'set forth' was a common contemporary idiom for 'publishing' a work, but 'setting.forth' also continues the 'Adventurer' metaphor.

13 T. T. i.e. Thomas Thorpe.

Sonnet 1

The first of a series (1–17) dealing with the duty of procreation, in which the youth here addressed is urged to obviate the idle waste of nature's treasure in 'fairest creatures' by marrying and perpetuating himself (i.e. giving himself a kind of immortality) through his offspring. Underlying this theme, as throughout the Sonnets, is the inexorable and ruinous action of 'Time the Destroyer' (see 19.1 n.). The marriage–procreation theme has classical roots in Plato's *Symposium* (206C–207E), and Shakespeare was familiar with several English treatments of it: Thomas Wilson, *The Arte of Rhetorique* (1553), pp. 95–140 – a translation of Erasmus's *Encomium Matrimonii*; Sir Philip Sidney, *Arcadia* (1590), pp. 137–40, the Geron–Histor eclogue, and pp. 376–81, Cecropia's 'shrewd temptations to love and mariage'; Marlowe, *Hero and Leander* (1598, but written before 1593), 1, 234–68; and perhaps Robert Greene, *Mamillia, Part I* (1583), II, 42–5. Shakespeare restates this theme in *Venus and Adonis*, 157–74 and 751–68, a poem in which the treatment of Adonis as a mere boy unresponsive to Venus's erotic advances (in contrast to Ovid's Adonis in *Metamorphoses* X, 503–39; Golding, 577–863) has been seen to parallel the attitude attributed to the youth in the Sonnets, and to Rosaline in *Rom.* 1.1.215–20.

1 fairest most beautiful (implying the neoPlatonic concept of the 'beautiful soul in the beautiful body'). Contrast 11.9–10. Compare Plato. *Symposium*, 206c: 'on reaching a certain age our nature yearns to beget. This it cannot do upon an ugly person, but only on the beautiful: the conjunction of man and woman is a begetting for both. It is a divine affair, this engendering and bringing to birth, an immortal element in the creature that is mortal' (Loeb).

1 creatures (1) all created things in what was called 'The Book of the Creatures'; (2) the human members of that creation.

1 increase fruit, offspring (through propagation). Compare 'bring forth fruit and multiply' (Gen. 1.22, 28 (Geneva)).

2 That So that.

2 beauty's rose The rose was commonly used as a symbol of youthful beauty. Compare 109.14 and Samuel Daniel's *Delia* (1592), 39.1–4, 50.5–8. Thomas Watson (*Hecatompathia* (1582), 4.11) says 'the Rose of flowres is best' (i.e. the 'king' flower) and Barnabe Barnes uses the phrase 'bewties rose' in *Parthenophil and Parthenophe* (1593), 45.1. Some see Q's '*Rose*', always capitalised but not elsewhere italicised in Q, as bearing special reference to the '*Idea*' or type of beauty in a Platonic sense. See Textual Analysis (p. 282 below) for Q's occasional use of italics. The first two lines are almost an epigraph for the series (1–17). The plant imagery is continued in lines 3–4, 11.

2 might may.

3 But So that. 'But' muddies the syntax of line 3, since it may be misread as meaning 'except' until clarified by line 4 (Booth).

3–4 riper . . . tender older, more mature . . . youthful, immature. Compare *Tit.* 3.2.50: 'tender sapling'. Mahood (p. 92) suggests a play on 'tender air' and quotes *Cym.* 5.5.446: 'The piece of tender air, thy virtuous daughter'.

4 bear (1) carry on, perpetuate; (2) contain; (3) give birth to.

5 contracted Literally 'betrothed', but here including the sense of 'confined' (in the narrow compass of your own eyes). The implied narcissism of lines 5–8 is thought to be suggested by Ovid's story of Narcissus (*Metamorphoses* III, 463–6; Golding, 582–7); compare *Venus and Adonis*, 161–2: 'Narcissus so himself himself forsook, / And died to kiss his shadow in the brook.'

6 Feed'st . . . fuel i.e. you feed upon yourself, like a candle that consumes itself as it burns.

6 self-substantial of one's own substance. Compare William Warner, *Albions England* (1612 edn), p. 215: 'Suns selfe-substance' (used in connection with the Narcissus story). On the suggestion here of autoeroticism, see 4.7–8 n.

9 fresh new, unsullied, 'green' (like the spring). Compare *John* 3.4.145: 'How green you are and fresh in this old world.'

10 only chief, peerless. 'only herald' = first bright flower of a new spring (Beeching). Compare Spenser's *Amoretti* (1595), 70.1: 'Fresh spring the herald of loves mighty king'. Hood suggests a witty play in 'herald' (= announcer) on 'King of Arms' (= principal herald; see *OED* King-of-Arms).

10 gaudy brilliantly coloured or clothed (without pejorative connotation). Booth notes a kind of cloth called 'gaudy-green'.

11 Within . . . content You, as a 'bud' with a potential for flowering (giving birth), bury (as in a 'grave'; compare line 14) your life-giving essence ('content' = semen) and appear to be 'content' to do so.

12 tender churl youthful miser; compare 'tender heir' in line 4.

12 mak'st . . . niggarding you (paradoxically) are prodigal ('mak'st waste') in acting like a niggard or miser. Compare 4.5–6, *Rom.* 1.1.209–10, and Michael Drayton, *Matilda* (1594), 771–7): 'Wrong not thy selfe, nor yet the worlde deprive, / Of that rare good which Nature freely lent, / Think'st thou by such base nygardize to thrive, / In sparing that which never will be spent? / . . . Playing the Churle, to hoord up Beauties pelfe, / And live, and dye, and all unto thy selfe.'

13–14 this glutton . . . thee be the kind of glutton (an unnatural eater, 'gluttony' being one of the Seven Deadly Sins) who will devour, by living Narcissus-like solely in yourself and dying (in the 'grave') without issue, the 'increase' (line 1) or offspring ('due') which you owe to others ('the world'). Compare *Venus and Adonis*, 757–60 (quoted in 3.7–8 n.).

14 by the grave and thee The apposition is deliberate: the young man's refusal to procreate compounds the destructive effect of death and makes him the grave of posterity (Hood).

Sonnet 2

There are thirteen known MS. versions of Sonnet 2; see 9–14 n., and Appendix, pp. 269–71 below.

1 forty An indefinite number frequently used to suggest what the Elizabethans thought of as the dangerously wrong side of middle age.

1 besiege The military metaphor continues in 'dig deep trenches' (compare 'time's furrows' (22.3)), 'field' (2), and 'livery' (3).

2 And dig . . . field Compare 22.3, 60.10; Michael Drayton, *The Shepheards Garland* (1593), Second Eclogue, 46: 'The time-plow'd furrowes in thy fairest field'; Fulke Greville, *Caelica*, 28.7: 'In beauties field you told me vertue dies'; and Samuel Daniel, *Delia* (1592), 4.8: 'Best in my face, how cares have tild deepe forrowes.'

3 youth's proud livery splendid physical appearance proper to the 'company' of youth. 'proud' suggests youthful arrogance; literally, 'livery' = a uniform or badge.

4 tottered weed (1) tattered garment (the 'livery' of line 3); (2) ragged 'weed' in 'beauty's field' (line 2). 'tottered' is a common variant form of 'tattered'; see 26.11.

6 lusty youthfully vigorous.

7 deep-sunken eyes Considered a mark of age, 'eyes' being here a metaphor for the 'grave'. With lines 6–8 compare 1.5–6, 14.

8 all-eating all-devouring (looks back to 1.13–14).

8 thriftless praise unprofitable commendation (because the youth has hoarded his 'treasure' (6) instead of putting it to 'use' (9)); contrast the socially responsible 'praise' of lines 9–12. Shakespeare seems to have the parable of the talents in mind (Matt. 25.14–30).

9–14 It has been suggested that Shakespeare is here (as elsewhere in the marriage–procreation series, 1–17) drawing on Wilson, pp. 127–8: 'Now again, what a joye shal this be unto you, when your moste faire wife, shall make you a father, in bringyng furthe a faire childe unto you, where you shall have a pretie litle boye, runnyng up and doune youre house, suche a one as shall expresse your looke, and your wives looke, suche a one as shall call you dad, with his swete lispyng wordes . . . You have them that shal comforte you, in your latter daies, that shall close up your iyes, when God shall call you, that shall bury you . . . by whom you shall seme, to bee newe borne. For so long as thei shall live, you shall nede never bee thought ded your self . . . For, what man can be greved, that he is old, when he seeth his awne countenaunce whiche he had beying a childe, to appere lively in his sonne?' Taylor argues persuasively that the version of this sonnet (see Appendix, p. 269–70 below) preserved in eleven manuscripts (titled '*Spes Altera*' in four) represents an earlier text which Shakespeare revised for the Q version, part of his argument turning on the closer verbal echoes from Wilson that appear in the '*Spes Altera*' text. The following passage from Sidney's *Arcadia* (1590; p. 379) may also have been working in Shakespeare's mind: 'O the sweet name of a mother . . . to see your children grow up, in whom you are (as it were) eternized: if you could conceive what a hart-tickling joy it is to see your own litle ones, with awfull love come running to your lap, and like litle models of your selfe, still cary you about them'. Shakespeare appears to draw on this chapter of the *Arcadia* in 5.10 and 8.9–10 (see notes).

9 deserved disguised subjunctive (see Abbott 361).

9 beauty's use (1) monetary interest ('use') accruing to, (2) proper 'use' of your 'beauty' (or 'trea-

sure' (line 6)) in procreation. For this play on 'use', compare *Venus and Adonis*, 767–8: 'Foul cank'ring rust the hidden treasure frets, / But gold that's put to use more gold begets.'

11 sum my count render a true audit (of my 'due' (1.14) to Nature). Compare 4.12.

11 make . . . excuse justify (through offspring) my old age. The syntax encourages misreading ('make my usual excuse' (Booth)); the adjective 'old' is made to stand for 'old age' and the noun 'excuse' given a verbal force with the legal sense of declaring him innocent of the crime of wasting his youth.

12 Proving (Thou thus) proving (because the child looks like you).

12 by succession by inherited right (in legal terms).

14 blood warm . . . cold It was then believed (1) that 'young blood' was fiery and hot, 'old blood', cold and sluggish; (2) that the blood in a son's veins was essentially the same as that in his father's (compare *R2* 1.2.11–21) (Kerrigan).

Sonnet 3

1 glass mirror, looking-glass.

3 Whose i.e. 'that face' (2) whose.

3 fresh repair condition unfaded, untarnished (by time). 'repair' is used in the sense of something ('that face') that is susceptible of restoration (*OED*); in this case it may be 'repaired' or 'renewed' only by reduplicating it in a male heir.

4 beguile the world cheat the world of its 'due' (compare 1.14).

4 unless deprive of happiness (in not having a child). The earliest citation in *OED* for the use of this word.

5 uneared untilled (hence 'unfruitful').

6 husbandry Literally, agricultural tillage, but referring to the sexual 'duty' of a 'husband' in marriage. Compare *MM* 1.4.43–4: 'even so her plenteous womb / Expresseth his full tilth and husbandry', and Wilson, p. 122: 'what punishement is he worthy to suffer, that refuseth to Plough that lande, whiche beyng tilled, yeldeth children'.

7–8 Compare 1.13–14 and *Venus and Adonis*, 757–60: 'What is thy body but a swallowing grave, / Seeming to bury that posterity / Which by the rights of time thou needs must have, / If thou destroy them not in dark obscurity?'

7 who . . . will i.e. what man is so foolish that he will, 'fond' may also mean 'selfishly loving' of himself.

7 tomb i.e. his own body.

8 Of his self-love Out of love for himself (narcissism).

8 stop posterity cut off a family line. Compare *Rom.* 1.1.210–11: 'For beauty starv'd with her severity / Cuts beauty off from all posterity', and Wilson, p. 121: 'The self same thyng [i.e. semen] that either withereth and drieth awaie in thy body . . . yea, that self same, which falleth from thee in thy slepe, would have been a manne, if thou thy self haddest been a man.' See also 13.14 n.

9 glass mirror (in which she sees herself reflected as she once was). Compare *Rape of Lucrece*, 1758–9: ' "Poor broken glass, I often did behold / In thy sweet semblance my old age new born." '

10 April . . . prime springtide of her perfection. April, the first month of spring, was proverbially associated with youth; see Tilley A310.

11 windows . . . age Metaphorically, aged eyes. See 24.5–8 n.

12 Despite of wrinkles i.e. despite the ravages of time (and the clouded vision suggested by 'windows of thine age' (11)).

12 golden time most flourishing age (youth) = 'April . . . prime' (10). Compare *Cym.* 4.2.262: 'Golden lads and girls . . .'

13 But . . . be i.e. but if you wish to live so as to die unremembered.

14 image (1) counterpart (i.e. a child); (2) mirror image; (3) remembrance; (4) *Idea* (of you). Compare Donne, '[Image and Dream]', line 1: 'Image of her whom I love, more then she'.

Sonnet 4

Sonnet 4 looks back, both in themes and language, to Sonnets 1 and, particularly, 2. In 4, and in the following nine sonnets, critics detect a probable debt (though some would reverse the direction) to Marlowe's *Hero and Leander* (1, 234–68, 317–28), which must have been written before May 1593, when Marlowe was killed.

1 Unthrifty Wasteful, profitless (because 'loveliness' is not put to 'use'; compare 2.8–9).

2 beauty's legacy (1) 'beauty' as inherited from your parents (the 'bounteous largess' of line 6), or possibly from Nature; (2) 'beauty' as a 'bequest' to be passed on, as Nature's 'due', through your offspring (see lines 2–4). Here, as throughout the Sonnets, 'beauty' is more than skin-deep and means much more than mere physical attractiveness; it implies inner 'beauty', the 'beautiful soul in the beautiful body', i.e. outward beauty was a reflection of inner beauty – a neo-Platonic concept. Compare 16.11: 'inward worth nor outward fair'.

3–14 Compare 2.8 and Matt. 25.14–30.

3 Nature's . . . lend Nature gives nothing without expecting a return ('interest', 'use') on her loan (in a sense, therefore, she acts like a usurer). Compare *MM* 1.1.36–40: 'Nature never lends / The smallest scruple of her excellence, / But like a thrifty goddess, she determines / Herself the glory of a creditor, / Both thanks and use.'

4 frank . . . free Synonyms for 'generous', though 'free' may also carry a suggestion of sexual licence.

4 those are those who are. See Abbott 244, on the not infrequent omission of the relative pronoun.

5 beauteous niggard beautiful (young) miser; compare 1.12. Misers were generally represented as old and ugly.

6 bounteous largess Since 'largess' means 'a liberal gift freely bestowed', the phrase, which rhetorically balances 'beauteous niggard' (5), is tautological and seems (in relation to 'given thee to give') to contradict the kind of 'giving' ascribed to Nature in line 3.

7–8 Profitless . . . live These lines present difficulties. 'Profitless usurer' seems an oxymoron, since a usurer lends money for profit ('interest', 'use') and the phrase is obviously intended, paradoxically, to echo 'beauteous niggard' in line 5, thus suggesting miserliness. The youth, however, is said to 'use' (i.e. put to 'use' in some way) the 'bounteous largess' of line 6 ('So great a sum of sums'), but in such a way that, as a 'usurer', he is denied a livelihood ('canst not live'), i.e. offspring and hence a kind of immortality in the world's remembrance. Despite the situation (a young man of superior social position, perhaps a nobleman, being addressed by an actor), Pequigney, following a suggestion derived from Partridge (see under 'spend', 'traffic', 'usury' (= sexual indulgence)) and Booth (pp. 142–3), believes that in Sonnet 4, and elsewhere in Sonnets 1–14, the poet is warning against autoeroticism on the youth's part.

8 sum of sums full total of all your many 'beauties'. Kerrigan derives the phrase from the Latin tag *summa summarum*. Compare *MV* 3.2.157–8: 'But the full sum of me / Is sum of something.'

9 traffic (1) trade, dealings; (2) intercourse.

10 of thyself by your own actions.

10 deceive cheat, defraud (of an heir).

12 àcceptable audit responsible reckoning or account (in the sense of showing 'profit' on Nature's investment in you). Compare Sidney, *Astrophil and Stella* (1591), 18.1–4.

13 unused unproductive, without 'increase' (compare 1.1).

14 usèd . . . be put to profitable use, will live in an heir (contrast 'not live' in line 8) who will be your legal agent ('th'executor') to administer your estate (the 'sum of sums' of your 'beauty').

Sonnet 5

Sonnets 5 ('man and the seasons'), 6 (continued), and 7 (man, day and night) appear to draw on Ovid's *Metamorphoses* xv, 176–236; Golding, 196–260 – lines which deal with ceaseless change, Time the Destroyer (see Sonnet 15 headnote and 19), and Death, Time's executioner.

1 hours Disyllabic, as frequently in Shakespeare; = time (compare 60.8: 'And Time that gave doth now his gift confound').

1 gentle work mild, seemingly tender ('gentle') action (of time in youth); to be contrasted with the harsh 'working' of time in age (see lines 3–8).

1 frame fashion, make.

2 gaze object of sight which draws 'every eye'.

3 tyrants The hours of time are, metaphorically, despotic rulers who exercise their power cruelly. See 19.1–2 n.

3 same = 'lovely gaze' (2).

4 unfair . . . excel deprive of beauty ('unfair') that which surpasses in fairness ('beauty'). Unique use of 'unfair' as a verb (*OED*). 'fairly' suggests overtones of (1) legitimately, (2) completely, (3) beautifully (Booth).

5 leads . . . on (1) guides; (2) lures (toward death, 'winter' being the 'dead' season).

6 confounds him spoils, corrupts summer ('him').

7 lusty healthfully vigorous, green.

8 o'ersnowed whitened as by snow (first citation in *OED* for this word; not found elsewhere in Shakespeare).

8 bareness Q's spelling 'barenes' (see collation) was also a contemporary spelling for 'barrenness' (see *OED*) which fits the context equally well, but is metrically awkward (compare 97.4).

8 every where Retained as two words (Q) to preserve final stress on 'where'.

9 summer's distillation summer's essence (both abstractly and as a perfume ('liquid prisoner' (10)).

9 left remaining.

10 liquid . . . glass 'summer's distillation' is imaged as a perfume extract or essence safely imprisoned ('pent') in a sealed glass 'vial' (see 6.3). Shakespeare seems to be indebted to Sidney's *Arcadia* (1590; p. 380): 'Have, you ever seene a pure Rosewater kept in a christal glas; how fine it lokes, how sweet it smels, while that beautifull glasse imprisons it? Breake the prison, and let the water take his owne course, doth it not imbrace dust, and loose all his former sweetenesse, and fairenesse? Truly so are we, if we have not the stay, rather then the restraint of Cristalline marriage.'

11 Beauty's . . . bereft Beauty's (generative) efficacy together with beauty's essence would be lost ('bereft').

12 Nor . . . no Emphatic double negative, common in Elizabethan English (see Abbott 406); 'no' = any (hence affirmative).

12 remembrance reminder.

13 flowers distilled i.e. flowers preserved in their essence ('substance' (14)) by being distilled as perfume. Compare 1.2 ('beauty's rose'), 54.11–12, and *MND* 1.1.76–8 ('rose distill'd' in relation to the marriage theme).

14 Leese Lose (variant form; not elsewhere in Shakespeare).

14 substance essence.

14 sweet (1) 'beautifully' scented; (2) uncorrupted, wholesome.

Sonnet 6

Sonnet 6 focuses the preservation theme of 5 on the youth (his 'summer' (2) or 'flower' (5.13)) by urging him to marry so that he may become 'fruitful and multiply' (Gen. 1.22, etc.; compare lines 5–12 below) and be a 'good' usurer.

1–3 The imagery ('winter's', 'summer', 'distilled', 'sweet some vial') establishes Sonnet 6 as a complement to 5.

1 ragged rough (perhaps with the force of 'making rough', though the active sense is otherwise unrecorded).

1 deface Kerrigan suggests a secondary play on 'face' ('deface' = unface, ravage the features); compare 3.1–2.

2 distilled essentialised (in progeny). Compare 5.13.

3 Make . . . vial Render some womb precious (because it would contain your 'beauty's treasure' (4)). There is obvious play on the bottle ('vial') of 'sweet' perfume as an image of marriage in 5.9–10.

3 treasure endow with treasure, enrich (first citation in this sense in *OED*).

4 self-killed See 4.7–8 n.

5 use (1) kind of using (with sexual suggestion); (2) interest, return.

5 not forbidden usury The Elizabethan attitude toward usury was ambivalent. The statute of 1571, while it declared that 'all usury, being forbidden by the law of God, is sin and detestable', legalised an interest rate of ten in the hundred (compare the emphasis on 'ten' in lines 8–10). Shakespeare is thus playing on the old idea (see Aristotle, *Politics*, 1.iii.23) that usury was considered 'unnatural', a kind of incest (metal breeding from metal) and at the same time glancing at the legal ten per cent return on an investment. See 4.7–8 n.

6 happies makes happy, fortunate (first citation as a verb; see *OED* Happy *v*).

6 those . . . loan (1) those who, like the youth, lend, in marriage, their essence (semen) voluntarily in hope of return (progeny); (2) those prospective mothers who gladly repay their husbands' investment ('loan') by bearing a child. Both senses may be present, but (1) is, I think, primary and leads into the explanation ('That's') offered by lines 7–8.

7–11 The ambiguity of Q's punctuation does not seem to have been noticed; Q punctuates these lines with terminal commas only, making the exact relations between the lines difficult to determine. The present punctuation is that adopted by editors since Malone, but it is arbitrary, and the following arrangement seems to me equally feasible: 'That's . . . thee;

/ Or ... one, / Ten ... art; / If ... thee, / Then ... depart,'.

7 That's Which is.

7 breed Usurers were similarly thought of as making their 'treasure' (4) breed and multiply.

8 ten for one i.e. ten in the hundred, the legal interest rate; but 'one' also = the youth, with a possible play on the numeral as a phallic symbol (compare 20.12, 'one thing'). On the phallic implication, see Sir John Davies, *Poems*, p. 138: 'When Marcus comes from Mins, he stil doth sweare / By, come on seaven, that all is lost and gone, / But thats not true, for he hath lost his hayre / Onely for that, he came too much on one.'

9 Ten ... art i.e. ten of your offspring would offer posterity a much more promising future ('happier') than you now do in your state of oneness.

10 ten times ... thee (1) reduplicated ('refigured') you ten times; (2) each one in turn reduplicated you ten times (thus, like Banquo's, his 'line [will] stretch out to th'crack of doom' (*Mac.* 4.1.116)). Booth suggests a play on the numerals 1–10 in 'refigured'.

11 depart die. Suggested perhaps by the phrase in the marriage service (Book of Common Prayer), 'till death us depart [i.e. separate]'.

12 Leaving thee living (1) Preserving you alive (through surrogates); (2) Bequeathing you, as a beneficiary of your 'will', a kind of life (the 'acceptable audit' of 4.12).

12 posterity (1) offspring and offspring of your offspring; (2) perpetuity.

13 self-willed obstinate, selfish in pursuing your own desires (compare the implications of 'self-killed' in line 4). Q's 'selfe-wild', though a common Elizabethan form, may also have suggested a play on 'licentiously self-destructive'.

13 fair (1) beautiful; (2) unblemished by time (hence death would be 'untimely'); and, perhaps, (3) equitable, fair-minded.

14 conquest (1) spoils (acquired by force, as in war); (2) in legal sense, property acquired by some means (here, force) other than inheritance (*OED* Conquest *sb* 4).

14 worms thine heir Worms or maggots were popularly believed to be self-generated from a corpse. In terms of the sonnet's reference, this *is* 'forbidden usury', a return ('worms') as lifeless as a dead usurer's 'treasure', promising only dissolution and oblivion.

Sonnet 7

Sonnet 7 offers several verbal parallels with *Romeo and Juliet*, but the direction of influence cannot be established.

1 gracious light regal, beneficent sun. The sun was considered king among the planets in the Ptolemaic system. Compare *Rom.* 1.1.118–19: 'the wor-

shipped sun / Peer'd forth the golden window of the east'.

2 Lifts ... eye Compare *Rom.* 2.3.5: 'Now ere the sun advance his burning eye'. Shakespeare personifies the sun as the Titan Helios or Phoebus Apollo (see Ovid, *Metamorphoses* II, and supplementary note in G. B. Evans (ed.), *Rom.*, 1984, 3.2.1–4), the 'eye' of *Rom.* (compare 18.5) figuring as the 'head', while the 'eye' image is transferred to earthly observers ('each under eye'), a phrase implying a servant–master relation between human beings and the sun; compare 'homage' (3), 'Serving' (4), 'Attending' and 'golden' (8), and *Rom.* 2.2.26–30; also *WT* 4.2.35, where Polixenes, a king, says: 'I have eyes under my service.'

3 new-appearing sight sight of his new appearance (dawn).

4 looks ... majesty adoring observance of (looking up to) his position as a divinity ('sacred majesty'). There is perhaps a glance at the Tudor doctrine of monarchs as God's vice-regents in 'sacred'. Compare line 7.

5 having climbed he having climbed (ellipsis; see Abbott 399). The sun has reached its zenith (noon).

5 steep-up rising precipitously. Compare *Passionate Pilgrim*, 9.5 ('steep-up hill') and *Oth.* 5.2.278 ('steep-down').

5 heavenly hill the hill of the heavens (i.e. the sky); 'heavenly' also = sacred.

6–10 Shakespeare seems to have in mind Ovid's description, which is preceded by a discussion of the changes from day to night, of the last two of man's four ages (*Metamorphoses* XV, 225–7; Golding, 247–9): 'he passeth foorth the space / Of youth, and also wearing out his middle age a pace, / Through drooping ages steepye path he ronneth out his race'.

6 Resembling ... age (1) Appearing like a man once young and strong who has entered upon middle age; (2) Appearing even in its ('his') middle age like a strong youth. The ambiguity in the referent of 'his' makes either reading possible; in immediate context (2) seems preferable, but 'Yet' (line 7) seems to call for (1), with the implication that the sun, unlike mortal men, even at its zenith ('middle age', 'highmost pitch' (9)) retains its power to attract 'mortal looks' (7). Strictly, the sun cannot really be said to decline until it has passed its zenith. Compare Donne's 'A Lecture upon the Shadow' in *Songs and Sonets*.

7 still (1) nevertheless; (2) continually.

8 Attending As courtiers did in the royal presence-chamber or following a royal progress.

8 golden pilgrimage brilliant, shining journey (as a pilgrim might visit a sacred shrine ('heavenly hill')). Gold as the king-metal was regularly associated with the sun as the king-planet; compare 18.6.

9 highmost pitch topmost height (i.e. zenith, noon).

9 weary car Metonymy for 'weary sun'; 'car' = chariot. Compare *R3* 5.3.19–21: 'The weary sun hath made a golden set, / And by the bright tract of his fiery car / Gives token of a goodly day to-morrow.'

10 reeleth from the day This reverses the image of sunrise in *Rom.* 2.3.3–4: 'And fleckled darkness like a drunkard reels / From forth day's path and Titan's fiery wheels.'

11 fore formerly (not merely an aphetic form of 'before', i.e. 'fore; see *OED Fore adv* and *prep*).

11 converted turned away. Compare *Tim.* 1.2.145: 'Men shut their doors against a setting sun' (proverbial, Tilley s979); and Daniel, *Civil Wars* (1595), II, i, 7–8.

12 tract track (variant form), path.

13 thyself ... noon yourself, being at your zenith ('noon') and on the point of declining ('outgoing').

14 get a son beget a male heir (with a play on 'sun', which will rise anew as you set).

Sonnet 8

1 Music to hear Vocative: O you, whose voice is music to hear (implying that the youth is music itself, subsuming all the perfectly integrated qualities attributed to music in the following lines).

1 sadly without pleasure, dully. The youth's inner harmonies are not attuned to outer social harmonies (see lines 9–12); in this sense he is actually out of tune or 'concord' (5). Compare *MV* 5.1.69: 'I am never merry when I hear sweet music.'

2 Sweets ... joy i.e. things affording pleasure ('Sweets', 'joy') do not fight against but complement ('delights') each other.

3–4 Why ... annoy Why (then) do you appear to love music ('that') since you listen to it without pleasure ('not gladly'), or, if indeed ('else'), what pleasure you do receive is accompanied by pain or boredom? 'with' = along with. Ingram and Redpath link 'annoy' with French 'ennui' (see Cotgrave's *Dictionarie* (1611), under 'Ennuy', where, as well as 'annoy', it = 'tediousnesse, irkesomenesse'). Compare Spenser, *The Ruines of Time* (1591), 613–14: 'Of the strings ... / That wrought both joy and sorrow in my mind'.

5 true concord true harmony, accord (etymologically, from Latin *concordia* = of one heart or mind). Looks forward to 'unions' (6). 'true' is merely intensive.

6 By unions married By joinings (of 'sounds' = notes, voices) made one (a unison). The phrase, in context with the following lines, suggests some reference to the 'mystical union that is betwixt Christ and his Church' of which marriage ('this mystery', as St Paul terms it) was considered an earthly symbol instituted primarily for the procreation of children (Book of Common Prayer).

7 sweetly chide (1) rebuke graciously or affectionately; (2) rebuke with sweet ('welltunèd' (5))

sounds. Compare Sidney, *Astrophil and Stella* (1591), first song, 18: 'Whose grace is such, that when it chides doth cherish', and Daniel, *Delia*, 4.7.

7 confounds (1) consumeth, wasteth (for second-person singular in *-s*, see Abbott 247, 340); (2) (in music) breaketh the harmony ('concord') by discord.

8 In singleness (1) Being single, unmarried; (2) (In music) failing to take your part in part singing or playing (singing your own tune in what should be concerted harmony).

8 parts (1) capacities (with possible play on 'genitalia'), roles (as a husband and father); (2) (in music) assigned melodies (as in performing a part-song). Since technically in part-singing or playing a person could perform only one part, Pooler's conjecture 'a part' (supported by a seventeenth-century MS. version of Sonnet 8) is tempting and fits (1) and (2) equally well.

8 bear (1) acquit yourself in, perform (as a husband and father); (2) (in music) carry (as a melody).

9–10 As in 2.9–14 and 5.10 (see notes), Shakespeare may here be drawing on Sidney's *Arcadia* (1590; p. 380): 'and is a solitary life as good as this [marriage]? then can one string make as good musicke as a consort'.

9–12 Allowing for ambiguities, these difficult and 'conceited' lines may be taken to mean: 'Observe how one (lute?) string, performing as a kind ('sweet'; musically, 'well-tunèd') husband (compare 'sire' (11)) in relation to another string (compare 'mother' (11)), when struck produces each through the other a reciprocally ('mutually') harmonious resonance, which, spreading to a third string (a 'child' (11)), reduces all three to one harmony ('all in one, one pleasing note' (12)). Compare Samuel Brandon, *The Virtuous Octavia* (1598), MSR, lines 2024–7: 'When any one doth strike a tuned string: / The rest, which with the same in concord be, / Will shew a motion to that senceless thing; / When all the other neither stirre nor play.' The musical imagery, here shifting from mainly vocal to instrumental and used to figure what St Paul calls the 'mystery' of marriage (Eph. 5.32–3), namely that 'two shall be one flesh' – a mystery that Shakespeare multiplies by making it 'three in one' – naturally contains sexual overtones, since, in addition to the meanings assigned above, 'husband' = 'one who by tillage fructifies the soil' (compare 'husbandry' (3.6 n.)) and 'Strikes' = to have sexual intercourse.

11 Resembling ... mother See 2.9–14 n.

12 all ... sing Some critics (see Baldwin, p. 175), detect here a reference to Southampton's family motto: 'Ung par tout, tout par ung' (see 105.4: 'To one, of one, still such, and ever so').

13 speechless wordless (because 'one pleasing note' (12)).

13 being many i.e. because produced in concord ('seeming one') by several.

14 single . . . none Plays on the proverbial idea (see Tilley O52) that one is no number ('none'). Compare 3.14, 136.8–10 n., and *Rom.* 1.2.32–3.

Sonnet 9

2 consum'st (1) waste; (2) destroy. See 3.8 n.

3 hap happen, chance.

4 The world . . . wife The world, like a mateless ('makeless') wife (i.e. a widow), will bewail thee. Thus, by not marrying and dying without offspring ('issueless' (3)), the youth will bring grief to the whole world instead of to one woman. This hyperbole implies the youth's noble position and importance to the future of the commonwealth ('world').

5 still always, continually.

6 form image (with possible reference to the Scholastic concept of something which contains the 'essential determinant principle' (*OED* Form *sb* 4)).

7 private individual (with a suggestion of 'ordinary' as compared with the widow of a noble). Booth proposes a secondary meaning derived from the Latin *privatus* = bereaved.

8 By children's eyes (1) By (looking into) her children's eyes; (2) Through the eyes of her children. In neo-Platonic doctrine the eyes were thought of as 'the windows of the soul'.

8 shape external image (compare 'form' (6)), with perhaps a suggestion of 'spectral form' or 'spirit'.

9–10 Look . . . it Whatever a prodigal wastes ('doth spend') here on earth merely, as it were, changes hands ('Shifts but his [i.e. its] place'), because the world continues to benefit from it ('still . . . enjoys'). For the idiom 'Look what', see *OED* Look *v* 4b.

11 beauty's . . . end i.e. the waste of beauty (unlike the dissipation of money or goods) yields no return ('hath . . . end') to others ('the world') unless put to proper 'use' (i.e. 'increase') in procreation. Compare the 'good' usurer theme in Sonnet 6, the parable of the talents (see 2.8 n.), and Marlowe, *Hero and Leander*, 1, 328: 'Beautie alone is lost, too warily kept.'

12 unused (beauty) not put to use, hoarded (with obvious play on 'not loaned out to earn interest', i.e. 'use').

12 user Difficult to explain in the context (appearing to contradict 'unused'); the best gloss is offered by Ingram and Redpath: '(1) "he who has the right to use", and probably (2) "waster" or "spendthrift"'. Taken in context with line 14 ('on himself such murd'rous shame commits'), one might also suggest that 'user' = 'one who uses himself autoerotically' (hence without 'use'); see 4.7–8 n. and Partridge under 'use' (verb). It was commonly believed

that each orgasm shortened life by a day; see Donne's 'Farewell to Love', 24–5, in *Songs and Sonets*.

12 so thus.

14 murd'rous shame (1) shameful murder (a kind of suicide); (2) killing disgrace. Compare Wilson, p. 137: 'you shalbe coumpted a parricide, or a murtherer of your stocke: that whereas you may by honest mariage encrease your posteritie: you suffer it to decaie for ever, through your wilful single lyfe'.

Sonnet 10

Sonnet 10 is the first to strike a personally involved note on the part of Shakespeare or his persona (see lines 9–13).

1 For shame Out of shame ('shame' and 'murd'rous' (5) look back to 9.14). See collation for different pointing.

2 unprovident improvident, failing to look to the future. For the common Elizabethan use of *un-* for modern forms with *in-* or *im-*, see Abbott 442.

3 Grant . . . wilt i.e. it may be granted if you wish to argue that.

5 possessed i.e. as by a demon, self-hate.

5 murd'rous hate Compare 9.14 n.

6 stick'st not dost not hesitate or scruple.

6 conspire plot secretly (against yourself).

7 roof (1) head (= whole body, by synecdoche); (2) house (= family, by synecdoche).

7 ruinate reduce to ruins, destroy (compare 'destroys' (9.12)). Compare 13.9, *Err.* 3.2.4, *TGV* 5.4.9–10. Kerrigan suggests that the image in line 7 was influenced by, among other possible sources (Wilson, Spenser), Marlowe's *Hero and Leander*, I, 239–42: 'Who builds a pallace and rams up the gate, / Shall see it ruinous and desolate. / Ah simple *Hero*, learne thy selfe to cherish, / Lone women like to emptie houses perish.'

8 repair renovate (= renew you and your 'house' in a son).

9 O change . . . mind O change your way of thinking (about marriage) so that I may be able to change the way I have been thinking (and writing) about your (selfish) attitude toward others ('the world' (9.9–11)) and particularly your 'house'). Kerrigan notes that this is the first time that Shakespeare (or the persona) alludes to himself ('my mind').

10 Shall . . . love? Should hate be lodged in a fairer (or more beautiful) dwelling than (my) gentle love is (i.e. I am no 'beauteous roof' (7), either physically or socially)? This is the first of many references to the persona's feelings of physical and social inferiority. An impersonal interpretation of the line has been assumed, but seems to me less immediate to the context.

11 Be . . . is Be as your appearance or demeanour shows you to be (i.e. be your (noble) self).

11 gracious and kind courteous or benevolent and generous (attributes of nobility, with play on 'kind' = acting according to 'nature').

12 Or ... prove Or (if you can't be generous for the sake of others) at least be generous ('kind-hearted prove') for your own sake ('to thyself').

13 for ... me (1) for my sake; (2) for the sake of my love

14 That So that.

14 still may ... thee may forever live in your heirs ('in thine') or continue to live in thee. There is some difficulty in 'or thee', since the continuance of the youth's beauty does not in itself really depend on the duplication of that beauty in an heir. Kerrigan suggests that 'thee' = 'your-children-who-are-you', which seems the best, if not very satisfactory, solution.

Sonnet 11

1–2 As fast ... departest The difficulty in these lines arises from the final clause ('from ... departest') and turns on the meaning given to 'departest'. Taking 'departest' as 'bestowest' (*OED* Depart *v* 2), we may paraphrase: '(Were you married), however quickly age might cause you to decline (physically and mentally), you would continue to increase ('grow'st') proportionally ('so fast') through your child ('In one of thine'), who is the product of that which (i.e. your seed) you have bestowed.' Taking 'departest' as 'separatest (from)' (*OED* Depart *v* 2b; *OED*, however, does not recognise an intransitive use), we may read: '(Were you married), however quickly age might cause you to decline from that which (i.e. your youth) time is separating from you, you would still increase proportionally through your child.' Critics are divided over which reading is preferable; but see 4 n. below.

3 fresh blood pure, invigorating blood (of youth, with suggestion of 'semen', as contrasted with the cold blood of age). Compare 2.14.

3 youngly as a young man.

4 from youth convertest decline from youth. Since line 4 essentially repeats line 2, if 'depart' (in 2) = separate from, 4 seems to support 'depart' = bestow; see above 1–2 n. 'convertest' would have been pronounced 'convartest' (compare 14.12); compare today's pronunciation of such spellings as 'clerk' (in English usage) and 'sergeant'.

5 Herein (1) In your fathering a child; (2) In the child itself (since your 'wisdom, beauty, and increase' (compare 'grow'st' (1)) will be preserved ('lives') in both of you); (3) In my advice. Compare 'truth and beauty' in 14.11 and 54.1–2.

6 Without this i.e. if you remain single (alone).

6 cold decay (1) in death; (2) in the grave.

7 If ... so If everyone thought in this way (referring to the alternative described in line 6).

7 times (future) generations.

7 should Elizabethan usage denoting contingent futurity (Abbott 322) where today we would use 'would'.

8 threescore Shortens the biblical limits ('The time [= span; 'days' in the Book of Common Prayer] of our life is threescore years and ten, and if they be of strength, four score years': Ps. 90.10 (Geneva)), but was probably suggested by them (compare 'times' (7)); the psalm, generally, describes the brevity of life.

8 year = years (collective plural, common in Elizabethan English; see Franz 190).

8 make ... away destroy mankind ('the world'). Compare Wilson, p. 133: 'Let it [marriage] bee forbidden ... and within fewe yeres, all mankynde must nedes decaye for ever ... Take awaie mariage, and howe many shall remain after a hundreth yeres.'

9 for store as a source of 'increase' (compare 1.1). Nature thus expects 'increase' only from those whom she has favoured (compare lines 11–12, 4.1–6, 14.12).

10 Harsh ... rude Uncouth, ill-featured (ugly, shapeless) ... coarse (unrefined, imperfect). Essentially synonyms; the earliest citation for 'featureless' in *OED*. Compare *John* 5.7.25–7: 'Be of good comfort, Prince, for you are born / To set a form upon that indigest / Which he hath left so shapeless and so rude.'

10 barrenly without offspring.

11 Look ... more Whomever Nature ('she') endowed most liberally, she also gave such individuals a potentially greater capacity ('the more') for 'increase' ('generative vitality' (Ingram and Redpath)). Without this extrapolated meaning for 'the more', the two parts of line 11 seem basically tautological. The Sewell–Capell emendation of Q 'the' to 'thee' ('thee' was sometimes spelled 'the' in Elizabethan usage) is tempting because it avoids this danger without extrapolation, i.e. 'However much Nature may have endowed all others, she has endowed you ("thee") with even more'; in other words, your endowment exceeds the 'best' that may be found in anybody else – an hyperbole certainly in tune with the general context. Most editors, however, retain 'the'.

12 in bounty cherish nourish by putting it ('beauteous gift') out to 'use' (i.e. increase). Booth notes: 'this phrase embodies the paradox of several preceding sonnets, that of keeping by giving, increasing by diminishing'. Kerrigan cites the parable of the talents (compare 2.8 and 4.3–14).

13–14 She ... die i.e. Nature created you in her own (perfect) image ('seal'), thereby intending that you should stamp ('print') your image, through procreation, on others (your heirs), not allowing that seal ('copy' = you as Nature's surrogate) to die in yourself alone and thus, in a sense, kill 'great creating Nature' (*WT* 4.4.88) herself. The youth is pictured as Nature's 'great seal' by which she validated (gave authority to) her highest creations, as a monarch did in appending a seal to documents of state. 'carved' = incised, as an intaglio-cut gemstone (mounted in a seal ring).

Sonnet 12

Dowden notes that Sonnet 12 gathers into one the themes of 5–7. Influence from Ovid's *Metamorphoses* XV, 199–216 (Golding, 221–37; see 7.6–10 n. and 73 headnote) and *Ars Amatoria* II, 113–20 (in lines 3–4) has been suggested.

1 **count the clock** number the strokes (= 'clock' by metonymy).

1 **tells** (1) records (to my hearing); (2) measures out. Both hearing and sight (lines 1–8) remind the speaker of the inexorable ('neverresting' (5.5)) march of Time the Destroyer against 'beauty'.

2 **brave** splendid, beautiful (as opposed to 'hideous night'). Compare 'summer' *v.* 'hideous winter' in 5.5–6.

2 **sunk** i.e. because the sun (= 'day') has set.

3 **past prime** past the perfection of full flowering. Compare *Venus and Adonis*, 131–2: 'Fair flowers that are not gath'red in their prime / Rot and consume themselves in little time.'

4 **sable** black (but probably used for dark brown as compared with fair hair).

4 **all silvered o'er** The most frequently adopted emendation of Q's 'or siluer'd ore' (see collation). But among recent editors Ingram and Redpath read (and defend) 'o'er-silver'd all' and Seymour-Smith, following Tucker, retains Q, paraphrasing the line as 'the golden tints in black hair silvered over with white' ('or' = the tincture of gold in armorial bearings). Sisson and Burto nearly complete the gamut by reading (with Gildon) 'are silver'd o'er' ('or' being taken as a misreading of 'ar', an occasional Elizabethan spelling of 'are'). I complete the gamut by conjecturing 'o'ersilvered are'. Compare 'Beauty o'ersnowed' (5.8) and *Ham.* 1.2.239–41: 'His beard was grisl'd, no? / *Hor.* It was, as I have seen it in his life, / A sable silver'd.' The form 'o'er-silvered', not illustrated in *OED*, occurs in Phineas Fletcher's *The Purple Island* (1633), Canto VII, St.47.7: 'And with untimely Winter earth's o're-silverèd.'

5 **barren** bare (but carrying the suggestion of 'barrenly perish' (11.10)).

6 **erst** (shortly) before.

6 **did canopy** served as a shelter for (earliest citation for 'canopy' as a verb in *OED*).

7 **summer's green** i.e. (by synecdoche) green stalks of wheat, barley, or rye (as yet unripened and uncut). Compare *MND* 2.1.94–5: 'and the green corn [= wheat] / Hath rotted ere his youth attain'd a beard'.

7 **girded up** tied tightly together (earliest citation in *OED*).

8 **Borne . . . bier** Carried on a framework or handbarrow (with strong suggestion of a funeral bier, since, once cut, the ripened stalks are like lifeless bodies incapable of growth or increase).

8 **white . . . beard** i.e. the ripened wheat, etc., when cut and dried, has sharp bleached ('white') kernels ('bristly beard'); but 'beard' continues the human reference (hair continuing to grow even after death). Thus the Harvest-home festival procession becomes a metaphor for a funeral procession.

9–10 **Then . . . go** Therefore I pose the problem as it pertains to ('of') your beauty, namely ('That'), you too must become one of time's ruins ('wastes'). For this sense of 'wastes', compare the title of Spenser's *The Ruines of Time* (1591). With lines 9–14, compare 5.11–14.

11 **sweets** See 8.2 n.

11 **do themselves forsake** lose (isolated in themselves) their essential qualities (through the action of time). Compare *Venus and Adonis*, 161: 'Narcissus so himself himself forsook.'

12 **die** move toward death, decay.

12 **others** i.e. 'sweets and beauties'.

13 **Time's scythe** Time (and sometimes Death) was pictured (in emblem books, for example) as bearing a scythe. Compare 60.12, 74.11 n., 100.13–14, etc.

14 **Save breed** Except offspring (by breeding).

14 **brave** defy, challenge.

Sonnet 13

Sonnet 13 is the first of thirty-four sonnets in which the youth is addressed as 'you' rather than by what has been considered the more usually intimate 'thou' (used among members of a family, when addressing inferiors, and in the (literary) language of lovers; see Franz 289a–g). But the distinction, in favour of 'you', was dying out by the end of the sixteenth century, and the same alternation between 'thou' and 'you' is found in most other contemporary sonnet writers (Sidney, Giles Fletcher the Elder, Constable, Daniel, etc.). No satisfactory explanation has been suggested to account for Shakespeare's vacillation between these forms from sonnet to sonnet in 13–126; in 127–52 (the Dark Lady series) only 'thou' is used (except in 145, an anomalous tetrameter sonnet; see Rollins, I, 35–6). Since Shakespeare can shift between 'thou' and 'you' in such closely linked sonnets as 79 and 80 (from 'thou' to 'you') and 98 and 99 (from 'you' to 'thou'), and even perhaps mix the two forms in 24, it seems to me very doubtful that, in general, such variation should be taken as signalling significant changes in attitude or tone. See Brian Vickers, *Returning to Shakespeare*, 1989, pp. 47–8, who agrees with this view, suggesting that euphony may be the basic factor.

1–2 **O that . . . live** I follow Ingram and Redpath's retention of Q's 'your selfe' (so throughout the sonnet in Q) in 1 and 7 as two words, 'self' being taken to mean 'soul' (i.e. essential self) and 'you' to mean 'the combination of soul and body' (i.e. 'yourself', as one word). To paraphrase: 'O if only the whole you were composed of soul ("self") and hence immortal (there would be no cause for concern), but "you" are a combination of soul and body and, as such, your bodily part is mortal and subject to death ("this coming end" (3)).'

3 Against To anticipate.

4 semblance image, copy (with the implication that this image would perpetuate both parts, spiritual and physical, of 'you').

5 beauty i.e. inner and outer 'beauty'.

5 in lease Legal: for a contracted (hence terminal) number of years (i.e. your life-span). Compare the phrase 'lease of life'; *Mac.* 4.1.98–100: 'Macbeth / Shall live the lease of nature, pay his breath / To time and mortal custom'; and 146.5–6.

6 determination end, termination (of the 'lease'). Continues the legal figure and picks up 'coming end' in line 3.

7 Your self i.e. your essential self or 'soul' (see 1–2 n. above). Tucker defends Q's 'You selfe' on the grounds that 'selfe' is an appositive for 'You' (i.e. 'You (selfe)' = 'you, the same over again'; compare 62.13), but, as Ingram and Redpath point out, the reading 'Your self' permits essentially the same interpretation with much less awkwardness.

7 yourself's decease the death of the mortal part of 'you'.

8 sweet form precious image (compare 'sweet semblance' (4)), with perhaps (as in 9.6) some reference to the Scholastic concept of something which contains the 'essential determinant principle'. The frequent and rather tiresome repetition throughout Shakespeare's Sonnets of 'sweet' (55 times), and its derivatives 'sweets' (7), 'sweetest' (6) and 'sweetness' (2), as in English sonnet writing generally, may be a legacy, direct or indirect, from Petrarch's continually repeated use of 'dolce', 'dolcemente', 'dolcezza', and other related forms in *Rime sparse*. Was Shakespeare perhaps parodying the cloying repetition of 'sweet' in this and other sonnets (e.g. 54) in *Tro.* 3.1.62–98?

9 Who lets i.e. would anyone allow.

9 house (1) body; (2) family. Compare 10.7 n. and Wilson, p. 119: 'you notwithstandinge can not wante greate rebuke, seynge it lieth in your handes to kepe that house from decaye wherof you lineallye descended'.

10 husbandry (1) good management; (2) tillage (compare 3.5–6).

10 in honour might uphold (1) might support in an honourable state; (2) might perpetuate through an 'honourable estate' of matrimony (compare Book of Common Prayer). 'in honour' can be taken with 'husbandry' or with 'might uphold'.

11 winter's day i.e. old age. Compare 6.1–2.

12 barren rage barren-making ravage (Ingram and Redpath). Abbott 4 cites 'barren' as an example of an adjective 'signifying effect . . . to signify the cause'.

13 O none . . . know The punctuation in this line is that usually adopted by most editors. However, Q's commas after 'unthrifts' and 'know' make it possible (as Simpson first observed) to read 'dear . . . know' with either 'O none but unthrifts' or line 14 ('You had a father'). Among other recent editors, Dover Wilson, Seymour-Smith, and Booth retain Q's pointing, leaving the choice open; Ingram and Redpath and Wells (subst.) read 'unthrifts, . . . know:' on the grounds that it is 'platitudinous' (Ingram and Redpath) to tell the young man that he knew he had had a father. I am not sure the present pointing is much less 'platitudinous'.

13 unthrifts prodigals, spendthrifts.

14 You had . . . so Some critics interpret this line to mean that the youth's father was dead (citing *AWW* 1.1.17–18: 'This young gentle woman had a father – O, that "had", how sad a passage 'tis!'), but probably it only means that the youth should follow his father's example and beget a son (compare Sidney, *Arcadia* (1590), p. 139): 'Thy father justly may of thee complaine, / If thou doo not repay his deeds for thee, / In granting unto him a grandsires gaine. / Thy common-wealth may rightly grieved be, / . . . If thus thou murther thy posteritie', and *Wiv.* 3.4.36–7: 'to her, coz. O boy, thou hadst a father!'). See also *Arcadia* (1590), p. 379, and 3.8 n. above.

Sonnet 14

1–2 Not . . . astronomy Shakespeare here does not necessarily repudiate judicial astrology ('astronomy'), but says: 'I do not draw or derive ("pluck", with possible suggestion of "steal") my conclusions ("judgement", "knowledge" (9)) from the stars (as astrologers claim to do), but even so it seems to me I possess the power of foretelling the future ("I have astronomy", "I read" (10), "I prognosticate" (13)).' Not until line 9 does the poet explain why. For Sidney's suggested influence, see 9–10 n. below.

3–8 These lines describe some of the sorts of prognostication astrologers claimed through the publication of almanacs (predicting plagues, weather, 'good' and 'evil' or 'infortunate' days, etc.) or the casting of horoscopes (foretelling the course and quality of a person's life and death). See Wayne Shumaker, *The Occult Sciences in the Renaissance*, 1972.

5 Nor . . . tell Nor can I foretell, to within short periods of time ('to brief minutes'), when good or bad chance or luck ('fortune') will befall.

6 Pointing . . . his Appointing (aphetic form) to each minute its ('his'). The rest of the line ('thunder, rain, and wind') seems to suggest that in fact 'each' should be taken with 'season's quality' in line 4 rather than with 'minutes' in 5, unless we interpret 'fortune' as referring only to good or bad weather. In other words, were it not for the rhyme-scheme, we might suppose that lines 5 and 6 had been transposed, since 6 follows more naturally on 4, and 5 could well serve as an introductory line to 7.

7 say with princes state in relation to princes.

7 it i.e. the future.

8 oft predict frequently occurring portents, omens, presages. A difficult phrase: 'oft' as an adjective is rare and 'predict' as a noun found only here (*OED*).

8 in heaven find i.e. read in the stars.

9–10 Suggested probably by Sidney's *Astrophil and Stella* (1591), 26.1, 11–14: 'Though dustie wits dare scorne Astrologie, / . . . And if these rules did faile, proofe makes me sure, / Who oft fore-judge my after-following race, / By only those two starres in *Stella's* face'; and *Arcadia* (1590), p. 375: 'O sweet *Philoclea* . . . thy heavenly face is my Astronomie' (compare 'astronomy' in line 2).

9 from . . . derive Compare *LLL* 4.3.298: 'From women's eyes this doctrine I derive.' The comparison of the beloved's eyes to stars is, of course, a commonplace; see e.g. Ovid, *Amores* II, xvi, 43–4; Petrarch, *Rime sparse*, 105.70; Sidney (9–10 n. above); Daniel, *Delia*, 34.1–6; Giles Fletcher the Elder, *Licia*, 43.1; *Rom.* 2.2.15–20. But John Dowland, *Third Book of Songs or Airs* (1603; ed. Bullen, p. 129), asks 'What poor astronomers are they, / Take women's eyes for stars.'

10 constant unmoved, unchanging (in distinction to the Circle of the Fixed Stars which, in the Ptolemaic system, rotated).

10 read such art discover such learning or knowledge (astronomy was one of the 'arts' studied in the quadrivium at the university).

11 As To the effect that.

11 truth and beauty Here the youth's inner qualities ('truth', or constancy) and his external qualities ('beauty') are differentiated. Compare 54.1–2 and 'wisdom, beauty' in 11.5.

12 If . . . convert If you would change your mind ('convert') and, out of ('from') your 'self', produce increase ('store'). Compare 11.9 n. 'from thy self' can also mean 'turning away from existing in your single (unmarried) state'.

14 doom and date final fate (= death) and end (= death), i.e. your end is the end of 'truth and beauty' (11). Compare *The Phoenix and Turtle*, 62–4: 'Truth may seem, but cannot be, / Beauty brag, but 'tis not she, / Truth and Beauty buried be.'

Sonnet 15

Sonnet 15, which leads into 16, first sounds the Horatian and Ovidian theme of immortality assured through poetry: Horace, *Odes* III, 30, 1–5: 'Exegi monumentum aere perennius . . .' ('I have finished a monument more lasting than bronze . . .' (Loeb));

Ovid, *Metamorphoses* XV, 871–9: 'Iamque opus exegi, quod non Iovis ira nec ignis / nec poterit ferrum nec edax abolere vetustas . . .' (Golding, XV, 984–95: 'Now have I brought a woork too end which neither *Joves* feerce wrath, / Nor swoord, nor fyre, nor freating age [i.e. time] with all the force it hath / Are able too abolish quyght . . .'). Ovid also promises such immortality to those celebrated in verse, including his own (see *Amores* I, X, 59–62, and I, XV, 25–30). Shakespeare, like Spenser in *The Ruines of Time* (1591), 253–9, 362–4, 400–6, and many other English and European poets (see notes on 18.9–14 and Rollins, I, 51), usually, as here, claims to confer immortality not so much on the author as on the subject addressed and combines this promise with a theme already emphasised in earlier sonnets (see, particularly 1, 5, 12), the Ovidian theme of Time the Destroyer: *Metamorphoses* XV, 234–6: 'Tempus edax rerum, tuque, invidiosa vetustas, / omnia destruitis vitiataque dentibus aevi / paulatim lenta consumitis omnia morte!' (Golding, XV, 258–60: 'Thou tyme, the eater up of things, and age of spyghtfull teene [i.e. injury, ruin], / Destroy all things. And when that long continuance hath them bit, / You leysurely by lingring death consume them every whit'). Compare *Rape of Lucrece* 925–59. In 16 and 17 Shakespeare plays the verse–immortality theme against the procreation theme, modestly urging that the latter is the better weapon against time and death, but in 18 and 19 he drops the procreation theme and promises the youth immortality through his verse.

1 consider every thing i.e. consider that every thing.

2 Holds in perfection (1) Remains at its prime; (2) Retains its perfection.

3–8 A somewhat confused theatrical metaphor in which the stars are pictured as spectators in the theatre governing the success or failure ('Cheerèd and checked' (6)) of the performance (i.e. the course of man's life).

3 That i.e. when I consider that (picking up the construction of the first clause (1–2), where, however, 'that' is omitted, a not uncommon usage in Elizabethan English when the first clause is clear without 'that'; see Abbott 285).

3 stage the world (frequently used for the earth). Compare *AYLI* 2.7.139–40: 'All the world's a stage, / And all the men and women merely players'; *MV* 1.1.77–9; *Lear* 4.6.182–3.

3 shows (1) imposing external images of reality (as in a play); (2) illusory appearances (because always waning toward, death). There are elements in lines 3–8 of Prospero's great lines on the mutability and evanescence of 'the great globe itself, / Yea, all which it inherit' (*Temp.* 4.1.148–58).

4 Whereon . . . comment Upon which the stars, through their occult or hidden ('secret') influence, make 'critical' decisions. It was generally believed that man's behaviour and events were influenced, though not determined, by the stars ('influence' is a technical astrological term = ethereal fluid flowing from the stars, affecting men and events), and such influence is described as 'secret' because, as Kerrigan suggests, it worked behind man's back ('unheard') like a political cabal or theatrical claque. Astrologers, of course, claimed to penetrate this 'secret influence'. Shakespeare's use of 'comment' has caused difficulty, since though spectators at a play may comment, the stars were believed to do much more than 'comment' in a passive sense. I have assigned a meaning to 'comment' (with support from *OED*) which suggests the action of a commentator or reviewer who makes crucial or 'critical' decisions that affect the future of a 'work'.

5 as plants increase i.e. grow as plants do, waxing and waning.

6 Cheerèd and checked Encouraged, solaced (by good fortune), or, possibly, applauded (as in the theatre; see the suggestion in *OED* Cheer *v* 7b) and hindered, cut short, reproved (by bad fortune), or cried down, taunted (as in the theatre). Booth notes that Jonson seems to echo the theatrical suggestion of lines 3–6 in his poem 'To the Memory of . . . Shakespeare' in the First Folio (1623), line 78: 'Or influence, chide, or cheere the drooping Stage'.

6 selfsame sky i.e. the stars, which at one and the same time seem to deal good fortune to some and bad fortune to others.

7 Vaunt . . . sap Act vaingloriously or ostentatiously (like actors) in their youthful vitality ('sap' = vital fluid). The subject of 'Vaunt' is 'men' in line 5, 6 being parenthetical. We might expect either 'And vaunt' or 'Vaunting'.

7 at height decrease decline, decay as soon as they touch their zenith (compare line 2).

8 wear . . . memory (1) wear away (in decay), forgotten ('out of memory'), what remains of their splendid zenith ('brave state'; compare 3.13, 'rememb'red not to be'); (2) wear away (in decay) what remains of their lives with only the memory ('out of memory') of their splendid zenith. According to Ingram and Redpath, 'brave' probably supports the theatrical metaphor with a secondary meaning of 'finely clothed', as actors were in their usual second-hand finery. Compare *H8* 2.4.228–31. Booth suggests an underlying metaphor in 5–8 of the rising and setting sun.

9 conceit thought, apprehension.

9 inconstant stay changing (i.e. declining, decaying) duration ('stay') of the life-span of 'every thing' (1) after reaching its 'height' (7).

10 rich in youth full of vitality, opulent, in your prime, as you are now (compare 'youthful sap' (7) and 'day of youth' (12)).

11 Where i.e. in which (= 'my sight' (10)) I see that (as in my mind's eye; compare 'conceit' (9)).

11 wasteful . . . Decay Time the Destroyer (1) fights against ('debateth') you through ('with') the action of Decay, (2) contests with Decay (i.e. there is competition between Time and Decay to ruin you), (3) engages in conspiratorial discussion with Decay (Hood).

12 your day . . . night i.e. as you decline or set (like the sun) from your prime ('day of youth') to tarnished ('sullied') old age and death ('night'). Compare 7.9–10 and *R3* 4.4.16: 'Hath dimm'd your infant morn to aged night'.

13 all . . . with in all-out war against.

13 for . . . you because of (my) love for you.

14 ingraft you new plant you anew, i.e. renew your life (by conferring immortality on you through writing about you as you are now (at your prime), thus, in one sense, stopping the ravages of Time and Decay). This early use of 'ingraft', a common variant spelling of 'engraft, is problematic. I treat it as an intensive form of 'graft', which was loosely used to mean 'plant' (*OED* Graft *v*¹ 4), a meaning not recognised by *OED* under 'engraft', which, like 'graft', basically means 'to insert (a scion of one tree) as a graft *into* or *upon* (another)', a meaning that does not seem applicable here. Seymour-Smith glosses 'ingraft' as 'engrave', a meaning that fits the context well but for which there is no other authority.

Sonnet 16

1 But Establishes the close link with Sonnet 15 and serves to reintroduce the procreation theme, which is continued in 17.

1 mightier way i.e. by marrying and producing a male heir; this is a more powerful and life-giving ('mightier'; compare 'more blessèd' (4)) method of proceeding or antidote against the ravages of Time and Death than trusting to the static kind of immortality my verses (see 'lines of life' (9)) can afford you.

3 fortify build defences for yourself against attack (the military metaphor being suggested by 'Make war upon' in line 2).

4 means i.e. the 'mightier way' of line 1.

4 blessèd prosperous, happy (because you will be 'blessèd' with children, i.e. a living future).

4 barren rhyme (1) fruitless verse (because it can bear no progeny); (2) poor, unattractive verse. Conventional modesty; compare 26.5–6, 72.13–14, and the dedications to *Venus and Adonis* and *The Rape of Lucrece*.

5 on . . . hours at the zenith of your fortunate or blessed time of life ('hours'). Compare 15.7, 10.

6 maiden . . . unset i.e. virgins (metaphorically described as potential 'gardens') as yet unseeded or unplanted ('unset'). Compare the same horticultural image in 3.5–6.

7 virtuous (1) chaste; (2) morally right (both meanings with reference to the married state).

7 living flowers i.e. children ('living' to contrast with the 'barren rhyme' (= 'flowers of poetry') of line 4).

8 liker more like (you).

8 painted counterfeit painted portrait. Until 'time's pencil' in line 10, the reader may be misled into interpreting 'painted counterfeit' as meaning 'the word-portraits that I have been "painting" of you in the preceding sonnets'.

9 lines of life The phrase has caused much debate (see summary of interpretations in Ingram and Redpath): (1) lineage; (2) descendants (children and children's children; compare *Rom.* 3.5.180); (3) lines drawn with a pencil (in painting) or pen (in verse writing); (4) lines in a genealogical table; (5) lines of a person's figure; (6) life-lines in the palms (palmistry). Of these, (1) and (2) would appear to be primary.

9 that life i.e. your life.

9 repair Compare 'ingraft you new' (15.14).

10 this time's pencil contemporary ('this time's') artist's small and fine paint-brush (like that used in painting miniatures). Among recent editions only Ingram and Redpath and Riverside (wrongly, I now think) retain Q's reading ('this (Times pensel or my pupill pen)'), which places 'Times . . . pen' in apposition to 'this'. But if 'this' is to be taken as referring to Shakespeare's 'barren rhyme' (4) or 'pupil pen', 'Time's pencil' cannot properly be considered a second appositive. I, therefore, find Ingram and Redpath's gloss of 'this' as 'this, namely' very strained, since the retention of Q's personification ('Times') contradicts the thrust of this and earlier sonnets which view Time as the Destroyer ('tyrant Time' (line 2)) not the Repairer.

10 pupil pen apprentice, novice verse (i.e. by metonymy, verse produced by a quill pen). Possibly a reference to Sonnets 1–16 as early work, but equally possibly merely conventional modesty (compare 4 n. above).

11 inward worth . . . outward fair i.e. the two aspects (inner and outer) of the *Idea* of 'Beauty'; see 4.2 n. 'fair' = fairness, beauty.

12 yourself i.e. both the inner and outer 'you'.

12 eyes of men i.e. both in men's physical eyes and in their 'minds' eyes'.

13 give away yourself (1) by marrying; (2) through marital intercourse (fathering a child). The phrase 'give away' may echo the marriage service ('Who giveth this woman to be married to this man?' (Book of Common Prayer)) with gender reversal.

13 keeps yourself still preserves 'you' (inner and outer) (1) without change, (2) always. Compare Donne, 'The Canonization', 26–7: 'Wee dye [i.e. at orgasm] and rise the same, and prove / Mysterious by this love.'

14 you must you will be able to. For this use of 'must', see Abbott 314.

14 drawn . . . skill i.e. you will be your own painter or poet (with a sexual suggestion, since both 'pencil' and 'pen' were slang terms for 'penis'; compare *Rom.* 1.2.39). Influenced perhaps by Sidney, *Arcadia* (1593), p. 74: 'With his sweet skill my skillesse youth he drewe.'

Sonnet 17

The last of the procreation sonnets, 17 combines the immortality-through-verse theme introduced in 15 and the procreation theme ('a mightier way' (16.1)) of 1–16, asserting that the hyperbolic praise showered on the youth throughout this series will seem beyond belief 'in time to come' unless such praise may be validated by the presence of one of his direct descendants, a living picture, 'drawn by [his] own sweet skill' (16.14), of his 'inward worth' and 'outward fair' (16.11). On the dangers of over-praise, compare Constable, *Diana* (1592), 13, and Drayton, *Ideas Mirrour* (1594), Amour 12.

1–4 The pointing in these lines is essentially that of Q. Ingram and Redpath, alone among recent editors, argue for Tucker's repointing (see collation), isolating line 1 as a question and making 3–4 parenthetical to avoid what they consider an unintelligible clash of tenses in 1 and 2, where today we would expect 'would' in 1 for Q's 'will' to accord with the subjunctive 'were' in 2. But Elizabethan usage in apparently subjunctive constructions was loose (see Abbott 103, 362–3), and the close paratactic linking Tucker's pointing sets up between 2–4 and 5–8 is somewhat awkward, if not misleading; for in 2–4 Shakespeare sadly admits that he has been unable adequately to render the youth's 'deserts', while in 5–8 he says that if he *could* do so, not only would his efforts not be believed but he would be branded openly as a liar.

2 deserts (1) good physical qualities; (2) spiritual merits.

3–4 it . . . life i.e. his (inadequate) verse ('it') hides, as in a tomb (which contains only the dead), your vital 'life' (your 'deserts' and 'parts'). The suggestion is that 'verse' only embalms the youth.

4 parts = 'deserts' (of line 2).

5 write express in words or verse.

6 fresh numbers lively, novel verses ('numbers').

6 number count up, reckon.

6 graces attractive innate qualities (compare 'deserts' (2); 'parts' (4)).

7 age to come i.e. the next generation.

8 touches strokes of the pen or brush.

8 touched left their imprint on.

8 earthly faces mortal beings (by metonymy). The implication is that the youth would thus have been described in terms proper only to a god ('heavenly').

9 papers manuscripts of his verses.

10 old . . . tongue Compare the proverb: 'Old men and travellers may lie by authority' (*ODEP*), and the character of Polonius in *Hamlet*.

10 tongue wordiness, garrulity (by metonymy).

11 true rights proper dues (which are owed to you).

11 poet's rage the inspiration (with a hint of madness) that was believed to seize upon a poet in the throes of composition (i.e. *furor divinus et poeticus*). Compare *MND* 5.1.12: 'The poet's eye, in a fine frenzy rolling . . .' Poets and poetry (particularly dramatic poetry) were under attack at this time by writers with strong Puritan leanings (e.g. John Northbrooke, Stephen Gosson, Philip Stubbes) on moral grounds because they considered a poet to be a liar (compare line 7, 'This poet lies'), banished by Plato from his ideal commonwealth (*The Republic*, x) a purveyor of fictions, not truth. The poet's defence was undertaken by Sidney in his famous *Apology for Poetry* (written *c.* 1579–80; published 1595).

12 strechèd metre (1) strained (by hyperbole) verse; (2) perhaps refers either to the formerly popular use of long verse lines such as the fourteener (couplets of seven stresses) and poulter's measure (couplets of seven and six stresses) or to the Latin hexameter, English imitations of which were in some vogue in the 1570s and 1580s.

12 àntique song old-time, ancient poem, not necessarily to be sung (with possible play on 'antic' = grotesque, bizarre).

13 that time i.e. 'age to come' (7).

14 rhyme verse.

Sonnet 18

Some critics include 18 and 19 as part of the series of procreation sonnets (1–17) because, even though the procreation theme is absent, both centre on the immortality-through-verse theme found in 15–17 and because 20, though addressed to the youth, clearly signals a change in Shakespeare's personal involvement in the relationship. Strictly considered, however, 18 and 19 flatly contradict the overriding procreation theme of 1–17 (hence perhaps their omission from Benson's 1640 *Poems*) and may be better thought of either as independent exercises on a traditional sonnet topos (finding a place here because of their theme) or as a kind of bridge to 20 in which Shakespeare as a poet asserts his independence from and mastery of 'Devouring Time' (19.1), thus placing himself in the new relation to the youth which is reflected in 20. Booth points out that 18 'plays on the proverbial comparative formula "as good as one shall see in a summer's day"', meaning "as good as the best there is"' (compare Tilley s967 and *MND* 1.2.86–7).

1 Shall . . . day? There is an underlying subjunctive force to 'Shall' (i.e. 'If I should . . .') which links line 1 to line 2 ('Thou art . . .') syntactically. Compare the use of 'will' in 17.1.

1 a summer's day The phrase may here be taken, by metonymy, as an equivalent for its later function as the 'season of summer' in lines 4–9.

2 temperate moderate, tempered (in character) as compared with summer days, which can be excessively hot, i.e. 'intemperate'.

3 darling much loved (because a sign of spring = 'May').

4 summer's . . . date i.e. the contract under which what may be called the 'summer season' is all too short-termed.

5 Sometime At times.

5 eye of heaven i.e. the sun. Shakespeare seems fond of this image; compare 7.2 n., *Rape of Lucrece*, 356, and *R2* 1.3.275, 3.2.37.

6 gold complexion golden-coloured face. The colour of the face was believed to reflect the 'temperament' or 'humour' (i.e. 'complexion'; see *OED* Complexion *sb* 4) of an individual. See 7.8 n.

6 dimmed i.e. overcast by clouds.

7 every . . . declines the beauty ('fair') of every beautiful thing or person ('fair') decays sooner or later ('sometime declines').

8 chance accident, bad luck (a stroke of external fortune).

8 nature's changing course natural decay (inherent in all things).

8 untrimmed despoiled of external ornament ('fair' (7)).

9 thy . . . fade i.e. your summer will never fade because my verses will make it eternal (compare 'eternal lines' (12)). The phrase 'eternal summer' is syntactically difficult, since the youth's summer is not 'eternal' in itself but only in so far as it is caught and preserved in Shakespeare's verses; 'eternal' thus anticipates the argument of lines 10–14.

10 lose possession be dispossessed.

10 fair thou ow'st beauty you own.

11 Death brag Compare *Ant.* 5.2.315–16: 'Now boast thee, death, in thy possession lies / A lass unparallel'd.'

11 wand'rest . . . shade Booth compares Ps. 23.3: 'Yea, though I walk through the valley of the shadow of death, I will fear no evil' (Bishops' Bible) and the *umbra mortis* of the Vulgate text (*OED* Shadow *sb* 1b). 'shade' = shadow (the darkness of death); compare 'gloomy shade of death' in *1H6* 5.4.89. 'wand'rest' was suggested perhaps by the ghosts (= 'shades') who are described as wandering in the classical underworld.

12 eternal lines (1) immortal verse; (2) 'lines of life' (16.9), but not, I think, here with reference to 'lineal descendants' (as Kerrigan suggests), though, as Booth notes, a reader might be tempted, in view of the preceding sonnets, so to read the line, a reading negated by lines 13–14. On the theme of immortality-through-verse, see Sonnet 15 headnote.

12 to time thou grow'st i.e. you become an organic part of time's 'eternal' span, being as it were 'ingraft' (15.14) and bound with 'eternal lines' (as by cords (= 'lines') used in grafting).

14 this i.e. this sonnet.

14 life immortality.

Sonnet 19

See 18 headnote.

1–2 Shakespeare is probably thinking of Ovid, *Metamorphoses* XV, 234–6 (see 15 headnote). Compare Spenser, *Amoretti*, 58.7–8: 'devouring tyme and changeful chance have prayd / her glories pride', and Daniel, *Delia*, 55.9–12: 'These are the Arkes, the Trophies I erect, / That fortifie thy name against old age: / And these thy sacred vertues must protect, / Against the darke [compare 18.11–12] and times consuming rage.' See Tilley T326: 'Time devours all things.'

2 make . . . brood i.e. cause the earth, through death, to absorb once again into itself its own precious ('sweet') progeny ('brood'). Compare the burial service in the Book of Common Prayer: 'earth to earth, ashes to ashes, dust to dust', though here there is no suggestion of a future state, either Christian or Ovidian (*Metamorphoses* XV, 158–9). Ingram and Redpath suggest that 'brood' refers specifically to flowers because of the modifier 'sweet'.

4 burn . . . blood A fabulous bird, of uncertain gender, the phoenix, of which there was only one at a time, was believed to live several hundred years (accounts differ as to how many); finally it immolated itself on a pyre of spices, and was reborn from its own ashes (see Ovid, *Metamorphoses* XV, 392–402). The legend thus makes it a symbol of immortality, the only 'creature' that could defy Time. Shakespeare, however, here places the phoenix, like other 'creatures', in Time's power and ignores its self-regeneration. Compare *Temp.* 3.3.21–4, where the legend is held up as incredible, and *1H6* 1.4.35–6, where it is treated conventionally.

4 in her blood alive (with possible play on 'in blood' = in full vigour, another contradiction of the legend).

5 Make . . . fleet'st Since without Time there would be no change of seasons, Time, as he flies quickly away ('fleet'st'; compare the Latin tag *Tempus fugit*, and 'swift-footed' in line 6), may be said to control seasonal changes, producing seasons which may be termed either happy and fortunate ('glad', i.e. spring and summer, when 'creatures' are in their prime and life flourishes) or sad and unfortunate ('sorry', i.e. autumn and winter, when life is beginning to decay or dies). See 5.5–6. Ovid compares the four seasons to the four ages of man (*Metamorphoses* XV, 199–213).

5 fleet'st Dyce's emendation to 'fleets' (a not uncommon contemporary second-person singular

form in verbs ending in *t* or *d* (see Abbott 340), and compare 'confounds' in 8.7) has been adopted by most editors for the sake of an exact rhyme with 'sweets' in line 7, but, as Kerrigan suggests, the *-st* form, followed by 'And', is more euphonious and accords with the play on *s* and *t* sounds in lines 5–7.

7 sweets = 'sweet brood' in line 2.

9 carve . . . brow. With this reference to the wrinkles of age (see 2.2, 3.12), compare Ovid, *Metamorphoses* XV, 231–3 (Golding, 255–6): 'And *Helen* when shee saw her aged wrincles in / A glasse, wept also' – a passage that immediately precedes the *tempus edax rerum* passage (234–6) which may have influenced the opening lines of this sonnet.

9 carve shape by cutting or engraving, incise (with reference to Time's symbolic scythe, described as a 'pen' or stylus in line 10). Lines 9 and 10 say essentially the same thing: don't cut (or write = 'draw' (10)) wrinkles in my love's brow.

10 Nor = And (no alternative is suggested). See perhaps Abbott 408.

10 àntique (1) so old as to be beyond memory; (2) old-making (in a causative sense); (3) producing monstrosities, grotesqueries (i.e. 'antic'), making beauty ugly. Compare 'àntique pen' in 106.7.

11 course (ever-onward) race, career.

11 untainted unimpaired, unblemished (from tilting, a 'taint' being a blow or hit; suggested by 'course').

12 pattern model, mould, 'beauty's pattern' may suggest the '*Idea* of Beauty' in neo-Platonic terms; compare Donne's 'The Canonization', 37–45.

13 Yet Nevertheless (reverses the argument).

13 wrong injury, damage, violation.

14 My love (1) the youth addressed; (2) my love of the youth.

Sonnet 20

Beginning with 20 and continuing through 126 (i.e. the rest of the series addressed to the youth), the sonnets take on a much more personally involved tone (notably more so than the slight evidence of such involvement in 13 or 15). As a result, the questions raised by the nature of Shakespeare's relationship to the young man inevitably become more pressing for those critics (the majority) who read the Sonnets as autobiographical. See pp. 11 and 105 above for an account of the problem this has caused critics and a discussion of the homoerotic issues involved. The sonnet owes something of its structure and development, I believe, to contemporary medical theory relating to physical differences between men and women. J. Huarte Navarro in his *Examen de Ingenios*, translated by Richard Carew as *The Examination of Mens Wits* (1594; pp. 268–9), observes: 'man (though it seem otherwise in the composition which we see) is different from a woman in nought els (saith *Galen*) than only in having his genitall members without his body. For if we make anotomie of a woman, we shall find that she hath within her two stones, two vessels for seed, and her belly of the same frame as a mans member, without that any one part is therin wanting. And this is so very true, that if when nature hath finished to forme a man in all perfection, she would convert him into a woman, there needeth nought els to be done, save only to tuine his instruments of generation inwards. And if she have shaped a woman, and would make a man of her, by taking forth her belly and her cods, it would quickly be performed.' Huarte adds (p. 269) that when, 'in the mothers womb', female children are converted into males it is 'afterwards plainly discovered, by certain motions which they retaine, unfitting for the masculin sex, being altogither womanish, & their voice shrill and sweet'. The portrait of the youth that emerges is strongly epicene, even though his physical and mental characteristics are throughout described as superior to those found in women. Compare the description of the youthful seducer in *A Lover's Complaint*, 92–8, and Sidney's description of Pyrocles (*Arcadia* (1593), p. 170): '*Pyrocles* of a pure [i.e. "fair" as compared with the "brownenes" of Musidorus] complexion, and of such a cheerefull favour, as might seeme either a womans face on a boy, or an excellent boyes face in a woman.' Both Shakespeare and Sidney may be recalling Ovid, *Metamorphoses* VIII, 322–3 (Golding, 434–6): 'Hir countnance and hir grace / Was such as in a Boy might well be cald a Wenches face, / And in a Wench be cald a Boyes.'

1 **woman's . . . painted** i.e. Nature, not art (as with women), is responsible for his complexion; his perfection is natural, women have to 'paint' even to approach it. 20 is the only one of Shakespeare's sonnets to use feminine rhyme throughout.

1 **with** by.

2 **master-mistress . . . passion** A phrase (with or without the hyphen) that has probably generated more heat than any other in the Sonnets, for obvious reasons. Some see in it a frank avowal of homosexual love or 'passion' ('master-mistress' = male mistress or 'masculine whore' as Patroclus is called in *Tro.* 5.1.17), others, taking 'passion' in the sense of 'poem' or 'sonnet' (*OED* Passion *sb* 6d), interpret 'master-mistress' as merely emphasising the situation in which a 'man' is being addressed in a way conventional to one of the many 'mistresses' (Delia, Idea, Laura, Stella, etc.) who are objects of 'passionate' adulation in other sonnet sequences. Various shades of opinion between these polar opposites have been suggested, depending on a reader's personal assessment of the kind of relationship Shakespeare is describing. Not generally noticed, I believe, is the way in which the phrase 'master-mistress' grows out of a witty play on the idea of a 'man' ('master') who has – though, of course, of a superior order – the complexion, heart, and eyes of a 'woman' ('mistress') –

the central conceit on which the sonnet turns until Nature's unfortunate addition of 'one thing' is finally admitted in line 12.

3–8 In parallel construction with lines 1–2; 'hast thou' is to be understood after 'heart' in line 3 and 'bright' in 5, and 'art thou' after 'hue' in 7.

4 **shifting change . . . women's fashion** Women were generally considered as being of a phlegmatic humour, which was governed by the moon, and therefore, as compared to men, of a shifting, fickle, and changeable nature. Compare Greene, *Mamillia, Part II* (1593), II, 221: '[Socrates, Plato, Aristotle] assigned this as a particular qualitie appertaining to womenkinde, namely, to be fickle and inconstant, alledging this Astronomicall reason, that *Luna* a feminine and mutable Planet hath such predominant power in the constitution of their complexion [temperament], because they be phlegmatike; that of necessitie they must be fickle, mutable and inconstant, whereas Choller [another of the four humours], wherewith men do abound, is contrarie, and therefore by consequence stable, firme and without change'.

5 **less . . . rolling** For the accepted psychological basis of this assumption, see the preceding note.

6 **Gilding** Tingeing with gold (like the sun). Compare *Tit.* 2.2.5–6: 'As when the golden sun salutes the morn, / And, having gilt the ocean with his beams . . .' (earliest citation in *OED*). Compare 33.3–4. One contemporary view held that light itself lay in the eye, which emitted 'beams' (compare 114.8) and hence had the power to transmute what is looked on (Tucker). See Sir Arthur Gorges, *The Vannetys and Toyes*, 3.1–2, and 114.8 n. below.

7 **A man in hue** Usually explained as meaning 'A man in form/shape, appearance' (the meaning 'colour' has been co-opted by line 1), but T. B. Baldwin (pp. 165–7) notes two passages in Hoby's translation (1561) of Castiglione's *Libro del Cortegiano* (1528) that suggest an abstract meaning for 'hue' of 'noble grace, air, bearing, or spirit' (not recorded in *OED*): (1) 'The Courtier, therefore, beside noblenesse of birth, I will have . . . by nature to have not onley a wit, and a comely shape of person and countenance, but also a certaine grace, and (as they say) a hewe, that shall make him at the first sight acceptable and loving unto who so beholdeth him' (Everyman edn, p. 33; Italian: 'ma una certa grazia, e come si dice, un sangue', trans. 'but with that certain grace which we call an "air"' (C. S. Singleton, Anchor Books, 1978, p. 29)); (2) 'Therefore when an amiable countenance of a beautifull woman commeth in his sight, that is accompanied with noble conditions and honest behaviours . . . hee woteth well that his hew hath an agreement with hers . . .' (pp. 312–13; Italian: 'conosca il sangue suo aver conformità con quello . . .', trans. 'feels that his spirit accords with hers' (Singleton, p. 346)). Castiglione's ideal

courtier, crowning all his other attributes, must do whatever he does with 'grace' (i.e. effortlessly) and Shakespeare attributes 'sweet graces' to the young man in 78.12. Some critics consider 'man in' to be textually corrupt (see collation).

7 all hues . . . controlling A richly ambiguous phrase: (1) challenging or overpowering (by his perfect grace/form) all other graces/forms; (2) having all other graces/forms contained in his grace/form (i.e. his is the ideal grace/form); (3) (though he looks like a man, or a mere man), he has the power to adopt any grace/form he chooses (Kerrigan); (4) (a fine-looking man) he enthralls everyone (Kerrigan; both (3) and (4) owe something to Booth); (5) (interpreting 'hue' as 'colour'), he has, through his complexion, power over all other complexions (i.e. causes others to blush or pale) (Booth, after Beeching). Q's spelling of 'hues' as '*Hews*' (though all italicised words in Q are capitalised) may imply some play on a proper name and various people called William Hughes have been dutifully dragged from deserved obscurity to figure as 'Mr. W. H.'; none had any known connection with Shakespeare (see Rollins, II, 180–5). See Textual Analysis (p. 265 below) for comment on Q's occasional use of italics.

8 Which May refer to 'hue' or 'controlling' (as a noun), or to 'his [hue]' (taking 'controlling' as a participle).

8 steals men's eyes Compare *Per.* 4.1.39–41: 'reserve / That excellent complexion, which did steal / The eyes of young and old'.

8 women's souls amazeth astounds or perplexes women's innermost feelings ('soul' = the seat of the emotions). Note that the youth's effect seems to be represented as less overpowering for men ('eyes') than for women ('souls'). In neo-Platonic terms, the eyes were thought of as the 'windows of the soul'. Men, therefore, may be thought of as viewing the youth intellectually, women, emotionally. For some discussion of neo-Platonism in the Sonnets, see 53 (headnote), 105.4 n., and Rollins, II, 131.

9 for a woman i.e. as a woman.

10 Nature . . . a-doting i.e. Nature as she formed you fell in love with you (being a woman, she became emotionally involved and therefore had to change you to a man). See 8 n. on 'women's souls'.

11 by addition In the obvious sense, this is rather awkwardly duplicated in line 12 by 'By adding', but 'addition' here may mean a 'mark of honour added to a coat-of-arms' (i.e. the title 'man' as compared to 'woman'). Some critics read lines 11–14 as decisive against any charge of homoeroticism.

11 defeated defrauded, deprived.

12 one thing 'thing' could vulgarly refer to male or female pudenda; here, of course, = penis (with possible play on 'one' as a phallic symbol; see 6.8 n.). Compare Wilson, p. 115: 'al men would thincke you were not worthye to have the thinge, if either you

coulde not, or you woulde not use it, and occupie it . . . it is not like that Nature slepte or forgate her selfe when she made this one thinge'.

12 to my purpose nothing of no 'use' to me as a man (unlike the female pudenda).

12 nothing Cercignani (as opposed to Kökeritz) denies that 'nothing' was regularly pronounced 'noting' and thus formed a perfect rhyme with 'a-doting' in line 10; thus a play on 'no thing' = not a vulva was probably intended.

13 pricked thee out marked you out (by giving you a 'prick' = penis). Compare *2H4* 3.2.152–5.

14 Mine be thy love Let thy love be mine (but in a spiritual, non-physical sense).

14 thy love's . . . treasure (1) let the sexual enjoyment ('use') and 'pleasure' (13) afforded by your 'loving' be the highly valued possession ('treasure') of women (with a new suggestion of promiscuity in 'women's'); (2) let the increase ('use') of your 'loving' (i.e. progeny) be for women a treasure-store (for future generations). Both (1) and (2) probably play on 'treasure' with bawdy reference to a woman's pudenda or male semen; compare *Tit.* 2.1.130–1: 'There serve your lust . . . / And revel in Lavinia's treasury.'

Sonnet 21

In Sonnet 21, Shakespeare seeks to distinguish his praise of the 'beloved' as true in properly human terms (lines 10–12) (compare John Davies of Hereford, *Wittes Pilgrimage*, Sonnet 74) from the grossly exaggerated, frequently supra-human, praise lavished on a 'painted beauty' by other writers of love poetry, particularly those writing in the Petrarchan sonnet tradition, who compare, or prefer, their mistresses to all the riches of heaven and earth. Compare, for example, Lodge, *Rosalynde* (1590), p. 186: 'In fluent numbers and in pleasant veines, / I rob both sea and earth of all their state, / To praise her parts.' Needless to say, Shakespeare is often, and effectively, capable of exactly the kinds of comparisons he here condemns (compare 33.9); the emphasis of 21 is thus, in part at least, a rhetorical device intended to imply his comparative veracity. On the other hand, it is not all a ploy, since it is Shakespeare's profound psychological insight into the comparative complexities of human character and motive that gives his work (including the Sonnets) the special stamp of poetic truth. On the theme of 'writing truly' and from the heart, compare George Herbert's 'Jordan (II)', in which line 6 ('Decking the sense, as if it were to sell') almost seems to echo Shakespeare's line 14 ('I will not praise that purpose not to sell').

1–2 So is . . . verse My inspiration as a poet is unlike that of the kind of poet ('that Muse') who is moved ('Stirred') to write verse by a beauty that tries to improve on nature ('painted'), since I am inspired by a 'beauty' 'with Nature's own hand painted' (20.1).

On 'painted beauty' compare 67 and 68. Despite the objections of certain critics, 21 seems to me closely linked with 20.1 by line 2 and by the method of comparison in 20, which illustrates the thesis of 21, namely, that human beings should most properly be compared with other human beings ('any mother's child'). Some critics detect an early reference in 'that Muse' to the 'rival poet (or poets)' (see Rollins, II, 277–94) who figures in 78–80, 82–6, but the 'Muse' in 21 refers specifically to love poets who address a 'painted beauty' (i.e. a mistress), not a young man.

3 heaven i.e. the heavenly firmament, but also with reference to the gods, goddesses, angels, etc. that were supposed to inhabit it.

3 itself Q's 'it selfe' may here (and elsewhere) retain the sense of 'its self' ('it' being used as a possessive); compare *Lear* 1.4.216: 'That it had it head bit off by it young'. See Abbott 228.

3 for ornament as embellishment, adornment (something extraneous to the thing itself).

4 every . . . rehearse cites or compares ('rehearse') his mistress ('his fair') as an example of each beautiful thing (stars, planets, etc.) or creature (with the implication that she is equal or superior). Compare *Rom.* 2.2.2–32.

5 complement pairing, union of pairs.

5 proud compare (1) exalted, magnificent comparison; (2) overblown, swollen comparison.

6 earth . . . gems the magnificent, opulent ('rich') treasures (or, literally, gems) of both earth and sea.

7 April's i.e. the spring's.

7 first-born earliest. Q's 'first borne' might just possibly mean 'the first flowers borne or carried by spring'.

7 all things rate (1) = 'every fair' (line 4); (2) all things exceptionally beautiful or good; (3) all scarce things.

8 heaven's air Here used for the 'macrocosm', the great world or universe, not merely for what, in the Ptolemaic geocentric system, was technically called the 'element of air', which was supposedly located above the elements of earth and water and below the element of fire, the spheres of the seven planets, and Circle of the Fixed Stars.

8 in this huge rondure hems confines in this huge circle ('rondure'). The universe was thought of as circular and round.

9 truly i.e. without the exaggerated comparisons of other love poets (as illustrated in lines 1–8).

10 And . . . me And as a result of which (i.e. my 'truth' in writing) believe me.

11 child Note the ungendered 'child' rather than 'son', again linking this sonnet to the epicene description of the youth in 20.

11–12 not so bright . . . gold candles (my love) is not so bright as the stars ('gold candles'). The implication is that 'that Muse' (line 1) would have claimed

his love to be as bright or brighter. Compare *MV* 5.1.220 ('blessed candles of the night'), *Mac.* 2.1.4–5, and the negative technique used in Sonnet 130.

12 fixed Refers to the Circle of the Fixed Stars (as distinct from planets, which rotated individually).

13 say more exaggerate, speak in hyperbole.

13 like of = like.

13 hearsay unverified report, gossip, rumour (as compared with 'facts').

14 I will . . . sell I will not overpraise (as a vendor would) since I have no intention of selling (my love as if he were a commodity). Proverbial, Tilley P546: 'He praises who wishes to sell.' Compare *LLL* 4.3.235–6. 'Fie, painted rhetoric! O, she needs it not. / To things of sale a seller's praise belongs', and 102.3–4. Does 'sell' perhaps carry also the sense 'dressing something up for public approval' (i.e. my verses are for my love only and need no heightening to catch others' eyes)? Compare 125.

Sonnet 22

Sonnet 22 turns on the conventional conceit of the 'exchange of hearts' by which lovers become 'one soul in two bodies'. Compare Petrarch, *Rime sparse*, 48; Malory, *Morte D'Arthur* (Everyman edn, I, 52): 'O Balin, two bodies thou hast slain and one heart, and two hearts in one body, and two souls thou hast lost', Sidney, 'My true love hath my hart, and I have his' (*Arcadia* (1593), p. 17); *LLL* 5.2.811–16; Sonnets 24, 36, 109.3–4, 133.9; and the proverb 'The lover [or heart, soul] is not where he [it] lives but where he [it] loves' (Tilley L565).

1 glass mirror, looking-glass. Kerrigan notes the shift in emphasis here from that in Sonnet 3. There the emphasis had been on the youth and the related procreation theme; here on the poet and the youth in terms of the 'complementariness of selves (something developed towards the extreme of 62.13)'.

1 old Shakespeare was probably between thirty and thirty-five when he wrote this sonnet, an age, to be sure, comparable to between fifty and sixty today in terms of life expectancy, but it was conventional for a sonneteer to describe himself as unworthily 'old' as compared to the youthful beauty of his mistress (compare Petrarch, Daniel, Drayton, etc.).

2–4 Since the youth and the poet have exchanged hearts (= loves), the poet, possessing the youth's heart, will remain young and will not allow his mirror to 'persuade' him (line 1) that he is 'old' until he sees, as in a mirror, the wrinkles of age ('time's furrows' (3)) in the youth's face. Lines 5–8 expand on this theme.

2 of one date coeval.

3 time's furrows See 2.2 n.

4 look . . . expiate I hope ('look') that death will bring my life ('days') to an end (*OED* Expiate *v* 7). Compare *R3* 3.3.24: 'Make haste, the hour of death is expiate.' Unlike Booth and Kerrigan, I see no reason here to take 'expiate' in a secondary sense of 'cleanse or purify from guilt' (*OED* Expiate *v* 2).

5 cover clothe (with the 'raiment' of line 6).

6 but merely.

6 seemly fair, handsome.

8 elder older (umlauted form; see Franz 223).

9–10 be . . . will guard yourself against harm ('be . . . wary') even as I will guard myself, not on my own account but on yours (because my breast contains your heart ('Bearing thy heart' (11))).

11 chary carefully, dearly cherished.

12 faring ill (1) experiencing ill fortune; (2) being ill fed.

13 Presume . . . slain Do not count on retrieving your heart (from my breast) when my heart (which is in your breast) dies (the result of your failure to cherish or nourish my heart as I have yours).

14 Thou . . . again i.e. once given, the heart (= love) is given absolutely and without reservations. The final couplet hints at the fear that the youth's love is less committed than the poet's. Booth suggests the influence in lines 5–14 of the vows taken in the marriage service (Book of Common Prayer) by which the bride and bridegroom promise each other to 'love, and to cherish, till death us depart'.

Sonnet 23

For the convention of the tongue-tied lover, see Petrarch, *Rime sparse*, 49, and Tottel (1557), no. 168, 35–8.

1 unperfect actor (1) actor who is not word-perfect in his lines or forgets them; (2) unskilled actor. Compare *Cor.* 5.3.40–2: 'Like a dull actor now / I have forgot my part, and I am out, / Even to a full disgrace.'

2 with as a result of.

2 besides out of. Elizabethan English used 'beside' and 'besides' as prepositions indifferently; see Franz 469.

3 replete gorged, sated, filled.

4 Whose . . . heart The superfluous power ('strength's abundance') of which (referring to 'rage' (3)) (1) overtaxes his heart, (2) limits his effectiveness in pursuing his purpose (= 'heart'). Compare *Ham.* 4.7.117–18: 'For goodness, growing to a plurisy, / Dies in his own too much.'

5 for fear of trust (1) fearing to trust myself (like an 'unperfect actor' (line 1)); (2) fearing the responsibility imposed on me. Lines 5–6 link with 1–2; lines 7–8 with 3–4.

5 say give expression to.

6 perfect ceremony word-perfect 'performance' or observance (such as would be given by the 'perfect actor' or lover).

6 rite ritual (Q's 'right', an interchangeable spelling of 'rite' at this time, would probably suggest a secondary meaning of love's 'due').

7–8 And in . . . might And would appear ('seem') to show a falling off in the capacity ('strength') of my love, being weighed down and 'weaken[ed]' (4) by the burden (compare 'too much rage' (3)) of my love's transcendent power. 'burthen' is a common variant form of 'burden'. Booth takes 'mine own love's might' to refer to the 'strength/might of my beloved'.

9 looks Sewell's emendation for Q 'books'; a much debated reading. Recent editors (Kerrigan does not even comment on 'looks') retain Q 'books' as referring to these sonnets, and, perhaps, to *Venus and Adonis* and *The Rape of Lucrece*. 'book' could be used to describe single written sheets; see *OED* Book *sb* 1, and compare *1H4* 2.1.221, 265, and *Cym.* 5.4.133. Earlier arguments, however (see Rollins, I, 66–7), favouring 'looks' (= glances of the eyes, facial expressions) convince me that, although 'books' may be a *possible* reading, 'looks' is the more *probable*, given the whole context. The principal stumbling-block for the proponents of 'books' lies in 'presagers' (10), not found elsewhere in Shakespeare, a word for which they are forced to invent, without lexical authority, such meanings as 'messengers', 'ambassadors', 'heralds', and 'presenters' (as in a dumb show), since Shakespeare's 'books', already written (or printed), cannot properly be said to prophesy or foretell (the only meaning of 'presage' and its compounds documented by *OED*, the meaning 'point to', attributed to Spenser, being, as Booth notes, due to a misreading of the passage). Moreover, since Shakespeare uses 'presage' (as noun and verb) elsewhere sixteen times with full understanding of its root meaning, it is difficult to argue that he would misuse such an obviously related, if rare, form as 'presager'. Some critics also see a less serious, though not entirely frivolous, objection to 'books' in the injunction of line 13 ('learn to read what silent love hath writ') on two grounds: (1) that 'learn to read', if interpreted literally, instead of metaphorically ('read' = understand), could be interpreted to suggest that the youth was illiterate; and (2) that 'silent' (like 'dumb' = silent, speechless in line 10) is strained if applied to written or printed words (i.e. 'books'), but perfectly natural if used to describe a lover's eloquent 'looks'. Finally, it is worth noting that a minuscule *l* in Secretary hand could very easily be misread as a *b* by the compositor.

9 eloquence rhetorically and artistically perfect speech (thus fitted to the expression of 'The perfect ceremony of love's rite' (6)).

10 dumb presagers silent, speechless portents or foretellers. See 9 n. for meanings if Q 'books' is retained in line 9.

10 my speaking breast i.e. the language of my heart ('breast' for 'heart' by synecdoche).

11 Who Refers probably to 'looks' (9) or possibly to 'presagers' (10). On the neuter use of 'who' (= which), which tends to personify irrational antecedents, see Abbott 264.

11 **look for recompense** (1) expect reward; (2) look in such a loving way as to hope for a similar return.

12 **More . . . expressed** Greater reward than that tongue (= poet, by synecdoche) which has given voice to more (vocal) praise of you more often or more lavishly. Shakespeare makes a distinction between the poet ('that tongue'), who can talk glibly about a shallow or imaginary love, and himself, whose love is so deep that he is tongue-tied and can only plead his case by silent looks. Like 'that Muse' (21.1), 'that tongue' has, wisely or not, been taken by some critics as a reference to the 'rival poet' who figures in 78–80, 82–6. As in 21.1, however, 'that' here can mean 'the' (*OED* That *adj* 3).

14 **hear with eyes** Compare Bottom's parody of 1 Cor. 2.9–10 (Bishops' Bible): 'The eye of man hath not heard' (*MND* 4.1.211), another example of Shakespeare's 'fine wit' (14); and John Davies of Hereford, *Wittes Pilgrimage* (*c.* 1605), Sonnet 62.

14 **belongs** is a proper function of.

14 **fine wit** acute, subtle intelligence (with perhaps a hint of over-subtle or attenuated in 'fine'). The 'wit . . . wiht' misprint in Q probably results from a compositor's error in misinterpreting a proof-corrector's attempt to remedy a first state which read 'wit . . . wit'.

Sonnet 24

Sonnet 24 is generally considered one of the most mechanically conceited and imitative of the sonnets; Mahood (p. 93) describes it as 'pure Bosch' (perhaps 'pure bosh' might be even more accurate). (See Sonnet 46 for further play on the eye/heart theme.)

1 **played** acted in the role of ('play' is symptomatic of the disengaged tone of the sonnet as a whole).

1 **stelled** (1) set, fixed; (2) portrayed (see *OED* Stell *v* 3). Both Capell's emendation (here adopted) and Q's 'steeld' have been strongly argued for, without much distinct advantage either way (see Ingram and Redpath, pp. 60–3, who, although favouring 'steeld', fairly weigh the arguments on both sides). Like the majority of editors, I have accepted Capell's emendation, mainly because, if we read 'steeled', it must be taken to mean 'engraved' or 'carved', as with a stylus (compare 'antique pen' in 19.10 and *Tit.* 4.1.102–3), a meaning of 'to steel' for which *OED* offers no support (admittedly not a conclusive argument, since Shakespeare is famous for his many neologisms), and because 'stelled' works more easily with the emphasis on painting here and elsewhere in the sonnet (see 'frame' (3), 'perspective' (4), and 'hanging' (as a picture (7))).

2 **form** shape, image (with possible reference to the Scholastic concept of something which contains

the 'essential determinant principle' (*OED* Form *sb* 4); compare 'image' in line 6, and 9.6, 13.8).

2 **table** tablet or board on which a picture is painted. Frequently used in association with 'heart'; compare *AWW* 1.1.95 ('In our heart's table') and Daniel, *Delia*, 13.6–7: 'I figurde on the table of mine hart, / The fairest forme, that all the world admires.'

3 **frame** (1) structure; (2) picture frame (earliest citation in *OED*). The right 'frame' gives depth and focus to a picture.

4 **And perspective . . . art** If 'perspective' is taken to mean 'the art' (= 'the art of delineating solid objects upon a plane surface so that the drawing produces the same impression of apparent relative positions and magnitudes, or of distance, as do the actual objects when viewed from a particular point' (*OED* Perspective *sb* 3; here used adverbially)), line 4 may be glossed as 'And in the use of perspective, it (i.e. "Thy beauty's form" (2)), as it is painted by "Mine eye" (1), is an example of the finest ("best") painter's (or painters') skill ("art").' This is, I believe, the primary meaning of line 4, but other plays on 'perspective' may also be intended: (1) And a perspective (= 'a picture or figure constructed so as to produce some fantastic effect; e.g. appearing distorted or confused except from one particular point of view, or presenting totally different aspects from different points' (*OED* Perspective *sb* 4b)) is itself the work ('art') of the finest painter(s) (i.e. 'thy beauty's form' can only be properly viewed from the correct angle by a lover's eye (= 'the painter' of line 1)); (2) And (an acute) sense of sight (*OED* Perspective *sb* 1) is a necessary adjunct ('art') of the best painter(s).

5–8 The opening lines of Sonnet 3 of Constable's *Diana* (1592) have been suggested as a possible influence:

> Thyne eye the glasse where I behold my
>   hearte
> Myne eye the windowe through the which
>   thyne eye
> May see my hearte and there thy selfe espie
> In bloudie coloures how thow paynted art.

Compare also Thomas Watson's *The Tears of Fancie* (1593), 45 and 46, and John Davies of Hereford, *Wittes Pilgrimage* (*c.* 1605), 86.

5–6 **For through . . . lies** i.e. because it is only through the uniquely acute eye of the painter (as here of the lover), who views objects from a correct 'perspective', that you will be able to 'see' or appreciate the perfection of his art and will thus discover where (i.e. 'in table of my heart' (2); 'my bosom's shop' (7)) your 'true image' ('Thy beauty's form' (2)) is 'stelled' (1) (i.e. 'pictured lies'). In other words, only the true lover, like the best painter, can 'see' the true essence of what is seen or loved.

5–6 **you . . . your** It has been suggested, to exculpate Shakespeare from mixing 'thou' and 'you' forms in the same sonnet, that 'you' and 'your' should here be understood in a general sense (= 'one' and 'one's'), but 'you' and 'your' work more naturally with lines 7–8 if taken to refer to the youth. Such confusion of forms in a single sonnet occurs not infrequently in other sonnet writers.

7 bosom's shop breast. Compare line 11 below (though 'shop' could also apply to the 'heart' as the seat of love and the emotions). Compare Breton, *The Toyes of an Idle Head* (1582), 'A dolorous Discourse', stanza 13: 'I winckte for feare, / And shut the windowes of my seeing shoppe.'

7 hanging i.e. as in a print-shop (though the commercial implications, if any are intended, are muted).

7 still always.

8 That . . . eyes Which (= 'bosom's shop') has its ('his') windows (i.e. the poet's eyes) glassed over ('glazèd', i.e. as a protection) with your eyes. There is perhaps a play on the phrase 'glasses of thine eyes' (= eyeballs); compare *R2* 1.3.208 and *Cor.* 3.2.117.

9 good turns Compare the proverb 'One good turn deserves another' (Tilley T616) and 47.2.

11 wherethrough through which.

12 thee i.e. your 'beauty's form' (2) or 'image' (6).

13–14 Yet eyes . . . heart But eyes (both the lover's and painter's) lack ('want') this essential knowledge ('cunning') to add the final touch ('grace') to their skill ('art'), namely, they can only draw what they 'see', but they cannot (as God can) know (see into) the heart. The final couplet strikes a note of doubt and undercuts all the high-flown nonsense of the preceding lines. Compare 92.14.

Sonnet 25

Sonnet 25 anticipates the tone of 29, though less bitterly; the first explicit comment on Shakespeare's apparently inferior social position.

1 are in favour . . . stars i.e. achieve worldly success because of propitious planetary influence (unlike Romeo and Juliet who were supposedly 'star-cross'd' (*Rom.* Prologue 6)). As Kerrigan notes: 'The astrological allusion scornfully severs advancement from merit, attributing success to chance.'

3 fortune (1) chance, accident (i.e. my stars); (2) position, status (in life).

3 of from (see Abbott 166).

4 Unlooked for (1) Unregarded, unnoticed (in the public eye); (2) (adverbially) Unexpectedly, surprisingly (considering my status or merit).

4 joy in that receive pleasure from what ('that' = our mutual love; compare line 13).

5–8 Compare *H8* 3.2.352–8: 'This is the state of man: to-day he puts forth / The tender leaves of hopes, to-morrow blossoms, / And bears his blushing honors thick upon him; / The third day comes a frost, a killing frost . . . / And then he falls as I do.'

5 fair beautiful, at least outwardly (as become 'favourites' = 'great men').

6 But Only, merely.

6 marigold The marigold was popularly known as the 'husbandmans Dyall, for that the same so aptlye declareth the houres of mornyng and evening, by opening and shutting of it' (T. Hill, *Profitable Art of Gardening* (1597), quoted Booth). Here used as a metaphor for a king's favourite: it flourishes in the 'sun's eye' (royal favour) and shrinks back into itself at nightfall (loss of royal favour, a 'frown' (8)).

7 pride (1) (of favourites) 'honour', ostentation, 'insolence of office' (*Ham.* 3.1.72), 'glory' (8); (2) (of marigolds) prime, flourishing state, 'glory' (8).

8 frown . . . glory See notes above on 'marigold' (6) and 'pride' (7).

9 painful warrior warrior who is painstaking in learning and practising his profession (with probable play on being 'full of pains' from the wounds he has incurred).

9 famousèd made famous, renowned, celebrated. Shakespeare's phrase (as here emended) was perhaps suggested by Marlowe or Nashe's 'famoused for armes' (*Dido* (1593), 1.2.264), a phrase that lends support to Theobald's conjecture of 'fight' for Q's 'worth' (see next note).

9 fight (success in) combat. Q's 'worth' makes good, if vague, sense in the immediate context, but violates the rhyme-scheme. Capell's reading 'might' is easier graphically ('worth' for MS. 'might'), but Theobald's conjecture 'fight' alliterates strongly with 'famousèd' and is more specific in relation to the 'thousand victories' of the next line. An alternative, also conjectured by Theobald, is to retain 'worth' and read 'forth' in line 11 for Q 'quite', an alternative rarely adopted by editors. Was Shakespeare recalling perhaps in this 'painful warrior' Sir John Fastolfe (metathesised to 'Falstaff' in the Folio text), who, in *1H6* 4.1.9–47, is stripped of his Garter and other honours and disgraced after his failure to participate in the battle of Patay?

10 thousand Poetic licence for 'many'.

10 once foiled defeated only once.

11 rasèd utterly erased, scratched out. 'rasèd' and 'razèd' (the form favoured by most editors) were variant spellings of 'rase' in Elizabethan English, but Ingram and Redpath point out that 'razèd' 'suggests the irrelevant association of a destroyed city' to modern readers.

12 toiled struggled, fought.

13–14 Then happy . . . removèd This final couplet, in contrast to that of Sonnet 24, seems to express a mutually assured love between the poet and the youth, unlike the situation of those who (lines 1–4) depend on 'fortune' (planetary influence), the changeable favour of princes (5–8), or the uncertainty of worldly reputation (9–12).

14 Where A situation in which.

14 remove . . . removèd separate myself from . . . be separated from (used with the implication of a

lover's constancy). Compare 116.1–4. The suggested
stressing of final -ed (as in Q) in lines 13 and 14,
coming as it does at the end of a verse line, may usually be considered optional metrically (though in line
7 above it is required for metre and rhyme); here,
though optional, the retention of Q's final stresses
gives weight and point to the couplet. Indeed, I
strongly suspect that syllabic -ed in this final position
was much more frequently stressed by Elizabethan
poets than modern editors (or readers) now allow for.
See also Sonnet 26.

Sonnet 26

Some critics see 26 as an envoy to Sonnets 20–5 (or
1–25). Capell first pointed out thematic and verbal
parallels with Shakespeare's dedication to *The Rape
of Lucrece* (1594) addressed to the Earl of Southampton (see 5–8 n. below), but such parallels are now generally dismissed as almost inevitable commonplaces
of the dedicatory mode.

1 Lord Master, sovereign (with perhaps some
suggestion of 'God'). Proponents of Southampton
or Pembroke as the addressee might take 'Lord' as a
title applicable to either.

1 vassalage allegiance, service (with some probable allusion to the relationship, in the feudal system,
between 'lord' or 'master' and 'vassal' in terms of the
'duty' (2) owed).

2 merit worth, excellence. Is a sense of social
position implied?

2 duty (1) moral obligation; (2) dutiful service
(both continuing the play on 'vassalage').

2 knit bound or tied. Compare the phrase
'bounden duty and service' in the Communion Service in the Book of Common Prayer.

3 ambassage message (variant of 'embassage'),
i.e. this sonnet or perhaps this group of sonnets (20–5
or, less likely, 1–25).

4 witness In legal terms 'witness' picks up the
implications of 'vassalage'; the sonnet is a 'witness'
of his 'duty' or service, a kind of signature to a 'bond'.

4 wit invention, ingenuity, cleverness. Rollins
quotes Thomas Nashe, *The Unfortunate Traveller*
(1594): 'truth it is, many become passionate lovers
onely to winne praise to theyr wits' (Nashe, *Works*,
II, 262). Booth's elaborate argument (pp. 176–8) on
the sexual implications of 'show' and 'wit' (= penis)
is strained in the present context.

5–8 Compare the dedication to *Rape of Lucrece*:
'The warrant I have of your Honourable disposition,
not the worth of my untutord Lines makes it [*Lucrece*]
assured of acceptance . . . Were my worth greater, my
duety would shew greater, meane time, as it is, it is
bound to your Lordship'; see also 16.4, 10–12, and
76.

5 wit (1) mental capacity; (2) skill.
5 poor ill-supplied, deficient (compare 'bare' (6)).

6 bare (1) worn thin (by triteness); (2) empty,
unfurnished (with words) (compare 'all naked' (8))
6 wanting lacking.
6 it i.e. 'Duty' (5).
7–12 Briefly put, the poet is here saying 'The
inadequacy of his "ambassage" (3) needs to be made
good by his lord's charitable acceptance of it until
more skilful wit or better fortune makes it more obviously worthy' (Hood).
7 But Unless.
7 some . . . thine some kind ('good') thought or
opinion ('conceit') of yours (for me).
8 soul's thought i.e. innermost feelings (of the
heart).
8 all naked . . . it it will store up 'this written
ambassage' (3; = 'it') even 'bare' (6) as it is (i.e. 'all
naked').
9 whatsoever star i.e. whatsoever star it may be
(with suggestion that his star is his beloved).
9 my moving (1) my sphere of life; (2) the movement of my life. Some detect a reference in 'moving'
to a projected 'journey'; compare Sonnet 27.
10 Points . . . aspect i.e. in astrological terms,
when 'his' star looks kindly (or points its rays) on
him in being at a fortunate conjunction ('fair aspect')
within the relative position of the planets (= stars).
11 puts apparel on clothes (figuratively, what is
'all naked').
11 my tottered loving (1) the 'ambassage' (line
3) as expressed by 'wit so poor as mine' (line 5); (2)
my love, poor in status and worldly fortune. 'tottered' = tattered (variant form), ragged, 'poor' (line
5); compare 2.4. Q's syllabic -ed form ('totterèd') has
sometimes been retained (as recently by Kittredge,
Neilson and Hill, Alexander, and Riverside), though
most editors now prefer the non-syllabic form as metrically smoother, if less emphatic. The editorial problem offered by internal syllabic -ed forms (frequent
in Shakespeare) raises the same questions and doubts
discussed in the note to 25.14.
12 show me worthy i.e. by accepting and clothing my lines (or my love).
12 thy Capell's emendation for Q's 'their' (see collation) is almost universally accepted (Sisson alone
argues for 'their'). Fourteen other examples of this
same compositorial misreading (not all accepted as
such by all editors) have been proposed as occurring
in Q, the last two appearing in Sonnet 128. For further discussion of this 'their/ thy' misreading and a
suggested scribal link with *Edward III* (see 94.14 n.),
see the Textual Analysis, pp. 263–5 below.
13 Then . . . thee Only then (when by acceptance
you have made my lines, and my love, worthy of your
acceptance) may I venture to glory in the full extent
of my love for you.
14 not show my head Kerrigan compares the
proverb 'He dares not show his head for debt' (Tilley
H246). This seems to carry the suggestion that the

poet is nothing but a 'poor debtor', unable to pay his debts (his homage to the youth) until authorised to do so.

14 prove me bring me to the test, put me to the touch (like a piece of gold).

Sonnet 27

Absence or separation from the beloved (as here and, for example, in Sonnets 28, 43–5, 48, 97–9) is, of course, one of the conventional themes of sonnet sequences from Petrarch onward; so, too, is the dreamlike apparition of the beloved during a lover's tormented sleepless nights. Compare Sonnets 43, 61; Sidney, *Astrophil and Stella* (1591), 38, 89; and Spenser, *Amoretti*, 87.

2 dear repose precious respite from 'toil' = 'bed' (line 1).

2 travel (1) journeying; (2) physical or mental labour, 'toil' (line 1). Though the primary meaning here seems best represented by the more modern distinction between 'travel' and 'travail' (see lines 3–6 and Sonnet 28), the Q spelling 'trauaill' could mean either (1) or (2) and the spelling 'travel' thus disguises the probable play on 'toil' in line 1.

3–4 But then . . . mind But then an imaginary journey ('journey in my head') begins to toil ('work') my mind.

4 body's work physical toil (compare line 1, 'Weary with toil').

4 expired ceased (with play perhaps on being able to breathe easily).

5 from . . . abide i.e. here, where I am at a great distance (from you).

6 Intend Proceed on, start out on (compare Latin *intendere iter*).

6 zealous fervent, emotionally driven.

6 pilgrimage Lovers often thought of themselves as pilgrims visiting the shrine of their 'saint'; compare the sonnet-wooing in *Rom.* 1.5.93–110.

8 see Paradoxically, the blind 'see' darkness.

9 Save Except.

9 my soul's imaginary sight my mind's ('soul's') imaginative ('imaginary') power of seeing ('sight'). Compare 113.1, *Ham.* 1.2.185: 'In my mind's eye, Horatio', and (with lines 9–12) the contrasting image in *John* 4.2.264–6: 'for my rage was blind, / And foul imaginary eyes of blood / Presented thee more hideous than thou art'. Shakespeare seems to be the first to use 'imaginary' in this sense (see *OED* Imaginary *a* 2).

10 thy shadow thy insubstantial image (with play on 'shadow' or 'shade' meaning 'spirit' or 'ghost'). Compare Sonnet 43. Sisson and Ingram and Redpath reject Capell's emendation of Q's 'their' to 'thy', arguing that 'their' refers back to 'thoughts' in 5; they may be right, but by line 10 the supposed referent is long out of a reader's mind and the Q compositor elsewhere misreads 'thy' as 'their' (see 26.12 n.).

10 sightless view blind seeing (picking up the paradox of 'see' in line 8). Compare 'sightless eyes' (43.12).

11 Which . . . night Like Dover Wilson, I have retained the Q pointing, though most editors prefer Capell's pointing or no pointing at all (e.g. Ingram and Redpath). Q makes a more direct association of 'jewel' (compare 131.4) with 'shadow' (line 10). Compare *Rom.* 1.5.45–6: 'It seems she hangs upon the cheek of night / Like a rich jewel in an Ethiop's ear.' It was believed that certain jewels glowed in the dark; compare *Tit.* 2.3.226–30.

11 ghastly frightful, horrifying (night was the time when spirits walked; compare *Ham.* 3.2.388–90).

12 old face Night is pictured as a wrinkled old woman; compare *H5* 4, Chorus 20–2: 'And chide the cripple tardy-gaited night, / Who like a foul and ugly witch doth limp / So tediously away'; and A.-J. Zwierlein notes (an even closer analogy) Sidney, *Astrophil and Stella* (1591), 98.9–11: 'While the blacke horrors of the silent night, / Paint woe's blacke face so lively to my sight, / That tedious leasure marks each wrinckled line'.

14 For thee On account of you (as the object of my love).

14 for myself (1) on account of myself (as toiler and separated lover); (2) on behalf of myself (i.e. to my benefit). Unless we assume the rhetorical figure called chiasmus (the order of 'by day' and 'by night' in line 13 being reversed in 14 so that 'For thee' may be taken with 'by night' and 'for myself' with 'by day'), there would seem to be the implication that the physical aspect of the poet's 'toil' (1) or 'body's work' (4) was being undertaken for the sake of the beloved, which is surely not Shakespeare's intention.

Sonnet 28

Sonnet 28 is closely linked with 27; a further stage on the same journey ('still farther off from thee' (8)).

1 happy plight good health (physical and mental).

2 debarred forbidden.

3 oppression burden, travail, 'toil' (7) (physical and mental).

4 But day . . . oppressed But 'day's oppression' (3) is weighed down ('oppressed') by night's mental distress and night's by day's (a never-ending cycle).

5 either's each other's. Ingram and Redpath prefer Gildon's emendation 'other's' for Q 'ethers' (see collation) on the grounds of its acceptance by editors from Gildon through Capell and because Shakespeare frequently uses 'other' to mean 'the other'; the meaning in either case is essentially the same.

5 reign dominion.

6 in consent shake hands by mutual agreement ('consent') seal a bargain ('shake hands').

7 toil i.e. 'day's oppression' (3), travail, labour.

7 the other to complain the other (i.e. night) by forcing me to bewail ('complain').

8 How far ... thee At what continually increasing distance ('still farther off') I labour separated from you (i.e. at a later and further stage of the poet's journey than that described in 27).

9 I tell ... bright In order to console or gratify ('please') the day I tell him that you (like him) are bright (*not*, that you are bright in order to please him). The implication is that the youth is even 'brighter' than day.

10 dost him grace (as a surrogate of the sun) (1) do him honour; (2) do him a favour.

10 clouds . . . heaven clouds obscure the sky. Compare 33.5–8 and *Venus and Adonis*, 184: 'like misty vapors when they blot the sky'.

11 flatter beguile, seek to please.

11 swart-complexioned black or dusky skinned.

12 twire peep, peer (prevented by clouds at night). Earliest citation in *OED*.

12 gild'st tinge with gold-coloured light. Q 'guil'st' (an aphetic form of 'beguil'st') is possible (compare 'flatter' (11)), but what is needed here is a parallel to 'dost him grace' (10), not a synonym for 'flatter', and Shakespeare nowhere else uses the aphetic form. Compare *MND* 3.2.187–8: 'Fair Helena! who more engilds the night / Than all yon fiery oes and eyes of light', and 33.4.

12 the even the evening. 'even' is dictated by the rhyme-scheme, but the context implies 'night', not 'twilight'. Since 'gild'st' is essentially monosyllabic, natural metrical stress calls for 'the' in place of Q's 'th' (see collation for Pooler's alternative, and compare 132.7). For 'even' as an acceptable rhyme for 'heaven', see Cercignani, p. 71.

13 day ... longer i.e. each passing day ('day doth daily') extends my sorrows (by increasing the length of my separation from you).

13–14 daily ... nightly i.e. day and night work 'in consent' to 'torture me' (6).

14 griefs' Editors, following Gildon, read 'grief's' for Q 'greefes', but 'griefs'' is equally possible and accords better with 'sorrows' in line 13.

14 length seem stronger the duration (of my grief) seems more overpowering. Capell's emendation of 'length' to 'strength' is tempting and has been adopted by a number of editors, but 'length' makes sense and continues the suggestion of extension in 'draw my sorrows longer' in line 13.

Sonnet 29

Sonnet 29 is the first of the great sonnets (excepting, perhaps, 18), followed immediately by the second (30).

1 disgrace disfavour (with no necessary connotation of 'shame').

1 men's eyes public estimation (i.e. as he is seen by other men).

2 outcast state condition or status, (1) rejected (by Fortune), (2) socially looked down on (as not a gentleman or perhaps as an actor).

3 trouble deaf heaven vex or importune God (= 'heaven' by synecdoche), who refuses to hear.

3 bootless unavailing, profitless. Compare Job 30.20: 'When I cry unto thee [God], thou dost not hear me' (Bishops' Bible). Lines 1–4 generally may owe something to the story of Job who also 'bewept' his 'outcast state' and cursed the day of his birth (Job 3.1–3; compare 'curse my fate' in line 4).

4–8 Compare Horace, *Satires* I, 1–22, particularly lines 1–3 as trans. by John Weever in *Faunus and Melliflora* (1600), sig. F3ᵛ: 'What is the cause that none content will live, / In that estate which choise or chance doth give, / But evermore a novell life pursues, / And praiseth that another man doth use?'

4 look upon myself i.e. consider my 'state'.

5 one That 'one' need not refer specifically to the youth's 'state' is suggested by the generality of line 7.

5 more rich in hope with better expectations.

6 Featured (1) Well proportioned or shaped; (2) Having (facial) features.

6 like him, like him The second 'him' may refer to the first 'him' or to another 'him' (i.e. a third person).

7 art (1) skill (perhaps with reference to poetic art); (2) learning.

7 scope mental range (again perhaps with reference to poetic power; see *OED* Scope sb² 6 (earliest citation in this sense) and 3).

8 what ... enjoy that in which I am most competent (and hence should take pleasure in). Shakespeare may be referring to his poetry.

9 Yet ... despising i.e. even as I think these thoughts, almost despising myself.

10 Haply Perchance (but with some sense of 'happily' = by happy chance).

10 state state of mind (but playing on 'state' as in line 2).

11–12 Like ... gate Compare *Cym.* 2.3.20–1: 'Hark, hark the lark at heaven's gate sings, / And Phoebus gins arise.' Here suggested perhaps by Lyly, *Campaspe* (1584), 5.1.37–9: 'None but the Larke so shrill and cleare; / Now at heavens gat[e]s she claps her wings.' The Q pointing, while making possible literal sense, makes the poet sing his 'hymns' 'From sullen earth' and fails to achieve the important psychological uplift inherent in the poet's exalted 'state' toward which the sonnet has been moving.

12 sullen (1) gloomy (the shades of night still lingering); (2) heavy, dull (earth was the heaviest of the so-called 'four elements'). The adjective also catches the earth-bound, dispirited mood of lines 1–8.

13 **wealth** happiness, well-being (with play on 'riches' such as 'kings' (14) enjoy).

14 **change . . . kings** exchange my 'state' (compare lines 2 and 10) for that of kings.

Sonnet 30

1–2 **When . . . past** Whenever I call up (as prisoners to the bar of thought) memories of the past to the councils or sittings ('sessions') of pleasant meditation ('silent thought'). Note the legal imagery ('sessions', 'summon up'), and how the serenity of line 1 is broken by the 'action' of lines 2–4. Ingram and Redpath suggest that Shakespeare is thinking in terms of a manorial court, presided over by the Lord of the Manor (i.e. thought), which is looking into the estate's losses and resources (the relevant words, including those in lines 1–2, are 'waste', 'dateless', 'cancelled', 'expense', 'vanished', 'tell o'er', 'account', 'pay', 'losses', 'restored'). Compare *Oth.* 3.3.138–41: 'Who has that breast so pure / But some uncleanly apprehensions / Keep leets and law-days and in sessions sit / With meditations lawful?', and Sidney, *Arcadia* (1593), p. 165: 'memorye . . . a print the senses have left of things passed'.

2 **remembrance of things past** Kerrigan compares Wisd. 11.10: 'for their grief was double with mourning, and the remembrance of things past' (Geneva). C. K. Scott Moncrieff, Proust's translator, borrowed this phrase for the English title of *A la Recherche du Temps Perdu*.

3 **lack** want, failure to achieve.

3 **sought** (1) tried to obtain; (2) desired.

4 **with old woes** i.e. in remembering past sorrows. Compare Spenser, *Shepheardes Calender*, 'May', 208–10.

4 **new wail** bewail afresh (making 'old woes' new).

4 **my . . . waste** (1) the ruin or decay ('waste') of my precious ('dear') time (i.e. the best years of my life); (2) the destruction of what my time (= life) holds precious (i.e. particularly my friends, though this special emphasis does not emerge until line 6, being carried on in Sonnet 31; compare Kerrigan). Lying behind this phrase there is probably some sense of Time the Destroyer.

5 **drown an eye** Periphrasis for 'weep'.

6 **precious** dear (compare 'dear' in line 4).

6 **dateless** timeless, unending.

7 **weep afresh** Compare 'new wail' (4).

7 **love's . . . woe** (1) sorrow, felt by me as a 'lover' ('love's') for the death of friends, which time ('long since'), as the healer, has (supposedly) terminated; (2) sorrow, originally borne by me as one who loved, which has long been forgotten.

8 **moan . . . sight** (1) bemoan or lament the loss ('expense') of many things now destroyed ('vanished') that I have seen (and valued); (2) lament the cost to me ('expense') of many a lost sigh ('vanished

sight'). 'Sight' for 'sigh' was archaic by Shakespeare's time and seems only to have been used for the sake of rhyme (see *OED* Sight *sb*²). Sighing was considered deleterious to health; compare *2H6* 3.2.61–3: 'blood-consuming sighs . . . / Look pale as primrose with blood-drinking sighs', and 47.4.

9–12 In these lines Shakespeare draws heavily on the figures of polyptoton (repetition of words derived from the same root) and diacope (repetition of a word with one or more between), perhaps to suggest, through iteration, the weight of his remembered 'woes'. See Joseph, pp. 83, 87, 306–7.

9 **Then . . . foregone** Then can I mourn deeply past injuries ('grievances foregone') (done to me or by me). If 'grievances' is taken to mean 'sorrows', line 9 essentially repeats 7.

10 **heavily** weighed down with sorrow, sadly.

10 **tell o'er** (1) repeat again (to myself); (2) reckon up again.

11 **sad account** (1) sorrowful, (2) burdensome, heavy reckoning (of debts).

11 **fore-bemoanèd moan** grief already lamented (in the past).

12 **Which . . . before** (A reckoning) which I again repay ('new pay') as if I had not already paid it before (in earlier 'sessions' (1)).

13 **But . . . while** Compare 29.9–10.

13 **friend** First use as referring to the young man.

14 **losses** i.e. 'many a thing I sought' (3), 'precious friends' (6), 'many a vanished sight' (8).

14 **restored** compensated for (because, as the next sonnet affirms, the 'friend' includes all these 'losses').

Sonnet 31

Sonnet 31 explains and develops the consolation for 'old woes' expressed in the final couplet of 30.

1 **Thy bosom . . . hearts** Your heart (='bosom' as the seat of thought and feeling) is (1) made (even more) precious ('endearèd') by all other hearts, (2) beloved of all other hearts (although *OED* does not record this use of 'endear' before 1622). Kerrigan suggests that behind this line lies the common conceit of the 'exchange of hearts', earlier employed in Sonnet 22. Retention of Q's comma after 'hearts' universalises the statement of line 1 before it is narrowed by the poet's personal application in line 2.

2 **by lacking** in missing, being deprived of.

2 **supposèd** mistakenly believed.

3 **there reigns . . . parts** in your bosom ('there') love reigns (as if enthroned) together with all its love-engendering ('loving') attributes or qualities ('parts'). 'parts' may also be taken to refer to 'all hearts' in line 1 and 'friends' in line 4. Q's apparent personification 'Love' and 'Love's', though rarely retained by editors since Capell, may indeed convey Shakespeare's intention (= God of Love, i.e. Cupid).

4 **And . . . friends** Supply 'reigns' from line 3.

5 **holy** (1) sacred; (2) dedicated.

5 **obsequious** dutiful in mourning (the dead). Compare *Tit.* 5.3.152: 'To shed obsequious tears upon this trunk'.

6 **dear religious love** love affectionate and (1) holy, (2) conscientious (perhaps with play on 'dear' = costly). The phrase 'religious love', used with a paradoxical twist, occurs in *A Lover's Complaint*, 250.

7 **interest of the dead** a return paid to the dead (on the debt incurred by their love for me).

7 **appear** seem (to me).

8 **things removed** things (= friends) moved from one place to another. 'thing' at this time did not necessarily mean an inanimate object (compare 30.2, 3).

8 **thee** Gildon's emendation of Q's 'there' is almost universally accepted, but Wyndham and Seymour-Smith defend 'there' as referring to 'Thy bosom' and 'there' in lines 1 and 3, a possible but comparatively flat reading. 'there' may be a compositorial misreading for 'thee'; compare Q's fairly frequent misreading of 'thy' as 'their' (see 26.12 n.).

9 **Thou art the grave** This (to us infelicitous) conceit would have been acceptable to an Elizabethan; compare Donne, 'The Autumnall' (13–14): 'Call not these wrinkles, graves: If graves they were, / They were Loves graves; for else he is no where.'

9 **doth live** (1) continues to live; (2) dwells.

10 **Hung ... gone** Decorated with the memorials ('trophies', i.e. their 'parts of me' in line 11) which my lost friends ('lovers gone') had won from me (by winning my love). Tombs were often 'hung' with wreaths, scrolls, etc. Compare *A Lover's Complaint*, 218–23: 'Lo all those trophies of affections hot, ... must your oblations be', and *Tit.* 1.1.387–8: 'There lie thy bones, ... / Till we with trophies do adorn thy tomb.'

10 **lovers** 'Lover' was frequently used as a term for 'friend', either male or female, though more often male, without any necessary sexual implications (see Rollins, I, 93).

11 **parts of me** shares of my love.

12 **due of many** debt owed to many (former friends).

13 **images** forms (of outer and inner qualities). Does 'images' perhaps suggest that in the past he has been giving his love and worship to false gods?

14 **thou (all they)** you, the beloved, who contains everything of worth in them (with the implication 'and more').

14 **all the all of me** i.e. the whole of my love ('me'), not just 'parts of me' (11). Compare Robert Chester, *Loves Martyr* (1601), p. 147: 'Thou art that All-in-all that I love best.'

Sonnet 32

Ingram and Redpath suggest that Sonnet 32 reflects Shakespeare's recognition that he was living in an age of extraordinary literary growth ('the bett'ring of the time' (5), 'this growing age' (10)) and was uncertain (as yet) of his future reputation. Perhaps so, but one should allow for the convention of an ironic personal depreciation or mock modesty common in the sonnet tradition.

1 **my well-contented day** i.e. the day I shall be well content to see (with play on 'content' = to pay in full, i.e. nature's debt, death).

2 **churl** rude low-bred fellow. Compare Hamlet's attitude (*Ham.* 5.1) to the grave-diggers.

2 **churl Death** Beeching suggests that Death is here pictured as a grave-digger.

2 **dust** i.e. earth. Compare the Burial Service in the Book of Common Prayer: 'earth to earth, ashes to ashes, dust to dust'.

3 **by fortune** by (happy) chance. Compare 29.10.

3 **re-survey** read over again (first used by Shakespeare in this sense; see *OED* Resurvey *v* 1).

4 **poor rude lines** mean or inadequate ('poor'), unpolished or artless ('rude') verses. Shakespeare, with conventional modesty (compare Petrarch, *Rime sparse*, 187), refers presumably to this or other sonnets, not to his plays (those who identify the youth as Southampton would probably include *Venus and Adonis* and *The Rape of Lucrece*). Contrast the mood here with that in 18.11–14.

4 **lover** friend. See 31.10 n. and line 10 below. 'lover' may here, of course, carry a suggestion of sexual involvement.

5 **bett'ring of the time** (literary) improvement of the age (since I wrote 'These poor rude lines'). Compare 'this growing age' (10) and 'poets better prove' (13). 'Bettering' in this sense was first used by Shakespeare; see *OED* Bettering *vbl sb* 2, and compare 82.8.

6 **outstripped** excelled, surpassed.

6 **every pen** every other poet (= 'pen' by metonymy).

7 **Reserve** Preserve.

7 **for my love** for the sake of (1) my love for you, (2) your love for me.

7 **rhyme** poetic art.

8 **Exceeded** = 'outstripped' (6).

8 **height** artistic superiority.

8 **happier** (1) more felicitous (as writers); (2) more fortunate (as living in this 'growing age' or in worldly terms).

9 **vouchsafe me** graciously grant me ('vouchsafe' probably carries a sense of condescension = deign).

10–12 The implication in these lines is clear: had the poet not been cut off by death, he would, like later poets, have benefited from 'this growing age', i.e. he too would have written better poetry.

10 growing age i.e. time in which literary skill and quality are flowering.

11 dearer birth ... brought his love (for me) had borne a more worthy offspring ('dearer birth') than this (= 'These ... lines' (4)). There is play perhaps on 'dearer' = costing more pains in the delivery.

12 march in ranks (1) walk in line with (keeping step); (2) move in unison on an equal footing with (with play on the movement of metrical 'feet' in verse). Compare *AYLI* 3.2.98: 'It is the right butter-women's rank to market' (describing monotonous verse). Shakespeare probably owes this figure to Nashe, who speaks of Thomas Watson as a poet 'whose *Amintas* ... may march in equippage of honour with any of our ancient Poets' ('Preface' to Greene's *Menaphon* (1589), in Nashe, *Works*, III, 320).

12 better equipage superior poetic endowment ('equipage' continues the military metaphor in 'march in ranks').

13 since he died because he died (too soon to benefit from the literary advances of 'this growing age' (10)).

13 poets better prove poets (now) turn out to be better (than they were when he wrote).

14 Theirs i.e. their (superior) lines.

14 style manner or quality of writing.

14 for his love for the sake of (1) his love for me, (2) his love in which I share.

Sonnet 33

Sonnet 33 is the first of what are called the 'estrangement' sonnets, a group that runs through 36 (there are later similar groups), and centres on some kind of 'sensual fault' (35.9), 'stain' (33.14), or 'strong offence' (34.12) committed by the youth. The poet feels himself to be a sharer in the resulting 'disgrace' (34.9–12, 35.9–14, 36.3–4); his love has been sullied by the youth's betrayal. As Adams points out, the emotional and pejorative tone of the language in 33 and 34 is strong ('ugly', 'disgrace' (twice), 'stain', 'base', 'salve', 'wound', 'shame', 'grief', 'repent', 'loss', 'offender', 'sorrow', 'strong offence', 'cross', 'tears', 'ill deeds'). Compare *Err.* 2.2.140–4: 'I am possess'd with an adulterate blot; / My blood is mingled with the crime of lust: / For if we two be one, and thou play false, / I do digest the poison of thy flesh, / Being strumpeted by thy contagion.' Sonnets of this kind are, of course, happy hunting-grounds for those critics who assume a homosexual liaison between Shakespeare and the youth. The sonnet plays on the proverb 'The morning sun never lasts the day' (Tilley s978).

1–4 Compare *Venus and Adonis*, 856–8: 'The sun ariseth in his majesty, / Who doth the world so gloriously behold / That cedar tops and hills seem burnish'd gold.'; and *John* 3.1.77–80: 'To solemnize this day the glorious sun / Stays in his course and plays the alchymist, / Turning with splendor of his precious eye / The meagre cloddy earth to glittering gold.'

1 Full Very.

2 Flatter ... eye (1) beguile, deceive, (2) honour the mountain tops with its kingly eye (= the sun as king-planet and the 'eye of the morning'). Compare 28.11 and *Edward III* 1.2.141–2: 'Let not thy presence, like the Aprill sunne, / Flatter our earth and suddenly be done.' For Shakespeare's possible hand in this anonymous play (*c.* 1590–5), see 94.14 n.

3 golden face The sun was regularly associated with gold as the king-metal.

4 heavenly alcumy celestial gold ('alcumy', here used figuratively, being the supposed chemical process by which alchemists claimed to turn base metals into gold). 'heavenly' may suggest that the sun is a true alchemist, not an 'earthly' con-man. 'alcumy' is a common variant form of 'alchymy' or 'alchemy'.

5–8 Compare *TGV* 1.3.84–7: 'O, how this spring of love resembleth / The uncertain glory of an April day, / Which now shows all the beauty of the sun, / And by and by a cloud takes all away'; *1H4* 1.2.197–203: 'Yet herein will I imitate the sun, / Who doth permit the base contagious clouds / To smother up his beauty from the world, / That when he please again to be himself, / Being wanted, he may be more wond'red at / By breaking through the foul and ugly mists / Of vapors that did seem to strangle him'; and *Mac.* 3.4.110–11.

5 Anon permit Soon allow. The subject of 'permit' is 'many a glorious morning' (1), in parallel construction with 'Flatter' (2) and 'hide' (7); we would expect 'And anon permit'.

5 basest (1) darkest; (2) most low-lying; (3) most foul (all contrasting with the sun's 'heavenly alcumy').

5 ride move (as if riding or sailing). Compare *Mac.* 4.1.138: 'Infected be the air whereon they ride'; and *Rom.* 2.2.31–2: 'When he bestrides the lazy puffing clouds, / And sails upon the bosom of the air.' There is perhaps some sexual suggestion in 'ride': compare 137.6 n.

6 rack cold mass, driven by the wind in the upper air (compare 'region cloud' in line 12). Compare *Ant.* 4.14.9–11: 'That which is now a horse, ... / The rack dislimns, and makes it in distinct / As water is in water.'

6 celestial heavenly (compare 'heavenly' in line 4).

7 forlorn abandoned, desolate.

7 visage i.e. the 'golden face' of line 3.

8 Stealing ... disgrace Sneaking away, out of sight ('unseen') toward the west as a result of ('with') permitting his glory to be 'stained' by 'this disgrace' (= disfigurement = loss of beauty). This sudden belittling of the sun under a cloud (compared to a sneak-thief) anticipates and leads into the application of the sun image in lines 1–8 to the youth ('my sun') in lines 9–14.

9 my sun i.e. the youth. Comparison of the beloved to the sun is a commonplace in the love poetry of the period – as Shakespeare notes disapprovingly in 21.5–6.

10 all triumphant full (and) (1) conquering, (2) glorious. Many editors prefer 'all-triumphant', but the hyphen limits the richer application of 'all'.

11 out alack alas ('out' being an intensifying interjection expressing anger or dismay).

11 he . . . mine i.e. he was mine for only ('but') a short time ('one hour').

12 region cloud = 'rack' (6); the 'region' was a division of the upper atmosphere.

12 masked concealed (but with suggestion that the 'region cloud' has 'disguised' the youth's essential nature).

13 this i.e. 'this disgrace' (8).

13 no whit disdaineth not in the least ('no whit') thinks (him) unworthy of me.

14 Suns . . . staineth Earthly great men ('Suns of the world', 'my sun' in line 9 being one; with obvious play on 'sons') may (be permitted to) lose lustre or colour ('stain'), when even the sun of heaven permits the same thing to happen to it. 'stain', however, also implies the transitive sense of 'to be stained' (i.e. blemished, soiled), which undercuts the primary meaning and gives the line an ambiguous twist by making us think of 'this disgrace' (8).

Sonnet 34

Sonnet 34 is closely linked with 33 (compare the morning/sun imagery which opens each and the repetition of the 'face/disgrace' rhyme climaxing both octaves). The conventional acceptance of the youth's 'fault' repeated by both final couplets belies the emotional turmoil realised so strongly (particularly in 34) in the first twelve lines. The importance of preserving relations with a friend, even when that friend has injured you (*Perfidus familiaris*), is popularly expressed by Geffrey Whitney in his *Choice of Emblemes* (1586), p. 142: 'But, if thou doe injoye a faithfull frende, / See that with care, thou keepe him as thy life: / And if perhappes he doe, that maye offende, / Yet waye thy frende: and shunne the cause of strife, / Remembringe still, there is no greater crosse, / Then of a frende, for, to sustaine the losse.'

1–2 The Aesopic fable of the Traveller, the Sun, and the Wind (see Stith Thompson, *Motif-Index of Folk-Literature*, 5 vols., 1955–7, V, L351) may lie behind these lines. Compare 'Although the sun shines, leave not thy cloak at home' (first citation 1640; Tilley s968).

1 beauteous day i.e. a time when the poet might bask in the rays of 'my sun['s]' (33.9) favour. Compare 'glorious morning' (33.1).

2 make me . . . cloak cause me (by your 'promise' of favour) to venture out without protection (against the elements). Figuratively, the poet is complaining that the youth by a brief show of favour has encouraged him to drop his defences ('cloak') against a sudden change in the youth's behaviour or attitude. Is there also a sense in which the poet feels that he has been beguiled into exposing himself publicly by dropping his mask of anonymity ('cloak')? The youth has encouraged him and then betrayed his confidence.

3 To Only to.

3 let Compare the implication of 'permit' (33.5).

3 base clouds Compare 33.5 n. Again, 'base clouds' may figuratively express the youth's action or the actions of others (in relation to the youth or to the poet).

4 brav'ry (1) splendour; (2) finery (carrying the pejorative sense of 'mere show'). Compare 15.8 n.

4 rotten smoke foul or unwholesome vapour. Compare *Rape of Lucrece*, 776–8: 'yet ere he [the sun] go to bed, / Knit poisonous clouds about his golden head. / With rotten damps ravish the morning air'.

5 thou break you do break (through). There is a hovering sense here and in 'thou repent' (10) of the conditional subjunctive mode (= shouldst thou break (or repent)); that the youth has 'shone' his favours on the poet and repented his 'strong offence' (12) is not completely clear until the final couplet.

6 To In order to.

6 rain (1) = the 'strong offence' (line 12); (2) figuratively = tears; compare the youth's 'tears' in line 13.

7 well favourably.

7 such a salve healing ointment of such a kind. Compare 'physic' in line 9.

8 That One that (retaining Q's comma after 'speak' in line 7).

8 heals . . . disgrace (1) heals the wound but leaves ('cures not') the disfigurement or scar ('disgrace'); (2) heals the outward wound (= the 'strong offence' (12)) but leaves the inner dishonour or shame ('disgrace') festering ('cures not'). Compare Tilley w929 ('Though the wound be healed yet the scar remains'); *Rape of Lucrece*, 731–2: 'Bearing away the wound that nothing healeth, / The scar that will in spite of cure remain'; Geffrey Whitney, *A Choice of Emblemes* (1586), p. 219, *In amore tormentum*: 'And suche as once doe feele this inwarde warre, / Thoughe they bee cur'de, yet still appeares the scarre.'

9 shame feeling of remorse, repentance.

10 Though thou repent Even if you do repent. See 5 n. above.

10 I have . . . loss I continue ('still') to bear the 'disgrace' (= 'loss' = the injury my image of you has suffered).

11 sorrow i.e. remorse, repentance.

11 **lends** bestows, imparts.

11 **weak** faint, little.

12 **bears . . . cross** The Sewell–Capell emendation 'cross' for Q's 'losse' (which repeats the rhyme in line 10, a licence found rarely in the Sonnets; but see, for other examples, 45 and 46) has been universally accepted (except by Seymour-Smith) because of its Christ-like association with 'bears' (compare John 19.17: 'And he [Christ] bare his cross' (Geneva)). The implication would seem to be that, like Christ, the poet is suffering affliction (= 'cross') for the sins of another. Compare 42.12. 'strong offence' contrasts with 'weak relief' (11); 'strong' = severe, grievous.

13 **tears** i.e. tears of repentance (implied by 'thou repent' (10)).

13 **pearl** Pearls were not only valuable ('rich' (14)) but, as Booth notes, when powdered were considered medicinal.

13 **thy love** i.e. your love for me.

13 **sheeds** sheds (variant form, preserved for the rhyme with 'deeds'). Compare *Rape of Lucrece*, 1549, 1551: 'sheeds', 'bleeds'.

14 **rich** valuable, precious (suitable for paying a 'ransom'). Compare *Oth.* 5.2.346–7: '(like the base Indian) threw a pearl away / Richer than all his tribe'.

14 **ransom all ill deeds** redeem or atone for all sins. The religious imagery (1 Tim. 2.5–6: 'Christ Jesus, Who gave himself a ransom for all men' (Geneva), the 'redeemer') here shifts from the poet (in line 12) to the youth, suggesting the oneness of their 'loves'.

Sonnet 35

Sonnet 35 is clearly linked with 33 and 34, picking up 'Th'offender's sorrow' (34.11) in 'No more be grieved' (1) and 'clouds' 'stain[ing]' the sun (33.5, 14) in 'Clouds . . . stain both moon and sun' (3).

1 **No more** (1) No longer; (2) No more greatly.

2 **Roses have thorns** Proverbial: 'No rose without a thorn (or prickle)' (Tilley R182). The youth has been called 'beauty's rose' (1.2; see note) and there may be a sexual play on 'thorn' = prick = penis, linking with 'sensual fault' in line 9. Compare *AYLI* 3.2.111–12: 'He that sweetest rose will find, / Must find love's prick and Rosalind.'

2 **silver fountains mud** i.e. fountains (or springs), which on the surface produce clear shining ('silver') water, are contaminated by mud. Compare *R2* 5.3.61–3: 'Thou sheer, immaculate, and silver fountain, / From whence this stream through muddy passages / Hath held his current and defil'd himself', and *Rape of Lucrece*, 577: 'Mud not the fountain that gave drink to thee.'

3 **stain** darken, dim (by losing their brightness or purity; with suggestion of adding a blot or blemish). Compare 33.14.

3 **moon** Perhaps a reference to the youth's 'infidelity' since the moon symbolised inconstancy. Com-

pare *Rom.* 2.2.109: 'O swear not by the moon, th'inconstant moon.'

4 **canker . . . bud** Proverbial: 'The canker soonest eats the fairest rose' (Tilley C56). The line may mean either (1) that cankers inhabit even the (a) most pleasing, (b) most fragrant, (c) best-tasting buds; or (2) that cankers choose particularly the 'sweetest' buds. In light of the proverb, 70.7 ('For canker vice the sweetest buds doth love'), and *TGV* 1.1.42–4 ('as in the sweetest bud / The eating canker dwells, so eating love / Inhabits in the finest wits of all'), (2) may be the sense primarily intended here. Compare also 95.1–3 and *Rape of Lucrece*, 848.

5 **make faults** commit wrongs, sins. Compare 121.14 n.

5 **even . . . this** just so, by doing what I am doing (= 'this', i.e. in attempting to exculpate you or in writing such verses), I am committing a 'fault' (against myself, as explained in lines 6–8).

6 **Authòrising** Sanctioning, justifying (as legal) (with probable play on 'author', i.e. the poet).

6 **with compare** by analogies (those cited in lines 1–4, which are false analogies because in a different category from moral 'faults' committed by a rational being) and by comparing you with other men.

7 **Myself . . . amiss** Debasing or perverting myself (i.e. my reason and integrity) by smoothing over ('salving') your fault.

8 **Excusing . . . are** A difficult and much discussed line. Most editors accept Capell's emendation of Q 'their . . . their' to 'thy . . . thy' or to some combination of 'their' and 'thy'. Some proposed glosses: (1) (reading 'thy . . . their') '(By) excusing your sins more (i.e. to a greater extent than their (i.e. other men's) sins are (excused by me))' (Vendler); (2) (reading 'thy . . . thy') '(By) excusing your sins to a greater extent than is warranted by the size of your sins ("more" modifying both "Excusing" and "sins")' (Booth); (3) (reading 'thy . . . thy') '(By) pleading excuses not only sufficient to cover your actual sins, but to cover them even if they were more (= greater: 23.12, 96.3)' (Tucker); (4) (reading 'thy . . . thy') '(By) giving excessive exculpation for his friend's misconduct by reducing it, through his analogies (lines 1–4), from a moral to a natural fault, his excuse for his friend's offence would be stretched so much wider than the offence itself that it would, if valid (which the poet knows it is not), exculpate all sins whatever' (Ingram and Redpath); (5) (reading 'their . . . their') '(By) exonerating those natural objects (the analogies of the first quatrain) from a moral turpitude they are incapable of (thus confusing the natural and moral orders)' (Ingram and Redpath); (6) (reading 'thy . . . their') '(By) excusing your sins which are more than the number of the sins enumerated already (as the sins or faults of roses, fountains, moon and sun, buds and men)' (Sisson). Given the obvious disagreement found among the

above glosses, I may venture to suggest that perhaps
the difficulty of the line lies in 'Excusing' rather than
in 'their . . . their' and that 'Excusing' is a compositor's misreading of a MS. 'Accusing' (graphically an
easy enough error to make in reading Secretary hand
and possibly influenced by 'salving' in line 7). Reading 'Accusing their   their sins are', the line would
then mean: '(By) accusing their sins (i.e. the "faults"
associated with "All men" (5) and by extension the
natural defects in nature listed in lines 1–4) of being
greater or more weighty ("more") than their "sins"
or defects in fact are'.

9 to to the defence of.

9 sensual fault (1) sin arising from one or more
of the five exterior senses (sight, taste, touch, hearing,
smell); (2) sin of lust.

9 bring in sense introduce sophistical (Kerrigan) reason (*OED* Sense *sb* 10b) (with play on 'sen
sual' and 'sense' = feeling; and probable further play
on 'incense' offered as to a god).

10 Thy . . . advocate The party standing in opposition to you ('Thy adverse part', i.e. reason) is acting,
paradoxically, as your defence counsel ('advocate').
The legal imagery is continued in lines 11 and 13.

11 lawful plea commence initiate a legally
sanctioned or just ('lawful') formal allegation or law
suit ('plea').

12 civil . . . hate intestine conflict between ('in')
my love (for you) and my hatred (for what you have
done). There is perhaps a play on 'civil' as referring to an action in civil rather than criminal law.
Compare *JC* 2.1.66–9: 'The Genius and the mortal
instruments / Are then in council, and the state of
man, / Like to a little kingdom, suffers then / The
nature of an insurrection.' 35, 71, 108, and 154 are the
only sonnets in which Shakespeare runs the syntax
on into the final couplet.

13 accessary accomplice.

14 sweet thief i.e. the youth. Compare 40.9.

14 sourly cruelly, bitterly.

14 robs from me i.e. steals away, deprives me of
my rational and moral integrity.

Sonnet 36

Booth suggests the influence of Eph. 5.25–33 (incor-
porated as part of the marriage service in the Book
of Common Prayer), particularly the 'mystery' by
which husband and wife 'shall be one flesh'. Pooler
questions the connection of this sonnet with 33–5
and connects it with 29 (see 11–12 n. below).

1 Let me confess I have to admit or own. 'confess' carries perhaps the legal sense of admitting to
the truth of the action charged ('bewailèd guilt' (10))
and the religious sense of confessing sins to a priest
(= the youth).

1 twain (1) two (not one, despite, paradoxically, our 'undivided loves'); (2) separate, parted.

Shakespeare plays on the same idea in *Tro.* 3.1.100–
1: 'she'll none of him. They two [Cressida and Paris]
are twain.'

2 undivided inseparable, not to be parted (compare 'separable' (6)).

2 one The 'oneness' of lovers, one soul in two
bodies, is a given premise of the sonnet tradition. Compare Petrarch, *Rime sparse*, 48, and the
'exchange of hearts' theme in 22.

3 blots (1) disgraces; (2) moral stains. The reference is uncertain: perhaps to the 'disgrace with
Fortune' in 29 or to the youth's action (whatever it
may have been), the 'stain' ('blots') of which, because
their 'undivided loves are one' (2), the poet, as he has
argued in 33–5, has taken upon himself ('by me be
borne alone' (4)) together with the resulting shame
or disgrace (later described as 'bewailèd guilt' in line
10), thus exonerating his friend from the burden of
guilt – an act of self-abnegation.

4 borne Compare 34.12: 'bears the strong
offence's cross' (with the same Christ-like implication).

4 alone (1) only; (2) in solitude (since we must be
'twain' (1)).

5 one respect single (hence mutual) regard (for
one another), i.e. we are united by a single consideration (our love).

6 Though i.e. though there is.

6 lives Note the alliterative play on 'loves' and
'lives' (the inner security versus the outer division).

6 a separable spite an injury (decreed by Fortune, and by fortune in the sense of 'wealth, social
status') which separates 'our lives'. For this active
use of 'separable', see Abbott 3.

7 it i.e. 'a separable spite'.

7 love's sole effect single, unified quality or
action of our love (compare 'one respect' (5)).

8 Yet . . . delight i.e. nevertheless (being no
longer 'one' but 'twain') it robs us (physically?) of
precious time spent together which is the delight of
true love.

9 not evermore not ever again (implying, 'as I
have acknowledged you in the past').

9 acknowledge (publicly) recognise. Compare
'public kindness' in line 11.

10 my bewailèd guilt i.e. the 'guilt' the poet
has 'bewailèd' as his in Sonnet 29 or the 'guilt' he
has accepted on the youth's behalf in 34 and 35. It
would be wrong, I think, to assume that the poet has
himself committed an act that would bring 'shame'
by association to the youth.

11–12 Nor . . . name These lines, and lines 6–
8, seem to link this sonnet with 29, since, unless we
associate the poet's 'guilt' (line 10) with some shameful act, publicly known, which he has committed, it
is difficult to interpret the implication of these lines
in terms of the transferred 'guilt' assumed by the
poet in 34 and 35, whereas the kind of 'guilt' (lack of

social position and opportunity) lamented in 29 fits the present context perfectly.

12 Unless . . . name i.e. unless (by honouring me) you bring dishonour ('take that honour from') your (family) name. Both the use of 'take that honour from' and 'name' implies that the poet is addressing a person of noble family and is playing on the title 'Right Honourable' as the proper form of address to such an individual. Compare the dedications in *Venus and Adonis* and *The Rape of Lucrece* (to Southampton) and in the First Folio (to Pembroke and Montgomery).

13–14 But . . . report This couplet is repeated as the concluding lines of 96. Various explanations for the repetition have been offered (see Rollins, I, 238, and Booth, p. 313), none very helpful, though most agree that the couplet is more integral in 36 than in 96.

13 But . . . so i.e. do not take the risk (of honouring me 'with public kindness' (11)).

13 in such sort in such a way (i.e. so deeply).

14 As . . . report That ('As'), since our 'undivided loves are one' (2) (i.e. 'thou being mine'), your good reputation ('report') is the equivalent of my good reputation (to dishonour one is to dishonour both).

Sonnet 37

1 decrepit old, feeble.

3 made lame . . . spite handicapped ('made lame') by the most grievous ('dearest') malice of Fortune. Compare 29.1, 'separable spite' (36.6), and (cited by Ingram and Redpath) *Lear* 4.6.221 (Q): 'A most poore man, made lame by Fortunes blowes'. Most critics wisely take 'lame' figuratively (here and in 89.3), but, since Capell first suggested it, some have insisted upon a literal interpretation – unwisely, since 89.3–4 essentially denies it.

4 comfort of consolation of or relief from.

4 worth and truth worthiness and honesty or constancy (with possible anticipation of 'worth' of 'birth' and 'wealth' in line 5, and in 'truth' of 'wit').

5 wit mental capacity, wisdom (with a suggestion of sharpness of intellect or fancy).

6 any i.e. any one (of these qualities).

6 or all or all of these taken together.

6 or more i.e. good qualities other than those listed in line 5 ('more' suggests perhaps 'better', not merely 'more' in number).

7 Intitled in thy parts Taking a rightful place ('Intitled') among your (virtuous) attributes ('parts'). 'Intitled' is a common variant of 'entitled'. The line has raised much discussion. Ingram and Redpath, rejecting Capell's emendation of Q 'their' to 'thy' and retaining (as here) the Q comma after 'parts' but inserting (as here) a comma after 'more' in 6, consider 'their' as referring to the attributes proper to the respective 'parts'. Seymour-Smith follows Q's pointing unchanged in lines 6 and 7 and glosses 'Inti-

tled . . . parts' as 'entitled to their positions in this hierarchy', limiting it specifically to 'or more' in line 6. He may be right.

7 crownèd sit i.e. like kings.

8 I make . . . store I graft my love (thus giving it life and strength) upon this abundant source ('store') (of virtues). 'Ingraft', a common variant of 'engraft', is Shakespeare's regular form.

10 shadow . . . substance A common Elizabethan contrast; compare Sonnet 53 and *1H6* 2.3.45–51.

10 shadow (1) reflection (of your virtues); (2) protection (from 'Fortune's dearest spite' (line 3)). Paradoxically, the 'shadow' here provides the 'substance' (= the *Idea* or reality) (Ingram and Redpath).

11 abundance = 'store' (8).

11 sufficed made sufficient, fulfilled.

12 by a part i.e. by participating in a portion.

12 glory merited honour (derived from your virtues).

12 live have a vitality worth calling 'life' (with a suggestion, perhaps, of monetary support) (Tucker).

13 Look what Whatever. See 9.9–10 n.

13 in as belonging to.

14 ten A conventional number, without specific significance.

Sonnet 38

1 my Muse Here restricted to the 'creative faculty' (Kerrigan). Shakespeare appears to make a distinction between 'my Muse' (and 'my slight Muse' in line 13) and the 'tenth Muse' (i.e. the youth) in line 9 (compare 'my Muse' in 78.1), who may inspire a better poet to write 'Eternal numbers' (12). Since, however, he says he owes whatever may be good in his poetry to the inspiration provided by the youth, the 'tenth Muse', the conventional modesty displayed in describing his Muse as 'slight' borders on the uncomplimentary. The distinction exists, but it is rather muddy.

2 that i.e. thou that.

3 argument i.e. yourself (as the 'subject' of invention).

4 every . . . rehearse any commonplace ('vulgar') paper-of-verses to set forth ('rehearse'). There is perhaps a play on 'vulgar', i.e. verses written in the 'vulgar tongue' – English not Latin.

5 in me i.e. in what I have written.

6 stand . . . sight i.e. stand the test of ('stand against') being seen (hence read) by you.

7 dumb destitute of words, tongue-tied (possibly, but probably not, 'stupid'). 'Dumb' offended eighteenth-century editors, who, until Capell, substituted Gildon's emendation 'dull'.

8 give invention light i.e. illuminate (and hence stimulate) even a 'dumb' writer's imaginative faculty.

9 tenth Muse The Nine Muses ('old nine' (10)), the daughters of Zeus and Mnemosyne (Memory), were regarded as the inspirers of learning and the arts, especially music and poetry (*OED* Muse *sb*¹ 1). Shakespeare may have been influenced by Michael Drayton (*Ideas Mirrour* (1594), Amour 8), who describes his mistress as a tenth muse – a sonnet ridiculed by Sir John Davies in *Epigrammes* (1599?), 25. See also Robert Chester, *Loves Martyr* (1601), p. 153.

10 invocate i.e. call upon for inspiration.

11 calls on thee i.e. invokes you as his muse (a literal translation of the Latin root of 'invocate' in line 10).

11 let him (1) may he; (2) allow him to.

12 Eternal numbers Everliving verses (Booth suggests a play on 'ten times' in line 9 and 'numbers').

12 to outlive long date i.e. which will live on after ('outlive') a distant ('long') period of time ('date'). The phrase contradicts 'Eternal', since no 'date' for 'Eternal numbers' is by definition possible.

13–14 Compare Daniel's dedicatory sonnet to the Countess of Pembroke (lines 13–14) in *Delia* (1594): 'Whereof, the travaile I may challenge mine, / But yet the glory, (Madam) must be thine'. The sonnet as a whole shows other thematic similarities with 38 and may have influenced it generally.

13 slight of small worth, humble.

13 curious days fastidious times (given to fault-finding in literary matters).

14 pain labour (as in giving birth).

14 praise i.e. because anything praiseworthy in my verses is derived from you.

Sonnet 39

Note the number of links with Sonnet 36, which, like 39, turns on the private *v.* public relations between the poet and the youth – the cruel necessity of maintaining the poet's anonymity so far as the world of society is concerned.

1 with manners with propriety (i.e. without praising myself).

2 all wholly.

2 better part of me better (= greater, nobler) half ('part') of me. There are underlying references to (1) the conventional theme of the oneness of lovers (see 22, 36.2 n. and line 6 below); (2) the proverb 'A friend is one's second self (another I)' (Tilley F696); (3) the phrase 'better half' commonly used of wife or husband as being 'one flesh' (Eph. 5.31). The phrase ('better part of me', repeated in 74.8) comes from Ovid, *Metamorphoses* XV, 875 ('parte tamen meliore mei'), and was translated by Golding as 'Yit shall the better part of mee' (989), where 'part', however, refers to the 'soul'.

3–4 What . . . thee i.e. to praise you brings me no reward, since in doing so I am only (unmannerly) praising myself. The implication of these weak lines, given the context, seems out of tune. Compare 104.2 n.

5 Even for this (1) For this very reason; (2) On this account also (looking back perhaps to 36.1–8).

6 dear (1) precious, heartfelt; (2) costly (in that it causes our 'separation' (7)).

6 name i.e. in public report only, not in reality or 'sole effect' (36.7).

6 single one indivisible oneness (the otherwise tautological adjective serving to emphasise the essentiality of the union). Compare 'undivided loves' in 36.2 and the similar seeming tautology of 'two must be twain' in 36.1.

7 separation Compare 'a separable spite' in 36.6. It is fruitless to argue over the kind or extent of the apparently physical 'separation' or 'absence' (9) here suggested.

8 That due to thee That which is your due or right.

8 which . . . alone which you only ('alone') deserve (thus solving the dilemma posed in lines 1 - 4, that in praising you publicly I improperly praise myself).

9 prove i.e. prove to be.

10 sour leisure In 'absence' time 'hangs heavy' and the enforced 'leisure' has a bitter ('sour') taste.

10 sweet leave sweet-tasting permission.

11 entertain the time occupy or beguile the time pleasantly. Compare *Rape of Lucrece*, 1361: 'The weary time she cannot entertain.'

12 Which time . . . dost deceive Q 'dost' is here retained, though most editors accept Malone's emendation 'doth'. Reading 'dost': 'The which time and thoughts (i.e. absence, "thou" being supplied and having as its antecedent "thou" in 9) dost so very (or, thus) pleasantly beguile ("deceive")'; reading 'doth': 'Which time and thoughts ("Which" having as antecedent "love" in 11) doth so pleasantly beguile'. For 'doth' used with a plural subject, see Abbott 334.

13 And that 'that' goes back to 'Were it not' in line 10, where 'that' is understood.

13 thou i.e. absence.

13 teachest how give (kindly) instruction by showing the way.

13 make one twain make the oneness of our love appear to be two (i.e. 'divided' (5)).

14 By praising . . . remain By praising him (i.e. the youth), who is removed from me ('doth hence remain'), (1) in these verses, (2) while I am absent ('here') (thus observing the terms of the called-for 'separation'). Compare *Ant.* 1.3.102–4: 'Our separation so abides and flies, / That thou residing here, goes yet with me; / And I hence fleeting, here remain with thee.'

Sonnet 40

Sonnets 40–2 are linked and deal with the youth's theft of the poet's mistress, a theme very similar to that handled in 133–4, 144 (part of the so-called

'Dark Lady' sequence (127–52)) and one that may also look back to the youth's 'sensual fault' treated in 34–6. Though usually assumed, any identification between the poet's mistress referred to in 40–2 and the 'Dark Lady' is purely speculative. It is possible, of course, that 40–2 are here misplaced and properly belong to the 'Dark Lady' sequence. Ingram and Redpath note that the full meaning of 40 is particularly dependent on ambiguities (turning in great part on the word 'love').

1 Take all my loves (1) Accept all the kinds of affection I can give; (2) Deprive me of all the affection I possess, your love of me; (3) Steal my mistress (my love, my beloved) (Booth).

1 my love i.e. the youth.

2 What . . . before i.e. in that case (or, in that time) (= 'then'), what have you added to what you already had?

3 No love (1) No kind of love; (2) No mistress.

3 true love constant, genuine love. Compare 'true-love' = a faithful lover (*TGV* 4.3.19–20).

4 All mine i.e. all my true love.

4 this more this 'No love' (i.e. my mistress, who has been false, therefore no true-love).

5 Then . . . receivest (1) Then (both senses, as in line 2) if for love of me you take ('receivest') my mistress ('my love'); (2) Then if you accept ('receivest') my mistress because she is a part of my 'love' (all of which you have by right). (1) suggests that the youth is a 'receiver of stolen goods'. See Booth for other possible glosses.

6 for . . . usest (1) because you 'use' (i.e. have sexual intercourse with) my mistress ('my love'); (2) because you make use of the love I have given you ('my love').

7 But . . . blamed Nevertheless you are blameworthy.

7 thou this self deceivest i.e. you betray me ('this self' = the poet's true self, an integral part of the lovers' essential two-in-oneness). Most editors accept Gildon's emendation of Q 'this selfe' to 'thy self' or 'thyself', an easier reading, but one that loses Q's apparent distinction between the effect of the youth's action both on the poet and on himself.

8 wilful (1) dictated by (wanton) will, not (controlling) reason; (2) sexually driven (with play on 'will' = male or female pudenda; see 135–6).

8 taste enjoyment, relish (again with strong sexual overtones).

8 thy self refusest i.e. your true self would not accept (the dictates of 'will' as opposed to 'reason'). Following Ingram and Redpath, I retain Q 'thy selfe' as two words to emphasise the special significance of 'self' and to balance 'this self' (7).

9 gentle (1) good-natured, sweet (compare 'sweet thief' in 35.14); (2) well-born (contrast 'my poverty' (10)).

10 steal thee steal for yourself (ethical dative; see Abbott 220).

10 all my poverty i.e. what little I possess, my poor all (echoing 'all' in line 1 and possibly referring to his mistress as a 'poor thing' (Booth, Kerrigan)).

11 And yet Even so.

11 love i.e. true love.

12 love's wrong i.e. an (unexpected) wrong committed against love.

12 hate's known injury i.e. the injury that may be expected from hatred.

13 Lascivious (1) Inclined to lust; (2) Inciting to wantonness.

13 grace attractiveness, charm (but probably carrying some suggestion of being, like God's 'grace', freely bestowed). 'Lascivious grace' = the youth, a phrase that in its combination of blame and praise anticipates the oxymoronic quality of 'all ill well shows' (= all evil appears to be good). Note the external limiting implication of 'shows' (= appears from your outward 'grace'). Compare *Ant.* 2.2.237–9: 'for vildest things / Become themselves in her [Cleopatra], that the holy priests / Bless her when she is riggish'.

14 spites injuries (psychological, not physical).

14 yet despite such 'spites'.

14 we . . . foes This singularly lame conclusion suggests that though the youth may 'kill' with 'spites', the poet will not fight back as a 'foe' would.

Sonnet 41

1 pretty wrongs (1) slight, petty injuries (ironic); (2) injuries arising from your natural attractiveness ('beauty' (3), 'grace' (40.13)); (3) injuries arising from your youth (compare 'Little things are pretty' (Tilley T188) and the common phrase 'a pretty child'). Pooler equates 'pretty wrongs' with 'Lascivious grace' in 40.13 (the implications of adjective and noun being reversed).

1 liberty licence, sexual indulgence (as in a 'libertine'). Compare *Edward III* 2.1.422–3: 'Why then, give sinne a pasport to offend, / And youth the dangerous reigne of liberty.'

2 sometime now and then, occasionally.

3 thy years i.e. as a youth (compare 1 n. above and 'straying youth' in line 10).

3 befits For the third-person plural in -*s* (still common in Elizabethan English), see Abbott 333.

4 still continually, always.

4 temptation i.e. both yourself and others are subjected to temptation (see lines 5–6).

5–6 Compare the proverb 'All women may be won' (Tilley W681); *1H6* 5.3.78–9: 'She's beautiful; and therefore to be wooed: / She is a woman; therefore to be won'; and similar phrasing in *Tit.* 2.1.82–4 and *R3* 1.2.227–8.

5 Gentle . . . won (1) You are well-born ('Gentle') and therefore worth winning; (2) You are kind-natured (hence susceptible) and therefore may be won. Compare 'gentle' in 40.9.

6 Beauteous . . . assailed i.e. because of your beauty you are naturally liable to be (1) wooed, (2) tempted, (3) besieged ('assailed').

7 woman's son i.e. any man.

8 sourly unkindly, cruelly.

8 till he have prevailed until (even though she is obviously willing) he has satisfied his male ego by *appearing* to have won her to intercourse ('prevailed') (picking up the love/war image inherent in 'assailed' in line 6). The majority of editors accept Malone's emendation of Q 'he' to 'she', on the grounds that it is the woman in line 7 that is wooing. This is an obviously easier reading, but misses the witty turn in 'he'.

9 Ay me Alas.

9 but yet even so.

9 my seat my place, chair, throne, private demesne (here with primary sexual overtones; compare *Oth.* 2.1.295–6: 'For that I do suspect the lusty Moor / Hath leap'd into my seat', and for the implied sexual play on 'riding', where 'seat' = saddle, see *H5* 3.7.45–59).

9 forbear abstain from, spare.

10 chide scold, rebuke.

10 straying youth Complements 'thy years full well befits' (3).

11 Who i.e. beauty and youth in line 10. The use of 'Who' rather than 'Which' tends to personify 'beauty' and 'youth' as the youth's licentious companions, thus in a sense separating them from the youth's 'true self', a separation further emphasised by 'their riot' instead of 'thy riot'.

11 riot debauchery, dissipation. The use of 'lead' with 'riot' suggests perhaps the idea of insurrection (compare *JC* 2.1.66–9: 'The Genius [i.e. rational soul] and the mortal instruments [i.e. the senses, etc.] / Are then in council, and the state of man, / Like to a little kingdom, suffers then / The nature of an insurrection').

12 forced i.e. forced by erring will against your rational faculty.

12 truth troth (as in 'plighted troth', the two forms being essentially interchangeable in Elizabethan English).

13 Hers, by Her troth being broken by.

14 Thine, by Your troth being broken by. The poet is thus doubly wronged: by his mistress and by the youth.

Sonnet 42

Sonnet 42 attempts a sophistical resolution or 'proof' (lines 6–14) of the situation treated in 40 and 41.

1 hast her i.e. have possessed her carnally. Compare 'hath' in line 3 and see 129.10 n.

2 loved Note the past tense.

2 dearly fondly, deeply (with probable play on 'dearly' = in a manner 'costly' to me).

3 is of . . . chief is the principal ('chief') cause of my mourning ('wailing').

4 loss in love lessening or diminution of (our) true love (caused by your apostasy).

4 touches hurts, injures (emotionally and physically).

4 nearly intimately (striking close ('near') to the heart).

5 Loving offenders Sinners who, paradoxically, sin by loving.

5 excuse ye find excuses for you (not really 'excuse' you). Note the game-playing force of 'thus'. Mahood (pp. 90–1) suggests an ironic play on 'excuse' = exculpate.

7 for my sake i.e. because she knows I love you.

7 even so for that cause.

7 abuse me wrong me by being unfaithful (the sexual connotation is strong; see Partridge).

8 Suff'ring Permitting.

8 for my sake i.e. because the friend and I are one.

8 approve try out, test (again with strong sexual suggestion and a possible play on 'approve' = commend).

9 thee i.e. the friend.

9 my love's i.e. my mistress's.

10 found recovered.

11 find (1) provide for; (2) discover.

11 and The form is perhaps ambiguous here; most probably = the coordinating conjunction, but possibly = 'if' ('and' was the usual spelling for 'an' (= if) at this time). Taking 'and' as 'if', 'and I lose' is in parallel construction with 'If I lose' in line 9. In either case his loss is double, the friend and mistress losing him (one), he losing the friend and his mistress (two).

11 both twain each of the two. The tautology is defensible as playing upon (and emphasising) 'Both' at the beginning of the line and 'both' in the following line. The phrase recurs in *LLL* 5.2.459.

12 for my sake (1) out of love for me; (2) using their mutual love for me as an excuse.

12 lay . . . cross burden ('lay on') me with this affliction ('cross'). As in 34.12, there is a suggestion of Christ-like self-sacrifice.

13 joy i.e. as contrasted with 'this cross' (12).

13 are one The 'oneness' of the youth and poet has already been expressed in 36, 37, 39, 40. Compare Nicholas Grimald in Tottel, I, 110: 'Who in pure love was so conjoynd with thee, / An other Grimald didst thou seem to bee.'

14 Sweet flattery Pleasing delusion. This bitter phrase puts the conventional and sophistical nature of lines 6–14 into sharp focus.

Sonnet 43

Compare the similar play on the ideas of sleep, sight, night, day, light, dark in Sonnet 27; see also 61. Booth comments: 'The recurring themes of this sonnet – things that are the opposite of what they would normally be expected to be, and the distinction between images or shadows of objects and the objects themselves – are played out stylistically in an intense display of antithesis and a range of rhetorical devices of repetition that make the language of the poem suggest mirror images.'

1 When . . . see A neat turn on the proverb 'Although I wink, I am not blind' (Tilley W500), which is illustrated by *Mac.* 1.4.52–3: 'The eye wink at the hand; yet let that be / Which the eye fears, when it is done, to see.' Here, however, 'wink' = close the eyes in sleep, and 'most I wink' = when I sleep most deeply, balancing 'best see'.

2 unrespected (1) not worthy of respect, unvalued; (2) unregarded, not carefully observed.

3 sleep, in dreams Contrast 27, where the poet is unable to sleep, but is haunted by the mental image of the youth when he tries to sleep.

4 darkly bright i.e. emitting clear light ('bright') although in darkness ('darkly') because my eyes are closed. It was thought that eyes gave off the light by which they saw.

4 bright in dark directed a point of light ('bright') focused in darkness. If 'bright' is taken adverbially = clearly.

5 Then (1) At that time; (2) In that case.

5 shadow mental image (in my mind's eye).

5 shadows . . . bright i.e. you make ordinary shadows (or other mental images) appear bright through your brightness.

6 thy shadow's form i.e. your real, physical shape ('form') which produces this mental image ('shadow').

6 form happy show produce a (comparatively) felicitous ('happy') appearance.

7 To the clear . . . light i.e. in the clear light of day, particularly given the advantage that your own light (or brightness) is much brighter ('clearer') than that of the day. Compare Sidney, *Arcadia* (1593), p. 5: 'Thy [i.e. Phoebus's = the sun's] beames I like, but her cleare rayes I love.'

8 unseeing eyes i.e. eyes closed in sleep (hence not 'seeing' in the usual sense). Compare 'sightless eyes' (12) and 'sightless view' in 27.10.

8 shade = shadow (as also in line 11).

8 so! i.e. so brightly. An exclamatory question mark (as here and in line 12 in Q) where we would employ an exclamation mark was common Elizabethan usage.

10 living day alive, active, creative day (as contrasted with 'dead night' in line 11; compare *Rape of Lucrece*, 162: 'Now stole upon the time the dead of night').

11 thy Capell's emendation 'thy' for Q 'their' (see 26.12 n.) has been universally accepted (with the exception of Porter).

11 imperfect i.e. being only the shadow of the reality.

11 shade shadow (but here, given the context, with possible play on 'ghost' or nocturnal apparition).

12 stay linger, remain (as imprinted).

13 All days . . . thee All days are like nights, dark and dismal to the sight ('to see'), until I see (the real) you.

14 thee me i.e. you to me. The final couplet suggests the poet's absence or separation from the youth, a theme picked up in 44.

Sonnet 44

Sonnets 44 and 45, a closely linked pair (compare 50 and 51 and the thematic and verbal connections with *H5* 3.7.11–79 in all four), are also linked to 43 by the theme of separation or absence (see 27 headnote).

1 dull substance slow-moving, heavy, comparatively inert matter (i.e. 'substance' lacking the lively, quick intelligence of 'thought').

1 flesh Man, like all created nature, was believed to be compounded of the so-called 'four elements': earth, water, air, and fire (see 11 n. below).

2 Injurious Hurtful, detrimental (in that 'distance' separates us).

2 stop my way bar my passage (to you).

3 For then Because in that case.

3 space 'Injurious distance' (2).

4 limits bounds, frontiers.

4 where i.e. to where (the ellipsis governed by 'From').

4 stay reside (at the time).

5 No matter then (1) It is of no concern (a) in that case, (b) at that time; (2) I could not then be mere 'dull substance' (line 1) (Hood).

6 farthest . . . thee separated from you by any of earth's most distant points ('farthest earth').

7 jump overleap.

7 sea and land i.e. water and earth, the lowest and least active of the 'four elements' (looking back to line 1 because his 'flesh', like sea and land, 'stop[s] his] way' (2)).

8 As soon as think As quickly as think of or imagine.

8 he i.e. 'thought' (7).

8 would be (1) wish to be; (2) should be.

9 thought kills me Here 'thought' probably carries the sense of 'melancholy musing', a connotation common in Elizabethan English (compare 'moan' in line 12).

9 I i.e. I in my flesh (see 1 n. above).

10 To In being able to.

10 large lengths of miles i.e. great distances.

10 **when . . . gone** when you are separated ('gone') from me.

11 **so much . . . wrought** i.e. being so largely ('much') compounded ('wrought') of earth and water (the two heaviest and least aspiring elements). Compare *H5* 3.7.21–3: 'He [the Dauphin's horse] is pure air and fire; and the dull elements of earth and water never appear in him, but only in patient stillness while his rider mounts him' (this scene shows other points of contact with Sonnet 44); *Ant.* 5.2.289–90: 'I am fire and air; my other elements / I give to baser life'; and Ovid, *Metamorphoses* xv, 239–43 (Golding, 263–7): 'This endlesse world conteynes therin I say / Fowre substances of which all things are gendred. Of theis fower / The Earth and Water for theyr masse and weyght are sunken lower. / The other cowple Aire and Fyre the purer of the twayne / Mount up, and nought can keepe them downe.'

12 **attend time's leisure** (1) wait upon the convenience of time; (2) wait upon time's leisureliness (time passes slowly for an absent lover). Personifying time, Ingram and Redpath suggest 'the image appears to be that of a petitioner waiting on a great man'.

12 **moan** complaint (i.e. this sonnet). 'Complaint' was a term commonly used to describe the poetic expression of a lover's grief; compare Shakespeare's own *A Lover's Complaint*.

13 **nought** i.e. nothing. Q's 'naughts' (= nothing, a worthless thing; see *OED* Nought *sb* 7a) is, since Gildon², retained and defended, perhaps rightly, only by Willen and Reed. Possibly a play on 'nought' (= o) and the shape of a tear-drop ('tears' (14)) may be intended.

13 **by** through the operation of.

13 **elements so slow** i.e. earth and water; see 11 n. above.

14 **heavy tears** 'heavy' because generated by the element of earth; 'tears' representing the element of water (see 11 n.).

14 **badges** distinctive signs, tokens.

14 **either's** i.e. of earth's and water's.

Sonnet 45

Sonnet 45 is essentially a continuation of 44, depending on 44 for its full meaning.

1 **two** i.e. elements.

1 **slight** thin, insubstantial, light (in contrast to 'dull' or 'slow' (44.1, 13), the qualities associated with earth and water as elements).

1 **purging** cleansing, purifying (see 3 n. below).

2 **Are both . . . abide** i.e. I am reduced to only two of my constituent elements (earth and water) because the other two (air and fire) are with you wherever I may be. Compare 'with two alone' (7). This apparently categorical statement of his complete physical (and impossible) division is almost immediately

refocused, not without some contradiction, by the paradox inherent in 'present-absent' in line 4 (see note) and by equating the physical elements (air and fire) with the mental and emotional faculties (thought and desire).

3 **first . . . other** i.e. air . . . fire.

3 **thought** Compare Sonnet 44 *passim*.

3 **desire** (1) love; (2) wish to be with you (the sexual implications, though inevitably present, seem secondary here; compare 'purging' in line 1, and 51.10: 'desire (of perfect'st love being made)'). Love and lust were frequently associated with fire; compare *Venus and Adonis*, 149–50: 'Love is a spirit all compact of fire, / Not gross to sink, but light, and will aspire', and *TGV* 2.7.18–20: 'Didst thou but know the inly touch of love, / Thou wouldst as soon go kindle fire with snow / As seek to quench the fire of love with words' (which is what the poet is attempting in this sonnet; the scene in *TGV* describes the agony of separation from the beloved). On the therapeutic 'endeavours of art', see Donne's 'The Triple Foole', 1–11.

4 **These** i.e. thought and desire.

4 **present-absent** i.e. (1) at one and the same time, here (with me) and elsewhere (with you) – a paradox (oxymoron) which, subversively perhaps, underlies the rest of the sonnet; (2) moving (compare 'slide') from here (where I am 'present') to you (being 'absent'), alternately back and forth. Malone's hyphen is accepted by almost all editors.

4 **swift** Swiftness is an attribute of thought (air) and desire (fire). Compare line 10.

4 **slide** pass from one place to another with a smooth and continuous 'motion', move effortlessly.

5 **For** Seeing that, since. The emendations 'So' (Ingram and Redpath) and 'Forth' (Tucker) make the apparently sequential relation to the first quatrain suggested by 'For' less awkward.

5 **quicker elements** more lively, volatile elements (air = thought, fire = desire).

6 **In tender . . . love** i.e. acting as gentle, affectionate ambassadors ('In tender embassy') for (my) love, 'tender' indicates that the 'embassy' is friendly, not hostile (which real embassies could be).

7 **life** (1) the composition of my living body; (2) my mental and emotional faculties ('thought' and 'desire').

7 **two alone** i.e. only ('alone') two elements (earth and water) remaining with me. The conceit tends to get out of hand here again, since 'thought' and 'desire', which have been equated with the elements of 'air' and 'fire', are obviously still present with him because otherwise he could not be 'oppressed with melancholy' (8). Again we have to seek some kind of solution in the first explanation of 'present-absent' (see 4 n. above).

8 **Sinks . . . melancholy** The line describes what may be termed a state of mental and emotional

depression, a state Keats refers to as being 'half in love with easeful Death' ('Ode to a Nightingale', 32).

8 melancholy melancholy thoughts and feelings. There is probable reference here to the Galenic doctrine of the 'four humours', or body fluids, which were distinguished as blood, choler, phlegm, and black bile, and were associated, in that order, with the 'four elements' (air, fire, water, and earth; see 44.1 n.). A combination of these 'humours', one being predominant, constituted the temperament (called the 'complexion') of men and women. Melancholy (or black bile) was considered the most dangerous humour when predominant, inducing depression, thoughts of death, even madness. Compare *John* 3.3.42–3: 'Or if that surly spirit, melancholy, / Had bak'd thy blood and made it heavy, thick'. See 91.5 n.

9 life's See 7 n.

9 composition be recured i.e. the elements that compose my 'life' (earth, water, air (thought), fire (desire)) are put back together again or restored ('recured').

10 messengers i.e. thought and desire (in their roles as air and fire).

10 thee Note the repeated rhyme on 'thee' (see line 6).

11 Who even but now i.e. which at this very moment. On 'Who' (= Which), see 23.11 n.

11 assured satisfied, reassured.

12 fair favourable, good.

12 recounting reporting, telling.

13 This told i.e. the good news being told.

13 then . . . glad i.e. because he is physically separated from his friend the relief is momentary (compare 'straight' in line 14).

14 them = the 'swift messengers' (see 10 n. above).

14 straight immediately.

14 sad melancholy (again).

Sonnet 46

The 'war' of the eyes (outer organs of sense) and the heart or mind (the inner 'closet' (6) where 'love' resides), the theme on which this sonnet (and its resolution in 47) turns, was a conventional conceit and may be found, stemming originally from Petrarch's *Rime sparse*, 75, as reworked by Ronsard, in Watson (1593), 19, 20, Barnes (1593), 20, Constable (1594), VI, 7, and Drayton (1594), 33. Shakespeare treats the theme again, with greater sophistication, in Sonnets 113–14. The interaction of eyes and heart in the pursuit of lust is described in *Rape of Lucrece*, 426–45. See Rollins, I, 128. Central to Shakespeare's handling of the conceit is the question of true 'seeing' ('sight' (2, 3)), and the final couplet apportions the spoils ('conquest' (2)) of war when the jury ('A quest of thoughts' (10)) – not seemingly an unprejudiced

one! – renders its verdict: to the eyes, the outward appearance of love (i.e. physical beauty); to the heart, the inward truth of love itself. The heart, then, 'sees' more truly than the eyes. Compare 24.13–14. Although legal imagery appears frequently in other sonnets, it is unusually concentrated in 46.

1 eye The use of the singular for the plural 'eyes' is common in Shakespeare and his contemporaries. Compare 24.1 and 113–14.

1 heart the seat of feeling, understanding, and thought.

1 mortal deadly, fatal (intentionally hyperbolic).

2 conquest (1) spoils of war (*opima spolia*); (2) acquisition of property (not through inheritance), a term in Scots law.

2 thy sight the sight of you (referring to an actual portrait, probably a miniature, of the youth in the poet's possession. See line 3 and compare 'my love's picture' and 'painted banquet' in 47.5, 6).

3 Mine eye . . . bar My eye would prohibit my heart from the sight of (i.e. from looking upon) your picture.

3 thy Capell's emendation of Q 'their', here and in line 8, is generally accepted.

4 My heart . . . right My heart (would 'bar') my eye the free exercise of its right to see the picture.

5 plead allege (in support of its case, as in a court of law).

5 thou . . . lie i.e. the true image or picture of the youth lies in the poet's heart. Compare 24.6–8.

6 A closet . . . eyes i.e. mortal eyes cannot see into the heart, only God or the 'mind's eye' of a lover. Compare 24.13–14.

6 closet (1) private room; (2) small box for valuables. Compare 'bosom's shop' (24.7).

6 pierced Eyes were believed to emit rays; compare the 'killing eye' of the fabulous basilisk and 43.4 n.

6 crystal clear, transparent (compare 'clear eye's' in line 12). Used perhaps derisively since it expresses the heart's view.

7 defendant i.e. the eyes (as, in a suit at law, the accused). The heart, therefore, is bringing an action against the eyes.

7 plea the suit (or action) being brought by the heart.

8 in him . . . lies i.e. your beauty ('fair appearance'), both outer and inner, is constituted ('lies') in him (= the eyes).

9 'cide Taken as an aphetic form of 'decide' (see Abbott 460 for a list of numerous other aphetic forms in Shakespeare). Gildon first read the Q spelling 'side' as ''cide' and has been followed by the great majority of later editors, even though ''cide' as an aphetic form of 'decide' is not recorded in *OED*, which interprets Q's 'side' as meaning 'assign to one of two sides or parties', a definition unsupported by any other examples. Given the uncertain authority of 'side' used in

this sense, '"cide", with its suggestion of a legal decision or judgement, should probably be preferred.

9 title legal right of possession.

9 impanellèd constituted, enrolled (in correct
legal procedure).

10 quest of thoughts jury made up of thoughts
(as in a sense all juries are).

10 all tenants to the heart (1) all of which owe
their tenure (as 'tenants') to the heart (as landlord);
(2) all inhabitants of the heart. Not surprisingly, the
jury is packed since the heart, here presented as
the organ of thought (compare 69.2) as well as the
'closet' of love, not the eyes, would be responsible for
choosing the jury. Compare Barnes's 'tenant' legal
metaphor in *Parthenophil and Parthenophe* (1593),
20.1–3: 'These eyes thy bewties tenants, pay dew
teares / For ocupation of myne hart thy free hold: /
In tenour of loves service . . .'

11 determinèd settled, apportioned (legally).

12 clear eye's moiety (1) keen eye's share; (2)
the share clearly belonging to the eye. 'moiety', here
disyllabic, as usual in Shakespeare, though legally
meaning a 'half', was loosely used to describe any portion or part of something, sometimes a 'small part'
(compare *Rape of Lucrece*, dedication. 'this Pamphlet . . . is but a superfluous Moity'), which may be
the implied meaning here, since the heart is obviously
given a greater 'part' by the 'determinèd' verdict.

12 dear heart's part (1) worthy, (2) valuable,
precious heart's share ('part'); (2) the heart's highly
valued (costly) share.

13–14 The final couplet sums up ('As thus') the
jury's verdict, which may be supposed to produce the
'league' between eyes and heart in 47. The rhyme-
scheme here is unique in the Sonnets, the first line
duplicating the rhyme in line 12 ('part . . . part'), the
second duplicating the rhyme in line 10 ('heart . . .
heart') – an unusual licence, which makes one wonder
whether what we have here is not a hasty first draft.
Compare the less extreme example of repeated rhyme
in 45.6, 10.

13 due legal claim or share.

13 outward part external physical beauty ('fair
appearance' (8), as reflected in the 'picture'). The
eyes are thus, despite what would appear to be a
packed jury, granted the exercise of their physical
attribute (i.e. 'sight'), which the heart had sought to
deny.

14 right = 'due' (13), but with perhaps a suggestion of 'natural right' making it a stronger word and
emphasising the superiority of the heart's claim.

14 thy inward love of heart i.e. the spiritual/
mental love of your heart (a 'part' of you in value far
beyond the 'due' accorded to the eyes because it is the
'essential' you, not merely the 'appearance'). Capell's
emendation of Q 'their' to 'thy' in lines 13 and 14 is
generally preferred to Malone's emendation 'thine'
(see also collation at 69.5), which some editors read

for euphony, because elsewhere the Q compositors
misread manuscript 'thy' as 'their' (see 26.12 n.) and
because Shakespeare, in undisputed readings in the
Sonnets (see e.g. 14.14, 56.2, 61.1, 79.1, 87.2) as well
as in his other poems and plays, sometimes employs
'thy' instead of 'thine' before words beginning with a
vowel which are metrically in an unstressed or unem-
phatic position (see Abbott 237).

Sonnet 47

Sonnet 47 grows out of 46, a 'league' having been
struck between the heart and eyes as a result of the
'verdict' rendered in 46.13–14.

1 league A compact for mutual assistance and
protection made between parties.

1 took taken, entered upon. For this strong form
of the past participle 'taken', compare 75.12 and see
Abbott 343; use of such strong forms here and elsewhere is often influenced by metre or rhyme-scheme.

2 now i.e. as a result of the 'league', contrasting
with their earlier behaviour in 46.

3 famished starving.

3 look glance (of, or from, the youth), i.e. the
opportunity to look upon or see the youth himself
(the reality). Compare 75.10 and *Err.* 2.1.88: 'Whilst
I at home starve for a merry look'.

4 in love with sighs (1) being in love, with sighs;
(2) addicted to melancholy thoughts (which give rise
to 'sighs').

4 himself itself.

4 smother suffocate. Sighs were considered
deleterious to health, each sigh taking a drop of
blood from the heart; compare *2H6* 3.2.61: 'blood-
consuming sighs', and 30.8.

5 With On.

5 love's picture Compare *A Lover's Complaint*,
134–5.

5 then at that time (when the eye is 'famished'
and the heart 'smothered').

6 painted banquet i.e. the youth's picture. A
'banquet' in Elizabethan usage often referred to a
special course of sweetmeats or other delicacies. In
'painted' Kerrigan suggests a reference to the story of
Zeuxis, the famous Greek artist, who painted a bunch
of grapes so realistically that birds came and pecked
at them (see Nashe, *Christes Teares over Jerusalem*
(1593); *Works*, II, 96). 'painted' is thus pejorative,
suggesting that the 'picture' is a poor substitute for
the reality, while 'banquet' together with 'feast' (5)
suggests a reference to what was called the 'Banquet
of Sense', a common food metaphor for sexual licence
(see Chapman, *Ovids Banquet of Sence* (1595), and
'sensual feast' in 141.8).

6 bids invites.

7 Another time On a different occasion.

7 guest Picks up the 'banquet' metaphor.

8 his its (i.e. the heart's).

8 thoughts of love i.e. the 'part' assigned as the 'heart's right' in 46.14.

9 by by means of, through.

9 my love i.e. my love of you (in the 'closet' of my heart, which under the 'league' may now be 'pierced' by the eyes (46.6)).

10 Thyself, away i.e. the real you, being absent.

10 are Sometimes used by Shakespeare for 'art' (the grammatically correct form here) before consonants for the sake of euphony (see Franz 152).

10 still constantly, always; nevertheless.

11 not Benson's emendation of Q 'nor' has been retained; a few editors (most recently Wells) prefer Capell's 'no'. I conjecture 'ner' (= ne'er), of which Q 'nor' would, graphically, be an easy misreading; the form 'ner' for 'ne'er' occurs twice in the *First Part of the Troublesome Reign of King John* (1591) 3.4.

11 farther . . . move i.e. you are always present in my thoughts.

12 still constantly, always.

13 sleep are dormant, inert (contrasts with 'Awakes' in line 14).

13 in my sight before my eyes.

14 Awakes Arouses, stimulates.

14 to heart's . . . delight to the pleasure of both heart and eye (i.e. both his heart's love and his senses are mutually gratified by the 'league').

Sonnet 48

There is no reason to think, as some earlier critics claim, that Sonnet 48 is addressed to the 'Dark Lady' and not to the youth. The uncertainty it expresses about the constancy of the youth's love for the poet, already expressed in 33–6, is again the theme: one can lock up one's 'jewels' (5) but one cannot lock up 'love'. Booth sees a play on two proverbs: 'Love locks no cupboards' (Tilley L520) and 'Love laughs at locksmiths' (a nineteenth-century proverb; *ODEP*, p. 491), but essentially expressed in *Venus and Adonis*, 575–6: 'Were beauty under twenty locks kept fast, / Yet love breaks through, and picks them all at last.'

1 when . . . way at the time I set out (on my journey).

2 truest bars most trustworthy fastenings (essentially = locks; compare 'sure wards of trust' (4)).

2 thrust push in (with a suggestion of last-minute haste).

3 That to . . . stay So that it ('Each trifle' (line 2)) might remain ('stay') unused and untainted (1) for my personal use, (2) for my profit (= 'use'). The sexual implications of 'use' here become resonant in lines 5–14. I have retained Q's hyphen in 'un-usèd' for its suggestion of stress on 'un-', thus emphasising the contrast with 'use' earlier in the line.

4 From hands of falsehood (Safe) from thieving hands (but 'hands' and 'falsehood' both look forward to the envisioned 'theft' of his most valued

'jewel', one that cannot be locked safely away 'in any chest' (9), i.e. the youth's love and constancy).

4 sure wards of trust safe ('sure'), trustworthy ('of trust') guards (with play on the ridges of a lock which permit only the right key to be used). Booth suggests some reference in 'wards' to 'prison walls', and Chipchase to 'ward' = court of a castle or stronghold: the outer ward and the inner ward (where the keep stood).

5 to whom compared to whom (i.e. 'thou').

5 jewels trifles are jewels are trifles, 'jewels' = prized possessions, and 'trifles', here repeated, explains the use of 'trifle' in line 2 (i.e. they are only 'trifles' when compared with 'thou'). Braunmuller suggests a sexual play on 'jewels' = testicles.

6 Most worthy comfort i.e. (my) most valued solace.

6 now . . . grief i.e. because now that he is journeying away he cannot place the youth (his love) in 'sure wards of trust' (4), as he has his other 'jewels' (5).

7 Thou best of dearest i.e. you who are (among my 'jewels') the most excellent ('best') of (1) the most precious, (2) the most loved, 'dearest' may also carry a negative suggestion of 'most costly'.

7 mine only care (1) the only jewel I really care about; (2) my only worry (because I cannot lock you up with my other 'jewels').

8 the prey of (1) as the spoils or plunder for; (2) as a victim for.

8 vulgar common, ordinary.

9 chest box, coffer (one that may be secured by a lock), with play on 'chest' = 'breast' or thorax; here used for 'heart', a 'chest' that cannot be locked. Compare the 'closet' of the heart in 46.6.

10 Save . . . not Except there where you are not (i.e. in my heart, because, taken literally, we are absent from one another).

10 though . . . art even though I believe emotionally ('feel') that you are.

11 gentle closure not harsh or strictly confining enclosure (because not locked), 'gentle closure' would appear to be an oxymoron, but is not, given the context. Compare *Venus and Adonis*, 782: 'the quiet closure of my breast'.

12 at pleasure i.e. as you may desire (with sexual suggestion in 'pleasure').

12 come and part i.e. enter or leave.

13 even (1) eventually, in time; (2) even from such a private place as the breast (i.e. 'thence').

13 stol'n stolen. Note the suggestion that since the youth is free to come and go 'at pleasure' (12) he may choose to be 'stol'n'.

14 For truth . . . dear Because (even) honesty ('truth') may become a thief to attain so precious (or costly, 'dear') a prize. Compare *Venus and Adonis*, 724: 'Rich preys make true men thieves'; *AYLI* 1.3.110: 'Beauty provoketh thieves sooner than gold';

and, proverbially, 'The prey entices the thief' (Tilley P570).

Sonnet 49

Sonnet 49, which appears to interrupt 48 and 50 (journey/separation sonnets; see, however, 9 n. below), may be misplaced, but it may also be taken as the sort of despairing meditation in which a lover might indulge when separated from his beloved (particularly when the lover, as in 48, feels uncertain of the beloved's constancy). For tone and theme, compare 88.

　1 **Against** In preparation for (as in lines 5 and 9).

　2 **defècts** deficiencies, faults (physical and spiritual).

　3 **Whenas** At the time that, when.

　3 **thy love** i.e. your love for me.

　3 **cast . . . sum** reckoned up its ('his') final 'utmost' total (i.e. has extended itself as far as it is possible for 'thy love', a finite love, to go, unlike the poet's which is, as always, infinite and without limit). The commercial image in 'cast' and 'sum' may thus be taken as a criticism of the quality of the youth's love.

　4 **Called . . . advised respects** Summoned to that official reckoning ('audit') by judicious or thoughtful considerations ('advised respects'). There is play perhaps on 'respect' = rank or social standing – his as opposed to that of the poet. This suggests that worldly 'respects' out-weigh the 'utmost sum' (3) of 'thy love' (reason *v*. feeling, mind *v*. heart). Compare *John* 4.2.213–14: 'when perchance it [i.e. majesty] frowns / More upon humour than advis'd respect'. The legal imagery, here begun, dominates the rest of the sonnet.

　5–7 Compare *JC* 4.2.20–1: 'When love begins to sicken and decay / It useth an enforced ceremony.'

　5 **strangely** i.e. as a stranger.

　6 **scarcely . . . eye** barely acknowledge me with a glance ('that sun, thine eye').

　7 **converted** changed, transformed.

　7 **thing it was** i.e. the kind of true love it had been. At best it is now a 'calculated' love, one 'cast' (3) on 'advised respects' (4).

　8 **of settled gravity** for (behaving) with staid propriety. The phrase echoes 'advised respects' (4) and carries a sense of being held in control by the constraining weight (= 'gravity') of the anti-love outcome of the 'audit' (4).

　9 **insconce** ensconce (variant form), fortify, shield ('sconce' = a small fort, with possible play on 'sconce' = head, where the 'knowledge' in line 10 is located).

　9 **here** Does 'here' suggest that he is separated by distance from the youth, i.e. here where I now am?

　10 **desert** Q 'desart' indicates the pronunciation, rhyming with 'part' in line 12. 'desert' may mean either (1) 'worth' (i.e. my good qualities) or (2)

absence of merit or worth (i.e. 'my defècts' (line 2)). The second meaning (2) was universally accepted until Ingram and Redpath proposed (1), a meaning endorsed by Kerrigan (Booth curiously ignores the problem), and it may fairly be asked why the poet would fortify ('insconce') himself with his 'demerits'. Kerrigan also suggests that (1) is necessary to certify the poet as a credible witness.

　11 **my hand . . . uprear** i.e. raise my (right) hand as a witness who swears to speak the truth in a court of law, even though I am bearing such witness in opposition to ('against') my own interests ('myself').

　12 **To guard . . . part** In order to protect the legal rights ('lawful reasons') on your side ('part'). As usual the poet is self-abnegating; even if it is against himself, he will uphold the youth's 'legal' position as explained in lines 13–14.

　13 **poor** (1) undeserving (because of 'my defècts' (line 2)); (2) pitiable; (3) needy (in terms of wealth and position).

　13 **strength of laws** power inherent in the law (with play perhaps on 'strength' = strongly fortified position as compared with the poet's 'sconce' = a small fort in line 9).

　14 **why to love** i.e. why you should love (me).

　14 **allege no cause** plead under oath ('allege') (1) no case in law, (2) no reason (i.e. no 'cause' necessitates the desired effect, namely that you should love me).

Sonnet 50

Sonnet 50 picks up the separation/journey theme of 48 and is closely linked with 51.

　1 **heavy** (1) sluggishly; (2) weighed down (by melancholy thoughts of my increasing distance from my 'friend' (4)).

　2–4 **When what . . . friend** i.e. when that which I seek – the end of my journey – makes me think ('teaches') that the comfort ('ease') and rest ('repose') I then anticipate will only remind ('say') me of how far the number of miles thus travelled ('measured') have separated me from my friend. For line 4, compare 28.8 and *R2* 1.3.268–70: 'every tedious stride I make / Will but remember me what a deal of world / I wander from the jewels that I love'.

　5 **beast** horse.

　5 **tirèd** The antecedent may be either 'me' or 'beast'; if 'beast', 'tirèd' would be linked to the sympathetic 'instinct' attributed to the 'beast' in line 7.

　6 **Plods** Trudges.

　6 **dully** sluggishly, heavily (compare 'heavy' (1)). Benson's emendation of Q 'duly' has been accepted by all editors, except Ridley, on the grounds that 'dully' fits the action of the horse as described in lines 6–11 (compare also 51.2, 'dull bearer') and that 'duly' is a possible Elizabethan spelling of 'dully'; however, 'duly' (= dutifully (Booth), methodically (Kerrigan), conscientiously) makes good, if less allusive, sense

and must be acknowledged as a possible reading. It may be, as Booth suggests, that Shakespeare intended a play on 'dully/duly'.

6 to bear in the act of bearing.

6 weight in me i.e. 'my woe' (5).

7 instinct Being irrational, the horse can only react to his rider's mood by instinct. Kerrigan points out that the doctrine of good horsemanship taught that horse and rider should function as one (i.e. that there was a sympathetic accommodation between them). See Sidney, *Astrophil and Stella* (1591), 49, a sonnet in which Sidney plays on this doctrine, a doctrine that suggests points of analogy with the conventional idea that lover and beloved are one (see 36.2 and *H5* 3.7.11–68 for the horse/mistress – rider/lover image).

7 wretch poor creature (without pejorative weight).

8 speed . . . thee i.e. swiftness which when effected ('being made') bears me further away from you.

9 bloody i.e. bloody from use.

9 provoke him on incite, stimulate him to a quicker pace.

10 anger The 'anger' here is not generated by the horse's slowness but by the poet's 'heavy' mood in being separated from the friend, an anger he takes out on the horse.

11 Which i.e. the action of spurring.

11 heavily mournfully, grievously (from the pain being inflicted).

12 More sharp More piercing or cutting.

13 doth put . . . mind i.e. gives rise to the following thought.

14 onward (1) ahead; (2) in forward movement (Hood).

14 joy (1) happiness; (2) the friend.

Sonnet 51

Sonnet 51 is closely linked with 50, reversing the conceit (while slow progress is acceptable when journeying away from the youth, the greatest 'speed' is demanded when returning to him). Booth (pp. 221–2) calls attention to a number of thematic and verbal echoes between this sonnet (as well as 44, 45, 50) and *H5* 3.7.11–79.

1 Thus In this way (referring to line 3).

1 my love i.e. my affection for my horse.

1 slow offence i.e. the fault ('offence') of slowness. Paradoxically, the 'offence' is considered a 'virtue' in 50.6–8.

2 my dull bearer i.e. the sluggish, plodding horse that bears me (compare 'Plods dully on' in 50.6).

2 speed i.e. his movement appears to the poet as 'speeding' (since he is unwilling to go) even though his progress is slow as described in 50.

4 I return i.e. I am returning (to you).

4 posting riding with great speed, post-haste.

5 what excuse . . . find i.e. what excuse could I offer or invent then on behalf of my sorry, inadequate horse ('beast'; compare 'jade' in line 12).

6 swift extremity extreme of swiftness, extreme speed.

6 but only.

7 I spur . . . wind i.e. even if I were mounted on the wind (instead of a 'poor beast') I would still use my spurs. Compare *2H4*, Induction 4: '(Making the wind my post-horse)'.

8 In wingèd . . . know (Because then) I shall be conscious of ('know') no motion even in my 'wingèd speed' (i.e. although mounted on the wings of the wind ('wingèd'), he will not feel that he is even moving so great is his 'desire' (9) for 'swift extremity' (6)).

10 desire the wish to be reunited (made one) with his beloved (with suggestion, underlined by 'neigh' in line 11, of sexual, physical desire).

10 perfect'st Dyce's emendation for Q 'perfects' is now generally accepted in preference to Gildon's 'perfect' (see collation), since the *s* in Q's spelling suggests an elided form of the superlative, a form I find vouched for in Drayton's *The Shepheards Garland* (1593), Fifth Eclogue, 147: 'But since unperfect are the perfects colours'; in Sir Arthur Gorges's *The Vannetys and Toyes* 26, 79: 'The perfects shape that ever yett . . .'; in Sir John Davies's 'A Songe of Contention', line 3: 'Women excell the perfects' men in this.' Thus, although 'perfect'st report' occurs in *Mac.* 1.5.2, an editor should perhaps retain Q 'perfects', reading it as 'perfects''. The use of a comparative or superlative form of an adjective that logically allows for no extension of quality is not uncommon in Shakespeare and his contemporaries (see Franz 215).

11 Shall neigh (no dull flesh) in his fiery race A celebrated crux. Most editors accept Q's 'naigh' (= neigh) and three different explanations have been proposed, depending on how the line is pointed: (1) making 'no dull flesh' a parenthetical appositive for 'desire' – (desire) shall neigh (being no inert or heavy ('dull') piece of horse-flesh) in its ('his') ardent, spirited course or career ('fiery race'); (2) with a comma (or dash) after 'neigh' – (desire) will neigh high-spiritedly, having no dull horse-flesh in its mettlesome breed ('fiery race'); (3) accepting, as here, Q's lack of internal pointing – (desire) will not neigh longingly after (= 'neigh') some piece of dull horse-flesh in its fiery course. In all three, 'neigh' is used to imply a state of spirited excitement or sexual arousal associated specifically with horses (compare the amorous stallion in *Venus and Adonis*, 265: 'Imperiously he leaps, he neighs, he bounds'; and 307: 'He looks upon his love, and neighs unto her'), and Kerrigan suggests that 'neigh' contrasts with the 'groan' of the poet's horse in 50.11. (1)

and (3) appear to have some slight advantage, since 'desire' has earlier been associated with the element of fire in 45.3 in its 'swift motion' (45.4), an association that may be echoed in 'fiery race' (i.e. fiery course). On the other hand, Shakespeare uses 'fiery' to describe a mettlesome and spirited horse (*R2* 5.2.8: 'Mounted upon a hot and fiery steed'), which may be adduced to support 'race' in the sense of 'breed' (as in (2)). Despite its obvious relevance to the other horse imagery, some few editors (most recently, Wells) consider Q's 'naigh' to be a compositorial misreading of some other word: 'wait' spelled 'waight' (= wait for); 'weigh' (= consider as a burden); 'rein' spelled 'raign' (= rein in). None of these, all taking 'race' in the sense of 'course' or 'career', offers an interpretation that is significantly better than those proposed for 'neigh' above. Compare, generally, Sir John Davies, 'On the Marriage of Lady Elizabeth Hatton to Edward Coke', Sonnet 2.1–4: 'Upon the Astrian hills the mountayne Mare, / Impregned by the breath of Westerne winde, / Bringes fourth her colte, not of dull stallions kinde, / Brave sprighted beast more swifter and more fayre.' For the most recent discussion of this crux, supporting Smith's emendation of Q 'naigh' to 'weigh' (see collation), see MacD. P. Jackson, 'How many horses has Sonnet 51? textual and literary criticism in Shakespeare's Sonnets', *ELN* 27 (1990), 10–19.

12 But love, for love (1) Nevertheless affection for his horse (compare 'my love' in line 1) because of its instinctive sympathy ('love') (in fitting his own mood by going 'wilful slow' (13)); (2) Nevertheless the *Idea* of Love itself (larger and more generous than 'desire' which is only a part of 'perfect'st love' (10)) for its own sake.

12 excuse find an excuse for (compare line 5).

12 jade sorry, poor nag.

13 wilful wilfully (i.e. by choice, thus fitting my mood).

14 I'll run i.e. I will ('mounted on the wind' of my 'desire') ride quickly (*OED* Run *v* 6; compare 'wingèd speed' (8)) in my imagination (i.e. my thoughts will ride post).

14 go walk, i.e. go at a walking pace, 'Plod' (50.6). Compare *TGV* 3.1.378–9: 'Thou must run to him, for thou hast stay'd so long that going will scarce serve the turn.'

Sonnet 52

1 So am . . . rich In this respect I am like the wealthy man ('the rich').

1 blessèd key i.e. the key (here, as often at this time, pronounced 'kay') is termed 'blessèd' because it gives him sole access to his 'treasure' (2), the 'sweet' (2) heaven of his delight. Booth compares the 'keys of the kingdom of heaven' given to St Peter (Matt. 16.19).

2 bring him Give him access to. The singular pronoun clarifies the ambiguity of 'the rich' in line 1. Line 2 also suggests that the 'rich' man in line 1 is being thought of as a miser.

2 sweet (1) precious, dearly loved; (2) yielding pleasure.

2 up-lockèd locked up (the only citation as a past participle in *OED* and probably the earliest example of the verb 'uplock').

3 ev'ry hour i.e. very often.

4 For blunting For fear of blunting (i.e. taking the edge off).

4 fine point (1) sharp, (2) sensitive; (1) moment, (2) height.

4 seldom rare, infrequent. Compare the proverb 'A seldom use of pleasure maketh the same the more pleasant' (Tilley P417), and *1H4* 1.2.204–7: 'If all the year were playing holidays, / To sport would be as tedious as to work; / But when they seldom come, they wish'd for come, / And nothing pleaseth but rare accidents' (see also 3.2.55–9 for the 'rare feast' image). The sexual undertones of the sonnet become more dominant in line 4, picking up the suggestions in 'key' (line 1) and 'sweet up-lockèd treasure' (line 2); see 75.6 n.

5 feasts (1) sumptuous banquets; (2) feast-days (as opposed to fast-days) as designated by church law (see the Book of Common Prayer).

5 solemn ceremonious, festively formal.

5 rare (1) few in number; (2) specially excellent.

6 seldom coming occurring infrequently. The number of feast-days had been reduced in the reformed Anglican calendar.

6 long year i.e. the year thought of as being long drawn out and tedious if not relieved by 'seldom coming' feasts.

6 set (1) placed; (2) ordained (by church or civil law). 'set' also looks forward to the 'setting' of jewels in lines 7–8.

7 stones of worth precious gemstones.

7 thinly widely spaced.

8 captain chief (i.e. the most valuable).

8 carcanet jewelled necklace or collar.

9 So is . . . chest Such are those moments of time (compare 'special instant' in line 11) which (1) hold you like a jewel in a treasure chest, (2) reserve you as though you were *my* treasure-box ('chest'). This parallels 'So am I' where the poet compares himself to 'the rich' in line 1 and focuses the comparison on himself and his relation to the youth. Figuratively, 'chest' may here be extended to mean 'breast' or 'heart' (*OED* Chest *sb*¹ 9b), since by the conventional exchange of hearts the beloved's heart is in the poet's 'chest'. Compare 48.9 n.

10 wardrobe room in which wearing apparel, or other costly gear, was kept under ward (= guard; compare 'garderobe'). 'Wardrobe' as a piece of movable furniture for a bedroom does not occur until the late eighteenth century; see *OED*. Q's spelling 'wardrobe' (see collation) helps to emphasise the security aspect and points up the play on 'robe'; it should perhaps be retained.

10 robe The comparison of the youth to a 'robe' suggests emphasis on the external, physical aspects of beauty, not its essential nature. Compare *1H4* 3.2.55–7: 'Thus did I keep my person fresh and new, / My presence, like a robe pontifical, / Ne'er seen but wond'red at.'

10 hide conceal (from 'ev'ry hour['s] survey' as in line 3).

11 To make The agent that 'makes' is 'the time' in line 9.

11 special instant special blest (1) exceptional, (2) particular moment of time especially blessed or pleasurable. Compare 'seldom pleasure' (4). In a sense 'the time' is the poet's 'blessèd key' (1), the 'blessing' being transferred directly to the youth by 'Blessèd' in line 13.

12 new unfolding newly revealing or disclosing ('unfolding' grows out of the 'robe' image in line 10).

12 his its (i.e. the time's).

12 imprisoned pride i.e. essentially, the 'uplockèd treasure' of line 2, but 'pride' may be taken to refer to the 'robe' which may be assumed to occupy 'pride of place' in the 'wardrobe' in line 10; 'imprisoned pride' may also suggest a reference to sexuality that has been held under restraint until the 'special instant' releases it (animals were described as being 'in pride' when sexually aroused).

13 worthiness inherent desert, merit (*OED* Worthy *adj* 6).

13 scope freedom of action, liberty of choice.

14 Being had . . . hope To glory or revel ('triumph') in you when you are present ('had'), to hope for reunion with you when you are absent ('lacked'). 'triumph' and 'hope' may also be construed as noun forms governed by 'to'. The implication of absence in 'lacked' serves as a slight link with the separation theme in 50 and 51. The phrase 'had, to triumph' can be taken as supporting the earlier sexual implications suggested by the imagery (see 129.10 n.).

Sonnet 53

Shakespeare here plays with some of the vocabulary of neo-Platonism ('substance', 'shadows', 'shade') to lend mystery and weight to his conceit: all other things in the natural order (i.e. all other parts of the 'Book of the Creatures') are but 'shadows' (*Idola*, poor imitations or reflections) of the youth's 'substance' (i.e. the *Idea* or essence of 'reality'). The youth, thus, equals 'truth' ('constant heart' (14)), both externally and internally (i.e. in body and in mind or soul). Kerrigan compares *AYLI* 3.2.135–54, which suggests that Nature created Rosalind as a combination of 'Helen's cheek', 'Cleopatra's

majesty', 'Atalanta's better part', and 'Lucretia's modesty'. The attitude here expressed toward the youth's constancy is apparently at odds with that expressed in 35 and 40–2, and Seymour-Smith argues that this sonnet should be read as ironic in its flattery, particularly the final couplet. The idea of comparing (and usually preferring) the beloved to various examples of classical beauty, power, wit, etc. was a commonplace in the sonnet tradition (compare Petrarch, *Rime sparse*, 260; Sidney, *Arcadia* (1590), p. 21, 'What length of verse can serve . . .'; Barnes, *Parthenophil and Parthenophe* (1593), 19).

1–2 substance . . . shadows Suggests the neo-Platonic distinction between the *Idea* ('substance' or essential reality) and the *Idola* ('shadows'), which, as in Plato's allegory of the Cave (*Republic*, VII), man takes for the 'real Good'. The youth is thus pictured as the essential *Idea* (the universal) of which everything else in Nature is merely a reflection or 'shadow' emanating from and attending upon him. Some critics see a play on 'material wealth' in 'substance'.

2 strange alien (i.e. other than his own shadow); exotic.

2 on you tend attend upon you (as servitors or vassals).

3 Since . . . shade Since every single creature has one shadow ('one shade') and only one. The repetition of 'every one' adds emphasis to both singularities (Hood).

4 And you . . . lend i.e. and you, although only a single creature, can cast or impart ('lend') images of all kinds of natural beauty or good ('every shadow'). That the youth should 'shadow forth' only 'good' or 'beauty' is implicit in the context, as 'blessèd shape' in line 12 and 'constant heart' in line 14 show.

5–7 Adonis . . . Helen's cheek Adonis and Helen of Troy represent classical types of male and female beauty, the youth combining the best of both, suggesting, as in Sonnet 20, an epicene quality.

5 Describe Adonis i.e. paint a word-picture of Adonis (as Shakespeare does in *Venus and Adonis*, 7–12).

5 counterfeit portrait (here verbal), with play on 'counterfeit' = imitation, i.e. a kind of 'shadow'.

6 poorly . . . you a poorly executed imitation modelled on ('after') you.

7 cheek face (by metonymy, the rhetorical figure where the part stands for the whole).

7 all art . . . set i.e. render or place ('set') all the art associated with depicting beauty.

8 And you . . . new i.e. the result will only be a freshly ('new') 'painted' portrait of you in Grecian dress.

8 tires apparel (aphetic form of 'attires'), with perhaps some reference to 'tire' = head-dress.

9 foison bountiful harvest (i.e. the autumn which brings to fruition the promise of spring).

10–11 The one . . . The other Spring . . . foison.

10 **shadow . . . show** i.e. reflects only a (poor) shadow or imitation of your beauty.

11 **bounty** (1) virtue, worth; (2) generosity (with perhaps a suggestion of 'financial largess' from a man of substance). Compare *Ant.* 5.2.86–8: 'For his bounty, / There was no winter in't; an autumn it was / That grew the more by reaping.'

12 **blessèd shape** holy, beautiful (i.e. 'good') form (in nature).

12 **know** are acquainted with.

13 **all external grace** all things of physical beauty (i.e. the outward as contrasted with the inward 'grace'). 'external' may also catch up the first sense of 'strange' in line 2 to suggest 'you have a part in all beautiful things beyond yourself' (Kerrigan).

13 **part** share (i.e. of the most excellent 'parts' of 'every blessèd shape').

14 **you like . . . heart** i.e. you are like none of the 'blessèd shape[s]', and none are like you, since you possess a 'constant heart' or mind, the inward sign of truth and virtue.

Sonnet 54

Sonnet 54 is linked to 53 by the opening two lines, in which the more 'constant heart' (53.14) that distinguishes the youth from all other 'creatures' becomes 'that sweet ornament which truth doth give' and makes the 'lovely youth' (13) appear even more beautiful, his inner beauty shining through his outward beauty – the beautiful soul in the beautiful body (see 1.1 n. and 4.2 n.). In 54 Shakespeare again returns to the immortality-through-verse theme found in 15–19 (see headnote to 15) and the flower-distilling-perfume imagery of 5–6.

2 **By** As a result of, through the agency of.

2 **sweet ornament** precious adornment (the inner reflected in the outward). On the fourfold repetition of 'sweet' in this sonnet, see 13.8 n.

2 **truth** fidelity, constancy (looking back to 'constant heart' in 53.14) and laying to rest now any hint of false cosmetic beauty in the 'painted' of 53.8). Compare 14.11–14.

3 **rose** Here, as elsewhere, a metaphor for the youth. Capitalised in Q, as always in the Sonnets; see 1.2 n.

3 **fair** beautiful.

3 **deem** consider, judge.

4 **For** Because of.

4 **odour** scent. Like 'truth' in line 2, an inner quality that enhances the rose's otherwise merely visual 'fairness'.

5 **canker blooms** blossoms of the canker- or dog-rose, which grew wild in hedges, but lacked any scent. Here used as a metaphor for ordinary men or women. Compare *Ado* 1.3.27–8: 'I had rather be a canker in a hedge than a rose in his grace.'

5 **dye** colour, hue.

6 **tincture** colour, tint, dye. In the sense of 'solution' 'tincture' anticipates the distillation image in line 14.

7 **such thorns** i.e. thorns like those of the domesticated rose.

7 **wantonly** sportively, playfully.

8 **summer's breath** warm winds of summer. Compare 65.5.

8 **maskèd buds** buds the beauty of which is concealed ('maskèd') until the corolla (= bud) is opened out into full bloom. Compare *LLL* 5.2.295–7: 'Fair ladies mask'd are roses in their bud; / Dismask'd, their damask sweet commixture shown, / Are angels vailing clouds, or roses blown.'

8 **discloses** opens up, unfolds.

9 **for** because.

9 **virtue** (1) excellence; (2) efficacy, worth (in healing or strengthening quality).

9 **only is their show** resides only in their appearance (i.e. they lack inner 'virtue', having only visual beauty and not perfume to accompany it).

10 **unwooed** unsought after, uncourted (in marriage, i.e. no 'increase' (compare 1.1) is sought from them since they are 'fair' only in 'show').

10 **unrespected** (1) unnoticed, (2) unesteemed, not held in respect.

11 **Die to themselves** i.e. perish without 'increase' or profit to others. Compare 94.9–10. Recalls the self-abortion theme of Sonnet 4, which is followed by the distillation imagery of 5 and 6, here repeated in line 14.

11 **Sweet** (1) Precious; (2) Sweet-smelling (continued in 'sweet' and 'sweetest' in line 12).

12 **deaths** i.e. dissolution on being crushed to distil perfume. There is also probably some play on 'death' (and on 'Die' in line 11) with reference to sexual orgasm in which the 'rose', unlike the canker-rose, does not autoerotically 'die' to itself, but produces issue ('sweetest odours').

13 **so of you** i.e. thus it follows in your case (identifying the youth with the 'Sweet roses' of line 11 rather than the 'canker blooms' of line 5).

13 **lovely** (1) lovable; (2) loving; (3) beautiful.

14 **that** i.e. external beauty, with its attendant loveliness and lovableness. The two qualities ('beauty' and 'truth') are distinguished in lines 1–2.

14 **vade** pass away, perish. 'vade' is a variant form of 'fade' (compare line 10), but also seems to have been treated in Elizabethan English as a distinct form related to the Latin *vadere* – to go (see *OED* Vade *v*² 1); it occurs five times in *The Passionate Pilgrim*, 10 and 13, two lyrics presumably by Shakespeare.

14 **by verse . . . truth** i.e. the essence of your 'truth' (see 2 n. above) or 'virtue' (9) is extracted drop by drop ('distils') as a perfume or 'sweetest odours' (12) by (my) verse (thus preserving it for posterity). Some earlier editors have preferred Capell's emendation of Q 'by' to 'my' (see collation), making 'distils'

transitive, because *OED* does not record an intransitive use of 'distil' in the sense 'is distilled' (i.e. 'is extracted'). Capell's emendation, therefore, is not without its attraction.

Sonnet 55

Not perhaps one of the great sonnets, but one of the best-known, 55 continues the immortality-through-verse theme resounded in the final couplet of 54 (see 54 headnote and compare Ovid, *Amores* I, xv, 31–42, Petrarch, *Rime sparse*, 104, and John Davies of Hereford, *Humours Heav'n on Earth* (1609), stanza 137).

1 gilded Carries perhaps a suggestion of specious ornamentation.

1 monuments Malone's emendation for Q 'monument' (see collation) is necessary for the rhyme with 'contènts' in line 3.

2 pow'rful potent, exerting generative influence.

2 rhyme (1) this sonnet; (2) the Sonnets generally.

3 these contènts i.e. what is contained in these verses (with reference to 'rhyme' (2) in either sense).

4 Than unswept . . . time Than in dust-covered (i.e. 'unswept') stone smeared over by unclean, slovenly ('sluttish') time ('time' being pictured as an untidy, lazy servant). The context requires 'in' after 'Than', parallel to 'in these contènts' in line 3.

4 stone (1) gravestone set in the church pavement on which the memorial inscription is rendered illegible by accumulated dust and the footsteps of the congregation; (2) uncared-for upright tomb or monument (the prey of dust and passing time). Compare 107.13–14 and *Cor.* 2.3.119: 'The dust on antique time would lie unswept.'

5 wasteful laying waste, causing devastation, ruin.

5 statues overturn bring memorial statues to ruin.

6 broils tumults, turmoils (usually internal disturbances as distinguished from foreign 'war[s]' (5)).

6 root out destroy, ruin.

6 work of masonry handiwork created by the mason's skill ('masonry').

7 Nor . . . nor Neither . . . nor.

7 Mars his i.e. Mars's (old form of the genitive; see Abbott 217). Compare *Tro.* 2.1.53: 'Mars his idiot!'

7 quick fast-acting, lively.

7 burn By a loose form of zeugma, 'burn' here serves as the verb for both 'Mars his sword' and 'war's', even though a sword cannot be said to burn anything. It may be argued, however, that Shakespeare considered 'Mars his sword' as a figurative attribute of 'war' which resulted in burning and destruction.

8 living record i.e. 'this pow'rful rhyme' (2).

9 all oblivious enmity i.e. all the hostile forces that work to produce oblivion (= the state of being forgotten).

10 pace forth stride out confidently (i.e. despite death and oblivion you will continue to 'advance', as it were, in the face of the enemy).

10 still (1) always; (2) nevertheless.

10 find room occupy a (secure) place.

11 Even An intensive or emphatic particle.

11 in the eyes . . . posterity in the opinion of all future generations (because you will be 'seen' in 'this pow'rful rhyme' (2) and thus read by the eyes of 'all posterity').

12 That Antecedent uncertain: (1) 'eyes' or 'posterity' (taken as a plural); (2) 'you' or 'praise' (linking 'That' to the person addressed). Syntactically, (2) is less likely than (1).

12 wear . . . doom will survive ('wear . . . out') in this world until the Day of Judgement ('ending doom', i.e. the 'ending' of the world; 'doom' = judgement). Perhaps 'wear out' involves a suggestion of 'exhaust to its final moment' (Hood).

13 So, till . . . arise Thus until the Day of Judgement when ('that') you arise as yourself (i.e. reunited in body and soul). See the burial service in the Book of Common Prayer: 'and when that dreadful day of the general resurrection shall come, make him to rise also with the just and righteous, and receive this body again to glory, then made pure and incorruptible'.

14 in this (1) in 'these contènts' (line 3); (2) in 'your praise' (line 10).

14 dwell Picks up 'find room' in line 10.

14 lovers' eyes (1) eyes of those who have experienced a love like ours; (2) eyes that in reading 'your praise' (10) will love you.

Sonnet 56

1 love i.e. 'The spirit of love' (8), not the beloved.

1 force strength, efficacy.

2 edge sharpness, keenness of desire. Lines 2–8 develop the common analogy between eating and sexual desire ('appetite', 'feeding', 'fill', 'hungry', 'fullness'). There is also a subsidiary analogy with the blade of a knife or weapon in lines 1–4 ('force', 'edge', 'blunter', 'sharp'ned', 'might') (Hood).

2 appetite lust. Compare 118.1–4.

3 Which i.e. appetite.

3 but only for.

3 allayed satisfied, alleviated.

4 Tomorrow sharp'ned i.e. (and) tomorrow is sharpened.

4 sharp'ned . . . might i.e. appetite is renewed in all its original ('former') strength ('might').

4 his its.

5 So, love, be thou i.e. love, behave like appetite. 'love' as in line 1 = 'The spirit of love'.

5–6 fill / Thy hungry eyes Compare the figurative expression 'to eat up (or devour) with the eyes'.

The eyes (i.e. the sense of sight) were thought of as the 'ports' through which love (or lust) was conveyed to the heart.

6 even Slurred as if monosyllabic.

6 wink with fullness close drowsily (as in sleep) with satiety ('fullness').

7 see again i.e. look once again with 'hungry eyes'.

7–8 kill / The spirit of love deaden the vitality of ('kill'; *OED* Kill *v* 3a) (1) love itself, (2) the vital principle ('spirit') which informs love. Compare lines 1–8 with *TN* 1.1.1–15 on the theme of satiety in 'the spirit of love'.

8 perpetual dullness continuing, permanent lethargy, sluggishness (with play on 'dull' = blunt, lacking sharpness or edge, as in the knife image in 'blunter' (2) and 'sharp'ned' 4).

9–12 This quatrain, while generally related to the renewal-of-love theme, is vaguely realised and its tone and intent stand in awkward relation to the first eight lines and the final couplet. There is a suggestion in these lines of the separation theme: a pair of newly betrothed lovers standing on the opposite banks of an ocean estuary renewing their love by casting longing looks toward each other, or in the direction where they think the other may be (suggested perhaps by the Hero and Leander story), but the separation theme does not arise naturally out of the appetite/love analogy of the preceding lines, where there is little or no suggestion of impeding temporal or spatial division, only the danger of satiety. Hood suggests there may well be some unfocused association between the renewal of the tide in the estuary and the renewal of love's force.

9 sad int'rim period of apathy. 'sad' carries both the sense of 'heavy' or 'dull' (compare 'dullness' (8)) and 'sorrowful', with, perhaps, some reference to the period of satiety or 'sadness' following sexual orgasm.

9 like the ocean be i.e. be compared to the ocean (or sea).

10 parts the shore i.e. divides the land bordering on the sea ('shore'), thus forming a bay or estuary by which the newly betrothed lovers ('two contracted new') are separated.

11 daily Picks up the 'daily' renewal of appetite and love in lines 4 and 7.

11 banks i.e. the opposite 'banks' of the bay or estuary.

11 that so that.

12 Return of love Echoes 'love, renew thy force' in line 1.

12 more . . . view i.e. when they see one another (or think of seeing one another) the 'view' from their respective 'banks' will be more greatly pleasurable or blissful ('blest'). Alternatively, when they see the tide renewed in the estuary, the prospect will be made more attractive by a sense of the corresponding renewal of love's force (Hood). 'view' picks up

the eye imagery in lines 6–7, and suggests a kind of reunion, though of a less physical nature than that urged in lines 1–8.

13 As call it (Or) as one might call it (i.e. 'this sad int'rim' (9)). Following Capell/Malone, Q's 'As' was usually emended to 'Or' or 'Else' (spelled as 'Els', graphically easier to explain than 'Or') until Sisson (*New Readings*, 1, 212) defended Q and glossed 'As we call it' as 'As (who should) call it'. Recent editors (except Wells, who reads 'Or') retain Q's 'As', though it must be admitted that 'Or' makes easier sense; my gloss takes 'As' as an ellipsis for 'Or as'.

13 winter i.e. the 'dead' season, an interim between autumn and spring or summer.

13 care grief, trouble, anxiety.

14 Makes summer's welcome i.e. the welcome given to the advent of summer (the height of the year compared to the height of love renewed).

14 thrice . . . rare i.e. more splendid ('rare', with play on 'rare' = unusual, special) because thrice more wished for (a reading supported, as Ingram and Red path note, by the Q comma after 'welcome'). Most editors (since Capell) omit the comma, thus making the two phrases parallel (i.e. 'thrice more wished' and 'more rare').

Sonnet 57

The tone of apparent servility in Sonnets 57 and 58 (a linked pair) is more distressing to a modern reader than it would have been to an Elizabethan, who would have recognised it as part of the conventionally sentimental submissiveness expected of a lover in the sonnet tradition. The 'you' of these two sonnets is probably the youth, not the unfaithful mistress referred to in 40–2 (see the implications of 57.10 and 58.9–12). Some recent critics read 57 and 58 ironically (see Mahood, p. 109, and P. J. Martin, pp. 71–2).

1–2 tend / Upon wait on (as a 'slave'). As Booth points out, the sonnet turns in good part on the theme of 'waiting' (in a temporal sense).

2 desire (1) wishes; (2) lust (both of which, as Kerrigan suggests, comparing the theme of 56, alter from 'time to time').

3 I have . . . spend i.e. no time is, in any way, 'precious' to me unless I spend it actively (not just 'waiting') in satisfying your 'desire' (2).

4 services to do duties to perform (with play on the sexual meaning of 'to do service' = to copulate).

4 require (1) command, (2) demand (them), i.e. 'precious time' and 'services'.

5 chide scold, rebuke.

5 world-without-end hour i.e. time that seems to be endless. Compare the service of Matins in the Book of Common Prayer: 'As it was in the beginning, is now, and ever shall be: world without end', and *LLL* 5.2.788–9: 'A time methinks too short / To make a world-without-end bargain in'.

6 my sovereign i.e. 'you' (Shakespeare uses the term for both men and women).
6 watch the clock i.e. wait impatiently, longingly (or as one might say 'A watched clock never strikes').
6 for you i.e. (1) until the time comes when you 'require' (4) my 'services' (4); (2) until you are present (anticipating the 'bitterness of absence' in line 7).
7 Nor think Nor dare I think (compare the construction in lines 5 and 9).
7 bitterness misery, pain.
7 sour (1) extremely unpleasant; (2) bitter-tasting (playing on the literal meaning of 'bitterness'). Compare 39.10: 'sour leisure'.
8 have bid . . . adieu i.e. whenever, on occasion ('once'), you may wish to say good-bye to your (1) slave, (2) lover ('servant'). The implication is that the poet must 'watch the clock' impatiently until 'you' are ready to return and acknowledge him again.
9 jealous suspicious, mistrustful (of any rival).
9 thought Probably carries, as often, the sense of 'melancholy thought'.
10 Where . . . be i.e. when you are absent from me.
10 or your affairs suppose i.e. or imagine ('suppose') what you may be doing ('your affairs'). 'affairs' may also suggest that the 'you' is a person of fortune or rank, a 'man of affairs'; 'affair' (or 'affaire') meaning a 'sexual liaison' is not recorded until the early eighteenth century.
11 sad (1) sorrowful; (2) trustworthy, steady; (3) earnest, serious.
11 stay wait.
12 Save where . . . those Except how happy or fortunate you make those who are in your presence (in contrast to the 'bitterness of absence' (7) then being felt by the poet).
13 So true a fool is love Love (i.e. my love for you or the *Idea* of love) is such a (1) complete, absolute (2) trustworthy, constant (a) dupe, (b) simple-minded attendant ('fool', in a general sense, one who serves his master (here 'you') faithfully under all circumstances). There is probably some irony in the shift from 'slave' to 'fool'. Compare 124.13 ('the fools of Time') and 137.1 ('Thou blind fool, Love'), and contrast 116.9 ('Love's not Time's fool'). Rosaline treats the lover/fool analogy in *LLL* 5.2.59–68.
13 will (1) choice of action; (2) sexual desire (compare 'desire' in line 2). Q reads 'Will' and some critics suggest Shakespeare is punning on 'Will[iam]' as he does in 135, 136, and 143, where, however, 'Will' is not only capitalised but italicised in Q. If a pun *is* intended, then 'that in . . . ill' (13–14) carries a secondary meaning: 'Love (i.e. "he" in line 14) in your Will (i.e. your Will Shakespeare) can think no evil of you, do what you please' (Dowden).
14 he i.e. love.
14 ill evil.

Sonnet 58

See headnote to 57. Sonnet 58 repeats a number of the key words and the 'waiting' theme of 57. Pooler suggests that the order of 57 and 58 should be reversed, the final couplet of 58 leading naturally into the first line of 57.
1–2 That god . . . I should May that god (probably Cupid, the god of Love), that first made me your slave, forbid that I should. Booth takes 'forbid' as an Elizabethan form of the past tense (see *OED*), i.e. 'That god that first made me your slave forbade I should' – a defensible reading, but one that loses what Kerrigan suggests is the poet's appeal (i.e. he feels that he may not be able, without Love's intervention, to master his desire to demand an accounting of the beloved's time and behaviour).
2 in thought (1) (even) in thinking; (2) in (my) melancholy (compare 57.9). There is perhaps a suggestion of 'think to' = presume to (Hood).
2 control (1) regulate, restrain; (2) call to account (in estimating).
2 times of pleasure Compare 'times of your desire' (57.2) – both with sexual suggestion.
3 at your hand i.e. personally from you.
3 account (1) reckoning, computation; (2) statement of personal responsibility (both picking up the image of financial accounting in 'control' (line 2)).
3 to crave For this construction with 'to' (which could be omitted or substituted for by repeating 'should' from line 2), see Abbott 416.
4 vassal (1) servant, retainer (i.e. one who owes feudal homage to his lord); (2) slave (compare line 1 above and 'Being your slave' in 57.1).
4 bound i.e. bound in duty (like a vassal).
4 stay your leisure wait for any moments of free time (when you are not busy with important 'affairs' (compare 57.10) or, perhaps, with my rivals).
5 let me suffer i.e. (with Love's aid) make it possible for me to (1) submit patiently to, (2) undergo the pain of.
5 beck nod, command.
6 imprisoned absence . . . liberty i.e. your absence, which grows out of your freedom of action or choice ('liberty'), is a prison (since it robs me of my only 'liberty', my freedom to contribute personally to your well-being or pleasure). Alternatively, the loved one's freely chosen absence makes him seem locked away in prison (Hood). Compare 'bitterness of absence' in 57.7. 'liberty' also suggests 'sexual licence' and 'libertine behaviour'; compare Jaques's demand in *AYLI* 2.7.47–9: 'I must have liberty / Withal, as large a charter [compare line 9 below] as the wind, / To blow on whom I please', and Duke Senior's rebuke: 'For thou thyself hast been a libertine, / As sensual as the brutish sting itself' (*AYLI* 2.7.65–6).
7 patience . . . sufferance, . . . check (let my) patience, being obedient and docile ('tame') to (1)

suffering, (2) endurance, tolerate ('bide') every rebuff and restraint. See the collation for the Q and other pointings of this line, none of which significantly changes the essential meaning.

8 injury wrong, injustice (to me).

9 where wherever.

9 list wish, desire. The clause 'Be where you list' implies not only place ('where') but also in whatever company.

9 your charter . . . strong i.e. your rights and privileges (granted by a 'charter') are so powerful and overriding. The financial 'account' of line 3 perhaps suggests the idea of a chartered company (Hood).

10–11 privilege . . . will use your time with freedom and licence ('privilege your time') to do whatever you wish ('To what you will'). Malone's emendation ('time: Do' and retaining Q comma after 'will'), formerly adopted by a number of editors, though it makes for neater syntax ('Do' paralleling the imperative 'Be' in line 9) and looks back to 'Though you do any thing' in 57.14, is unnecessary, since 'To' may be taken to imply 'to do'.

12 self-doing (1) done by yourself; (2) done to yourself; and, perhaps, (3) done to me (i.e. whatever you do to yourself you do to me, lovers being 'one').

12 crime sin, wrong-doing (compare 'injury' (8)), here probably used without any intended sense of an illegal act. Hood compares Spenser, *Faerie Queene*, II, xii, lxxv, 6–9: 'Gather therefore the Rose, whilest yet is prime, / For soone comes age, that will her pride deflowre: / Gather the Rose of love, whilest yet is time, / Whilest loving thou mayst loved be with equall crime.'

13 I am to wait i.e. I must await your pleasure (as your 'slave' I have no other choice).

13 so under such circumstances.

14 Not blame Not to find fault with.

Sonnet 59

The theory of cyclical recurrence, a generally Pythagorean and Stoic concept, underlies the theme of this sonnet, but it was most probably suggested to Shakespeare by the well-known passage in Eccles. 1.9–10: 'What is it that hath been? that that shall be: and what is it that hath been done? that which shall be done: and there is no new thing under the sun. Is there any thing, whereof one may say, Behold this, it is new? It hath been already in the old time that was before us' (Geneva). Compare Tilley T147: 'There is no new thing under the sun', and 123.2–4. Ovid (*Metamorphoses* XV, 252–8; Golding, 282–4) has also been suggested as an influence, though Ovid dwells on never-ceasing change and the inviolability of prime matter rather than on recurring cycles of sameness. Note, however, that Ovid's influence is clear in 60.1–4, and see 126.5 n.

2 how are . . . beguiled to what an extent are our mental faculties deceived or deluded. Compare

108.1 and *A Lover's Complaint*, 209 ('deep-brain'd sonnets').

3 labouring i.e. as with birth pains (compare 'bear', 'burthen', 'child' following). Literary composition is often referred to in terms of childbearing.

3 invention (1) selecting topics or arguments for apt treatment (a term in rhetoric); (2) something new or original (to say).

3 bear amiss (1) mistakenly give birth to (i.e. under the misapprehension that the 'child' is a 'new' conception); (2) carry the weight of abortively (i.e. without reward).

4 second . . . child the second brain-child ('burthen') is exactly like the first ('former') child (i.e. a mere refrain or repetition). In other words, nothing 'new' has been created, all the poet's 'birth pains' having been suffered twice for the same 'child'.

5 recòrd (1) memory; (2) historical witness. The word was accented on the first or second syllable, depending on metrical considerations; compare 55.8.

6 Even of To the extent of.

6 five hundred . . . sun Perhaps this simply means 'five hundred years' (an indefinite number for a long, long time), but Ingram and Redpath, following a hint from Pooler, find here a reference to the 'Great Year': 'the period (variously reckoned) after which all the heavenly bodies were supposed to return to their original positions. To those who believed in stellar influence on human affairs this would naturally seem to cause a corresponding recurrence in human affairs. The periods assigned to the Great Year included 540 and 600 years as well as longer periods.' Booth and Kerrigan accept this interpretation, Kerrigan adding that 'hundred' (Q 'hundreth', a common variant form at this time) should be taken as meaning 'great' or 'long hundred' (i.e. six score or 120; see *OED* Hundred *sb* 3) and that 'five hundred' thus refers to a period 600 years ago, 'when the heavens last held their present astrological configuration'.

7 image written description (not here pictorial).

7 àntique ancient.

8 Since At any time since.

8 mind . . . done thought was first expressed ('done') through writing ('in character').

9 say record (in writing, underscoring the verbal rather than pictorial nature of the 'image' (7) being sought).

10 To (1) In response to; (2) In comparison with.

10 this composèd . . . frame this wonderfully articulated composition ('composèd wonder') which is (1) your bodily structure, build, (2) your mental and emotional form. The use of 'frame' in sense (2) (as in 'frame of mind') is not recorded before the Restoration (see *OED* Frame *sb* 6). For the transferred adjective/noun relation in 'composèd wonder', compare 9.14 n.

11 mended amended, improved.

11 whe'er whether (see collation). Booth retains Q 'where', even though it is a common Elizabethan elided spelling of 'whether', and glosses it as 'in what respects' (they are better).

12 Or whether . . . same i.e. or whether recurrence from cycle to cycle (i.e. 'revolution') involves complete qualitative similarity (Ingram and Redpath). See 6 n. above. Taken more generally, the line may mean: 'Or whether time in its course (i.e. "revolution") produces the same things, same qualities, same kinds of men, etc.' (Verity).

13 O sure I am i.e. O indeed I am quite certain (whether or not 'there be nothing new' (1)).

13 wits men of outstanding intellect.

13 former days earlier times (compare 'old world' in line 9).

14 subjects worse men or topics less worthy (than you). The phrase, however, does not entirely escape the ironic implication of 'subjects even worse than you are', an implication that resonates with some earlier and later criticism of the youth.

14 admiring wondering. The final couplet changes the focus of the sonnet and rather weakly reverts to the commonplace idea that the youth is superior to 'subjects' celebrated by writers of the past (see headnote to 53).

Sonnet 60

Sonnet 60 returns to the themes of Time the Destroyer and the immortality promised through the poet's verse. See 15 (headnote) and 19.1–2.

1–4 Like as . . . contend Compare Ovid, *Metamorphoses* xv, 178–85 (Golding, 198–205): 'Things eb and flow, and every shape is made too passe away. / The tyme itself continually is fleeting like a brooke. / For neyther brooke nor lyghtsomme tyme can tarrye still. But looke / As every wave dryves other foorth, and that that commes behynd / Bothe thrusteth and is thrust itself: Even so the tymes by kynd / Doo fly and follow bothe at once, and evermore renew. / For that that was before is left, and streyght there dooth ensew / Anoother that was never erst.'

1 Like as Just as (see Franz 583c).

1 make press strongly. A nautical term for the tide coming to the full (see *OED* Make *v* [1] 72 – in the intransitive use, which this example clearly predates) (Hood).

2 minutes The use of 'minutes' rather than 'hours' or 'years' (both of which can be disyllabic in Shakespeare) emphasises the shortness and fleetingness of life.

2 end Although lines 3–4 turn out to be an independent clause, retaining the Q comma after 'end', instead of the usual editorial semicolon, 'hasten[s]' (2) the 'forwards' (4) movement so integral to this quatrain.

3 An extension of the idea of one wave replacing another. As Booth (*An Essay*, pp. 153–4) points

out, the line does not make literal sense: 'waves don't exchange places with each other'.

3 Each i.e. each wave (though a combined referent to 'waves' and 'minutes' is just possible).

3 goes before precedes (it).

4 In sequent . . . contend (They) strive, labouring successively one after another ('In sequent toil'), ever onward (i.e. the waves like time ('minutes' (2)) never turn back). Perhaps, however, 'all' should be taken as an adjective modifying 'Each (wave)', i.e. 'they all strive'. 'contend' may also suggest 'fight' or 'combat', thus preparing for 'fight' in line 7.

5–12 Nativity . . . mow Once again Ovid's *Metamorphoses* (xv, 218–36; Golding, 240–60) seems to be working in Shakespeare's mind: 'Dame Nature put too [i.e. to] conning hand and suffred not that wee / Within our moothers streyned womb should ay distressed bee, / But brought us out too aire, and from our prison set us free. / . . . Within a season tho / He [i.e. the child] wexing fowerfooted lernes like savage beastes too go. / . . . From that tyme growing strong and swift, he passeth foorth the space / Of youth, and also wearing out his middle age a pace, / Through drooping ages steepye path he ronneth out his race. / This age dooth undermyne the strength of former yeeres, and throwes / It downe . . . / And *Helen* when shee saw her aged wrincles in / A glasse, wept also . . . / Thou tyme, the eater up of things, and age of spyghtfull teene, / Destroy all things. And when that long continuance hath them bit, / You leysurely by lingring death consume them every whit.'

5 Nativity (1) The new-born child (abstract for concrete); (2) The moment of birth (in astrology a child's 'nativity' or horoscope was reckoned in terms of the planetary configurations of the 'heavens' at the precise moment the child was born).

5 once . . . light i.e. when once (or at the time that) 'Nativity' is released from the darkness of the womb into the broad expanse ('main') of light (i.e. the realm of earth under the sun and the vast expanse of the heavens). The sea imagery in lines 1–4 suggested 'the main of light', since Shakespeare most often associates 'main' with the sea or ocean (compare 64.7 and *MV* 5.1.97: 'the main of waters').

6 Crawls Moves slowly (as a child on all fours). Looks back to the first meaning of 'Nativity' in line 5.

6 being Treated here as a monosyllable.

6 crowned blessed by a successful outcome (i.e. in achieving 'maturity'). The suggestion of royal status in 'crowned' and 'glory' (7) gives the general metaphor of human growth, failure, and decline a momentous political dimension and application (Hood).

7 Crookèd Malignant (which, joined with 'eclipses', picks up the astrological suggestion in the second meaning of 'Nativity' (5)).

7 **eclipses** (1) obscuration of the sun, moon, etc.; (2) obscuration, loss of splendour, generally. Compare 35.3 and *Rape of Lucrece*, 1224: 'Why her two suns [i.e. eyes] were cloud-eclipsed so.'

7 **glory** (1) splendour; (2) state of life being at its height or prime ('maturity'). This description of the child's slow growth to 'maturity' is couched in terms of the sun ('main of light') rising, moving up to the meridian at noon (its 'crown'), and setting, suffering 'Crookèd eclipses' as it declines into night (i.e. death).

8 **Time that gave** i.e. Time which contributed the 'minutes' (2) leading to 'maturity' (6).

8 **confound** destroy, ruinate. Compare 5.5–6.

9 **transfix** (1) pierce through (as with a dart; compare 'delves' (10)); (2) remove, unfix (meanings for which *OED* offers no authority, but which are felt by some critics to be called for by the context). J. Poole, *English Parnassus* (1677), p. 571, reads 'ungloss' for 'transfix', a word which, though unknown to *OED*, would mean 'remove the gloss from' – possibly, at some stage, a Shakespearean revision.

9 **flourish set on youth** (1) blooming or blossoming condition which nature sets on the prime of youth; (2) ostentatious embellishment with which youth decorates ('set on') itself (Ingram and Redpath suggest a possible reference to cosmetic painting).

10 **delves the parallels** digs the wrinkles (literally, 'parallels' = military trenches, compare 2.2: 'And dig deep trenches in thy beauty's field', and 'time's furrows' in 22.3). Connecting this with 'transfix' and 'flourish', Hood detects an allusion to the tracks made by the horses on either side of the central bar in jousting.

11 **rarities of nature's truth** choicest creatures produced by the perfection ('truth') of nature. Compare 1.1: 'fairest creatures'.

12 **stands** (1) flourishes; (2) exists; (3) remains upright.

12 **but** except.

12 **scythe** Compare 12.13: 'And nothing' gainst Time's scythe can make defence' (see note).

13 **to times in hope** unto ages ('times') expected but yet unborn ('in hope').

13–14 **stand, / Praising . . . hand** (Unlike created things in nature, which cannot 'stand'), the poet's verse, honouring your excellence ('worth'), will endure unchanged ('stand') in spite of Time's merciless hand. 'hand' picks up the agent in the scythe/mowing image in line 12.

Sonnet 61

See also Sonnets 27 and 43 for the theme of sleep and dreaming – a common topic of love sonnets; Sidney's *Astrophil and Stella* (1591), 38 and 39, were especially influential. Booth suggests that 61 is a 'perverse play' on the proverb 'One friend watches for [i.e. cares for, looks after] another' (Tilley F716).

1 **Is it thy will** i.e. do you wish that.

1 **image** form. Compare 'shadow' in 27.10 and 43.5, 6, and 'shadows' in line 4.

1–3 **open . . . broken** An imperfect, if assonantal, rhyme, very rare in the Sonnets (see 120.9, 11). Shakespeare repeats this rhyme in *Venus and Adonis*, 47, 48.

2 **heavy eyelids** Compare 'drooping eyelids' in 27.7.

2 **weary** (1) tired; (2) irksome, tedious, burdensome. The night is 'weary' because (a) it is the natural time of weariness (Hood) and (b) it reflects the poet's mood.

4 **shadows like to thee** mental images in your likeness.

5 **spirit** spiritual essence, soul (with suggestion of 'ghostly apparition').

6 **far from home** Touches on the separation theme in 27 and 43, etc. Compare 'From me far off' in line 14.

7 **find out . . . me** discover (through prying) the shameful deeds ('shames') committed by me in my leisure time ('idle hours'). Thus interpreted, 'shames and idle hours' may be taken as an example of hendiadys. Compare *Venus and Adonis* (dedication): 'I . . . vow to take advantage of all idle houres.'

8 **scope . . . jealousy** aim, end ('scope') and purport ('tenure') of your suspicion ('jealousy'). 'Tenure' is a common variant form of 'tenour' in Shakespeare and his contemporaries, and, as Hood suggests, this makes possible here an ironic play on the idea of 'jealousy' as central to the agreement between landlord and tenant (*OED* Tenure 2). 'scope and tenure' refers back to 'shames and idle hours', not to 'me'.

9–10 **thy love . . . my love** your love for me . . . (1) my love for you; (2) the beloved (i.e. 'you'). The poet feels that he has flattered the youth in suggesting that his love is 'great' enough (unlike the poet's) to be emotionally disturbed by what the poet may do or not do in his 'idle hours' – only 'true love' (11) cares enough to be jealous.

11 **Mine own true love** = 'my love' in line 10 (in both senses).

11 **my rest defeat** destroy my repose (i.e. sleep).

12 **To** In order to.

12 **play the watchman ever** always act the role of watchman (i.e. one who never sleeps when on 'watch'). In lines 12 and 13, Shakespeare plays on 'watchman' and 'watch' meaning (1) remain awake, (2) look out for, (3) attend upon, and on 'wake' meaning (1) remain awake, (2) hold nightly revel. Sense (3) of 'watch' links lines 12–14 with the 'tending' and 'waiting' theme of Sonnets 57 and 58 (compare 'I am to wait' (58.13) with 'For thee watch I' in 13 below, and the common phrase 'to watch and wait').

13 **For thee** (1) For your sake, on your behalf (because of my 'great' love I 'play the watchman', i.e. 'watch I'); (2) Because of you.

13 **watch ... wake** For the wordplay here, see 12 n. above.

14 **with others ... near** The implication is that the youth (when he should be asleep) is bestowing sexual favours on the poet's rivals (while the poet is 'far off' the 'others' are 'too near', the latter phrase strongly suggesting physical contact). The Q spellings, 'of' (for 'off') and 'to' (for 'too'), are common enough at this period.

Sonnet 62

In Sonnet 62 Shakespeare plays again (see 22, 36, 39) with the question of 'identity': is his real self more or less real than the 'self' he possesses in the beloved? In terms of the convention, the answer is 'less real'. What he thinks he admires in himself is really only what he admires in the beloved.

1 **self-love** arrogant belief in one's own superiority, both physical ('eye' (1), 'face' (5), 'shape' (6)) and spiritual–intellectual ('soul' (2), 'heart' (4), 'truth' (6), 'worth' (7)).

1 **possesseth** engrosses, dominates.

1 **all mine eye** my whole seeing, my sight.

2 **all my every part** all and every part of me. Compare *John* 2.4.38: 'all and every part', and Drayton, *Mortimeriados* (1596), 1169: 'Shee's all in all, and all in every part.'

3 **remedy** cure ('sin' being considered as a disease).

4 **grounded inward in my heart** firmly fixed in the innermost parts ('inward') of my (1) heart (as the seat of the emotions), (2) mind. Compare the phrase in one of the collects of the Communion Service in the Book of Common Prayer: 'grafted inwardly in our hearts'.

5 **Methinks** It seems to me.

5 **gracious** attractive, pleasing (with, perhaps, a suggestion of 'condescendingly kind', where 'face' = 'look').

6 **shape so true** bodily form so perfect. Compare *Lear* 1.2.8: 'my shape as true'.

6 **truth of such account** (1) constancy, (2) honesty of so great ('such') value or estimation.

7 **And for ... define** And (I) personally ('for myself') (1) decide upon, (2) fix the amount of my own merit ('worth', i.e. physical and spiritual 'value'). The line has raised problems because there is no stated subject for 'define', but the majority of editors have felt that the 'I' (supplied above) is sufficiently suggested by 'Methinks' (5) to render any of the proposed emendations unnecessary.

8 **As I ... surmount** So that, as a result of such 'defining', I suppose myself to surpass ('surmount') all others ('other') in all meritorious qualities ('worths'). Compare *1H6* 5.3.191: 'Bethink thee on her virtues that surmount'.

9–14 **But when ... days** The sestet absolves the poet of the 'Sin of self-love' by declaring that it is

not his 'self' he thus praises and values so extravagantly but his 'other self' (i.e. the beloved), who is 'all [his] every part' (2) of him (lovers being two in one; compare 39.1–2).

9–10 Compare Daniel, *Delia* (1592), 38.9–10: 'When, if she grieve to gaze her in her glasse, / Which, then presents her winter-withered hew'.

9 **glass** mirror.

9 **indeed** in actual fact.

10 **Beated** Beaten, battered (by time) (an irregular but possible past-participial formation; see Abbott 344). See collation for suggested emendations.

10 **chopped** chapped (variant form), cracked by wrinkles.

10 **with tanned antiquity** by browned or sunburned age. 'tanned' was probably suggested by 'Beated', since beating the hides was part of the tanning process.

11 **quite contrary I read** I interpret ('read') in a way entirely different or opposite.

12 **Self ... iniquity** i.e. to be so much in love with one's self ('Self so self-loving') would be a sin ('iniquity'). Recapitulates the theme of the octet – the 'Sin of self-love', and suggests some reference to the Narcissus myth (Ovid, *Metamorphoses* III, 341–510).

13 **'Tis thee (my self) ... praise** i.e. (Since you and I are one) it is you, the essence of my 'self' ('thee (my self)'), that I am praising when I seem to be praising (merely) myself. The retention of Q's first 'my selfe' as two words (as by Ingram and Redpath) emphasises a significant distinction in relation to 'myself'. In view of 'iniquity' in line 12 and the play on 'my self' and 'myself', the following passage in *R3* (3.1.82–3) seems worth noting: 'Thus, like the formal Vice, Iniquity, / I moralize two meanings in one word.'

14 **Painting** (1) Depicting; (2) Adorning; (3) Flattering (with the implication of cosmetic deception).

14 **age ... days** i.e. old age (reckoned in years) ... youth (reckoned in days). Compare 'youthful morn' in 63.4.

14 **beauty** i.e. both physical and spiritual 'beauty' or 'worth' (7).

Sonnet 63

Though the opening line is closely linked to 62.9–10, Sonnet 63 returns to the themes, last heard in 60, of Time the Destroyer and its antidote: Time and Death defeated by verse. There are indeed, as Hood notes, close conceptual and verbal parallels between 63 and 60. Compare 63.3–4, 4–7, 9–12, 13–14 with 60.9–10, 5–8, 9–12, 13–14 respectively. Compare Daniel, *Delia* (1592), Sonnets 38, 42.

1 **Against** In preparation for the time when.

1 **my love** i.e. the youth. Lines 1–8 are a series of subordinate clauses, restated in 9 by 'For such a time'.

2 **injurious** unjustly hurtful.

2 **crushed and o'erworn** broken down, creased (as if crumpled) and worn out. Compare 'Beated and chopped' in 62.10, Spenser, *Ruines of Rome* (1591), Sonnet 27.6: 'The which injurious time hath quite outworne', and Daniel, *Civil Wars* (1595), III, 14: 'And seeke t'oppresse and weare them out with time'.

3 **hours** i.e. the passing hours (= time).

3 **drained his blood** Time here is pictured as 'draining away' the heat of young blood and replacing it with the cold blood of age (see 2.14 n.).

3 **filled** The contrast with 'drained' almost certainly guarantees that Q 'fild' should be interpreted as 'filld' (i.e. the past tense of 'to fill'), but, as Kerrigan observes, Q 'fild' could also be the past tense of 'to file' (i.e. = defiled, sullied, corrupted). Note, however, that 'fild' is the regular spelling of 'filld' elsewhere in the Sonnets (see 17.2; 86.13).

3 **brow** forehead.

5 **travelled** (1) moved, journeyed; (2) laboured, toiled. Since 'travail' and 'travel' were then interchangeable spellings for both verbs, the Q spelling 'travaild' allowed for both meanings, a choice which 'travelled' (without a special note) might seem to limit.

5 **age's steepy night** i.e. the precipitous ('steepy') descent into the darkness (and death) of old age (contrasted with 'youthful morn' in line 4). Compare Ovid, *Metamorphoses* XV, 225–7 (Golding, 247–9): 'he passeth foorth the space / Of youth . . . / Through drooping ages steepye path he ronneth out his race' (see also 'wrinkles' in line 4 and 60.5–12 n.).

6 **king** (1) ruler; (2) highest example.

7 **vanishing, or vanished . . . sight** i.e. (all his 'beauties' are) in the process of disappearing from sight (like the sun after noon), or have disappeared (like the sun after setting into night).

8 **Stealing . . . spring** (1) Robbing, (2) stealthily, secretly pilfering the precious store ('treasure') of his youth ('spring'; compare 'morn' in line 4).

9 **For** In preparation for (repeats 'Against' in line 1).

9 **such a time** i.e. the time or moment described in lines 1–8.

9 **fortify** build defences.

10 **Against** In opposition to.

10 **confounding** destroying, defeating.

10 **age's cruel knife** i.e. the merciless, savage knife wielded by Time as exemplified in old age. Though classical allusions in the Sonnets are rare (see Sonnet 53), the word 'knife' here, followed as it is by 'cut from memory' in line 11, suggests the operation of the Parcae, the three goddesses of destiny, who wove and cut the thread of human life.

11 **That he** So that Time.

11 **memory** living or future record.

12 **love's beauty** i.e. the beauty of my loved one. There may also be a hint of 'the beauty of my feelings of love' (Hood).

12 **though my lover's life** i.e. even though Time may have cut off my beloved's physical life.

13 **black lines** 'black' because written or printed in ink (compare 'in black ink' in 65.14). 'black', though conventionally treated as antithetical to 'beauty' (compare 127.1–2), here serves to heighten and set off 'beauty' by contrast; compare *MM* 2.4.79–81: 'as these black masks / Proclaim an enshield beauty ten times louder / Than beauty could, displayed', and *Rom.* 1.1.221–2.

13 **seen** In contrast to 'vanished out of sight' in line 7.

14 **still green** ever, always alive and flourishing ('green', as in the 'spring' (8) of his life). Compare *LLL* 1.2.86: 'Green indeed is the color of lovers.'

Sonnet 64

For the themes of Time and change in lines 1–8 compare *2H4* 3.1.45–53: 'O God, that one might read the book of fate, / And see the revolution of the times / Make mountains level, and the continent, / Weary of solid firmness, melt itself / Into the sea, and other times to see / The beachy girdle of the ocean / Too wide for Neptune's hips; how chance's mocks / And changes fill the cup of alteration / With divers liquors!'; and Ovid, *Metamorphoses* XV, 261–7 (Golding, 287–93): 'Even so have places often-tymes exchaunged theyr estate. / For I have seene it sea which was substanciall ground alate, / Ageine where sea was, I have seene the same become dry lond, / . . . Deepe valleyes have by watershotte beene made of levell ground, / And hilles by force of gulling oft have intoo sea beene worne.' See also the headnotes to 15 and 55.

1–12 A periodic sentence, built on a series of subordinate 'When' clauses, and only resolved by lines 11–12. This structure confirms that Q's pointing of line 11 (see collation) is inadequate.

1 **fell** savage, ruthless, destructive (conveys something of the sense of 'to fell' = to cut down, kill). With 'Time's fell hand' compare 'age's cruel knife' in 63.10, 'hand' and 'knife' being essentially interchangeable as the instruments of Time.

2 **rich** splendid, sumptuous, costly.

2 **proud** lordly, prideful.

2 **cost** (1) financial outlay; (2) costly things or objects. Compare 91.10: 'Richer than wealth, prouder than garments' cost'.

2 **outworn buried age** i.e. antiquity lost in oblivion, 'buried age' being consumed or worn out (by time). See 63.2 and 68.1. There is, perhaps, a suggestion of an extremely costly funeral monument that has been 'defaced' (1), perhaps literally, by the operation of 'Time's fell hand'; compare 55.1–4. Hood

compares Daniel's reflections in *Musophilus* (1599), 325–90, on 'gorgeous tombs' generally and Stonehenge specifically as the destroyed 'mockers of vain glory'. As J. C. Ransom (*The World's Body*, 1938, p. 283) notes, the line 'strongly resists paraphrase'.

3 When sometime . . . I see (1) When I see formerly lofty towers; (2) When on occasion I see lofty towers.

3 down rased levelled to the ground ('down' is intensive).

4 brass eternal slave i.e. (1) (even) everlasting brass (or bronze) being a slave; (2) (even) brass (or bronze) being forever ('eternal') a slave. 'Brass eternal' (with its Latinate inversion) recalls Horace's famous 'aere perennius' (see 15 headnote), referring to his writing as a 'monument more lasting than bronze', the implication being that 'bronze/brass' is otherwise the most time-proof of things. Compare 'brass impregnable' in *R2* 3.2.168. The reference to 'brass' here may be to the kind of brass funeral memorial laid into the floor of churches, which 'in time' was 'defaced' (line 1) by being continually walked on.

4 mortal rage (1) deadly destruction; (2) human destructiveness.

5–6 gain / Advantage on improve its position in relation to (i.e. win territory from the shore like a conqueror).

6 kingdom royal territory.

7 firm soil i.e. *terra firma*. Compare Ovid's 'solidissima tellus' (see headnote above).

7 win of (1) prevail upon; (2) gain from.

7 wat'ry main great expanse of waters (i.e. the ocean). See 60.5 n.

8 Increasing . . . store Increasing the plenty ('store') of the ocean with the loss of the land, and contrariwise the loss of the ocean with the plenty of the land's gain on it (a continuing cycle of reciprocal depletion and growth; compare *2H4* 3.1.45–51).

9 interchange of state reciprocal exchange (1) in condition, (2) of territory.

10 state itself i.e. the very concept of greatness, rank, magnificence, political order (picking up and expanding the meanings of 'state' in line 9).

10 confounded to decay wasted to (1) a decayed state, (2) death.

11 Ruin i.e. all the examples of Time's decay, destruction, and change cited in lines 1–10.

11 thus in such a way, as a result.

11 ruminate muse, ponder.

12 That Such.

12 my love i.e. my beloved.

13–14 This thought . . . lose This thought, which cannot refrain from weeping because it now has what it fears to lose (in the future), is like (the stroke of) death (i.e. the thought that Time will some day come and take his beloved from him is for the poet a killing thought). Compare *AWW* 1.3.213–15: 'O then give pity / To her whose state is such that

cannot choose / But lend and give where she is sure to lose.'

Sonnet 65
Sonnet 65 shows obvious links with 63 and 64 in both theme and language.

1 Since Since there are neither (elliptical; see Abbott 403).

1 brass . . . sea Recapitulates the objects on which Time wreaks its ruin in 64.1–8: 'brass' (= 'brass eternal' (4)), 'stone' (= 'lofty towers' (3)), 'earth' (= 'firm soil' (7)), 'boundless sea' (= 'hungry ocean' (5)).

2 But sad . . . power But their strength or capacity ('their power') is prevailed over by (1) sorrowful, calamitous, (2) determined, inescapable ('sad') dissolution or ruin ('mortality') (i.e. they, like man, are 'mortal' by nature and subject to Time). For 'sad' = 'determined, firmly established in purpose', see *OED* Sad *adj* 2.

3 with against.

3 this rage Compare 'mortal rage' (64.4).

3 beauty If seemingly indestructible things like 'brass, nor stone', etc. cannot withstand the ravages of Time, what chance has something as fragile as 'beauty'?

3 hold a plea be able to plead its case or suit.

4 action (1) operation; (2) legal suit (picking up the legal terminology in 'plea' (line 3) and anticipating in the sense of 'military action' the battle and siege imagery of line 6).

4 stronger (1) more enduring; (2) more powerful; (3) more resistant.

4 flower Often used as a symbol of the shortness of human existence; compare, for example, Job 14.1–2: 'Man that is born of woman is of short continuance . . . He shooteth forth as a flower, and is cut down: he vanisheth as a shadow, and continueth not' (Geneva).

5 summer's honey breath (1) the sweet ('honey') warm winds of summertime (which bring 'flowers' to maturity); (2) the sweet perfume of the summer flower (Hood). Compare 54.8.

5 hold out endure, resist.

6 wrackful destructive, ruinous (variant form of 'wreckful').

6 siege . . . days besieging by the crushing blows ('batt'ring') of time ('days' here = the hours of passing time).

7 impregnable able (seemingly) to 'hold out' (6) against all attacks (continuing, as does 'gates of steel' in line 8, the 'siege' imagery from line 6). See 64.4 n. The unqualified use of 'impregnable' here intensifies the idea of Time's irresistible power (Hood).

7 stout strong (in resistance).

8 but Time decays but Time nevertheless decays (them, i.e. 'rocks' and 'gates'). The omission of the object of the verb 'decays' gives a sense of

Time's destructive power as absolute and indeterminate (Hood).

9 fearful meditation contemplation full of dread and terror ('meditation' referring to the contents of lines 1–8). Compare a meditative poem like Spenser's *The Ruines of Time* (1591) and his translation, *Ruines of Rome* (1591), of Du Bellay's *Antiquitez de Rome*.

9–10 Where, alack, / Shall . . . hid Where, alas, shall Time's most precious jewel (= 'beauty', with special reference to the poet's beloved) hide itself in safety from (being cast into) Time's chest (here conceived of as (1) a miser's coffer; (2) a coffin, where it will be lost in oblivion). The jewel may be called 'Time's jewel' because it is generated *in* time; Time thus first gives and then takes back its gift (the idea of 60.8). Compare *Tro.* 3.3.145–7: 'Time hath, my lord, a wallet at his back, / Wherein he puts alms for oblivion, / A great-siz'd monster of ingratitudes.'

11 hand Booth suggests a play here on 'hand' = handwriting, which anticipates the poet's hand *writing* verses in 'black ink' in line 14.

11 swift foot Time pictured as a 'swift runner'. See 19.5 n.

12 spoil of beauty spoliation of, injury to, beauty (with play on 'spoil' = plunder taken from an enemy in battle, picking up the earlier military imagery in lines 6 and 8) Capell's emendation of Q 'or' to 'o'er' is graphically closest, but almost all editors prefer Malone's 'of' (see collation); recently, Booth alone has retained Q's 'or' and glosses the line as 'no one can prohibit time's ravages or exclude the beloved's beauty from time's ravages'.

12 forbid (1) rule out, prohibit; (2) restrain, hinder.

13 miracle Refers here primarily to the idea that 'black ink' can make beauty 'shine' in opposition to the conventional idea that 'black' and 'beauty' were antithetical (see 63.13 n.); underlying this, however, is the usual claim (also a 'miracle') that the beloved will be immortalised by the poet's verses.

14 black ink See 63.13 n.

14 my love i.e. the beloved (with possible suggestion of 'his love for the beloved').

14 still always, eternally.

14 bright clear and unsullied by decay or death.

Sonnet 66
The world-weary, 'tired' tone of this sonnet has been compared with that of *Rape of Lucrece*, 848–924 (particularly 904–7), *MV* 2.9.41–9, and Hamlet's 'To be, or not to be' soliloquy (*Ham.* 3.1.55–87; particularly 69–75). The rhetorical structure, unique in the Sonnets, represents an extreme use of the figure of repetition called anaphora (here, ten consecutive lines beginning 'And'), with the result that, though the conventional rhyme-scheme is preserved, the usual movement of quatrain construction is submerged.

1 Tired with all these (1) Worn out, exhausted, (2) satiated by (observing and experiencing) all the following evils ('these').

1 cry (1) call out loudly; (2) supplicate.

2 As Such as, as for example.

2 to behold i.e. in beholding, when I behold.

2 desert merit, worth. An editor has the choice of capitalising the numerous personifications in this sonnet (as do Ingram and Redpath) or not (as almost all editors); Q capitalises only 'Nothing' (3), 'Folly' (10), 'Truth' and 'Simplicity' (11).

2 desert a beggar born a meritorious person born destitute (and therefore with little chance of success or happiness).

3 needy nothing a person worth 'nothing' and lacking in moral qualities – the opposite of 'desert'. Compare *Cym.* 3.4.132–3: 'With that harsh, noble, simple nothing, / That Cloten'.

3 trimmed decked out.

3 jollity (1) splendour, finery; (2) carefree, exuberant revelry. Line 3 suggests a court jester (i.e. a kind of 'nothing') dressed in motley.

4 faith (1) constancy, fidelity; (2) belief; (3) obligation.

4 unhappily (1) sinfully; (2) unfortunately.

4 forsworn (1) denied, repudiated; (2) broken.

5 gilded honour golden-appearing ('gilded') rank or position. 'gilded' does not here suggest false seeming, as it often does in Shakespeare (Hood).

5 misplaced wrongly bestowed or borne (by someone not worthy).

6 maiden virtue i.e. virginity, maidenhead.

6 rudely strumpeted violently prostituted or whored.

7 right perfection true, genuine perfection (where 'perfection' probably = 'beauty'; see Tucker).

7 disgraced (1) dishonoured, discredited; (2) disfigured.

8 strength (1) power; (2) authority.

8 limping sway halting, ineffectual rule, authority.

8 disablèd rendered incapable of effective action (compare 'limping'). The pronunciation is quadrisyllabic – 'disab(e)lèd'; see Abbott 477.

9 art letters, learning, science (the exercise of intellect), with possible reference to the 'art of the theatre'.

9 tongue-tied by authority made speechless (hence ineffective) by (1) the 'powers that be' (political, social), (2) perhaps, the stultifying power of earlier precedent.

10 doctor-like i.e. posing as a man of learning and wisdom.

10 skill (1) knowledge; (2) cleverness, expertness.

11 simple truth guileless, artless (1) adherence to principle or belief, (2) honesty, innocence.

11 miscalled pejoratively misnamed.

11 **simplicity** (1) ignorance; (2) foolishness (such as that displayed by a 'simpleton').

12 **captive good . . . ill** imprisoned, enslaved goodness waiting upon ('attending' as a servant) the worst kind ('captain' = chief) of evil. Note the underlying military image set up by 'captive' and 'captain'. Compare 'captain jewels' in 52.8.

14 **Save that to die** Except that in dying.

14 **my love** i.e. my beloved.

14 **alone** solitary. It is unnecessary, I think, to find plays on 'only' (i.e. 'only my love') (Booth) or 'alone' = all one (i.e. 'my love a single thing, one') (Kerrigan).

Sonnet 67

The opening line of Sonnet 67 appears to link it with the evils of the age treated in 66. Sonnet 67 also anticipates the theme of 'false Art' in 68, here figured (line 5) as cosmetic painting ('false painting'). Hood notes that despite a possible hint in line 1 of his collusion with them, the youth is presented as their innocent victim until finally complimented as the enduring model of beauty and virtue. There is also, perhaps, a secondary reference, as Wyndham suggests, to the excessive flattery lavished on the youth by friends and rival poets (see 69).

1 **Ah wherefore . . . live** O why should he have to live in a corrupt and diseased age (the kind of world pictured in 66)? But there may also be a suggestion in lines 1–4 of less flattering questions: 'Why should he (i.e. the youth) who is inwardly infected live to encourage and strengthen sin through his outward beauty?' (compare 69.5–14); or 'Why should he hang out with bad company?' (Vendler).

2 **grace impiety** adorn, set off to advantage sin or wickedness.

3 **That sin by him** So that sin through ('by') him (his 'presence' (2)).

3 **advantage** (1) benefit, profit; (2) superiority.

4 **lace itself with** (1) fasten itself securely with; (2) interlace itself with; (3) trick, trim itself up through.

4 **society** (1) presence; (2) associates.

5 **Why should . . . cheek** Why should those who use cosmetics ('false painting') be able to imitate (the rosy colour of) his cheek? The use of cosmetics by young gallants was not uncommon at this period. Compare 127.5–8.

6 **dead seeming of** lifeless appearance or semblance from or belonging to ('of'). Cosmetics produce only a lifeless imitation of his natural complexion. Capell's emendation of Q's 'dead seeing' to 'dead seeming' (graphically explained by a MS. 'dead seẽing', where the tilde over the second 'e' (= 'em') was missed by the compositor) is here adopted because there is no lexical authority (in or out of Shakespeare) for 'seeing' in the sense of 'appearance' or 'semblance', though editors (the majority) who

retain 'seeing' so define it (see Booth). It is always possible, of course, that 'seeing' here is a Shakespearean neologism.

6 **hue** (1) complexion, colour; (2) form.

7 **poor beauty** (1) beauty of a lesser degree; (2) poor old Beauty (which is inferior to the beauty of the youth) (Kerrigan).

7 **indirectly** (1) deceitfully; (2) artificially (i.e. by cosmetic painting).

8 **Roses of shadow** Imitation roses (i.e. rosy painted cheeks).

8 **since . . . true** i.e. only because he is in himself the *Idea* (the essence) of the true rose. Compare the youth as 'beauty's rose' in 1.2.

9 **bankrout** bankrupt (variant form), without resources.

10 **Beggared of blood** Impoverished of (good red) blood (i.e. Nature is 'bankrout' in the sense of being drained, its blood thin and pale, by the 'infection' (1) of the age). Alternatively, Hood suggests, if 'Beggared' is in apposition to 'he' in line 9, then the youth is deprived of vigorous blood by the thieving of those obliged to 'steal' it cosmetically from him (line 6).

10 **blush** show rosy red.

10 **lively veins** veins full of life (i.e. pulsing with strong, not weak and pale, red blood).

11 **For she . . . but his** Just because she (Nature) has no (other) treasure-hoard of beauty ('exchequer') except ('but') the youth's. Some editors place a question mark after 'veins' in line 10 and treat lines 11–12 ('For (= Because) . . . gains') as an answer to the question then posed in lines 9–10.

12 **proud of many . . . gains** (1) swollen by, or falsely proud of, the many existing examples of inferior beauty (the only kind she is now able to produce), she (Nature as a creating principle) now survives ('lives') only by drawing upon the interest ('gains') still paid out by the youth's perfect beauty (outer and inner); (2) (nostalgically) proud of the many 'beauties' she had produced 'In days long since' (14), she (Nature) now survives, etc.' The phrase 'proud of many' is obscure and has led to much discussion. Kerrigan adopts Ridley's conjecture ''priv'd' (an apheotic form of 'deprived' used nowhere else by Shakespeare), pointing out that it picks up the financial imagery in 'bankrout' (9), 'Beggared' (10), and 'exchequer' (11), and 'provides a neat paradox when set against *gains*'. There is a suggestion that Nature is herself responsible for the kind of weakening 'infection' referred to in line 1, because, in creating the youth as the *Idea* of outer and inner 'beauty', she has bankrupted ('Beggared' (10)) her 'exchequer' (11) and can now produce only inferior ('painted') copies.

13 **stores** keeps, reserves for future use.

13 **show . . . had** show (as an example) what her 'wealth of beauty' had once been. Compare 68.1–2, 13–14.

14 **since** past. Compare 'days outworn' (68.1).

14 **these last so bad** i.e. these present degenerate days. Douglas Bruster (privately) suggests that Shakespeare may here be recalling 2 Tim. 3.1–4: 'This know also, that in the last days shall come perilous times. For men shall be lovers of their own selves, covetous, boasters, proud, cursed speakers, disobedient to parents, unthankful, unholy, Without natural affection, truce-breakers, false accusers, intemperate, fierce, despisers of them which are good, Traitors, heady, high-minded, lovers of pleasures more than lovers of God' (Geneva).

Sonnet 68

See 67 headnote. Sonnet 68 deals with the distinction between false art and the youth as the epitome of natural beauty.

1 **Thus** For this reason (linking directly with lines 13–14 in 67).

1 **his cheek . . . outworn** i.e. his cheek (= the whole beauty of his form, inner as well as outer) serves as the epitome or very picture ('map') of ages past. Compare 63.2 n., 64.2 n., 'days long since' (67.14), and *Rape of Lucrece*, 1712: 'The face, that map which deep impression bears / Of hard misfortune . . .'

2 **When beauty . . . now** i.e. when, as flowers do now, beauty was content to live and die unadulterated by adventitious 'ornament' (10) (cosmetics and false hair). Compare 127.5–8.

3 **bastard signs** illegitimate, spurious (heraldic) badges or tokens. The 'signs', therefore, are not 'an outward and visible sign of an inward and spiritual grace' (Book of Common Prayer (1604), 'A Catechism'), but a 'sign' of inward and spiritual 'disgrace'.

3 **fair** beauty.

3 **borne** (1) carried about; (2) worn. Compare *Tro.* 3.3.103–4: 'The beauty that is borne here in the face / The bearer knows not.' Until recently most editors read Q's 'borne' as 'born' (= produced, given birth to, thus linking with 'bastard'); the two spellings were interchangeable in Elizabethan usage and allowed a contemporary reader a choice of (or a play on both) meanings.

4 **durst** dared.

4 **inhabit** dwell, live.

4 **living brow** forehead of any living person (anticipates the shift from cosmetics to false hair in the following line).

5 **golden tresses of the dead** The hair of corpses was sometimes bought to furnish material for wigs or hairpieces. 'golden' thus refers not only to colour but to monetary value. Compare lines 5–8 with *MV* 3.2.88–101 (particularly 92–6): 'So are those crisped snaky golden locks, / . . . often known / To be the dowry of a second head, / The skull that bred them in the sepulchre.'

6 **right** proper due.

7 **To** So to.

7 **live . . . life** Used ironically.

8 **Ere** Before (compare line 3).

8 **fleece** hair (suggesting 'woolly'; compare *Tit.* 2.3.34: 'My fleece of woolly hair'), Kerrigan suggests that in 'fleece' and 'golden tresses' (5) there may be some submerged reference to the legendary Golden Fleece of Colchis stolen by Jason with Medea's help.

8 **gay** (1) lively-looking, showy (especially in colouring); (2) speciously attractive.

9 **holy àntique hours** (1) blessed, (2) sinless age ('hours') of long ago ('àntique' = 'days outworn' (1) and, perhaps, the Golden Age).

9 **are seen** may be observed, witnessed.

10 **all ornament** any decoration, embellishment.

10 **itself and true** its essential and true self. Ingram and Redpath, perhaps rightly, keep the Q form 'it self', referring 'it' to 'beauty' (2 and 8) and interpreting 'self' as 'the same throughout'.

11 **Making . . . green** i.e. not, as others do, making use of another's youth ('green') to give him the appearance of being in a flourishing state ('summer').

12 **no old** (1) nothing used or second-hand; (2) no former beauty (Hood).

12 **dress . . . new** deck out, adorn, as others do, his (fading) beauty afresh.

13–14 **And him . . . yore** A variation on the final couplet of 67.

13 **as for** to serve as.

13 **map** See 1 n. above.

13 **store** keep, reserve for future use (compare 67.13).

14 **false Art** i.e. the embellishments, ornaments (= 'bastard signs' (3)) of cosmetics and false hair.

14 **of yore** in past ages.

Sonnet 69

The idea of the youth as a blameworthy contributor to the ill of which he is a victim, suppressed in Sonnet 68, comes to the fore here. See headnotes to 67 and 68.

1 **parts** (1) abilities, attributes; (2) positions (i.e. those 'outward' (5) 'parts' that 'the world's eye doth view').

1 **world's eye** mankind generally.

2 **Want nothing . . . mend** Lack nothing that man's deepest thoughts ('thought of hearts') can improve upon or surpass.

3 **All tongues** i.e. (by synecdoche) all men who speak or write (about you).

3 **souls** = 'hearts' in line 2 (as the seat of the emotions and sentiments in man).

3 **due** proper right. The Q reading 'end' (see collation) is an easy misreading of a MS. 'due', since *d* and *e* and the minim strokes in *u* and *n* are often difficult to distinguish in Secretary hand.

4 **bare** least possible, simple.

4 even so . . . commend i.e. even as in the same 'bare' way foes are forced (by 'truth' and despite themselves) to praise.

5 Thy See collation and 46.14 n.

5 outward external appearance (see line 1, 16.11, and *Venus and Adonis*, 435).

5 outward praise (1) praise of your outward appearance (with a suggestion in 'outward' that the praise lacks the proper substance that would include the 'whole man', inner and outer); (2) public praise (contrasting perhaps with 'their thoughts' in line 11). Ingram and Redpath suggest a possible play in 'outward' on 'uttered'.

5 crowned given regal status (i.e. the highest praise, properly due only to a 'king').

6 those same tongues = 'All tongues' in line 3 and hence includes the poet among the 'churls' (11) as 'seeing farther' (8) (as he had already done in 33–6, 40–2).

6 so thine own (1) in this way, (2) to this extent your proper due (compare 'due' in line 3).

7 In other accents With different ('other') (1) words or language, (2) emphases (the 'difference' being now pejorative instead of laudatory).

7 confound (1) confuse; (2) nullify, destroy.

8 seeing farther penetrating more deeply (i.e. seeing past outward appearance).

8 shown revealed.

9 beauty of thy mind i.e. your inner spiritual and moral qualities (which should reflect the perfection of your outward 'beauty' so evident to the 'eye').

10 that in guess . . . deeds they, by guessing, appraise or estimate ('measure') that (i.e. 'the beauty of thy mind' (9)) by your actions ('deeds').

11 churls i.e. men (= 'They' (9)) who are niggardly or grudging (in awarding praise; compare 'as foes commend' in line 4). Pooler, placing a comma only after 'churls', makes 'their thoughts', not 'they', the referent of 'churls'.

11–12 their thoughts . . . weeds i.e. (inwardly) in their thoughts, although they were willing (or forced by 'truth') to give 'outward praise' (= 'their eyes were kind'), they associate ('add') the grossly offensive smell of weeds with you as 'beauty's rose' ('thy fair flower'), which is, or ought to be, sweet-smelling. 'rank' also suggests 'lustful'. See 1.2, 54.3–4, 67.8, and 109.14. Compare the vegetal degeneration metaphor in 93.13–14 and 94.13–14. As Booth notes, 'thy fair flower' may at first seem to mean 'your prime of youth', a meaning that is submerged (though not perhaps entirely lost) by the botanical imagery of the remaining lines.

13–14 But why . . . grow Taken in conjunction with line 12, these lines appear to be saying (following the theme and imagery of 54) that the youth is in danger of becoming a 'common' weed like 'canker blooms', whose 'virtue only is their show' (54.5, 9), instead of a 'rose' which not only 'looks fair' but

which we prize 'For that sweet odour which doth in it live' (54.3–4).

13 But why But the reason why.

13 odour (1) smell, scent; (2) reputation.

13 show = 'Thy outward' in line 5 as described in lines 1–2.

14 soil A much debated crux. Among the various proposed emendations of Q 'solye' (a non-word), 'soil' (spelled, as commonly, 'soyle') is now generally accepted, but with disagreement as to its meaning: (1) ground, foundation ('soil' as 'earth' or 'ground', either in itself or as determining the development of the flower, fitting well into the botanical imagery); (2) blemish, stain; (3) solution of a problem (taking 'soil' as an aphetic form of the noun 'assoil' (= solution), for which *OED* offers no support apart from its use here, citing only one example of 'assoil' as a noun). Thus (1), with play on (2), appears most likely.

14 thou dost common grow (1) you are becoming publicly accessible (as (a) common lands, (b) a prostitute); (2) you are becoming inferior in quality (like weeds, which flourish ('grow') in common lands). 'grow' continues the botanical imagery of lines 12–13. Compare 102.12 and Fulke Greville, *Caelica* (*c.* 1590), 38.13–14: 'While that fine soyle, which all these joyes did yeeld, / By broken fence is prov'd a common field.'

Sonnet 70

The attitude toward the youth's 'deeds' expressed in 70 is very different from that in 69 (and from the criticisms offered in 33–6, 40–2), particularly the statement about his 'pure unstainèd prime' (lines 8–10); nevertheless 'slander's mark' (2) seems to look back to the 'churls'' thoughts in 69.11 and to deny those thoughts, even though the couplet in 69 suggests that there is some substance to what the 'churls' had 'guessed' from the youth's 'deeds'. However, as Hood notes, the pivot of the argument here is the conditional phrase 'So thou be good' (5) and much depends on the degree of confidence with which that is proposed. It will eventually become not just a preliminary condition but an admonition – in 94 and 95 for example.

1 That thou are . . . defect i.e. the fact that you are censured ought not ('shall not') to be taken as evidence of any fault or flaw in you. For the occasional use of 'are' with 'thou' for euphony before a consonant, see 47.10 n. and Franz 152. Compare Jonson, *Epigrammes*, 72.1: '. . . thou are started up'.

2 For slander's . . . fair Because beauty ('the fair', both inner and outer) has always been the target or butt ('mark') of slander (= false or malicious statements, calumny). Proverbial: 'Envy (calumny) shoots at the fairest mark' (Tilley E175).

3 ornament . . . suspèct suspicion (of inner evil) is automatically associated (by envious churls and slanderers) with anyone who is physically 'fair' (i.e.

bears 'The ornament of beauty'). Compare 69.12–13 and 'envy' in line 12 below. 'Suspèct' is used by Shakespeare only as a noun (see line 13 below). Compare Tilley B163: 'Beauty and chastity (honesty) seldom meet.' This statement contrasts with the underlying theme of the sonnet – the neo-Platonic concept of the 'beautiful soul in the beautiful body'.

4 crow The antecedent is 'suspèct'. The crow was considered a dirty, raucous, thievish, malicious, and ill-omened bird and was associated with the Devil. Tucker suggests that the crow is here shown as preferring to fly 'in heaven's sweetest air' in order to pollute it.

4 heaven's sweetest air Metaphorical for the youth ('thou'); compare 'sweetest buds' in line 7.

5 So So long as, provided that.

5 doth but approve only proves or confirms.

6 Thy See collation and 26.12 n. on the misreading of MS. 'thy' as 'their'.

6 worth high moral and intellectual quality.

6 being wooed of time (1) being tempted by ('wooed of') the promptings of your youth ('time'); (2) being solicited and allured by ('wooed of') the immorality of the present age ('time'; compare 66 and 67). As Hood notes, in either case, the idea is of being importuned but resisting ('So thou be good' (5)). The phrase has given rise to much discussion (see collation, Rollins, 1, 184, and Booth, p. 256).

7 For Because.

7 canker vice vice as an ulcer or cancer (with special reference to the 'canker worm' which devours 'the sweetest buds'). See 35.4 n. and 95.1–3.

8 present'st offer (by your 'beauty', like 'sweetest buds', a perfect prey for 'canker vice').

8 a pure unstainèd prime a youth ('prime' = spring of youth) unadulterated and unblemished (by 'canker vice'). 'unstainèd' may also suggest 'undimmed in lustre'.

9 passed by (1) successfully avoided (while still in your 'prime'); (2) outgrown (i.e. you are now older and more mature).

9 ambush of young days hidden traps or temptations that lie in wait for youth ('young days').

10 assailed . . . victor . . . charged A continuation of the military metaphor in 'ambush' (9).

10 charged attacked, assailed.

11–12 Yet this . . . enlarged But even the fact that you are 'pure' and 'unstainèd' ('this thy praise') cannot be sufficient in itself ('so thy praise') to restrain envy, which (as slander) will always continue to (1) increase, (2) be at liberty. In other words, being 'good' is never enough in itself to shut envy's mouth. Compare the proverb 'Envy never dies' (Tilley E172) and Err. 3.1.105–6: 'For slander lives upon succession, / For ever hous'd where it gets possession.'

13 suspèct of ill suspicion of ill-doing.

13 masked not did not disguise the real nature of. Compare the sun/cloud image in 33 and 34.

13 show appearance (as beauty's paragon). Compare 69.13.

14 Then thou . . . owe Then you, uniquely, would possess ('owe' = 'own') the sovereignty of all hearts ('kingdoms of hearts').

Sonnet 71

In Sonnets 71–4 the poet considers how, after his death, he wishes to be thought of (or not thought of) by the youth (compare 32). As in the plays, consideration of human mortality moves him deeply and inspires two of the great sonnets (71 and 73).

1–3 Compare 2H4 1.1.101–3: 'and his tongue / Sounds ever after as a sullen bell, / Rememb'red tolling a departing friend'.

2 hear . . . bell hear the sternly imperious ('surly') and mournful or solemn-sounding ('sullen') passing-bell. The so-called 'passing-bell' was, for a fee, tolled once for each year the deceased had lived.

4 vildest A frequent variant form of 'vilest', used four times by Shakespeare; 'vilest' only once. The 'd' form seems to extend the force and weight of even the superlative.

5 line line of verse (synecdoche for 'this sonnet', i.e. the part for the whole; compare 'this verse' in line 9, and 74.3).

6 so i.e. so much, so deeply.

7 would be forgot would rather be forgotten.

8 on about.

8 then at the time (of my death).

8 make you woe cause you sorrow.

9 verse i.e. the whole sonnet. See 5 n. above.

10 perhaps This parenthetical 'perhaps', taken with the rest of the line, suggests that the poet is now speaking about a longer period of time after his death, whereas lines 1–8 deal with the time immediately following his death. Hood suggests that the word 'perhaps' is wittily placed to qualify both 'compounded' and 'look upon' (9): 'if you perhaps look upon', 'when I perhaps am compounded'.

10 compounded am with clay blended, mixed with the dust of the earth (i.e. his body has become one with the element of earth). Compare 2H4 4.5.115: 'Only compound me with forgotten dust.'

11 poor (1) humble; (2) insignificant; (3) unfortunate (with possible play on 'poor' meaning 'late' or 'deceased' in common English speech; see OED Poor adj 6).

11 rehearse repeat.

12 let your love . . . decay allow your love (for me) to dwindle away or rot in the same way as ('even with') my life (i.e. die with my dying).

13 wise world i.e. those persons ('world') who know me (and hence my shortcomings), but with a suggestion of irony in 'wise' = 'know-it-alls', people who think they know more than they do.

13 should look . . . moan might investigate the cause of your sorrow. Hood notes that there is

probably a suggestion of over-minute scrutiny by the malicious know-it-alls of the 'wise world' and detects the underlying idea of an over-fastidious coroner's inquest. See also 72.1 n.

14 mock you with me i.e. (1) use me (in my unworthiness) to deride you; (2) add mockery of you to their already established mockery of me (Vendler).

Sonnet 72

Part of the sequence 71–4; see 71 headnote.

1 world Picks up 'wise world' in 71.13 and continues its note of irony.

1 task you to recite (1) force, (2) burden, tax you to rehearse or declare (with, perhaps, a play on 'recite' in the legal sense of 'make a legal statement regarding'; *OED* Recite *v* 2b)

2–4 The Capell–Staunton pointing of lines 2–4 (see collation), here adopted, makes it clear that the youth is being challenged to explain not why he should continue to love the poet's memory *after* his death, but why he had loved the poet while he 'lived' ('After my death' goes with 'forget', not 'love'). On the other hand, the Q lack of pointing after 'love' (followed by a majority of editors) supports the 'after' interpretation and may, perhaps, be what Shakespeare intended. The remainder of the sonnet may be interpreted in either way. Staunton's pointing of lines 3 and 4, linking 4 with 5 instead of 3 with 4, clarifies the sequential relation of 'unless' in line 5 and avoids the awkward syntactical break which the Q period after 'prove' (lowered to a semicolon by Malone and adopted by the majority of editors) entails.

2 should love (1) should have loved (as here pointed); (2) should continue to love (as pointed in Q).

3 quite completely.

4 prove attest to, bring forward as evidence.

5 would were to.

5 devise feign, invent.

5 virtuous lie (1) potent, (2) heroic, valiant untruth. The inherent oxymoron in 'virtuous lie' is further emphasised by the implication in 'virtuous' that the 'lie' will assign to the poet 'virtues' that he does not possess.

6 To do . . . desert In order to (1) praise me more highly ('do more for me') than my personal merit warrants, (2) credit me with doing more ('do more for me') than my own merit has accomplished.

6 desert Pronounced 'desart', as usually at this time, to rhyme with 'impart' in line 8.

7 hang Perhaps with reference to the custom of hanging laudatory verses on the bier at a funeral, the dead being here 'deceasèd I'.

7 more greater.

8 niggard parsimonious, miserly (truth as 'truth' can't be generous in his favour).

8 willingly impart voluntarily bestow, grant a share of.

9 your true love . . . this the truth of your love may seem to falsify itself in devising such a 'virtuous lie' (5) (i.e. 'in this').

10 That Namely that.

10 for out of.

10 untrue untruly.

11 My name be Let my name be.

12 no more no longer.

12 nor . . . nor neither . . . nor.

13 shamed put to shame (perhaps by comparison with others, looking back to 32 and forward to 76 and the following 'rival poet(s)' sonnets).

13 by that . . . forth (1) by what (i.e. my sonnets and, perhaps, my plays) I give birth to ('bring forth'); (2) by what I do ('bring forth', i.e. my 'deeds' (61.6; 69.10) or actions). On the conventional modesty in (1), see 16.4 n. and 32.4–8.

14 And so . . . love (1) And, as a result, you would ('should') be 'shamed' by loving ('to love'); (2) And for the same reason, you ought ('should') to be ashamed to love.

14 things nothing worth (1) works, (2) deeds or actions ('things' = 'that which I bring forth' in line 13) of no value.

Sonnet 73

Part of the cluster 71–4; see 71 headnote. As in 7.6–10 and in 12 (see headnote), the influence of Ovid's *Metamorphoses* XV, 199–216 (Golding, 221–37), has been discerned in lines 1–8: 'What? seest thou not how that the yeere as representing playne / The age of man, departes itself in quarters fowre? first bayne [supple] / And tender in the spring it is, even like a sucking babe. / Then greene, and voyd of strength, and lush, and foggye [puffy] is the blade, / . . . Then all things florish gay. / The earth with flowres of sundry hew then seemeth for too play, / And vertue small or none too herbes there dooth as yit belong. / The yeere from springtyde passing foorth too sommer, wexeth strong, / Becommeth lyke a lusty youth. For in our lyfe through out / There is no tyme more plentifull, more lusty whote [hot] and stout. / Then followeth] Harvest when the heate of youth growes sumwhat cold, / Rype, meeld [? spotted;? mild], disposed meane [half-way] betwixt a yoongman and an old, / And sumwhat sprent [sprinkled] with grayish heare. The ugly winter last / Like age steales on with trembling steppes, all bald, or overcast / With shirle [rough] thinne heare as whyght as snowe. Our bodies also ay / Doo alter still from tyme too tyme, and never stand at stay. / Wee shall not bee the same wee were too day or yisterday.' Spenser (*The Shepheardes Calender* (1579), 'January', 19–42) develops the image, as in 73, of winter's ruin and desolation as 'a myrrhour to behold my [i.e. Colin Clout's] plight' (line 30) in love. For further discussion, see John C. Coldeway, '"Bare rn'wd quiers": Sonnet 73 and poetry, dying', *PQ*, 67 (1988), 1–9.

1 **time of year** i.e. late autumn or early winter. The poet's assumption of old age is conventional; compare 62.9–10.

2 **yellow leaves** For this metaphor, grounded in literal observation, compare *Mac.* 5.3.22–3: 'my way of life / Is fall'n into the sear, the yellow leaf' (where such leaves are associated with 'old age'), *Cym* 3.3.42–4, 60–4, and *Tim.* 4.3.263–7.

3 **against** (1) in relation to; (2) in opposition to.

4 **Bare ruined choirs** A celebrated and much discussed emendation of Q's 'Bare rn'wd quiers' (see collation, the spelling 'choirs' for 'quires' (= Q 'quiers') being an eighteenth-century sophistication (see *OED* Choir *sb*) now generally adopted). The phrase may be taken as operating more or less simultaneously on several levels of meaning (pictorial, historical, metaphorical). Pictorially, it summons up the ruined remains of a church choir (i.e. the chancel, that part of the church where the service was read and sung, east of the nave and masked off from it by the rood screen) in which only the branching, bough like arches are left standing open to the elements. Historically, it may, perhaps, be taken as a reference to the despoiling and destruction of the monasteries under Henry VIII. And metaphorically, it may refer to 'those [leafless] boughs which shake against the cold' in line 3. It further resonates, however, with two wordplays on 'choirs': (1) = the organised body of singers who perform the choral parts of the church service (immediately brought to focus by the singing of the 'sweet birds' in the second half of the line); (2) = (possibly) quire, a gathering of leaves in a manuscript or printed book (referring back to 'yellow leaves' in line 2 and metaphorically to copies of the poet's manuscript verses (the sonnets) to the youth, which, like the poet, have become 'aged' (i.e. yellowed; compare 17.9: 'my papers (yellowed with their age)')). The modernised spelling 'choir' disguises (2) except to the ear. Compare *Cym.* 3.3.43.

4 **late** lately.

5 **twilight of such day** i.e. only as much ('such') faint light as remains of the day (= life) 'after sunset' (6). On the relatival constructions in lines 5–7 and 9–11, see Abbott 279.

7 **Which** The antecedent is 'twilight of such day' (5).

7 **by and by** (1) straightway; (2) soon.

7 **black night** death (metaphorically).

8 **Death's second self** In apposition to 'black night', i.e. the 'sleep of death' (compare *Ham.* 3.1.59–67). From classical times, 'sleep' was often referred to as 'the brother of death'; Shakespeare here identifies death and sleep. Contrast *Mac.* 2.2.32–7, where, though sleep is the 'death of each day's life', it is celebrated as 'Chief nourisher in life's feast'.

8 **seals up** (1) closes up, shuts up (as in a coffin), a metaphor from placing a seal on something to prevent unauthorised opening; (2) shuts up in the darkness

(of night or death, a metaphor derived from falconry, in which a hawk's eyelids were 'seeled' (i.e. stitched shut), 'seal' being a common Elizabethan spelling of 'seel'). Booth compares *Mac.* 3.2.46–7: 'Come, seeling night, / Scarf up the tender eye of pitiful day.'

8 **rest** Enforces the sense of death as sleep.

9 **glowing . . . fire** such faint remains of fire.

10 **That . . . lie** As ('That') lie on top of the ashes of its ('his') youth (i.e. when the fire of life burned at its height).

11 **death-bed . . . expire** i.e. the bed of ashes on which it (= fire = life = love) must (soon) die.

12 **Consumed with** Wasted away or eaten up (1) by, (2) together with.

12 **that** the poet's love for the youth, which, in *its* 'youth', has fuelled the fire (of life) to flame so brightly.

12 **which . . . by** by which it (= the fire of life and love) was fed or nurtured. Thus both fire and fuel die simultaneously. Compare the implications of 1.6: 'Feed'st thy light's flame with self substantial fuel'.

13 **This** i.e. the approaching demise of the poet and of his love as described in lines 1–12.

13 **thou perceiv'st . . . strong** you understand or recognise, the perception of which causes *your* love (for me) to grow stronger.

14 **To love that well** (Causing you) to love or prize (1) my love for you, (2) me faithfully or constantly ('well'), (3) your youth.

14 **leave ere long** forgo, lose before long (i.e. soon). Malone's pointing (a colon after 'long' rather than Q's full stop) insists in an unnecessary orthographic way on the intimate relationship of thought with 74.

Sonnet 74

The last in the cluster 71–4; see 71 headnote. Kerrigan notes that the Ovidean overtones, relating man's life-span to the seasons in 73.1–4, gradually give way to imagery drawing on the Bible (Job 17.11–15) and the burial service (in the Book of Common Prayer) in the later development of 73 and 74, though both sonnets may still be read in essentially secular terms.

1–4 The pointing of these lines is that of Q, except for the omission of a comma after 'arrest' in line 1. Until recently, most editors have broken line 1 with a heavy stop after 'contented' (see collation), taking 'when . . . away,' as a subordinate clause governed only by 'My life . . . stay.', but, as Ingram and Redpath point out, such an abrupt break in the first line is found nowhere else in the Sonnets.

1 **But** Serves to link 74 directly to 73.

1 **be contented** i.e. accept the situation (= my death) without undue sorrow or complaint. Hood thinks it a parenthetical phrase meaning 'rest assured', 'be satisfied'.

1–2 **fell arrest / Without all bail** ruthless, cruel seizure ('fell arrest') without any chance of being bailed (i.e. gaining temporary release on security). Death is pictured as an officer of the law, a sergeant, one of whose duties it was to arrest debtors and consign them to debtors' prison, where they would remain until they arranged bail or satisfied their creditors; Death's arrest, however, is 'without bail'. Compare *Ham.* 5.2.236–7: 'as this fell sergeant, Death, / Is strict in his arrest'.

2 carry me away i.e. as to prison (until the Day of Judgement). Is there, perhaps, some reference to the morality play Vice (a surrogate for the Devil), who conventionally sometimes carried a sinner away to Hell on his shoulders at the conclusion of the play?

2–3 away, / My life The retention of the Q comma (rather than the semicolon inserted by most editors who follow Q's lack of pointing after 'contented') more clearly links lines 3–4 with 1–2 as a 'because' clause explaining why the youth should be 'contented'. Alternatively, Hood suggests, if 'be contented' is a parenthetical phrase meaning 'rest assured', the linkage still holds, though line 3 is then the main clause rather than a subordinate causal clause. See 1 n. above.

3 My life . . . interest (Because) I continue to have some claim upon or share in 'life' (i.e. living memory or fame) through my verses. 'in this line' may refer to this sonnet or to the Sonnets generally as the 'living' expression of 'My spirit'; see lines 7–8. Compare 'lines of life' (16.9) and 'read this line' (71.5).

4 for memorial (1) as something preserving my memory; (2) as a reminder (of me).

4 still . . . stay will always remain ('stay') with you. There is also a suggestion here that the kind of 'life' (i.e. immortality through 'this line' or 'memorial') will 'stay' with the youth forever ('still') even after the youth's death, i.e. the poet's verses will immortalise them both (see 15 headnote).

5 reviewest . . . review reread . . . see again. Although the repetition of 'review' in two slightly different senses may be defended as an example of one of the 'figures of repetition' (exactly which one is not clear to me; see Joseph, pp. 99, 78–89), the effect, if effect was intended, is surely rhetorically flat. I would suggest, therefore, that Q 'reuew' may be a compositorial misreading of a manuscript 'renew', the compositor, influenced by Q 'reuewest', mistaking the minim strokes of the *n* for *u* (a very easy error to make in reading Secretary hand). In context, 'renew' (= revive, give new life to (*OED* Renew *v*¹ 7b); compare *3H6* 5.4.52–4) points both back and forward and hence affords a richer and more integrated sense in lines 5–6 than 'review': When you reread ('reviewest') this (i.e. 'this line' (3)), you revive or give life to ('renew') the true or better part of me ('very part') that was 'consecrate' to you (i.e. the share or 'interest' I retain in 'life' (3) and 'My spirit . . . the better part of me' (8), as it was preserved in my

verses). The reading of his verse (dead if unread) thus, in one sense, restores the poet to new life. For other uses by Shakespeare of 'renew' in interpersonal relationships, see 3.3, 56.1, 111.8, and *Rape of Lucrece*, 1103.

6 The very . . . thee See preceding note.

6 consecrate consecrated. See Abbott 342.

7–12 Compare the burial service in the Book of Common Prayer: 'I commend thy soul to God the Father almighty, and thy body to the ground, earth to earth, ashes to ashes, dust to dust, in sure and certain hope of resurrection to eternal life.' See also Job 19.25–7 and 1 Cor. 15.53–5 (both quoted in the burial service).

7 his its.

8 spirit volatile, spiritual, and intellectual nature (as it is preserved in his verse); see 5 n. above. 'spirit' is often slurred as if a monosyllable in Elizabethan English.

8 better part of me Refers back to 'very part' in line 6; see 39.2 n.

9 but only, nothing more than.

9 dregs of life i.e. what had remained of his physical nature (his body), with reference to the poet's loss of 'vitality' in the 'twilight' of his assumed old age (see 73). For the metaphor, compare *Mac.* 2.3.95–6: 'The wine of life is drawn, and the mere lees [= dregs] / Is left this vault to brag of.'

10–11 The prey . . . wretch's knife A much discussed and controversial passage. I would paraphrase: My dead body has become food ('prey' = plunder, spoils, booty) for worms because of its cowardly seizure ('coward conquest'), under the knife, by Death (or his alias, Time). The seizure is described as 'coward' (= cowardly) because (a) it is like that of an assassin who steals up on his victim unawares and stabs him in the back, and (b) mankind is defenceless against either Death or Time. Compare 6.14: 'To be death's conquest and make worms thine heir'; and 63.10: 'Against confounding age's cruel knife'.

10 worms Compare Job 19.26: 'And though after my skin *worms* destroy this body, yet shall I see God in my flesh' (Geneva); the Book of Common Prayer (see 7–12 n. above) follows the Bishops' Bible version, which omits the reference to worms (though it includes it in a marginal note).

11 coward conquest See 10–11 n. above.

11 wretch's knife i.e. Death's (or Time's) knife. Shakespeare's figure was inspired, I suggest, by the many representations of Death to be found in the Dance of Death (mural paintings, woodcuts, etc.), popular in the late Middle Ages and the Renaissance, in which Death is shown making his 'fell arrest' (as in lines 1–2). In such depictions Death is frequently shown flourishing a dart or spear (compare Milton, *Paradise Lost*, II, 672), and, though I have found only one instance where Death is shown grasping a knife (see Francis Douce, *Holbein's Dance of Death*, 1833,

p. 162), Sidney (*Arcadia* (1590), p. 349) refers to 'deaths sharpe knife'. These illustrations also establish Death's role as the agent of Time by showing Death holding an hourglass (as in Hans Holbein's famous woodcut series, Nos. 11, 19), or a scythe (see J. M. Clark, *The Dance of Death*, 1950, p. 32), and Shakespeare, in 100.14, describes Time's scythe as his 'crooked knife'. The term 'wretch' as applied to Death or Time may be seen as looking back to the underlying image of Death in lines 1–2 as a sergeant, such under-officers having had a very unsavoury reputation, as the names Fang and Snare, two sergeants in *2H4*, testify. Line 11, much less persuasively, has also been taken by some commentators as referring to (a) Marlowe's murder in a tavern brawl in 1593; (b) a particular assassination attempt on Shakespeare; (c) Shakespeare meditating suicide; (d) a dissecting anatomist. Of these, only (a) deserves more than passing consideration; see the suggested reference to Marlowe's murder in *AYLI* 3.3.14–15.

12 Too base ... rememberèd Too mean, worthless (because not of the 'spirit') to be remembered by you.

13 The worth ... contains The value or excellence of the body ('that') is what it embodies (i.e. its spiritual or intellectual essence).

14 that is this what it contains ('that') is these lines ('this', i.e. 'My spirit . . . the better part of me' (8)).

14 with thee remains (1) stays with you; (2) endures, giving you (and me) a kind of immortality that defies Death's 'fell arrest'.

Sonnet 75

Sonnet 75 echoes the ideas of love's feast and love's treasure found in earlier sonnets (47.2–5, 48.5–8, 52.1–4, and 56.1–6).

1 So are you ... life As food to the body (sustaining its 'life') so are you to my mind and spirit ('thoughts').

2 seasoned (1) tempered; (2) ripening; (3) scented.

3 for (1) in order to achieve, ensure; (2) for the sake of; (3) because of; (4) instead of, in place of (the meaning depending on how the following enigmatic and cloudy phrase 'the peace of you' is interpreted).

3 the peace of you (1) your tranquillity or peace of mind (taking 'for' as in (1) or (2) above); (2) the enjoyment (compare 'enjoyer' in line 5) or contentment ('peace') I should find in your love (taking 'for' as in (1), (2), or (3) above); (3) the tranquillity or contentment which you exemplify (taking 'for' as in (4) above). The clear antithesis between 'peace' and 'strife' in this line has deterred editors from accepting any of the proposed emendations (see collation), though Booth suggests a play on 'piece', looking back to 'ground' in line 2 and forward to the 'pieces of money' that constitute the miser's 'wealth' in line 4.

3 hold such strife entertain such conflicting feelings.

4 As 'twixt ... found i.e. as is found in a miser in relation to ("twixt') his ambivalent feelings toward his treasure (the youth being thought of as the miserpoet's 'wealth').

5–12 This series of subordinate clauses illustrates the poet's continually shifting and ambivalent feelings toward the youth and his love for the youth, feelings that mirror those of a miser toward his 'wealth'. The reversals of mood are signalled by 'Now . . . anon', 'Now . . . Then', 'Sometime . . . by and by'.

5 proud as an enjoyer taking pride in, or being gratified by, the enjoyment (of my 'wealth'). There is probable play on 'proud' = sexually aroused and 'enjoy' = have sexual relations with. Earliest use of 'enjoyer' (*OED*).

5 anon (1) at once; (2) soon.

6 Doubting Fearing.

6 filching robbing, pilfering.

6 treasure i.e. you (as my beloved and as my inspiration ('my Muse' (78.1)) for writing verse). As Hood notes, 'his' here refers to the miser with whom the poet identifies; by line 8 the identification has become complete. This looks forward to the rival poet(s) sonnets (78–80, 82–6), where the poet complains that his 'treasure', in both senses, is being 'filched'. Like 'proud' and 'enjoyer' in line 5, 'treasure' may have sexual implications; see 52.4 n. and 136.5 n.

7 counting best thinking or reckoning it most happy ('best'). 'counting' carries on the image of the miser in line 4, who experiences both pleasure and fear' in counting up his 'wealth'.

8 Then bettered ... pleasure i.e. then thinking (as an 'enjoyer') that that 'best' would be bettered if other people ('the world') might see my happiness.

9 Sometime At one moment.

9 all full completely satisfied (with a suggestion, emphasised by 'feasting', of being gorged or satiated). The eating/food imagery is continued in lines 10–14.

9 on your sight i.e. upon the sight of you ('you' figured as a 'feast').

10 by and by straightway, presently (compare 'anon' (5)).

10 clean utterly, entirely ('clean starvèd' being the antithesis of 'all full' in line 9).

10 for a look (1) for the sight of you; (2) for a glance from you.

11 Possessing . . . delight Owning or seeking after no pleasure or happiness.

12 Save what . . . took Except what (in 'Possessing') I have had ('is had') from you or what (in 'pursuing') must yet be received ('took') from you. For the use of 'took' (= taken), see Abbott 343. Both 'have' and 'take' may carry sexual implications; see 129.10 n. and Partridge.

13 pine (1) suffer unhappiness; (2) starve (picking up 'clean starvèd' (10)).

13 surfeit indulge (or feed) to excess. Compare *Venus and Adonis*, 602: 'Do surfeit by the eye and pine the maw'.

13 day by day (1) every day; (2) changing from one day to another.

14 Or gluttoning ... all away i.e. either feeding to excess ('gluttoning' = surfeiting like a glutton) on you as my 'all' (compare 'all full with feasting on your sight' (9)) or starving (compare 'clean starvèd for a look' (10)) when my 'all' is away (i.e. absent or unkind). For 'all' = you (i.e. the youth) compare 109.13–14: 'For nothing this wide universe I call / Save thou, my rose; in it thou art my all', and 112.5: 'You are my all the world.' *OED* (Glutton *v*) cites 'gluttoning' here as the earliest verbal use of 'glutton'.

Sonnet 76

Compare 32, 105, and 108. Shakespeare's concern here (as in 32.5–14) to defend what he professes to consider his old-fashioned style and language as compared with the 'new-found methods' and 'strange compounds' of his more up-to-date and, in some cases, younger contemporaries, may be seen as leading up to the rival poet(s) group (78–80, 82–6). That his concern here (and in 78–80 and 82–6) may arise in part from a genuine feeling of uncertainty about the comparative merit of his verses, despite the conventional modesty expected of a sonneteer, should not be discounted, but it should also be recognised as, in a sense, a metaphor to express an underlying and stronger concern: the fear that a rival (or rivals), whether of superior poetic genius or not, may steal from him the youth's 'love', and all that such 'love' implies. This is a 'filching age' (75.6).

1 barren (1) bare; (2) unproductive, fruitless.

1 new novel, strange.

1 pride splendid (with suggestion of 'ostentatious') adornment or display (of rhetorical fireworks). Compare 103.2.

2 So far from So lacking in.

2 variation variety or varying (in style, figures of speech, language, syntax, metrics, verse forms).

2 or quick change or what might be called 'alteration' that is lively and sudden (i.e. 'quick change' being itself an example of linguistic 'alteration'). See Puttenham, *The Arte of English Poesie* (1589), p. 159: 'Figurative speech is a noveltie of language evidently (and yet not absurdly) estranged from the ordinarie habite and manner of our dayly talke and writing and figure it selfe is a certaine lively or good grace set upon wordes, speaches and sentences to some purpose and not in vaine, giving them ornament or efficacie by many maner of alterations in shape, in sounde, and also in sence, sometime by way of surplusage, sometime by defect, sometime by disorder . . . in this or that sort tuning and tempring them, by ampli-

fication, abridgement, opening, closing, enforcing, meekening [mitigating, lowering] or otherwise disposing them to the best purpose.' Shakespeare is, of course, commenting on what he suggests are excessive, disproportionate, and misapplied 'variations', what Puttenham called 'the vices or deformities in speech and writing' (pp. 138, 249 ff.). The kinds of vices Puttenham and Shakespeare are attacking are perfectly illustrated by Anthony Copley's *A Fig for Fortune* (1596), which is cluttered with neologisms and 'compounds strange' (see 4 n. below).

3 with the time i.e. as is now the fashion.

3–4 glance aside / To change course and look favourably upon.

4 new-found This is an established 'compound', not one of the 'compounds strange' here criticised.

4 methods ways of arranging or ordering thoughts and topics (a term used in discussions of rhetorical (and medical) procedure). Puttenham observes that 'Poesie' only became an 'Art' when it was 'fashioned and reduced onto a method of rules and precepts' (p. 5).

4 compounds strange unknown and hence potentially 'barbarous' or adventitious (1) compound words, or, possibly, neologisms, (2) mixtures (in verse forms and rhetorical decorum). There is some possible suggestion here, picking up the medical sense in 'methods', of life-threatening (hence art-threatening) 'compounds'; compare *Cym.* 1.5.8: 'these most poisonous compounds'. Shakespeare uses two unique 'compounds strange' in 82.8, 12; on his use of 'compounds' generally, see Abbott 428–35. Joseph Hall (*Virgidemiarum* (1599), VI, i, 255–62) calls 'compounds' a 'new elegance', at least when used by a Sidney, and claims, exaggeratedly, that Sidney, who earlier had praised the use of 'compounds' in English (*An Apology for Poetry*, pp. 85–6), 'fetch't [them] of late from *France*'. Shakespeare's implied criticisms are tantalisingly vague if he has particular writers in mind. Possibly he is thinking of Barnes's *Parthenophil and Parthenophe* (1593) (Barnes is fond of new compounds) or the anonymous *Zepheria* (1594), which is pestered with legal imagery and racked language, or perhaps the intentional obscurity and difficulty of George Chapman's earlier poems (*The Shadow of Night* (1594) and *Ovids Banquet of Sence* (1595)). See also 2 n. above, and the criticisms levelled against Nashe (*Works*, II, 183). It has been suggested that if the sonnet was written after 1597 or 1598, Joseph Hall and John Marston might have been suitable targets. Whoever may have been aimed at (if anyone), one thing needs to be emphasised: Shakespeare is far from the 'simple poet' he pictures himself as being (compare 82.9–12) and he uses all the 'tricks' of rhetoric (see Joseph, *Shakespeare and the Arts of Language*, 1947) and has his full share of 'variation and quick change' (including neologisms and compounds). His criticism is really levelled at what he claims to be newfangled excess and disproportion, the 'vices' of rhetoric – a claim he may, indeed, be using merely as a defence mechanism.

5, 10, 14 still (1) continually; (2) always.

5 all one Glossed by the following phrase 'ever the same' (i.e. 'without variation or quick change' in topic (you), form (sonnet), or style). Compare 105.4–5.

6 keep (1) maintain; (2) contain (in the sense of 'limit').

6 invention Technically, in rhetoric, 'invention' (the finding out or selection of topics) was the first requirement of an orator or writer, the second, 'disposition', and the third, 'elocution' (the application of 'apte wordes and sentences to the matter'; see Wilson, pp. 31–2). Shakespeare here uses 'invention' more generally to mean 'free exercise of the imagination'.

6 noted weed commonly recognisable, well-known dress or garb. The clothing metaphor (compare 'dressing' in line 11) was often used to describe the 'art of writing' (compare Puttenham, pp. 137, 159).

7 almost tell my name very nearly reveal or speak my identity ('name') (because 'every word' is characteristically 'all one, ever the same'). Capell's emendation of Q 'fel' has been adopted by all editors (see collation).

8 birth parentage, descent.

8 where from where, whence.

9 know Booth suggests a possible play on 'no'; compare 123.1.

10 argument subject, theme (of my 'invention').

11 dressing old words new i.e. (through the use of the various figures of speech) clothing the (same) old words (and topics) in a new guise ('new' = anew).

12 Spending . . . spent Again paying out, expending what (i.e. 'old words') is already worn out or exhausted (by repetition = 'still telling' in line 14). Is there an element of self-criticism in lines 11–12?

13–14 For as . . . told i.e. even as the (same old) sun daily seems to be 'spent' when it sets but rises at the next dawn in new strength and brightness, in the same way ('So') the expression of my love for you is continually ('still') given new vitality by 'dressing old words new' (= 'telling what is told', ringing the changes in a new way on what has been said before).

Sonnet 77

Booth suggests that Sonnet 77 is in the *memento mori* tradition. The poet may be pictured as sending the youth, along with this sonnet, a new and unused notebook or table-book of some kind, which, when the youth has filled its 'blanks' (10) with his thoughts ('mind's imprint' (3)), will, like his 'glass' and 'dial', serve to remind him of the inescapable ravages of Time and Death's 'fell arrest' (74.1). See 122, where

the poet gives away a table-book apparently given to him by the youth.

1 glass mirror, looking-glass.

1 wear (1) waste away, decay; (2) last, resist Time's attrition. Gildon's emendation for Q 'were' has been universally accepted by editors. Booth's suggestion of a play on 'wear' and 'were' (a common variant spelling of 'wear') is forced: a mirror does not show what *was*, but what *is*.

2 dial sundial (probably of a pocket variety). Some critics argue that the 'glass' and 'dial', like the 'book', are part of the poet's gift; most, however, find the supposition unnecessary (as well as unlikely), and Ingram and Redpath point out that 'Thy' modifying both (instead of 'The' to match 'The vacant leaves' in line 3) strongly supports the single gift interpretation. Kerrigan notes how the underlying, if unexpressed, idea of 'face' (the youth's reflected face in the 'glass' and the dial's face reflecting the passing of time) metaphorically ties lines 1 and 2 together.

3 The vacant leaves i.e. the leaves of the 'book' are 'vacant' (= empty) because 'blanks' (10). This continues, perhaps, the underlying 'face' metaphor in lines 1 and 2, since the 'faces' of the leaves are 'vacant' (i.e. characterless, with play on 'character' = written or printed symbol) until written upon by the youth's 'mind's imprint' (= his thoughts and feelings), at which time they will serve the same function as the 'glass' and 'dial'. Capell's reading, 'These' for Q 'The' (see collation), has understandably tempted later editors, clarifying, as it does, the immediate reference to the 'gift book', but no recent editor has succumbed.

4 of from (reading).

4 this learning . . . taste i.e. the knowledge and experience gained from your thinking ('thy mind's imprint' (3)) about the lessons taught by your 'glass' and 'dial' may be recalled or savoured ('taste') in 'this book', which, like a diary, will record your thoughts about growth and decay as time passes.

5 truly faithfully, without flattery.

6 mouthèd graves i.e. graves gaping to swallow you. Compare 'wrinkles' (line 5) as 'trenches' (2.2), 'furrows' (22.3), 'parallels' (60.10), and 'wrinkle graven' (100.10); see also 31.9 n. and *3H6* 5.2.19.

7 shady stealth shadowy, almost imperceptible movement. 'shady' plays on the 'shade' or 'shadow' cast by the sun on a 'dial' and 'stealth' (i.e. theft) suggests 'Time's thievish progress' in line 8.

7 know understand, recognise.

8 Time's . . . eternity Time's ever-onward movement ('progress'), like that of a stealthy thief, 'steals' on forever ('to eternity'). See 104.9–10 n.

9 Look what Whatever. See 9.9 n.

9 thy memory . . . contain i.e. (thoughts) you are afraid may be forgotten.

10 Commit . . . blanks Entrust to these blank pages ('blanks') which are barren or profitless ('waste') 'vacant leaves' (3), i.e. 'blanks' ('waste' until they have been put to use as the repository of 'thy mind's imprint' (3)). Q 'blacks' (see collation) results from the compositor's failure to observe a tilde over the 'a' (i.e. 'blăcks' = blancks).

11 **Those children . . . brain** Those children (= your thoughts) cherished and fostered ('nursed' = given strength to grow and mature), which your mind has given birth to.

12 **To take . . . mind** Will refresh your memory (with these thoughts otherwise forgotten) in such a way as to make them seem new and fresh (i.e. as 'new acquaintance', they will appear to be new and more mature because you will be more mature when you read them).

13–14 **These offices . . . book** These duties as performed ('offices', i.e. in properly observing yourself in your 'glass' and 'dial') will, as often as you look upon them, profit you and (by recording such timely observations) make your 'book' more valuable (as another source of moral instruction). Hood suggests that there is a play on the idea of observing or noting the effects of time in the 'glass' and 'dial' and noting them down for continuing consideration in the 'book', 'offices' also suggests, as Tucker notes, that the three meditational aids to morality (and mortality) are being imaged in terms of a religious 'office-book' (like the Book of Common Prayer).

Sonnet 78

Sonnet 78 is the first of a group of sonnets (78–80, 82–6) that focuses on a 'rival poet' (or 'rival poets'), who is/are challenging and threatening Shakespeare's special relationship with the youth, his 'lovely boy' (126.1). Something of the poet's defensive uneasiness, leading up to this group, had already been sounded in 76. Much ink has been spilled in attempting to identify the rival (or rivals) (see Rollins, ii, 277–94). We will probably never know his identity, though, if we must guess, George Chapman seems to me the most likely candidate (see 86.5–12 n.).

1 **So oft** So many times.

1 **invoked . . . Muse** called upon or appealed to you (1) as, (2) to be my source of poetic inspiration ('Muse'; see 21.1 n.). 'Invocation of the Muse' was a much imitated convention of classical poetry.

2 **fair assistance** generously favourable (with play on 'fair' = beautiful) support or inspiration (with further play on 'assistance' = your 'presence' attending on me).

2 **in my verse** i.e. in the composing of my verse.

3 **As** That (see Abbott 109).

3 **every alien pen** each strange writer (= 'pen' by metonymy). The 'pens' are 'alien' or 'strange' because, like foreigners, they appear to be trying to intrude into the 'oneness' of lover and beloved by invoking the poet's private 'Muse'. For more on 'pen', see 7 n. below.

3 **hath got my use** i.e. has appropriated my practice (of invoking you). There is also, perhaps, a suggestion of 'use' in the sense of 'interest' or 'return' (i.e. the 'fair assistance' (2) the poet has received as a result of his invocation and which 'every alien pen' is now trying to cheat him of).

4 **under thee** (1) in your service; (2) under your influence; (3) under your patronage (Ingram and Redpath).

4 **disperse** (1) publish in printed form; (2) circulate in manuscript. Both practices were common.

5 **taught . . . sing** taught (me) in my speechlessness ('the dumb') to sing (i.e. express myself in verse) (1) in a high strain, (2) aloud. 'on high to sing' suggests angelic choirs or the lark that 'sings hymns at heaven's gate' (29.12). The concept of poets as 'singers' rests on a long classical and bardic tradition.

6 **heavy ignorance** ignorance (contrasted with the knowledge possessed by 'the learnèd' in line 7) that is sluggish and weighed down by mental torpor – an attribute (compare line 14) that, like 'dumbness' in line 5, the poet, with ironically conventional modesty, ascribes to himself. The phrase recurs in *Oth.* 2.1.143. 'heavy' is used to contrast with the vital, upward movement in 'aloft to fly'.

7 **Have added** Have (even) added.

7 **added . . . wing** The metaphor is drawn from falconry or hawking, the damaged wing of a hawk being 'imped out' by the engrafting or 'adding' of new feathers. Booth suggests that Shakespeare may here be playing on 'feathers' in relation to 'pen' in line 3 (i.e. a quill or feather pen, a word derived from Latin *penna* = feather) and to 'style' in line 11 (its literary sense being derived from Latin *stylus* = a writing instrument). We may add, I think, that *penna* in classical Latin could also, by extension, mean both 'wings' and 'flight' and may thus resonate with 'aloft to fly' (6) and 'wing' (7).

7 **learnèd's wing** i.e. even 'learnèd' poets are enabled to rise to a higher flight by having their wings imped (= 'added feathers to') by the inspiration of 'Thine eyes' (5).

8 **given grace . . . majesty** i.e. have given 'the learnèd's' verses, already possessing beauty and elegance ('grace'), a twofold magnificence of expression ('majesty'). Some critics see here a reference to a particular 'learnèd' poet-rival (a 'university wit' like Marlowe and Nashe, or Chapman), but 'every alien pen' (3) and 'others' works' (11) suggest that Shakespeare, though he may already have one 'learnèd' poet in mind, is here using the term more generally.

9 **Yet** Nevertheless.

9 **be most proud** i.e. value most highly.

9 **compile** compose. Compare 85.2 and *LLL* 4.3.131–2: 'Longaville / Did never sonnet for her sake compile.'

10 influence infusion of moral or divine power (a term from astrology describing the supposed 'influence' of the stars (= 'Thine eyes' in line 5, a commonplace equation) on men and events). There is perhaps some play on 'grace' (8) and 'graces' (12) in the theological sense of 'divine influence' (*OED* Grace *sb* 6b).

10 born of thee brought forth or generated (as a child) by you. Given the Q spelling 'borne' (see 68.3 n.), the phrase may also possibly convey an underlying sense of 'carried by you as a natural attribute'.

11 but mend the style only or merely (1) augment, improve, (2) correct, remedy the manner of expression (i.e. adding external embellishment, which has little to do with the true substance of what is said, unlike the 'style' of my verses which comes not from the head but the heart). For possible play on 'style' = pen, see 7 n. above.

12 arts (1) learning, scholarship; (2) rhetorical skills.

12 with thy . . . be are adorned ('gracèd be') by your delightful and pleasing (as well as influential) charms ('graces'). 'sweet graces' is essentially tautological. Is it merely fanciful to suggest an underlying allusion to the 'Three Graces' of Greek mythology who were believed to bestow beauty and charm, they themselves being exemplars of female beauty? Compare 20.7 n. Note how deliberately Shakespeare, in lines 12–13, employs the figure of antanaclasis (the repetition of a word that shifts from one meaning to another) in playing on 'art' and 'grace'.

13 thou art all my art i.e. you (as my Muse) are the sole source of my knowledge and skill.

13–14 and dost advance . . . ignorance and raise up my barbarous ('rude') ignorance (i.e. lack of learning) to a state of knowledge as high as that of 'the learnèd' (7). Compare lines 5–14 with Berowne's speech (*LLL* 4.3.315–51) in which he argues that 'women's eyes' (see 'Thine eyes' in line 5) are 'the books, the arts, the academes, / That show, contain, and nourish all the world', and *1H6* 5.3.192: 'And natural graces that extinguish art' (see 62.8).

Sonnet 79

Sonnet 79 is the second of the group focusing on the rival poet(s). See 78 headnote.

1 I alone I only. The poet here claims that he was the first to celebrate the youth in verse, a claim that need not, perhaps, be taken too literally.

1 call upon invoke (compare 78.1).

1 aid Poets regularly invoked the Muse for 'aid' (i.e. inspiration), but where, as here and in 78.1, the Muse is a fellow mortal, 'aid' may also carry the suggestion of patronage or financial aid.

2 had all . . . grace Ingram and Redpath suggest a triple play on 'grace': (1) was fully possessed of the same elegance as that of your person and character; (2) gave full expression to your excellence;

(3) received the whole of your favour (the last picking up the financial undertone of 'aid' in line 1). It should be added, however, that 'gentle' (not accounted for above), besides meaning 'mild' or 'courteous', also carried for an Elizabethan the senses of 'wellborn' (at least of the rank of gentleman) and 'generous'.

3 gracious numbers graceful, pleasing verses ('gracious' because they embody 'thy gentle grace' (2)).

3 are decayed (1) have deteriorated, lost their vitality; (2) have lost favour (with you). 'decayed' may suggest the operation of Time, which has rendered the poet's verses old-fashioned (compare the theme of 76) and out of favour.

4 And my sick . . . place The primary meaning is clear: 'And my ailing poetic ability ("sick Muse") gives up its place to another's poetic ability or "Muse".' But the line may also be interpreted to imply a criticism of the youth as his Muse (see line 1 and 78.1): 'And you, my Muse, are unfaithful ("sick") in allowing another (poet) to usurp my place.'

5 sweet love i.e. the youth.

5 thy lovely argument i.e. you as a theme which confers love and beauty ('lovely').

6 travail mental labour (with suggestion of birth-pains). Hood suggests that Benson's 'travell', the alternative contemporary spelling, may pick up an intended play on the traverse or movement of the pen in bestowing praise.

7 what of thee whatever quality of yours.

7 thy poet This may refer to any poet (including Shakespeare) or to 'another' poet referred to in line 4. If to both, as Hood notes, then the implied distinction is that Shakespeare would recognise the debt whilst the rival poet in his pride would not.

7 invent find out, discover (by mental 'travail').

8 He robs thee of He (only) steals from you (i.e. he 'invents' nothing original).

8 pays . . . again i.e. what praise he bestows as your due ('pays') only pays back again what was already yours. The same idea is essentially repeated in line 14.

9–10 He lends . . . behaviour He imputes 'virtue' to you, a word or moral quality (and all it implies) he stole from you by observing your conduct (i.e. bearing and actions). Contrast 69.9–14.

11 cheek face (by synecdoche).

11 can afford is able to give.

12 live (1) dwell, inhabit; (2) flourish (in a vital state).

13–14 Then thank . . . pay He ('thy poet' (7)), then, deserves no thanks or patronage (as 'interest' on the praise he 'lends' (9) you), for, whatever he may say, he *owes* such praise to your spiritual and physical 'beauty' – the 'principal' from which he borrows. He gives you nothing that you have not already paid for in being yourself.

Sonnet 80

Sonnet 80 is the first sonnet unquestionably to identify the rival poet as a single individual ('a better
spirit').

1 faint lose courage, grow weak, become
depressed.

2 a better spirit a poet of superior genius (one
who writes with greater spirit = stronger, more vital
poetic effect). Contrast 'faint' in line 1 and compare 'able spirit' in 85.7. 'spirit' is here, as often in
Shakespeare, slurred as a monosyllable, though not,
I think, meant to be pronounced as 'sprite' (a variant
form).

2 use your name i.e. (1) invoke you as his Muse
(his source of inspiration); (2) address you personally as a patron (as Shakespeare did Southampton in
the dedications to *Venus and Adonis* and *The Rape of
Lucrece*). Other, generally pejorative, senses of 'use'
may also be at work: (1) frequent another's company,
haunt; (2) have sexual relations with; (3) manipulate
for one's own purposes.

3 spends all his might (1) expends, pays out,
(2) utters all his poetic strength or power. But 'spend'
could also mean 'waste', 'exhaust', sometimes with
sexual implications.

4 To make me (1) With the result that I become;
(2) (omitting the Q comma after 'might' (3)) In order
to make me.

4 fame (1) honour, renown (i.e. your greatness);
(2) reputation.

5 worth high merit, excellence (with possible play
on 'pecuniary value', 'possessions').

5 wide extensive, essentially unbounded.

6–13 The humble . . . cast away Compare the
nautical imagery in *MV* 1.1.8–14 (where 'argosies' –
the 'rich burghers on the flood' – 'overpeer the petty
traffickers / That cur'sy to them') and *Tro.* 1.3.33–45
(where, in a storm, the safety of 'shallow bauble boats'
and 'the saucy boat' with 'weak untimber'd sides' is
contrasted with ships 'of nobler bulk' and a 'strong-
ribb'd bark' that can 'through liquid mountains cut').

6 humble 'humble' is accorded the force of 'hum-
blest' by the following superlative 'proudest' (for
other examples of this elliptical construction, see
Abbott 398).

6 proudest sail (1) most stately and magnificent,
(2) 'haughty', 'arrogant' ship. Compare 'of goodly
pride' in line 12 and 'the proud full sail of his great
verse' (86.1), referring probably to the same 'better
spirit' as in line 2.

6 bear hold up (compare 'hold me up' (9)).

7 saucy bark presumptuous, 'cheeky' (here
small) boat.

8 broad main wide ocean (compare 'wide as the
ocean' (5)).

8 wilfully (1) voluntarily, deliberately; (2) obsti-
nately, perversely. Possible play on Will(iam) has been
suggested (see 57.13 n. and 135–6).

9 shallowest help slightest aid ('shallowest'
playing on the idea of being kept 'afloat' even in 'shal-
lows'). The poet suggests that the youth's smallest
favour will keep him buoyed up (contrast 'faint' in
line 1).

10 soundless deep unplumbable depths ('deep'
= ocean).

10 ride sail or lie at anchor (with possible sexual
suggestion). Compare 137.6 n. Is Shakespeare hint-
ing that the 'better spirit', unlike himself, only skims
the surface ('ride') of the 'soundless deep', never
plumbing the youth's rich depths?

11 Or (being wracked) Or if I should be wrecked
(variant form of 'wracked').

11–12 I am . . . pride i.e. I am only a small,
contemptible boat and will therefore be destroyed
by being wrecked (i.e. losing your favour), while he
(the 'better spirit'), being a vessel of strong and high
construction ('of tall building') and large and comely
magnificence ('of goodly pride'), will survive. There
is play, perhaps, on 'worthless' = lacking in excellence or social and financial position (see line 5 n.
above), on 'goodly', used ironically, and on 'pride' =
arrogance.

13 thrive prosper (i.e. win your favour).

13 cast away wrecked (i.e. lose your favour, continuing the nautical imagery of lines 8–12).

14 The worst i.e. the worst that can happen.

14 my love (1) my love for you; (2) you as my
beloved.

14 my decay the cause of my progressive decline
or ruin (looking back perhaps to 'faint' in line 1 =
loss of vital energy). As a whole the line may also be
glossed: 'The worst aspect of the situation for me will
be that it was my *love* that did me in' (Vendler).

Sonnet 81

Sonnet 81 seems to interrupt the 'rival-poet(s)'
series, representing, perhaps, a sudden up-swing in
mood. Its confident, almost boastful, tone associates
it with 18 and its preoccupation with the poet's death
with 71–4.

1–2 Or . . . . Or Whether . . . Or. See *OED* Or
conj[2] 3b and compare *MV* 3.2.63–4: 'Tell me where
is fancy bred, / Or in the heart or in the head?'

1 epitaph verses lamenting and praising the dead
(literally, an inscription on a tomb).

2 make write, compose. 'Maker' was a term frequently used for 'poet' at this time (see Sidney, *Apology for Poetry*, pp. 12–13).

2 rotten, Until recently most editors replaced the
Q comma with a semicolon or period, thus making
'Or' in line 1 = 'Either'; such pointing, however, as
Ingram and Redpath note, reduces lines 1–2 to 'a
platitude of high banality'.

3 From hence (1) From the world, now and to
come; (2) As a result of my verses (a hint anticipating
'Your monument' in line 9). Note that the specific

reason why death cannot 'take' (= seize upon and, hence, destroy) the youth's 'memory' (= exemption from oblivion (Johnson)) is intentionally held as it were in suspension until the sestet, which thus serves as a key to unlock the unresolved hints of the octave.

4 in me . . . forgotten in my case ('in me') I will be totally lost to 'memory' ('forgotten'). 'each part' = all parts, both physical and spiritual. Restated in line 6.

5 Your name i.e. you (in 'each part'). Taken literally, this line is supremely ironic, since the youth's 'name' remains, and probably will always remain, a matter of mere conjecture.

5 from hence (1) from henceforward; (2) from my verses (another hint, as in line 3).

6 once gone i.e. dead.

6 world i.e. mankind generally.

7 The earth . . . common grave (1) The ground, (2) the world of man (considering my humble 'worth') will grant me only an ordinary, undistinguished grave (with a suggestion in 'common' of a 'mass' or 'general grave' of the kind provided for paupers or necessarily resorted to during visitations of the plague). The further irony of this line, given the distinction of Shakespeare's burial (in the chancel) as a man of wealth and substance and the handsome memorial celebrating him as a poet, on the north wall of Holy Trinity church, Stratford, has been pointed out by Ivor Brown and G. Fearon (*Amazing Monument*, 1939, pp. 27 ff.).

8 When you intombèd . . . lie While ('When') you will lie entombed (1) in the (admiring) eyes (and minds) of men (i.e. you, 'laid out' in full-length effigy, will be kept 'alive' and honoured in 'men's eyes' by a costly and ornate funeral 'monument'; see line 9), (2) in 'my gentle verse' (9) when it is read by 'men's eyes'. Compare *Ham.* 1.2.185: 'In my mind's eye, Horatio'. The connotations of 'intombèd' (a variant form of 'entombed') emphasise the stark contrast with the poet's 'common grave', undistinguished, perhaps, even by a headstone.

9 Your monument . . . verse This line suddenly resolves the true reason for the youth's promised immortality hinted at in lines 3, 5, and 8. For the play on 'monument', see 8 n. above.

9 gentle verse i.e. 'gentle' because it derives from the youth's courteous and noble character, his 'worth' (see 80.5 n.).

10 o'er-read read over (with a suggestion of 'read again and again').

11 to be i.e. 'not yet created' (10).

11 being (1) existence (as if alive); (2) essence.

11 rehearse tell of, recite.

12 all the breathers . . . dead all those now alive and breathing are dead. 'this world' = the present age. This is the earliest citation for 'breather' in *OED*. The Q pointing of lines 11–12 ('rehearse, . . . dead,') leaves it unclear whether 12 should syntac-

tically be read with 11 or with 13. Almost all editors, as here, adopt Sewell's pointing, thus making an arbitrary decision, even though Gildon's pointing (also arbitrary) makes acceptable sense. Booth retains Q's unprescriptive pointing, arguing that 'the syntax of lines 11–13 is similarly [as in 'the urgent parallelism between lines 10 and 11'] demonstrative of the almost supernatural "virtue" of the speaker's pen: the lines expand as they are read so that each in effect speaks twice'. Perhaps so, but the implied finely balanced intentionality on Shakespeare's part hangs on a very slender thread – the Q pointing, which is frequently uncertain, particularly in the indiscriminate use of commas. See Textual Analysis, p. 278 below.

13 still always, forever.

13 virtue power, strength (with a suggestion, perhaps, of 'divine' or 'supernatural').

13 pen i.e. what I write.

14 breath (1) life (i.e. the breath of life); (2) speech.

14 breathes (1) lives; (2) speaks (*OED* Breathe *v* 7 cites *Wiv.* 4.5.2 as earliest use in this sense).

14 even in . . . men namely ('even') in men's mouths (i.e. you 'still shall live' because, when they 'o'er read' 'my gentle verse', you will always be in their 'mouths', and they will talk about you, keeping your 'memory' (3) alive).

Sonnet 82

Sonnet 82 returns to the 'rival poet(s)' theme, though here the emphasis (unlike 80) is on several 'writers' ('they' in line 9) who write about, or dedicate their works to, the youth.

1–4 I grant . . . book The general idea is that since the youth has no formal obligation to the poet, he may without dishonour enjoy the work of other writers who celebrate him.

1 I grant . . . Muse I admit that you were not indissolubly wedded to me (i.e. my poetic talent = 'my Muse') as your (sole) praiser. Shakespeare is playing on the vows taken in matrimony by husband and wife 'to have and to hold from this day forward, for better or for worse, for richer, for poorer, in sickness, and in health, to love and to cherish, till death us depart' (Book of Common Prayer).

2 without attaint without stain of dishonour or unfaithfulness (since you took no vow not to do so).

2 o'erlook peruse, read over (with, Tucker suggests, possible play on 'casting an appraising eye over women', since you are 'not married').

3 dedicated words (1) language of devotion (in the 'book' as a whole); (2) words used in the 'dedication' of a 'book' to a potential patron.

4 Of Concerning.

4 fair subject i.e. your 'beauty' (inner and outer), the 'subject' of which they write.

4 blessing every book consecrating, making blessed, every book. The subject may be either 'writers' (3) or 'fair subject' (4).

5 as fair ... hue as excellent or 'beautiful' in mind ('knowledge', i.e. character) as in external appearance or form ('hue'; see 20.7 n.).

6 Finding thy worth . . . praise (1) (You in) judging ('Finding') that your merit was beyond the bound or height ('limit') I could attain in my praise of you; (2) (I in) discovering that your merit . . . The antecedent of 'Finding' is unclear, though lines 7–8 seem to favour 'you' as in (1) rather than 'I' as in (2).

7 inforced . . . anew enforced (variant form), or compelled to seek out once more.

8 Some fresher . . . days Something (or someone) carrying the newer stamp or imprint of these improved times ('time-bettering days'). Compare 'the bett'ring of the time' and 'this growing age' in 32.5, 10. In view of the sestet, the line should be taken ironically. Both 'time-bettering' and 'truetelling' (12) are unique to Shakespeare and might qualify as the very 'compounds strange' which he criticises in 76.4.

9 And do so, love The poet magnanimously grants, since the youth is not 'married to my Muse' (1), that he may 'o'erlook' (2) other 'writers' (3) of 'fresher stamp' (8) whose 'dedicated words' (3) are addressed to him, but the 'yet' that immediately follows sets up the poet's claim as the only 'true-telling friend' (12), because his rivals only 'word' the youth with 'strainèd touches' of 'rhetoric' (10).

9 devised contrived (from the head, not the heart).

10 strainèd touches artificial, wrested, forced strokes (of wit), tricks.

10 rhetoric i.e. the 'art of rhetoric' as explained, for example, in Puttenham's *The Arte of English Poesie* (1589) or Wilson's *The Arte of Rhetorique* (1553).

10 lend impart, afford (with a suggestion that the 'touches' are merely borrowed, external ornaments).

11–12 Thou, truly . . . friend Note the self-conscious and artful play on 'truly' and 'true' using the figure polyptoton (repetition of words derived from the same root but with different endings or forms); see Joseph, p. 306. Hood notes that Shakespeare here shows that he at least can employ rhetoric in the service of genuine feeling.

11 truly . . . truly (1) naturally; (2) in all truth.

11 fair (1) beautiful; (2) excellent (both in body and mind).

11 sympathised (1) represented (to the life); (2) mentally apprehended (by the poet's 'true plain words' (12)). The poet's 'truth' responds by innate sympathy to the youth's 'truth' without any art of rhetoric. Ironically of course, these two lines are extremely 'artful'; see 11–12 n. above. Compare the use of 'sympathised' in *Rape of Lucrece*, 1112–13, and *LLL* 3.1.51–2.

12 true plain words Contrasted with 'strainèd touches' (10) and 'gross painting' (13). The repetition of 'true', like 'truly' in line 11, underscores again the oneness of the youth and his 'friend' who speaks and writes truly ('true-telling').

13 gross painting flagrant, palpably apparent (verbal) daubing. The underlying image in lines 13–14 is that of a 'face with Nature's own hand painted' (20.1), which other writers are falsifying by a kind of cosmetic art – 'beautied with plast'ring art' and 'painted word[s]' (*Ham.* 3.1.50–2); their 'painting' only conceals 'truth'.

14 Where In those cases where.

14 blood The youth's natural complexion needs no adventitious 'red' (= 'blood'). Compare 67.10. There is perhaps, as Ingram and Redpath suggest, some play here on what were called the 'colours (i.e. figures) of rhetoric', abuse of which was described as 'larded (i.e. fattened) rhetoric'.

14 in thee in your case.

14 it i.e. 'gross painting' (13).

14 abused misused. Compare *LLL* 2.1.226–7: 'This civil war of wits were much better used / On Navarre and his book-men, for here 'tis abused.'

Sonnet 83

The 'rival poet(s)' group of sonnets continues; see 78 headnote. The opening lines of 83 are clearly linked to the closing couplet of 82 by the 'painting' metaphor, but despite 'others' in line 12 (which could be loosely used for 'other'), Sonnet 83, unlike 82, is generally taken to refer to a single rival poet, 'both your poets' (14) being interpreted as referring to Shakespeare and one other, even though the phrase is ambiguous and could possibly refer to two rival poets. Lines 5–14 seem to suggest that the poet has been 'silent' for a while, neglecting to address the youth as he had in the past.

1–2 I never ... set Compare *LLL* 2.1.13–14: 'my beauty, though but mean, / Needs not the painted flourish of your praise', and 82.13–14.

1 saw (1) perceived visually; (2) apprehended mentally.

1 painting (1) verbal embellishment; (2) cosmetic 'art'. See 82.13 n.

2 And therefore As in 82.2, 7, this coordinating, explanatory phrase is repeated in line 5; such obvious repeated transitions are not common in the Sonnets and establish a structural set of mind between 82 and 83 (compare 123.1 n.).

2 fair fairness, beauty (outer and inner).

2 painting Here, only 'verbal embellishment'.

2 set (1) applied, laid on (as verbal paint); (2) grafted (compare 'barren tender' (4), 'doth grow' (8), 'give life' (12), 'lives more life' (13)). In this second sense, the phrase 'painting set' becomes almost a witty oxymoron bringing together the opponents of natural propagation and the artifice of cosmetics

(Hood). It is possible, I think, that Shakespeare wrote 'fet' (= fetched, as if from some esoteric source), a form he uses in *Richard III* and *Henry V*, and an easy misreading in Secretary hand. The line is a calculated understatement, intended as a compliment (i.e. implying the 'truth' of what he has said), since in the preceding sonnets Shakespeare has lavished a good deal of rather fulsome 'painting' on what he claims to be 'unpaintable'.

3 **found** (1) discovered; (2) determined (i.e. bringing in a mental verdict). The sense of inner apprehension is underscored by 'or thought I found' and contrasts with the primary sense of 'saw' in line 1. Hood notes the legal sense of 'finding' invoked in 82.6 for another specific link between the two sonnets.

3 **exceed** transcend the limits of, surpass. Compare 82.6.

4 **barren tender** unproductive, unprofitable offering (hence 'worthless', since, being 'barren', it is not 'life-giving'). This phrase seems to deny the poet's claim, last made in 81, that his verse will confer immortality on the youth, but 'barren' may here carry the sense of 'failing to enhance something', since the youth is by nature superior to anything that can be said about him.

4 **debt** obligation (what a poet owes to his 'patron').

5 **slept** been quiescent, inactive (resulting in 'This silence' of line 9).

5 **in your report** in commendation of you (i.e. your 'worth' (8)). Only other use of 'report' in this sense cited in *OED* (Report *sb* 3b) is in *LLL* 2.1.63.

6 **That** So that.

6 **extant** alive and publicly visible (with play on 'conspicuous', 'prominent').

7 **modern quill** (1) present-day, contemporary, (2) ordinary, commonplace pen (i.e. writer, by metonymy). Although Shakespeare's use of 'modern' elsewhere (nine times) would seem to favour (2), (1) makes better and stronger sense, since an 'ordinary' or 'commonplace' writer would inevitably fall short ('come too short'), and, as Hood suggests, there would be more wit in exposing the hollow pretensions of the thoroughly up-to-date 'better spirit' of 80.2 or the perpetrator of 'strainèd touches' of rhetoric of 82.10. Behind it may lie a sense of the comparative superiority of what Shakespeare, in 106.7, calls an 'àntique pen' (i.e. a classical writer), which, though it too must of necessity fall short of expressing the youth's perfection, might come closer to doing so.

8 **Speaking** In speaking (i.e. writing).

8 **worth** value, merit.

8 **what worth** the value or merit which. As Kerrigan notes, however, the awkward syntax in 'worth, what worth' suggests some hesitation on the poet's part, and the whole clause ('what worth in you doth grow') may be taken to imply some question about the extent to which 'worth' does indeed flourish ('grow') in the youth.

9 **This silence** i.e. when the poet 'slept in your report' (5).

9 **for** as.

9 **impute** consider, charge as being.

10 **Which** i.e. the 'sin of silence'.

10 **shall be . . . dumb** shall be, (I) being silent ('dumb'), my highest praise ('most my glory'). The poet, unlike others, recognises that the youth's 'worth' is such that it needs no 'report' to make it 'live'; his 'silence' is therefore his greatest virtue. Compare 84.1–2 and Cordelia's comparative 'silence' in *Lear* 1.1. For the elliptical omission of 'I' before a present participle ('being') preceded by a pronominal adjective ('my'), see Abbott 379.

11 **impair** diminish, injure.

11 **being mute** (I) being silent. See 10 n. above.

12 **When others . . . tomb** When others (not 'mute'), who intend (by their praise) to give you 'life' or immortality, only succeed in burying you in the grave ('bring a tomb'). Thus their 'strainèd touches' (82.10) give death, not life. 'tomb' suggests a large, showy (rhetorical) monument.

13 **more life** i.e. greater potentiality for immortality.

14 **both your poets** See headnote.

14 **devise** (1) invent, contrive; (2) bequeath (as by will).

Sonnet 84

See 78 headnote. Sonnet 84 is non-committal on the question of whether Shakespeare is addressing one or more rival poets. Ironic self-deprecation has here become a more aggressive insistence on the self-defining beauty of the youth which needs only accurate transcription rather than the 'painting' of 'strainèd touches' of rhetoric; see 83.2, 82.10 (Hood).

1–4 The opening quatrain is syntactically confusing and, abetted by Q's unrestrictive pointing (all commas), forces an editor into making arbitrary choices in punctuation and hence meaning. As here pointed, the lines may be roughly paraphrased as: 'Who is there that praises you most extravagantly who can offer more unstinted praise than this – that you are unique, and that you, within whose compass is locked up Nature's stock of beauty and worth, in the (unlikely) event that anyone equal to you came to exist, would have to serve as the exemplar?' Until comparatively recently, most editors adopted the Malone–Gildon pointing (' . . . most? . . . you? . . . grew.'; see collation), which though it tends to disguise the immediate relation between 'Who' and 'which' (= who) in line 1, gives essentially the same sense as the pointing here adopted. Knight, however, while keeping the Malone–Gildon pointing in lines 1–2, turns lines 3–4 into a separate question (reading 'grew?' with Capell), thus shifting the antecedent of 'whose' in line 3 from 'you' (i.e. the youth) to anyone who may write about 'you'. Paraphrased, 3–4 would then mean something like: 'What poet's mind, given its natural limits, encloses or locks up such an abundant store (of invention) that it could imagine another example in which your equal might be found?' Booth, who favours this interpretation of lines 3–4, tries to leave a reader's decision open by his pointing – not, as he would admit, very effectively. Ingram and Redpath and Kerrigan ignore this second reading of lines 3–4, because, I suppose, the use of 'immurèd' (= literally, 'walled in', i.e. wholly restricted to, imprisoned in) favours the first of the above interpretations, since it better fits the context of the youth, who subsumes 'alone' (2) in himself the sum or 'store' (3) of all perfection, than when it is associated with the admittedly less inclusive mind-store of the poet.

2 rich abundant, unstinted.

3 confine compass, bounds.

3 immurèd See above. Ingram and Redpath suggest that the underlying image in this line is that of a walled garden in which grows a unique plant (= 'you alone' (2) or 'beauty's rose' (1.2)). This conjecture seems to be confirmed by 83.2 ('to your fair no painting set') since *OED* Fair *adj* 1h confirms that 'fair' is an element of several plant names, whilst 'set' has the secondary horticultural sense of 'graft', 'propagate' (Hood). See 83.2 n.

5 Lean penury (1) Scanty, mean poverty or dearth; (2) Infertile lack (of invention).

5 pen writer, poet (by metonymy).

6 his its (though the metonymic use of 'pen' as 'writer' may make the masculine form acceptable in this context).

6 subject i.e. any ordinary subject, the youth being beyond even slight praise or honour ('some small glory'). The implied limitation on 'subject' is made clear by 'But' in line 7.

6 lends (1) bestows; (2) loans (even if 'some small glory' is not warranted).

7 of about.

7–8 can tell / That you are you i.e. is able to express or reveal you as you are.

8 so dignifies his story by this means and no other ('so') honours and ennobles his account (i.e. 'his story', since he can't, by definition, add anything to perfection).

9 but copy merely transcribe.

9 what in . . . writ what is already delineated ('writ') in you by nature (with possible play on (a) 'what is spelled out ('writ') in the word 'you'; (b) Holy Writ (taking 'writ' as a noun), which, like 'you', is divinely inspired and beyond 'praise'). Compare Sidney, *Astrophil and Stella* (1591), 3.12–14: 'in *Stella's* face I reed, / What Love and Beautie be, then all my deed / But Copying is, what in her Nature writes'.

10 making worse impairing, injuring (by needless, and hence false, praise).

10 clear free from fault, perfect.

11 counterpart exact copy.

11 fame his wit make his genius or skill ('wit') famous (i.e. widely recognised).

12 style (1) mode of expression; (2) literary composition (with play on 'style' = pen, stylus; compare 'pen' in line 5).

12 every where Retained as two words (Q) to preserve the equal stress on 'every' and 'where'.

13–14 These lines, regardless of how they are interpreted (see below), suddenly and unexpectedly undercut lines 1–12 by asserting that the youth's 'perfection' is flawed.

13 beauteous blessings (1) good qualities that make you 'beautiful' (outwardly and inwardly); (2) generous bestowal of praises or patronage.

13 add a curse join or attach a blighting, bad quality ('curse' suggesting the opposite of 'blessing'). Does this perhaps look back to the garden image in 'immurèd' (see 3 n. above)? As Eden (= a walled garden) contained its serpent (= potential 'curse'), so does the youth as a type of Eden.

14 Being fond . . . worse Being foolishly in love with flattery ('praise'), either (a) that lavished on you or (b) that dispensed by you, which renders the praises you (a) receive or (b) give the poorer ('worse'). They are a 'curse' because (a) the kinds of indiscriminate praises you so greedily lap up are false (you being beyond praise) or (b) the praises you indiscriminately dispense are given to those unworthy of them. Choice between interpretations favours (a) in each case.

Sonnet 85

Sonnet 85 adopts a rather more defensive position than 84: Shakespeare gives ironic approval to the ornate elegancies of compliment by the rival poet(s) but claims a superiority for the depth and quality of his unspoken admiration. Sonnet 85 makes reference to more than one 'rival poet' (i.e. 'other' (5), 'others' (13); see also 7 n. below). See 78 headnote for this group of sonnets.

1 tongue-tied Compare 80.4.

1 Muse See 82.1 n.

1 in manners decently, with propriety. Compare 39.1.

1 holds her still restrains or keeps herself in quiet (i.e. remains silent; compare 'This silence' in 83.9). There is a play, perhaps, on 'still' = constantly, always. A 'Muse' was usually addressed as feminine ('her') because the Nine Muses of classical mythology were thought of as beautiful young women.

2 comments of your praise eulogising remarks or glosses made about or on you (as if on a sacred text). Literally, 'comments' = expository treatises, which suggests prose, but the emphasis here is on 'poetical comments'.

2 richly compiled composed in a lavish, elaborately ornamented style (with a suggestion in 'richly' of being overfattened). Compare 78.9 n.

3 Reserve their character A much debated phrase, the first two words of which have been busily emended (see collation). The majority of editors have retained the Q reading, as here, which, without too much straining, may be paraphrased as: '(These "comments" praising you) preserve, retain, store up (for posterity) their (1) imprint (i.e. written or printed stamp ("character") of essential quality), (2) individual nature (as reflecting moral qualities).' Recently, however, Kerrigan and Wells (but not Booth) have accepted the emendation of Q 'their' to 'thy' and explain 'thy character' as '(1) your nature; (2) the writing which you are' (Kerrigan). This is certainly tempting and affords an easier, less involved sense (as Booth admits). Even so, it has the disadvantage, not admittedly insuperable (compare 24.5–6 n.), of making Shakespeare confuse the use of 'your' (in line 2) and 'thy' (in line 3) in a single sentence. There is fairly frequent compositorial misreading of 'thy' as 'their' in Q (see 26.12 n.). If an editor feels that emendation is necessary, then 'your' rather than 'thy' would seem preferable (see collation), Q 'their' being a misreading of 'y^r' or 'yor' (= your), the 'y' being read as 'th' (see 26.12 n.), the second form regularly employed by Hand D (generally agreed to be Shakespeare's) in Addition II of *Sir Thomas More (STM)*. It might even be argued that Q 'their' reflects a slip on Shakespeare's part; Hand D makes an identical slip (Addition II, 136), first wrongly writing 'their', then cancelling it and interlining 'yor' above.

3 character See above. Kerrigan, mistakenly I believe, sees a reference in 'character' to the short Theophrastan prose 'characters' that became popular in England in the first decade of the seventeenth century, basing his argument in good part on the fact that Q spells the word with a capital C. Such evidence is meaningless, since in Secretary hand capital C was very frequently used, to obviate misreading as Secretary *r* or *t*, for initial lower-case *c* (as, for example, by Hand D in *STM* and reproduced by compositors in Q in 69.4, 70.4,7). Moreover, unless we date 85 shortly after 1600, the concept of the Theophrastan prose character would not have been understood (see B. Boyce, *The Theophrastan Character in England to 1642*, 1947).

3 with golden quill i.e. by writing in aureate, splendidly rhetorical ('golden') style ('quill' by metonymy). A pen or 'quill' of gold may also suggest that what is written will be preserved for posterity (deeply incised, as it were, by a metal stylus).

4 precious phrase costly, fine language or diction (with an underlying suggestion in 'precious' of 'over-refined' or 'affected'). Compare 'strainèd touches' in 82.10.

4 all the Muses i.e. the Nine Muses of classical mythology, especially as they relate to poetry and music (see 1 n. above).

4 filed polished, refined. See line 8.

5–6 Rollins compares 1 Cor. 14.16: 'Else, when thou blessest with the spirit, how shall he that occupieth the room of the unlearned, say Amen, at thy giving of thanks, seeing he knoweth not what thou say'st' (Geneva).

5 I think . . . words Compare 83.9–12. The line suggests that thoughts are true and words are cheap; however 'good' the words may be, they need not come from the heart as the poet's thoughts do. 'other' = others.

6 like unlettered . . . 'Amen' i.e. like an unlearned ('unlettered') parish clerk who always leads the congregation in responses (e.g. saying 'Amen') even though he may not really understand what he is responding to. Compare William Warner, *Albions England* (1612 edn), p. 115: 'By tale [i.e. rote] we say Orysons, and to words unknowne Amen.' The conventional modesty in 'unlettered' looks back to 78.7, 13–14, and the 'learnèd' implications of 'better spirit' (80.2) and forward to 'able spirit' in line 7.

7 hymn song (or poem) of praise. Proponents of George Chapman as the 'rival poet' see in Q's capital H ('Himne') a specific reference to his *The Shadow of Night: Containing Two Poeticall Hymnes* (1594). But Spenser, also advanced as one of the many candidates for the role of rival poet, published *Fowre Hymnes* in 1596. See, however, 86.5–12 n.

7 that able spirit affords which (any) capable or lively capacity offers. It is unlikely that 'that' is adjectival, thus referring to a particular 'able spirit', since a singular form would then fall between two plural forms ('other' (5); 'others' (13)). 'able' may be somewhat patronising, meaning merely 'clever', 'capable', 'competent', or it may mean 'powerful', 'talented'. Compare Christopher Lever, *Queene Elizabeths Teares* (1607), p. 70: 'O let my verse moove indignation, / And stir the blood of better ablèd wit . . . Our love is in our heart, not in our phrase' (compare line 5 above).

8 In polished form In a smooth, refined ('polished' = 'filed' (4)) (1) style, (2) ordering of constituent parts (with perhaps some suggestion of merely 'formal' or 'lacking in intrinsic sincerity or truth').

8 well-refinèd pen i.e. polished writer (by metonymy).

9 'Tis so, 'tis true Picks up and translates the Hebrew word 'Amen' (= so be it; truly) in line 6.

10 most of praise highest, most exalted praise. Compare 84.1.

10 more even higher or greater.

11 But that But that 'something more' (which I add).

11 thought Compare 'I think good thoughts' (5). It is disingenuous, of course, since by writing the sonnet the poet is doing essentially what he claims 'that able spirit affords' – lavishing excessive praise (if excess is possible where the youth is concerned) and in fact adding to it.

11 whose love to you i.e. my thought's love as it is directed toward you.

12 Though words . . . before Though (my) words bring up the rear (i.e. I am a laggard in putting my love into words), my 'love to you' maintains its ('his') position in the first rank (among those who praise you). There is perhaps a suggestion of conventional modesty in 'Though . . . hindmost' (i.e. his words when they 'come' are of comparatively inferior quality).

13–14 Then others . . . effect Then value ('respect') others for their windy, insubstantial words ('breath of words'; compare *Mac.* 5.3.27, 'mouth-honor, breath'), me for my silent ('dumb') thoughts which express you truly ('in effect' = in reality as opposed to appearance). Compare *Tro.* 5.3.108–9: 'Words, words, mere words, no matter from the heart; / Th'effect doth operate another way.'

Sonnet 86

Sonnet 86 is concerned with a single rival poet, generally accepted as the same rival referred to as 'a better spirit' in 80.2. The designation of the rival poet as a 'spirit' in 80 seems to be echoed here in the play on 'his spirit' and 'spirits' (5), and the metaphor of the rival as a 'tall' ship in 'full sail' (1–2) repeats the same figure used to describe the 'better spirit' in 80.6, the last of the 'rival poet(s)' sonnets, is closely linked to 85, offering a fanciful explanation of why the 'good thoughts' of 85.5 remain inarticulate.

1 proud full sail Compare 'proudest sail' (80.6 n.); there, as here, 'proud' carries a strongly ironic edge. 'sail' = (1) ship; (2) sailing.

1 great (1) grand, magnificent; (2) grandiloquent, puffed up (full of wind; compare 'proud'), swollen (as in 'great with child'; compare 'full' and *MND* 2.1.128–34).

2 Bound . . . you The image is that of a privateer (e.g. Sir Francis Drake) setting forth to seize a 'prize' (i.e. a ship laden with Spanish gold from the New World) on the high seas, an intentionally denigrating image that implies a mercenary goal on the rival's part and undercuts the seeming 'magnificent' tone of line 1.

2 all-too-precious you you who are altogether ('all-too') precious (i.e. like pure gold, the 'king' and most 'precious' of metals and the desired 'prize' of a privateer). May the phrase also suggest that the youth's favour is 'too costly', i.e. more demanding perhaps than the effort is worth? Compare 'too dear' in 87.1. The Q parentheses (see collation), though explained by Simpson as a contemporary device to

indicate a compound, could also be used to achieve a special kind of rhythmic emphasis that is lost without them; they should perhaps be retained.

3 ripe matured, ready to be born (in speech or verse).

3 inhearse shut up, enclose (as in a coffin). Earliest citation in *OED* (Enhearse *v*).

4 Making . . . grew Making the womb (= 'brain' (3)) in which they were conceived and matured ('grew') their grave (i.e. his thoughts are stillborn). Compare *Rom.* 2.3.9–10: 'The earth that's nature's mother is her tomb; / What is her burying grave, that is her womb.'

5–12 These lines (together with 85.7; see note) have been claimed as particularly supporting the case for George Chapman as the principal rival poet (an identification first suggested by William Minto in 1874; see Rollins, II, 284–8). It is, indeed, generally, if cautiously, agreed, despite the lack of anything approaching conclusive evidence, that of all the other candidates proposed (Spenser, Marlowe, Daniel, Nashe, Barnes, etc.) these lines seem best to fit certain of Chapman's characteristics and pretensions as a poet. He claims, for example, a special affinity with 'night' in *The Shadow of Night* (1594; see title page motto 'Versus mei habebunt aliquantum Noctis', and 85.7 n.), and says, in his dedication, that knowledge 'will scarcely be lookt upon by others but with invocation, fasting, watching; yea not without having drops of their soules like an heavenly familiar' (compare 'affable familiar ghost' in line 9). Years later, in *Euthemia Raptus* (1609), he boasts (a boast he may have been making as early as 1594 when he is believed to have begun work on his famous translation of the *Iliad*, seven books of which were published in 1598) that he was inspired by the 'spirit' of Homer: 'I am (sayd hee [Homer]) that spirit *Elysian*, / That . . . did thy bosome fill, / . . . When (meditating of me) a sweet gale / Brought me upon thee; and thou didst inherit / My true sense (for the time then) in my spirit; / And I, invisiblie, went prompting thee, / To those fayre Greenes, where thou didst english me' (75–85); and later in the same poem (944–8) he says: ' . . . these are dreames, of my retired Night; / That, all my Reading; Writing; all my paines / Are serious trifles; and the idle vaines / Of an unthriftie Angell, that deludes [compare the 'ghost / Which nightly gulls him' in lines 9–10] / My simple fancie'. Chapman also speaks of being 'drawne by strange instigation' to complete Marlowe's *Hero and Leander* (1598) and of communing with spirits (III, 183–7). It is even possible that Chapman echoes 86.5–6 in his 1611 *Iliad* (II, 419–21): 'That great worke, unlesse the seed of Jove / (The deathlesse Muses) undertake, maintaines a pitch above / All mortall powers.' Such evidence and the further considerations that Chapman laboured to project the image of a 'learned' poet 'by all the Muses filed' (85.4), and that his manner might be described, in various senses, as 'proud' and 'full' (especially the fourteeners of his *Iliad*), constitute the case for Chapman. Many readers will probably prefer to allow the identity of the rival poet to remain an unsolved mystery. See also 76.4 n.

5 spirit (1) vigour of mind; (2) informing genius, daemon.

5 spirits supernatural, incorporeal beings (compare 'ghost' in line 9).

5 write compose (verses).

6 Above a mortal pitch i.e. in a manner beyond the highest reach of an ordinary mortal (because 'taught' by 'spirits'). Strongly ironic (compare lines 7–10).

6 struck me dead i.e. forced me to be silent, 'tongue-tied' (85.1).

7 compeers comrades, fellows (i.e. the 'spirits' of line 5).

7 by night i.e. those spirits who commune with him at night (compare 'nightly' in line 10 and see 5–12 n. above).

8 astonishèd paralysed, stunned (picks up 'struck' in line 6, the root meaning of 'astonish' being 'to be struck by a thunderbolt').

9 He, nor For the ellipsis of 'neither' before 'nor', see Abbott 396.

9 affable familiar ghost courteous, civil spirit intimately associated ('familiar') with him (with play on 'familiar spirit' or 'demon', a witch's 'familiar'). Under the terms of Protestant theology 'ghosts' were almost always emissaries of the Devil (see Lewes Lavater, *Of Ghostes and Spirites Walking by Night* (1572), ed. J. D. Wilson, M. Yardley, 1929, p. 196, and compare *Ham.* 1.4.40–1: 'Be thou a spirit of health, or goblin damn'd, / Bring with thee airs from heaven, or blasts from hell').

10 gulls (1) deceives, dupes; (2) gorges.

10 intelligence news, information (here false information, such as might be conveyed by an 'intelligencer' or informer who 'gulls' his client).

11 As victors ... boast i.e. neither the rival ('He') nor his 'familiar ghost[s]' can boast of being 'victors' in the sense that they have forced me to be silent. For the double negative in 'cannot', see Abbott 406.

12 sick of ... thence weakened mentally ('sick', i.e. reduced to silence) by any anxiety arising from such sources ('thence').

13 countenance (1) face, appearance; (2) favour, support, patronage.

13 filled up (1) wholly pervaded, dominated; (2) lent support to (by favouring). Some editors, following Steevens and Malone, read 'fil'd up' (Q 'fild vp') with the meaning 'polished', but 'file up' in that sense is otherwise unrecorded and 'fild' for 'fill'd' is common at this time (compare 17.2 and *Rape of Lucrece*, 1804).

13 line verse.

14 lacked I matter i.e. I was deprived of a subject (because my rival had wholly appropriated my 'matter' with the youth's 'countenance', in both senses).

14 that i.e. (1) the rival's (and youth's) action implied in line 13; (2) the absence or lack of matter (Vendler).

14 infeebled enfeebled (variant form), weakened (compare 'sick' in line 12).

14 mine i.e. my verse.

Sonnet 87

Though not concerned directly with a rival poet, 87 may have grown out of the situation suggested by the rival poet(s) sonnets – a feeling that the speaker can no longer compete – and a suggestive link with 86 may be seen, perhaps, in 'too dear' in the first line and 'all-too-precious' in 86.2 (see note). Note the preponderance of feminine rhymes, ten of the twelve ending in -*ing*. The lines, though end-stopped throughout, thus convey a kind of hovering though on-going, if tentative, movement. Other, probably earlier, examples of sonnets playing on the -*ing* rhyme may be found in Watson, *The Tears of Fancie* (1593), 28, and Daniel, *Delia* (1592), 27 (eight each); Daniel, however, disliking the tonal/metrical effect, replaced all of them with masculine rhymes in his 1594 revision. The heavy use of legal language in lines 1–12 here has the effect of reducing 'love' to a kind of *quid pro quo* transaction, at least so far as the youth's is concerned.

1 dear (1) precious, of great worth (with perhaps a suggestion of 'high rank'); (2) costly (see 86.2 n.).

1 for my possessing i.e. for me to consider you as my exclusive possession or 'property' (as I used to before others trespassed on my right with your permission). Compare 'Thy self thou gav'st' in line 9.

2 like enough probably. Note the hint of doubt.

2 thy estimate (1) your actual value or worth; (2) the value or price which you set on yourself.

3 charter of thy worth (1) privilege or right, (2) legal document which your worth (= (1) worthiness, value; (2) social and financial position) confers on you.

3 releasing freedom to (1) withdraw, (2) transfer (your favour or 'countenance' (86.13)).

4 My bonds in thee i.e. the mutual ties that bound you to me (or me to you). 'bonds' plays on 'legal bonds' and continues the underlying legal imagery in 'possessing', 'estimate', 'charter', and 'releasing' in lines 1–3.

4 all (1) every one; (2) entirely.

4 determinate (1) terminable; (2) outdated (legal language picking up 'bonds', etc.; see 13.6 n.). For the participial form in -*ate*, see Franz 159.

5 For how ... granting In reading, the stress should probably fall on 'I', 'thee', and 'thy'.

5 hold thee retain my (legal) right in you.

5 **but by thy granting** except through your consent or favour (with play on 'grant' = legal deed of conveyance).

6 **for that riches** to warrant ('for') the possession of that wealth. 'riches' was still frequently used as a substantive singular at this time.

6 **deserving** (comparable) desert, merit.

7 **cause of** motivating reason for (with play on 'cause' = legal case).

7 **fair gift** = 'that riches' (6). 'fair' = (1) beautiful, unblemished; (2) (legally) equitable; (3) (perhaps) flattering.

7 **wanting** lacking.

8 **so** therefore.

8 **patent** licence, exclusive privilege (with suggestion of a legal licence).

8 **back again is swerving** reverting again (to you who granted the 'patent'). Compare 'Comes home again' in line 12.

9 **Thy self** Retained as two words (Q). 'self' = whole essence (inner and outer), the referent of 'it' in line 10 (Tucker).

9 **thy own worth** i.e. extent of the worth which is properly yours. See 3 n. above.

9 **knowing** realising.

10 **Or** For the ellipsis of 'either' before 'thy own worth' in line 9, see Abbott 396.

10 **Or me . . . mistaking** Or, on the other hand ('else'), making a wrong 'estimate' of me (i.e. 'mistaking' my 'worth') to whom you gave it (= 'self' (9)).

11 **So** Therefore.

11 **upon misprision growing** growing out of (i.e. being based 'upon') a mistake or error (in judgement on your part either in undervaluing yourself or in overvaluing me). *OED* credits Shakespeare with the earliest use of 'misprision' in this sense. Another interpretation of the phrase is possible, though less likely, if 'misprision' is taken in a legal sense: 'resulting from (my) neglect of duty (i.e. in failing, through my lack of "worth" or "silence" (see e.g. 83.9–12), to fulfil the terms of the "bond" on which your "great gift" was originally granted)'.

12 **Comes home again** See 8 n. above.

12 **on better judgement making** on making a better judgement or more accurate 'estimate' (of yourself and of me).

13–14 Compare *Rom.* 5.1.1–2: 'If I may trust the flattering truth of sleep, / My dreams presage some joyful news at hand'; and 2.2.140–1: 'all this is but a dream, / Too flattering-sweet to be substantial'.

13 **Thus have . . . flatter** Thus I have possessed ('had', with probable sexual overtones; compare 129.6, 10 nn.) you only in the way in which one is flattered in a dream (where desires *appear* to be fulfilled).

14 **In sleep** i.e. in the dream world.

14 **waking** i.e. in the real world.

14 **no such matter** nothing of the sort.

Sonnet 88

Sonnet 88, as Verity notes, sounds like an echo of 49; here the poet does what he had there promised. The readiness to betray the self in the cause of the faithless loved one and the idea of a strange satisfaction of love to be found in doing so are striking (Hood).

1 **be disposed** feel inclined.

1 **set me light** value me little, hold me cheap.

2 **place** (1) set (with a suggestion of 'expose'); (2) rank.

2 **my merit** (1) my worth; (2) my deserving (such as it may be, much or little).

2 **in the eye of scorn** within the view or gaze ('eye') of contempt or mockery. It is not clear whether the 'eye' is the youth's or the 'public eye'; if the former, one would expect 'an eye' rather than 'the eye'. Compare *2H6* 2.4.45–7: 'whilest I . . . / Was made a wonder and a pointing-stock / To every idle rascal follower'; and *Oth.* 4.2.53–5: 'but, alas, to make me / The fixed figure for the time of scorn / To point his slow unmoving finger at!'

4 **prove** The 'proof' follows in lines 5–12.

4 **virtuous** morally justified.

4 **forsworn** perjured (in breaking your 'faith' to me).

5 **weakness** (1) moral or physical liability; (2) vulnerability.

6 **Upon thy part** In your defence.

6 **set down a story** (1) reckon up an account (i.e. draw up a schedule); (2) make a sworn statement; (3) tell a (fictitious) tale.

7 **faults concealed** hidden (1) defects, (2) offences (against my 'faith' to you).

7 **wherein . . . attainted** (1) by which I am tainted or infected; (2) of which I am accused. As Booth notes, however, lines 6–7 are perhaps intentionally ambiguous and may be read to mean 'I can tell about faults on your part, concealed by you, of which I am accused.'

8 **That** So that (as a result of the derogatory nature of the 'faults concealed' revealed in my 'story').

8 **thou in losing me** (1) by your ceasing to possess me; (2) by your destroying or ruining (a) me (compare *Ham.* 3.2.195), (b) my estimation in others' eyes (compare 2 n. above and *Lear* 1.1.232–3); (3) by your forgetting me (compare *MND* 1.1.113–14). Booth points out, however, that, although the following 'win' establishes 'losing' as the primary sense, the Q form 'loosing', at this time a common spelling for 'losing' (or vice versa), may at least suggest a play on 'loose' and 'lose'; in which case the phrase carries the sense of 'by releasing me' or, more strongly, 'by casting me off (i.e. by undoing the ties that bound you to me)'.

8 shall For the occasional use of the plural form with the second-person singular, see Franz 152, and compare 47.10 and 70.1. 'shall' may, of course, be a simple misprint for 'shalt'.

8 win much glory gain or earn great praise (by common consent).

9 a gainer one who derives advantage (see line 12), a winner.

10 For Because.

10 bending . . . on directing, concentrating . . . upon. There is perhaps an admission of perverseness in thus turning 'away' the instinct of self-preservation (Hood).

11 injuries i.e. those caused by reckoning up his 'faults'.

12 Doing thee vantage In doing you a benefit (i.e. in supporting my argument to 'prove thee virtuous' (4)). 'vantage' is an apheptic form of 'advantage'.

12 double vantage me doubly benefit me (first, because you and I are (or were) *one* in love (compare 22.14 n. and 36.2 n.), second, because I (as myself) have been honest in revealing the 'truth' about myself (compare 'Open confession is good for the soul' (Tilley C592)), and, third (Hood), any way of gratifying you, even at my own expense, is an additional gratification to me). There is perhaps an ironic edge to the phrase, since 'double' can also carry the sense of 'false', 'duplicitous', an irony implied in 'injuries' (11) and 'wrong' (14).

13 Such is my love So great is my love (for you).

13 to thee . . . belong I am so (totally) 'possessed' by you ('to you belong' as a possession). In other words, I am unlike you, who are 'too dear for my possessing' (87.1).

14 for thy right for the sake of putting *you* in the right (Tucker) (i.e. giving you the reputation for being 'virtuous' (= 'right'), even 'though thou art forsworn', as the poet promised in line 4).

14 bear all wrong (1) carry the responsibility for all blame (that may arise from your 'forswearing' me; compare 40.11–12); (2) suffer the injustice of taking part against myself in defence of your faithlessness.

Sonnet 89

Sonnet 89 seems to follow naturally from 88 and is clearly linked with 90. The emphasis here is on the readiness to sacrifice the self, however innocent, to the interests of the false beloved.

1 Say that (1) State or argue that (parallel with 'Speak' (line 3); (2) Suppose that.

1 for because of.

1 fault See 88.7 n. That the 'fault' or 'offence' (2) is not true is implied (see 6 n. below).

2 comment upon (1) make unfavourable remarks about; (2) (Hood) provide explanatory notes about. Compare 'set down a story' (88.6) and *TGV* 2.1.40–1: 'not an eye that sees you but is a physician to comment on your malady'.

3 lameness Figuratively: weakness, deficiency (with probable play on 'lame' or 'limping' metrical feet in verse). Compare *TGV* 2.1.87–91 and *AYLI* 3.2.167–71: 'the feet might bear the verses. / *Ros.* Ay, but the feet were lame, and could not bear themselves without the verse, and therefore stood lamely in the verse.' Shakespeare seems to be the first to use 'lameness' and 'lamely' in this figurative sense; see *OED*. On the discredited literal interpretation of 'lameness', see 37.3 n.

3 straight immediately.

3 halt limp (also used figuratively to describe metrically defective verse; compare *Ham.* 2.2.324–5: 'and the lady shall say her mind freely, or the blank verse shall halt for't').

4 reasons i.e. the reasons you allege ('Speak' (3))

5 disgrace disparage, discredit (by withdrawing your favour). There may be play on 'disgrace' = 'disfigure', considering the earlier charge of 'lameness'.

5 ill badly (i.e. to my disadvantage).

6 To set (1) In order to set; (2) In setting.

6 set a form . . . change i.e. set a specious appearance of propriety, i.e. set up an outwardly good model (or 'form') upon a wished for ('desired') change (of heart and favour).

7 disgrace, . . . will: The pointing here follows Q and Capell; Q reads 'disgrace, . . . wil,', leaving it possible to take 'knowing thy will' either with 'As . . . disgrace' or with the following 'I will acquaintance . . .' in line 8. Until Kittredge, however, most editors followed Gildon, placing a semicolon after 'disgrace' and treating 'knowing thy will' as a phrase introducing line 8. Either pointing makes perfectly acceptable sense, but, as Ingram and Redpath point out, the Capell–Kittredge pointing (see collation) seems to accord better with Shakespeare's usual handling of the line unit by not breaking line 7 with a heavy caesural stop after 'disgrace'.

7 knowing thy will knowing what you desire. Sexual suggestions have been detected in 'know' (= have carnal knowledge of) and 'will' (= (a) sexual desire; (b) the male and female pudenda), and some even see 'will' as a pun on 'Will[iam]' (i.e. Shakespeare) as in 135 and 136, sonnets in which all these meanings resonate.

8 acquaintance . . . strange deny any knowledge of you (literally, 'kill my acquaintance with you') and (if we meet) look upon you as I would a stranger. Compare *Ant.* 2.6.120–2: 'the band that seems to tie their friendship together will be the very strangler of their amity'.

9 walks haunts (i.e. where you are usually to be found). Compare *MND* 3.1.165.

9 in my tongue i.e. when I speak.

10 dwell find room, live (as your 'name' formerly did).

11 too much profane too greatly impious, blasphemous (with play perhaps on Latin *profanus* describing 'one who by entering desecrates a sacred precinct'). Considering lines 9–10 and the use of 'hate' in line 14, Shakespeare may, I think, have been recalling the opening lines of Horace's famous ode (III.i): 'Odi profanum vulgus et arceo: / favete linguis.' ('I hate the uninitiate crowd and keep them far away. Observe a reverent silence!' (Loeb)). 'profane' fits the context, but it does not seem to have been noticed that Q's reading 'proface' in the uncorrected state also makes a more difficult though possible sense in the same context. 'proface' (related to Latin *proficere* = to advantage, promote) was a salutation used in eating and drinking and meant 'May it do you good!' (*OED*); it is used by Shakespeare in *2H4* 5.3.28. Thus the phrase 'too much proface', taken in the context of lines 9–10, might be interpreted to mean 'being overly familiar in saluting you by your "sweet belovèd name"'. On the principle of *lectio difficilior*, then, some sort of case might be made for considering 'proface' as Shakespeare's reading and Q's 'prophane' as a proof-corrector's substitution for a word he did not understand.

11 **it** i.e. 'Thy sweet belovèd name' (10).

12 **haply** by chance, accidentally.

12 **of our . . . tell** reveal our former ('old') relationship.

13 **For thee** For your sake, in your defence.

13 **against myself . . . debate** (1) I'll bind myself to argue or dispute (as in a 'debate') against myself ('vow' suggesting 'devotion' as to a saint); (2) I'll declare war ('vow debate') against myself.

14 **For I . . . hate** Compare 149.5–6 and *Ado* 5.2.70–1: 'for I will never love that which my friend hates'.

14 **For** Because.

14 **him** i.e. one like myself.

14 **hate** The conventional opposite of 'to love', but here used in the sense of 'disprize' or 'repudiate' (compare 'set me light' (88.1)) rather than in the stronger sense of 'bear hatred toward'.

Sonnet 90

Sonnet 90 is clearly linked with 89 by the opening line, but more emotionally charged – perhaps as a result of some serious misfortune that has befallen the poet (see lines 2–3), the nature of which is, of course, unknown. Hood, however, suggests that the youth's hypothesised rather than actual hate ('if ever') may signal that 88–90 dramatise and explore in a calculatedly artful way possible rather than 'real' states of love – though, of course, the *idea* of the sacrifice of self volunteered here could be no less meaningful for that.

1–2 The retention of the Q pointing allows line 2 to be read with both 'hate' (1) and 'Join' (3).

1 **Then** Therefore (some suggestion of a temporal sense, however, is implied by 'now, / Now while' (1–2)).

1 **hate** disprize, repudiate. See 89.14 n.

1 **if ever, now** i.e. if you are ever going to 'hate' me, 'hate' me now (at this moment).

2 **world** mankind generally.

2 **bent** determined, resolved (as if 'couched to spring') (*OED* Bent *ppl a* 2).

2 **my deeds** i.e. whatever I do or may attempt to do.

2 **cross** thwart, run counter to.

3 **Join with** i.e. join forces with (a military metaphor picked up in 'rearward', 'conquered' (6), 'overthrow' (8), and 'onset' (11)).

3 **the spite of Fortune** Fortune's malice or injury. Compare 37.3.

3 **make me bow** force or bend me into submission (i.e. humble or cast me down, as the goddess Fortuna was thought of as doing when she turned her wheel adversely).

4 **drop in . . . after-loss** fall upon (me), crushingly, (1) as, (2) to achieve a future (final?) defeat or woe ('after-loss'). Kerrigan compares *Ant.* 3.13.158–62: 'Ah, dear, if I be so, / From my cold heart let heaven engender hail, / And poison it in the source, and the first stone / Drop in my neck; as it determines, so / Dissolve my life!' Although *OED* (Drop *v* 27b) glosses 'drop in' in the sense of 'come in unexpectedly or casually' and cites line 4, this sense is otherwise unattested before 1667.

5 **scaped** Aphetic form of 'escaped'.

5 **this sorrow** i.e. the misfortune referred to in lines 2–3.

6 **Come in . . . woe** Attack with a rearguard action after a victory has been won over an earlier grief ('conquered woe' = 'this sorrow' (5)). Compare *Ado* 4.1.126–7: 'on the rearward of reproaches, / Strike at thy life'.

7 **Give not** Do not impose.

7 **windy night** Metaphorical for 'a darkly turbulent state of mind'.

7 **rainy morrow** Metaphorical for 'a morrow that brings (further) tears'. On the relation of 'rain' (as 'tears') following 'windy tempest', compare *Rape of Lucrece*, 1788–92. Line 7 begs the youth not to reverse the proverb 'A blustering night [promises] a fair day' (Tilley N166).

8 **To** In order to.

8 **linger out** prolong, draw out.

8 **purposed overthrow** intended, planned destruction or ruin (by (a) the youth, (b) Fortune, (c) both).

9 **thou wilt leave me** i.e. you are determined to abandon or forsake me.

9 **do not . . . last** i.e. do not be the last of my claims to happiness or good fortune to do so.

10 **When** After that time when.

10 **other petty griefs** i.e. other comparatively small sorrows ('petty' compared to the loss of you).

10 have . . . spite have already inflicted their injury.

11 onset vanguard (i.e. as in the first line of an attacking army).

11 so in this way.

11 taste experience, feel ('taste' suggesting the 'bitterness' of the 'worst' in line 12).

12 might power, strength.

13 strains of woe (1) kinds, degrees, (2) stresses of grief or sorrow. Compare *Ado* 5.1.11–14: 'Measure his woe the length and breadth of mine, / And let it answer every strain for strain, / As thus for thus, and such a grief for such, / In every lineament, branch, shape, and form.'

13 seem may appear to be.

14 will not seem so will not (in comparison 'with loss of thee') seem to be such ('so', i.e. 'woe' (13)).

Sonnet 91

1 glory in (1) rejoice in; (2) boast of.

1 birth i.e. exalted social position (compare 'high birth' in line 9).

1 skill knowledge, cleverness, art.

2 body's force physical strength. Capell's 'body's' for Q 'bodies' is adopted by most editors (see collation), but the plural possessive 'bodies'' makes equally good sense.

3 new-fangled ill i.e. badly ('ill') tailored in the most extreme new and foppish fashion. 'ill' is somewhat tautological since 'new-fangled' always carried a pejorative force.

4 horse i.e. horses. For 'horse' as a plural, see Abbott 471. The singular is possible, but, taken with the plural in 'hawks and hounds' and 'horses' in line 11, unlikely. Q capitalises all three (and two again in line 11) and Wyndham suggests that Shakespeare is using the words generally to characterise the pursuits of hawking, hunting, and manège (i.e. horsemanship) – three of the principal gentlemanly 'delight[s]' (11) of the period. For the probable tone, Hood compares Thomas Campion's *Third Book of Ayres* (1612?), xxvii, 13–16: 'Men when their affaires require, / Must a while themselves retire: / Sometimes hunt, and sometimes hawke, / And not ever sit and talke.'

5 every humour (1) each mental disposition, temperament; (2) each whim. 'humour' refers to the 'four humours' which were believed to circulate in the body and govern its psychological bent (see 45.8 n.).

5 hath his adjunct pleasure has its ('his') own enjoyment or delight peculiarly connected or associated ('adjunct') with it. It was believed that *one* of the four humours, each with its special inherent tendencies, nearly always predominated in a person's bodily and psychological make-up, a 'balanced humour' – Horatio in *Hamlet*, for example – being a great rarity. Shakespeare is the first to use 'adjunct' as an adjective (see *OED*).

6 it finds . . . rest the individual 'humour' ('it') discovers or experiences a pleasure ('joy') (1) peculiar to it, (2) beyond its other joys.

7 these particulars i.e. (1) the 'pleasures' or 'joys' listed in lines 1–4 which particularly 'delight' (11) some people; (2) the limited individual components of the total experience of 'delight' (11; 'one general best' (8)).

7 are not my measure (1) are not adequate to satisfy me (i.e. my 'humour'); (2) do not constitute a standard or limit for me; (3) do not fit me (i.e. like the 'garments . . . new-fangled ill' in line 3, 'these particulars' are not 'made to my measure').

8 better surpass, improve upon.

8 one general best a single, all-embracing, and superlative 'joy' (i.e. 'Thy love' (9), which, in 'one', contains the 'best' of all possible sources of happiness because you are the 'essence' of perfection).

9–12 Recapitulates in the comparative mode the various 'particulars' (7) of lines 1–4, a conventional structural device, omitting, however, 'skill' (1), 'body's force' (2), and 'hounds' (4).

10 Richer than wealth Plays on 'riches' = 'wealth'.

10 prouder . . . cost i.e. a source of pride greater than costly or splendid garments. Compare 64.2 and *Cym.* 3.3.23–4: 'Richer than doing nothing for a bable [i.e. trifle]; / Prouder than rustling in unpaid-for silk'.

11 Of more delight Giving greater pleasure or joy.

11 be are capable of giving.

12 And having . . . boast And in possessing you (with a possible suggestion of 'having' you carnally) I may boast (compare 'glory in' (1)) of possessing that which would be the most prized possession ('pride') of all men (if they could aspire to it).

13–14 Contrast the mood of confidence in the concluding couplet in 25.

13 Wretched in this alone Only unhappy or to be pitied in this (i.e. the possibility that 'thou mayst take / All this away' (13–14)).

14 All this Refers to the riches of 'Thy love' described in lines 9–12.

Sonnet 92

Sonnet 92 is an answer to the fears expressed in 91.13–14: the poet cannot be made 'most wretched' by the loss of the youth's love because such a loss (or even a hint of such a loss) will kill him at once. The idea is conventional. Booth compares *LLL* 5.4.108–20 for themes and language. For the critical tone of 92–6, compare 33–6.

1 But Nevertheless.

1 do thy worst go to the most extreme lengths (by repudiating your love for me; see 5 n. below). As Hood notes, however, the mood of 'do' may well be subjunctive and mean 'suppose you did'.

1 **steal thyself away** i.e. rob me of your love
(with a strong suggestion in 'steal . . . away' of 'withdraw surreptitiously', 'convey stealthily', 'sneak off',
implying a gradual appearance of withdrawal of the
youth's love (= little hints of coldness; compare 'the
least of them (i.e. "wrongs")' in line 6), when in fact
he has already decided to abandon the poet).

2 **term of life** duration of (my) lifetime (a legal
term, like the following 'assurèd' = pledges, guaran-
teed by deed, with a play on 'betrothed' in marriage).

3–4 **And life . . . thine** i.e. the poet will die immediately upon losing the youth's love.

3 **stay** remain steadfast.

4 **For** Because.

4 **depends upon** is contingent on, hangs on.

5 **worst of wrongs** i.e. the complete loss of
your love. Focuses the implications of 'worst' in
line 1.

6 **in the least of them** i.e. in (suffering) the
slightest hint of coldness or inconstancy ('them'
referring to 'wrongs' in line 5). Contrast 89.5–6.

7 **I see** I perceive or understand that. The Q
comma after 'see' may have been intended to emphasise the ellipsis of 'that'.

7–8 **a better state . . . which** (I perceive that) I
am in or possess ('to me belongs') a (psychological)
condition or state better than that which.

8 **humour** (1) whim, caprice; (2) mental disposition, character.

9–10 **Thou canst . . . lie** You can't make me
wretched ('vex me'; compare 91.14) by being inconstant ('with inconstant mind') because my life hangs
('doth lie') upon your inconstancy ('revolt'). In other
words, the minute you are inconstant I will die and
therefore will not live long enough to suffer vexa-
tion. Compare *John* 3.1.322: 'O foul revolt of French
inconstancy!'

11 **happy title** (1) title to happiness; (2) fortunate
legal title (that 'assurèd' for 'term of life' in line 2
above).

11 **find** discover (myself to be possessed of).

12 **Happy . . . happy** (1) Joyful; (2) Fortunate;
(3) Blessed.

12 **have thy love** possess your love (for the 'term'
of my life).

12 **to die** i.e. for your love, if I have lost it. There
is possibly some sexual innuendo in 'have' (= possess
carnally) and 'die' (= experience orgasm).

13 **But what's . . . blot** But what condition or
state of being (my 'better state' of line 7) is so happily fortunate (and) beautiful ('blessèd-fair') that it
fears no blemish? The antecedent of 'what' is thus
presumably 'happy title' in line 11, and 'blot' is the
'fly in the ointment' of that 'happy title', a 'blot' that
is, however, transferred to the youth in line 12. It
is tempting to take 'blessèd' as a quasi-adverb (=
blessedly), but *OED* (Blessed *ppl a* 6) cites only this
line as authority for such usage. Although, to my

knowledge, no one has here questioned the Q text,
it may be possible, I think, that Q 'feares' may be a
compositorial misreading (or simple typographical
error) for 'beares' (= carries with it), a reading that
allows 'what' to refer to the youth, obviates the awkwardness of describing 'a happy title' (11) as 'fair'
(an adjective often applied to the youth), and links
'blot' directly with the youth without the necessity
of transference in line 12. The line would then mean:
'But what is so blessèd (and) fair in appearance that
does not carry with it a blemish?' Both readings may
be supported by *Rape of Lucrece*, 853–4: 'But no perfection is so absolute, / That some impurity doth
not pollute' (referring to the belief that all sublunary
creation was of mixed, not pure, composition); the
second, by 95.9–12, where 'beauty's veil doth cover
every blot'.

14 **mayst** i.e. now or hereafter.

14 **yet** (1) nevertheless, for all that; (2) still (now
or hereafter). The present–future temporal uncertainty (whether the youth already is or may later be
'false' and whether the poet can now or later recognise
('know') such falsity under 'beauty's veil' (95.11)) is
skilfully conveyed.

Sonnet 93

Sonnet 93 continues the theme of fear and uncertainty announced in 92.13–14: the 'face' (outward
appearance) of love may not change even though the
'heart' (inner reality) of love may be dead. Compare
Mac. 1.4.11–12: 'There's no art / To find the mind's
construction in the face', and *Cym.* 5.5.62–6. At two
places 93 is syntactically awkward and potentially
confusing: lines 5 and 11 are so phrased that at first
they appear respectively to modify lines 4 and 10, and
that each is syntactically the beginning of a new construction does not register fully until lines 6 and 12
(see collation for the pointing here adopted). Booth
retains the Q comma at the end of line 10, arguing
that 11 does double duty, first modifying 10 and then
modifying 12.

1 **So shall I live** For this reason (i.e. the uncertain, imperceptible status of the youth's love for me)
I shall continue to live (even though I would be happy
to die (92.12) if I 'knew' that I had lost his love).

2 **deceivèd husband** i.e. husband who fears his
wife may have been unfaithful (not one who *knows*
he is a cuckold).

2 **so** with the result that.

2 **love's face** i.e. the outward appearance of love
as it may be registered by the face (not the actual face
of the one loved).

3 **still seem love to me** i.e. continue to appear
like (true) love to me. 'seem', as often in Shakespeare,
carries overtones of hypocrisy.

3 **though altered new** even if (your love) may be
newly changed (i.e. it is not the 'face' (2) or 'looks' (4)
of your love that may be newly altered, but your 'love'

itself). For the ellipsis of 'it is' ('it' here referring to
'love') after 'though', see Abbott 403.

4 Thy looks . . . place i.e. the outward appearance or expression ('looks') of your love thus remains
unaltered so far as I am concerned ('(are) with me'),
but the inner reality ('heart') of your love may be
placed elsewhere ('in other place').

5 For Because

5 can live . . . eye i.e. your eye (= your face) is so
perfect in beauty that nothing ugly such as 'hatred'
can inhabit there.

6 in that i.e. by looking into your eyes, observing
your 'looks' (4).

6 know thy change i.e. know whether your love
for me has changed or not.

7 false heart's history story of the heart's falsity.

8 writ in clearly revealed (as if inscribed) by.

8 moods feelings (of anger).

8 wrinkles strange unusual or uncharacteristic
grimaces (such as sneering, grinning, etc., including
'frowns').

9 in thy creation i.e. when you were created (by
'heaven').

9 decree ordain.

10 sweet love (apparently) (1) charming, gracious, (2) precious love (i.e. 'love' having the appearance of 'true love').

10 should would.

11 heart's workings be operations of the heart
(as the seat of thought, feeling, and love or hatred)
may be (in fact). Compare *LLL* 4.1.33.

12 looks See 4 n. above.

12 should nothing . . . tell i.e. would ('should')
report or reveal nothing from 'Thy looks' except graciousness or affection (thus reflecting *apparent* constancy in your love for me).

13–14 The question posed by the couplet suddenly and powerfully undercuts the conventional
nonsense of lines 5–12 by giving true expression to
the poet's 'heart's workings'.

13 like to.

13 Eve's apple The *outward* beauty of 'Eve's
apple' is vouched for by Gen. 3.6: 'So the woman
(seeing that the tree was good for meat, and that
it was pleasant to the eyes' (Geneva). For its *inner*
poison (sin and death) compare *MV* 1.3.101–2: 'A
goodly apple rotten at the heart. / O, what a goodly
outside falsehood hath!' The apple image may have
been suggested to Shakespeare by a kind of apple
known to the Elizabethans as a 'sweeting'; note the
repeated emphasis on 'sweet' (10), 'sweetness' (12),
and 'sweet' (14).

13 grow (1) become; (2) flourish.

14 virtue moral character (with play perhaps on
'chastity').

14 answer not thy show does not accord with
your outward appearance ('show'; compare 'face' in
lines 2 and 10). Compare 69.13–14.

Sonnet 94

Sonnet 94 is one of the most enigmatic and most
discussed of the Sonnets. Critics have tended to fall
roughly into two camps: (1) those who view the poet's
treatment of the kind of individuals sketched in lines
1–10 as conveying his approval (lines 11–14 furnish-
ing a warning of what can happen to such individuals if they abuse the 'graces' that 'heaven' has given
them); (2) those who read the poem as a sustained
piece of irony conveying condemnation. There is,
however, more than enough ambiguity in the sonnet (see the notes below) to make any single view
highly questionable. Although seemingly an impersonal and abstract 'meditation' (note the absence of
'I' (= the poet), 'thou/you' (= the youth), and the
'love' theme), one that might appear to be an essentially detached (and detachable) poem, 94 evidences
close links, in theme, imagery, language, and structure with the poet's unhappiness over his relations
with the youth as expressed in 93 (and hence in
91–2). Consider, for example, the distinction drawn
between two kinds of men in 93.1–6 and 7–8 with
the similar distinction in 94.1–7 and 3, 8, the play on
'face' in 93.2, 10 and 94.7; the hand of 'heaven' in the
creation of the youth (93.9–10) and of 'They' (94.5);
and the concluding horticultural metaphors, 'apple'
in 93.13–14 and 'flow'r–Lilies' in 94.9–14, the first
directly applied to the youth, the second implying
the youth. Thus, however detached and impersonal
94 may seem to be in itself, the youth and the poet's
involvement with the youth furnish the generating
sub-text and support the Q ordering at this point.
Compare, perhaps, *A Lover's Complaint*, 190–6.

1 They that . . . none Proverbial; see Tilley H170
('To be able to do harm and not to do it is noble'),
deriving presumably from the Latin tag *Posse et nolle,
nobile*. As Tilley points out, Shakespeare also uses
variants of the idea in *LLL* 2.1.56–8, *AYLI* 4.3.128–
30, *MM* 2.2.107–9, and *Cor.* 5.1.18–19, originally
influenced perhaps by Sidney, *Arcadia* (1590), p. 246:
'but the more power he [Plangus] hath to hurte, the
more admirable is his praise, the he wil not hurt'.

1 will do desire or will to do (though the simple
future may also be operative).

1 none i.e. no hurt. Schmidt comments on this
as an example of Shakespeare's habit 'of abstracting
nouns from preceding verbs'.

2 That do not do . . . show i.e. that do not exercise ('do not do') the 'pow'r' (= 'the thing') that
they so abundantly ('most') appear to possess ('do
show'). It later becomes clear that the 'pow'r' here
referred to is primarily that of physical beauty. Taken
by itself, without the controlling context of line 1,
line 2 is ambiguous and can be read as an accusation:
'(They) that fail to do what they make most show
of doing'. In either case, however, there is the ominous echo of 'show' (= mere outward appearance)
from 93.14.

3 moving (1) influencing; (2) tempting, inciting. Compare 41.4 and 96.11–12.

3 as stone i.e. as immovable and fixed as a rock (inanimate matter). Booth suggests a play on 'lodestone', which, like a magnet and 'They', has 'attractive' qualities. See next note.

4 cold i.e. of a cold 'humour' or 'complexion', lacking in passion or feeling. Compare the adjective 'stone-cold' and *H5* 2.3.25–6: 'and all was as cold as any stone'.

4 to temptation slow i.e. not easily or quickly tempted ((a) to exercise their 'pow'r' over 'others'; (b) to indulge their senses and appetite). This phrase allows some measure of 'life' to the 'dead' implications of 'stone' (3), 'Unmovèd', and 'cold'. Lines 3–4, in contrast to the general tone of lines 1–2, are ice-cold, and, though they may be read favourably, may also, in Pope's words, be said to 'damn with faint praise'.

5 rightly (1) properly, truly; (2) by right.

5 do inherit are the heirs to (in a right line of succession).

5 heaven's graces God's favours or gifts (moral, intellectual, and physical).

6 husband save by prudent use (like a good steward).

6 nature's riches (1) abundant endowments given (them) by nature ('nature' thus becoming a surrogate for 'heaven' in line 5); (2) wealth of created nature (like 'They', also the inheritor of 'heaven's graces').

6 expense waste, loss (perhaps with reference to sexual 'spending'; compare 129.1). The tone of lines 5–6, although possible criticism has been seen in 'husband' (i.e. a suggestion perhaps of miserliness), seems approving, reflecting the comparative warmth of lines 1–2.

7 They are . . . faces They are the (sole) controllers ('lords and owners') of the appearance ('faces') they exhibit (to the world). This strange line appears to undercut all the apparently favourable comments about 'They' in lines 1–6, reducing them to a mere mirage of self-control, and suggests that below the surface (i.e. their 'faces'; compare 93.2, 10–12) lies something much less beautiful and admirable (i.e. although they may control others, 'They' don't, in fact, control themselves, a charge directly levelled in the savage concluding couplet). As in the case of the youth, in 93.10–12, no one, then, including the poet, can judge their true nature ('heart's workings' (93.11)) from their outward appearance: 'meet it is I set it down / That one may smile, and smile, and be a villain!' (*Ham.* 1.5.107–8).

8 Others but . . . excellence i.e. ordinary men ('Others' when compared to 'They') are only ('but') like stewards, who, lacking in themselves the rich endowments ('excellence') of their 'lords' (= 'They'), can only participate at second hand in these endowments as faithful administrators or dispensers (i.e. 'stewards') of such 'excellence' (as the poet may be said to have done in most of the preceding sonnets). This would seem to be the primary meaning, taking 'lords and owners' as the antecedent of 'their', but there is ambiguity since 'their' may also be taken as referring to 'stewards', in which case the line would mean: 'Other ordinary men only hold their "excellence" in trust (as "stewards") and, unlike "They", are not the "owners" of it.' Empson (*Pastoral*, p. 93) suggests a play in 'excellence' on the titular form of address 'Your excellence' or 'Your excellency'.

9 is to . . . sweet affords sweet fragrance to summer. Compare 54.3–4.

10 to itself . . . die i.e. it may live and die only in (and for) itself (without making any 'conscious' contribution). For the transposed use of 'only', see Abbott 420. Compare 54.9–11, where, however, the idea of 'dying to itself' is pejoratively applied to 'canker blooms' (= 'weeds') as compared with 'roses' (= 'flow'r[s]') which give of their 'sweet odour' to 'summer's breath' (note the reference to the 'fragrant rose' in 95.2). In 54, as elsewhere, the 'rose' is a metaphor for the youth and thus links the present 'flow'r' image to those earlier uses by implication. The praise of the 'flow'r' that lives and dies 'to itself' contradicts, of course, the general theme of the 'procreation sonnets' (1–17); compare 5.9–14.

11 with base infection meet i.e. become contaminated ('meet' = come in contact) with a loathsome disease. 'base infection' may suggest venereal disease. Compare 35.4: 'And loathsome canker lives in sweetest bud'.

12 basest weed meanest, lowliest weed (with play on 'weed' = garment, clothing, implied in 'outbraves'). The phrase occurs in *Edward III* 2.1.164; see 14 n. below.

12 outbraves surpasses or outrivals in splendid appearance or 'show'.

12 his dignity its worth, excellence (compare 'excellence' in line 8). 'dignity' also suggests 'rank' or 'social status' of the kind associated with 'They' as 'lords and owners' in line 7.

13 For sweetest . . . deeds Proverbial; see Tilley c668: 'The corruption of the best is worst' (compare the Latin tag: *Optimi corruptio pessima*), and N317: 'Nothing so good but it (the best things, everything) may be abused'. Compare *Rom.* 2.3.19–20: 'Nor aught so good but, strain'd from that fair use, / Revolts from true birth, stumbling on abuse', and *Rape of Lucrece*, 1006: 'For greatest scandal waits on greatest state.' A similar collocation of 'sour' and 'sweet' occurs in *Edward III* 4.4.3 (see line 14 n. below).

13 deeds i.e. faults, bad actions (the pejorative connotation being governed by context). Compare 69.9–14 and *Rape of Lucrece*, 1002–3: 'The baser is he, coming from a king, / To shame his hope with deeds degenerate.'

14 Lilies that fester . . . weeds A variation of the proverb 'The lily is fair in show but foul in smell' (Tilley L297) and connected with Tilley C668 (see 13 n. above). The line appears verbatim in the anonymous *Edward III* 2.1.451 and is followed by two lines which are a variant statement of line 13 above: 'And every glory [compare 'sweetest things'] that inclynes to sin, / The shame is treble by the opposite.' The play, written perhaps as early as 1591, was entered in the Stationers' Register on 1 December 1595, published by Cuthbert Burby in 1596, and attributed to Shakespeare by Capell in his *Prolusions* (1760). Until quite recently, however, later critics argued for Shakespeare's hand only in 1.2.90–166, 2.1–2 (the 'Countess scenes', in which line 14 occurs), and 4.4 (see Kenneth Muir, *Shakespeare as Collaborator*, 1960). There is no firm evidence to establish priority between *Edward III* and Sonnet 94, though most would agree, I think, that *Edward III* is probably the earlier. Other verbal parallels with the Sonnets are pointed out in the notes to 33.2, 41.1, 94.12, 13, and 142.6, and a hitherto unnoticed link between the Sonnets and the 'Shakespearean' parts of *Edward III* (the rare compositorial misreading of 'thy' as 'their' (see 26.12 n.) which they have in common) is discussed in the Textual Analysis, pp. 263–5 below.

14 Lilies The lily was known for its external beauty; see Tilley L297 (quoted above) and Luke 12.27: 'Consider the lilies how they grow: they labour not, neither spin they: yet I say unto you, that Solomon himself in all his royalty was not clothed like one of these' (Geneva) Note that, in both, the lily is a symbol of outward beauty ('show', 'clothed') and hence a fitting flower metaphor for 'They', whose 'deeds' (13) do not always 'answer . . . [their] show' (93.14). Compare Brandon, *The Virtuous Octavia* (1598), 'Octavia to Antonius', lines 438–441 (MSR): 'Nor are the fayrest alwayes found, / The best, (as I suppose) / Some noysome flowers, do seeme as faire, / As doth the fragrant Rose.' See 10 n. above.

14 fester rot. 'fester' suggests internal disease, a 'rot' that might not 'show' except as a doubly noisome 'smell', the scent of a healthy lily being already noisome; see 95.2 n. and 69.12–13, where 'thy odour matcheth not thy show'.

14 weeds (1) weeds generally; (2) even weeds that 'fester'.

Sonnet 95

Sonnet 95 focuses on the youth the criticism implicit in 94's seemingly generalised and impersonal comments about 'They'. It also shows thematic and linguistic links with 69, and 40.13 ('Lascivious grace, in whom all ill well shows') might be taken as an epigraph for the sonnet as a whole.

1 sweet Echoes 'sweetest things' in 94.13 and is re-echoed in 'sweets' (4).

1 sweet and lovely i.e. in appearance because your physical 'beauty' remains untarnished by your 'deeds' (94.13).

1 shame disgrace.

2 canker . . . rose i.e. the 'canker worm' or caterpillar which destroys the bud of the rose. There is also play on the 'fragrant rose' and the 'canker rose', the inferior, scentless dog-rose or wild rose. See 35.4 n. and 70.7. The image picks up the internal disease (compare line 4) suggested by 'fester' in 94.14 (see note); despite the hidden 'canker', however, the rose is described as 'fragrant'. The 'flow'r–Lilies' metaphor of 94.9–14 here becomes the 'rose', the usual metaphor for the youth.

3 spot blemish.

3 beauty . . . budding name i.e. your external, physical 'beauty' and your youthful ('budding') reputation for or as a result of it.

4 sweets delectably 'sweet' outward appearances (with suggestion of sexual pleasures; compare Francis Beaumont, *Salmacis and Hermaphroditus* (1602), lines 342, 467 (ed. N. Alexander, 1968).

4 inclose enclose (variant form). 'Inclose' suggests that the youth's 'sins' are hidden behind a 'face' of 'sweets' (compare 54.8, 93.12).

5 tells . . . days gives an account ('tells the story') of your life ('days'). Hood notes that this sense of 'closes the account' is found in a poem attributed to Raleigh, 'Nature that washt her hands in milke' (31–7): 'Oh cruell Time . . . When we have wandred all our wayes / Shutts up the story of our dayes.'

6 Making lascivious . . . sport Making lewd, wanton remarks ('lascivious comments') about your (1) diversions, (2) amorous dalliance, sensual self-indulgence ('sport'; compare 'sportive blood' (121.6), 'gentle sport' (96.2), and *Oth.* 2.1.226–7: 'When the blood is made dull with the act of sport').

7–8 Cannot dispraise . . . report As here pointed (following Q; see collation) these lines may be paraphrased: '(That tongue) is unable to censure or disparage (even though it makes "lascivious comments on thy sport"), but (instead), by a "kind" of praise, (in) naming your name (i.e. associating you with the censure), turns the intended "ill report" into a benediction ("blesses").' Most editors, until recently, have preferred the Capell–Malone pointing (see collation), reading 'but' in line 7 as meaning 'except' and making 'Naming thy name' the subject of 'blesses' in line 8. This, admittedly, tightens the rather parenthetical 'meandering flow' of lines 5–8 (Ingram and Redpath), and allows the quatrain to end with a strong independent summary statement, though it does not materially alter the meaning of lines 5–8. Since the Q pointing is certainly for the most part not authorial (see Textual Analysis, p. 280 below), choice must rest with the individual reader.

8 ill report (1) = 'lascivious comments' (line 6); (2) bad repute. Compare 96.4 and *Ant.* 2.2.237–9: 'for vildest things / Become themselves in her, that the holy priests / Bless her when she is riggish'; and see 'all things turns to fair' in line 12.

9 what a mansion...got Compare *Rom.* 3.2.84–5: 'O that deceit should dwell / In such a gorgeous palace!' (the preceding lines (73–83) also deal with the appearance–reality theme) and 3.3.107–8 in which 'mansion' = body.

9 mansion large and stately residence, manor house. As Hood notes, this is the kind of house imagined in 94 where the 'lords and owners' (7) could employ 'stewards'. The connection with 94 is further strengthened by the biblical association of 'mansions' with places of 'heaven's graces' (5); see John 14.2: 'In my father's house are many mansions' (Book of Common Prayer, Gospel for Saint Philip and James Day).

9 those vices i.e. the 'sins' in line 4 (lines 9–10 being essentially a rephrasing of line 4).

10 for their . . . thee i.e. selected ('chose out') you for their dwelling place ('habitation'). Compare 'resort' in 96.4.

11 beauty's veil i.e. the skin, or flesh, the outer covering of beauty. Compare Tilley B170 ('Beauty is but skin-deep') and Heb. 10.20 (Geneva), where 'veil' = flesh.

11 blot blemish, sin, vice.

12 all things i.e. everything, including sins and vices.

12 turns to fair converts to (an appearance of) beauty. The subject of 'turns' is probably 'veil' (11), though it is also possible to take 'turns' as an example of the old third-person plural in -*s*, still common in Elizabethan English (see Abbott 333 and 41.3 n.), in which case 'all things' would be the subject.

12 eyes can see Eyes can see only the outer appearance; they cannot penetrate below the surface or 'veil' (11).

13 Take heed . . . of Be careful how you use (or abuse).

13 dear heart i.e. the youth, used as a term of endearment, but with a suggestion in 'heart' (= one's moral being, spirit) that the youth should consider his moral health and look into how he uses his 'heart'.

13 this large privilege this great personal superiority or advantage which the perfection of your physical beauty accords you (with perhaps a suggestion in 'large' that 'privilege' can become an excuse for mere 'licence').

14 The hardest . . . edge The hardest knife (i.e. one made of the best steel) if misused loses its ('his') cutting edge. 'knife' refers figuratively to the youth's 'large privilege' (13) and may be intended to convey a phallic suggestion. The line sounds proverbial but is unrecorded by Tilley or *ODEP*. Nashe, however, in *Christs Teares over Jerusalem* (1593), offers

what seems to be a close parallel, which also sounds proverbial: 'No sword but wil loose his edge in long striking against stones' (Nashe, *Works*, II, 37). Hood notes that the warning complements in personal terms that given at the end of 94 in terms of 'They'.

Sonnet 96

Sonnet 96 continues the theme of 95: the youth's outward beauty is such that it makes sins ('faults') appear like virtues ('graces').

1 thy fault is youth your sin or folly is of the kind commonly incident to youth. In the 'Homily against Whoredom and Uncleanness', Part 1 (*Book of Homilies* (1547)), those who make light of such sins are accused of treating adultery as 'a pastime [compare 'sport' in line 2], a dalliance, and but a touch of youth'.

1 some i.e. some others say.

1 wantonness (1) lechery; (2) frivolity; (3) high-spirited extravagant behaviour. The primary emphasis, however, seems to be on (1), thus contrasting with the more generally sympathetic view taken by the first 'Some'. The second 'some' may glance back at 'That tongue' that made 'lascivious comments on thy sport' in 95.5–6.

2 Some i.e. a third group.

2 thy grace . . . sport i.e. your charm ('grace') lies in your youthfulness ('is youth') coupled with the behaviour (sexual and otherwise) befitting a gentleman ('gentle sport'; compare 95.6). For the attitude here expressed toward the behaviour of upper-class or aristocratic young men, compare Polonius on Hamlet: 'For Lord Hamlet, / Believe so much in him, that he is young, / And with a larger teder [i.e. longer tether] may he walk / Than may be given you [Ophelia]' (*Ham.* 1.3.123–6).

3 Both grace . . . less i.e. both your 'grace' and 'faults' are loved by high and low ('more and less', i.e. everybody, from nobles to commoners).

4 mak'st faults graces i.e. give to sins attractive qualities, making them seem like virtues.

4 that i.e. the 'faults' which.

4 resort Compare 'chose out thee' (95.10). The youth may be said to suffer from the 'vice' of 'attractiveness'.

5 thronèd queen i.e. a queen seated in her royal state (= throne).

6 basest least valuable.

6 well esteemed valued highly (only because 'on the finger of a thronèd queen').

7 So In the same way. Applies the simile begun with 'As' (5) to the youth.

7 errors i.e. a somewhat softened synonym for the 'faults' attributed to the youth in lines 1–4 and the 'sins' and 'vices' mentioned in 95.4, 9.

8 To truths translated Transformed into virtues ('truths') (*not*, shown to be the 'truth' about you). Since Knight, the Q comma after 'seen' (7) has usually been omitted; it is possible, however, to take 'To truths translated', as parenthetical (i.e. 'Being transformed to virtues') and to read line 7 as meaning 'In the same way those errors are (well esteemed) that are observed ("seen") in you.'

8 true things deemed (are) judged to be virtuous actions ('true things').

9 lambs . . . wolf The wolf (as despoiler) and lamb (as innocent victim) are a commonplace of Aesopic literature (compare *Rape of Lucrece*, 677: 'The wolf hath seiz'd his prey, the poor lamb cries').

9 stern cruel, merciless.

9 betray entrap, ensnare, seduce.

10 like a lamb to resemble a lamb.

10 looks translate appearance transform. Bottom was 'translated' to an ass (*MND* 3.1.18–19). Compare the proverb 'A wolf in a lamb's (sheep's) skin' (Tilley w614).

11 gazers i.e. those who see only your lamblike appearance.

11 lead away mislead, seduce (compare 'betray' in line 9, 'Who, moving others' in 94.3, and 41.4).

12 strength of all thy state (full) power ('strength') of all your greatness, magnificence, and, perhaps, rank. See 64.2 n. and compare the apparently contrasting implications of 94.1–2).

13–14 These lines repeat, *verbatim ac literatim*, the couplet of 36.13–14, where they seem more integral to the argument. In the present context, the couplet furnishes a flat, if intelligible, conclusion to a rather flat sonnet, though, as Kerrigan points out, both couplets conclude groups of sonnets (33–6 and 92–6) critical of the youth: 'The common couplet makes the two groups rhyme, as it were.' This may seem fanciful, but, if we assume that Shakespeare is responsible for the repetition, it is as good an 'explanation' as any that has been offered (see Rollins, I, 238).

13 But do not so i.e. do not use 'the strength of all thy state' (12) to mislead or seduce others.

13–14 I love . . . report See 36.13–14 nn. Did the 'ill report' in 95.8 perhaps recall to Shakespeare's mind the 'good report' of 36.14?

Sonnet 97

Sonnet 97 begins a group of 'separation' sonnets (97–9; compare 27–8, 43–5) and offers no clear links with 92–6, though some critics suggest that 'absence' represents an emotional estrangement, reflecting the poet's unhappiness with the youth's behaviour criticised in 92–6, rather than a physical separation.

1–4 Compare 5.5–8 for theme (the 'deadness of winter').

1 winter i.e. the dead, sterile season.

1 absence separation (probably physical; see headnote).

2 the pleasure . . . year the source of joy and delight throughout the swiftly passing seasons

('year') (a 'pleasure' that would be constant even in 'winter' if you were present to me). Q employs question marks at the ends of lines 2, 3, and 4 (see collation); the use of what may be called 'exclamatory question marks' (where we would use an exclamation mark) was common in this period, the exclamation mark being a comparative newcomer and rarely used in Q.

3 What Exclamatory, suggesting extreme or unbearable 'freezings', 'dark days', 'bareness' (4).

4 old December's i.e. by December the 'fleeting year' (2) is approaching its demise, 'Sans teeth, sans eyes, sans taste, sans every thing' (*AYLI* 2.7.166). Compare Ovid, *Metamorphoses* XV, 212–13 (Golding, 233–4): 'Then ugly winter last / Like age steales on with trembling steppes.'

4 bareness every where The same phrase appears in 5.8; see there the notes on 'bareness' and 'every where'.

5 And yet . . . summer's time Despite all this, this period of absence or separation ('this time removed') was (in fact) the summer season. Compare *R2* 2.3.79: 'To take advantage of the absent time'.

6–10 The teeming autumn . . . fruit Ingram and Redpath were the first to explain satisfactorily what at first sight (by the sudden introduction of autumn) had here seemed to be a confusion in the time-scheme, i.e. that 'summer's time' (5) offers all the burgeoning *promise* of autumn's 'issue' (9), and it is the poet's subjective reaction to the fecund *promise* of autumn (birth or harvest is yet to come), not its actual 'issue', that generates the melancholy tone dominating these lines. Summer is flourishing, but by contrast – a contrast that only increases his unhappiness now and in the prospect of a rich autumn – the poet's mood reflects the cold sterility of winter. Compare the persona's reaction to spring in Petrarch's *Rime sparse*, 310, and Donne's 'Twicknam Garden'. Note the extended use of the imagery of parturition throughout these lines.

6 teeming fertile, prolific. Shakespeare seems to be the first to use 'teeming' in this sense; compare *R2* 2.1.51.

6 big pregnant (as with child). Compare *MND* 2.1.112: 'The childing autumn'.

6 rich increase abundant, unstinted (number of) progeny. Compare 'abundant issue' in line 9.

7 Bearing . . . prime Carrying ('Bearing' like a woman 'big with child') the (1) frolicsome, (2) luxuriant, (3) amorously sportive ('wanton' as glossed by Ingram and Redpath) progeny or increase ('burthen') of the spring ('prime', the season of generation). Compare *R2* 1.3.214: 'Four lagging winters and four wanton springs', and Spenser, *Faerie Queene*, III, vi, 42.4: 'And with fresh colours decke the wanton Prime'.

8 Like widowed . . . decease The 'teeming autumn' is here compared to the wives of deceased 'lords' who have left their widows ('widowed wombs') pregnant. Shakespeare may have intended us to read 'widowèd' and 'unfatherèd' (10); see collation.

9 Yet Nevertheless (despite all this rich promise of 'increase' (6)).

9 issue i.e. nature's potential or promised progeny.

10 But hope . . . fruit A difficult line, though the general sense of a false or hollow hope is clear (Hood). The sense seems to be either: (1) 'Only ("But") the promise of offspring ("fruit"), yet to be born, who will be orphans and fatherless ("unfathered") (because their nurturing father (i.e. the poet's beloved), being absent, is in one sense dead)'; or (2) (Hood) 'Only that kind of hope of prosperity which an orphan or fatherless child might expect ("hope of orphans").' 'Orphan' could be used of a child one of whose parents was dead (see *OED* Orphan *sb* 1); the mother here implied is 'The teeming autumn' (6), the father, the 'prime' (7) or spring. 'hope' may echo Ovid (*Metamorphoses* XV, 203: 'spe delectat agrestes'), who describes how spring 'cheeres the husbandman with hope' (Golding, 225).

11 For Because.

11 his pleasures its delights (though Shakespeare treats summer as masculine in 5.6).

11 wait on attend upon (as servants or courtiers).

12 thou away i.e. you being absent.

12 the very birds are mute even the birds (who ordinarily express their joy in summer) are silent.

13 with so . . . cheer with such subdued mirth, so cheerlessly.

14 That That as a result.

14 leaves look . . . near the leaves (i.e. the green leaves of summer) look pallid and wan ('pale', like leaves in autumn) fearing (mistakenly) that winter is at hand ('winter's near'). Compare 73.2–3.

Sonnet 98

Perhaps his summer's 'absence' from the youth as it was described in 97 may have recalled to the poet's mind an earlier 'spring' absence, one that saddened him, but was not, as the lighter and more delicate tone of 98 suggests, *as* 'wintry' and dark. 99 is obviously a continuation of 98, as Malone indicated (see collation).

2 proud-pied splendidly, gorgeously particoloured (with a suggestion in 'proud' of 'highspirited', even 'arrogant').

2 April The month most commonly associated with spring and the renewal of vital spirits and generative activity.

2 dressed i.e. dressed up, clothed.

2 his Describes the personified April (compare 'him' in line 4); therefore not, as so often elsewhere, to be understood as 'its'.

2 trim array, adornment (= gay clothing). Compare *Rom.* 1.2.26–8: 'Such comfort as do lusty young men feel / When well-apparell'd April on the heel / Of limping winter treads'.

3 spirit of youth On the 'spirit of youth' in spring as described in lines 2–12, compare Ovid, *Metamorphoses* XV, 204–7 (Golding, 225–9): 'Then [in spring] all things florish gay. / The earth with flowres of sundry hew then seemeth for too play, / . . . The yeere from springtyde passing foorth too sommer, wexeth strong, / Becommeth lyke a lusty youth'.

3 every thing Retained as two words (Q) to preserve final stress on 'thing'.

4 That So that (even) (Vendler).

4 heavy Saturn Among the 'four humours' which were thought of as governing man's temperament or 'complexion', the 'melancholy humour' was under the planet Saturn, a symbol of ponderous gravity and physical lethargy and associated with old age (compare the adjective 'saturnine').

4 leapt danced, skipped.

5 Yet Nevertheless.

5 nor . . . nor neither . . . nor.

5 lays songs.

6 Of different flowers in i.e. of flowers different in. See Abbott 419a.

6 hue (1) colour; (2) form, appearance.

7 Could make . . . tell i.e. would be able to make me give any happy or promising account ('summer's story') (of the spring when I am separated from you). 'summer's story' may be taken, perhaps, as anticipatory (hence 'promising'), like the sudden introduction of 'autumn' in 97.6–10.

8 their proud lap i.e. the richly burgeoning earth.

8 grew i.e. were growing.

9–12 Nor did I . . . those These lines play with uncommon brilliance and economy on the conventional floral conceit in which flowers are compared to, or merely imitate, the beloved's red (rosy cheeks) and white (skin). Compare, for example, Richard Barnfield, *The Affectionate Shepheard* (1594), p. 1: 'His Ivory-white and Alabaster skin / Is stained throughout with rare Vermillion red, / Whose twinckling starrie lights do never blin / To shine on lovely *Venus* (Beauties bed:) / But as the Lillie and the blushing Rose, / So white and red on him in order growes', and *LLL* 1.2.90–1: 'My love is most immaculate white and red.'

9 wonder marvel.

9 white whiteness.

10 deep vermilion dark red or scarlet.

11 but . . . but only, merely . . . only, merely.

11 sweet (1) pleasing, agreeable; (2) fragrant. See collation for various proposed emendations. My conjecture 'sweets' offers a plural noun form to balance 'figures'; compare, for example, 'sweets' in 95.4 and 102.12.

11 **figures of delight** shapes, images, symbols (i.e. not the essential things themselves) of pleasure. Compare 'shadow' in line 14.

12 **Drawn after you** Copied from you.

12 **you pattern of all those** i.e. you being the model for all lilies and roses ('those'). Compare 19.12 and *Oth.* 5.2.11: 'Thou cunning'st pattern of excelling nature'

13 **Yet seemed . . . still** During this time ('Yet') it appeared (to me) a continual winter ('winter still'). Compare 97.1.

13 **and, you away** and, you being absent. Compare 'And thou away' (97.12).

14 **As with your shadow** As if with your (1) image, portrait; (2) phantom, shade.

14 **these** i.e. the lily and rose.

14 **play** amuse myself, sport (as the poet has done in lines 9–12; also with possible sexual suggestion).

Sonnet 99

Sonnet 99 is obviously a continuation of 98, as Malone indicated by a colon at the end of 98.14; see the headnote to 98. Among Shakespeare's sonnets, 99 is an anomaly, having fifteen lines instead of the regular fourteen (126 is not technically a sonnet, its twelve lines rhyming in couplets). The majority of the first 46 sonnets in Barnes's *Parthenophil and Parthenophe* (1593) are in fifteen lines, but the extra line (13) always introduces the final couplet and rhymes with lines 10 and 12. Barnes's sonnets and one in B. Griffin's *Fidessa* (1596) – No. 60, based on a single rhyme-word – have been cited to show that fifteen-line sonnets were not unknown in the period, but this does little or nothing to explain the anomalous 99. Without line 1, 99 is perfectly regular, with marked breaks at the end of each quatrain, or, if we accept 1 as integral, line 5 would be extraneous in terms of the usual rhyme-scheme. As the sonnet presently stands, however, both 1 and 5 are essential to sense and syntax. Two explanations seem possible: (1) Shakespeare intentionally wrote a fifteen-line sonnet, employing line 1 as structurally introductory to the sonnet proper; or (2) and more likely, the sonnet as we have it represents a first or early draft which he failed to revise. Some evidence for (2) may perhaps be seen in the weakly plodding and tautological second line, the syntactical confusion in the relation of lines 6 and 7, and the confused pointing of Q in lines 2–5 (see collation).

1 Analogues to this sonnet have been noted in Petrarch's *Rime sparse*, 127, Spenser's *Amoretti* (1595), 64, and Thomas Campion's lyric, 'There is a Garden in her face', but many critics feel that Shakespeare was consciously reworking the following sonnet in Henry Constable's *Diana* (before 1592), Sonnetto decisette (pointing added):

> My Ladies presence makes the roses red,
> Because to see her lips they blush for shame.

The lilies leaves, for envy, pale became,
And her white hands in them this envy bred.
The marygold abroad the leaves did spread,
Because the suns and her power is the same.
The violet of purple coloure came,
Dy'd with the bloud she made my heart to shed.
In briefe, all flowers from her theyre vertue take;
From her sweet breath theyre sweet smells doe proceed;
The living heate which her eybeames doe make
Warmeth the ground, and quickneth the seede.
The rayne, wherewith she watereth these flowers,
Falls from myne eyes, which she dissolves in shewers.

On the 'theft motif' compare 79.5–14. See 106.9–10 n. for another suggested debt to Constable.

1 **forward** (1) flowering early; (2) presumptuous (as suggested in lines 2–5).

1 **chide** scold, rebuke.

2 **Sweet** (1) Fragrant; (2) Charming, delightful.

2 **thy sweet** your fragrance, scent.

3, 5 **love's** i.e. the youth's (assuming that 97–9 are addressed to the youth).

3 **purple pride** i.e. the purplish-blue ('purple') splendour ('pride') that adorns or clothes the violet (with a suggestion of 'overweening self-esteem' in 'pride'). Etymologically, 'purple' meant 'crimson' or 'scarlet' and was loosely used for various shades of red, particularly a mixture of red with blue, and to describe 'blood' (hence the reference to 'my love's veins' in line 5; 'purple' (i.e. scarlet) was also associated with the robes proper to emperors, kings, and men of high rank or 'pride' (compare the saying 'He was born to the purple'). Compare *Venus and Adonis*, 1168–70 (describing the metamorphosis of Adonis): 'A purple flow'r sprung up, check'red with white, / Resembling well his pale cheeks and the blood / Which in round drops upon their whiteness stood'; and 'blue-vein'd violets' (*Venus and Adonis*, 125).

4 **soft cheek** i.e. the petals of the violet.

4 **for complexion** for (facial) colouring.

4 **dwells** exists, lives.

5 **veins** i.e. the blood in his 'love's' veins.

5 **grossly dyed** (1) excessively, (2) obviously coloured. The object of 'dyed' is 'purple pride' in line 3. Hood notes here an awkward reversal of idea. Having been accused of stealing its properties from the youth, the violet is now seen as contributing them to the youth in a grossly exaggerated way. Just possibly a thought may be developing in which the violet is accused of misrepresenting by too gross an imitation the delicacy of colour of the youth's veins. See the headnote for the possibility that such awkwardness results from a more or less unrevised draft.

6 The lily . . . hand Taken in conjunction with line 7, 6 is usually glossed as: 'I condemned or censured the lily for stealing its whiteness from your hand' (thus anticipating 'stol'n' in line 7), but, taken independently, line 6 can also mean: 'I censured the whiteness of the lily when compared with ("for") the whiteness of your hand.' Compare 98.9.

7 And buds . . . hair i.e. and (I condemned) marjoram buds because they had stolen your hair. The syntactical relation of lines 6 and 7 is at best awkward and confusing.

7 marjoram A pleasingly aromatic plant ('sweet marjoram'), which, according to John Gerard (*The Herbal* (1597), quoted by Kerrigan), was 'of a whitish colour and marvellous sweet smell . . . the flowers grow at the top in scaly or chaffy spiked ears, of a white colour'. Thus, the 'spiked ears' of the flower when a bud *might* be said to look something like hairs. But it is not clear whether the comparison with marjoram is really to the youth's hair as such or only to its fragrance.

8 fearfully anxiously (perhaps fearing retribution for their theft). Any sense of 'threateningly' seems unlikely.

8 on thorns did stand i.e. were full of fears (proverbial; see Tilley T239). The more literal meaning ('grew on thorny stalks') may also be present.

9 One Q 'Our' makes no sense in the context and is an easy misreading of 'One' (see collation).

9 One blushing . . . despair i.e. one (a red rose) symbolising 'blushing shame', another (a white rose) symbolising pale 'despair' (or, possibly, 'another white' (rose) symbolising 'despair').

10 A third i.e. a third rose.

10 nor red nor white neither red nor white (i.e. 'damasked', a mingling of red and white; compare 130.5).

10 stol'n of both stolen (its mixture of red and white) from the red rose and the white rose ('both'). At first reading, line 10 seems to contradict line 14, which insists that all flowers had stolen their colours from the youth, but Shakespeare may have been thinking of the third rose as a product of grafting; thus its colours would still (though indirectly) be 'stol'n' from the youth.

11 to his robb'ry in addition to its (first) theft.

11 annexed joined (the theft of).

12 for his theft as a result of its theft (i.e. because through its triple theft (of red, white, and odour ('thy breath') (Vendler)) it had made itself particularly beautiful and fragrant, the kind of rose most attacked by a canker worm (see line 13; compare 35.4 n. and 70.7 n.)).

12 in pride . . . growth in the splendour ('pride') of full bloom ('of all his growth'). 'pride' carries the same pejorative suggestion as in line 3. Technically, cankers only attacked buds and killed them before they could bloom.

13 vengeful canker vindictive canker worm. Why the canker should be harbouring revenge is not clear, perhaps Shakespeare is thinking of the canker as Nature's revenge for the third rose's triple theft. *1H6* 2.4.60–71 combines the red/white rose and canker images.

13 eat ate (Elizabethans pronounced both the present and past tenses as 'et').

13 eat him . . . death i.e. devour and kill ('to death') it ('him'). Compare *Rom.* 2.3.30: 'Full soon the canker death eats up that plant.'

14 More flowers I noted i.e. I observed other ('More') flowers.

15 But sweet Except scent, fragrance.

Sonnet 100

This is the first of four sonnets (100–3) which, like 83 and 85, offer apology and excuses for a period of silence on the poet's part. 100 is an extended 'complaint' addressed to the poet's 'Muse', an obvious, self-excusing ploy by which he attributes his silence to his 'forgetful' and wandering Muse ('truant Muse' (101.1)); thus his Muse is ordered to assume the function proper to the poet. Many critics feel that 100–3 lack any sense of conviction or emotional involvement.

1 so long Does this imply a considerable period of time?

2 that i.e. the youth and the youth's 'beauty'.

2 might power, strength.

3 Spend'st thou Are you using up, wasting?

3 fury i.e. *furor poeticus* (compare 17.11: 'poet's rage').

3–4 worthless song . . . base subjects Note that lines 3–4 are couched as a hypothetical question, not a statement of fact; his Muse *may* have been wasting its powers on 'base subjects'. It would seem unlikely, then, that Shakespeare intends any specific reference (to his plays, for example) in these conventionally modest and pejorative phrases. Any 'song' would inevitably be 'worthless' and all 'subjects' mean, low, or degrading ('base') when set against his Muse's proper subject – praise of perfection (i.e. the youth).

4 Dark'ning Clouding, depriving of light.

4 pow'r might, strength (compare line 2).

4 lend . . . light i.e. deprive yourself ('lend') of your inner visionary illumination ('light') in order to bestow it on 'worthless' or 'base' subjects (see preceding note).

5 Return, forgetful Muse i.e. come back to your proper 'subject' which you seem to have forgotten.

5 straight redeem at once, immediately compensate for. Compare *1H4* 1.2.217: 'Redeeming time when men think least I will' (the rationalising purpose and tone of Prince Hal's whole speech (195–217) seems to resonate in this sonnet; see also 102.12 n.).

6 gentle numbers noble verse (in contrast to the 'base' 'numbers' described in lines 2–4).

6 **idly** vainly, carelessly, frivolously (with perhaps a suggestion of 'indolently' (*OED* Idly *adv* 2), since it was much less demanding to write 'worthless song[s]' etc. than to exercise the Muse's full 'pow'r' (4) in praising the youth).

6 **spent** wasted, dissipated (compare 'Spend'st' (3)).

7 **ear** i.e. the youth's ear.

7 **lays** songs (here = sonnets).

7 **esteem** value at their proper worth.

8 **skill** (1) understanding, knowledge; (2) art; (3) ability, wit.

8 **argument** subject-matter.

9 **Rise** Rouse yourself.

9 **resty** (1) sluggish, indolent, lazy; (2) intractable, refractory, erring (both senses frequently transferred from the behaviour of horses).

9 **survey** examine in detail.

10 **If** i.e. in order to see if.

10 **have** may have.

11 **If any** i.e. if you discover any wrinkles.

11 **be a satire to decay** become a satirist against (Time's) destruction or ruin. Perhaps the earliest use of 'satire' (= satirist); see *OED* Satire 4. Compare William Rankins, *Seven Satyres* (1598), Satire 1, 40: 'I am a Satyre savage is my sport.'

12 **Time's spoils** booty, plunder, *opima spolia* seized by Time (as the Destroyer; see headnote to 15).

12 **despisèd** held in contempt.

12 **every where** Retained as two words (Q) to preserve the final stress on 'where'.

13 **my love** (1) the youth; (2) my love for the youth.

13 **fame** honour, renown (for now and for the future).

14 **So** In this way.

14 **prevent'st** take action in anticipation of, forestall, frustrate. I follow Gildon's emendation of Q 'preuenst', despite the tempting reading 'prevene'st' proposed and adopted by Wells (as by Kerrigan). 'Prevene' is a distinct lexical form (see *OED*) and in the present context carries the same meaning as 'prevent', but there are two problems (neither of them considered by Wells or Kerrigan) which make the acceptance of 'prevene'st' at least questionable: (1) 'prevene' as a verb occurs nowhere else in Shakespeare, whereas he uses various forms of 'prevent' 57 times (compare an identical use of 'prevent' in 118.3); (2) more significantly, 'prevene' was used only by Scottish writers (including James I) in the sixteenth and seventeenth centuries, no examples of clearly English usage being recorded in *OED* for those periods. The first objection is, of course, not in itself insuperable (many words are used by Shakespeare only once), but when combined with (2) the case against accepting 'prevene'st' is, I think, a strong one.

14 **scythe and crookèd knife** Most simply taken as a not very happy example of hendiadys (= crooked scythe (Pooler), i.e. 'crookèd' because the blade was curved; on 'scythe' and Time, see 12.13 n.). It is generally agreed that 'crookèd' refers not only to shape but to 'malicious intent' (compare 'crookèd fortune' (*1GV* 4.1.22); 'crookèd malice' (*H8* 5.2.79); 'Crookèd eclipses' (60.7)). 'crookèd' applied to a knife and meaning 'curved' is supported by Marlowe's translation of 'obliquoque . . . cultro' (Lucan's *Pharsalia* 1, 610), there used to describe a sacrificial knife. Tucker disputes the use of hendiadys and suggests that 'crookèd knife' refers to a 'pruning-knife', which, unlike a 'scythe', 'only lops away portions during life', adding 'The line would thus mean that the Muse will ensure the record of the beloved's personality both after death and after the loss of the beauty of his prime.' To this, Ingram and Redpath object that a pruning-knife 'is properly used only to promote desirable growth' (a legitimate if perhaps over-literal objection given the confused context). Shakespeare further confuses the point at issue by twice referring to Time's conventional scythe as a 'sickle' in 126.2 and a 'bending sickle' in 116.10 (the second example suggesting another kind of 'crookèd knife', doubly 'crookèd' in being crescent-shaped and having a serrated blade).

Sonnet 101

See 100 headnote.

1 **truant** (1) idle, lazy; (2) wandering.

1 **what shall . . . amends** i.e. what kind of reparation will you be able to offer.

2 **truth in beauty dyed** The metaphor is of beauty lending colour (dye) to a perfect idea: beauty and truth (Gibbons). The inner and outer qualities of 'truth' are permanently 'fixed' (compare line 6 and the neo-Platonic idea of the 'beautiful soul in the beautiful body'). Compare 14.11 n. and 54.1–2, 13–14.

3 **Both . . . depends** As Ingram and Redpath note, this line undercuts the Platonic implications of line 2, 'reversing the dependence of the temporal on the eternal'. Vendler suggests, however, that in a 'worldly' sense truth and beauty do depend on the good.

3 **on my love depends** is contingent upon or conditioned by my beloved (= the youth). Compare 14.11–14. For the then still not uncommon third-person plural in *-s*, see Abbott 333.

4 **therein dignified** i.e. by being similarly dependent on 'my love' (3) you too are ennobled and made more worthy (because you draw your inspiration from him).

5 **Make answer . . . say** Retaining the Q comma after 'Muse', I interpret as: 'If you, Muse, should attempt a defence ("Make answer"), will you not perhaps ("haply") say'. Most editors, however, adopt

Capell's semicolon after 'Muse' (see collation), treating 'Make answer' as an imperative.

6 Truth needs . . . fixed i.e. truth needs no adventitious or specious painting ('colour'), already having its own perfectly constant and true 'complexion' ('colour' = mixture of unimprovable attributes). Proverbial; compare Tilley T585 ('Truth needs no colors') and T575 ('Truth has no need of rhetoric (figures)').

7 Beauty Supply 'needs' from line 6.

7 pencil painter's fine brush.

7 beauty's truth to lay i.e. in order to (1) lay on or overlay (as a painter lays on colours), (2) express in words ('lay') the intrinsic constancy of the *Idea* of beauty.

8 But best . . . intermixed i.e. but the best (= truth and beauty) remains the 'best' (only) if its constituents remain pure and unadulterated ('never intermixed'). In neo-Platonic thought all 'matter' below the Moon was 'intermixed'; compare Donne, 'A Valediction: forbidding Mourning', 13–16: 'Dull sublunary lovers love/ (Whose soule is sense) cannot admit / Absence, because it doth remove / Those things which elemented it.'

9 he i.e. the youth, 'my love' (3). Note Benson's attempt (his first, but not last) to turn the person referred to into a woman (see collation on lines 11 and 14).

9 needs no praise i.e. (he) is like truth and beauty.

9 dumb silent, tongue-tied. Contrast 83.9–11 and 85.13–14.

10 so in such a way.

10 for't lies in thee because it rests with you.

11–12 To make . . . be The poet, though the youth 'needs no praise' *now* (indeed is beyond praise), conjures his Muse, nevertheless, to praise his perfection 'as he shows now' (14) so that the memory of that perfection may be preserved for the ages to come ('yet to be') after the youth's death and thus 'outlive a gilded tomb'. Compare 'gilded monuments', 'outlive', and 'Even in the eyes of all posterity' in 55.1–2, 11.

13 office duty.

13 I teach thee how i.e. I am instructing you how such eternising of the youth may be accomplished. Ingram and Redpath take 'I . . . how' as parenthetical (see collation), in which case 'To' (14) would mean 'In order to'.

14 seem give the appearance of being.

14 he shows now i.e. his appearance as it is now to be seen. Implied criticism of the youth may possibly be intended if the pejorative connotations of 'seem' and 'shows' are taken as undercutting the 'seemingly' positive thrust of the line; note, however, that the same two words recur, without any pejorative suggestion, in the first two lines of 102.

Sonnet 102

See 100 headnote.

1 My love . . . seeming My love for you is (actually) stronger even though (it appears to be) weaker in outward show ('seeming') (i.e. as a result of the poet's silence).

2 I love . . . appear Essentially a gloss on line 1. See 101.14 n.

2 show = 'seeming' (1).

3–4 That love . . . where Compare 21.14 n. and *LLL* 2.1.15–16: 'Beauty is bought by judgment of the eye, / Not utt'red by base sale of chapmen's tongues.'

3 merchandised i.e. treated as a commodity for sale.

3 whose rich esteeming the costly value or worth ('esteeming') of which.

4 publish (1) announce publicly; (2) advertise for sale.

4 every where As two words (Q), to ensure final stress on 'where'.

5 new (1) of recent growth; (2) fresh, green, budding (promising growth, 'Our love' being 'then but in the spring', the season of renewal). There is no necessary implication that 'Our love' began in the spring.

6 I was wont i.e. it was my habit.

6 lays songs (i.e. sonnets).

7–14 Compare Breton, *The Passionate Shepheard* (1604), Sonnet 1, p. 10:

And when I heare the Nightingale recorde,
The Musicke, wherein Nature pleaseth Arte:
To trie how love can with her tune accorde,
To sound the passions of a panting hearte:
And when that shee her warbling Tunnes doth ease,
And shades her selfe from parching sommer's heate,
Then learne of her, how I may holde my peace,
While lesser Birdes, the idle ayre doe beate.

7 Philomel i.e. the nightingale, so termed from Philomela, daughter of Pandion and sister of Procne, who was raped by Tereus, Procne's husband; in revenge the sisters slew Procne's son, Itys, and fed him to his father at a 'bloody banquet', after which Philomela and Procne were metamorphosed into a nightingale and a swallow and Tereus into a hoopoe (see Ovid, *Metamorphoses* VI, 424–674). Shakespeare adapts the Philomela story in *Titus Andronicus*.

7 in summer's front at the beginning of summer (earliest citation of 'front' in this sense; see *OED* Front *sb* 7b). Compare 'Flora / Peering in April's front' (*WT* 4.4.2–3).

8 stops his pipe ceases his song ('pipe'). Compare 'hold my tongue' in line 13.

8 his The Q reading 'his' seems clearly wrong, since Philomel was a woman, but the error may well be Shakespeare's, who, it is argued, at this point is thinking of himself as Philomel, an error that he, perhaps unconsciously, adjusts to 'her' in lines 10 and 13. Nor does it solve the gender problem to take 'his' in the then commonly used neuter sense of 'its'; Shakespeare elsewhere always properly refers to Philomela and (though improperly) to the singing nightingale as 'she'. 'his', however, is not a common misreading in Secretary hand of 'her', and similar pronominal confusion of 'his' for 'her' (perhaps Shakespeare's) occurs in *LLL* 5.2.148, *AYLI* 5.4.114, and *1H6* 5.3.57, and of 'her' for 'his' (again perhaps Shakespeare's) in *AYLI* 3.2.145, *Tit.* 3.1.146, *Ham.* 2.2.143, and *Lear* 2.4.148. 'his' is thus kept as quite possibly Shakespeare's own slip, even though the majority of editors since 1835 has emended to 'her'.

8 in growth of riper days i.e. when (summer) days produce more fully matured growth or increase (i.e. as summer advances from its 'front' (7)).

9 is less pleasant i.e. gives less pleasure.

9 now i.e. in its maturity.

10, 13 her i.e. the nightingale's (= Philomel's). Elizabethans, probably influenced by the Philomela story, usually associated the song of the nightingale with the female (compare *Rom.* 3.5.4; *Passionate Pilgrim*, xx, 7–10); technically, it is the male who sings 'mournful hymns'.

10 mournful hymns sad songs (in praise of early summer). 'mournful' reflects the tragic events surrounding Philomela.

10 hush (1) soothe; (2) make quiet (ready to listen).

11 But that But because.

11 wild music . . . bough tumultuous, unrestrained bird-songs weigh down every bough (i.e. all the other birds are singing 'wildly'). Shakespeare is here probably glancing back at the 'rival poet' (or poets), whom he accuses of 'burthening' the youth with their 'songs' in 78–80, 82–6, and of trying to steal the favourable moment (= summer season).

12 sweets grown common sweet things, pleasures (of all kinds) having become (1) too easily available, (2) too publicly shared. Compare 69.14 and *1H4* 1.2.204–7.

12 dear delight (1) beloved, (2) precious power to give pleasure ('delight').

13 sometime from time to time.

14 would not do not wish to.

14 dull you (1) render your 'dear delight' (12) less intense (i.e. satiate you, by making 'my song' too 'common', as the other 'birds' (= 'poets' in line 11) have done); (2) dim your lustre (= render you common, a common property (Vendler)).

14 my Should be stressed in reading to emphasise the contrast with the 'dulling' effect of others' 'songs'.

Sonnet 103
See 100 headnote.

1 Alack Alas. Booth sees a delayed pun on 'a lack' and 'poverty'.

1 poverty inferior matter, poor stuff. Compare 40.10 n. and 76.1.

2 That, having In as much as she has. See Franz 552.

2 scope wide range of opportunity (in which) (i.e. the youth as 'subject' (10)).

2 show her pride exhibit, display her (rhetorical) splendour (with, perhaps, a suggestion in 'pride' of 'ostentatious display').

3 argument all bare subject ('argument' = the youth) without any 'added praise' (4). 'all bare' = naked, in its natural state without ornament.

3 more worth greater value, estimation.

4 hath my . . . beside is accorded, in addition, my increased ('added') praise. 'added' and 'beside' are essentially tautological.

4 my Note that the poet now suddenly identifies himself with 'my Muse' (1); contrast the pretended distinction between the poet and his Muse in 100 and 101.

5 if I . . . write (1) if I am unable to write any more (hence his 'silence' treated in 100–2); (2) if I am unable to write better or with greater effect ('more').

6 glass mirror, looking-glass.

7 overgoes (1) excels; (2) overpowers.

7 blunt (1) dull; (2) barren; (3) rude; (4) plainspoken.

7 invention exercise of mind, imagination, inventiveness.

7 quite entirely, completely.

8 Dulling my lines Making my verses torpid and lacking in edge, vigour, and wit ('Dulling'). Compare 'blunt' in line 7.

8 doing me disgrace (1) dishonouring me; (2) doing me injury. For 'me' as an ethical dative (= to me), see Abbott 220.

9 Were it not Would it not be.

9 striving in trying.

9 mend improve.

10 To mar . . . well To impair, disfigure the subject (= 'argument' (3) = the youth) that originally was exactly as it should be ('well'). In other words, one should not try to gild the lily; compare *Lear* 1.4.346: 'Striving to better, oft we mar what's well', and the proverb 'Let well alone' (Tilley w260).

11 For Because.

11 pass issue, end.

11 tend (1) are directed; (2) serve (as if 'my verses' were your servants).

12 graces . . . gifts charms, attractive qualities . . . natural endowments (of mind and body). Both words, however, may also carry the sense of 'voluntary favours bestowed'.

12 tell report (with, perhaps, a sense of 'reckon up').

13 And more . . . sit i.e. and more 'graces' and 'gifts', many more, than are able to find a place ('can sit') in my verse. Almost all editors follow Lintott in placing a comma after 'much more' (see collation), but this limits 'And more' to what the poet's 'verse' can contain. For this use of 'sit', compare 37.7 and *Rape of Lucrece*, 288–9.

14 shows you (1) shows you to be; (2) reveals to you. Both senses carry, perhaps, a critical edge, suggesting that the 'more' which his glass 'shows' reveals the youth in his 'true colours', not all of them necessarily worthy 'graces' and 'gifts' (compare 'show her pride' (2)).

Sonnet 104

Together with 107, 104 is one of the most discussed so called 'dated sonnets', but there is wide disagreement among critics who look for actual historical allusions about when the three-year friendship between the poet and the youth is supposed to have begun, such dating frequently turning on whether the critic is a proponent of Southampton (earlier 1590s) or Pembroke (later 1590s) as the youth addressed in 1–126 (see Rollins, II, 59–61). Lee, moreover, suggests (see Rollins I, 255) that 'three' may be not a specific historical allusion but a poetically conventional number for commemorating such meetings, and cites, in support, poems by Ronsard, Desportes, Fresnaie, and Daniel (*Delia* (1592), 31.6); it should, however, be noted that Daniel's 'three' becomes 'five' in the revised edition of 1594.

1 fair (1) beautiful to the eye (see line 2); (2) desirable, attractive (with possible play on having 'fair' (as opposed to 'dark') complexion or hair; compare 19.9 n.).

1 friend Could be used to refer to either a man or a woman, though apparently Benson didn't think so (see collation).

2 your eye I eyed (1) we saw each other (my eye encountering your eye); (2) I saw you (i.e. your 'I' = you as a whole person, outer and inner). See 39.3–4 n. As Booth notes, Shakespeare here plays on three figures of rhetoric: the pun ('eye', 'I'); polyptoton ('eye', 'eyed' – repetition of different forms of words derived from the same root); and a form of epizeuxis ('eye I eyed' – contiguous repetition of sounds). An Elizabethan reader would doubtless have found the 'witty' result more pleasing than we do. Behind Shakespeare's 'eye' figure may lie two neo-Platonic concepts: (1) the eye as the window of the soul; (2) the beautiful soul in the beautiful body.

3 Such i.e. 'as you were' (line 2) (when I first saw you).

3 seems appears (with an almost inevitable suggestion of outward 'seeming', since, in the Q arrangement, we must recall the poet's criticism of the youth's moral nature in earlier sonnets (33–6, 92–6)). Shakespeare could, had he wished, have

avoided an ambiguity by writing 'is' instead of 'seems'.

3 still now as before.

3 Three winters cold i.e. three cold winters. The noun/adjective inversion would seem to be dictated by the rhyme with 'old', though a few editors accept Knight's possessive form 'winters'' (see collation) and, taking 'cold' as the subject, defend the use of the plural 'Have' (in line 4) as 'perfectly Elizabethan', if not perfectly Shakespearean. If we take this 'Three winters' and the following 'three's literally, the poet seems to suggest that he and the youth first encountered each other in the season of spring three years ago. Leishman (p. 161, crediting L. P. Wilkinson) compares Horace, *Epodes* XI, 5–6 ('The third December, since I ceased to rave for Inchia, is now shaking their glory from the woods').

4 shook shaken down, scattered (through the action of cold and wind).

4 three summers' pride the splendour ('pride' = magnificent arboreal growth) generated (1) by three summers, (2) by 'the forests' in three summertimes. It is not clear whether 'pride' belongs to the 'forests' or to the action of summer, though *Rom.* 1.2.10 ('Let two more summers wither in their pride') would seem to favour (1).

5 yellow The colour usually associated with autumn; compare 73.2 and *Mac.* 5.3.23.

6 In process . . . seasons In the regular progress or course of the four seasons.

6 seen witnessed.

7 Three April . . . burned The sweet scents of three Aprils (1) scorched, (2) destroyed in the heat of three Junes ('three hot Junes' = three hot summers).

8 fresh i.e. in full vigour or bloom of youth (with an echo, picking up 'first' earlier in the line and in line 2, of 'for the first time').

8 which yet who still, even now (three years later). For 'which' = who, see Abbott 265.

8 green (1) vital, fresh; (2) young (with perhaps an undertone of 'inexperienced' or 'immature').

9–10 Ah yet . . . perceived Compare the proverb 'To move as the dial hand, which is not seen to move' (Tilley D321) and see 77.7–8 n.

9 yet nevertheless.

9 dial hand Usually glossed as 'the hand of a clock or watch', but, as in 77.7 ('shady stealth'), the 'hand' of a sundial seems more apposite since it may be said to 'shadow' (= dim, cast a shadow over) the 'face' of the 'dial' as Time 'shadows' the 'face' of 'beauty'.

10 Steal from his figure i.e. (beauty) imperceptibly degenerates ('steal[s]' away) from its original appearance ('figure') (as a result of 'Time's thievish progress' (77.8)). But 'his' can also be read as 'his' instead of 'its', if 'beauty' (in line 9) is taken as equivalent to the youth himself, and 'figure' is taken as playing on one of the numerals on the face of a 'dial'.

10 and no pace perceived and yet (in this 'stealing') no movement or motion be observed. Compare Lyly, *Euphues and his England* (1580), in *Works*, II, 176: 'The tongue of a lover should be like the poynt in the Diall, which though it go, none can see it going.'

11 So In the same way.

11 sweet hue (1) beloved, (2) precious, charming physical form or appearance. See 20.7 n.

11 methinks it seems to me.

11 still doth stand (1) remains motionless; (2) always remains unchanged. Compare 'my verse shall stand' (60.13). Kerrigan suggests a play on 'stand' (= stand still) and 'pace' in line 10 (= move forward).

12 Hath motion i.e. is subject to Time's 'pace' (10).

12 mine eye . . . deceived Picks up the 'eye/seeing' theme and the deceptiveness of 'sight' which judges by appearances and has difficulty penetrating to the underlying reality (compare 93.9–14). There is perhaps an answering pun on 'your eye' (= your I) in 'mine eye' (= mine I); see note on line 2.

13 For fear of which Out of a fear that this may be true (i.e. that your beauty will, despite present appearances, decay).

13 hear this Compare 'Oyez' (= Hear ye), a command used by the public crier to demand silence for the reading of a proclamation.

13 age unbred generation(s) yet unborn (only citation in this sense in *OED* (Unbred *ppl a* 1)). 'unbred' meaning 'ill-bred' or 'unmannerly' is not recorded before 1622, but Shakespeare may also be playing on that sense here.

14 Ere Before.

14 you i.e. any members of the 'age unbred'. The switch from 'thou' (in 'thou age' (13)) to 'you' may be explained by taking 'age' as a collective singular and 'you' as 'any of you' in that 'age' (Tucker).

14 was beauty's summer dead i.e. the height of beauty ('beauty's summer' = the youth's beauty) was perished. In other words, 'you' will never see perfect beauty, since the youth's beauty is, and will remain for all ages to come, unique.

Sonnet 105

In 105 the poet argues that he should not be charged with 'idolatry' (i.e. polytheism, the worship of many gods) because his repeated and obsessive praise is always directed to *one* god, the youth (monotheism, 'To one, of one, still such, and ever so' (4)) – a god, moreover, not only 'one' but 'three . . . in one' (14). As Adams points out, there are, behind this sophistical argument, probable allusions to the first two of the Ten Commandments ((1) 'Thou shalt have none other Gods but me'; (2) 'Thou shalt not make to thyself any graven image . . . thou shalt not bow down to them, nor worship them', 'A Catechism',

Book of Common Prayer) and to the doctrine of the Trinity. If so, the poet conveniently forgot the Third Commandment ('Thou shalt not take the name of the Lord thy God in vain'); unorthodox monotheism is in Christian terms blasphemous. Booth suggests that the 'idolatry' theme may refer to the Protestant claim that in praying for the intercession of the saints and the Virgin Mary Roman Catholics were in effect practising idolatry; he quotes from the *Book of Homilies* (1563), 'An Homily against Peril of Idolatry': 'images in churches be indeed none other but idols, as unto the which idolatry hath been, is, and ever will be committed'. 105 echoes 76 in theme and language; see notes below. A parallel to 105 has been noticed in Nicholas Breton's 'An Odde Conceit' in *Melancholike Humours* (1600), p. 15, though the direction of influence is uncertain:

> Lovely kinde, and kindly loving,
> Such a minde were worth the moving.
> Truly faire, and fairely true,
> Where are all these, but in you?
>
> Wisely kinde, and kindely wise,
> Blessed life, where such love lies:
> Wise, and kinde, and faire, and true,
> Lovely live all these in you.
>
> Sweetely deare, and dearely sweete,
> Blessed, where these blessings meete:
> Sweete, faire, wise, kinde, blessed, true,
> Blessed be all these in you.

1 Let not . . . idolatry Compare *Rom.* 2.2.113–14: 'swear by thy gracious self, / Which is the god of my idolatry', and 110.12, where the 'friend' is described as 'A god in love, to whom I am confined' (compare 'confined' in line 7 below).

2 show seem, appear (intransitive).

3 Since Because (either (a) giving reason for the charge, or (b) offering a defence against the charge). 'Since' may be taken in either way (even perhaps both ways), but the implied deification of the youth as 'one' and 'Three . . . in one' which follows seems to favour (2).

3 all alike (1) each the same as the other; (2) all one (compare 76.5 and line 4 below).

3 my songs i.e. my earlier sonnets in the series.

4 To one . . . so 'One' and 'one' = the youth; 'still such' = always to and of the same; 'ever so' = always thus (i.e. always constant). Compare 76.5. 'still . . . so' seems to modify both the poet's 'songs and praises' and 'one' (i.e. the youth). Some critics see in 'one' a reference to the Platonic *Idea* (the *summum bonum*) and compare the neo-Platonic phrase 'tota in toto, et tota in qualibet parte'; others find echoes of the *Gloria Patri* ('Glory be to the Father, and to the Son, and to the Holy Ghost. As it was in the beginning, is now, and ever shall be: world without end'). Booth notes the echo of the *Gloria* in the passage from the *Homilies* quoted in the headnote. For a suggested connection with Southampton's family motto, see 8.12 n.; as Baldwin notes (p. 176), Pembroke's advocates have countered by citing the Pembroke motto, 'Ung je servirai' – so the game plays on!

5 Kind See 9 n. below.

5 my love = 'my belovèd' (2). The reader may momentarily mistake this as referring to the poet's love for the youth.

6 Still constant Always, ever (1) unchanging, (2) faithful, (3) true.

6 in a wondrous excellence in (possessing) an unsurpassed merit or virtue ('excellence') that is a cause for wonder ('wondrous').

7 Therefore For that reason.

7 to constancy confined being bounded or limited ('confined') by that 'truth' ('constancy') (which is exemplified by 'my belovèd' (2)).

8 One thing i.e. 'my belovèd' and his 'constancy'.

8 leaves out difference admits of no 'variation or quick change' (76.2) in being 'confined' to 'constancy' (i.e. no 'difference' or embellishment is allowable or necessary when 'expressing' truth). Compare 76.5–14.

9–12 Compare *MV* 3.6.53–7.

9 'Fair, kind, and true' These three 'words' (10) or 'themes' (12), individually and 'in one' (12), constitute the 'wondrous excellence' (6) of 'my belovèd' (2). 'Fair' = beautiful, lovely, desirable, attractive; morally unstained; gentle, etc.; 'kind' = naturally well-disposed, good-natured, sweet, affectionate, friendly; generous, liberal, etc.; 'true' = constant, faithful, steadfast; honest, virtuous; sincere, genuine, etc.

9 all my argument my whole subject. As Kerrigan notes, 'all', though restrictive in one sense, suggests that the 'argument' includes 'everything'.

10 varying to other words i.e. using synonyms of 'Fair', 'kind', and 'true' (see 9 n. above and 76.11).

11 change variation ('varying' (10)).

11 invention See 76.6 n.

11 spent (1) exhausted, used up; (2) expended, paid out. Compare 76.12.

12 Three themes in one Three topics (= topoi, i.e. kindness, fairness, truth) in 'one' 'argument' (9), a trinity. Compare 'three . . . in one' in line 14, and see 4 n. above and headnote.

12 which Modifies either 'Three . . . one' as a singular subject or 'one' (i.e. a one which), alternatives allowing for the singular form in 'affords'.

12 scope range, opportunity.

13 'Fair' . . . alone i.e. these three qualities have often existed ('lived') singly (in different individuals).

14 never kept . . . one i.e. never before resided ('kept seat') in a single person ('in one' = in 'my belovèd' (2)).

Sonnet 106

In integration of theme, structure, and imagery, 106 is one of the most perfectly realised of the Sonnets. Kerrigan (pp. 8–9) points out, despite the various attempts of the reorderers to disassociate them, a significant number of verbal and thematic links between 106 and 107–9.

1 chronicle written record.

1 wasted time (1) ages turned to ruin by time; (2) time spent unprofitably. Compare *R2* 5.5.49: 'I wasted time, and now doth time waste me.' An element of witty reversal may be present in 'wasted', since Time is regularly described as the 'waster' or 'destroyer'.

2 fairest wights most beautiful men or women ('wight' could be used for either sex). The context suggests that the use of 'wights' is a conscious (perhaps Spenserian) archaism.

3 And And (when I see).

3 beauty . . . rhyme i.e. the 'beauty', of which the poet reads in the 'descriptions' (2), imparting its beauty to the verse of earlier ages ('old rhyme').

4 dead Modifies both 'ladies' and 'knights'.

4 lovely (1) beautiful, attractive, lovable; (2) amorous (like a lover; compare *Passionate Pilgrim*, 4.1–3: 'Sweet Cytherea . . . / Did court the lad with many a lovely look').

5 Then in . . . best Then in the portrayal of such virtues and excellencies (depicted, as in a heraldic 'blazon' or coat-of-arms, in sharp, fine 'colours' of rhetoric) the best (past examples) of delightful, precious beauty. Compare (a poetic form of 'blazon') *TN* 1.5.292–3: 'Thy tongue, thy face, thy limbs, actions, and spirit / Do give thee fivefold blazon'; see 6 n.

6 Of hand . . . brow Parenthetical, enumerating some of the 'parts' of beauty.

6 brow forehead.

7 I see I see that.

7 their Refers to the writers of 'the chronicle' (1) and 'old rhyme' (3), though syntactically without an antecedent.

7 àntique pen i.e. the pen(s) employed by ancient or earlier writers (probably without any suggestion of 'antic' as in 19.10).

7 would have expressed i.e. would have wished to portray or represent (had their pens been capable of doing so).

8 Even such a i.e. the very kind of.

8 you master you have at your disposal, possess. In this sense, the three earliest instances (*OED* Master *v* 6) are by Shakespeare. The use of 'master' suggests that the 'you' referred to is masculine (i.e. he is the 'master' of 'such beauty'). Compare 63.6: 'all those beauties whereof now he's king'.

8 now = 'this our time' (10).

9–10 So all . . . prefiguring Critics are generally agreed that these lines (if not indeed the sonnet as a whole) are indebted to a sonnet of Henry

Constable's preserved only in the Todd MS. (date uncertain, but probably not later than 1591; see Constable, *Poems*, p. 133): 'Miracle of the world I never will denye / That former poets prayse the beautie of theyre dayes / But all those beauties were but figures of the prayse / And all those poets did of thee but prophecye' (1–4). Moreover, as Kerrigan observes, Constable's final line ('Which onlye we withoute idolatrye adore') suggests a link with 105.1–2. See 24.5–8 and 99 (headnote) for other probable debts to Constable.

9 So For this reason.

9 but prophecies merely foretellings, anticipations. Some element, though perhaps secondary, of divine inspiration (*furor poeticus*) is suggested; see 'divining' in line 11 and 17.11 n. Compare *Ham.* 1.5.40: 'O my prophetic soul!', and 107.1.

10 all you prefiguring all ('their praises' (9)) foreshadowing you (with play on the use of rhetorical 'figures'; compare 'figured' (108.2)).

11 for because

11 but with divining eyes only with (1) the eyes of conjecture or speculation ('divining eyes', i.e. the eyes of the mind), (2) the insight of inspiration (because, before 'this our time' (10), they had never been able to look upon the perfection of 'beauty' = 'you'). Compare *3H6* 4.6.68–9: 'If secret powers / Suggest but truth to my divining thoughts'.

12 skill enough sufficient knowledge or understanding (of perfect beauty). Capell's emendation of Q 'still' has been adopted (see collation), though not without hesitation, even though 'skill' is supported by two relatively early MS. versions (see Appendix, p. 288 below). Following Wyndham (*New Readings*, 1, 213) defends Q 'still', explaining lines 11–12 as meaning 'The old poets had poetic talent, but not having seen you were not fully equipped, had not *yet* [i.e. "still"] enough to sing you perfectly.' Objections against the retention of 'still' are: (a) there is no noun for 'enough' to modify (Beeching); (b) 'still' in the sense of 'as yet' or 'nevertheless' is not cited in *OED* before 1632 and 1722 respectively; (c) 'still' turns the couplet into a *non sequitur*, since there is no logical connection between modern poets lacking talent and ancient poets lacking a model (Ingram and Redpath); and (d) 'For' in line 13 should be 'But' if, as Sisson insists, the couplet introduces an antithesis (i.e. the ancient poets 'had tongues, but no eyes' (only 'divining eyes'), while 'we have eyes, but no tongues') (Ingram and Redpath). Cumulatively, the number of objections makes a strong case, even though none of them may be individually decisive.

12 worth worthiness, excellence (as the type of perfect beauty).

12 sing i.e. praise.

13 For we So long as we are concerned, we (*OED* For *prep* 26). Tucker's gloss 'Even we' is tempting, but appears to be without lexical support.

13 these present days i.e. now (when we, unlike earlier writers or poets, can see, not merely 'divine', 'you').

14 Have eyes to wonder i.e. we are in a position, since we can see it, to (1) marvel at, (2) desire to comprehend your beauty.

14 but lack . . . praise i.e. (even having 'you' as a model) we lack the power of expression ('lack tongues') to praise you adequately (i.e. give 'tongues' to the full extent of your beauty).

Sonnet 107

Grandly evocative, 107 is the most industriously 'dated' of the so-called 'dated sonnets' (see 104 and 123 headnotes). The various dates argued for range from 1579 (absurdly improbable) to 1609, the majority falling between 1592 and 1603. Although most critics agree that Shakespeare (particularly in the second quatrain) is enigmatically and covertly referring to certain historical events, there has been wide disagreement about exactly which events he is 'shadowing forth' – hence, of course, the startling range in the dates proposed. In this connection, we may compare a sonnet by Michael Drayton (written 1605, published 1619, No. 51) which it has been suggested was written under the influence of 107 (and possibly 105): 'Calling to minde since first my Love begun, / Th'incertaine Times [compare 'Incertainties' (107.7)] oft varying in their Course' – opening lines which are then followed by explicit references to, among others, the Essex rebellion (1601), the 'quiet end of that Long-living Queene' (1603), and 'This Kings faire Entrance [1603] and our Peace with *Spaine* [1603–4]'. If, indeed, Drayton's sonnet was influenced by Shakespeare's, he must have thought that he detected historical allusions in 107. See Rollins (11, 263–8) for detailed summaries of the various theories advanced before 1942, and Kerrigan (pp. 313–19) for more recent contributions to the ever-ongoing discussion.

1 The postulated historical references are essentially confined to lines 3–8:

(1) lines 3–4 'Can yet . . . doom': historical only if taken as referring to (1) Pembroke's release from the Fleet prison in March or April 1601; (2) Southampton's release from the Tower in April 1603; acceptable only to those who identify the youth addressed in the Sonnets as either Pembroke or Southampton.

(2) lines 5–6 'The mortal moon . . . presàge': variously interpreted as referring (a) to the defeat ('eclipse endured') of the Spanish Armada ('mortal moon') in the latter part of July 1588, because, during part of its disastrous encounter with the English fleet, it sailed, as a protective measure, in a half-moon or crescent-shaped formation, a manoeuvre frequently commented on then and later (an interpretation now generally discredited); (b) to Queen Elizabeth as the 'mortal moon' (poets continually

paid court to her as Diana or Cynthia, the moon goddess) and to her escape ('eclipse endured') from the alleged Dr Lopez poisoning conspiracy in 1594; to her survival, despite illness, in her sixty-third year (1596), her Grand Climacteric, astrologically considered a very dangerous age, being compounded of the mystic numbers 7 and 9; to the false rumours (the Queen was not ill) which circulated in 1599–1600 that she was near death or even dead; to her safe weathering of the Essex rebellion (1601); and to her death in 1603, when she was peacefully succeeded by James I, despite the widespread fears expressed by 'sad augurs' of possible civil war (see 7 n. and 8 n. below).

1 (3) lines 7–8 'Incertainties now crown . . . age': the theme of 'peace' as here envisioned and celebrated lends itself generally, if vaguely, to the aftermath of any crisis successfully survived, but it has been more specifically associated with (a) the defeat of the Spanish Armada (1588); (b) the negotiations for the treaty of Vervins between France and Spain (1596); (c) the negotiations for peace, following another threat of Spanish invasion, between England and Spain (1599–1600); and (d) the bloodless accession of James I (1603), despite the rights of succession claimed by some eleven other contenders, and the widely hailed promise of an enduring peace, a theme that James, who coveted a popular reputation as *Rex pacificus*, especially stressed in his first address to Parliament (1604).

Of some thirteen year-dates proposed, only three (1596, 1599–1600, and 1603) have received serious attention from later scholars. Considering the veiled nature of Shakespeare's postulated allusions, no single date can ever be taken as incontestable, but the majority of recent critics strongly favours 1603 as the most likely date. Indeed, the case for 1603 (or a little later) is so brilliantly presented by Kerrigan that one is dangerously tempted to cry 'Q. E. D.'

1–2 Not mine . . . come, Editors run the gamut in pointing these lines (see collation). The majority follow Capell–Malone, omitting the Q comma after 'world' (2), probably under the influence of Lintott's supposedly diplomatic reprint of Q, but this lack of pointing limits 'dreaming on things to come' to 'the prophetic soul / Of the wide world', whereas the Q pointing allows the phrase to modify both 'mine own fears' and 'the prophetic soul / Of the wide world'.

1 fears (1) fears (compare 'Incertainties' (7)) of death, physical decay (compare line 10); (2) fears of insurrection and civil war (compare lines 5–8).

1–2 nor the prophetic soul . . . come nor (the fears) augured or foreboded by men's minds (i.e. 'the prophetic soul / Of the wide world') as they (like myself) envision as in a dream future events ('dreaming on things to come'). Compare 'prophecies / Of this our time' and 'divining eyes' in 106.9–10, 11.

The 'soul', as the seat of man's intellect and emotions, was, by its intuitive, introspective nature, 'prophetic'. Compare, as in 106.9, *Ham.* 1.5.40: 'O my prophetic soul!'

3 yet (1) after all, even so (i.e. admitting my own fears and those of others); (2) as yet.

3 lease . . . control i.e. (are able) to set limits to the length of time ('lease') that my unchanging, constant love (for you) will survive (the 'lease' is for life and beyond, without 'date'; see lines 9–14).

4 Supposed as forfeit . . . doom i.e. (that 'lease' or 'my true love' (3)) being misconceived of ('Supposed') as terminable ('forfeit' = liable to being forfeited) and, in merely legal terms, subject to a prescribed fate (i.e. terminal date = 'confined doom'). Even more than usual, any attempt at paraphrase of the opening quatrain completely loses the metaphorically evocative power and sense of macrocosmic implications generated by these lines. For the suggested Pembroke/ Southampton reference, see headnote (1).

5–6 The mortal moon . . . presàge Some thematic and verbal links between this sonnet, particularly in these lines, and *Hamlet* (1.1.112–25; written 1600–1) are striking: 'A mote it is to trouble the mind's eye [compare 'dreaming on things to come' (2)]. / In the most high and palmy state [compare 'most balmy time' (9)] of Rome, / . . . Disasters in the sun; and the moist star [compare 'mortal moon' (5)] / Upon whose influence Neptune's empire stands / Was sick almost to doomsday [compare 'confined doom' (4)] with eclipse [compare 'eclipse endured' (5)]. / And even the like precurse [compare 'presàge' (6)] of fear'd events [compare 'fears' (1), 'things to come' (2)], / As harbingers preceding still the fates / And prologue to the omen coming on [as they would be interpreted by 'mine own fears' (1), the 'prophetic soul / Of the wide world' (2–3), and 'sad augurs' (6)], / Have heaven and earth together demonstrated / Unto our climatures and countrymen.' A curious passage in Donne's *Ignatius His Conclave* (1611), p. 85, suggests that he may have recalled line 5: (referring to Elizabeth, whom he later (p. 87) wittily calls 'this *Lunatique* [i.e. influenced by the moon] *Queene*'), 'why should wee doubt of our fortune in this *Queene*, which is so much subject to alterations, and passions? she languishes often in the absence of the Sunne, and often in *Ecclipses* falles into swounes, and is at the point of death'.

5 mortal moon Usually taken as referring to Queen Elizabeth (see headnote (2) (b)). The adjective 'mortal' (= subject to death) renders unlikely a literal reference to the moon (only matter below the moon was subject to decay in terms of the Ptolemaic cosmology), even though the moon was thought of as changing and inconstant, admittedly 'mortal' or human characteristics. Compare *Ant.* 3.13.153–5: 'Alack, our terrene [earthly] moon [Cleopatra] /

Is now eclips'd, and it portends alone / The fall of
Antony!'.

5 hath her eclipse endured (1) has survived
('endured') her eclipse (= anything that obscures or
threatens her 'light'; eclipses were generally considered ominous); (2) has suffered or been subjected
to ('endured') her eclipse (i.e. has permanently lost
her 'light' in death). The dating theories, for those
interested in them, require a choice to be made
between (1) and (2). Although *OED* offers little support (see *OED* Endure *v* 3b) except for (1), the proponents of a 1603/4 date argue that both 'endure'
and 'eclipse' allow for a terminal interpretation and,
for 'endure', cite *Lear* 5.2.9–11 ('Men must endure
/ Their going hence even as their coming hither, /
Ripeness is all') in support. The *Lear* passage, however, proves nothing, since 'endure' there carries the
sense of 'wait patiently (for death)', Edgar here arguing against Gloucester's suicidal wish. *OED* (Eclipse
v 3b) records only a single example of 'eclipse' used
in a terminal sense in *1H6* 4.5.52–3: 'Then here I take
my leave of thee, fair son, / Born to eclipse thy life
this afternoon', though other examples could easily
be cited.

6 sad augurs (1) pessimistic, mournful,
(2) grave, solemn prophets (either professional
astrologers or people generally).

6 mock deride, laugh at (forced to do so because
their dire forebodings were in the event proved
wrong). Compare Drayton, *To the Majestie of
King James* (1603), 149–50: 'Whilst such as rightly
propheci'd thy raigne, / Deride those Ideots held
their words for vaine'.

6 presàge prediction, foreboding.

7 Incertainties . . . assured Matters of doubtful issue or outcome ('Incertainties' = uncertainties)
now honour themselves by eventuating in fortunate
certainties ('assured'). For the application of lines 7–
8 to the unexpectedly peaceful accession of James I,
see headnote (3) (d).

8 peace proclaims . . . age peace makes (official) proclamation of everlasting concord ('olives of
endless age'). Olive leaves or branches ('olives') were
an ancient emblem of 'peace' or security (see Gen.
8.11); the tree was also well known for its extraordinary longevity. Both 'crown' (7) and 'proclaims' may
be taken to suggest regal authority. Compare Dekker,
The Wonderfull Yeare. 1603, pp. 96–7: whereas 'Civill
Sedition, Uproares, Rapes, Murders, and Massacres'
were feared, 'up rises a comfortable Sun out of the
North [James I], whose glorious beames (like a fan)
dispersed all thick and contagious clowdes. The losse
of a Queene, was paid with the double interest of a
King and Queene. The Cedar of her government
which stood alone and bare no fruit, is changed now
to an Olive, upon whose spreading branches grow
both Kings and Queenes'; and Gervase Markham,
Honour in His Perfection (1624), sig. D4ᵛ: James I

'enters not with an Olive Branch in his hand, but
with a whole Forrest of *Olives* round about him; for
he brought not Peace to this Kingdome alone, but
almost to all the Christian Kingdomes of Europe'.

9 Now Emphasises the 'now' of line 7.

9 with (1) in accord with; (2) as a result of

9 drops of . . . time (nourishing) dews or the
essences distilled by peace (i.e. extracts of 'olives'
(8)) of this most (1) refreshing, soothing, healing,
(2) pleasant, delightfully promising time. Kerrigan,
arguing for 1603, sees in 'balmy' a covert reference
to the anointing with 'balm' which was part of the
coronation ceremony (compare 'crown' (7)). Compare *R2* 3.2.54–5: 'Not all the water in the rough
rude sea / Can wash the balm off from an anointed
king.'

10 My love (1) the youth; (2) my love for the
youth. Either (1) or (2) is possible: 'looks' would seem
to favour (1), particularly if a reference to Southampton is accepted in 3–4; 'me', however, instead of 'him'
in the second half of the line seems to favour (2) and
avoids a switch between clauses from the youth to the
poet.

10 fresh new, untarnished by time, blooming (as
in the spring).

10 subscribes capitulates, submits to.

11 spite of in spite of.

11 I'll live i.e. I'll defeat Death and Time.

11 poor rhyme verse of slight or little worth (the
usual conventional modesty; compare 26.5, 32.4).

12 insults o'er . . . tribes arrogantly triumphs
over stupid, slow-thinking races ('tribes') lacking in
(the power of) poetic utterance ('speechless').

13 in this i.e. 'in this poor rhyme' (11).

13 find thy monument come to have or receive
your memorial.

14 crests armorial insignia (decorating the
'tombs' of 'tyrants'). A crest was technically that part
of a coat-of-arms placed above the central shield.

14 spent wasted away (by Time). Compare 55.1–
4. Any covert reference to a projected 'tomb' for
Queen Elizabeth (as some critics have suggested)
seems most unlikely, because Elizabeth was certainly
not perceived as a tyrant.

Sonnet 108

Sonnet 108 plays on the theme of the inescapable
necessity for simple repetition imposed on the poet
by the youth's 'dear merit' (4); compare 76, 105.

1 character write, inscribe (i.e. in 'characters' =
letters of the alphabet).

2 figured (1) portrayed, represented; (2) imaged
in the mind (both with play on the use of rhetorical
'figures', i.e. 'figures' of speech).

2 true spirit (1) constant, loyal, (2) truthful
inward disposition, character.

3 What's new to speak What is there left to say
that is novel or fresh?

3 what now to register what now (as I write) remains to record (that the poet has not already recorded about your 'dear merit' (4))? Until recently most editors, unnecessarily, preferred Malone's emendation 'new' for Q 'now' (see collation), partly, as Booth suggests, to balance 'old thing old' in line 7.

4 my love my love for you (but, as Booth notes, with a suggestion of 'my beloved' as being contained in that 'love').

4 dear merit precious worth or excellence.

5 sweet boy Richard Barnfield uses the phrase in *The Affectionate Shepheard* (1594), p. 16, a poem with clearly homosexual overtones; compare 126.1 ('lovely boy'). Note Benson's attempt to neutralise the sex of the person addressed (see collation).

5 yet nevertheless.

5–6 prayers divine . . . same Probably with some reference to the comparatively recent Acts of Uniformity (1549, 1552) limiting the 'prayers divine' to be used in churches to those contained in the Anglican Prayer-Book. See 'The Preface' in the Book of Common Prayer: 'And where heretofore, there hath been great diversity in saying and singing in churches within this realm: . . . Now from henceforth, all the whole realm shall have but one use.' Note the echo from the Lord's Prayer in line 8.

6 say o'er repeat.

6 the very same i.e. without departing from the prescribed form. The poet here daringly implies an equivalence between the praise of God ('prayers divine') and his praise of his 'god' (= the youth; compare 110.12 and 105.1–2).

7 Counting no old thing old Accounting nothing that has been earlier said ('old thing') as 'old' (i.e. worn threadbare, just because it has been said before).

7 thou mine, I thine A parenthetical example of an 'old thing' which has, as a basic theme, been repeated again and again in earlier sonnets – the exchange of hearts by which lovers become 'one'. Ingram and Redpath compare Song of Sol. 2.16: 'My well-beloved is mine, and I am his' (Geneva).

8 Even as Just as.

8 hallowèd thy fair name An obvious echo of the Lord's Prayer ('hallowed be thy name'), continuing the daring analogy begun in lines 5–6. Q's trisyllabic 'hallowèd' has been retained because it represents the common accenting of the word (certainly until recently) as spoken in the Lord's Prayer.

8 hallowèd sanctified, made holy.

8 fair name (1) name of honour and distinction; (2) reputation, (a) unblemished, clear, (b) honoured for 'beauty'. Compare 89.10.

9 So that (1) In the same way; (2) Thus that (taking 'that' as pronominal adjective modifying 'eternal love').

9 eternal constant, undying.

9 in love's fresh case A much debated phrase. Kerrigan notes four possible readings: '(1) in the (constantly) fresh circumstances of (truly true) love; (2) contained in affection's sprightly (though *old*) argument (meaning "my love poetry"); (3) covered by affection's youthful vigour (*case* suggesting "skin", and thus the *wrinkles* of l. 11); (4) clad in affection's sprightly garb (common meaning of *case* in the period)'. A fifth possibility is perhaps worth considering: (5) in the case of a newly conceived love (i.e. in a particular case of 'thou mine, I thine', which, though 'fresh', is, if 'true', as 'eternal' as the *Idea* of love itself; compare 'first conceit of love' in line 13). Any choice (or choices) among these five readings is finally impossible, but (2), which may be said to grow out of the 'writing theme' in lines 1–4, may be said to be working at some level. (2) might, indeed, be more rhetorically restated as: clothed in new 'character[s]' (1) or 'figure[s]' (2) expressing (see line 4) love (i.e. the poet's verses). The 'case' is 'fresh' because in 'expressing' true ('eternal') love anything that may properly be said about such a subject can never be considered 'old' ('no old thing old' (7)) but constantly 'new' ('fresh'). Compare 'My love looks fresh' (107.10).

10 Weighs not i.e. gives no weight or serious consideration to.

10 dust and injury of age i.e. disintegration ('dust') and damage or ruin ('injury') caused by (1) old age, (2) Time.

11 Nor gives . . . place i.e. nor finds any room for recognising wrinkles (in the beloved) even though such wrinkles are inevitable ('necessary') in 'age'. Vendler reads lines 11–12 as: 'Nor does he admit any ageing in "eternal love" (9), but constantly makes old books the pages that he reads (i.e. makes his staple reading the pages of antiquity).'

12 But makes . . . page But (by doing so) turns (1) old age, (2) old things ('antiquity'), including what has been said about love or the beloved, forever into its ('his', i.e. 'eternal love' (9)) servant. Love and the beloved will thus always remain in 'fresh case' (9). Booth suggests a play in 'page' on 'leaf' (i.e. a manuscript or printed page containing the poet's verses).

13 Finding the first . . . bred Discovering (or recovering) the original conception or idea ('first conceit') of love as it had there (i.e. 'in love's fresh case' (9) or in 'antiquity' (12)) been conceived.

14 Where (1) Whereas; (2) There where (if Q comma is omitted after 'bred'; see collation).

14 time and outward form the passage of time and external appearance.

14 would show (1) would appear to show; (2) would wish to show.

Sonnet 109

Sonnet 109 sounds again the theme of absence from the beloved, last heard in 97 and 98, but, particularly in view of 110, it is not clear whether this 'absence' (2) is literal or figurative (representing some kind of emotional rift between the poet and the youth). The theme of the 'traveller returned' (6) may owe something to the parable of the Prodigal Son in Luke 15.11–32.

1 false of heart untrue to my love (the heart being the seat of feeling and thought).

2 seemed may have appeared.

2 flame passion (of love).

2 qualify moderate, lessen the intensity of.

3 easy easily, without pain or difficulty.

3 from my self depart divide, separate myself from my essential or true self ('my self'). As Ingram and Redpath suggest, retaining the Q 'my selfe' as two words preserves the larger implications of, 'self' that are obscured by modernising to 'myself'. Compare 'my true spirit' (108.2).

4 soul (1) the essential, animating part; (2) heart.

4 breast heart. Compare 22.5–7, 24.5–7.

5 my home of love the proper, fixed centre of my affections. 'home' refers to (1) 'thy breast' (line 4), (2) 'my soul' (line 4), equivalents in the sense of 'thou mine, I thine' (108.7).

5 ranged wandered, strayed, roamed. Compare 'gone here and there' (110.1). Gibbons compares Wyatt, 'They fle from me' (37, 6–7): 'and nowe they raunge / Besely seking with a continuell chaunge'.

6 Like him . . . again (Even if I have seemed to wander), I am, nevertheless, like ('him') that travels, who, though he may roam widely, always means to return home. With lines 1–8 compare Donne, 'A Valediction: forbidding Mourning', 21–32: 'Our two soules therefore, which are one, / Though I must goe, endure not yet / A breach, but an expansion, / . . . If they be two, they are two so / As stiffe twin compasses are two, / Thy soul the fixt foot, makes no show / To move, but doth, if the other doe. / And though it in the center sit, / Yet when the other far doth rome, / It leanes, and hearkens after it, / And growes erect, as it comes home.'

7 Just to the time Exactly punctual (with play on 'Just' = faithful, constant).

7 not with . . . exchanged not changed (1) by the passage of time (during my 'absence' (line 2)), (2) by the influence of the present time or age.

8 So that . . . stain (1) So in this way, (2) Providing that (i.e. by returning 'Just to the time' (7)) I ('myself') bring water (i.e. perhaps = tears of repentance) to wash away my offence ('stain'). 'bring water for' may also be taken to mean 'make excuse for'. Contrast the less sophistical argument in 34.5–12 and the irony contained in Lady Macbeth's 'A little water clears us of this deed' (Mac. 2.2.64).

9 though even if in fact.

9 nature (1) inherent character, disposition; (2) natural qualities.

9 reigned ruled, predominated.

10 frailties moral weaknesses, flaws.

10 besiege lay siege to, assault.

10 all kinds of blood i.e. all men and women (with play on 'blood' = the sensual nature of man, animal passion). Lines 9–10 suggest some connection with Malcolm's (false) self-accusation of being given to all kinds of moral vices in Mac. 4.2.44–100.

11 it i.e. 'my nature' (9).

11 preposterously perversely, unnaturally (i.e. inverting the order of nature).

11 stained blemished, defiled.

12 To As to.

12 leave for . . . good relinquish, abandon you (as the total sum of all that is good) for something of no value or worth ('nothing').

13 For Because.

13 nothing this . . . call I proclaim ('call') this vast, broad world ('wide universe') to be (such a) nothing.

14 Save With the exception of.

14 my rose See 1.2 n.

14 in it . . . all in 'this wide universe' ('it') you are (1) everything (worthy of love), (2) the totality of my 'self' (you and I being one). Compare 112.5 and A Lover's Complaint, 264–6.

Sonnet 110

Sonnet 110 seems to grow naturally out of 109, offering some (rather vague) examples of how far the poet has 'ranged' (109.5). Some critics read 110.2–3 (see notes below) as a bitter rejection by Shakespeare of his profession as actor/dramatist (see 29.2 n. and 111.3–7). The latter lines, by their close juxtaposition with 110.2–3, lend some measure of support, at least so far as line 2 is concerned, to such an interpretation.

1 Alas 'tis true Sisson points out how the omission of Q's comma after 'true' (frequently omitted following Dyce) significantly alters the tone from that of a definite confessional statement to one more self-palliating, i.e. 'Alas it is true' becomes 'Alas it may (perhaps) be true'. Moreover, the Q pointing here is supported by the emphatic 'Most true it is' at the beginning of the second quatrain.

1 here and there Suggests a somewhat promiscuous 'going'.

2 made myself . . . view turned myself into a fool or jester ('motley') in men's eyes ('to the view'), 'motley', of course, refers to the parti-coloured dress worn by professional fools on and off the stage, and while it is possible that Shakespeare is here derogating his profession as an actor/dramatist (i.e. all actors and dramatists are 'fools' because they never 'play' or 'write' themselves and hence are never 'true' to themselves), it is equally possible that, using a theatrical metaphor, he is simply saying he has made a public fool of himself by some personal (not theatrical) actions or, perhaps, by some social pretensions.

3 Gored (1) Wounded; (2) Vitiated (by, metaphorically, wearing a motley fool's baggy breeches, which were gaudily ornamented by inset 'gores', i.e. triangular patches of brightly coloured cloth); (3) Dishonoured (by, metaphorically, allowing a 'gore' (= (in heraldry) a shaped area between two charges in a coat-of-arms, indicating some loss of honour) to be inserted in his scutcheon). Compare *Tro.* 3.3.227–8: 'I see my reputation is at stake, / My fame is shrewdly gor'd.'

3 mine own thoughts my own rational nature (by allowing the senses to overrule reason).

3 sold cheap . . . dear bartered away for little or nothing ('sold cheap') what is most precious (i.e. both his 'truth' (5) or integrity and the object of his love, the youth, with play on 'cheap' and 'dear' = costly). With 'sold cheap' compare 'leave for nothing' (109.12). Attempts to read this line as an indictment of Shakespeare's 'role' as actor and dramatist are strained.

4 Made old . . . new i.e. repeated the same old sins in forming new emotional attachments. The principal 'offence' is presumably infidelity.

6 Askance Asquint, distortedly (avoiding looking at 'truth' directly and honestly).

6 strangely i.e. as a stranger (one unaccustomed to looking 'truth' in the face).

6 by all above by by heaven (a milder way of swearing 'By God').

7 blenches (1) side glances (only citation in this sense: *OED* Blench *sb* 2); (2) swervings (from the narrow path of 'truth'; compare 'Askance' (6)).

7 gave my . . . youth i.e. made me think I was young again.

8 worse essays (1) much inferior, (2) more morally reprehensible, (3) more painful, unlucky trials, experiments.

8 proved thee . . . love proved (by trial and error) that you were (1) the highest expression of love's ideal for me, (2) the best of all my loves.

9 Now all is done i.e. I have now finished with all that (going 'here and there' (1), 'blenches' (7), 'worse essays' (8)).

9 have what . . . end be assured of ('have') my constant and unending love (i.e. 'what is most dear' (3)).

10 appetite (1) affection; (2) (sensual) craving, inclination.

10 grind sharpen, whet (with 'blenches' (7)).

11 On newer . . . friend On newer examples of 'friendship' (using them as assaies or trials, i.e. 'proof') in order to test the value of a friend of older standing (i.e. the youth). He will thus cease to use 'newer proof' to 'try' his 'older friend', because his 'worse essays' (8) have shown the 'older friend', like

gold 'tried' by a touchstone, to be pure gold as compared with base metal.

12 A god in love . . . confined i.e. the very deity of Love itself (its highest expression; compare 'my best of love' (8)), to the worship of whom I am wholly devoted ('confined'; compare 105.7). There is perhaps, however, a suggestion in 'confined' of 'imprisoned' or 'constricted', since the sonnet as a whole implies that 'constancy' has become something of a burden for the poet. Dowden notes that the line may contain an echo of the First Commandment: 'I am the Lord thy God. Thou shalt have none other gods but me.'

13 Then give me welcome i.e. like the Prodigal Son (compare 109.6).

13 next my . . . best (1) (you who are) the best (refuge or haven) for me next to heaven (i.e. God's promise of immortality); (2) 'the nearest thing for me to a welcome into heaven' (Ingram and Redpath). There is perhaps some play in 'heaven' on 'haven'; see 129.14 n. and *Cym.* 3.2.60–1: 'Tell me how Wales was made so happy as / T'inherit such a haven!'

14 breast In a sense the poet thus returns to his 'true self' since his 'heart' or 'soul' is in the breast of the beloved. Compare 109.4–5.

Sonnet 111

See headnote to 110.

1 for my sake on my behalf.

1 do you . . . chide i.e. rebuke Fortune (imperative). This reading adopts Gildon's emendation of Q 'wish' to 'with', universally accepted (except for Seymour-Smith) until very recently. Shakespeare elsewhere uses 'chide with' (*OED* Chide *v* 2b) twice (*Oth.* 4.2.167 (Q1), *Cym.* 5.4.32). Randall McLeod ('Unemending Shakespeare's Sonnet 111', *Studies in English Literature* 21 (1981), 75–96), however, argues that the compositor must have intended to set 'wish' because *sh* was a ligature (as *th* was not) and occupied a box in the printer's case nowhere near either *t* or *h* (making a possible missort extremely unlikely). Booth (in the 1978 reprint of his *Shakespeare's Sonnets*) restores 'wish' and declares the substitution of 'with' to be a 'presumption and folly' (p. 580). If 'wish' is retained, what does the line mean? Seymour-Smith glosses as (1) 'It is for my sake that you wish fortune to scold'; or (2), more colloquially, 'You are correct when you say that I, or what I have represented, deserve this criticism' (surely a very strained interpretation). McLeod glosses as (1) 'Wish for my sake that Fortune chide' (which, as Kerrigan points out, makes 'The guilty goddess' in line 2 'an independent deity'); (2) 'You wish Fortune to chide me for my own good.' Kerrigan adds another variation: 'O, surely you don't for my sake wish Fortune to chide me (don't you know what she has done to me already)?' Despite all this *wish*ful ingenuity to preserve Q 'wish', Kerrigan concludes (and Wells agrees with him) that 'None of the senses that can be squeezed from Q seems quite satisfactory.' The sonnet as a whole is a 'chiding' of or 'with' Fortune for what she has done (or failed to do) for the poet. We should, therefore, I think, consider Q 'wish' as either a possible compositorial misreading of a manuscript 'with' or a *lapsus memoriae*, perhaps through some confusion with the use of 'wish' in line 8.

2 The guilty . . . deeds i.e. the goddess (= Fortune) who is responsible for ('guilty') whatever deeds I have done that may be injurious or wrongful ('harmful'; compare 'blenches' (110.7)). In other words, 'I'm not guilty, merely a victim of circumstances imposed by an unfriendly Fortune.' On the transposed adjective 'guilty', see Abbott 419a.

3 That Relative pronoun; antecedent is 'Fortune' (1). See Abbott 258–9.

3 better (1) more generously, (2) more suitably (in my relations with you).

3 life living, livelihood.

4 public means (1) resources, livelihood, (2) way of attaining open to public approval (with play perhaps on 'mean' = inferior, demeaning).

4 which public manners breeds (a 'means') that fosters low-bred or vulgar ('public') (1) behaviour, (2) morals. Like 'means', 'breeds' may be either singular or plural; see Abbott 333. In lines 2–7, if anywhere in the Sonnets, it is possible, but not necessary, to suppose that, as Malone first pointed out, 'The author seems . . . to lament his being reduced to the necessity of appearing on the stage, or writing for the theatre.' That Shakespeare in his plays spoke warmly and approvingly of the theatre (e.g. in *Ham.* 3.2.16–28) is beside the point here. Actors, as well as those who wrote for the public theatres, might be applauded in the theatre, but they were, particularly by the rising Puritan groups, widely considered moral pariahs, if not rogues and vagabonds, and 'vile esteemed' (121.1) by the middle and upper levels of society generally. This is the 'brand' (5) or social stigma about which Shakespeare so bitterly complains. A passage in John Davies of Hereford's *Microcosmos* (1603), p. 82, which has been described as 'a reply' to this sonnet, may be taken as supporting the view that Shakespeare is here referring to his 'low' position as a man of the theatre: '*Players*, I love yee, and your *Qualitie* [i.e. profession], / As ye are Men, *that* pass-time not abus'd: / And some [marginal note refers to 'W.S. R.B.' i.e. William Shakespeare and Richard Burbage] I love for *painting, poesie*, / And say fell *Fortune* cannot be excus'd, / That hath for better *uses* you refus'd: / . . . And though the *stage* doth staine pure gentle *bloud*, / Yet generous yee are in *minde* and *moode*.' Later (1605) Davies again refers to 'W.S. R.B.' as players whom Fortune 'guerdond not, to their desarts' (*Humours Heav'n on Earth*, 'The Second Tale', stanza 76), and in 1610/11 (*The Scourge of Folly*, Epigram 159), in an epigram addressed 'To our

English Terence Mr. Will: Shakespeare', he writes: 'Some say good *Will* . . . / Had'st thou not plaid some Kingly parts in sport, / Thou hadst bin a companion for a *King*; / And, beene a King among the meaner sort.'

5 Thence comes it that As a result of which it happens.

5 name reputation.

5 brand stamp, mark, stigma (of infamy). Compare 112.1–2.

6 almost thence . . . subdued my (good) natural qualities ('nature') are, as a result, almost subjected or overpowered. Note 'almost'.

7 To what . . . hand To (or by) that which it (i.e. 'my nature' (6)) practises or labours in (i.e. the world of the theatre), like the hand of a dyer (which becomes indelibly stained by what it 'works in').

8 Pity me then i.e. have compassion for me, therefore.

8 I were that I might be.

8 renewed restored (to spiritual and moral health).

9 Whilst Meanwhile.

9 willing patient i.e. one who wishes to be cured.

10 Potions Medicinal draughts.

10 eisel vinegar. A mixture of vinegar and honey was prescribed by many doctors for victims of the plague; that it was a 'bitter' remedy is suggested by Hamlet ('Woo't drink up eisel, eat a crocadile?' (*Ham.* 5.1.276)).

10 'gainst . . . infection i.e. to combat my severe or potent ('strong') disease. The poet, metaphorically, describes himself as a victim of the bubonic plague, a disease then considered highly infectious, epidemic outbreaks of which occurred in London in 1592–4, 1603, and 1609. On the danger of 'infection', compare 36.9–12.

11 No bitterness (There is) no bitterness (= mental anguish). 'bitterness' picks up and plays on 'eisel' (10).

12 double penance . . . correction i.e. the same, or perhaps additional, punishment repeated ('double penance') in order to remedy any lack of amendment (= repentance) remaining after its first imposition ('correction' = a double dose of the same medicine). Kenyon's emendation 'too' for Q 'to' (a not infrequent spelling of 'too' at the time) is worth noting (see collation); it treats 'correct' as an adjective, the line then meaning '(I will think) no "double penance" to be an excessive ("too correct") rebuke ("correction").'

13 ye you (singular). See Abbott 236.

14 Even . . . pity i.e. your pity or compassion alone (without other remedies).

Sonnet 112

Sonnet 112 describes the therapeutic results of the 'pity' asked for in 111.8–14. Booth (pp. 369–70)

believes that 112 may be 'an unfinished poem', thus suggesting a reason for the difficulties posed by lines 7–8 and 14.

1 love and pity i.e. love as expressed through compassion.

1 doth Earlier southern form of the plural in *-th*; see Abbott 334.

1 th'impression fill heal over the wound ('impression' = mark, stamp, i.e. the indented scars left by a branding iron; compare 111.5).

2 vulgar scandal public rumour, malicious gossip.

2 stamped . . . brow The poet, metaphorically, describes himself as a convicted (Roman) felon branded ('stamped') with a hot iron on the forehead ('brow').

3 For Because.

3 calls . . . ill speaks of me as good or bad.

4 So So long as.

4 o'er-green give a fresh, unblemished appearance to (only citation in *OED*; compare 'renewed' (111.8)).

4 allow approve.

5 my all the world Compare Constance on her son, Prince Arthur: 'My life, my joy, my food, my all the world!' (*John* 3.4.104), and 109.13–14.

6 To know . . . tongue To be aware of and understand my bad ('shames') and good ('praises') as you determine them ('from your tongue'). You are, in other words, the arbiter of what is good or bad in me.

7–8 None else . . . wrong Steevens (in Malone), not unfairly, calls these lines 'purblind and obscure stuff'. In the context of lines 5–6 and 9–11, they may be roughly paraphrased: 'For me, as I love, there is no one else except you alive (compare line 14) that is able to change my hardened sensibilities ("steeled sense") by judging (in me) what is either right or wrong (= "well/ill" (3), "bad/good" (4), "shames/praises" (6)).' 'sense' is here (but less certainly, I think, in line 10) a collective (= senses); the poet's 'sense' is 'steeled' because he has been forced to braze himself to 'others' voices' (10) to such an extent that he is no longer sure of the difference between right and wrong, or what in him is praiseworthy or shameful. See collation for proposed emendations and Booth's long note, pp. 364–70.

9 In so profound abysm Into such a deep or bottomless pit. There is some suggestion, perhaps, of telling 'others' voices' (10) to 'go to hell' (= 'abysm').

9 throw cast away.

9–10 care / Of (1) serious consideration of; (2) concern or worry about.

10 others' voices i.e. the judgements 'voiced' by those who spread 'vulgar scandal' (2), his 'critic[s]', and those who 'flatter' (11).

10 my adder's sense i.e. my senses, particularly that of hearing. Adders were believed to possess an extraordinarily acute sense of hearing; when they

wished to 'turn a deaf ear' (as the poet says he is doing) they were said to lay one ear on the ground and stick the tip of their tail into the other ear, thus 'stopping' it. Compare Tilley A32 ('As deaf as an adder') and *Tro.* 2.2.171–3: 'for pleasure and revenge / Have ears more deaf than adders to the voice / Of any true decision'.

11 critic censurer.

11 stoppèd are See 10 n. above. The use of 'are' seems to demand that 'sense' (10) be taken (as in line 8 above) as a collective (= senses), not only as the sense of hearing, but the exigencies of rhyme (with 'care') may have dictated 'are' instead of 'is'.

12 Mark how . . . dispense Observe how I excuse or pardon my indifference ('neglect') to 'others' voices' (those of critics and flatterers). Compare *Rape of Lucrece*, 1278–9: 'The more to blame my sluggard negligence. / Yet with the fault I thus far can dispense: [an "excuse" follows]'. Given the immediate context, it seems unlikely that 'my neglect' should be taken to refer to the poet's lack of constancy, his 'ranging', treated in 109 and 110.

13 You are . . . bred You are so strongly engrafted ('bred') in my thoughts (i.e. you are so very much a part of me that my 'purpose' (= intent, the result of thought) is essentially determined by your opinion of me).

14 That all . . . dead A much debated and emended line (see collation). The difficulties arise from how an editor interprets Q 'me thinkes' and 'y'are'. The reading here adopted (substantially following Malone²) means: 'That all the people in the world, apart from you ("besides"), are, it seems to me ("methinks"), (as if) dead (i.e. they might as well be dead so far as influencing my life or "purpose" is concerned)'. This reading takes Q 'me thinkes' as 'methinks' (usually printed as two words at this time and always in the Sonnets), and interprets Q 'y'are' as 'th'are' (= they're, taking the Q 'y' as a compositorial reading of 'y' (= 'th'), a degenerate form of the Old English thorn, which was still frequently used by writers and printers (e.g. 'yᵉ' = the; see 26.12 n.). 'th'are' is here preferred to 'they're' (Dyce) as representing the more Shakespearean form (compare *Ham.* (Q2) 4.7.11, *Tro.* (Q) 3.3.120, *H8* 2.2.53), 'they're' being (except for *Per.* (Q) 2.1.25, 2.2.16 – a reported text) confined to those of his plays printed after 1620. Capell's reading, adopted by a number of editors, by simply deleting Q 'y', gets rid of the redundant 'y' (= th' = they = 'all the world') but fails to account for its presence in Q. A very few editors have defended the Q line *literatim*, paraphrasing as: 'That everybody else in the world, except for me ("besides me"), thinks ye are ("y'are") dead'. Such a reading is nice and straightforward so far as the line in itself is concerned, but it requires extraordinary mental gymnastics (see Seymour-Smith's noble attempt) to validate it in the context of the sonnet as a whole, whereas the reading here adopted fits that context perfectly – if somewhat repetitiously (see lines 5–8 and notes above).

Sonnet 113

113 and 114 are paired sonnets. On the conflict between eye and mind, compare the similar conflict between eye and heart (= mind) in 46–7 (see 46 headnote) and 141.

1 **Since I left you** This may refer to the 'absence', actual or figurative, lamented in 109.1 (see headnote).

1 **mine eye . . . mind** i.e. I 'see' only with my mind's eye (my imagination). Compare *Rape of Lucrece*, 1426: 'save to the eye of mind'; *Ham.* 1.2.185: 'In my mind's eye'; and 27.9 n.

2 **that** i.e. 'mine eye' (1).

2 **governs . . . about** guides me as I move or walk ('go') around.

3 **part his function** (1) divide, separate, (2) give up, abandon, (3) (taken adverbially) in part, partly its ('his') proper mode of action (i.e. in first seeing and then conveying what is seen to the mind; see line 5). Given the second half of the line, (1) and (3) seem most likely. Compare *Mac.* 1.3.139–42: 'My thought, whose murther yet is but fantastical, / Shakes so my single state of man that function / Is smother'd in surmise, and nothing is / But what is not.'

3 **partly** Plays on 'part' as taken in (1) and (2) above.

4 **Seems seeing . . . out** i.e. (my eye) appears to be fulfilling its 'function' (= 'seeing'), but so far as performing its office adequately ('effectually') it is blinded ('is out', extinguished like a snuffed candle conveying no light to the mind or 'heart' (5))

5 **For it . . . heart** Because it communicates no essential image or picture ('form') to the mind ('heart').

6 **shape** form, body.

6 **latch** take hold of, grasp, catch sight of. Capell's emendation of Q 'lack' has been universally accepted (except by Seymour-Smith, who, ignoring the question of rhyme, argues, unconvincingly, that 'it' in line 6 refers not to the 'eye' but to the 'heart' in line 5). Compare *Mac.* 4.3.193–5: 'words / That would be howl'd out in the desert air, / Where hearing should not latch them'.

7 **Of his . . . part** The mind has no share of its ('his', i.e. the eye's) rapidly sensed images ('quick objects', e.g. 'bird', 'flow'r', 'shape' (6)). 'quick' may also carry some suggestion of 'alive' or 'living', referring to things of the real world as compared with the bodiless 'objects' of the mind.

8 **Nor his . . . catch** (1) Nor does the mind's own eye ('his own vision') preserve or retain what it apprehends or 'sees' ('doth catch'); (2) Nor does the eye itself retain what it sees. There is disagreement about the antecedent of 'his' and 'it' (i.e. whether 'mind' or 'eye'), but surely 'it' in lines 9 and 12 tends

to support 'mind' as the antecedent, since it is the mind and not the eye that may better be said to 'shape' things 'to your feature' (12); the eye merely 'sees', the mind 'transforms'. (1) thus seems preferable.

9 **For** Because.

9 **it** (1) the mind; (2) the eye (see 8 n. above).

9 **rud'st** (1) most uncivilised or barbarous (with suggestion perhaps of low social status); (2) most ill-shaped; (3) most rugged, roughest.

9 **gentlest** (1) noblest, most excellent (with suggestion perhaps of 'well-born'); (2) tamest, least violent; (3) tenderest. 'gentlest' is treated as a disyllable.

10 **most sweet favour** most (1) pleasing, delightful appearance, (2) agreeable, charming face or countenance (implying something morally 'good'; compare 'gentlest' (9)). Kerrigan, for the first time, restores Q 'sweet-fauor', arguing, as first suggested by Brooke, 'that Q's hyphen implies an adjectival form with the "–ed" assumed from "deformèd'st" (i.e. 'sweet-favour' = sweet-favoured; compare Delius's conjecture in collation). He may be right, but there is no other instance recorded, in or out of Shakespeare, of this idiosyncratic construction (the kind of superlative ellipsis found in 86.6 is not relevant here; see Abbott 398). Wells, though he notes the above argument for retaining the Q hyphen, reads 'sweet favour' (without acknowledgement to Benson) in his modern-spelling Oxford text, but, rather confusingly, 'sweet-fauor' in his old-spelling text. If an adjectival form is felt to be necessary, we should, I think, accept Delius's conjecture ('sweet-favour'd'), curiously enough never adopted by any editor. It would have been very easy for a compositor to misread 'sweet-fauord' as 'sweet-fauore' (final *d* and *e* in Secretary hand are frequently and easily confused), and, because by the last decades of the sixteenth century the spelling 'fauore' or 'fauoure' had become rare in printed works (see citations in *OED*), he dropped what he mistook for an old-fashioned, unfunctional *e*.

10 **deformèd'st creature** most misshapen, monstrous, ugly, ill-favoured (with an implication of moral ugliness) work of God's creation. 'creature' may be either animate or inanimate, part of the Great Chain of Being or 'The Book of the Creatures'. Compare 114.5.

11–12 **The mountain . . . dove** Most editors, since Lintott and Gildon, omit the Q commas after 'mountain', 'day', and 'crow', thus giving three presumably contrasting pairs as examples of 'most sweet favour' as opposed to 'deformèd'st'. The Q pointing, here retained (first restored by Capell), although not necessarily restrictive, seems to suggest treating the six items listed as separate entities. Behind these lines lies, I think, a recollection of the widely known canticle *Benedicite omnia opera domini domino* (in the Book of Common Prayer), in which 'all ye works [=

creatures] of the Lord' are called on to praise Him, including 'nights and days', 'mountains and hills', 'seas and floods', and 'fowls of the air'. Two pairings do seem to offer definite contrasts, 'good' or 'bad': 'day' (light and fair), 'night' (black and ugly; compare *Rape of Lucrece*, 764–805, and *H5* 4. Chorus 4, 21: 'the foul womb of night . . . a foul and ugly witch'); 'crow' (carrion crow or raven, of ill omen, black like the Devil; compare Tilley c846: 'Breed up a crow and she will peck out your eyes'), 'dove' (emblem of peace, comfort, loving; compare Tilley D572: 'As innocent (harmless) as a dove') – chiasmic reversal of order to 'bad' and 'good'. But in these terms, how are we supposed to take 'mountain' and 'sea'? 'Mountain' may be considered either as *terra firma*, solid and dependable, or as a wart on the face of the earth, threatening, barren, and misshapen; 'sea', as either a reservoir of life or as treacherous and unstable (compare Tilley s170: 'As mad as the troubled sea').

12 **it** (1) the mind's eye; (2) my eye (see 8 n. above).

12 **shapes . . . feature** fashions or frames them to your form or shape (with possible play on 'feature' = face).

13 **Incapable** Unable to take in or hold (earliest citation in this sense in *OED*).

13 **replete with** filled up with (with perhaps a suggestion of 'gorged'; compare 'confined' (110.12 n.)).

14 **My most true mind** This paradoxically suggests that, though the poet's mind falsifies what his eye sees by turning whatever it sees into the 'shape' of the beloved, his mind performs the essential and higher function of 'truth' ('most true'). Compare, in some respects, the theme of 98 and 99.

14 **maketh mine eye untrue** i.e. falsifies my sense of sight. Among the numerous emendations offered for Q 'maketh mine untrue' (see collation), Keightley's has been adopted here because it supports the antithesis between mind and eye, the theme of the sonnet, with, assuming a dropped word, a minimum of textual meddling. Collier's 'maketh my eyne' would, out of context, be tempting (Q 'mine' being taken as a compositorial misreading of 'my eyne' or possibly of 'm'eyne'), but 'eye' is throughout treated as singular and always modified by 'mine' (as in the following linked sonnet, 114). Editors who retain Q unemended treat 'untrue' as a substantive (= untruth, for which *OED* offers no support) and follow Malone in paraphrasing the line as 'The sincerity of my affection is the cause of my untruth', a strained, rather flat, but possible interpretation.

Sonnet 114

Sonnet 114 continues the 'eye/mind' theme of 113, but now argues that it is the 'eye', not the 'mind', that 'shapes' all 'objects', even 'Creating every bad a perfect best' (7), to the image of the beloved because the 'eye well knows' (11) what the 'mind' most relishes.

Compare Marlowe and Nashe, *Dido* (1594), 2.2.32–3: 'Thy mind, *Aeneas*, that would have it so, / Deludes thy eye sight.'

1, 3 **Or whether . . . Or whether** Poses two alternatives as questions: 'Is this the case? . . . Or is that the case?' On the idiom 'or whether' (where modern usage would omit one of the two conjunctions), see Abbott 136.

1 **being crowned with you** i.e. being made a king ('crowned') by the consciousness of possessing you as my friend (Tucker). Compare 69.5 n. As in 60.6, 'being' is treated as a monosyllable.

2 **Drink up** Swallow down (greedily).

2 **monarch's . . . flattery** i.e. the practice of flattery or false praise, a kind of poison, to which (1) a monarch is continually subjected and which (2) becomes a deadly sickness ('plague') in the monarch if he (or she) allows it to poison his (or her) mental vision. Both Queen Elizabeth and James I suffered from this 'plague' in both senses, especially James.

3 **saith true** i.e. 'speaks' the truth (does not 'flatter' what it, the eye, sees).

4 **your love . . . alcumy** my love for you taught my eye ('it') this miraculous power of transmutation, 'alcumy' is a variant form of 'alchemy'. One of the principal aims of the alchemist was to transmute base metals into pure gold (i.e. 'a perfect best' (7)). Compare 'heavenly alcumy' in 33.4 and note.

5 **To make of** Namely, to make out of.

5 **monsters . . . indigest** malformed or unnatural births (compare 113.9–10) and shapeless, ill-formed objects. Compare *John* 5.7.25–7: 'you are born / To set a form upon that indigest / Which he hath left so shapeless and so rude'. The line may owe something to Ovid (*Metamorphoses* 1, 7), who describes the unformed universe as 'rudis indigestaque moles' ('a rough, unordered mass of things' (Loeb)) and the earth (1, 87) as 'rudis sine imagine' ('a rough and formless thing' (Loeb)).

6 **cherubins** (1) literally, the second order of angels after seraphim; (2) 'creatures' beautiful in form and/or intellect 'cherubin' or 'cherubim' (a variant form, historically more correct), though etymologically a plural form of 'cherub', was at this time frequently treated as singular; hence the present plural with -*s* (see *OED* Cherub).

6 **resemble** symbolise, typify (with perhaps a suggestion of the likeness being outward only).

7 **every bad** every bad thing, such as the 'monsters', and things indigest' (5).

7 **a perfect best** i.e. the 'cherubins' in line 6, for example. The apparent tautology is used for emphatic heightening; compare our frequently used phrase 'the very best'.

8 **fast as objects** Compare 'his quick objects' in 113.7.

8 **his** its (i.e. the eye's).

8 **beams** i.e. beams of light. For the theory of vision behind this line, see 20.6 n. Compare *Venus and Adonis*, 1051–2: 'And being open'd [i.e. Venus's eyes], threw unwilling light / Upon the wide wound', and Castiglione, *The Courtier* (1561), p. 247: 'the eyes shoote, and . . . send their glistering beames into the eyes of the wight beloved'.

8 **assemble** come together.

9 **first** i.e. the correct answer is that posed, in lines 1–2, by the first question.

9 **flatt'ry in my seeing** i.e. it is my eye, not my mind, that deceptively transmutes everything it sees into your superlative image, 'a perfect best' (7). Compare *TN* 1.5.308–9: '[I] fear to find / Mine eye too great a flatterer for my mind.'

10 **great mind most kingly** The poet's mind is playfully said to be 'great' and acting in a 'kingly' manner because it is 'crowned with you' (1).

11 **with his . . . greeing** is agreeing with its ('his', i.e. the mind's) taste (i.e. what it wishes eagerly to 'Drink up' (2, 10)). 'Gree' is an independent aphetic form of 'agree' (see *OED* Gree *v*).

12 **to his palate . . . cup** i.e. as a 'royal taster', whose office it was to taste, in advance, the sovereign's food and drink to guard against poison, might season a cup of wine or other drink to please or suit his lord's palate. There is a suggestion here (and earlier) that the poet's eye, as 'taster', is falling in its duty and, in fact, serving its sovereign (the mind) with a poisoned cup ('flattery' being a kind of poison; compare 'If it be poisoned' in line 13, and see 2 n. above).

13 **it** i.e. the contents of the cup.

13–14 **'tis the lesser . . . begin** i.e. the sin committed by my eye is of a lesser nature (venial, not mortal) because (1) my eye truly loves what it offers to my mind and (2) it first 'tastes' the 'poison' itself ('doth first begin'). Booth notes that there is a suggestion of neo-Platonic theory underlying 'lesser sin', sins of the senses being considered less grave than sins of the mind. The colloquial phrase 'to begin to' meant 'to pledge or toast a person'.

Sonnet 115

Critics often compare Donne's 'Loves Growth', especially lines 1–12, though, as we would expect, Donne treats the theme differently.

1–2 **Those lines . . . dearer** Compare 'Loves Growth', 5–6: 'Me thinkes I lyed all winter, when I swore, / My love was infinite, if spring make'it more.' Strictly speaking such 'lines' do not occur in the sonnets to the young man and it has been argued that this means that Shakespeare is referring to a sonnet or sonnets now lost, but something of the same claim ('I could not love you dearer') may be extrapolated, as Brooke notes, from 25, 29, 31, 37, 75, and 91. We cannot always expect Shakespeare to 'speak by the card'.

2 **Even** Namely.

3 **judgement** mental discernment, belief.

4 **My most full flame** i.e. the flame of my love (then) burning (1) most (2) very intensely. Love was often described as a 'fire'; compare *Rom.* 1.1.190–1: 'Love is a smoke made with the fume of sighs, / Being purg'd, a fire sparkling in lovers' eyes', and 109.2.

4 **clearer** more brightly, more purely.

5–8 Generally considered syntactically hanging lines (see, however, note on line 5), since if the subject is taken as 'Time', modified by three relative clauses, it is left without a predicate, line 9 apparently beginning a new syntactical unit. The Q text has been allowed to stand, with a dash after 'things' (8) for the Q colon, but Capell's emendation (first recorded in Rollins and ignored by later editors) of 'Divert' (8) to 'Diverts' ('Divert' being an easy compositorial slip, followed as it is by the *s* in 'strong') deserves at least some consideration, since 'Diverts' thus becomes the main verb, with 'Time' as its subject, and lines 5–7 ('whose millioned . . . intents') may be treated as parenthetical examples of Time's 'reckoning' (5).

5 **But reckoning Time** Yet Time that calls everything to account (by its destructive action; compare 'Time's tyranny' in line 9). Most editors thus take 'reckoning' as a participial adjective modifying 'Time' as subject. It is possible, however, to understand the phrase as meaning 'Yet considering Time (and its destructive action)', in which case, as Beeching suggests, the syntactical construction is resumed in 'fearing of Time's tyranny' in line 9.

5 **millioned** numbered by the million. *OED* (no other citation before 1747) suggests that Q 'millioud' may be only a form of 'million' formed on the analogy of 'hundred' or 'thousand'.

5 **accidents** (1) events, seen or unforeseen, fortunate or unfortunate; (2) effects.

6 **Creep . . . vows** i.e. steal in between the taking of vows and their fulfilment (causing such vows to be broken).

6 **decrees** ordinances, edicts (as handed down by the Court of Equity, which was under the control of the sovereign).

7 **Tan sacred beauty** Make beauty, which is worthy of being worshipped ('sacred'), dark or leathery-looking ('Tan'). 'sacred' was suggested perhaps by 'kings' (6), who, as God's vice-regents, were sometimes addressed as 'your sacred majesty'.

7 **blunt . . . intents** dull or render inoperative the most keenly held ('sharp'st') intentions or purposes. Compare *Ham.* 3.4.110–11: 'This visitation / Is but to whet thy almost blunted purpose.'

8 **Divert . . . things** i.e. cause firm and constant ('strong') minds to be deflected (from their true direction) by the (eddying) current ('course') of anything undergoing change ('alt'ring things'). The mind is thus being influenced or subverted by merely temporal and external changes. Compare *Ham.* 3.2.200–1: 'This world is not for aye, nor 'tis

not strange / That even our loves should with our fortunes change.'

9 fearing of being afraid of. See Abbott 178.

9 Time's tyranny Compare 'this bloody tyrant Time' in 16.2.

10 then say i.e. at that time when I said 'I could not love you dearer' (2). It is possible, however, to take 'then' = therefore; see the same ambiguity in line 13.

10 'Now . . . best' i.e. my love is at its highest (no increase possible). Compare 'My most full flame' (4).

11 When (1) Then when; (2) Since.

11 I was . . . incertainty I was utterly sure (of the full growth of my love for you) beyond all question ('o'er incertainty'). But 'o'er incertainty' may also suggest, anticipating 'doubting of the rest' (12), 'rising above ('o'er') the fear of an uncertain future'. Q's form 'in-certainty' may be taken to indicate initial and contrasting stress on 'in-'. See 107.7 n.

12 Crowning the present Investing the present moment (i.e. the 'then' of line 10) as with a crown (a symbol of the highest and 'best' (10)).

12 doubting of the rest fearing what the future ('the rest') might hold (compare 'fearing of' in line 9).

13 Love is a babe Love = (1) Cupid (from classical times, Love or Cupid was pictured as a (frequently chubby) male infant; compare 151.1 and 154.1); (2) a baby. Ingram and Redpath first ignored the generally accepted reference to Cupid and glossed 'babe' as simply 'baby', and Booth has pointed out that 'baby' should be the primary meaning because Cupid as 'babe' could never grow any older and hence as 'Love' cannot properly be said to mature or 'still . . . grow' (14). Even if Shakespeare had been conscious of the somewhat technical objection raised by Booth, I suspect that, nevertheless, the association here of 'Love' with Cupid probably remained primary in his mind; that Shakespeare seems to have thought of Cupid as capable of growth is suggested (as Tucker notes) by *LLL* 5.2.10–11: 'That was the way to make his godhead wax, / For he hath been five thousand year a boy.'

13–14 then might . . . grow therefore (since 'Love is a babe'), I may not say as I said ('so' = 'Now I love you best'), for to say 'so' would be to ascribe full growth to that (= Love) which, now and always ('still'), continues to grow (i.e. I would be stunting or limiting it). As in line 10 (see note) 'then' is somewhat ambiguous; it here most probably means 'therefore' (as interpreted above), but it can also be taken to mean 'at that earlier time'. The couplet is difficult and was misunderstood by editors from Gildon to Rolfe (Capell being an exception), who interpreted 'then might I not say so' interrogatively (an interpretation encouraged by the word-order), and 'To give' as 'Thereby giving', substituting a question mark for the Q period after 'grow'. Such a reading, as Wynd-

ham remarks, 'defeats the sense of the whole sonnet. The *ictus* or stress on "not", l. 13–(cf. the *ictus* on "then" and "now" in l. 10) – shows that the couplet *refutes* the argument of the third quatrain.'

Sonnet 116

Sonnet 116 is one of the best known and most admired of Shakespeare's Sonnets– a meditation on the potential ideality and constancy of human love (compare 124). Recent criticism, however, finding an uneasy ambiguity in what appears to be its confident tone, holds that the sonnet has all too often been 'mawkishly' misread and that, in addition to the implied limitations suggested by lines 7–8, 'The convoluted negatives of the last line . . . show the poet protesting too much, losing confidence in his protestations, or at least inviting disagreement with them (by anticipating rebuttal), at their climax' (Kerrigan, p. 53). Thus Shakespeare, it is argued, admits, consciously or unconsciously, that the perfection of the abstract *Idea* of Love can never be realised in merely human terms ('Whose worth's unknown' (8)). Such a view, as Kerrigan wisely allows, while it adds a human dimension to the poem, does not, paradoxically, lessen the poet's commitment to his '"unknown" absolute'; it therefore makes 'a sceptical reading available' (Kerrigan, p. 54), but does not deny the essential thrust of the more traditional and less ambiguous reading which celebrated the poem (Wordsworth called it Shakespeare's 'best sonnet') as the noblest expression of the constancy and strength of human love in conflict with the assaults of Time and 'millioned accidents' (115.5). See Booth's long and perceptive, if sometimes over-ingenious, critical discussion (pp. 387–92) of this sonnet.

1–2 Let me not . . . impediments i.e. (1) never let it be thought I (or *I*) acknowledge, (2) may I (or *I*) never be forced to acknowledge that any obstacles can alter the spiritual union ('marriage') of constant and faithful ('true') minds. 'impediments' is thus taken as referring to Time's 'millioned accidents', which 'Divert strong minds to th'course of alt'ring things' (115.5, 8). Three echoes from the marriage service in the Book of Common Prayer seem to be combined here: (1) marriage was considered a 'mystical union' through which a man and a woman become 'one flesh' (compare the 'exchange of hearts (or minds)' by which lover and beloved become 'one'; see 36.1–2 and headnote); (2) 'I require and charge you (as you will answer at the dreadful day of judgement, when the secrets of all hearts shall be disclosed) that if either of you do know any impediment [*previously stated as* if any man can show any just cause], why ye may not be lawfully joined in matrimony, that ye confess it'; (3) 'Those whom God hath joined together: let no man put asunder.' Compare also the proverb (Publilius Syrus) *Conjunctio animi maxima est cognatio* (The marriage of minds is the strongest of ties).

See C. G. Smith, *Shakespeare's Proverb Lore*, 1963, p. 86.

2 love is not love i.e. love cannot be considered as true love. Compare *Lear* 1.1.238–40: 'Love's not love / When it is mingled with regards that stands / Aloof from th'entire point.'

3 alteration finds i.e. (1) encounters the changes (= 'millioned accidents' (115.5)) which Time, events, or persons bring about in 'th' course of alt'ring things' (115.8); (2) discovers a loss of physical beauty in lover or beloved (compare lines 9–12).

4 bends with . . . remove turns awry ('bends') under the influence of 'alteration' ('with the remover') to change its true course ('remove'). 'remover' may also refer to subversive human agency. Compare 25.14, Constable, *Diana*, 1, 5, 5–6: 'but sith resolved love cannot remove / As longe as thy devine perfections stay', and Sir John Davies's parody of the theme in *Gulling Sonnets* (c. 1594), 3.5–10: 'I chaunges prove, yet still the same am I, / The same am I and never will remove, / Never remove untill my soule dorhe flye, / My soule dothe fly and I surcease to move; / I cease to move which now am mov'd by yow, / Am mov'd by yow that move all mortall hartes . . .'

5 mark sea-mark (such as a beacon or other highly visible object set up to warn mariners of shoals or dangerous rocks). Compare *Cor.* 5.3.74–5: 'Like a great sea-mark, standing evey flaw [compare 'tempests' (6)], / And saving those that eye thee', and Fulke Greville, *Caelica* (c. 1590), 43.9–12: 'So I because I cannot choose to know, / How constantly you have forgotten me, / Because my Faith doth like the Sea-marks show, / And tell the strangers where the dangers be . . .'

6 looks on observes (without fear because it is 'ever-fixèd' (5) and can never be 'shaken' (6)).

7 star i.e. probably referring to the North or pole-star, used by mariners, as most dependable, to get their bearings. Compare *JC* 3.1.60–2: 'But I am constant as the northern star, / Of whose true-fix'd and resting quality / There is no fellow in the firmament.'

7 to every wand'ring bark i.e. to guide ('to') any vessel that is off its course.

8 Whose worth's . . . taken i.e. the occult virtue and potential influence of which can never (like love's) be fully understood or realised (by imperfect human beings), even though its ('his') altitude ('heighth') can be reckoned ('taken') (as by a sextant reading in the sky, calculating height and position by angles). Although lines 7–8 recognise that human love is necessarily limited and thus 'admit' an 'impediment' – that such love cannot fully reach the constant perfection of ideal love – they nevertheless set up that ideal as one to which, like a guiding star, mankind can aspire; mankind can 'take' love's measure (i.e. have a rational understanding of its 'worth') and be inspired by it – even as mankind is inspired

by the equally 'unknowable' concept of God's love.

8 heighth This common variant form of 'height' (compare *John* 4.3.46, *Ant.* 3.10.20) accords better with the Q spelling 'higth' than 'height', the usually adopted form, and is easier for modern readers than Capell's 'highth', which is also historically recognised (see collation and *OED* Height *sb*).

9 Love's . . . fool i.e. Time will never make a fool or (Vendler) slave (= one whose moral and mental faculties are (1) deficient, (2) subjected) of true love. See 124.8, 13, and *1H4* 5.4.81–3: 'But thoughts, the slaves of life, and life, time's fool, / And time, that takes survey of all the world, / Must have a stop.'

9–10 though rosy . . . come even though physical beauty ('rosy lips and cheeks') may fall within the sweep ('compass') of his (1) curved sickle, (2) sickle that bends or mows down (compare 'bends' (4)). In other words, Time's destruction of mere physical beauty in lover or beloved creates no 'impediment' to the constancy of true love. Compare lines 11–12, and see 100.14 n. and 126.2 n.

11 with his under the influence of, in accordance with, Time's.

11 brief short-lived, fleeting (hence continually changing, unlike true love).

12 bears it out endures defiantly (Ingram and Redpath). Booth compares 1 Cor. 13.7: '[Love] endureth ["beareth" in AV] all things' (Geneva).

12 edge of doom brink of (1) death, (2) Doomsday or the Last Judgement. The phrase suggests an image of being poised on the edge of an abyss (Tucker) Compare 14.14 n. and *AWW* 3.3.5–6: 'We'll strive to bear it for your worthy sake / To th'extreme edge of hazard.' Booth compares 'till death us depart' from the marriage service (Book of Common Prayer).

13 If this be error If this claim that I have made (concerning the fidelity of true love) should be mistaken (i.e. in 'error'). There is a possible play on 'writ of error' = a legal writ brought to procure the reversal of a judgement, on the ground of error (*OED* Error 4c), anticipating, perhaps, the implications of 'writ' in line 14.

13 and upon me proved and is proved against me (by what I have said and done).

14 I never . . . loved i.e. anything I have written ('writ') (referring presumably only to earlier sonnets) is false, and no man (including me) ever truly loved (with the strong implication, underscored by the use of emphatic negatives, that what he has written *is* true and that his love *is* true). Greville (*Caelica* (c. 1590), 75.51–8; see 5 n. above) offers an interesting parallel construction and use of negatives on the theme of true love: 'Deare, if ever in my dayes, / My heart joy'd in others praise: / If I of the world did borrow, / Other ground for joy or sorrow: / If I better wish to be / But the better to please thee; / I say, if this false be proved, / Let me not love, or not be loved.' Indeed, some influence from Greville's *Caelica*, which Shakespeare could have known in manuscript, may perhaps be argued for here and elsewhere in 116 (compare 'Let me not' (1) and 'mark' (5 n.)). For a different view of the 'convoluted negatives' of line 14, see headnote.

Sonnet 117

Considering the playful hypocrisy of the couplet, it is somewhat surprising to find so many thematic and verbal contacts between 117 and 116. As Booth points out, 117 'picks up on 116's topics (e.g. constancy, departure, accusation, proof, value, writing, ties between people, measuring worth), its metaphors (e.g. navigation, trials at law, the range of weapons [116.10: *Within... compass*, 117.11: *within the level*]), and its language (e.g. *minds* and *unknown* in 116.1, 8 and *unknown minds* in 117.5; *error* in 116.13 and *errors* in 117.9); but 117 uses them to entirely different effect (in 116 the speaker is grand, noble, general, and beyond logic; in 117 he is petty, particular, and narrowly logical)'. The theme of self-accusation in lines 1–12 also links 117 with 109 and 110 and is continued in 118–21.

1 Accuse me thus Charge me as follows (as if before the bar of justice). The 'charges' follow (1–8), in a form resembling an itemised legal writ, each charge introduced by 'that' clauses.

1–2 I have ... repay I have neglected or slighted everything ('scanted all') by which I should repay your great merits ('deserts', with some play perhaps on 'good deeds' or 'patronage'). *OED* Scant *v* 7 cites *Oth.* 1.3.267 as the earliest use of 'scant' in this sense. It is possible that 'all' should be taken adverbially, 'scanted all / Wherein' then = 'utterly neglected or slighted (matters) wherein'.

3 Forgot ... call i.e. (and) forgot to invoke ('upon ... to call') your most precious love ('dearest' has possible undertones of 'costliest'). Compare 100.1–2 and 101.9–10, describing the poet's 'silence'. This seems a better reading than to take 'upon ... to call' as = 'to draw upon (the riches of)'.

4 Whereto all ... day To which all ties (i.e. 'bonds' of affection) bind me every day ('day by day', implying 'forever' or 'even to the edge of doom' (116.12) – unlike legal 'bonds' which had a 'due date', after which, if met, they were abrogated). 'bonds' in the sense of 'legal documents' picks up the legal metaphor implied in line 1. Is there a hint here that the poet is feeling inescapably 'fettered' or 'confined' by his love (compare 110.12 n.)?

5 frequent been with been in company with, familiar with (earliest citation in this sense: *OED* Frequent *a* 6c). It is possible that Shakespeare intends 'frequent' adverbially (= often), even though *OED* Frequent *a* 7 gives 1614 as the earliest example of such usage.

5 unknown minds strangers, persons whose moral and intellectual 'worth' is 'unknown' to me (unlike 'your great deserts' (2) so well 'known' to me).

6 given to time i.e. wasted in idle pursuits of the moment ('time').

6 your own ... right the proper ('own') right or claim (to my constancy) which you have acquired with so much cost (1) to you, or (2) (more cynically) to me.

7 hoisted sail ... winds i.e. set my sails to catch each and every wind (like 'every wand'ring bark' (116.7)). Compare 109.5–8 and 110.1–6.

8 should would.

8 from your sight i.e. where I would not be under your eye (hence avoiding an immediate feeling of guilt). Compare 'Out of sight out of mind' (Tilley S438).

9 Book ... down Record ('Book ... down', as a summary of the charges against me) both my wilfulness (i.e. actions against reason) and (1) transgressions, (2) wanderings. Compare *2H4* 4.3.46–7: 'let it be book'd with the rest of this day's deeds'. Vendler suggests a possible name-pun between 'wilfulness' and 'Will[iam]' (compare 80.8).

10 And on ... accumulate And, in addition to what true evidence ('just proof' of my 'errors') you may have, pile up (unjust) suspicion ('surmise').

11 Bring ... frown i.e. take true aim at me ('Bring ... level of') in your anger or displeasure ('of your frown'). The metaphor in 'level' is from the practice of gunnery, continued in 'shoot' (12).

12 wakened hate i.e. the hatred or aversion aroused in you (by my 'errors' (9)). Compare *Oth.* 3.3.363: 'my wak'd wrath'.

13 Since ... says Because my defence plea ('appeal') claims or states (that). Picks up the legal frame begun in line 1.

13 prove test. The couplet employs the same 'clever' excuse that Jachimo uses to Imogen after he has tried to seduce her by lying about Posthumus's loose sexual behaviour while absent in Rome ('I have spoke this to know if your affiance / Were deeply rooted' (*Cym.* 1.6.163–4)).

14 virtue of your love (1) strength or power, (2) moral and physical purity of your love (for me).

Sonnet 118

Sonnet 118 is built around a purging metaphor; for a similarly extended use of the same metaphor, see *2H4* 4.1.54–66. The sonnet asks to be read on several levels: (1) as an expanded conceit, witty if shallow (like the couplet of 117); (2) as a veiled statement that the poet has become uneasily 'sated' ('being full of' (5), 'sick of welfare' (7), 'rank of goodness' (12), 'so fell sick of you' (14)) by his 'love' (compare 117.4 n.) and has thus felt the need for a 'purge' (4); (3) as a kind of confession of promiscuous sexual activity, playing on such words as 'appetites' (1), 'eager compounds' and 'palate urge' (2), 'sicken' and 'purge' (4), 'bitter sauces' and 'feeding' (6), 'diseased' (8), 'faults assured' (10), 'to medicine' (11), 'rank' (12), 'Drugs poison' and 'fell sick' (14) – several of these words even suggesting perhaps treatment for venereal disease. Tobin notes that something of the idea behind 118 may have been suggested by the story of Mithridates VI, King of Pontus, who intentionally took poisons to immunise himself against being poisoned (he was stabbed to death!); compare Martial, *Epigrams* v, 76.1–2: 'Proficit poto Mithridates saepe veneno / toxica ne possent saeva nocere sibi' ('Mithridates, by often drinking poison, achieved protection against deadly drugs' (Loeb)).

1–3 Like as to ... As to Just as in order to ... (And) as in order to.

1 appetites (1) natural inclinations; (2) lusts. See 56.2 n.

1 keen sharp, eager, biting.

2 eager compounds (1) tart, pungent, biting mixtures (of food and drink to heighten a cloyed appetite); (2) aphrodisiacs (compare 'bitter sauces' in line 6). See *Ham.* 1.4.2: 'It is a nipping and an eager air.'

2 our palate urge stimulate, excite (1) our sense of taste, (2) physical or mental desires. Compare, partly for tone, *Tro.* 3.2.18–22: 'I am giddy; expectation whirls me round; / Th'imaginary relish [compare 'sauces' (6)] is so sweet / That it enchants my sense; what will it be, / When that the wat'ry palates taste indeed / Love's thrice-repured nectar?' Here 'palates' means 'senses'.

3 prevent forestall.

3 maladies unseen ailments, diseases of which no symptoms are yet apparent.

4 We sicken ... sickness We make ourselves sick (e.g. by inducing vomiting) in order to avoid ('shun') sickness (through repletion). Compare *TN* 1.1.1–3: 'If music be the food of love, play on, / Give me excess of it; that surfeiting, / The appetite may sicken, and so die.'

4 purge (1) cleanse ourselves by 'purgation' (i.e. ridding the system of potentially harmful elements); (2) have sexual intercourse. In one sense, both 117 and 118 might be described as metaphorical 'purges'.

5 Even so In just such ways (picking up 'Like as' (1) and 'As' (3)).

5 ne'er-cloying sweetness never-surfeiting graciousness, delightfulness ('sweetness', with play on 'something pleasant to the senses'). Compare *Ant.* 2.2.235–7: 'Other women cloy / The appetites they feed, but she makes hungry / Where most she satisfies.' Benson's reading 'neare' for Q 'nere' (a common spelling of both 'ne'er' and 'near' at this time; see *OED* and collation), even if mistaken, is understandable in the context of 'being full of'; Q 'nere cloying' would have thus offered an Elizabethan reader

a suggestive ambiguity that is lost in modernising to 'ne'er'.

6 To bitter ... feeding i.e. for (1) food, (2) company, I resorted ('frame[d] my feeding') to (1) sharp sauces or relishes, (2) inferior companions ('sauces' which, when 'tasted', though intended to stimulate, turned out to be 'bitter' = injurious, painful). Compare Sidney, *Old Arcadia*, p. 216: 'And specyally those sawcy pages of Love, Doubtes, greeffes, Languisshing hopes and threateninge dispayres, came all nowe to his [Pyrocles'] mynde in one Ranck, to beutify this after followyng blisfullnes, and to serve for a moste fitt sauce, whose sowernes mighte give a kynde of Lyfe to the delightfull chere [the rape of Philoclea] his Imaginacyon fedd uppon.'

7 sick of welfare sick as a result of being well or healthy (in 'being full of your ne'er cloying sweetness'). The oxymoron, like 'rank of goodness' (12), consciously or unconsciously, undercuts 'ne'er-cloying' and suggests that the poet is actually feeling 'o'ercloyed' (*R3* 5.3.318).

7 found ... meetness thought I had discovered a kind of fitness or propriety ('a kind of' implying 'a partial excuse for').

8 To be diseased In being (1) infected, sick, (2) made uneasy (physically or mentally).

8 true needing i.e. any real cause (for fearing such 'disease').

9–10 Thus policy ... assured As a result (what had seemed) a prudent or shrewd course to pursue in matters concerning love, namely, to forestall potential (1) diseases, (2) ill effects, produced ('grew to') real diseases or ill effects ('faults assured').

11–12 And brought ... cured i.e. and reduced to the necessity of seeking medicinal aid ('brought to medicine'), a completely healthy ('healthful') state (of mind and body), which, being gorged with your goodness ('rank of goodness'; compare 'sick of welfare' (7)), sought (mistakenly) to be cured by making use of ill or evil (remedies). 'medicine' may be taken either metaphorically or literally. Compare some of the 'remedies' suggested by lines 2 and 6 above and 117.5–6.

13 thence i.e. from the 'lesson' learned from the 'policy' practised in lines 5–12.

14 Drugs (1) Medicinal purges; (2) 'eager compounds' (line 2), 'bitter sauces' (line 6); (3) 'unknown minds' (117.5).

14 so fell ... you became (1) so deeply, (2) in such a way infected ('sick') by you (i.e. by your 'sweetness' (5)), a 'disease' for which there are no remedial 'Drugs').

Sonnet 119

Sonnet 119 is closely linked with 118, describing the 'benefit of ill' (9) and 'gain by ills' (14), which poisonous 'Drugs' (118.14) and 'potions' (1) may, paradoxically, effect – a threefold bonus!

1 potions (1) poisonous draughts (looking back to 'Drugs poison' in 118.14); (2) medicinal draughts (looking back to 'purge' and 'bitter sauces' in 118.4, 6).

1 Siren tears Deceitfully, destructively alluring tears (metaphorically referring to the kind of 'unknown minds' (see 117.5 n.) with whom the poet has been associating). The Sirens were mythological creatures, part woman, part bird, who lured sailors to destruction by their sweet singing. Compare *A Lover's Complaint*, 288–9: 'O father, what a hell of witchcraft lies / In the small orb of one particular tear!'

2 Distilled Extracted (as an essence).

2 limbecks foul as hell within distilling vessels (alembics) or retorts, the insides or contents of which ('within') were as polluted or filthy as hell itself. Though the imagery of lines 1–2 may be traditional (compare Chaucer, *Troilus and Criseyde*, IV, 519–20: 'Troylus in teris gan distille, / As licour out of a lambic ful faste', and Barnes, *Parthenophil and Parthenophe* (1593), Sonnet 49.6–9: 'A Syren which within thy brest doth bath her . . . / From my loves lymbeck still still'd teares, oh teares!'), Shakespeare gives the context strongly sexual implications by introducing 'foul' and 'hell', the second of which, here associated with 'limbecks' (= from their shapes, the male or female genitalia), has a long history as a slang term for the female pudenda. See Boccaccio, *The Decameron*, Day Three, Story Ten, in which the young monk, Rustico, teaches the innocent virgin, Alibech, how 'to put the devil back in hell'; and compare 129.14 and *Lear* 4.6.124–9: 'Down from the waist are they Centaurs; / Though women all above; / But to the girdle do the gods inherit, / Beneath is all the fiends': there's hell, there's darkness, / There is the sulphurous pit, burning, scalding, / Stench, consumption.' Something of Lear's extreme sexual nausea seems to be caught up in this line. As Booth notes, though the main reference here seems to be to women (compare 'Siren tears' (1), 'hell' (2)), a homosexual application is possible.

3 Applying fears . . . fears Checking the sanguine hopes with draughts of fear, and cheering with draughts of hope too desperate fears (Ingram and Redpath). 'Applying', used in the medical sense of 'administering a remedy', together with 'potions' (1), continues the medical imagery of 118.

4 Still Always, continually.

4 saw myself to win thought of myself as winning (by 'Applying' the means described in lines 1–3).

5 wretched errors contemptibly base sins or mistakes (committed in ignorance of the truth).

5 heart the seat of the inmost thoughts and feelings (= mind).

6 thought itself believed itself to be.

6 so blessèd never never before so happy or fortunate.

7 eyes out . . . fitted The eyes are compared to stars (in the Ptolemaic system) which have been pulled out of their proper spheres by some disruptive force (i.e. the poet's eye only 'seems seeing' (113.4), and has 'looked on truth / Askance and strangely' (110.5–6)). *OED* Fit *v*² defines 'fitted' as 'forced by fits or paroxysms', a nonce-use of 'fit' in this sense; see collation. Compare *Ham.* 1.5.17: 'Make thy two eyes like stars start from their spheres [i.e. sockets]', and Sidney, *Arcadia* (1590), p. 183: 'the agony of *Dorus* giving a fit to her selfe' – a step toward Shakespeare's coinage.

8 distraction mental derangement (literally = a forced division; compare 'out of . . . fitted' (7)). Compare *Ham.* 2.2.555: 'Tears in his eyes, distraction in his aspect'.

8 madding fever i.e. a fever (here = the burning of mental and physical desire) that makes one mad. Earliest citation of 'madding' in this sense (*OED* Madding *ppl a* 2). A high fever can have the effect of making the eyes especially prominent as if 'fitted' 'out of their spheres' (7).

9–12 O benefit . . . greater As Booth points out, some reference to the doctrine of the *felix culpa* or 'fortunate fall' of Adam may lie behind these lines: compare Milton, *Paradise Lost*, XII, 469–78. Shakespeare restates the case for 'benefit of ill' in *MM* 5.1.439–41: 'They say best men are moulded out of faults, / And for the most, become much more the better / For being a little bad.'

9 benefit Booth suggests a play on Latin *bene fit* (= it is made well).

9 find true discover to be true. Compare 'find the lesson true' in 118.13.

10 That better . . . better That something already superior ('better') is made (1) even, (2) constantly ('still') more superior, stronger ('better') by the action of evil. Compare the implications of Tilley B515: 'A broken bone (leg) is the stronger when it is well set', and see *2H4* 4.1.220–1 and *Oth.* 2.3.322–5.

11 ruined love love that has been reduced to ruins.

11 built anew rebuilt afresh, newly restored.

12 Grows fairer Comes to be more beautiful, desirable, pure (i.e. unblemished in both a physical and moral sense).

12 than at first i.e. than it originally was before being 'ruined' (11). Compare Tilley F40: 'The falling out of lovers is the renewing of love.'

12 strong (1) durable, lasting; (2) powerful.

12 far greater much greater in degree and capacity (hence, more compelling).

13 So I . . . content Thus, reproved, chided ('rebuked', for my 'wretched errors' (5)), I come back again to my (true source of) happiness and contentment (i.e. the 'you' of 118.14; compare 'my home of love' and 'I return again' in 109.5–6).

14 And gain . . . spent And earn, as a result of my 'wretched errors' ('ills'), three times more than I (1) paid out, (2) wasted ('spent', with probable play on 'sexual expenditure'). In other words, the poet's 'investment' in 'ills' has paid a threefold dividend by making his 'love' 'fairer', 'more strong', 'greater' (12). Malone's reading 'ill' for Q 'ills' (to accord with 'ill' in line 9; see collation), though adopted by a number of earlier editors, is unnecessary; as Brooke points out, 'ill' in line 9 is abstract, 'ills' here personally concrete.

Sonnet 120

Sonnet 120 is linked to 117–19 by a common theme – the poet's 'transgression' (3) or 'unkindness' (5), which he now argues may be considered as redeemed by a similar earlier 'crime' (8) on the part of the young man ('That you were once unkind' (1)). Shakespeare may here be looking back to 33–5, which lament the 'wound' (34.8) the poet received when the youth was guilty of some 'sensual fault' (35.9), to 57–8, in which he half-heartedly defends the youth's right to 'times of pleasure' and 'self-doing crime' (58.2, 12), or to 92–6, in which he laments the youth's 'inconstant mind' (92.9) and his 'shame / Which . . . / Doth spot the beauty of thy budding name' (95.1–3). There are verbal echoes in 120 from both 33–5 and 57–8 (see notes below). On the other hand, the reference may be to some other unrelated (perhaps more recent) incident.

1 That The fact that.

1 once (1) the only time; (2) one of several possible times.

1 unkind (1) hurtful, injurious (to me); (2) lacking in kindness (to me) (with play on trespassing against your true nature (= 'kind')).

1 befriends favours (i.e. is to my advantage).

2 for that . . . feel as a result of that grief that I then suffered. Compare 34.9.

3 Needs must . . . bow i.e. I must of necessity be beaten down by the weight of my transgression (i.e. feel guilty, because I remember the weight of pain 'which I then did feel' (2) when you were 'unkind' (1) to me). Lovers, being 'one', should theoretically be expected to have an equally intense reaction to 'unkindness' on the part of either lover. 'transgression' refers, presumably, to the 'wretched errors' confessed in 119.5.

4 Unless my nerves . . . steel Unless (indeed) my sinews were made of brass or beaten iron ('hammerèd steel'). Shakespeare may perhaps have been thinking of Spenser's Talus, the stern and unbending type of Justice, who, with classical precedents, is described as 'An yron man' (*Faerie Queene* v, i, 12). Compare *Rape of Lucrece*, 951: 'To spoil antiquities of hammer'd steel'. I have retained Q's syllabic *-ed* in 'ham-

merèd' for its possibly intentional onomatopoeic effect.

5 For Because.

5 unkindness = 'transgression' (3) and, probably, 'wretched errors' (119.5). See 3 n. above.

5 shaken emotionally disturbed.

6 y'have passed . . . time you have gone through a period of time the pains of which were like those of hell. Compare 58.13; *Rape of Lucrece*, 1287: 'And that deep torture may be call'd a hell'; *Oth.* 3.3.169–70: 'But O, what damned minutes tells he o'er / Who dotes, yet doubts; suspects, yet strongly loves!'; and *Tro.* 4.1.58: 'such a hell of pain'.

7 tyrant i.e. one who is pitiless and cruel.

7 have no leisure taken have not taken the time, used the opportunity.

8 weigh consider.

8 in your crime as a result of your offence or sin. See line 1 and 58.12.

9 O that . . . woe Would that our dark period of sorrow or estrangement. That this refers to the present situation (i.e. the result of 'my transgression' (3) and not to the youth's earlier transgression ('that you were once unkind' (1)), seems probable from lines 10–12. Compare the mystical state known as the 'dark night of the soul'.

9–10 rememb'red / My deepest sense reminded my innermost feelings and thoughts (i.e. by making me recall my sorrow when you were 'unkind' (1)). Compare *R2* 3.4.14: 'It doth remember me the more of sorrow.'

10 hard cruelly, violently.

10 hits strikes.

11 soon (as) quickly, without delay. See Abbott 276 on the omission of the first 'as' in an 'as . . . as' construction.

11 to me then, tend'red at that time ('then', referring to 'once' in line 1) offered to me. Some editors have placed the comma (lacking in Q; see collation) after 'me', thus making 'then' refer to the present 'night of woe' (9), which, given the general context, seems less likely, 'then' more probably echoing 'then' in line 2.

12 humble salve An apology or healing remedy offered with a humble and contrite heart (compare Isa. 57.15). Contrast the use of the 'salve' image in 34.7–9.

12 wounded i.e. as if by a blow (compare 'hits' (10) and 34.8).

12 fits (1) restores to health or fitness; (2) befits, is suitable for.

13 that your trespass that trespass or 'crime' (8) of yours.

13 fee payment (in kind).

14 Mine i.e. 'my transgression' (3).

14 ransoms . . . ransom provides recompense for . . . pays for the release of, redeems (Kerrigan).

14 yours i.e. 'your crime' (8). Compare 34.13–14.

Sonnet 121

Sonnet 121 is rather tenuously connected to 117–20 by the theme of the poet's 'frailties' (7) and 'abuses' (10); he repudiates the right of prurient-minded 'others' to judge the morality of his behaviour – 'I am that I am' (9).

1–2 'Tis better . . . being It is better to be of despicable character or morally depraved than to be adjudged vile, since, though innocent, one is (nevertheless) censured as being vile ('of being'). Compare Tilley D336: 'There is small difference to the eye of the world in being nought and being thought so.' There is perhaps an element of Hamlet's dilemma ('To be, or not to be' (*Ham.* 3.1.55)) in these lines.

3–4 And the just . . . seeing And the (1) legitimate, (2) appropriate pleasure is lost, which is thus judged to be vile ('so deemed'), not by how we feel about it (i.e. we may consider it 'just') but by how others view it. In other words, as a somewhat later proverb puts it, 'As good be hanged for an old sheep as a young lamb' (Tilley S293), since we stand to lose both the 'pleasure' and our reputation for virtue. 'pleasure' probably refers here primarily to sexual enjoyment. It is possible, particularly if the Q comma is retained after 'deemed', to take 'so' as referring not to 'vile' but to the 'pleasure' as being 'just' in the eyes of the poet. A second reading of these lines is perhaps possible: 'And the legitimate pleasure which attaches to not being "vile" is lost, when it is thus deemed "vile", not by how we evaluate or feel about it but by how others view it.' Vendler offers a third reading: 'And there are two kinds of pleasure we take in uprightness – one our own approval of our conduct, the second, the approval of us by others; when I'm "vile esteemed" (though not vile), I lose the just pleasure, which I deserve to enjoy, of being thought well of by others.'

5 For why Possibly Shakespeare meant us to read 'Forwhy' = Why (see collation).

5 false adulterate eyes eyes (= persons) that see and interpret falsely because they themselves are wantonly corrupt (i.e. they interpret what they see in terms of their own corruption; compare lines 8 and 12). 'adulterate' carries a suggestion of 'adulterous'. Compare Samuel Brandon, *The Virtuous Octavia* (1598), 'Antonius to Octavia' (MSR, lines 901–904): 'O how can he be ever brought, / To thinke another true: / Who through the guilt of his owne minde, / The others life doth view?', and 'false adulterate heart' in *A Lover's Complaint*, 175.

6 Give salutation . . . blood (1) Greet or hail me (as a fellow sinner), assuming that my sexual inclinations ('sportive blood') are as 'adulterate' as theirs; (2) Assume my sexual inclinations are corrupt ('vile'). (1) may carry with it a suggestion that the 'false adulterate eyes' (5) hope to tempt or incite the poet to lecherous feelings (his feelings are free of lechery, though to such spies that is not imaginable).

See *OED* Salute *v* 5, and *H8* 2.3.102–3: 'Would I had no being / If this salute my blood a jot.' For 'sportive blood', see 95.6 n. and compare *A Lover's Complaint*, 162–8, generally, with lines 3–8: 'Nor gives it satisfaction to our blood . . .'

7 Or on . . . spies i.e. or why should those (= 'adulterate eyes' (5)), who are subject to 'frailties' greater than mine (i.e. 'frailer spies'), spy upon (and interpret) my frailties? Or, more literally, 'Why, on the subject of my frailties, are (there) spies who are frailer (than I am)?' The elliptical construction is awkward. Gibbons suggests that the difficulty lies in the poet's admission that he has 'frailties' 'straight' (11). He acknowledges that mankind is subject to original sin (frailty); nevertheless he asserts that sexual desire is not always merely lechery; it may be a noble and commendable thing, and in his case is so – integrity governs his feelings, whatever vile assumptions certain vile people may project upon him with their 'false adulterate eyes'.

8 Which Who. See Abbott 265.

8 in their . . . good in terms of their 'adulterate' desires or appetites what I think good or moral to be bad or immoral.

9 I am that I am Though there may be undertones of Exod. 3.14 (where God identifies himself to Moses as 'I AM THAT I AM' (Geneva)) and even of Richard of Gloucester's 'I am myself alone' (*3H6* 5.6.83) and Iago's 'I am not what I am' (*Oth.* 1.1.65), more recent criticism suggests this seemingly arrogant statement probably means nothing more presumptuous than 'I have an independent standard of character, and when others do not find theirs fitting it, the crookedness (l. 11) may be theirs' (Alden). However, it is difficult not to feel here some suggestion of a Renaissance confidence in the union of the highest pleasure and beauty in goodness (Gibbons) and a concept of man's relatively godlike sense of his autonomy, as expressed by Hamlet in 'What a piece of work is a man, how noble in reason, how infinite in faculties . . . how like a god!' (*Ham.* 2.2.303–7).

9 level take careful aim (i.e. getting me in their sights in order to score a direct hit – a metaphor from gunnery). Compare 117.11 n.

10 abuses faults, errors, 'frailties' (7), i.e. those *ascribed* to him as such by 'false adulterate eyes' (5) (Tucker).

10 reckon up their own i.e. measure my 'abuses' by their own 'abuses'. Lines 5–10 suggest comparison with Duke Senior's rebuke to Jaques, the would-be satirist: 'Fie on thee! I can tell what thou wouldst do. / . . . Most mischievous foul sin, in chiding sin: / For thou thyself hast been a libertine, / . . . And all th'embossed sores, and headed evils, / That thou with license of free foot hast caught, / Wouldst thou disgorge into the general world' (*AYLI* 2.7.62–9). Compare also Sidney, *Arcadia* (1593), p. 135: '*Timantus* rayling speech (who whatsoever he findes

evill in his owne soule, can with ease lay it upon
another)'.

11 **straight** honest, virtuous (in following the
'straight' (= direct) or 'strait' (= narrow) way of
morality).

11 **be bevel** are crooked, biased (in deviating from
the 'straight' or 'strait' way); earliest citation in this
sense. *OED* Bevel *adj* 2. Compare Matt. 7.13: 'Enter
in at the strait gate: for it is the wide gate, and broad
way that leadeth to destruction' (Geneva). 'bevel' is
also a heraldic term describing a broken line made up
of two parallel parts joined to each other by a slanting
line that makes an acute angle with each of the two
main lines; a kind of zig-zag (*OED* Bevel *adj* 1).

12 **By** According to, in terms of.

12 **rank** (1) corrupt; (2) licentious.

12 **deeds** actions.

12 **shown** (1) interpreted, explained; (2) exhib-
ited (to the world).

13–14 **Unless this ... bad** Unless (indeed) they
can support this general proposition regarding the
innateness of evil, (namely) all men are wicked. Compare *Ham.* 3.1.128: 'We are arrant knaves, believe
none of us.'

14 **and in ... reign** (1) and rule (the world)
through their wickedness; (2) and flourish or prosper (*OED* Reign *v* 2d) in their evil ways. The couplet requires us to keep in mind the relative degrees
of 'badness' distinguished in lines 5–12. Since the
doctrine of 'original sin', so strongly stressed by St
Augustine, held that all men inherited the sin of
Adam and are therefore inherently sinful (compare
35.5), the poet is not claiming that he is without sin;
like all men he is 'bad'. His claim is that men more
guilty of sexual sin than he ('frailer spies' (7)), who
'maintain' that the world is dominated by the power
of 'general evil' (13), insist on their right to interpret
his feelings through the dark glass of their own sins.
Compare Greville, *Caelica* (*c.* 1590), 101.29–30: 'So
that when Power and Nature doe oppose, / All but
the worst men are assur'd to lose'.

Sonnet 122

The central conceit in 122 (that a lover's 'brain and
heart' (5) are better than any table-book ('tables' (1))
in preserving the 'true image' of the beloved) occurs,
as Lee notes, in Ronsard's *Les Amours diverses* (1578),
Sonnet 4: 'Il ne falloit, Maistresse, autres tablettes /
Pour vous graver, que celles de mon coeur, / Où de
sa main Amour nostre veinqueur / Vous a gravée,
et vos graces parfaites.' 122 reverses the situation in
77, where the poet presents the youth with a similar
'book', urging him to fill it with 'what thy memory
cannot contain' (9).

1 **Thy gift, thy tables** Your gift, the table-book
or memorandum book that you gave me. Compare
Ham. 1.5.107: 'My tables – meet it is I set it down /
That one may smile, and smile, and be a villain!' It is

fruitless to speculate, as some critics have, about the
exact nature of the 'tables' (see Ingram and Redpath
and Kerrigan). Like the 'book' in 77, it was most
probably made up of 'vacant' or blank leaves. If it,
indeed, contained writings by the youth (the 'book'
which figures in 77 has been suggested) or even by
the poet himself, it is most unlikely that the poet
would have given it away, and accidental loss seems
to be ruled out by line 11. That the poet would part
with any 'gift', even a blank table book, given him by
the youth may perhaps be interpreted, considering
the position of 122 near the end of the young man
series (1–126), as evidence, along with earlier hints,
of a gradually cooling friendship.

1 **are within my brain** i.e. anything such 'tables'
might have contained is already (and better) stored
in my mind and 'heart' (5). The verb ('are') is plural
by the attraction of 'tables', which though here singular in meaning is grammatically treated as a plural;
compare 'them' in line 11.

2 **Full charactered** Fully inscribed, written out
(in 'characters' = letters). Compare *Ham.* 1.3.58–9:
'And these few precepts in thy memory / Look thou
character.'

2 **with lasting memory** as an enduring record.

3 **Which** i.e. 'lasting memory' (2).

3 **shall above ... remain** i.e. will continue
unchanged and superior to ('above') rows of trifling
or plodding verses (such as mere 'tables' might contain). The link between 'idle rank' and the writing of
mechanically accurate but dull verses, as Ingram and
Redpath note, may be found in *AYLI* 3.2.96–8: 'I'll
rhyme you so eight years together ... It is the right
butter-women's rank to market.'

4 **Beyond all date** Unrestricted by time, time-
lessly.

4 **even to eternity** i.e. namely, forever.

5–8 In the second quatrain the poet suddenly
leaves the timeless and eternal world of the ideal, in
which the 'life' of the mind alone is capable of realising the 'true image' of the beloved – a 'truth' that
words can barely approximate (compare 83.9–14) –
and descends to harsh reality – the mind's record is
after all mortal. The unmediated and stark opposition of two essentially different views tends to frac-
ture the sonnet because it leaves the 'poor retention'
(9) of 'that idle rank' (3), slightingly dismissed in the
first quatrain and line 9, as the only 'record' (8) or
'memory' (2) that can truly be said to be 'Beyond all
date' (4).

5 **at the least** at any rate.

5 **so long as** during the (limited) time that.

5 **brain and heart** i.e. centres of thought and
feeling.

6 **Have faculty ... subsist** i.e. (brain and heart)
have the power or capacity ('faculty') to function
('subsist') as physical nature allows them. 'by nature'
is limiting and looks forward to 'razed oblivion' (7).

7 **each** i.e. brain and heart.

7 **to razed oblivion** to an oblivion that totally erases and destroys (the 'faculties' of brain and heart), i.e. death.

7 **yield his part** shall surrender up its share, portion.

8 **thy record** i.e. the 'lasting memory' (2) of you.

8 **missed** lacking, lost.

9 **That poor retention** i.e. the 'tables' (1), which are an inferior ('poor') receptacle for thought and feeling (when compared with 'brain and heart' (5)).

9 **could not . . . hold** could not contain so much (either in quantity or quality).

10 **Nor need . . . score** I do not need any merely mechanical means ('tallies') to reckon up ('score') the true value of your precious love. Tallies were notched wooden sticks on which debts were reckoned or scored, the number of notches indicating the amount of the debt. 'dear' may also carry a negative suggestion of 'costly'.

11 **Therefore** For the reasons given in lines 9–10.

11 **to give . . . bold** I dared ('was I bold') to give away 'thy tables' (i.e. 'them'; see 1 n. above).

12 **To trust . . . more** In order to (1) have confidence in, (2) commit to the safety of those tables (i.e. 'tables of the brain and heart') which are able to contain the real 'you' more truthfully. Contrast the 'tables' of line 1.

13 **an adjunct . . . thee** an aid to memory (i.e. 'thy tables' (1)) by which to keep you in mind.

14 **import** imply, betoken.

Sonnet 123

Sonnets 123–5 are closely interrelated (see 1 n. below). In 123 the theme of the poet's unchanging love in defiance of Time recalls, as Tucker notes, 108.9–12 and 116.9–12. Attempts have been made to date 123 by suggesting specific examples of 'pyramids' to which Shakespeare might be referring: (1) St Peter's in Rome, nearing completion by the late 1590s (Tucker); (2) Egyptian obelisks, dug up, transported, restored, and then re-erected in Rome by Pope Sixtus V between 1586 and 1589 (Leslie Hotson, *Shakespeare's Sonnets Dated and Other Essays*, 1949); and (3) pyramidal structures (referred to as 'pyramids') ornamenting some of the seven triumphal arches temporarily erected in honour of James I's first state progress through London on 15 March 1604 (Alfred Harbage, 'Dating Shakespeare's Sonnets', *SQ* 1 (1950), 62–3). Only (3) gives anything resembling a *terminus a quo* (compare the arguments for dating 107 as 1603–4 in the headnote to that sonnet), but it is difficult to see the propriety of describing such temporary and presumably rather flimsy structures as being 'built up with newer might' (2) or as representing 'What . . . that is old' (6). Both phrases, however, fit the resurrected Egyptian obelisks of (2) well enough, but such an identification only tells us

that 123 could have been written at any time after about 1590. Perhaps Shakespeare was reminded of the Egyptian obelisks by seeing the newly erected triumphal arches.

1 **No! Time** The Q exclamation mark (rare in Q) after 'No' gives a strong, ringing emphasis that a comma, usually substituted in more recent editions (see collation), considerably diminishes. Both suggests (as in 76.9) a possible play on 'Know'. Note the perhaps intentionally graduated 'No' pattern which links 123–5: in 123 'No!' begins the first quatrain and dominates the whole sonnet; in 124 'No' introduces the second quatrain; and in 125 'No' introduces the third quatrain – a gradation that finally focuses the poet's (the 'I') generally meditative discussion of the nature of his 'love' directly and personally on his commitment to the youth (the 'thou').

1 **shalt not boast** will never be able to brag or vaunt.

1 **I do change** I do alter (in my allegiance to true love). 'I' should here be given special emphasis, preparatory to distinguishing 'I' from 'we' in the second quatrain, where the poet, disassociating himself, is talking about the general run of mankind. They may be fooled by Time, but 'I' am not. Compare 116.2–4, 11–12.

2–4 These lines restate the theme broached in 59.1–2 – that there is nothing new under the sun (see 59 headnote for the suggested influence of Ecclesiastes and Ovid). Old 'pyramids' may be renovated or new 'pyramids' may be built on stronger principles, but the essential concept in either case is 'nothing novel, nothing strange'; in the same way, the poet's 'love', despite the 'wilfulness and errors' (117.9) he admits to in 117–21, remains unchanged in essence, is, in fact, like 'pyramids built up with newer might', 'built anew . . . fairer than at first, more strong, far greater' (119.11–12) – no real 'change' has taken place, only 'dressings of a former sight'. In a sense, the poet is challenging the very idea of change (Pooler).

2 **Thy pyramids** For suggested specific references, see headnote. In the sixteenth century, 'pyramid', apart from its common reference to the even then famous Egyptian pyramids, was somewhat loosely used to refer to 'Any structure of pyramidal form, as a spire, [steeple,] pinnacle, obelisk, etc.' (*OED* Pyramid *sb* 3) – a definition that supports Hotson's identification of 'pyramids' as referring to the Egyptian obelisks re-erected in Rome by Sixtus V. Dowden, however, offers a more general, metaphorical interpretation of line 2: 'all that Time piles up from day to day, all his new stupendous erections'. There is a certain paradox in referring to such 'pyramids' as belonging to Time (i.e. 'Thy'); though indeed the product of Time, they were for the most part built in an abortive attempt to defy Time.

2 **built . . . might** (1) restored, rebuilt in such a way that they are stronger than they originally were;

(2) erected by more recent, hence enduring, technical methods.

3 To me So far as I am concerned.

3 nothing novel, nothing strange in no way new, in no way unfamiliar or surprising. 'nothing' may also be understood as a noun (= nought).

4 dressings dressings up, trimmings, deckings (i.e. exterior 'shows' not affecting the basic 'idea' of 'pyramid'). Some play may be intended on 'dress' = cure a wound, restore to health (*OED* Dress *v* 10). As Kerrigan notes, pejorative use of clothing imagery is typical of Shakespeare.

4 a former sight something seen before (i.e. not in any real sense 'new').

5 Our dates are brief Man is short-lived (and his experience is hence limited). Compare 116.11.

5 we admire we wonder at, consider astonishing. See 1 n. above on the distinction between 'we' and 'I'.

6 What thou . . . old Whatever old thing you palm off ('foist') upon us (as 'novel' and 'strange' (3)) (Kerrigan). As Booth notes, 'foist' resonates with Time, suggesting that he is a 'foist' (= a cheat), and with 'old', in the sense that old things are very often 'foisty' (= musty, mouldy, fusty).

7 rather make . . . desire i.e. (we) prefer to give a new birth (in our minds) to 'old things' as if we thought them 'new' out of our desire (for novelty). The great majority of editors read 'born' for Q 'borne' (see collation) as preferable in the context of lines 6 and 8, but, as Wyndham argues, 'borne', then a common variant spelling of 'bourn' (= aim, goal, bounds), also makes good sense (i.e. 'bourn to our desire' would mean 'the aim or goal of our wishful thinking'). On the theme of wishful self-deception compare 138.1–4.

9 registers (1) (written) 'records' (11), chronicles; (2) the evidences of decay which Time leaves behind in its 'thievish progress to eternity' (77.8). Looks forward to 'the past' in line 10 and 'records' in 11.

9 thee i.e. Time as he continues to function now and in the future. Looks forward to 'the present' in line 10 and 'what we see' in 11.

10 wond'ring at being astonished by, marvelling at. Compare 'admire' (5).

10–11 present . . . past . . . records . . . what we see See the notes on line 9.

11 doth For 'doth' with a plural subject, see Abbott 332, 334.

12 Made more or less Rendered greater in significance or more prominent than the things 'recorded' deserve or denigrated and belittled (alternatives that may refer to both the 'past' and 'present' action of Time as we interpret his action).

12 by . . . haste i.e. Time moves so swiftly that we lose any chance of settled judgement or stable perspective. Compare 'swift-footed Time' (19.6

and note). The rhyme 'past/haste' (spelled 'hast' in Q) was acceptable, *a* in 'haste' varying at this time between *ă* and *ā* (see Cercignani, pp. 175–6, and compare 'haste/fast' in *Rape of Lucrece*, 1332, 1334).

13 This Looks forward to the 'vow' in line 14 and back to the poet's statement in line 1.

13 shall . . . be i.e. for as long as I live.

14 true constant, unchanging (in 'my dear love' (124.1)).

14 scythe See 12.13 n. and compare 116.9–10.

14 thee See 9 n. above.

Sonnet 124

One of the most difficult of the sonnets, 124 continues the theme of the unalterable nature of the poet's love for the youth, moving from the threat posed by Time in 123 to the threats to true love posed by 'the way of the world' and the 'fashion' of the times (8). Pooler notes that the subject of 124, undisguised by changing metaphors, may be found in 25. Again, as in 123, there are strong echoes of 116 (see notes below). Attempts to identify possible references to more or less specific political/religious events in 124 are once again confusingly inconclusive; see Rollins, I, 311–14, and the notes to lines 5, 6–7, and 13–14 below.

1 If my . . . but If my deeply-felt and precious love were only ('but'). The momentary ambiguity of 'my dear love' as referring to the youth himself is immediately clarified by the neuter pronoun 'It' in line 2.

1 the child of state the offspring of worldly position or circumstance (unlike 'my dear love', which grows not out of any mere hope of worldly advantage to be derived from its object, the youth). 'state' may suggest that the object of his affection is of high rank (= 'state'). Compare 29.1–4, 9–12.

2 It might . . . unfathered (If my dear 'love' were merely a 'child of state',) it might well find itself an anonymous by-blow ('bastard') of Fortune's caprice and without a legal parent (i.e. I love the youth not for his 'state' but for himself – whatever Fortune may inflict upon him; my 'love' is a legitimate 'child', not built on 'Policy' (9)). 'Fortune' also plays on 'fortune' = the pursuit of gain. Compare 97.10 and *2H4* 4.4.122: 'Unfather'd heirs and loathly births of nature'.

3 As subject . . . hate Because (it would then be) open ('As subject') to Time's (hence Fortune's) caprice, one moment favourable ('love'), the next malicious ('hate'). Q's spelling 'times' (see collation) carries a suggestion of how unstable a 'love' that was 'but the child of state' (1) would be if it depended on the 'fashion' of the moment (i.e. the immediate 'time'; compare line 8). Compare 115.5–8 and *Coriolanus*, whose 'virtues / Lie in th'interpretation of the time' (*Cor.* 4.7.49–50).

4 Weeds among . . . gathered i.e. the poet's 'love', if it were 'but the child of state' (1), would be a mere weed among other weeds, if the object of its affection suffered from 'Time's hate' (3), or a flower, temporarily preserved, in a bouquet of flowers ('flowers gathered'), if the object of its affection flourished or bloomed under 'Time's love' (3). In other words, such 'love', depending for its sustenance only on the uncertain warmth of 'smiling pomp' (6), would have no inner centre of constancy but would fluctuate (a flower or a weed) according to changing weather – it would be a mere time-server, 'Time's fool' (116.9), in contrast to 'true love' (116.9–12). The use of the plural 'weeds' and 'flowers' to refer back to 'my dear love', while at first sight awkward, merely suggests that Shakespeare is here generalising his statement to include all 'loves' that grow out of politic self-interest. Pooler suggests that 'flowers' and 'weeds' are metaphors for courtiers or suitors who are either in ('flowers') or out ('weeds') of favour. See 125.5–8.

5 No, it No, my dear love (see lines 1–2, and 123.1 n.).

5 builded built (an alternative form of the past participle; see Franz 160). Shakespeare's usual form is 'built' (e.g. 123.2); he uses 'builded' only twice elsewhere (*A Lover's Complaint* 152, and *Ant.* 3.2.30), both, as here, employed for metrical reasons.

5 far from accident out of the reach of chance or unforeseen circumstances. Compare Time's 'millioned accidents' in 115.5.

6 It suffers . . . pomp It remains unaffected and unchanged ('suffers not') when prosperity or greatness smiles upon it (i.e. the poet's love is no greater (see line 12) because he, or the object of his love, is enjoying good fortune). 'pomp' looks back to 'state' in line 1, and Booth suggests an element of the hypocrisy of power in 'smiling'. It is tempting to see in 'smiling pomp' some reference to James I's triumphal progress through London on 15 March 1604, since 'pomp' was also used to mean 'a triumphal or ceremonial procession or train; a pageant' (*OED* Pomp *sb* 2) and 'smiling' might be a suitable epithet for that particular 'pomp'. Shakespeare was presumably a part of that procession, having been granted four yards of red cloth for the occasion as a leading member of the King's Men, by then the official title of Shakespeare's acting company. The phrase 'bore the canopy' in 125.1 may also recall the same occasion (see 125.1 n.).

6–7 nor falls . . . discontent nor falls off or decreases (when Time and Fortune frown) under the blow(s) of thralling or imprisoning distress ('thrallèd discontent'). For the active use of the passive participle 'thrallèd', see Abbott 374. Proponents of Southampton as the 'youth' would perhaps interpret lines 6–7 as a veiled reference to his imprisonment in the Tower for his role in the Essex conspiracy.

8 Whereto . . . calls Toward which the allurements or opportunities of the times ('th'inviting time') influence ('calls') our behaviour ('fashion' = way of life).

9 fears not . . . heretic is unafraid of (hence uninfluenced by) Policy, that self-interested, cunning time-server. 'Policy' is called a 'heretic' because it departs from 'true faith' for worldly advantage. Though 'policy' could mean 'lawful polity', 'prudence' or 'sagacity', Shakespeare more often employs the word in a pejorative sense; compare *1H4* 1.3.108–9: 'Never did bare and rotten policy / Color her working with such deadly wounds.' But see 'hugely politic' in line 11.

10 Which The kind of creature that. Compare 'Which' in line 14 and see Abbott 266.

10 works on . . . hours operates on short-term commitments (i.e. Policy's commitments are of short and uncertain duration (= of 'short-numb'red hours'), unlike those of the poet's 'true love', which 'alters not with his [Time's] brief hours and weeks' (116.11)). As Booth notes, Shakespeare is perhaps playing on 'leases' = leasings, untruths (*OED* Lease *sb*²; see 'leasing' (= lying) in *TN* 1.5.97, *Cor.* 5.2.22) – an apt description of 'politic commitments'.

11 all alone (1) entirely by itself, on its own feet; (2) itself alone among all other things.

11 stands hugely politic remains firmly fixed (as something) immensely, vastly prudent or sagacious, unaltered and 'far from accident' (5). Compare 116.5–6 (true love as 'an ever-fixèd mark').

12 That it . . . show'rs So that it (= true love) neither increases under the influence of (nurturing) heat (= the warming rays of patronage, when Time/Fortune smiles) nor sinks or is decreased ('drowns') under the effects of inclement weather ('show'rs', when Time/Fortune frowns). Looks back, in different metaphorical terms, to lines 6–8.

13–14 Teasingly enigmatic lines, in which critics have seen various specific references: Protestant martyrs (under Queen Mary), Roman Catholic martyrs (under Queen Elizabeth and James I), the execution of Essex (1601) or Guy Fawkes (1606) and some of his followers, even references to the deaths of Greene (1592), Marlowe (1593), Peele (1596), and Nashe (1600–1) as supposed competitors of Shakespeare, several of them admittedly men of questionable life-style. Considering the mature, knotty style of the sonnet and its several links with other sonnets from at least 115 on, specific reference to any particular event before 1600 would seem unlikely – if, indeed, Shakespeare has any persons or events in mind. See Booth's note on the difficulty of these lines (pp. 423–6).

13 To this . . . Time To this (i.e. what lines 6–12 have said about the difference between the value to be found in the constancy of 'true love' and the ephemeral, at best short-term, rewards arising out of

'love' based on 'Policy'). I call to witness the fools of
Time (i.e. time-servers who have 'loved' only out of
'Policy'). Compare 116.9: '[true] Love's not Time's
fool'.

14 Which die... crime The kind of men who die
(1) repentant and in a state of grace, (2) for the public
good, (3) true to their faith, but who have formerly
lived lives of sinful or criminal activity. Compare the
death of Cawdor, *Mac.* 1.4.3–11. 'crime' may here
mean either a 'criminal act' or simply 'wrong-doing'
or 'sin'; compare 58.12 and 120.8. The line seems to
hint at some specific 'fools of Time', but remains tantalisingly vague. (1) refers to ordinary sinners, all of
whom are inevitably 'fools of Time', who make a sincere death-bed repentance for 'the foul crimes done
in [their] days of nature' (*Ham.* 1.5.12) and die in a
state of grace as promised by Anglican doctrine (see
the opening quotation from Ezek. 18.27 in the Book
of Common Prayer (1552) in the Order for Morning
Prayer); (2), Tobin suggests to me, may be taken to
refer to political criminals like Essex or Guy Fawkes
whose executions were doubtless generally considered as being for the good of the state and who thus
could have been described as dying 'for (i.e. in the
interests of) goodness'; (3) may refer to religious martyrs (most probably Roman Catholics) who died for
and in their faith, being executed for real or supposed
crimes against the political/religious establishment.

Sonnet 125

Sonnet 125 continues the theme of the poet's 'true
love', which 'knows no art' (11), contrasted with the
expedient 'love' of 'dwellers on form and favour' (5).
Landry (*Interpretation*, pp. 121–2), picking up a hint
from Steevens, notes that Iago, a supreme example of
the time-server, frankly admits to Roderigo the pure
expediency of his 'love' for Othello (1.1.41–65) and
characterises two kinds of followers: 'honest knaves',
who serve long and faithfully only to be cast off without reward; and clever time-servers, who, 'trimm'd
in forms and visages of duty', serve only to advantage themselves, 'not for love and duty'. Apart from
the relevance of Iago's lines for the counter-theme of
'time-serving love', which runs through 124 and 125,
several contextually suggestive words are common
to these lines and 125: 'obsequious' (9), 'forms and
visages' (compare 'form and favour' (5)), 'outward'
(2), and 'extern' (2). See also the suggestive collocation of 'soul' and 'suborned' (13) in *Oth.* 3.4.152–3
(Tobin).

1 Were't aught... canopy (1) What importance
or worth would it be to me if I should bear the canopy;
(2) What would it matter to me that I (once) bore the
canopy. A 'canopy', if taken literally in the present
context, was a protective cloth covering, held up on
poles by four or more individuals, over a king, or other
person of special eminence, when he (or she) walked
(or was carried) in an official procession. Since to

'bear the canopy' was a mark of honour reserved for
influential courtiers or members of the aristocracy,
(1) seems the more likely interpretation. Some critics, however, suggest that 'canopy' should be read
metaphorically as referring in a pejorative sense to
the kind of demeaning service forced on an individual by the demands of 'smiling pomp' (124.6), or to
the act of writing time-serving praise to an individual, either, or both, of which charges might have been
levelled (unfairly, of course) against the poet by some
'suborned informer' (13). For a suggestion why the
phrase 'to bear the canopy', unique in the canon, may
have occurred to Shakespeare, see 124.6 n.

2 With my... honouring Honouring (here =
pretending to honour, flattering) with my outward
behaviour ('extern', not heartfelt or sincere) the mere
outward appearance or show of others (unconcerned
whether such individuals possess any 'inner' worth).
The line perfectly describes the kind of 'honour'
practised by time-servers whose 'love' is 'but the
child of state' (124.1). Earliest use of 'extern' as a
noun (*OED* Extern *sb* 1).

3 Or laid Or ('Were't aught to me I') laid down
or sought to establish.

3 great bases for eternity large, strong founda-
tions made to last forever ('for eternity'). 'bases' may
be taken as a plural of either 'base' or 'basis'.

4 Which proves The antecedent of 'Which' may
be either 'great bases' (taking 'proves' as an example
of the not uncommon third-person plural in -*s*; see
Abbott 333) or 'eternity'.

4 Which proves... ruining Which (i.e. either
'great bases' or 'eternity'), in the event, prove (or
proves) to be less lasting ('more short') than the usual
objects of Time's decay or destruction ('waste or
ruining'). Some critics interpret lines 3–4 metaphorically, seeing in 'laid great bases for eternity' a veiled
reference to (a) the poet's love for the youth, which,
though 'builded far from accident' (124.5), has in a
comparatively short time suffered 'waste or ruining';
or (b) the poet's verses to the youth ('laid' could
then mean 'expressed in writing' (*OED* Lay *v*[1] 40)),
which, though promising immortality ('eternity') to
both the youth and himself, had all too soon suffered
the ravages of Time.

5–8 There are, I think, two possible, though different, ways of interpreting these allusively difficult
lines. They may refer to those who build the world
in which they dwell on mere externals (i.e. 'form' =
outward shape, physical beauty; 'favour' = appearance, a beautiful face) and who, because they live only
on the surface and waste their substance in riotous
living, 'Lose all' in the sense that they never penetrate the veil of illusion, bankrupting themselves
by paying an exorbitant 'rent' for values that are at
best ephemeral ('compound sweet'), never experiencing the true values (e.g. true love) that constitute the essential meaning of life ('simple savour');

they are 'pitiful thrivers' because, though they may to worldly eyes *appear* to prosper, they are only spectators ('gazing') and should be pitied. Or, picking up again the time-server theme of 124 and 125.2, they may refer to those who set their store only on outward ceremony ('form' = self-serving and expedient behaviour aimed at pleasing those in positions of power) and patronage ('favour' = the smiles of the great; compare 'smiling pomp' (124.6)), who 'Lose all', despite their costly and extravagant efforts to ingratiate themselves ('paying too much rent'), when Fortune frowns or the smiles of the great cease; they are 'pitiful thrivers' because, even when they seem to thrive, their house is built on sand and *not* 'far from accident' (124.5), and because like those in the first gloss, they have wasted or exhausted ('spent') their lives looking myopically ('gazing') on only the appearance of good. In either case, they are unlike the poet who 'dwells' in a world of real or constant values, 'A true soul' (13).

5 dwellers . . . favour See preceding note. 'dwellers on' may also suggest those who insist upon observing, make it a matter of 'policy' to observe.

6 Lose all, and more See 5–8 n. above. As Booth notes, the phrase if taken literally is a contradiction in terms, but Kerrigan points out that it may be based on intensifying idioms like 'all and whole' and 'all and some', both meaning 'absolutely all' and glosses as 'run through their wealth and into debt'. Taking the second inter-pretation suggested in the note to 5–8 above, 'and more' may refer to 'death' (i.e. they lose not only their livelihoods but their lives as well).

6 rent Suggested by 'dwellers' (5) in the sense of 'tenants', those who are dependent on a 'landlord' or 'land Lord'.

7 For compound . . . savour In exchange for mixed (compare 11 n. below), hence adulterated, pleasure or 'sweets' ('compound sweet'), forsaking or neglecting the pure, unadulterated taste of essential virtue ('simple savour'). Note the metaphor drawn from food and eating: sweetmeats, which soon cloy the appetite, as opposed to nourishing diet. Compare *A Lover's Complaint*, 259 ('compound love').

8 Pitiful thrivers An oxymoron; see 5–8 n. above.

8 in . . . spent See 5–8 n.

9 No, let me be No (in contrast to those described in lines 5–8), rather let me be. On 'No', see 123.1 n.

9 obsequious . . . heart dutiful, obedient (in loving) to your innermost being, the 'true you' (not your outward appearance or position). 'heart' = mind, the seat of feeling, understanding, and thought; 'obsequious' in the pejorative sense of 'servilely compliant, sycophantic' glances back to 'dwellers on form and favour' (5) and may perhaps resonate even in the present context.

10 take accept, receive.

10 oblation, poor but free offering, sacrifice, of little worth but freely given (i.e. without any thought of self-interest). 'oblation' carries religious overtones and would have reminded a contemporary reader of a prayer near the end of the Communion Service in the Book of Common Prayer (1552), in which Christ's death is celebrated: 'who made there (by his one oblation of himself once offered) a full, perfect and sufficient sacrifice, oblation, and satisfaction, for the sins of the whole world'; and Landry (*Interpretations*, p. 126) compares Lev. 1.13: 'it is a burnt offering, an oblation made by fire for a sweet savour unto the Lord' (Geneva); note 'savour' in line 7. Shakespeare's only other use of 'oblation' occurs in *A Lover's Complaint*, 223, in a stanza that uses 'render' as a verb ('where I myself must render' (221)); see line 12.

11 mixed with seconds adulterated by inferior qualities or considerations. Compare 'compound sweet' in line 7.

11 knows no art knows or practises no (1) skill, (2) artful wile or manipulative device (i.e. his 'oblation', like Christ's, is 'free', not offered out of self-interest).

12 But Except, only.

12 mutual render . . . thee 'only me for thee' glosses 'mutual render': 'render' = (1) return, recompense; (2) surrender; 'mutual' emphasises the oneness of lover and beloved; 'only' = simply (compare 'simple' in line 7).

13 Hence, thou Get thee hence. See Abbott 41.

13 suborned informer bribed informer (i.e. one who bears false witness or makes a business of reporting offenders, real or supposed, to the authorities). Shakespeare may have a specific individual in mind, or merely tale-bearers generally, who out of jealousy or for other motives have sought to undermine his relationship with the youth. See 1 n. above.

13 A true soul i.e. the poet, whose love is 'true', unadulterated by the pursuit of worldly advantage, unlike that of an 'informer'.

14 impeached (1) challenged; (2) (falsely) accused of treason (against love); (3) (seemingly) discredited.

14 stands . . . control is least subject ('stands least') to the (subversive) power of an informer.

Sonnet 126

Usually taken as an envoy to the young man series (1–125), 126, as Kerrigan notes, treats a number of the dominant themes in the series (love, mortal beauty, treasure, finance and its growth, Time and its inexorable destruction, death). The tone is valedictory: the 'boy' may be 'lovely', but, despite Nature's attempt to preserve him as the paragon and pattern of her creative power, Time will demand a final accounting in death. One theme is notably absent – there is no hint of the immortality that the poet has earlier (e.g. in 63, 65) promised to bestow on the 'boy' as 'great bases for eternity' (see 125.3 n.). Formally, like 99 and 145, 126, though in a different way, is an anomaly; instead of the usual fourteen-line sonnet in three alternately rhymed pentameter quatrains and final couplet, it is a twelve-line poem in six pentameter couplets. But 'sonnet' was loosely used at this time for any short lyric poem, and several examples of twelve-line 'sonnets' occur in other sonnet series in which the fourteen-line form is the norm, only one of them, however, in rhyming couplets (William Smith, Chloris (1596), 27; see Rollins, I, 319), and none of them as an envoy. Despite its couplet rhyme-scheme, however, 126 retains its feeling for the three-quatrain-plus-couplet structure of the regular Shakespearean sonnet – the first and second four lines forming clearly integrated units and the last four lines being broken by a heavy stop after the first couplet, thus giving the last two lines much of the summary effect of the usual final couplet. Editors and critics, since Malone, generally accept 126 as a complete twelve-line poem, even though Q indicates that two final lines are lacking (see collation), Q's device being explained as an attempt by Thomas Thorpe or one of George Eld's compositors to accommodate 126 to fit into Shakespeare's usual fourteen-line form. This is a reasonable hypothesis, but the possibility remains that Thorpe intentionally omitted a final couplet, perhaps because it gave too obvious a clue to the identity of the 'lovely boy'.

1 lovely boy (1) beautiful, (2) lovable, (3) loving boy or youth. Compare 'lovely youth' (54.13). Benson omits the poem, perhaps because of this phrase; see 108.5 n. Wrong-headed, if well intentioned, attempts have been made to identify 'thou, my lovely boy' as Cupid, the little god of Love, an identification which, though it could conceivably fit with lines 1–4, obviously cannot be applied to the same 'thou', who, in lines 5–12, is declared to be subject to Time's 'sickle': Cupid, as a god, was immune to Time.

1 power control, command.

2 Dost hold ... hour A much discussed and variously emended line (see collation). I have retained the Q reading because there is considerable disagreement about what needs to be emended and because the Q reading, though elliptical and ambiguous, may, nevertheless, bear two different, but possible, interpretations: (1) 'Holds time's ever-changing ("fickle") mirror (a "glass" in which ordinary mortals are forced to view Time's depredations), his sickle or scythe (which cuts them down), (and his) hourglass (which measures out their life-spans)'; (2) 'Holds Time's ever-running ("fickle") hourglass, his sickle or scythe, (and his) hour (i.e. the moment when he summons his accomplice Death to take ordinary mortals)'. As (1) and (2) illustrate, one principal difficulty lies in the different meanings that may be attached to

'glass' and 'hour'. Kerrigan has noted that 'glass' for 'hourglass' may be paralleled in WT 4.1.16, where Time, acting as the Chorus, says 'I turn my glass.' 'hour' for 'hourglass', though hitherto unrecorded in that sense, occurs in George Peele's (?) Histrio-Mastix (1610; revised by John Marston c, 1599), 3.1.19–20: 'Then thus, (as soveraigne Empresse of all sinnes) / Pryde turnes her houre, and heere her Sceane beginnes.' While the Q pointing apparently gives Time three characteristic attributes (though a mirror, unlike the hourglass and scythe/sickle (compare 116.10), is not conventionally associated with pictorial representations of Father Time), most recent editors reduce these to two and read Q's 'sickle, hower' as either 'sickle hour' or 'sickle-hour' (see collation), both of which may be interpreted to mean 'the moment when Time cuts us down in death'. On Shakespeare's use of noun-compounds, see Abbott 430. If emendation is considered necessary, these readings, among the various others proposed, seem most acceptable.

3 Who hast ... grown i.e. who, experiencing Time's decaying action ('waning', which ordinarily results in the loss of beauty, strength, etc.), has only grown more 'lovely' (1). The 'waning/growing' paradox may have been suggested by the shape and action of an 'hourglass', in which as the sand 'wanes' in the upper part it 'grows' in the lower and is ready to be reused, unchanged by the passage of 'time', when the 'glass' is turned (Tobin). The influence of Ovid, Metamorphoses xv, 178–83 (Golding, 198–203), has been suggested: 'Things eb and flow, . . . / Even so the tymes by kynd / Doo fly and follow bothe at once, and evermore renew.' Kerrigan compares lines 3–6 in George Peele's (?) 'sonnet' attached to Polyhymnia (1590): 'His youth 'gainst time and age hath ever spurn'd, / But spurn'd in vain; youth waneth by increasing: / Beauty, strength, youth are flowers, but fading seen; / Duty, faith, love are roots, and ever green', and notes how the poem, generally, resonates with A Lover's Complaint, 59–60, and many of the underlying themes in the Sonnets.

3 show'st shows up, reveals (by contrast).

4 lovers withering (1) friends, (2) lovers (with sexual implications) suffering from the decaying effects of Time ('withering'), 'lovers' is doubly ambiguous, in meaning (see 31.10 n. and 32.4 n.) and form. It is possible to interpret Q 'louers' as simply plural, or as 'lover's' or 'lovers'', since the use of an apostrophe to indicate the possessive form was almost never used at this time. Without exception, however, editors have retained 'lover's' as a simple plural, even though 'lover's' as referring specifically to the poet may be, as Dover Wilson admits, attractive.

4 as even as, while.

4 grow'st increases (in beauty, strength, etc.). Picks up 'grown' (3).

5 If Nature (sovereign . . . wrack) If Nature, who is the supreme ruler over ruin. Compare 'great creating Nature' (*WT* 4.4.88). The seeming paradox by which Nature is declared to rule over Time's 'wrack' but is finally subject to Time (see lines 9–12) may be resolved by viewing Nature as Ovid does in *Metamorphoses* xv, 252–5 (Golding, 276–9): 'No kind of thing keepes ay his shape and hew. / For nature loving ever chaunge repayres one shape a new / Uppon another, neyther dooth there perrish aught (trust mee) / In all the world, but altring takes new shape.' Nature, then, is endlessly creating new forms out of the old, thus renewing Time's 'wrack'; in this sense she is preeminent; but Time inexorably produces the very 'wrack', she renews, and, though for a while she may seemingly delay Time's action (or even reverse it), she, like her creations, is sooner or later subject to Time. Note the conditional construction ('If'): if Nature acts as she appears to do in lines 6–8 she does so only from self-interest, not for the sake of 'my lovely boy', but because she wishes to *use* him, for as long as she is able, as a kind of pawn to 'disgrace' (8) Time.

6 As thou . . . back Q's lack of pointing ('onwards still will') allows 'still' to be taken either with 'pluck thee back' or with 'goest onwards'. Until recently editors have arbitrarily adopted Malone's comma after 'onwards', but since either reading is equally possible, it is better to leave the choice of reading open.

7 keeps . . . purpose (1) preserves, (2) reserves, (3) controls you for this purpose or reason. 'keeps' may also suggest that Nature is treating the 'lovely boy' as a 'kept man' for her pleasure; compare 'pleasure' in line 9 and the phrase 'a kept woman'. 'this purpose' suggests the earlier designation of the youth as a pattern/ paragon of Nature's creative power in 19.11–12 and 98.11–12.

7–8 that her . . . disgrace so that her (1) cleverness, (2) cunning may (appear to) discredit Time.

8 and wretched minutes i.e. and ruin or destroy Time's power to make life's (fleeting) minutes miserable. Capell's emendation 'minuits' (= minutes) for Q 'mynuit' has been almost universally accepted. There is, I think, a good possibility that Q 'mynuit' is the result of compositorial miscorrection, i.e. under the influence of 'skill' in line 7, the compositor originally set 'mynuit skill' for 'mynuits kill', the *s* getting omitted in the process of correction. Note that the *k* in 'kill' prints heavily, suggesting adjustment of the type, and that 'skill' in line 7 is followed, wrongly, by a period (see collation), suggesting further confusion possibly linked to the postulated press-correction in line 8.

9 Yet fear her Nevertheless distrust or beware of her.

9 minion of her pleasure (1) favourite, darling, (2) servile dependant, plaything for her enjoyment

or gratification. 'minion' looks back to 'sovereign mistress' (5) and was frequently used pejoratively to describe a king's (or queen's) favourite.

10 may detain . . . treasure may be able to withhold (for a while) her treasure (= 'thou minion' (9)) but never permanently ('not still') (1) preserve, (2) maintain it (against Time's power). See note on 'keeps' (7).

11 Her audit . . . be Her accountability (to Time), though it may be delayed, must (sooner or later) be met ('answered').

12 her quietus . . . thee her acquittance ('quietus') is to settle her account ('audit' (11)) by surrendering you (to the tyranny of Time). 'audit', 'quietus', and 'render' suggest a kind of legal action and give a hard and minatory edge to the final couplet. Note that 'render' echoes 'mutual render' in 125.12; the word (as verb or noun) occurs nowhere else in the Sonnets. Although 'quietus' in the figurative sense of 'release from life' (i.e. death; compare *Ham.* 3.1.74–5: 'When he himself might his quietus make / With a bare bodkin') cannot properly be applied to Nature herself, there is a reflected or transferred sense in which its use here signals the 'death' of Shakespeare's 'lovely boy', both metaphorically and literally. If we accept 126 as a valediction, 'quietus' may also be seen as a suitable word on which to conclude the young man series – Shakespeare's 'acquittance', by which he legally 'renders' his *final* debt of praise to his 'belovèd' (105.2).

Sonnet 127

Sonnet 127 is the first of what is often called the 'Dark Lady series' (127–52); all are addressed to a woman ('My mistress' (127.9, 130.1, 8, 12, 153.9, 14, 154.12)), except 129 and 146, which are in the nature of general meditations on a theme, although both may be seen as related to the poet's relations with his 'mistress'. Like the identity of the 'youth' in 1–126, the identity of the Dark Lady is not known despite various attempts by an army of critics and commentators to give her 'a local habitation and a name' or to treat her as an allegory (see, for further discussion, the awe-inspiring index entry under 'dark woman' in Rollins (II, 480) and Samuel Schoenbaum, 'Shakespeare's Dark Lady: a question of identity', in *Shakespeare's Styles: Essays in Honour of Kenneth Muir*, ed. Philip Edwards *et al.*, 1980, pp. 221–39). Two candidates are perhaps worth mentioning (among the many): (1) Mary Fitton, one of Elizabeth's Maids of Honour and the mistress of William Herbert, himself a candidate for the 'youth' to whom the Sonnets may be addressed; (2) Emilia Lanier (a late-comer first proposed by A. L. Rowse in 1973), the mistress of Henry Carey, first Lord Hunsdon, the patron of Shakespeare's company, the Chamberlain's Men. It is usually assumed that the same woman is addressed throughout 127–52, an assumption like that generally made about the single identity of the 'youth' or 'friend' in 1–126. But in neither case can such assumptions be proved (see 145 headnote). For possible connections with events described in the first series (1–126), see the headnote to 40.

Critics have suggested that Shakespeare's conception of the Dark Lady was influenced by some of the attributes that Sidney assigns to Stella in *Astrophil and Stella* (1591), particularly in Sonnet 7 (see notes below to lines 9–10), a paradoxical 'praise of black'. Shakespeare himself repeats (or anticipates) the 'praise of black' theme in a passage, strikingly similar to 127, in *Love's Labour's Lost* (4.3.245–61) when Berowne defends his lady, Rosaline (one of Shakespeare's several 'dark ladies' in the plays – Anne Page, Kate, Hero, Phoebe, Cleopatra), against the King's charge that 'thy love is black as ebony' and that 'Black is the badge of hell.' Shakespeare may also have had Ovid's *Amores* II, 4, 41–2, in the back of his mind. Such suggested literary connections do not mean, as Kerrigan points out, that the Dark Lady of the Sonnets does not allude to a historical person.

1 In the old . . . fair In former times black was not accounted beautiful ('fair', with play on having a 'light' complexion and fair or golden blonde hair). Compare *LLL* 4.3.258–61: 'Her favor [Rosaline's] turns the fashion of the days, / For native blood is counted painting now; / And therefore red, that would avoid dispraise, / Paints itself black, to imitate her brow.' The exact meaning of 'black', as Shakespeare and his contemporaries sometimes used it when describing hair, eyes, or complexion, is confusing for a modern reader. Although 'black' was most often used literally, it was also used loosely to mean 'dark-coloured' or brownish, as opposed to 'light-coloured' or gold/blonde, and to describe what we would now call a brunet or brunette (compare *Ado* 3.1.61–4: 'If fair-fac'd, / She would swear the gentleman should be her sister; / If black, why, Nature, drawing of an antic, / Made a foul blot'). From early times the ideal of beauty (particularly in women) was to be 'fair' or blonde. Petrarch's Laura, for example, had blonde or golden hair, eyes 'white and black', and a complexion that mingled white and red, though her eyebrows are described as 'ebony'. Shakespeare's Dark Lady may indeed be imagined as having black hair (see 130.4), black eyes (see notes to lines 9–10), and a dark or swarthy complexion (see 130.3, 5–6, 144.4), or as a brunette, like Hero in *Much Ado*, 'too brown for a fair praise' (*Ado* 1.1.172), the adjective 'black' being chosen because it allowed Shakespeare to talk in terms of paradox (compare the King's charge: 'O paradox! Black is the badge of hell' (*LLL* 4.3.250)) with its wide field of possible pejorative connotations and wordplay.

2 it bore . . . name i.e. (even if something 'black' were then accounted 'fair' or beautiful) it never carried the repute ('name') of beauty.

3 beauty's successive heir beauty's heir by (rightful) succession (i.e. 'black' has replaced 'fair' by a kind of primogeniture). Ingram and Redpath note that Daniel's Delia has golden hair in 1592 but that in the 1601 revision her hair has become sable!

4 slandered . . . shame discredited, defamed with the disgrace associated with giving birth to a bastard (i.e. that Nature's 'heir' is a bastard; see 6 n. below).

5 each hand . . . power every (mortal) hand has (1) assumed, (2) usurped the (creative) power of Nature.

6 Fairing . . . face Making the foul or ugly fair or beautiful by giving it the *appearance* of 'fair' (i.e. 'false' and 'borrowed') through human skill ('art'). Compare *Mac.* 1.1.11.: 'Fair is foul, and foul is fair', which catches perfectly the general theme of the sonnet. Shakespeare is obviously thinking primarily of cosmetic 'art' ('painting', 'false hair'; see 20.1, 67.5, and 68.3 ('Before these bastard signs of fair were borne'), 5–8), but he may also be thinking of the 'art' of grafting (see *WT* 4.4.79–103, where 'Nature's bastards' produced by 'art' are dismissed by Perdita and compared to the products of cosmetic art).

7 Sweet Beloved, prized, precious

7 no name . . . bower no good repute, no sacred abode or shrine (in which beauty is properly worshipped).

8 But is profaned But, on the contrary, (beauty) is desecrated or abused. Some editors, following Capell (see collation), omit the Q comma after 'bower' and interpret 'But is' as 'That is not', thus making 'bower' the antecedent of 'profaned'.

8 if not . . . disgrace i.e. even if not profaned, beauty lives in disfavour (with play on 'disgrace' = disfigurement; see 33.8 n.).

9 Therefore i.e. as a result of the new status of 'black' as opposed to 'fair'. This seems to suggest that his mistress had some choice, but it may also suggest that the poet chose her as his mistress because she was 'black' – the new 'ideal' of beauty.

9 eyes are raven black eyes are as black as a raven (both the raven and crow were considered types of blackness; see Tilley C844). 'black' here refers to the iris, which might be either black or dark-coloured (see *OED* Black eye 1). Berowne refers to Rosaline's eyes as 'two pitch-balls stuck in her face for eyes' (*LLL* 3.1.197), and compare Sidney, *Astrophil and Stella* (1591), 7.1–2: 'When Nature made her chiefe worke, *Stella's* eyes, / In colour blacke, why wrapt she beames so bright?' Stella, however, had golden hair and a 'fair' complexion.

10 Her eyes so suited Her eyes clothed or dressed (1) in this way, (2) in accord, congruently (i.e. in black; with a possible play on 'sooted' = smudged with black; compare *Oth.* 1.2.70: 'sooty'). The repetition of 'eyes' in lines 9 and 10 has led many editors to emend one or the other, and 'hairs' or 'brows' have been proposed for either line – 'brows' (or 'brow' in line 10) being favoured because it seems to be supported by *LLL* 4.3.254: 'O, if in black my lady's brows be deck'd'. Admitting the rather weak tautology of Q's text and the strong probability of some kind of error either in line 9 or line 10 (either Shakespeare's, a scribe's, or a compositor's), an error that may indeed lie not in line 10's 'eyes' but in the following 'and', I have nevertheless retained the Q text because, tempting as the proposed emendations may be, there is no finally compelling reason, given the context, that makes the emendation of 'eyes' in line 10 much more likely than the emendation of 'eyes' in line 9. See Ingram and Redpath's analysis of the case for emendation.

10 and they mourners seem It has been suggested that 'and' is a misreading of a manuscript 'as' or perhaps 'that' (written 'yᵗ'; see collation); the line could then be read as meaning 'Her eyes thus dressed (in black) appear to be like mourners.' The black/mourning conceit appears in Sidney, *Astrophil and Stella* (1591), 7.12–14; *LLL* 4.3.254–7: 'O, if in black my lady's brows be deck'd, / It mourns that painting and usurping hair / Should ravish doters with a false aspect: / And therefore is she born to make black fair'; see 132.3–12.

11 At Over the case of (Ingram and Redpath).

11–12 such who . . . esteem i.e. such (women) who, although they were not born (1) beautiful, (2) with blonde hair and a light/white complexion, lack no (so-called) beauty (because they have rendered themselves 'fair' by 'Fairing the foul with art's false borrowed face' (6)), thus defaming or demeaning ('Sland'ring') true beauty naturally created by being esteemed for their false beauty. The poet's mistress thus appears to mourn for some women who are naturally beautiful in their 'blackness' (like herself) but who have falsified their beauty by trying, unnaturally, to make themselves 'fair'.

13 Yet so they mourn But they mourn in such a way.

13 becoming of their woe gracing their mourning appearance. Compare *Ant.* 1.1.48–9: 'Fie, wrangling queen! / Whom every thing becomes.' On 'becoming of', see Abbott 178 and compare 115.9.

14 every tongue i.e. everybody (by metonymy).

14 beauty . . . so beauty ought to, or would wish to look like – or be coloured like – my mistress (in her mourning/black appearance). Note how 'so' picks up and balances 'so' in line 13.

Sonnet 128

Sonnet 128 was presumably suggested to the poet by having seen his 'mistress' playing on the virginal, a cased instrument resembling a spinet but without legs, in which the sound was produced by devices that plucked rather than struck the strings.

The strings/fingers conceit is used, for pathos, in *Tit.* 2.4.44–7: 'O, had the monster seen those lily hands / Tremble like aspen leaves upon a lute, / And make the silken strings delight to kiss them, / He would not then have touch'd them for his life!', and Jonson uses the conceit to ridicule Fastidious Briske, an 'affecting Courtier', in *Every Man out of His Humour* (1599) 3.9.102–6 (describing his mistress playing on the viola da gamba): 'Oh, shee tickles it so, that . . . shee makes it laugh most divinely . . . I'le tell you a good jest now, and your selfe shall say it's a good one: I have wisht my selfe to be that instrument (I thinke) a thousand times, and not so few, by heaven.'

1 my music Compare 'Music to hear' (8.1).

2 blessèd wood i.e. the keys ('wood') made (1) happy or fortunate, (2) consecrated by the touch of his mistress's 'sweet fingers'. Does 'blessèd' carry a parodic suggestion perhaps of the 'laying on of hands' by the bishop in the rite of Confirmation (Book of Common Prayer)? The context determines the meaning 'keys' for 'wood' (compare 'chips' in line 10), but such a figurative use is unrecorded. Tucker suggests that 'wood' implies that the keys were not, in this instance, plated with ivory.

2 whose motion sounds the movement of which (1) makes sounds, resounds (intransitive), (2) causes to sound (transitive; 'The wiry concord' being the object of both 'sounds' and 'sway'st' in line 3) (Booth). Though not recorded until 1674 (*OED* Motion *sb* 12a), 'motion' was a musical term used to describe tempo (quick or slow).

3 With (1) Through the mediation of, by means of; (2) In harmony or concord with.

3 gently sway'st (1) softly, delicately, (2) elegantly controls or directs. 'gently' may perhaps carry some sense of 'as a gentlewoman'.

4 The wiry concord The harmony produced by the strings or wires of the virginal under expert fingering.

4 confounds overwhelms with wonder, delights, amazes. Compare 'amazeth' in 20.8. This is surely the primary meaning, but 'confounds' inevitably implies 'confusion', and in context with 'concord' suggests something of the complexity of the metaphysical concept of *discordia concors*.

5 Do I envy Syntactically picks up 'How oft' in line 1. As a verb, both 'envy' and 'ènvy' were current at this time (see Cercignani, p. 39); Shakespeare uses 'envy' only once again (*Shr.* 2.1.18).

5 jacks keys of the virginal. Technically, Shakespeare is misusing the word, 'jacks' being upright pieces of wood fixed to the back of the key-lever and fitted with a quill which plucked the string as the jack rose on the key's being pressed down (*OED* Jack *sb*¹ 14). The MS. version (see Appendix, p. 271 below) reads 'kies' here and in line 13. It has been suggested implausibly that the lady is tuning the instrument and holding the jacks down with the palm of her hand, but the first line makes it clear that she is playing 'music', not tuning or tinkering. Much more cogently it has been suggested that Shakespeare is using 'jack' metonymically for the whole key/jack mechanism because it allows him to play on 'jacks' meaning 'common fellows' (compare *R3* 1.3.71–2 and 'saucy jacks' in line 13), thus implying that such 'common fellows' may kiss his mistress's fingers (Kerrigan), a situation that he is finally (lines 13–14) willing to countenance so long as he only may kiss her lips.

5 nimble leap jump up and down nimbly. As Booth notes, this phrase seems more appropriate to the actual jacks than to the keys. 'nimble', however, may be taken to refer as much to the dexterity of his mistress's playing as to the keys themselves.

6 To kiss … hand Though 'tender inward' seems most naturally to refer to the palm, it can also be taken to mean the underside of the fingers. Tucker notes that the Elizabethans made an important distinction between the formal kiss on the back of the hand and the kissing of the 'inward', which was proper only to love and intimacy, either licit or illicit. Compare *WT* 1.2.115: 'But to be paddling palms and pinching fingers', and 1.2.125–6: 'Still virginalling / Upon his palm?', *Oth.* 2.1.253–4: 'Didst thou not see her paddle with the palm of his hand?'; and *LLL* 5.2.806: 'And by this virgin palm now kissing thine', 'kiss' now begins to make more explicit the underlying sexual innuendos of the 'virginal-playing' conceit so neatly caught in one of the above quotations from *Winter's Tale*.

7 poor hapless, unfortunate (asking to be pitied).

8 At the wood's … stand i.e. ('my poor lips') are left watching you as (helpless) bystanders ('by thee … stand') blushing at the key's impudence ('wood's boldness'). The 'lips' are described as 'blushing' from shame or anger even though they are already naturally red.

9 tickled lightly touched (used of a stringed instrument; *OED* Tickle *v* 6). Like 'kiss' (6), 'tickled' is sexually suggestive.

9–10 change … situation exchange their high status (as living things) and their physical position (i.e. trade places).

10 dancing chips With 'dancing' compare 'nimble leap' (5); 'chips' = 'wood' (2) = 'jacks' (5).

11, 14 See collation and 26.12 n.

11 walk … gait move with delicate 'steps' (figurative for 'finger the keys'). See 'gently' (3 n.).

12 dead wood … lips Compare Constable, *Diana* (1594), Second Seven, Sonnet 4.9–10.

13 saucy jacks (1) impertinent, presumptuous keys; (2) wanton, insolent common fellows (see 5 n.).

13 happy Compare 'blessèd' (2 n.) and 'blest' (12).

14 Give them Let them have.

Sonnet 129

Sonnet 129, partly because of its apparently emotionally charged and involved tone, is one of the best-known and most widely discussed sonnets. Like Tarquin in *The Rape of Lucrece* (734–5), it appears to most readers to bear 'the burthen of a guilty mind', expressing a kind of 'extreme' sexual nausea comparable to that of a Hamlet (*Ham.* 1.5.55–7; 3.4.65–94, 180–91), a Timon (*Tim.* 4.3.134–66), and, especially, a Lear (*Lear* 4.6.109–31). The theme of lust is also treated in *Venus and Adonis* (799–804) and centrally in *The Rape of Lucrece* (211–15, 239–40, 687–735, 867–924), the *Lucrece* passages offering a number of verbal links with 129. Various non-Shakespearean influences have been suggested, among them: (1) two lines from a short poem ascribed to Petronius (*Poetae Latini minores*, ed. E. Baehrens, 5 vols., 1879–83, IV, 99): 'Foeda est in coitu et brevis voluptas / Et taedet Veneris statim peractae' (translated by Ben Jonson in *Underwoods*, 88: 'Doing, a filthy pleasure is, and short; / And done, we straight repent us of the sport', referring to the Latin tag *omne animal post coitum triste*); (2) a sonnet of Sidney's (no. 31 in *Certain Sonnets*), first published in 1598, which begins: 'Thou blind man's marke, thou foole's selfe chosen snare, / Fond fancie's scum, and dregs of scattred thought, / Band of all evils, cradle of causelesse care, / Thou web of will, whose end is never wrought; / Desire, desire I have too dearely bought, / With price of mangled mind thy worthlesse ware …'; (3) an eclogue in Thomas Lodge's *Rosalynde* (1590), p. 184, the direct source of *As You Like It*: 'In errours maske I blindfolde judgements eye, / I fetter reason in the snares of lust, / I seeme secure, yet know not how to trust; / I live by that, which makes me living die … / Ah Lorrell lad, what makes thee herry love? … / A heaven in shew, a hell to them that prove … / A minutes joy to gaine a world of greefe, / A subtill net to snare the idle minde / A seeing Scorpion, yet in seeming blinde, / A poore rejoyce, a plague without releefe'; (4) Wilson's *The Arte of Rhetorique* (1553), pp. 405–7, from which Shakespeare may have taken hints for his use of various forms of syntactic variation (sentences 'Like emong themselfes', 'Gradacion', 'Regression'; see Douglas L. Peterson, *English Lyric from Wyatt to Donne*, 1967, pp. 227–31). Compare also two poems on the same general theme by Robert Southwell: 'Loves servile lot' and 'Lewd Love is Losse' and his description of 'sin' in *St Peters Complaint* (1595), lines 637 ff.

1 Th'expense of spirit The waste of (1) vital energy, (2) semen, 'spirit' most probably refers to one or more of the 'spirits' (animal (associated with the brain), vital (with the heart), and natural (with the liver)), highly subtle fluids or vapours, which were thought of as acting as intermediaries between body and soul (compare Donne, 'The Extasie', 61–8). Shakespeare's use of the phrase may have been suggested by Timothy Bright's *A Treatise of Melan-cholie* (1586), pp. 250-1: 'the excessive travaile of animall actions, or such as springe from the braine, waist and spende that spirit . . . which spirite being consumed, or empaired, leaveth the Massy patrs [*sic*] more heavie, grosse, and dull . . . In other-some by lavish waste, and predigall [*sic*] expence of the spirite in one pasion, which dispensed with judgement, would suffice the execution of many wor-thy actions besides' (the phrase occurs twice earlier, pp. 63, 244; see Mary J. O'Sullivan, 'Hamlet and Dr Timothy Bright', *PMLA* 41 (1926), 671). Bacon much later employs the phrase in connection with sexual overindulgence (*Sylva Sylvarum* (1627), sec-tion 693). It was generally believed that each orgasm shortened life by a day (compare Donne, 'Farewell to Love', 24–5).

1 **in a waste of shame** in a desolation or desert of painful regret (with play on 'in a shameful waist', i.e. having intercourse with a whore). For the sex-ual implications in 'waist', compare *Ham.* 2.2.232–6: '*Ham.* Then you live about her [Fortune's] waist, or in the middle of her favors? / *Guil.* Faith, her privates we. / *Ham.* In the secret parts of Fortune? O, most true, she is a strumpet', and *Lear* 4.6.118–29 (see 14 n. below).

2 **lust in action** i.e. the act of sexual intercourse. 'lust', not 'expense', is the subject of 'Is'.

2 **till action** until the act is consummated.

3 **perjured, murd'rous** i.e. lust will lie or kill to gain its end. Compare *Rape of Lucrece*, 918–19: 'Guilty thou [i.e. Opportunity] art of murther and of theft, / Guilty of perjury and subornation', and the Latin tag *penis erectus non habet conscientiam* (see 151.1–2 n.).

3 **full of blame** (1) most blameworthy; (2) filled with faults.

4 **extreme, rude** excessive, beyond rational or moral limits ('extreme'), violent, brutal.

4 **not to trust** not to be trusted (unlike 'true love'). See Abbott 359 for this use of an active infini-tive where we would use a passive. Compare *Venus and Adonis*, 793–804: 'Call it not love, for Love to heaven is fled, / Since sweating Lust on earth usurp'd his name . . . / Love surfeits not, Lust like a glutton dies; Love is all truth, Lust full of forged lies.'

5–12 Compare *Rape of Lucrece*, 211–14: 'What win I if I gain the thing I seek? / A dream, a breath, a froth of fleeting joy. / Who buys a minute's mirth to wail a week? / Or sells eternity to get a toy?'; 688: 'And he hath won what he would lose again'; 867–8: 'The sweets we wish for turn to loathed sours / Even in the moment that we call them ours'; and *Tro.* 5.10.38–9.

5 **Enjoyed . . . but** No sooner enjoyed (sexually) than. To 'enjoy a woman' meant to have sexual inter-course with her.

5 **straight** immediately.

6, 7 **Past reason** Beyond reason. Lust is an expression of man's animal, not his rational nature. Compare *A Lover's Complaint*, 166–8.

6 **hunted** pursued, chased (suggests that lust is a huntsman pursuing his 'game' for the pleasure of killing it).

6 **had** i.e. possessed sexually, 'Enjoyed' (5). See 10 n. below and compare *1H4* 3.3.127–30: '*Fal.* Why? she's neither fish nor flesh, a man knows not where to have her. / *Host.* . . . . Thou or any man knows where to have me', and 87.13.

7 **hated** 'despisèd' (5), loathed. The revulsion from lust 'had' is, equally, or more, irrational and 'extreme'.

7–8 **as a swallowed . . . mad** as an (all-too-greedily) swallowed and enticing morsel ('bait'), a lure purposely set ('On purpose laid') in order to make the taker mad (= 'Past reason' (6)). This is the first suggestion that lust is not wholly self-generated, but may be intentionally incited by an outside agency (e.g. the wanton art, physical and cosmetic, prac-tised by a whore). In a sense, then, both 'setter' and 'taker' are 'angler[s] in the lake of darkness' (*Lear* 3.6.7). 'bait' may also carry a sense of 'food' for lust, thus suggesting the 'sensual banquet' image (com-pare *Venus and Adonis*, 803 (quoted above in 4 n.) and 547–8: 'Now quick desire hath caught the yielding prey, / And glutton-like she feeds, yet never filleth'). Kerrigan appositely compares *MM* 1.2.128–30: 'Our natures do pursue, / Like rats that ravin down their proper bane, / A thirsty evil, and when we drink we die.' Compare also Ovid, *Amores* II, iv, 5–6 (as trans-lated by Marlowe): 'I loathe, yet after that I loathe, I runne: / Oh how the burthen irks, that we should shun' (compare 'shun' in line 14 below).

9 **Mad** The Gildon–Capell emendation for Q 'Made' has been universally accepted since Capell–Malone (Gildon² reverted to 'Made'), even though, as Booth points out, the Q line may be read as mean-ing 'Made so (i.e. "mad") both in pursuit and in pos-session'. It seems probable, however, that Q 'Made' is a compositorial misreading of 'Madd' (a common spelling of 'Mad'), final *d* and *e* being easily and often confused in reading Secretary hand. The anomalous capital I in Q 'In' probably evidences some compos-itorial confusion at this point, possibly, as has been suggested, the omission of 'Made' from the line as originally set.

9 **pursuit . . . possession** Compare 'hunted' (6) and 'in quest' (10) and 'had' (6, 10), 'pursuit' and 'in quest' picking up the image of lust as a huntsman (see 6 n. above).

9 **so** i.e. also 'mad'.

10 **Had, having . . . have** The line rings the changes on the sexual implications of 'to have (a woman)'. 'having' = sexual intercourse (i.e. 'lust in action' (2)).

10 **extreme** See 129.4 n. above.

11 A bliss . . . woe A delight or joy in the experiencing ('in proof', i.e. in the 'having') and experienced ('proved', i.e. 'had'), an extreme ('very') grief or misery. The emendation of Q 'proud and' to 'proved, a' has been universally accepted since Capell–Malone. It is possible, I think, given the standard convention by which, in most scripts and printing, internal *u* was used for either *u* or *v*, that the compositor misinterpreted the ambiguous form 'proud' as an adjective (influenced perhaps by context, 'proud' = sexually excited) and then compounded the problem by misreading a Secretary *a* as an ampersand (&). Compare Thomas Lodge, *A fig for Momus* (1595), 'The Anatomie of Alchymie', sig. I1ᵛ: 'Divine in show, in proofe, a subtill drift'.

12 Before, a joy . . . dream Beforehand, anticipated as a delight, afterwards, a deceitful trick of fleeting fancy (a bad 'dream' or nightmare). For 'dream' in this context, compare *Rape of Lucrece*, 211–12 (quoted in 5–12 n. above).

13–14 Compare Samuel Brandon, *Virtuous Octavia* (1598), 'Antonius to Octavia' (MSR, lines 605–12): 'I know the safe, and perfect way, / Which reason saith is best: / Yet willingly I follow that, / Which wisdom liketh least. / What reason will, that same would I, / And wisdom would so too. / But some thing greater than us all, / Will not consent thereto.'

13 the world mankind generally.

13 none knows well no one knows effectively or successfully (how).

14 shun eschew, abstain from.

14 heaven the height or place of bliss, paradise. Booth suggests a play on 'haven' = the female pudenda (compare 'bay' (137.6) and George Turbervile, *Eglogs* (1567), fol. 8ᵛ), toward which a man directs his 'quest' (10), and perhaps on 'havin'' as in line 10. 'heaven', the realm of light, looks back to 'bliss' in line 11 and forward, as an extreme contrast, to 'hell', the realm of palpable darkness (compare 147.14).

14 hell the depth or place of punishing pains and misery (with, again, reference to the female pudenda). Compare *Lear* 3.6.7: 'the lake of darkness', and 4.6.124–9 (quoted in 119.2 n.). Also note the heaven/hell image in 'A description of Love' (anonymous, in *The Phoenix Nest* (1593), ed. Rollins, p. 98): 'it is that fountaine and that well, / Where pleasure and repentance dwell, / It is perhaps that saucing bell, / That tols all in to heaven or hell, / And this is Love as I heare tell.'

Sonnet 130

Sonnet 130 picks up the paradoxical praise of black from 127 and develops the anti-Petrarchan stance of 21 (see headnote) by denying to the poet's mistress the metaphorically hyperbolic attributes conventionally associated with any woman being addressed by a lover (eyes that rival the sun, lips that are redder than coral, breasts as white as snow, hair that outshines gold, etc.), thus claiming, as in 21, to be speaking the truth, unlike other love poets who lie extravagantly. Having made his point in 130, Shakespeare proceeds to compare his mistress to the rising sun and the evening star in 132. The tone, which suggests a love/hate, attraction/ repulsion relationship, is generally cool, clinical, and negative (more so than in 21), cleverly telling us what his mistress is *not*, little of what she *is*, except that she is *not* conventionally 'fair' or beautiful. Even the complimentary twist of the final couplet fails to override entirely the wittily negative, if playful, impact of the quatrains.

1 nothing . . . sun in no way comparable to the sun (i.e. 'the eye of heaven' (18.5)). The sun was regularly associated with 'gold' (see 33.1–4 n.), which in turn was associated with 'fair'; the poet's mistress had 'black' eyes (127.9). Spenser runs the conventional gamut on his mistress's eyes in *Amoretti*, 9. The *brightness* of a mistress's eye – brighter than the sun itself – is a commonplace love-poet's hyperbole, one even remembered by Pope in *The Rape of the Lock* (Gibbons).

2 lips' red i.e. the red of her lips. Since Capell first introduced the possessive plural 'lips' (see collation) editors (except Tyler) have followed suit, but Q may equally well be taken to mean 'than her lips (are) red', or even, possibly, 'lip's red' (i.e. 'lip is red'). Contrast Adonis's 'sweet coral mouth' (*Venus and Adonis*, 542) and Lucrece's 'coral lips' (*Rape of Lucrece*, 420).

3 If snow be white i.e. if snow is to be considered white (as it proverbially was; see Tilley S591).

3 dun dull greyish brown.

4 If hairs be wires i.e. if hairs be thought of as wires (as they regularly were by Elizabethan poets, usually, however, as 'golden wires', hence the implied contrast with 'black wires'). Compare Spenser, *Epithalamion*, 154: 'Her long loose yellow locks lyke golden wyre'. The extremely common hair/wire image may owe something to the frame of wires used to support or control the more extravagant hair styles adopted by fashionable ladies at this time. See Spenser, *Amoretti*, 37.1–4: 'What guyle is this, that those her golden tresses, / She doth attyre under a net of gold: / and with sly skill so cunningly them dresses, / that which is gold or heare, may scarse be told?'

5 damasked . . . white having the hue of the damask rose, a mingling of red and white (with, as Ingram and Redpath suggest, a possible reference to the softness of silk damask cloth). Contrast the cheeks of the youth which *are* 'damasked' (99.10). Ingram and Redpath compare Barnes's *Parthenophil and Parthenophe* (1593), Ode 16, 34–8: 'Her cheekes with *rose*, and *lillyes* deck'te, / . . . Her cheekes to *Damaske roses* sweet / In sent, and colour, weare so like.'

6 no such roses . . . cheeks This suggests that his mistress's complexion was dark or swarthy. Compare 144.4.

7 more delight greater sensory pleasure, gratification.

8 reeks is exhaled, emitted. It should be noted, however, that although the strongly pejorative sense of 'reek' meaning 'to emit an unwholesome or disagreeable vapour or fume; hence, to smell strongly and unpleasantly; to stink' (*OED* Reek *v*¹ 3) is apparently unrecorded before 1679 or 1710, the various forms of the word had much earlier frequently carried unpleasant connotations (of smoke, sweat, marsh vapour, blood, etc.); compare *Cor.* 3.3.120–1 ('You common cry of curs, whose breath I hate / As reek a'th'rotten fens'), *JC* 3.1.158 (Now, whilst your purpled hands do reek and smoke'), and *Tim.* 3.6.92–3 ('and sprinkles in your faces / Your reeking villainy'). 'reeks', therefore, is not so neutral as it is generally considered by most commentators.

9–10 Compare 141.5.

11 grant admit.

11 goddess go goddess walk. Shakespeare may have been thinking of Aeneas's encounter with Venus (*Aeneid* 1, 405): 'et vera incessu patuit dea' ('and in her step she was revealed, a very goddess' (Loeb)). As Rollins notes, Shakespeare describes how a goddess 'goes' in *Venus and Adonis*, 1028: 'The grass stoops not, she treads on it so light.'

12 My mistress . . . ground i.e. his mistress is a real down-to-earth woman, not the sort of idealised fiction imagined by other love poets.

13 by heaven (1) by all that's holy; (2) by the place of bliss (looking back perhaps to the sexual implications of 'heaven' in 129.14; see note). Compare the implications of Nashe's sonnet in *The Unfortunate Traveller* (1594), in *Works*, II, 262–3, which concludes: 'Into heavens joyes none can profoundly see, / Except that first they meditate on thee.' See 131.11 n.

13 my love i.e. my mistress.

13 rare splendid, excellent, choice.

14 any she . . . compare any woman ('she') described untruthfully ('belied') through mendacious, improper, artificial comparisons ('false compare'). The compliment is somewhat tempered, perhaps, because not only beautiful women but relatively plain women (e.g. Queen Elizabeth) could be, and were, 'belied with false compare'.

Sonnet 131

Sonnet 131 continues the love/hate tone of 130, finally claiming, paradoxically, that 'black is fairest' (12) and that the poet's mistress is truly 'black' only in her 'deeds' (13).

1 tyrannous despotic, pitilessly cruel. A woman's 'cruelty' (see 'cruel' in line 2) traditionally

referred to her refusal to accede to a lover's amorous desires.

1 so as thou art i.e. even in your 'blackness' (a state that conventionally should be suppliant, not tyrannical).

2 those whose beauties i.e. those women who are 'fair' or conventionally 'beautiful', not 'black'.

2 proudly (1) arrogantly; (2) presumptuously (out of unwarranted pride). As Booth notes, syntactically 'proudly' modifies and tends to personify 'beauties'.

3 For . . . know'st Because you know only too well.

3 dear (1) affectionate, loving, fond; (as adverb) affectionately, lovingly, fondly; (2) earnest; earnestly. 'dear' may also carry some suggestion of 'costly' in terms of the 'pains' his 'heart' (= love) has suffered.

3 doting loving to a foolish extreme.

4 fairest (1) most beautiful (with play on 'fair' *v*. 'black'); (2) most desirable, most admirable.

4 most precious jewel most highly valued (1) treasure, (2) gem, (3) costly ornament (metaphorically = the poet's mistress). 'precious' looks back to 'dear' (3), though with a meaning not there directly applicable. In 65.10, the youth is described as 'Time's best jewel'. It was a commonplace to describe one's mistress as a 'jewel'; compare Sidney, *Poems*, p. 68, no. 33, lines 27–8: 'Thus nature's Diamond, receave thy conquest, / Thus pure pearle, I do yeeld, my senses and soule.'

5 in good faith (1) indeed; (2) in all honesty.

5 that who. See Abbott 258.

6 Thy face . . . groan i.e. your face lacks the ability or attraction ('power') to make love or a lover express unrequited longing in groans of desire.

7 To say they err To assert (publicly) that they are wrong.

7 bold daring, courageous (perhaps, presumptuous).

8 Although I . . . alone i.e. even though I privately ('to myself alone') assert ('swear') that 'they err' in saying it.

9 And to be sure . . . swear And in order to (1) make it certain, (2) reassure myself that what I swear 'to myself alone' is not a lie ('false').

10 groans See 6 n. above.

10 but thinking on only thinking about.

11 One on another's neck In rapid succession. Rollins notes the same phrase in *The Unfortunate Traveller* (1594), in Nashe, *Works*, II, 262: 'Passion upon passion would throng one on anothers necke, he wold praise her beyond the moone and starres, and that so sweetly and ravishingly as I perswade my self he was more in love with his own curious forming fancie than her face; and truth it is, many become passionate lovers onely to winne praise to theyr wits.' I quote the whole passage because it may suggest something about Shakespeare's ambivalently witty treatment of the Dark Lady. *The Unfortunate Traveller*, the first edition of which was dedicated to the Earl of Southampton, Shakespeare's patron, was well known to Shakespeare – a number of verbal echoes from it appear, for example, in *Hamlet* (see Tobin, 'More elements from Nashe', *Hamlet Studies* 5 (1983), 52–8). Indeed, Nashe's picture there of a certain married lady called Diamante (*Works*, II, 261–3), with her 'blacke eie browes' and 'licorous roulling eie', and of her would-be lover, the Earl of Surrey (she is eventually seduced by his page, Jack Wilton), may have been somewhere in the back of Shakespeare's mind.

12 Thy black Your blackness (physical and, perhaps, moral).

12 fairest See 4 n. above.

12 in my judgement's place to my mind, in my opinion. The mind is the 'seat' or 'place' of 'judgement' (compare 'judgement-seat' and the legal link with 'I swear' (8, 9) and 'witness bear' (11). Booth observes that 'The phrase also carries a self-mocking echo of "in place of my judgment" and suggests "which has displaced my judgment and now acts in its stead."' Lines 7–12 express a noticeably rationalised and uncertain commitment on the poet's part: he refuses to assert his mistress's 'black beauty' publicly and then, in order to reassure himself of the truth of his private opinion (which we may note is that of his 'judgement', not his 'heart'), he works himself into a paroxysm of a 'thousand groans' as 'evidence' 'to be sure that is not false I swear'.

13 In nothing . . . black In no way are you 'black' (since, paradoxically, to me you are 'fairest' (4, 12)).

13 save in thy deeds except in the morality of your actions. Compare 69.6–12, where the youth's outward 'fairness' is contrasted with his 'deeds'. This is the first time in the Dark Lady series that the morally pejorative connotations of 'black' (as dirty, ugly, malignant, baneful, evil) are openly played on.

14 thence i.e. as a result of your 'deeds'. Compare 147.14.

14 this slander Refers to line 6 (i.e. because of your 'blackness', 'Thy face hath not the power to make love groan').

14 as I think With or without Gildon's commas, this parenthetical clause (*pace* Ingram and Redpath) strikes a tentative note. Kerrigan glosses 'think' as 'presume', nicely catching this tentative tone.

14 proceeds springs, arises. Ironically, the couplet is considerably more 'slanderous' than the 'slander' of line 6.

Sonnet 132

Like 128, 132 is more conventional and less openly critical in tone than most of the Dark Lady series – an exercise on the Dark Lady's black eyes which *appear* to mourn, despite her 'heart' (compare 127.10), 'pitying' 'with pretty ruth' the poet's 'pain'. The nature

of that 'pain' presumably lies in the 'deeds' generally alluded to in 131.13 and particularised by his mistress's implied liaison with the poet's 'friend' described in 133.

1–2 These lines have been variously pointed (see collation); the pointing here adopted accepts the Abbott-Tucker argument that 'torment' in line 2 is to be understood as an infinitive (= to torment), as e.g. in 'I have known her torment him' (see Abbott 340). Until recently, however, most editors have preferred the easier reading 'torments' introduced by Benson (1640).

1 as as if.

2 heart i.e. the seat of the emotions, feelings.

2 torment (to) torture, pain. See 1–2 n. above.

2 disdain scorn, contempt.

3 Have put on black Have clothed themselves in black (like mourners). The phrase 'Have put on' would seem to suggest that this was a voluntary act on the part of the eyes, even though, as the poet has told us (127.9), his mistress's eyes are naturally black.

4 pretty ruth (1) pleasing, agreeable, (2) comely, proper pity (with perhaps ironic undertones: the eyes are putting on a 'pretty' show of 'ruth' that has no emotional basis in real feeling).

4 pain See headnote.

5–8 Despite the truth-telling protestations of 130 these lines, with their comparison of the lady's eyes to the sun and evening star, revert to the most commonplace hyperboles in the conventional sonneteers' repertory from Petrarch on. Indeed, these metaphors are so trite and threadbare that a reader may be tempted to suspect an underlying parodic intention. Compare Mercutio's parody (*Rom.* 2.4.38–43) of 'the numbers that Petrarch flow'd in'. Whether or not, as I have suggested, there is an element of parody here, Ingram and Redpath are probably correct in saying that 'these lines make clear that the poet saw the chief beauty of his mistress as her eyes' and in noting that 'the apparent parallel between "grey cheeks" (line 6), "sober west" (line 8), and "thy face" (line 9) may even suggest that without the animation of her eyes the mistress's face might have been dull'.

5 morning sun of heaven i.e. the sun as it begins to rise (with probable play on 'mourning'; see line 9).

6 Better becomes Is more becoming to.

6 grey cheeks of the east Compare *Rom.* 2.3.1–2: 'The grey-ey'd morn smiles on the frowning night, / Check'ring the eastern clouds with streaks of light.' Metrical considerations support the emendation of Q 'th' to 'the' (see collation).

7 full star i.e. Hesperus, the evening star. 'full' seems to mean something like 'plentifully charged or richly stored with bright light', a sense that may be generally supported by *OED* Full *adj* 2a and d. Of light, 'full' meaning 'intense' is not recorded before 1664.

7 even For the rhyme with 'heaven', see 28.12 n.

8 Doth half that glory Affords half as much (1) honour, (2) splendour.

8 sober not bright or colourful, subdued (as a result of the loss of the sun's light). *OED* cites Milton, *Paradise Lost*, IV, 598–9: 'Now came still Eevning on, and Twilight gray / Had in her sober Liverie all things clad.'

9 mourning Reverses the probable play on 'morning' in line 5. Given the context, Gildon's reading 'mourning' for Q 'morning' (see collation) has been almost universally adopted, 'morning' being a common variant spelling of 'mourning' at this time.

9 become are becoming to.

10 let it then permit it therefore ('it' anticipating the action of mourning, i.e. 'To mourn' (11)).

10 as well beseem (1) also, (2) equally become (by suiting it in a mourning appearance).

11 doth thee grace (1) is becoming to you; (2) is a creditable or worthy act on your part.

12 suit thy . . . part i.e. let every part of you (not just your eyes) show your pity (for me) by suiting or clothing itself alike (i.e. in mourning black). There is perhaps, as in 127.10, a play on 'to suit' and 'to soot' (= blacken).

13 Then Should you do so.

13 beauty herself i.e. the *Idea* of beauty.

14 all they foul all others ugly or loathsome. Shakespeare here may be said to be 'fouling the fair' in contrast to 'Fairing the foul' (127.6).

14 complexion facial colouring (with perhaps some reference to 'complexion' = general temperament or nature). The couplet essentially repeats the couplet of 127.

Sonnet 133

Sonnet 133 continues the 'tyranny' theme of 131 and the 'tormenting heart' theme of 132, introducing for the first time in the Dark Lady series any direct mention of the poet's 'friend' and setting up a triangular relationship (poet, friend, mistress) similar to that treated in the young man series in 40–2, including perhaps 34 and 35.

1 Beshrew Probably to be taken in the weakened sense 'A plague on' or 'Fie upon', not the more literal sense 'Curses on'. Compare, for example, *MND* 5.1.290: 'Beshrew my heart, but I pity the man.'

1 that heart Referring back to 132.2, 9–12.

1 groan See 131.6 n.

2 deep wound The nature of the 'wound', a liaison between the poet's 'friend' and his mistress, is revealed in lines 3–8. Compare 'the wound' in 34.8.

3 torture Picks up 'torment' (132.2) and 'pain' (132.4).

3 alone only.

4 But slave . . . be But in addition my (1) most precious, dearest, (2) most desirable friend must be made a slave to the kind of slavery (that you impose

on me). In 57 and 58 it is the poet who describes himself as the young man's 'slave'.

5 Me from . . . taken i.e. you have stolen my 'heart' from me (without giving me yours in return) through the attraction of your pitiless, hard-hearted ('cruel') eye (an eye that no longer appears to mourn 'as pitying me' (132.1)).

6 my next self my nearest, dearest self (i.e. the 'friend'). Compare 'that other mine' (134.3).

6 harder hast engrossed more (1) severely, cruelly, (2) securely, completely have monopolised (thus leaving in the friend's heart no place for the poet). Shakespeare may have intended us to read 'engrossèd' and 'crossèd' (8) as indicated by the Q forms.

7 myself i.e. 'Me' (5).

7 forsaken (1) abandoned; (2) deprived (Kerrigan).

8 A torment (Which is) a torment. Line 8 is appositional.

8 thrice threefold Literally, 'A torment' multiplied by nine. The poet's loss is indeed 'threefold' or triple (his friend, himself, and his mistress); 'thrice' is used as an intensifier to triple the extent and weight of his loss.

8 thus to be crossed to be thwarted in this way. Compare *Wiv.* 4.5.125–6: 'Sure, one of you does not serve heaven well, that you are so cross'd.' It is possible that 'crossed' may also carry some sense of 'crucified', though *OED* records no examples after 1550; see the notes on 'cross' and its implied Christ-like association with the poet in 34.12 and 42.12.

9 Prison Imprison, confine (imperative).

9 my Here and in line 10 'my' carries special stress.

9 steel bosom's ward obdurate heart's (1) keeping, care, (2) jail cell. 'Prison', 'steel', and 'keeps' (line 11, a prison warder being known as a 'keeper') all intensify the sense of solitary confinement in 'ward'.

10 then (1) in that case; (2) at that time.

10 my friend's . . . bail permit my (1) humble, inferior, (2) unfortunate, suffering heart to (1) go bail for, redeem, (2) confine my friend's heart. 'bail' in the sense of 'confine' only becomes operative with lines 11–12.

11 Whoe'er Whoever it may be that.

11 keeps me (1) possesses, (2) confines, imprisons me (i.e. my heart).

11 guard guard-house, place of confinement (but also carrying implications of 'defence' and 'protection').

12 use rigour . . . jail i.e. if his friend's heart is safely confined in his heart ('in my jail'), the poet's mistress ('Thou') cannot exercise her severe cruelty ('rigour') upon his friend's heart.

13 And yet thou wilt But nevertheless you will ('use' such 'rigour').

13 pent confined, imprisoned. Looks back to 'Prison my heart . . . ward' (9).

14 Perforce Out of necessity (with a suggestion of 'forcible constraint'; compare 134.2).

14 all everything (including his friend's heart).

Sonnet 134

Sonnet 134 continues 133, lines 1–2 commenting on the conclusion reached in the couplet of 133. Compare 46 for the heavy use of legal imagery throughout.

1–2 So now I . . . And I Therefore now that I . . . And that I. Most editors, following Capell (see collation), insert a comma after 'So', making it an absolute meaning 'Well! that being so' (Ingram and Redpath); this is, admittedly, a more dramatic reading, and may be paralleled in *JC* 5.3.47, but the Q text makes perfectly acceptable sense without the comma.

1 confessed acknowledged (as a fact admitted in legal terms). There may also be some suggestion of a 'religious confession'.

1 thine, The retention of the Q comma allows line 2 to be taken either as part of the 'confession' or as a related but discrete statement; omission of the comma (adopted by some editors; see collation) makes line 2 necessarily part of the 'confession' (see Ingram and Redpath's note).

2 mortgaged . . . will pledged to comply with your (1) volition, (2) wilfulness, (3) carnal lust (and liable to forfeiture in case of failure) (Ingram and Redpath). The introduction here of 'will' initiates the tiresome and increasingly bawdy play on the word in 135 and 136.

3 Myself I'll forfeit I'll make a forfeit of myself (i.e. lose all property rights in myself under the terms of the 'mortgage' (2) or 'bond' (8) subscribed to between us).

3 so (1) provided that; (2) in order that.

3 that other mine i.e. my other self, 'my friend' (133.2), 'my next self' (133.6). Is there perhaps a play on 'mine' in the sense of 'treasure hoard'? The 'friend' is so described in 52.1–2.

4 restore to be give back so that he may be.

4 my comfort still always my (1) support, consolation, (2) pleasure, delight (in return for the poet's self-forfeiture).

5 wilt not i.e. accede to the terms laid down in lines 1–4.

5 will not does not desire to. Until the second half of line 6 'will not be free' can be taken as meaning '(he) won't be free because you won't permit it'.

6 covetous greedily possessive, unwilling to give up anything you think belongs to you. Ironically, 'covetous' may equally be applied to the poet, who desires sole possession of his 'friend' and his 'mistress'.

6 kind (1) by nature kindhearted, gentle, benevolent; (2) affectionate, loving (with some suggestion perhaps of 'overly kind' or 'fondly doting').

7–8 He learned . . . bind Under the guise of a legal transaction these lines, as Tucker suggests, seem, metaphorically, to describe a situation in which the poet's 'friend' had undertaken, as a proxy or underwriter ('surety-like'), to woo the lady on the poet's behalf (see line 11) and then found himself unwittingly but as securely ('as fast') bound 'Under that bond' to the lady because, instead of wooing for the poet, he had wooed the lady for himself (or was seduced by her), thus becoming her 'bond' slave. This is the lesson his 'friend' presumably 'learned', a learning process equally costly to both the poet and the friend. Compare the proxy wooings, though with happier outcomes, in *Much Ado* (Don Pedro–Claudio–Hero) and *Twelfth Night* (Viola/Cesario–Orsino–Olivia).

9 The statute . . . take i.e. you will exact the full terms of the 'bond' (8) or 'statute' which your beauty has imposed (on the 'friend'). The lady is pictured as a she-Shylock who insists, though with a difference, on her 'pound of flesh'.

10 Thou usurer . . . use You usurer, who lends out for your own profit ('use') all your physical capital (i.e. your body). 'use', like 'hast' in line 13, carries strong sexual overtones. Line 10 is parenthetical, commenting on the implied action in line 9.

11 sue (1) bring legal proceedings against (if the 'friend' fails to meet the full terms of the 'bond'); (2) pursue, hold in, chase; (3) woo, court. (1) must be understood metaphorically in terms of (2) and (3).

11 came debtor . . . sake who (only) became a debtor on my behalf.

12 So So that.

12 lose The common variant spelling 'loose' in Q might have suggested to a contemporary reader a secondary sense of 'set free (from me)'.

12 through my unkind abuse as a result of (1) your unnaturally harsh ill-treatment of me, (2) my unloving ill-usage (of the 'friend' in using him as a proxy). (1) is surely the more likely gloss.

13 hast For the sexual implication, see 129.10 n.

14 He pays the whole He, as 'debtor' (11), is responsible, under the 'bond' (8), for payment of the whole debt (principal and 'use'). Bawdy play is probably intended on 'whole' and 'hole' (compare *Rom.* 2.4.98–100).

14 yet am . . . free i.e. (1) even so, (2) at the same time I am not liberated or exempt from my obligations to you ('free') because, as I have confessed, I 'am mortgaged to thy will' (2).

Sonnet 135

In 135 and 136, closely linked sonnets, Shakespeare abandons himself (and his readers) to two frankly bawdy and frenetically witty exercises in which he obsessively exploits (and exhausts) various denotative and connotative shades of meaning that Elizabethans associated with the word 'will', both as noun and verb. Six senses of 'will' (each usually playing on one or more of the others) have been distinguished (see Tucker, Booth, Kerrigan): (a) wish, desire, choice, intent (in both noun and associated verb forms), wilfulness – as, for example, in 'Will' (line 1); (b) carnal desire, lust – as in 'Will' (line 2) and 'rich in Will' (line 11); (c) shall (expressing definite intention) – as in 'will fulfil' (136.5); (d) penis – as in 'hide my will in thine' (line 6) and 'Will will fulfil the treasure of thy love' (136.5; compare *AWW* 4.3.16 – 17: 'he fleshes his will in the spoil of her honor'); (e) vagina – as in 'thou, whose will is large and spacious' (line 5) and 'thy large Will' (line 12); (f) the Christian name 'Will[iam]' (i.e. William Shakespeare and probably at least one other 'William') – as in 'Will' (lines 1, 2, etc.) and 'my name is Will' (136.14).

Other contemporary writers also liked to quibble on 'will' (see Rollins, I, 345), but some verses in Breton's *Melancholike Humours* (1600), p. 15, not elsewhere cited, seem especially relevant because they appear immediately preceding another poem of Breton's in some way connected with 105 (see headnote) and may even suggest points of contact with 143:

> Childrens Abs and Womens Ohs,
> Doe a wondrous griefe disclose;
> Where a dugge the one will still,
> And the t'other but a will . . .
>
> Let the childe then sucke his fill,
> Let the woman have her will;
> All will hush, was hearde before;
> Ah and Oh, will cry no more.
>
> (lines 1–4, 17–20)

For the possible biographical questions raised by 135 and 136, see Rollins, II, 133–65.

1 Whoever . . . Will Whoever other women desire and get, you have your Will. 'wish' plays on 'will' in senses (a) and (b) (see headnote); 'Will', on senses (b), (d), and (f); 'hath' and 'hast' may also carry sexual implications (see 129.10 n.). Compare the proverbs 'Women will have their wills' (Tilley w723) and, looking forward to line 2, 'Will will have will though will woe win' (Tilley w397). Compare Sidney, *Arcadia* (1590), p. 339: '*P[assion]*. Will hath his will, when *Reasons* will doth misse. / *R[eason]*. Whom *Passion* leades unto his death is bent.'

2 And Will . . . overplus This teasingly ambiguous line, and 'thy Will' in line 1, has given rise to various speculations as to how many different 'Will's Shakespeare may be juggling with (see Rollins, I, 345–7). Critics are agreed on only one point: that, among the several suggested possibilities, most of the 'Will's (all printed in italics and capitalised in Q; see collation) refer primarily to the poet, Will[iam] Shakespeare ('my name is Will' (136.14)), and a few even argue that only Shakespeare is thus referred to. Most critics, however, favour two or more 'Will's.

Some, particularly in lines 1–2, argue for two 'Will's: Shakespeare and the 'friend' of the first series (1–126), whom they claim was also named 'Will[iam]', possibly to be identified with the elusive 'M^r. W. H.' of Thorpe's dedication to the 1609 Q. Others argue for three 'Will's: the two suggested above, plus a third 'Will', the Dark Lady's husband, who, it is postulated, must also have been named 'Will[iam]'. For some slight evidence that the Dark Lady was married, see 152.3 n. There is, of course, considerable disagreement, here and throughout 135 and 136, about which 'Will' refers to which 'Will', unless one accepts the minority view that they all refer to the poet himself. But, as Dowden noted, 'Will in overplus' (line 2) seems to anticipate 'More than enough am I' (line 3) and should, therefore, probably be taken to refer to Shakespeare. As usual, the various views summarised above are influenced by which candidate the critic is supporting for the role of the 'friend' or 'youth'. For the continuing wordplay on 'Will' and 'will' in 135 and 136, with a few exceptions, the reader is referred to the headnote and the notes to lines 1–2.

2 to boot in addition (with play perhaps on 'booty' = spoils).

2 in overplus in excess, 'More than enough' (3).

3 More than . . . still i.e. I alone (without any other 'Will') am more than enough, continually, and no less than I have done in the past ('still'), to trouble or importune you (with my demands for 'love'). Kerrigan notes that 'vex' (= agitate, stir) may have sexual implications. If so, is the poet here (and in 136.5, 'Will will fulfil') suggesting that his 'will' (= lust or penis) is large enough ('More than enough') to satisfy the Dark Lady, 'whose will is large and spacious' (5)?

4 thy sweet will your will (see headnote (a), (b), (e)) which yields (me) pleasure.

4 making addition thus i.e. in such a way adding to your pleasure ('sweet will'). Compare 'to boot' (2) and 'in overplus' (2). The sonnet is, indeed, thematically concerned with 'addition' (see also lines 10, 11), i.e. addition as it pertains to 'increased sexual pleasure' for both the Dark Lady and the poet himself.

5 will For wordplay, see headnote (a), (b), (e). Compare *Lear* 4.6.271: 'O indistinguish'd space of woman's will'.

5, 7 spacious . . . gracious Trisyllabic. Usually disyllabic in Shakespeare, but compare *Tit.* 2.1.114: 'The forest walks are wide and spacious', and *Ado* 4.1.108: 'And never shall it be more gracious' (both, as here, used terminally).

6 once vouchsafe deign just once.

6 hide . . . thine The primary bawdy reference here is obvious (see headnote (d) and (e)), with secondary play on (a) and (b)).

7 will For wordplay, see headnote (a), (b), (d).

7 right gracious very (1) acceptable, (2) attractive, pleasing.

8 in my will . . . shine i.e. in my particular case why does my will not (1) stand out brightly among, (2) excel ('shine') in receiving your favourable ('fair') acceptance? For 'will', see 7 n. above.

9 yet . . . still nevertheless, always and constantly ('still') gives 'fair acceptance' (8) to rain. Compare *TN* 1.1.9–11: 'O spirit of love, how quick and fresh art thou, / That notwithstanding thy capacity / Receiveth as the sea . . .', and the proverb 'The sea refuseth no river' (Tilley S179).

10 in abundance . . . store i.e. (despite) already having a great plenty of water ('in abundance'; compare 'all water' (9)) is still willing to increase its ('his') natural stock ('store'). 'in abundance' thus modifies 'sea' (9), but it can also be taken to modify 'addeth' adverbially (= abundantly).

11 So thou In the same way you should.

11–12 being rich . . . more These allusively difficult lines are generally ignored by commentators, but may be taken to mean something like 'having an abundance of "Will"s, add to your stock of "Will"s my single "will" in order to make your already large stock of "Will"s greater or more in number'. For equivoques on 'Will' and 'will', here and in line 14, see headnote (a), (b), (d), (e), (f). For the possible phallic implications of 'one' here and in line 14, see 6.8 n., 20.12 n., and 136.6–12.

13 Let no . . . kill (1) Do not allow an unkind one (i.e. the poet's mistress), or unkindness, to kill (figuratively) any (a) handsome, (b) desirable, (c) gentle suppliants or wooers (who, like me, seek your sexual favours); (2) (reading as in Tucker and Ingram and Redpath; see collation) Do not allow a harsh or ungenerous 'No' or refusal to kill, etc. (1) allows for a substantival use of 'unkind' (= unkind one, unkindness), a use not recorded by *OED*, but an example, hitherto unnoticed, occurs in Chapman's *Ovids Banquet of Sence* (1595), 24, 3–4: 'Not able to endure earthes rude unkindes [*rhymes with* mindes] / Bred in my soveraigns parts too tenderly'.

14 Think all . . . Will i.e. think of all the 'Will's as a single 'Will', and thus include me as one among the other 'Will's.

Sonnet 136

See the headnote to 135; (a), (b), etc. refer to the wordplay on the various shades of meaning of 'Will' and 'will' there listed and illustrated.

1 soul Here (and in lines 2 and 3) used as the seat of intelligence and its resulting emotions, without any necessary suggestion of 'spiritual' qualities. See 107.1–2 n.

1 check . . . near (1) reproach, (2) restrain you because I (i) come so close to the truth in what I say about you (as, for example, in 135), (ii) seek to come so close to you sexually (i.e. to 'bed' you).

2 blind soul A difficult phrase that is variously explained: the 'soul' is considered 'blind' because (1)

it is within the body and hence lacks eyes to 'see' or judge correctly (Tyler); (2) (taking 'blind' as proleptic) it becomes 'blind' by deliberately closing its eyes (Tucker); (3) its sensibilities are blinded by love (Booth); (4) it is heedless and ignorant (Kerrigan – a definition derived from (1) above).

2 thy Will For wordplay, see 135 headnote (a), (b), (d), (f).

3 will For wordplay, see 135 headnote (b), (d), (f).

3 is admitted there (1) is accepted as an inmate (Elizabethans accepting 'reason' and 'will' as the two rational faculties of the soul (Willen and Reed)) by your soul; (2) is accepted as a companion in your bed ('there' looking back to the second meaning inherent in 'I come so near' in line 1).

4 Thus far for love To this extent for love's sake.

4 my love-suit, sweet, fulfil satisfy (by granting your favours), sweet one, my love-suit. Following Capell's pointing (see collation), 'sweet' thus refers to the lady and has been adopted by most editors, but Q reads 'my louesute sweet fullfill', which may be taken to mean 'satisfy my love-suit which is so precious to me'. The present context, however, seems to favour Capell's pointing (but see an identical choice offered by 'sweet' in line 12).

5 Will i.e. Will[iam] (italicised in Q). For wordplay, see 135 headnote (b), (d), (f).

5 treasure . . . love i.e. the precious storehouse of your love (with play on 'love' as 'lovers' and on 'treasure' = pudenda; see 20.14 n.). Compare 'store's account' in line 10.

6 Ay Yes (with play perhaps on 'aye' = 'ever'). The Q spelling 'I' for 'Ay' was standard at this time; Capell's modernised form, universally accepted, loses the play on the pronoun 'I' as referring to the 'Will' of line 5, a reference tacitly assumed by the earlier eighteenth-century editors.

6 fill it full Plays on 'fulfil' in line 5, with obvious bawdy innuendo on the following 'wills' and 'my will [being] one' (see 135 headnote (b), (d)).

7 In things of great receipt In regard to things of large (1) reception or capacity, (2) size. There is a bawdy play on 'things' (= both vulva and penis; see 20.12 n.), and 'of great receipt' looks back to 'thou, whose will is large and spacious' (see 135 headnote and line 5 n.).

7 with ease we prove i.e. we can easily establish it as a truth that.

8–10 Among . . . be These lines play on the old argument that 'one' is no number (i.e. 'none'); see 8.14 n. – here used with a special twist: 'Since there are already "a number" of "Will"s and "will"s involved ("thou being rich in Will" (135.11)), one more "Will" or "will" will make no discernible difference among so many others.'

9 pass untold be treated as uncounted (as only 'one', i.e. 'none', among 'the number').

10 in thy store's account in the inventory ('account') of your store (of 'Will's and 'will's).

10 I one must be i.e. I will (nevertheless) figure as 'one' (even though I will not 'count' as 'one'). See 6.8 n. and 135.11–12 n. for the possible phallic suggestion in 'one', and Abbott 314 for 'must' used to indicate definite futurity. There is also perhaps further play on 'I' and 'one' as a numeral.

11–12 For nothing . . . thee i.e. you may reckon me to be a nothing ('one' being 'reckoned none' (8)) just so long as you continue to esteem ('hold') that 'nothing', which is me, as a 'something' that is precious to you. There is obvious play on 'nothing' as 'no-thing' and 'something' as 'some-thing' (see collation). Some editors, perhaps correctly, follow Capell in taking 'sweet' as a vocative referring to the lady (see 4 n. above), but the argument from context does not seem as compelling here, 'a something sweet' balancing 'That nothing me'.

13–14 Make but . . . Will Make only my name your love (i.e. what you most desire, your 'Will' and 'will' in senses (a), (b), (d), (f) – see 135 headnote), and love my name always ('that still'), and then you will love *me* because ('for') my name is Will. Most editors adopt Sewell's 'lov'st' for Q 'louest', but 'lovest', though metrically less easy, helps to throw stress on 'me' (i.e. the 'man', not the 'name').

Sonnet 137

In 137 Shakespeare returns, after the wittily bawdy but comparatively disengaged exercises of 135 and 136, to the more personal and emotionally charged love/hate or attraction/repulsion theme of 131–4: Why do I, who know what 'beauty' and 'truth' are, nevertheless love a woman who is neither 'beautiful' nor 'true', who is indeed promiscuous – 'the bay where all men ride' (6) and 'the wide world's common race' (10)? In 113 the 'mind' is accused of misleading the 'eyes' (as the 'heart' is in 141); here, in contrast, the 'eyes' are accused of misleading the 'heart' or 'mind'. The argument is continued in 148 and touched on in 152.11–14.

1 Thou blind fool, Love Most editors, as here, personify Q 'loue' as 'Love', a reading which may be interpreted as (1) the passion of sexual love generally or (2) Cupid, the 'little Love-god' (154.1), who is described as either blind or blindfolded (see *Ado* 1.1.254 and *Rom.* 1.4.4) and who delights, like a professional 'fool', in playing wanton tricks, randomly shooting his arrows in a childish and mischievous way (compare *AYLI* 4.1.213–14: 'that blind rascally boy that abuses every one's eyes because his own are out'). Tucker, however, though admitting a secondary allusion to the Cupid legend, suggests that Q 'loue' (uncapitalised) should be retained and should be taken as referring primarily to the poet's 'love' for the Dark Lady, which is both 'blind' and a 'fool';

he compares 'So true a fool is love' in 57.13. In (1) and (2) above, and in Tucker's interpretation, 'fool' may perhaps carry the adjectival force of 'foolish' (compare 'this fool gudgeon, this opinion' and 'the fool multitude that choose by show' (*MV* 1.1.102, 2.9.26)).

1 eyes The eyes were conventionally thought of as the 'entry-ports of love'; see, for example, Petrarch, *Rime sparse*, 84.

2 That they . . . they see i.e. so that in beholding (objects) they do not see truly what it is they are seeing. In a sense, then, 'Love' makes the eyes 'blind'. Compare 113.3–4.

3 They know . . . lies They know what true beauty is and where such beauty ('it') may be seen (because the poet's eyes have seen, and hence 'know', the perfection of beauty so often attributed to the youth in 1–126).

4 Yet what . . . be Nevertheless (they) mistake or esteem the worst (i.e. what is ugly) to be the best (i.e. what is beautiful).

5 corrupt corrupted. For this form of the past participle, see Abbott 342.

5 by over-partial looks i.e. by looking too favourably (upon 'the worst' (4)).

6 Be anchored Are held fast, fixed (as by an anchor). Compare *R3* 4.4.232: 'Till that my nails were anchor'd in thine eyes'. For a sexual suggestion in 'anchored', see the anonymous play, *A Warning for Faire Women* (1599), sig. B3ᵛ: 'He must not thinke to anker where he hopes, / Unlesse you [i.e. a bawd] be his pylot.'

6 in the bay . . . ride in the wide-mouthed inlet where all men ride at anchor (with obvious sexual innuendo in 'bay' (= female pudenda; compare 135.5) and 'ride' (= engage in coitus)).

7 eyes' falsehood i.e. the lies my eyes are telling (being 'corrupt by over-partial looks' (5)).

7 thou i.e. Love (in line 1).

7 forgèd hooks The 'hooks', like grapples (i.e. small anchors), which, in line 8, 'tie' or anchor the 'judgement' of the poet's 'heart', are termed 'forgèd' because, paradoxically, they are both (1) weak counterfeits being made of 'eyes' falsehood' and (2) compelling 'ties' being, figuratively, 'forgèd' of hammered steel. Compare *Ham.* 1.3.63: 'Grapple them unto thy soul with hoops of steel.'

8 judgement of my heart the faculty of judging by which my heart makes its choice (between 'the best' and 'the worst' (4)).

8 tied made fast, grappled.

9 that a several plot that (place = woman) as a privately owned, fenced piece of land.

10 knows knows to be.

10 wide world's common place unfenced, public or 'common' land which is open for use by all men. The intended sexual wordplay on 'several plot' and 'common place' is obvious. Compare Thomas

Heywood (?), *Tom a Lincoln* (*c.* 1615), lines 240–6 (in MSR).

11 Or mine . . . this Or why should mine eyes seeing this (i.e. that the woman concerned is 'the wide world's common place' (10))?

11 say this is not assure me this is not so.

12 To put . . . face In order to attribute (1) an unstained, (2) attractive, (3) specious appearance of virtue, constancy, chastity to a face that is so ugly or disgusting. The woman (= 'face') is thus described as 'foul' not only physically but morally – a foul soul in a foul body – and appears as a contrast to the youth, who, in 1–126, is often thought of as the supreme example of the neo-Platonic concept of the 'beautiful soul in the beautiful body'. Compare 'The worser spirit' contrasted to 'The better angel' in 144.

13–14 The couplet offers a rather lame answer to the preceding series of questions.

13 In things right true In concerns or persons that are genuinely (not speciously) (1) virtuous, (2) constant, faithful.

13 erred (1) gone astray; (2) sinned.

14 this false plague (1) this sickness of seeing and feeling falsely; (2) this (a) mendacious, (b) inconstant, (c) treacherous woman (taking 'plague' as a figurative term describing the kind of woman revealed in lines 3–12).

14 they i.e. 'heart and eyes' (13).

14 transferred (1) handed over (as captives to); (2) shifted (in so far as a proper focus on 'things right true' (13) is concerned).

Sonnet 138

A variant version of 138 (and 144) was printed in *The Passionate Pilgrim* (first edn, 1599; second edn, 1599; third edn, enlarged, 1612), a small collection of twenty poems published by William Jaggard and described as being '*By W. Shakespeare.*' (only five poems are otherwise vouched for as being by Shakespeare and another five are almost certainly by other hands). The rather extensive textual variants between Q (1609) and *The Passionate Pilgrim* (see collation) are generally thought of as resulting from Shakespeare's revision, the *Passionate Pilgrim* text probably representing an earlier version. A manuscript copy (Folger MS. 2071.7, fol. 197ᵛ), dating from about 1630 to 1640 and closely related to the *Passionate Pilgrim* text, offers three variants (see collation, lines 6, 11, 14).

1 my love i.e. my beloved, my mistress.

1 made A pun may perhaps be heard on made/maid (Booth).

1 truth faithfulness, constancy.

2 lies For the possible sexual equivoque in 'lies', see 13 n. below. The sonnet turns on 'lies': being lied to and lying to oneself.

3 That (I believe her) so that.

3 might may.

3 untutored simple, unsophisticated. According to *OED* 'untutored' is a Shakespearean coinage (see *2H6* 3.2.213 and *Rape of Lucrece*, dedication).

4 Unlearnèd in Ignorant of, unskilled in. Compare *Passionate Pilgrim*, 'Vnskilful in' and 'untutored' (3).

4 false subtleties deceitful guiles, tricks, cunning. Compare *Passionate Pilgrim*, 'forgeries'.

5 vainly (1) foolishly; (2) conceitedly, out of vanity.

6 my days . . . best i.e. physically, sexually, I am no longer young.

7 Simply (1) Foolishly, weakly; (2) Without condition, absolutely.

7 tongue Note that the rhyme 'young/tongue' is repeated in *The Passionate Pilgrim* in lines 9 and 11, an indication perhaps that the *Passionate Pilgrim* version is an earlier unrevised draft (see 46.13–14 n.).

8 On both sides thus In this way on either side (i.e. by you and me).

8 simple truth suppressed plain, unmixed truth (1) overpowered, defeated, (2) undisclosed, (3) denied.

9 But wherefore . . . unjust But why does she not admit that she is (1) unfaithful, (2) full of deceit, (3) dishonest (i.e. not 'honest' = chaste). 'unjust' looks back to lines 1–2; in *Passionate Pilgrim*, line 9 introduces a different twist – that the woman concerned is herself 'not young' (see collation).

11 love's best . . . trust love's most effective (1) attire, guise, (2) settled practice, policy lies in giving the appearance of faith or constancy ('seeming trust', with possibly a play on 'seeming' = seemly). The effectiveness of this 'policy' in love is illustrated by lines 1–2. *The Passionate Pilgrim* substitutes 'in a soothing toung' for Q's 'in seeming trust', a reading that even more obviously looks back to lines 1–2.

12 age in love i.e. older persons who fall in, or are infatuated by, love (like the poet who claims 'I am old' (10)). Lines 11 and 12, though generalised, have, respectively, immediate reference to the woman involved and the poet.

12 t'have years Almost all editors substitute *Passionate Pilgrim*'s 'to have' for Q's 't'have'; Q's reading, however, throws emphasis on 'years' (taken as disyllabic) where, I think, it properly belongs.

12 told (1) counted; (2) recounted, reported.

13 I lie . . . me (1) I lie to her and she lies to me; (2) we indulge in sexual intercourse with each other. Dekker devotes some eight pages in *The Seven deadly Sinnes of London* (1606), '2. Lying', to ringing the same changes on 'lie'.

14 in our faults through our (1) defects, failings, (2) offences.

14 flattered be are (1) deceived, beguiled, (2) gratified, pleased (even though improperly). *The Passionate Pilgrim*'s reading of the line (see collation), by substituting 'smother'd' for 'flattered', limits the meaning to (1). Compare Ovid, *Amores* II, xi, 53–4 (as translated by Marlowe): 'Ile thinke all true, though it be feigned matter. / Mine owne desires why should my selfe not flatter?'

Sonnet 139

Sonnet 139 reflects a sonnet convention: the lover pretends to find a justification or excuse (see lines 9–12) for his mistress's unkindness. It has been compared with Sidney, *Astrophil and Stella* (1591), 48.

1 call not me i.e. do not ask me.

1 justify (1) acquit you of; (2) defend as right and proper; (3) approve of. Suggested perhaps by 'she is unjust' (138.9); neither word occurs elsewhere in the Sonnets.

1 wrong The 'wrong' and 'unkindness' (2) refer not to the conventional 'coldness' of a desired mistress but to the unfaithfulness of the poet's mistress in loving 'elsewhere' (5) and in, unblushingly, allowing the poet to witness her roving eye (see lines 5–6). Thus, in terms of the conventionally cold and chaste mistress celebrated by most sonnet writers, her behaviour may be considered 'unkind' (i.e. unnatural).

2 heart i.e. the seat of feeling, understanding, and thought (= mind).

3 Wound . . . eye i.e. by glancing aside or eyeing other men (see line 6). Compare *Rom.* 2.4.13–15: 'Alas, poor Romeo, he is already dead, stabb'd with a white wench's black eye, run through the ear with a love-song.' According to one theory of vision at this time, the eyes emitted 'beams' of light; hence a lover could be 'wounded' or 'stabbed' by the eyes. The poet has already been 'wounded' by his mistress's 'black' eye; now she is doubly wounding him by faithlessly 'wounding' others (particularly his 'friend').

3 but with thy tongue i.e. rather speak out honestly and 'Tell me thou lov'st elsewhere' (5).

4 Use power . . . art Use your power (over me) with forthright force ('power') and do not kill me through indirect strategy or 'cunning' (7).

5 elsewhere (1) someone else; (2) other men.

5 in my sight i.e. when I am present and can see your actions.

6 Dear heart Precious love (a common term of endearment). 'Dear' may perhaps carry a suggestion of 'overpriced'.

6 forbear . . . aside refrain from casting sidelong (amorous) looks or oeillades (in order to entice other men). Compare *Lear* 4.5.25–6: 'She [Goneril] gave strange eliads and most speaking looks / To noble Edmund.'

7 What Why. See Abbott 253.

7 with cunning = 'by art' (4).

7 might = 'power' (4).

8 Is more . . . bide Is greater than my (1) overburdened, oppressed, (2) overwhelmed power of resistance ('defence') is able to endure or sustain ('bide').

9 Let me excuse thee Having in lines 1–8 refused to offer any excuse 'to justify the wrong' that his mistress is doing him, the poet now, rather weakly, tries to invent one (lines 9–12).

9 my love i.e. my beloved.

10 pretty looks (1) artful, wanton glances (see line 6); (2) agreeable, pleasing appearance (with probably more than a touch of irony in 'pretty'). As a term of seeming approbation, 'pretty' tends to 'damn with faint praise'; see 41.1 n.

11 therefore . . . foes for that reason (as a kindness to me) she turns her 'pretty looks' (= 'foes' = 'enemies' (10)) away from me ('from my face').

12 That So that.

12 elsewhere might may on others.

12 dart their injuries shoot out (like arrows) their mischiefs or harms. See the note on 'Wound' (3).

13 Yet do not so i.e. nevertheless do not transfer your 'injuries' (12) to others (in order to spare me). Compare 'But do not so' (36.13).

13 but since . . . slain rather because I am (already) nearly killed (by your 'unkindness' (2) and 'pretty looks' (10)).

14 outright on the spot, immediately (and don't linger out my 'pain'). The same wish for quick and final action occurs in 90. Compare Sidney, *Astrophil and Stella* (1591), 48.13–14: 'Deare Killer, spare not thy sweet cruell shot: / A kind of grace it is to slay with speed', and Constable, *Diana* (1594), Fourth Decad, 5.5–8, in *Poems*, p. 195: 'It is some mercie in a black-mouth'd Judge, / to haste his prysoners end, if he must die. / Deere, if all other favour you shall grudge, / doe speedie execution with your eye.'

14 rid my pain (1) free me from, (2) take away my physical and mental suffering.

Sonnet 140

In 140, which shows thematic and verbal links with 139, the idea that a lover too much and too openly despised may be driven to despair, hatred, and possible revenge is interestingly paralleled in Donne's sixth elegy, entitled 'Recusancy' by Gardner (lines 35–44):

> Yet let not thy deepe bitternesse beget
> Carelesse despaire in mee, for that will whet
> My minde to scorne; and Oh, love dull'd with
>   paine
> Was ne'r so wise, nor well arm'd as disdaine.
> Then with new eyes I shall survay thee, 'and
>   spie
> Death in thy cheekes, and darknesse in thine
>   eye.
> Though hope bred faith and love; thus taught,
>   I shall
> As nations do from Rome, from thy love fall.

My hate shall outgrow thine, and utterly
I will renounce thy dalliance.

1 wise as (1) as wise as; (2) wise, since (Booth).

1 press oppress, weigh too heavily upon. Compare 'lays upon' and 'o'erpressed' (139.2, 8). Booth suggests a reference to a form of torture known as 'peine forte et dure', in which a person who refused to plead 'guilty' or 'not guilty' was pressed to death (*OED* Press v^1 1b).

2 My tongue-tied patience i.e. my patient silence (which, 'pressed' too far, I will break and speak out against your 'unkindness' or 'disdain').

2 disdain (1) scorn, contempt; (2) aversion, hatred.

3 Lest For fear that.

4 The manner . . . pain The true character or nature ('manner') of my (1) unpitied, (2) pity-craving mental (and perhaps physical) suffering. 'pity-wanting' may also carry a suggestion of 'hate-breeding', since the poet's 'pain' is so great that it threatens him with madness (see lines 9–10), a madness in which he 'might speak ill' (10) and 'express' (3) his love turned to hate.

5 If I . . . wit If I could teach you wisdom or discretion.

6 Though not . . . so i.e. even though, my love, you do not love me, tell me that you do love me ('tell me so'). This gives a new twist to the poet's request in 139.5.

7–8 As testy sick men . . . know As (1) peevish, irascible, (2) contentious sick men, near death, hear only (false) reassurances of returning health from their physicians (so the poet, near 'madness' (10), needs his physician's (i.e. his mistress's) lies to comfort him in his extremity). The implied analogy is flawed because the sick men are going to die regardless of their physicians' comforting reassurances, while the poet claims that he may be saved from 'madness' by his mistress's lies.

9 if I . . . mad if I were to lose all hope (of my mistress's love, i.e. 'despair'), I would become mad.

10 speak ill of (1) say unkind, wicked, harmful things about; (2) speak malevolently about (i.e. 'speak' as a madman of 'ill' or unsound mind). Ironically, of course, 'speaking ill' of his mistress is exactly what the poet has been doing, and will continue to do, in most of the Dark Lady sonnets.

11 Now In these times. The following 'is grown' renders 'Now' somewhat superfluous. Is 'Now' perhaps a compositorial error for 'Know' (imperative)?

11 ill-wresting interpreting whatever is said or done in a bad sense (i.e. twisting the truth and believing the worst).

12 Mad slanderers That mad slanderers (like the poet in his mad ravings).

12 mad ears i.e. 'ill-wresting' hearers (by metonymy).

13 be so i.e. (1) be 'believed' by 'mad ears'; (2) be reduced to madness and hence slander you.

13 belied (be) calumniated or slandered (by my mad lies).

14 Bear . . . straight i.e. cast loving looks, when in company, directly and only on me (at least giving the appearance to others that you love me) and 'forbear to glance thine eye aside' (139.6; see note). Compare 93.4.

14 though thy . . . wide i.e. even though your (1) arrogant, disdainful, (2) lascivious heart (= feelings, desires) may wander from the 'straight' path of virtue ('go wide'). Compare 'glance thine eye aside' (139.6). Ingram and Redpath suggest that an image from archery underlies line 14.

Sonnet 141

Sonnet 141 changes the subject from the cooperation of his mistress's eyes and heart asked for in 140.13–14 back to the conflict between the poet's eyes and heart earlier treated in 113. See 137 headnote.

1 In faith Verily, truly. Without the added comma after 'faith', which makes 'In faith' an interjection, the phrase may be taken to mean 'In (my) constancy or faithfulness in love'.

2 errors (1) physical faults, blemishes; (2) wrong or errant behaviour (as when the poet's mistress glances aside at others in his presence; see 139.6 n.).

3 heart i.e. the seat of the innermost feelings (= mind).

3 despise view with contempt, disdain, repudiate. Ingram and Redpath suggest a 'phonal play' on 'despite' in line 4, a 'phonal play' which, I would suggest, echoes 'disdain' and 'despair', two key words in 140.2, 9.

4 Who Which (as again in line 11). On this neuter use of 'Who', see 23.11 n.

4 in despite of view in spite of what is seen (by the eyes).

4 is pleased to dote is happy to, desires to love foolishly (as if his 'heart' were deranged). 'dote' thus picks up the 'madness' motif in 140.9–12.

5, 6, 7 Nor Neither. This series of negatives, relating to four of the senses (hearing, touch, taste, smell), continues the negative construction set up in line 1, where it refers to the fifth sense ('eyes' = sight).

5 thy tongue's tune sound or tone of your voice. Compare the slightly more complimentary reference to his mistress's voice in 130.9–12. 'tune', with its musical association, seems to me ironic, and I question the 'covert compliment' which Kerrigan suggests it implies.

6 Nor tender . . . prone Neither (is my) sensitive, delicate sense of touch ('tender feeling') desirous of, or inclined toward (your) low, degrading caresses (i.e. my 'tender feeling' only deserves or reacts to something finer than your 'base touches'). There is obvious sexual implication in 'tender feeling', 'base touches' and 'prone'. Booth suggests an underlying musical image, arising out of 'tune' (5): the touching or fingering of a viol or harp (see *R2* 1.3.161–5), an image frequently used with sexual innuendo (see *Per.* 1.1.81–5, and 128.6 n.). Many editors, following Malone, place a comma after 'feeling' and thus give a different turn to the line: 'Neither (is my) sensitive sense of touch, which is naturally inclined to enjoy "base touches"'.

8 sensual feast 'Banquet of Sense' (in which all 'five senses' (9) are fed to repletion). See 47.6 n. and compare *LLL* 4.3.330–5: 'It [love] adds a precious seeing to the eye: / A lover's eyes will gaze an eagle blind. / A lover's ear will hear the lowest sound, / When the suspicious head of theft is stopp'd. / Love's feeling is more soft and sensible / Than are the tender horns of cockled snails. / Love's tongue proves dainty Bacchus gross in taste.'

8 with thee alone (1) with you and you solely (among other possible choices); (2) (perhaps) with you in private.

9 But Nevertheless neither. For the ellipsis of 'neither' before 'nor', see Abbott 396.

9 five wits i.e. the five intellectual, interior 'senses': common wit, imagination, fantasy, estimation, memory – a rather vaguely conceived concept formed as analogous to the five physical, exterior senses. Though Shakespeare is careful to make a distinction here, the two terms were often confused, 'five wits' being used to refer to the 'five senses' (as in *Rom.* 1.4.47).

10 foolish heart Compare 'dote' (4).

10 serving i.e. as a servant serves his master or mistress (with play on 'servant' = lover).

11–12 Who leaves . . . be Which reduces him to the mere semblance of a man, ungoverned ('unswayed') by either his 'five wits' or his 'five senses' (9), a subserviently miserable slave ('vassal wretch') to your 'proud heart' (compare 58.4). The poet has become an automaton without any mind or 'heart' of his own – a 'hollow man'. Shakespeare seems to be the first to use 'vassal' as an attributive adjective (see *OED*).

13 Only my plague . . . gain To this extent ('thus far') only do I reckon my (love-)sickness to be to my advantage ('my gain'). See 'false plague' in 137.14, where, as here, 'plague' may be taken as a figurative term for his mistress. Vendler suggests a play on Latin *plaga* (= wound), from which 'plague' is derived, and that 'wound' may be taken as metaphor for 'vulva'.

14 That Namely, that.

14 sin The nature of the poet's 'sin' is described in lines 1–12 and glossed by 142.1 ('Love is my sin').

14 awards me pain (1) determines (as in law) the proper extent of my punishment (i.e. in a sense, the poet suffers justly for his 'sin' and therefore may

'count' his present 'pain' as his 'gain' – a kind of 'credit' to his account after death); (2) rewards me with the kind of suffering found only in hell (see *OED* Pain *sb*[1] 2b). Gibbons notes the intense bitterness of this paradox.

Sonnet 142

Sonnet 142 follows naturally from 141, the first line explaining the nature of the poet's 'sin' referred to in 141.14.

1–2 Love . . . loving Love (of you, not the idea of love itself) is my sin, and your precious, prized, or costly (to me) essential character ('dear virtue') is hate (= 'disdain' (140.2)), masquerading as 'chastity' (= virtue), namely hatred of my sin, (1) a sin that grows out of the wrong kind of love (i.e. mere sensuality), (2) a hatred that arises from your own 'sinful loving' (i.e. your promiscuity and adultery). As Booth notes, 'grounded on' may be taken to modify either 'my sin' or 'Hate'; if 'sin' (as in (1) above), the harshness of the poet's criticism is softened by offering his mistress an excuse for her hatred. But the ambiguity may have been intentional, forcing a reader to consider both (1) and (2), since (2) looks forward to the charges levelled against his mistress in lines 5–8 as in earlier sonnets.

3 O but . . . state O only ('but') compare my state of being (spiritual and physical) with your own.

4 it i.e. my 'state'.

4 merits not reproving does not deserve censure.

6 profaned desecrated, defiled (by lying and promiscuous kissing = 'false bonds' (7)).

6 scarlet ornaments scarlet attire or adornments (the pure and natural red which has been 'profaned' by 'seal[ing] false bonds' (7), and, perhaps, by cosmetic painting). The phrase recurs in the anonymous *Edward III* 2.1.10: 'His cheekes put on their scarlet ornaments.' For Shakespeare's probable hand in this scene, see 94.14 n. As used in the play 'scarlet ornaments' clearly means 'blushes', something embellishing the cheeks, whereas in the present context it is a rather redundant way of saying 'redness'. 'Scarlet' often carried a strongly pejorative connotation (see Isa. 1.18 and *Rape of Lucrece*, 1650, 'scarlet lust'), and Booth suggests that the context and diction here may draw resonance from the idea of the Scarlet Woman, the Whore of Babylon (identified with the Pope and Catholicism by Protestants), who figures so prominently in Rev. 17–19. This association may have led to the 'sealing' image in line 7, since Rev. 5–10 deals with the opening of the 'seven seals' on the 'Book' containing God's 'counsels and judgements' (Geneva).

7 sealed . . . love set a seal (i.e. a kiss) to false promises of love. The underlying image, the 'sealing' of a legal agreement ('bond') by affixing a red wax seal, may have been suggested by 'scarlet ornaments' (6). The literary association of 'seals' and 'kisses' was common; compare *TGV* 2.2.7: 'And seal the bargain with a holy kiss', and *Venus and Adonis*, 511–12: 'Pure lips, sweet seals in my soft lips imprinted, / What bargains may I make, still to be sealing?'

7 as oft as mine as often as mine (i.e. my lips).

8 Robbed . . . rents (And) unlawfully deprived other women of the profits properly belonging to their marital beds ('beds' revènues') and hence of their legal returns ('rents', i.e. sexual satisfaction and potential children) The charge is clearly not only of promiscuity but of adultery. Compare *Oth.* 4.3.87–8. 'Say that they slack their duties, / And pour our treasures into foreign laps.' Tucker argues, on syntactical grounds, for the omission of the Q comma after 'mine' in line 7, thus making line 8 apply to the poet's behaviour – a possible but not generally accepted alternative reading.

9 Be it . . . those Let it (then) be permitted that I may love you in the same way as you love those (others). Booth observes that 'as' (i.e. the 'way' of loving) implies either passionate, if shortlived, infatuation or casual, unscrupulous lust. Willen and Reed gloss 'Be it lawful' as 'If it is permissible' (on analogy with 'An't please you', as Booth notes). Taken in this sense, lines 9–10 may then be read as a conditional statement introducing the main clause ('Root pity . . . be'), the Q comma after 'thee' in line 10 being retained (as by Dover Wilson) in place of the colon, semicolon, or period adopted by most editors since Gildon (see collation). This close syntactical linking of lines 9–10 and 11–12 may perhaps convey Shakespeare's intention more clearly.

10 thine eyes woo Compare 139.5 and note.

10 impòrtune (1) solicit; (2) pester, annoy. Always accented on the second syllable by Shakespeare, at least in verse.

11 Root pity Fix pity firmly, plant it deeply. 'pity' (as again in line 12) probably refers, as Ingram and Redpath suggest, more to the active kind of 'pity' conventionally pled for by lovers in songs and sonnets (i.e. the acquiescence of the beloved to the lover's desires) than to mere passive sympathy.

11 that when it grows so that once it achieves growth (i.e. burgeons).

12 Thy pity . . . be i.e. (1) your pity, (2) your need for pity may deserve to be pitied in return.

13 what i.e. 'pity'.

13 hide (1) refuse to show; (2) withhold.

14 By self-example . . . denied By your own example (1) may you (as I wish), (2) you may be refused (pity). The optative sense of 'mayst', as in (1), is probably the more likely.

Sonnet 143

Sonnet 143 is the third (and last) of the so-called 'Will sonnets' (see 135 and 136). Booth, adapting a suggestion of Dowden's, notes that 143 'resembles 142.9–12 in presenting a situation in which "A" vigorously

seeks "B" while "C" seeks "A" with equal vigor'. Shakespeare here employs an 'epic' or extended simile (lines 1–8, applied in lines 9–12) for serio-comic or mock-heroic effect.

1 Lo, as Behold, even as.

1 careful huswife (1) attentive, provident, (2) anxious, aggrieved housewife. 'huswife' is Shakespeare's regular form (pronounced 'hussif', here with play on 'hussy' = light woman = the poet's mistress).

2 feathered creatures barnyard animals (chicken, ducks, geese). Booth suggests that 'feathered creatures' may be metaphorical for the 'dandified rivals – the popinjays' who vied with the poet for his mistress's favours. It has also been suggested that the 'feathered creature' who tries to break away may refer to the poet's 'friend' (see 133–4), the 'better angel' of the following sonnet.

2 broke away that had broken away, escaped (from an enclosure). For the metaphorical implications, see 7 n. below. On 'broke' as a past participle, see Abbott 343.

3 Sets . . . babe i.e. abandons or neglects her child (= the poet) in order to chase after other more attractive interests.

3 all swift dispatch all possible speed or haste. 'swift' is merely intensive, being implicit in 'dispatch'.

4 the thing i.e. the 'feathered creature' (2). 'thing' was frequently used of animate creatures at this time, but it may be used here intentionally to derogate and generalise the object of her 'dispatch'.

4 would have stay wishes to retain (in her control).

5 holds . . . chase chases or hunts after her (a hunting idiom).

6 Cries (And) calls out (the 'child' weeping as he 'cries').

6–7 busy care . . . follow (1) active, (2) anxious concern or solicitude is intent upon pursuing. 'busy' may also carry a suggestion of undue activity. Compare 'careful' (1).

7 that i.e. 'the thing' (4). Compare 'that' in line 9.

7 flies . . . face flees or runs away ahead of her as she advances in pursuit. As Kerrigan notes, following a suggestion of Booth's, Shakespeare here 'mixes two stock idioms – "flee from the face of" and "before the face of" (meaning "in the sight of") – to suggest the fowl's ability to stay in sight but out of reach'. On a metaphorical level (i.e. a lover trying to escape from his former mistress's toils or a new but unresponsive lover), I think the phrase may also be taken as carrying some sense of 'flees from the sight of her face', a 'face' that has been described as 'so foul' in 137.12. As Booth notes, 'flies' has special relevance to the 'flight' of a 'feathered creature'.

8 Not prizing Not caring about or valuing (as she should).

8 poor needy, dependent.

9 So In the same way (syntactically answering 'as' in line 1).

9 that i.e. a former or, perhaps, a prospective lover, who is trying to escape.

10 afar from far, at a great distance.

11 catch thy hope (1) capture your hoped-for quarry; (2) satisfy your sexual desires or 'will' (anticipating 'have thy Will' in line 13).

12 play the mother's part perform the duty proper to a mother. In terms of common theatrical idiom, however, the phrase suggests that she should at least 'play the role of a mother' even if she is only acting a 'part', dissimulation being characteristic of the poet's mistress.

12 kind gentle, generous, nurturing (as a natural (= 'kind') mother should be).

13 So Under such circumstances. The couplet, summarising lines 9–12, cravenly admits that the poet is content to cast himself in the role of the often satirised 'happy cuckold'.

13 have (1) possess; (2) enjoy sexually. See 129.6, 10 nn.

13 thy Will (1) your Will (the person referred to as 'that' in line 9, whose name is Will[iam]); (2) me, your poet (whose 'name is Will' (136.14)); (3) your carnal desires, lust. See the headnote to 135 and 135.2 n.

14 still silence, quiet. Compare the couplet with the poem by Breton quoted in the headnote to 135 – the woman's 'Ohs' and the child's 'Ahs' are both 'hushed'.

Sonnet 144

Although 144, like 143, treats a triangular love relationship (here specifically poet, mistress, and 'friend' as in 133–4 and, much earlier, in 41–2), the intensity of mood and tone is startlingly different, linking it with the emotional ferocity of 129. 144, however, focuses 129's more general indictment of lust in a directly personal way and introduces the corrosive element of sexual jealousy, which, like Othello's, threatens to devour the poet. Leslie Fiedler ('Some contexts of Shakespeare's Sonnets', in *The Riddle of Shakespeare's Sonnets*, 1962, pp. 60–6) discusses 144 as 'the thematic key to the entire sequence'. Adams suggests (see Rollins, I, 370) that 144 is imitated or parodied by Samuel Rowlands in *The Letting of Humours Blood* (1600), Epigram 15.

The case for considering the version of 144 printed in *The Passionate Pilgrim* (1599) as representing an earlier Shakespearean version of the Q text is generally less persuasive than that for 138. The differences are comparatively slight (see collation), of a kind often found in careless transcriptions, but the likelihood that Jaggard, the publisher, derived it from the same manuscript source as 138 may perhaps be admitted as strengthening the argument for Shakespeare's revising hand.

1 Two loves . . . despair i.e. I have two beloveds, of whom one affords me (1) happiness, solace, (2) support, the other, hopeless grief.

2–3 Shakespeare here is clearly thinking in terms of the morality play or psychomachia tradition, in which Mankind, as the central character, is subjected to the promptings of personified Virtues and Vices, a tradition that received its most famous development in Marlowe's *Dr Faustus* (*c.* 1592), in which (1.2, etc.) a 'Good Angel' and an 'Evil Angel' try to influence Faustus's thought and action, the 'Good Angel', unlike the earlier moral Virtues, without success. Compare Henry Porter, *The Two Angry Women of Abington* (1599), sig. E4ᴾ: 'They say, every man hath two spiritis attending on him, eyther good or bad.'

spirits incorporeal, supernatural beings, capable, under certain circumstances, of making themselves visible to mortal sight; here used figuratively to refer to the essential inner characters of the poet's 'Two loves'.

2 suggest me still continually ('still') tempt, prompt, or solicit me (to good or evil).

3 better angel i.e. the better of the 'two spirits' (2) in a moral and intellectual sense. Compare 'worser' (4).

3 man right fair i.e. most probably the same as the 'friend' referred to in 133–4 and the young man addressed in 1–126. 'right fair' = very or uprightly beautiful, just, equitable, gentle, morally unblemished, light or pale complexioned, blond.

4 worser spirit i.e. the 'female evil' of line 5 and 'bad angel' of line 14 (= the poet's mistress addressed in most of the sonnets beginning with 127 and perhaps the same woman referred to in 41–2). 'spirit' is here, as often, monosyllabic. Compare *Temp.* 4.1.26–8: 'the strong'st suggestion [compare 'suggest' in line 2] / Our worser genius [= bad angel] can, shall never melt / Mine honor into lust'. 'spirit' may here be intentionally pejorative (in contrast to 'angel' in line 3), since 'spirit' was often used to mean an 'evil spirit', an emissary of the Devil.

4 coloured ill of an ill or bad complexion (i.e. of a 'black' or swarthy colouring, the Dark Lady; compare 130.5–6). The woman's 'ill' colouring, however, should be understood as an outward and visible sign of an inward evil disposition, which, by a kind of metonymy, is used as a foil to the 'fair[ness]' of the 'better angel' in all its several senses (see 'better angel' 3 n. above).

5 To win . . . hell In order, betimes ('soon'), to subdue or reduce me to a state like that of hell (i.e. arouse my jealousy, make me endure 'a hell of time' (120.6)). Compare *Wiv.* 2.2.291: 'See the hell of having a false woman!' For a possible reference here to the game of barley-break, see 12 n. below.

6 side So *The Passionate Pilgrim* and all later editors (except Lintott); Q reads 'sight', which in the immediate context makes possible, if weaker, sense, but affords an unacceptable rhyme with 'pride' in line 8. 'sight' may be merely a compositorial misreading of 'side' (graphically difficult to explain), but I conjecture that 'sight' preserves an early stage in the composition of the sonnet when Shakespeare rhymed 'sight' with some word like 'slight' (= sleight = cunning, deceit), a word that fits the context perfectly, and that the manuscript from which Q was printed, though corrected to 'pride' in line 8, retained 'sight' through carelessness or unclearly marked substitution.

7 would wishes to.

7 saint (1) angel (in biblical usage); (2) beloved (compare *Rom.* 1.5.97–105). The usual roles are reversed, the 'beloved' being a man. Compare Sidney, *Astrophil and Stella* (1591), Song 5, 81: 'I say thou art a Devill, though Clothd in Angel's shining.'

8 purity innocence, chastity (fitting to a 'saint' (7)). An allowable hyperbole, given the stark distinction being drawn between the poet's 'better angel' and his 'worser spirit' or 'female evil'.

8 foul (1) ugly, 'coloured ill' (4), i.e. not 'fair' (3); (2) wicked, evil. *The Passionate Pilgrim* reads 'faire pride', 'faire' being used ironically, implying a 'fairness' that disguises an evil 'pride'. 'foul' may represent Shakespeare's second thoughts.

8 pride (1) ostentation; (2) sexual desire, lust; (3) arrogance. For 'lust' compare *Oth.* 3.3.404: 'As salt as wolves in pride'. As Booth observes, Pride (the worst of the Seven Deadly Sins) was 'preeminently the Devil's sin'.

9 And whether that And whether or not it is true that.

9 fiend devil, a 'worser spirit' (4), like the woman who is trying to seduce the poet's 'better angel' (3).

10 Suspect...tell I may suspect but not know for certain ('directly tell'). 'directly' may also carry the sense of 'immediately'. Compare Othello's anguished uncertainty when faced with Iago's charges of unfaithfulness against Desdemona (3.3.333–90).

11 But being...friend But both being (1) alienated, (2) absent from me (and) both being a friend to the other. Compare 61.14. *The Passionate Pilgrim* reads 'For being both to me; both, to each friend,', a reading that changes the meaning to 'Because both being a friend to me (and) both a friend to each other' and loses (or at least blurs) the immediate reason for the poet's 'guess' in line 12. Rather than a Shakespearean first-thought, the *Passionate Pilgrim* version here suggests a rather fumbling attempt to recall (or perhaps clarify) the rather packed and difficult Q line.

12 I guess . . . hell I think or imagine ('guess') my 'better angel' (3) to be having sexual inter-

course with my 'worser spirit' (4) (i.e. his penis in her vulva = 'hell'; see 119.2 n. and 129.14 n.). As Massey first suggested, Shakespeare may also be playing (as in line 5) on the term 'hell' as used in the game of barley-break. Ringler (Sidney, *Poems*, p. 495) describes the game: 'In the country game of barley-break the two couples at either end of the field attempt to change partners without being caught by the couple in the middle (called hell). The couple in the middle must hold hands while chasing the others, and if they catch any one member of an opposing couple before they meet as partners, that pair must take their place in hell.' Contemporary accounts indicate that the game was often made the pretext for sexual indulgence (see Rollins, I, 371).

13 This line essentially rephrases line 10.

14 fire my...out i.e. infect my 'good angel' with the burning pain of venereal disease (Rollins). This is surely the primary meaning, though 'fire out' may partially disguise this under the much less pejorative sense 'cast out' or 'drive away'. The idiom probably derives from the common practice of smoking foxes out of their holes; compare *Lear* 5.3.22–3: 'He that parts us shall bring a brand from heaven, / And fire us hence like foxes.' For the association of 'fire' and 'burning' with venereal disease, compare *Lear* 4.6.124–9 (quoted in 119.2 n.) and Everard Guilpin, *Skialetheia* (1598), Epigram 39, 'Of Chrestina'.

Sonnet 145

Formally, like 99 and 126, though in a different way, 145 is an anomaly; it is written in tetrameters and in this respect seems to be unique among English sonnets of the period, unless we admit Sir Arthur Gorges's Sonnet 60 written in a four-stress non-English metre. But 145 has proved an embarrassment to critics and editors for more substantive reasons. A playful, neatly turned trifle, 145 conveys no sense of serious emotional involvement or complication, and the richly ambivalent associative language we commonly find in Shakespeare's sonnets is notably absent. Moreover, its sudden 'intrusion' between 144 and 146 (both weighty and 'serious' sonnets) is difficult to explain or justify, particularly so because the normal, kindly disposition attributed to the woman addressed (see lines 4–7) seems so inappropriate to the Dark Lady as she is usually characterised in earlier and later sonnets. One solution to account for the comparative inferiority of this sonnet (aside from denying Shakespeare's authorship – an easy way out embraced by a number of earlier critics) has been proposed by Andrew Gurr ('Shakespeare's first poem: Sonnet 145' in *Essays in Criticism*, 21 (1971), 221–6), who argues that 145 is a piece of juvenilia, dating from 1582, in which Shakespeare addresses his future wife, Anne Hathaway, and puns on her name in line 13 ('hate away'). That Anne was indeed of a 'merciful' disposition Shakespeare's hastily arranged marriage testifies. Both Booth and Kerrigan find Gurr's argument persuasive, and Booth carries it further by tentatively suggesting a play on 'Anne' in 'And saved my life' ('And' being often pronounced 'an' at this time in informal speech). Even if we accept 145 as Shakespeare's prentice work, its inclusion among the Dark Lady series still remains a problem. It is possible, of course, to spin various hypothetical answers as to how and why, but only one point, as Booth and Kerrigan stress, is clear: whoever was responsible for its present position must have known the Sonnets intimately and chose the place where 145's light and conventional amatory use of the theme of damnation and salvation might seem to set up superficial, if misleading, resonances with the same theme, treated with strong emotional engagement, in 144 and 146 (145 echoes three key words in 144 – 'fiend', 'heaven', 'hell').

1 Love's i.e. Venus's (rather than Cupid's).

2 'I hate' Compare 142.1–5, where 'lips' are also accused of expressing 'hate'.

3 The use of a heavy stop (a colon in Q) at the end of line 3, which fractures the first quatrain and attaches line 4 as a dependent clause to the second quatrain, occurs elsewhere only in 154.4–5 and may, perhaps, suggest early work. Such fracturing does occur, however, very occasionally in the second or third quatrain (see 35.11–12, 89.7–8, 99.7–8, 111.7–8, 112.11–12, 154.11–12).

3 languished pined, suffered. Lovers conventionally 'languished' from the effects of unrequited love.

4 state condition. The first quatrain has been criticised for its monosyllabic rhymes, all rhyming on the same vowel sound, an infelicity that has been seen as another indication of early work. Perhaps so, but the same kind of vowel repetition in monosyllabic rhymes, though rare, may be paralleled elsewhere in the Sonnets (see 9.1–4, 12.1–4, 122.9–12).

5 Straight Immediately, directly.

5 mercy compassion, forbearance. In conventional sonnet parlance the request for the beloved's 'mercy' usually implied the desire for sexual favours.

6 ever sweet always (1) kind, generous, (2) sweetly or kindly (with play on 'sweet' = melodious, pleasing).

7 Was used in giving (1) Was employed in granting; (2) Was accustomed to give.

7 gentle doom not harsh or severe (i.e. mild or merciful) judgement.

8 it i.e. 'that tongue' (6).

8 anew to greet speak in a new (hence friendly or loving) way (to me).

9 altered with an end changed by adding a conclusion or ending (i.e. the 'not you' of line 14).

10–11 gentle day . . . fiend 'gentle' here carries the sense of 'not threatening', the clear light of 'day'

being contrasted with the black terrors of the 'night', which, like a 'fiend', flees to its home in hell with the coming of dawn. Compare *Rape of Lucrece*, 1081–3: 'And solemn night with slow sad gait descended / To ugly hell, when lo the blushing morrow / Lends light to all fair eyes that light will borrow.' As Booth notes, the regular progression of night and day was often used to express inevitability (compare *Ham.* 1.3.79) or, as here, hope (compare Tilley N164: 'After night comes the day', and *Mac.* 4.3.240).

12 is flown fled ('flown' suggesting the winged flight of an evil spirit (= 'fiend' = devil; compare *Shr.* 1.1.88: 'fiend of hell')).

13–14 'I hate' . . . 'not you' i.e. she cast off, or distanced herself from, the concept 'hate', inherent in the two words 'I hate', by joining them with two other words, 'not you', thus saving my life. In other words, 'I hate' now implies 'I love'. Shakespeare plays a similar word-game in *Rape of Lucrece*, 1534–40. Michael Drayton (*Mortimeriados* (1596), lines 2871–7) offers a rather striking parallel, which probably owes something to the passage just cited in *Lucrece* (compare line 2872 with *Rape of Lucrece*, 1536), to the final conceit in lines 9–14:

Now shee begins to curse the King her Sonne,
The Earle of *March* then comes unto her mind,
Then shee with blessing ends what shee begun,
And leaves the last part of the curse behind,
  Then with a vowe shee her revenge doth bind:
Unto that vowe shee ads a little oth,
Thus blessing cursing, cursing blessing both.

For the suggested puns in 'hate away' and 'And', see the headnote.

Sonnet 146

Sonnet 146 is generally acknowledged to be one of the great sonnets. Clearly related to a long medieval literary tradition of 'debates' or dialogues between the Soul and Body (for contemporary examples, see 'A Dialogue betweene the Soule and the Body' in Francis Davison's *A Poetical Rhapsody* (1602), ed. H. E. Rollins, 1931, 1, 197, the opening lines of which read 'Ay me, poore Soule, whom bound in sinful chains / This wretched body keepes against my will' (compare line 1); and Sidney's debate between Reason and Passion, beginning 'Thou Rebell vile [i.e. Passion], come, to thy master yelde', in *Arcadia* (1590), pp. 339–40), it draws, as they do, from various New Testament Pauline passages on the proper relations to be observed between spirit and flesh (deny or moderate the flesh to nourish and save the spirit). For a treatment of body and soul in neo-Platonic terms, see Castiglione, *The Courtier* (1561), pp. 304 ff. Many critics have seen 146 as Shakespeare's most explicit expression of orthodox Christian values and most of his contemporaries would surely have accepted it as such. But, as nearly always in the Sonnets, there are

possible ambiguities that have led more recent criticism to find in it a complex mingling (not perhaps
entirely fused) of both early Christian and human-
ist attitudes (see Michael West, 'The Christian basis
of Shakespeare's Sonnet 146', *SQ* 19 (1968), 355–
65, and Booth, pp. 507–17). Like 121, 146 is a personal meditation (i.e. 'my sinful earth', not 'our sinful earth'), here, however, involving issues of life
and death, salvation and possible damnation; as a
result the appropriateness of its position in the Dark
Lady series has been questioned. If, however, we
admit that 145 is, for whatever reason, an 'intrusion' (see headnote), it may be argued, I think, that
146 follows 144 naturally enough and focuses the
comparatively external conflict between the poet's
'better angel' and his 'worser spirit' in 144 on his
own inner spiritual and moral conflict – that, in a
sense, the poet's 'soul' and 'body' are internalised
projections of his 'better angel' and 'worser spirit'.
Moreover, the 'soul' and 'rebel pow'rs' of 146 may be
seen as anticipating, respectively, the 'reason' and the
'uncertain sickly appetite' of 147.5, 4 (see also 147.3
n.). In tone and manner 146 has been felt to show
affinities with the style of Donne. Specific influence
has also been suggested from Sidney's famous sonnet 'Leave me O Love, which reachest but to dust'
(not published until 1598) and, by Kerrigan, from a
mediocre sonnet (No. 28) in Bartholomew Griffin's
Fidessa (1596).

1 Poor soul . . . earth The poet here addresses his
'soul' as the vital, spiritual, and rational entity which
was generally believed to distinguish man from the
lower creation. As God-infused and immortal (Gen.
2.7: 'a living soul'), the soul was thought of as the
governing and informing 'centre' of man's physical,
hence mortal, body ('my sinful earth' = 'the dust of
the ground' (Gen. 2.7)), which, through the demands
of the bodily senses (i.e. the 'rebel pow'rs' of line
2), shared in common with the lower animals, kept
the two essential sides of man's nature (spiritual and
physical) in a state of constant conflict (see Rom.
7.22–4). 'Poor' = asking for or deserving pity (with
play on 'impoverished' as suffering 'dearth' (3)). For
a similar use of 'earth' and 'centre', compare *Rom.*
2.1.2: 'Turn back, dull earth, and find thy centre
out.'

2 [. . .] these . . . array It is generally agreed
that the compositor (or possibly the manuscript from
which Q was printed) inadvertently repeated the last
three words of line 1 at the beginning of line 2, thus
producing an extra-metrical (hexameter) and essentially unintelligible line. Some word or words, metrically disyllabic, which express some kind of interaction or relationship between the soul and the 'rebel
pow'rs' of the body seem to be called for, and editors, since Malone, have guessed valiantly, proposing
almost a hundred different readings (see collation for
a selection). Rather than privilege any one of these

emendations, it is better, I think, to indicate a textual
hiatus at the beginning of the line.

2 rebel pow'rs rebellious forces (i.e. the five bodily senses). 'rebel' implies civil insurrection against
a lord or master (= the soul). J. C. Maxwell (*N&Q*
14 (1967), 139) suggests that Shakespeare borrowed
the phrase from Daniel's *Cleopatra* (1594), ed. M.
Lederer: 'And sharply blaming of her rebell powres,
/ False flesh (sayth shee), and what dost thou conspire / With *Caesar* too . . .?'

2 array (1) clothe (the body being the 'clothes' of
the soul); (2) afflict, defile; (3) besiege (without lexical
authority in this absolute sense, but supported by the
military metaphor in 'rebel pow'rs'). The war/siege
metaphor is frequently used to figure the conflict
between spirit (or reason) and body. See, for example,
Spenser, *Faerie Queene*, II, xi, stanzas 1–2, and *Rape
of Lucrece*, 722–3: 'She [the soul] says her subjects
[the senses] with foul insurrection / Have batter'd
down her consecrated wall.'

3 pine within waste away, starve spiritually
within yourself.

3 suffer dearth submit painfully to privation or
famine (like the inhabitants in a besieged city (Kerrigan)). Booth suggests a possible phonal play on 'suffer death'.

4 Painting . . . gay Adorning, decking your body
('outward walls') at such dear cost ('costly') in a manner so showy, brightly-coloured, and (speciously)
attractive ('gay'). Both 'Painting' and 'gay' suggest
the duplicity of cosmetic art (compare 82.13 n.), and
the line as a whole images the sensual flourishing of
the 'outward' at the expense of the 'inner' (compare
'within' (3, 12)). It is important to note, however,
that the body does not act alone. 'Painting' modifies 'thou' (i.e. the soul) in line 3, thus making the
soul an accomplice of the body, a lord or governor
who has failed to exercise his rational faculties and
has pandered to the demands of the body instead
of controlling or moderating them. The faculties of
the soul, then, have allowed the body to usurp their
power and, in a sense, are responsible for the soul's
'dearth' (compare 151.7–8). Unless the soul is going
to suffer the pains of damnation for eternity, it must
nourish itself even though such nourishment has to
come at the expense of the body (see lines 9–14).

5 so large cost such excessive expense, expenditure. Compare 'this excess' (7).

5 having . . . lease The body, unlike the soul,
has a 'short lease' on life (i.e. its contract (= 'lease')
having a terminal date in death).

6 fading mansion i.e. ageing (hence, decaying)
body. 'mansion' looks back to 'outward walls' (4), the
body being the 'house' of the soul. Compare *Rape of
Lucrece*, 1170–2: 'Her [i.e. Lucrece's soul's] house is
sack'd, her quiet interrupted, / Her mansion batter'd
by the enemy, / Her sacred temple spotted, spoil'd,
corrupted . . .'

6 spend (1) expend, lay out; (2) waste, squander.

7 Shall worms ... excess i.e. shall worms (which will devour the body after death), the heirs ('inheritors') of this intemperance ('excess'; compare 'so large cost' (5), and 74.9–10). The worm was thought of as a symbol of degradation and the most contemptible of all creatures; see Ps. 22.6: 'But I am a worm, and not a man: a shame of men, and the contempt of the people' (Geneva).

8 charge (1) cost, expense; (2) ward in trust (i.e. the body, for which you act as guardian); (3) troublesome burden.

8 end (1) final reason or purpose (i.e. does the body exist only to become food for worms?); (2) dissolution in death; (3) aim (to consume the soul's substance in riotous or 'rich' (12) living). One answer to the question posed by 'Is this the body's end?' is 'no', since, according to Catholic and Anglican church doctrine, the body also had a kind of delayed immortality, being reunited with the soul at the Day of Judgement and becoming once again a 'whole man', the blessed, 'pure and incorruptible', in heaven, the damned in hell (see 1 Cor. 15.20–58, quoted in the burial service in the Book of Common Prayer). It is not clear, however, to what extent, if indeed any, Shakespeare allows for this doctrine in 146.

9–11 Compare Matt. 6.19–20: 'Lay not up treasure for yourselves upon the earth, where the moth and canker corrupt, and where thieves dig through, and steal. But lay up treasures for yourselves in heaven, where neither the moth nor canker corrupteth, and where thieves neither dig through, nor steal' (Geneva).

9 Then, soul ... loss i.e. in such circumstances, soul, nourish yourself on what you have in the past squandered on your servant, the body (this action constituting 'thy servant's loss'). Since the soul and body were thought of as interdependent, unequal but necessary to each other, a profligate body placed the soul in danger of eternal damnation (i.e. a kind of 'death').

10 that Refers to 'servant' (9).

10 pine Compare *LLL* 1.1.25: 'The mind shall banquet, though the body pine.'

10 aggravate thy store increase (literally, give added weight to) your (depleted) stock (of virtues). In other words, turn 'dearth' (3) to 'plenty' (= 'store').

11 Buy terms ... dross (1) Purchase, (2) gain ages of immortality ('terms divine') in exchange for ('in selling') hours (i.e. short periods) of worthless or impure pleasures ('dross' = literally, scum thrown off from metals in smelting). Compare *MV* 2.7.20: 'A golden mind stoops not to shows of dross.' As Booth notes, 'terms divine' may also suggest 'making a deal (= "terms") with God'.

12 fed nourished.

12 rich (1) sumptuously arrayed; (2) sensuously luxurious; (3) costly (at the expense of the soul).

Compare *Cym.* 1.6.15–17: 'All of her that is out of door most rich! / If she be furnish'd with a mind so rare, / She is alone th'Arabian bird.' Despite 'pine' in line 10, Shakespeare should not be interpreted as advocating that the soul revenge itself on the body by starving it, but that the body should be restored to its proper subordinate position as servant to the soul, a position that would benefit both of them, here as well as in the life to come.

13–14 Compare 1 Cor. 15.52–5 (in the Book of Common Prayer version): 'For the trump shall blow, and the dead shall rise incorruptible, and we shall be changed ... When this corruptible hath put on incorruption, and this mortal hath put on immortality: then shall be brought to pass the saying that is written: Death is swallowed up in victory: Death where is thy sting? Hell where is thy victory?'; and 1 Cor. 15.26: 'The last enemy that shall be destroyed, is death.'

13 So shalt ... men i.e. in nourishing or feeding itself by bringing the body into subjection (i.e. 'thy servant's loss' (9)), the body being Death's staple diet ('feeds on men'), the soul will thus feed on (and, on the Last Day, destroy) Death. Note that 'feed on' echoes 'swallowed up' in 1 Cor. 15.54 and is repeated in 147.3.

14 And Death ... then See the note on lines 13–14. Donne's famous sonnet (later than 146) 'Death be not proud ... Death thou shalt die', and Giles Fletcher the Younger, *Christ's Victory* (1610), stanza 76: 'But thus long Death hath liv'd, and now Death's selfe shall die.'

Sonnet 147

For suggested links between 146 and 147, see 146 headnote. On love as a sickness, compare 118.

1 My love The poet's passion for his mistress. See, however, 13–14 n. below.

1 longing still yearning, desiring incessantly (i.e. burning with the 'fever' of desire).

2, 3 that which i.e. the poet's burning desire (= 'My love' (1)) for his mistress.

2 nurseth nourishes, feeds.

3 Feeding on In parallel construction with 'longing' (1). 'Feeding on' here means 'devouring', 'eating up', not 'nourishing', and may be seen as looking back to the way 'worms' 'Eat up' the body in 146.7–8 as contrasted with the healthy 'feeding' of the soul in 146.11–12. Vendler suggests that 'Feeding' here makes 'Feeding' the most plausible reading with which to begin line 2 of 146.

3 preserve the ill protract the illness (= 'longer nurseth the disease' (2)).

4 Th'uncertain ... please (In order) to pamper ('please') the capricious, fickle, unhealthy, and corrupt ('uncertain sickly') desires of the body ('appetite').

5–12 Compare 129.6–9.

5 **reason** the rational faculty of the soul.

5 **physician to my love** i.e. the healing agent that should control or moderate the desires of 'My love' ((1) = sensual passion). Compare *Wiv.* 2.1.4–6: 'for though Love use Reason for his precisian, he admits him not for his counsellor'.

6 **prescriptions** . . . **kept** directions, injunctions are not observed, followed.

7 **Hath left me** Has abandoned me (to the delirium of 'a fever' (i.e. 'My love' (1)).

7–8 **I desperate** . . . **except** I, driven 'frantic mad' (10) and hopeless ('desperate'), now find by experience ('approve') that (sensual) desire, which medical science ('physic', in the role of 'reason') proscribed ('did except'), leads to death. A less likely, though possible, reading of line 8 would be to take 'physic' as the object of 'did except' and interpret as 'Desire which rules out physic is death.'

9–12 Like Dover Wilson and Booth, I retain the Q comma after 'unrest' in line 10 in place of the semicolon introduced by Capell (see collation) and regularly followed by later editors; syntactically, this makes line 10 introductory to lines 11–12. To clarify the construction I have inserted a comma after 'And' in line 10 to indicate that 'frantic . . . unrest' is to be taken as a phrase modifying 'My thoughts . . . discourse'.

9 **Past cure** . . . **care** I am beyond curing now that reason is beyond caring. Proverbial (see Tilley C921 and *LLL* 5.2.28), but, as Pooler notes, Shakespeare here inverts the proverb to mean 'Past care is past cure.'

10 **frantic mad** deliriously, wildly mad (in my love-fever).

10 **with evermore unrest** from everlasting, constant (inner) turmoil (the poet being 'Past cure' (9)). The Q form 'euer-more' appears to authorise this adjectival use of 'evermore' (not found elsewhere in Shakespeare or recorded by *OED*; compare 'oft predict' (14.8 and note)); as two words, 'ever more' (see collation), meaning 'constantly greater', would offer an easier, more idiomatic, reading.

11 **discourse** speech, talk (the expression of 'My thoughts').

12 **At random** . . . **expressed** Foolishly, idly ('vainly') uttered in a (1) haphazard, heedless, (2) uncontrolled, violent manner ('At random') at variance with ('from') the truth. Q's 'randon' (= random) at this time was still a commonly used variant form and is etymologically justified (from Old French *randon*); see *Venus and Adonis*, 940. The poet's frenzied state of mind is illustrated by the harshly extreme indictment of his mistress in the following couplet. Compare 140.9–10, where the poet fears that in his mad 'despair' he may 'speak ill' of his mistress.

13–14 The couplet suddenly shifts the earlier focus to a direct attack on his mistress ('thee'), 'My

love' (1) becoming, ironically, 'My beloved', an identification, however, that has been implicit in lines 1–12. The couplet also looks back to 131.12, 132.13–14, and 138.1–2; forward to 150.4 and, particularly, 152.13–14.

13 **For I . . . bright** (I have violated 'truth') because I have sworn that you are (1) beautiful, (2) desirable, (3) morally unblemished, (4) just, and thought of you (morally and physically) as a clear shining light ('bright', like day as contrasted with night). See preceding note.

14 **black . . . night** Proverbial: compare Tilley H397; *LLL* 4.3.250–1: 'Black is the badge of hell, / The hue of dungeons, and the school of night'; *Ham.* 3.3.94–5; and see 145.10–11 n. In 'black' and 'dark' the poet is, of course, not only referring to his mistress's moral nature, but playing on the 'blackness' of her physical appearance (see 127 headnote).

Sonnet 148

Sonnet 148 returns to the rather tiresome eye/mind theme last heard in 141 (see 137 headnote).

1 **O me!** Alas for me!

1 **what eyes . . . head** i.e. what has the passion of love done to my eyes? 'what eyes' = what kind of eyes.

2 **have no . . . sight** i.e. my seeing ('sight') does not correspond or agree with the truth of what it views. Compare 'false eyes' (5) and 150.3. 'have no correspondence' also suggests a failure in 'communication' on the part of the eyes.

3 **if they have** i.e. if my eyes do indeed see truly.

3 **where is . . . fled** where has my rational faculty ('judgement') withdrawn itself to. Compare 147.5–7: 'My reason . . . Hath left me.'

4 **censures** estimates, evaluates (without pejorative connotation).

4 **aright** justly, truly.

5 **that** i.e. my mistress.

5 **fair** See 147.13 n.

5 **false eyes dote** The eyes are 'false' because they 'dote' (= see in a deranged, love-sick way and 'have no correspondence with true sight' (2)).

6 **What means . . . so?** What does the rest of mankind ('the world') mean by saying that it (i.e. that my mistress is 'fair', physically and morally) is untrue ('not so')?

7 **If it be not** i.e. if it be not true that my mistress is 'fair'.

7 **well denote** clearly indicate or demonstrate (the truth) that.

8–9 **Love's eye . . . it?** Love's (doting) eye is not as trustworthy or honest ('so true') in judging (the beloved object) as (the eyes of) everyone else ('all men's' = 'the world' (6)); no, how can it be ('so true')? The Q pointing of line 8 (here followed, as by the majority of editors) has been criticised as being uncharacteristic of Shakespeare in the Sonnets (allowing a second heavily stressed caesura so near the end of a line) and as sacrificing, here, if not in line 9, a possibly intended pun on 'eye' = ay = yes. To meet these objections some editors have adopted Lettsom's conjecture (with slight variations; see collation) and read 'Love's eye is not so true as all men's no [*or* "No"]' – a reading that removes the late caesura and allows for the 'eye/ay' pun, though demanding from a reader some mental acrobatics. Such a reading is tempting, but Q's pointing, otherwise unexampled though it may be, makes clear sense and seems more likely to reflect manuscript copy than compositorial interference.

10 so vexed . . . tears so deeply distressed or afflicted by wakefulness and weeping. Sleeplessness and tears were conventionally the hall-mark of unrequited love.

11 No marvel then (It is) no wonder therefore.

11 mistake my view i.e. see reality falsely, misinterpret what I see. Compare 141.3–4 (where the 'heart' dotes despite the eyes' 'view').

12 The sun . . . clears i.e. even the sun itself ('the eye of heaven' (18.5)) is unable to see (the earth) till the overarching firmament ('heaven') is cleared of masking clouds. Compare 33.5–8 n.

13 cunning love clever, crafty passion of love (shading into a reference to his mistress in 'thy foul faults' in line 14).

13 blind i.e. unable to see truly (hence 'blind' to the truth).

14 well seeing i.e. seeing truly or 'aright' (4).

14 foul faults morally and physically ugly defects. Compare 'thy defect' (149.11).

Sonnet 149

Sonnet 149 continues the love/blindness theme of 148.13–14 – the poet loves his mistress despite her unworthiness in the eyes of the 'world' (148.6), a theme further developed in 150.

1 O cruel O cruel one (i.e. the poet's mistress). See 131.1 n.

2 When I . . . partake When I take your part against myself (i.e. against my own best interests). Compare 88.3 and 89.13–14, where the poet argues against himself on behalf of the youth.

3–4 Do I . . . myself Do I not think about you (so obsessively) that I (1) am oblivious to, (2) neglect myself (and my best interests)?

4 all tyrant . . . sake i.e. acting like a complete tyrant against myself on your behalf. The Q pointing (here retained) makes 'all tyrant' modify 'I' in line 3. Most editors, however, following Malone, treat 'all tyrant' (like 'O cruel' (1)) as a vocative addressed to the poet's mistress (= 'wholly tyrannous one'). A third possibility, suggested by Sewell and Capell, treats 'tyrant' as a vocative but takes 'all' as meaning 'wholly (forgot of myself)'. Since there is little to

choose among these readings, it seems best to keep the Q pointing.

5–6 Compare *H8* 2.4.27–34: 'When was the hour / I ever contradicted your desire? / Or made it not mine too? Or which of your friends / Have I not strove to love, although I knew / He were mine enemy? What friend of mine / That had to him deriv'd your anger did I / Continue in my liking?'

5 Who hateth . . . friend i.e. whoever hates you is no friend of mine. Compare Ps. 139.21: 'Do I not hate them, O Lord, that hate thee?' (Geneva).

6 fawn upon grovel before (for favours, like a dog).

7 lour'st frown, look angrily upon (= 'frown'st' (6)).

7–8 spend / Revenge . . . moan expend punishment ('spend Revenge') on myself by an immediate expression of grief ('with present moan') (for whatever it was that I had done to offend you). 'spend' may also convey the sense of 'revenge' wasted or squandered so far as its effect on his mistress is concerned.

9–10 What merit . . . despise What worthy quality do I (1) discern, (2) esteem in myself which is so (1) splendid, (2) presumptuous as to scorn your service (i.e. being your 'servant' = lover).

11 all my best i.e. all my finest qualities.

11 worship Conventionally a lover was supposed to 'worship' his mistress as though she were a divine being. Compare *Rom.* 1.5.93–107.

11 defect lack of worthy qualities and, perhaps, of beauty.

12 Commanded Controlled, compelled, dominated.

12 motion (1) movement; (2) bidding, instigation. Compare *Cor.* 5.6.39–40: 'He wag'd me with his countenance as if / I had been mercenary.'

13–14 As Tucker notes, commentators have been singularly silent on this enigmatic couplet (Rollins's Variorum, for example, records no comments on the lines). Tucker dismisses the couplet as 'either very obscure or impotent' and Booth notes that it 'seems inappropriate – uncalled for by what precedes it'. Commenting on line 14, Kerrigan says: 'The lady loves those who see and admire her, but the poet so admires that he cannot really see (compare Sonnet 148); he is, because uncritical, *blind* (as in 148.13), and (in her mind at least) to that extent unlovable. The psychology of shallow loving.' Excellent as this may be for line 14, it fails to account for the implications of 'But, love, hate on' in line 13. I would suggest a slightly different interpretation, one that takes the couplet as a whole as dismissive, expressing a (perhaps momentary) 'I don't care any more' attitude, an attitude that arises out of the poet's realisation that he has sunk so low in his abject subservience to his mistress that 'all [his] best' qualities. 'nobler part' (151.6), are submerged and that he has lost any feeling of self-respect (see lines 9–12). If taken in this sense, the couplet may be paraphrased as follows: 'Yet, love (i.e. his mistress), continue to disdain me, since I now realise what kind of a person you really are ("I know thy mind"): you (paradoxically) desire ("lov'st") only those who see clearly your "foul faults" (148.14 and compare 143.9), not someone like me who is "blind" to those faults and thus, too easy a mark, one who offers no challenge to your roving eye (139.6).' Like Shakespeare's Cressida, she is one of the 'daughters of the game' (see *Tro.* 4.5.54–63). Compare Lyly, *Euphues and his England* (1580), p. 66: 'But this is incident to women to love those that least care for them, and to hate those that most desire them.'

Sonnet 150

See the headnote to 149.

1 pow'r (1) (seemingly) supernatural authority (with possible reference to Cupid, the knavish god of Love; see 151.1); (2) innate capacity.

1 pow'rful might Essentially tautological ('might' = great power), but 'pow'rful' may be intended as an intensifier meaning 'overpowering' or 'insuperable'.

2 insufficiency defects, lack of worthy qualities (physical and moral). Compare 'thy defect' (149.11) and 'thy unworthiness' in line 13 below.

2 sway rule, command. Compare 'Commanded' (149.12).

3 give . . . sight Compare 148.2.

4 swear . . . day swear that a bright, 'fair' light does not set off or adorn (the beauty of) the day (by contrast with the powerful 'darkness' of the poet's mistress). Or, as Pooler puts it, 'swear that black is white, that you are lovely'. Compare 147.13–14 and *Rom.* 3.5.18–19: 'I am content, so thou wilt have it so. / I'll say yon grey is not the morning's eye.'

5–8 Compare *Ant.* 1.1.48–9: 'Fie, wrangling queen! / Whom every thing becomes . . .', and 2.2.235–9: 'Other women cloy / The appetites they feed, but she makes hungry / Where most she satisfies; for vildest things / Become themselves in her, that the holy priests / Bless her when she is riggish.'

5 Whence hast . . . ill From what source do you derive the power to make ill things seem becoming in you? 'Whence' looks back to 'from what pow'r' in line 1. The same thing is said of the youth in 40.13 and 96.7–8.

6 That in . . . deeds So that in the very worst of your actions ('refuse' = scum, dregs).

7 strength power, might (looking back to line 1).

7 warrantise of skill warranty or assurance of expertise (Ingram and Redpath) (i.e. you are always so clever or cunning in the way you exercise your 'strength').

8 thy worst . . . exceeds your worst (= 'refuse' (6)) transcends all the best qualities to be found in

others. Compare 114.7, where the poet's love for the youth creates 'every bad a perfect best'.

9–10 Malone compares Catullus, carmen 85: 'Odi et amo. quare id faciam, fortasse requiris. / nescio, sed fieri sentio et excrucior' (I hate and love. Why do I so, perhaps you ask. I know not, but I feel it, and I am in torment (Loeb)).

10 just cause of hate proper or valid reason for hating (what I 'hear and see' of you).

11 abhor shrink from in disgust, despise. Booth suggests a play on 'whore' (= bewhore, treat as a whore) and cites *Oth.* 4.2.161–2: 'I cannot say "whore." / It does abhor me now I speak the word.'

12 With others In company with others (who 'abhor' me).

12 my state my mental and emotional condition (made 'frantic mad' (147.10) by unrequited love). There is also perhaps some reference in 'state' to the poet's comparatively low social position (see 29.2 n.).

13–14 The couplet is open to two interpretations: if your very unworthiness caused me to love you, (1) I should be beloved by you for my generous nature (in loving one unworthy of love); (2) I am all the *more* a fit lover for you, since *I* am doing an unworthy thing in loving you (Tucker). The first sense (1) should probably be considered primary. There is perhaps some sexual innuendo in 'raised love in me', anticipating the obviously sexual implications of 'rise' and 'stand' in 151.9, 12, 14.

Sonnet 151

Possible, though slight, links, between 151 and 150 are suggested in the notes to 150.1, 13. The frankly open bawdry of 151, particularly lines 5–14, seems an admission that the poet's 'love' for his mistress, never clearly defined, is essentially nothing but lust, an 'expense of spirit in a waste of shame' (129.1). See lines 5–6 and note below.

1 Love . . . young (1) Cupid (compare 'Love is a babe' (115.13) and 'The little Love-god' (154.1)); (2) the passion of love in its early stage of irrational, amoral infatuation.

1–2 conscience . . . conscience Plays (as in line 13) on two senses of 'conscience': (1) moral sense, scruple, compunction; (2) knowledge (in the present context primarily 'guilty knowledge' associated with sex, i.e. 'born of love'). Compare the condition of Adam and Eve after the Fall (Gen. 3.7): 'Then the eyes of them both were opened, and they knew they were naked' (Geneva). Booth suggests that underlying line 1 there is some reference to the proverbial Latin tag, *penis erectus non habet conscientiam*, and to the proverbs 'It is impossible to love and be wise' and 'Love is without reason' (Tilley L558 and L517).

2 not not that.

3 gentle cheater i.e. the poet's mistress. For a similar oxymoron, compare 'tender churl' (1.12).

Like 'sweet' in line 4, 'gentle' may be dismissed as conventionally complimentary or as used with an intentionally ironic edge.

3 urge not my amiss (1) do not charge (me) with, (2) do not provoke or incite offence or sin (in me) (Willen and Reed). (1), as Booth observes, is primary in the context of line 4, but (2) is called into play by line 5.

4 Lest guilty . . . prove Lest your sweet self prove to be responsible ('guilty . . . prove') for my faults (= 'amiss' (3)). The line may also be read to mean: 'Lest your sweet self turn out to be guilty of the same faults as mine' (compare 142.3–4), but in context with lines 5–6 the first reading seems primary. For other examples of apparent 'endearments' (like 'sweet self' (4)) in generally pejorative contexts, see 35.14, 40.9, 95.13, and 139.6.

5–6 For thou . . . treason Because when you betray my love ('me'), I betray my 'soul' (7) or mind ('nobler part') by allowing my coarse, overfed ('gross') body to commit treason (by turning my 'love' to mere lust, the spirit (as in lines 7–14) being swamped in sense). Compare the treatment of 'soul' and 'body' in 146.

7 soul spiritual being, mind.

7 he The body is personified as being addressed.

8 Triumph in love Be victorious or glory in reaping love's spoils (with probable reference to a Roman 'triumph' celebrating a victorious commander's return to Rome with the spoils of war).

8 flesh the body with its sensual appetites (which, by metonymy, in lines 9–14 figures as the penis and is personified as 'He' in line 11).

8 stays . . . reason does not wait to be told anything further ('reason' = speech, telling, or grounds for action).

9–14 The openly sexual implications here given to 'rising/rise', 'point', 'Proud', 'stand', and 'fall' are obvious. For the libertine attitude to 'love' as sensual gratification, compare Mercutio's lines in *Romeo and Juliet* (2.1.17–38), particularly, for the present context, lines 23–9: 'This cannot anger him [Romeo]; 'twould anger him / To raise a spirit in his mistress' circle, / Of some strange nature, letting it there stand / Till she had laid it and conjur'd it down. / . . . My invocation / Is fair and honest; in his mistress' name / I conjure only but to raise up him.'

9 rising at thy name The overt reference is to sexual erection, but, as Booth notes, underlying the phrase is a strong suggestion of the black art of conjuring, through which the conjuror could supposedly raise up a diabolic spirit by calling on certain potent names associated with the powers of darkness (compare Marlowe's *Dr Faustus* 1.3). Mercutio, in his mock conjuration (see preceding note), playfully summons Romeo to appear by invoking 'his mistress' name' ('I conjure thee by Rosaline's bright eyes' (2.1.17)).

9 point out thee Kerrigan suggests that as the penis stiffens it points (like the needle of a compass) unerringly at the poet's mistress (with play on 'point' = prick = penis).

10 triumphant prize triumphal spoils (see 'Triumph' (8 n. above)).

10 Proud of this pride (1) Aroused or swollen with this sexual desire; (2) Glorying in this 'triumphant prize'. With (1) compare the term 'proud flesh' (= swollen flesh) and *Rape of Lucrece*, 705: 'While Lust is in his pride'. See above, pp. 10–11.

11 poor drudge abject servant (in satisfying his mistress's sexual demands).

12 To stand . . . side The sexual meaning is primary: 'fall', as opposed to 'stand' (= have an erection), = become limp after having 'died' ('die' = to experience orgasm; compare *Tro.* 3.1.116–24). But in a less sexually laden context the line might be read to mean that the poet will champion his mistress's side in all matters of concern to her ('stand in thy affairs'), and if she 'falls' he will die in her company ('by thy side').

13 No want . . . it Do not consider it (in me) a lack of (1) moral scruple, (2) knowledge, understanding (of what kind of person my mistress really is).

13–14 I call / Her 'love' I give her the name '(my) love'. This, following Dyce's pointing, is the most commonly accepted reading. Q reads 'I call, / Her loue,' and the comma after 'call', isolating 'Her loue,', may have been placed there to indicate a similar sense. It is possible, however, if again omitting the comma after 'call', that Shakespeare intended us to read 'I call / Her love' as meaning 'I call upon (or invite) her love', thus picking up the conjuring metaphor in line 9 (compare *1H4* 3.1.52: 'I can call spirits from the vasty deep').

14 for whose dear love for the sake of whose (1) precious, (2) costly, debilitating love.

14 rise and fall See 12 n. above. The couplet suggests that nothing is left of the poet's 'love' but the mechanical act of coition.

Sonnet 152

As apparently the last of the 'Dark Lady' series, and in contrast to the cynically sensual, Mercutio-like 'love' expressed in 151, 152 may be taken as the poet's final statement of moral revulsion against a 'love' that has led to the loss of 'all my honest faith' (8). A kind of microcosm, it concentrates and indicts as 'so foul a lie' against 'truth' (14) the whole process and present status of the poet's 'love' for the Dark Lady, gathering together most of the informing themes in 127–51 (love/hate, constancy/inconstancy, truth suborned, oaths/vows sworn and forsworn, blindness of soul/mind/heart, and false-seeing eyes). More than any other of the Sonnets, 152 hammers home its theme (false swearing, perjury) through syntactical and verbal repetition.

1 **I am forsworn** I am perjured (1) in having broken my marriage vow by committing adultery (i.e. 'In loving thee'), (2) in having broken the vows of constancy sworn to my 'friend' (see 133, 134). The poet may be referring to either (1) or (2), even perhaps to both, in which case, like his mistress, he is 'twice forsworn'. But in the context of the specific reference to 'bed-vow' in line 3, (1) should perhaps be considered as primary.

2 **to me love swearing** in swearing that you (1) did love me, (2) do love me.

3–4 **In act ... bearing** These lines multiply the ambiguities of lines 1–2 and are open to different interpretations depending on who is being referred to. As here pointed (see collation), and considering 'twice forsworn' (2) and 'two oaths' (5), they may be read as referring to the actions of the woman in relation to her husband and the poet: 'In committing adultery you have broken your marriage vows to your husband (by loving me), and you have torn up your newly contracted vow of constancy to me by resolving to harbour, after having professed this new love ("after ... bearing"), a newly conceived hatred toward me (i.e. you not only don't love me anymore but now hate and despise me).' Or alternatively, 'after new love bearing' may be taken to introduce a fourth party (e.g. the 'friend' or another lover), and thus to mean: 'after carrying on a new love affair with some other person'.

3 **In act** Refers here specifically to sexual intercourse; compare 'lust in action' (129.2) and 'act of sport', 'act of shame' (Oth. 2.1.227, 5.2.211).

3 **bed-vow broke** marriage vow broken (by adultery) Compare Rape of Lucrece, 809: 'The impious breach of holy wedlock vow'. For the form 'broke', see Abbott 343.

3 **new faith torn** The image, as Tucker suggests, may be that of tearing up or rending a legal contract signed under oath. Compare LLL 4.3.281: 'Our loving lawful, and our faith not torn', 'faith' = sworn constancy, faithfulness.

4 **In vowing** By resolving to harbour (see OED Vow v¹ 3).

4 **bearing** (1) professing; (2) carrying on (with probable play on 'bearing the weight' of a new lover).

5–14 These lines shift the focus of the poet's bitter indictment from the Dark Lady's inconstancy to the poet's complete moral bankruptcy in having for so long allowed himself to reiterate 'so foul a lie' against 'truth' (i.e. 'true love'). Compare Tilley F107: 'He finds fault with others and does worse himself', and LLL 4.3.129–30: 'Come, sir, you blush; as his your case is such; / You chide at him, offending twice as much.'

6 **most** most greatly (though possibly meant to be understood as 'more greatly of the two').

7 **For** Because (as again in lines 9 and 13).

7 **but to misuse thee** merely in order to (1) deceive for the purpose of debauching you, (2) revile you, (3) falsely make use of such terms as 'love', 'truth', and 'constancy' (see line 10) in describing you (i.e. misrepresent you as praiseworthy). As Booth observes, the underlying primacy of (3) only becomes clear in lines 9–12.

8 **all my ... lost** i.e. I have lost all my moral integrity ('honest faith') through my relationship with you. A possible alternative reading ('I have lost all my sincere belief in you') does not fit the context.

9 **deep oaths ... deep kindness** solemn, strong, weighty oaths ... great, sincere kindliness, affectionate nature (with ironic suggestion). Compare 'deep oaths' (LLL 1.1.23). 'deep kindness' may also carry a sexual innuendo as in Per. 4.6.6–7: 'do me the kindness of our profession [i.e. prostitution]'.

10 **Oaths ... constancy** i.e. oaths affirming the sincerity ('truth') and steadfastness ('constancy') of your love. Ironically, except for some general 'oaths' relating to the Dark Lady's physical charms (e.g. 127.13–14, 130.13–14, 132.13–14), 'oaths' praising her moral qualities are essentially lacking (see, however, 147.13); usually the poet attacks his mistress for 'inconstancy' and want of 'truth'.

11 **to enlighten thee** in order to make you appear as a clear, bright, shining light (i.e. not 'black' or 'dark' in moral or physical terms). Lines 13–14 are the poet's bitter comment on such 'enlightenment'. Note that 'enlighten' looks back to 'and thought thee bright' in 147.13, a recollection of the couplet of 147 expressly picked up again in lines 13–14 below.

11 **gave eyes to blindness** (1) gave away, sacrificed (my) eyes and became blind (refusing to see his mistress as she really was); (2) in (my) blindness (to your faults) I gave free rein to my imagination (thinking what I wanted to believe). Lines 11–14 pick up the false eye/heart theme treated in 137, 141, 148.

12 **made them ... see** (my mind/heart) forced the eyes to deny the truth ('swear against') of what it was ('the thing') they were seeing. Often used neutrally of entities or persons, 'thing' (here = the woman) may be intended to convey a sense of contempt (compare Ham. 4.2.28–31).

13 **For I ... fair** Repeats verbatim the opening words of the couplet in 147, but the statement is now used to introduce a significantly different conclusion: the poet's own, not his mistress's, moral culpability. For the possible shades of meaning in 'fair', see 147.13.

13–14 **more perjured eye ... lie** (1) (my) eye (particularly my 'mind's eye') is all the more deeply perjured in having sworn such a grossly shameful lie against the truth (i.e. for swearing that 'Fair is foul, and foul is fair' (Mac. 1.1.11)); (2) (my) eye is more perjured (than yours) in having sworn such a grossly shameful lie against the truth. For (2), compare 'I am perjured most' (6). Until recently, the majority of editors, following Sewell (see collation), have read 'more perjured I', a reading that may, indeed, clarify the obvious pun in 'eye' on 'I' and, probably, on 'ay' (see 136.4 n. and 148.8–9 n.), but fails to emphasise (as the Q text does) the special relevance of the 'eye' metaphor in relation to lines 11–12, where the 'eyes' have specifically been accused of being 'perjured'. Moreover, 'eye' must surely have been the reading in the manuscript copy, compositorial conversion of 'I' to 'eye' being extremely unlikely.

Sonnet 153

Sonnets 153 and 154, anacreontic in character, are ultimately alternative variations on the central conceit of an epigram in the Greek Anthology (Planudean Anthology, IX, 627) attributed to Marcianus Scholasticus (fifth century A.D.). Since, however, it is highly unlikely that Shakespeare drew directly on Marcianus's epigram (first printed in 1494; first known Latin translation, 1603) other possible intermediate sources have been sought among a significant number of Latin (of which an early one, by Regianus, may be independent of Marcianus), Italian, and French adaptations of the epigram, some of which offer occasional details that seem to be closer to Shakespeare's treatment than to that of Marcianus (see James Hutton, 'Analogues of Shakespeare's Sonnets 153–54: contributions to the history of a theme', *MP* 38 (1940–1), 385–403). After an exhaustive examination of all known analogues, however, Hutton is forced to conclude that 'Shakespeare's immediate source still eludes us' (p. 403). Marcianus's epigram (in Hutton's translation) is as follows: 'Beneath these plane trees, detained by gentle slumber, Love slept, having put his torch in the care of the Nymphs; but the Nymphs said one to another: "Why wait? Would that together with this we could quench the fire in the hearts of men." But the torch set fire even to the water, and with hot water thenceforth the Love-Nymphs fill the bath.' Hutton also argues persuasively (pp. 400–2) that Shakespeare probably composed 154 before 153. Shakespeare's authorship of both sonnets has been questioned by a number of earlier critics, a claim generally discounted by recent criticism. For discussion of the inclusion and placement in Q of 153 and 154 and their probable underlying relation to the Dark Lady series (127–52), see the Introductory Note, p. 107 above, and 7–14 n. below.

1 **Cupid** i.e. 'The boy' (10), 'The little Love-god' (154.1). See 151.1 n.

1 **brand** Cupid was sometimes pictured as bearing a flaming torch (see Ovid, *Remedia Amoris* 699–700), here described as 'love-kindling' (3) and 'heart-inflaming' (154.2). Clearly a phallic symbol = *penis erectus*.

2 **A maid of Dian's** One of the virgins attending on Diana, the goddess of chastity.

2 **this advantage found** took advantage of the opportunity offered.

3 **quickly steep** hastily souse, quench (extinguishing the 'fire'). Compare 154.8.

4 **valley-fountain** i.e. fountain in a valley (probably with play on the female pudenda; (compare 'well' (154.9)).

4 **ground** place (i.e. 'nearby', where Cupid was sleeping; compare 'by' (154.9)).

5 **borrowed** took (strictly, 'borrow' implies intention to repay, but see 'dateless' and 'still' in line 6).

5 **holy fire** 'holy' because Cupid was a god.

5 **Love** i.e. Cupid (as again in line 9). Some editors prefer to keep the unpersonified form (as in Q 'loue'), thus leaving specific reference open.

6 **dateless lively heat** endless and life-generating heat. Compare 'heat perpetual' (154.10). Some editors prefer to read 'dateless-lively', taking 'dateless' as adverbial. In the context of the underlying metaphor of coition in lines 3–7, 'heat' and 'fire' (in lines 3, 5) suggest 'heat of lust' (*Rape of Lucrece*, 706) or 'hot desire' (154.7, *Rape of Lucrece*, 691).

6 **still to endure** to last forever, 'dateless' renders 'still' essentially redundant.

7–14 These lines introduce the special turn that Shakespeare gives to the original conceit (see headnote): hot medicinal baths as a cure for disease, here the 'disease of love' (compare 154.11–14), with, however, probable covert reference to so-called 'sweating tubs' used in the treatment of venereal disease (see *MM* 3.2.57 and *Tro.* 5.10.55), a disease the poet seems to be suggesting he has contracted from his mistress (see the implication of 'fire out' in 144.14 n.). Shakespeare may have taken a hint from Sonnet 27 (imitated from Angeriano) in Giles Fletcher the Elder's *Licia* (1593) on his mistress bathing: 'The fountaine smoak'd, as if it thought to burne: . . . / I searcht the cause, and found it to be this, / She toucht the water, and it burnt with love, / Now by her meanes, it purchast hath that blisse, / Which all diseases, quicklie can remoove.' John Davies of Hereford (*The Scourge of Folly* (1610/11), 'Upon English Proverbes', No. 380. 1–4 (p. 49)) associates fire and water with venereal disease: '"Luce beares fire in th'on hand and water in th'other:" / But in her chaffendish beares both together; / Shee's "ambodexter, with both hands shee playes:" / But yet with both leggs she workes nights and dayes'; see also Guilpin cited in 144.14 n.

7 **grew** became. Compare 'Growing' (154.11).

7 **seething** boiling.

7 **which . . . prove** which to this day men find by experience to be.

8 **Against strange . . . cure** A potently effective remedy ('sovereign cure'; compare 'healthful remedy' (154.11)) against (1) extreme, (2) unusual,

exotic diseases ('strange maladies'). Compare *Venus and Adonis*, 916:"'Gainst venom'd sores the only sovereign plaster', 'strange' may also carry the sense of 'alien' or 'foreign', since Elizabethans tended to consider venereal disease a European (particularly Italian) import (see Chapman, *All Fools* 3.1.362–4).

9 new fired (being) freshly kindled (his mistress's eye being the prime source of 'love-kindling fire' (3)).

10 for trial . . . touch as a test of (the 'brand new-fired') felt it necessary ('needs would') to touch.

11 withal therewith (as a result of being touched).

11 the help . . . desired wished for the cooling (or warm medicinal) relief (or cure) of a bath (i.e. the poet was 'seething' (7) with the 'fire of Love' (5)). The Capell–Steevens suggestion that 'bath' here refers to the famous hot springs of Bath may be questionable, but cannot be entirely dismissed. Some of the Marcianus analogues, influenced by the early Latin epigram of Regianus, specifically localise the hot springs at Baiae.

12 hied hastened, hurried.

12 sad distempered guest (1) grieving, (2) heavy, morose (1) sick, diseased, (2) mentally deranged visitor. For the poet's mental derangement, compare 147.5–12.

13 But . . . cure The implication would seem to be that the poet's love passion, unlike Cupid's brand, only succeeded in making cool water hot or hot water boiling, without any alleviation of his infection (compare 154.13–14). Compare *Venus and Adonis*, 94: 'She [i.e. Venus weeping] bathes in water, yet her fire must burn.'

13 for my help to relieve or cure me.

14 my mistress' eyes His mistress's eyes are seen as a curative 'bath', which, when weeping in sympathy, look 'with pretty ruth upon my pain' (132.4). Almost all editors accept Benson's reading 'eyes' for Q 'eye' for the sake of the rhyme with 'lies' in 13, even though 'my mistress' eye' occurs in line 9. The same switch from 'eye' to 'eyes' appears, however, in 46.6, where again its use is governed by a rhyme with 'lies'. It is possible that the compositor's own eye was caught by the 'eye/lie' rhyme in 152.13–14. A play on 'eye' = ay (see 148.8–9 n. and 152.13–14 n.) may, even with the plural 'eyes', have been intended, i.e. the poet's cure is dependent on his mistress's assent(s) to his love suit.

Sonnet 154

See 153 headnote. The use of mid-line breaks, as in the fourth line of both the first and third quatrains (thus running the sense into the second quatrain and the couplet), occurs nowhere else in the Sonnets and is in marked contrast to the normal handling of the

quatrain structure in 153 (for similar breaks in one quatrain only, see 145.3 n.). This rather 'unbound' structure, as well as the sonnet's comparative inferiority, may suggest that 154 represents a trial draft – even perhaps an early piece of prentice work – that Shakespeare revised to serve as an intended tail-piece to the Dark Lady series, adding, as an intentionally associative link with 152.11–14, the 'eye' motif (absent in 154) in lines 9–14. In such a view, of course, 154's inclusion in the collection would have to be considered as accidental.

1 little Love-god i.e. the 'boy' Cupid (153.1, 10), 'the general of hot desire' (7).

2 Laid (Having) laid. Taken literally, as Hutton notes (p. 401), 'Laid' seems to imply that Cupid placed his brand by his side after falling asleep, an awkwardness corrected in 153.1, which compresses lines 1–2 into a single line, one of several such economies in 153.1–8.

3 Whilst . . . keep This line is neatly compacted in 'A maid of Dian's' (153.2). 'nymphs' suggest a connection with the Marcianus tradition (see 153 headnote); in classical mythology, *nymphae* were thought of as guardian spirits who presided over rivers or fountains.

5 votary one bound by religious vows (here, to 'chaste life' (3)).

6 legions . . . hearts thousands of true lovers.

7 general of hot desire supreme commander (i.e. Cupid) of burning (sexual) passion (i.e. it is Cupid's sole prerogative to 'fire' men and women with the flames of love; compare 'heart-inflaming brand' (2) and 'love-kindling fire' (153.3)).

8 disarmed Continues the military metaphor in 'general' (7), with a suggestion perhaps of emasculation; see note on 'brand' (153.1).

9 cool well See 153.4 n.

9 by nearby. Compare 'of that ground' (153.4).

10 Love's Cupid's (as in line 14; see (153.5 n.)).

11 Growing Becoming (compare 'grew' 153.7)).

12 thrall slave, prisoner. Compare 141.12.

13 this by that 'this' = the gnomic statement of line 14; 'by' = by means of; 'that' = (1) the poet's failure to find a 'cure' (13) or 'healthful remedy' (11), a failure made explicit in line 14; (2) his state of thraldom.

13 prove cite as proof, demonstrate.

14 The first half-line, as Kerrigan notes, recapitulates lines 1–12 (through 'diseased'), which offer a fanciful explanation of how a certain medicinal hot spring was created; the second half-line complains that, although such a spring (or 'bath' (11)) may cure other diseases, it fails to alleviate or cure the disease of love ('cools not love'). Compare 'But found no cure' (153.13).

TEXTUAL ANALYSIS

The first edition: Sonnets (1609)

After duly entering 'a Booke called Shakespeares *sonnettes*' in the Stationers' Register at Stationers' Hall on 20 May 1609, Thomas Thorpe published, some time before 19 June of the same year (see Rollins, II, 54), the first and only substantive edition of the Sonnets in a quarto volume (= Q) entitled 'SHAKE-SPEARES / SONNETS. / Neuer before Imprinted.'[1] Q collates as follows: 4° [A]², B–K⁴, L² (unpaged). The two unsigned leaves ([A]1 and [A]2), containing the title page (verso blank) and Thorpe's enigmatic dedication to 'Mʳ. W. H.' (verso blank), were probably printed as part of sheet L (along with sigs. L1 and L2). The Sonnets occupy sigs. B–K1 and are followed by 'A Louers complaint.', sigs. K1ᵛ–L2ᵛ.

Thomas Thorpe, a freeman of the Stationers' Company, was a publisher,[2] not a printer or (except for a short period in 1608) a bookseller. He employed the services of George Eld, a well-established printer, to print the volume, and arranged for its sale with two booksellers, William Aspley and John Wright. The Q title page occurs in two states reflecting this division, one imprint reading 'AT LONDON / By *G. Eld* for *T. T.* and are / to be solde by *Iohn Wright*, dwelling / at Christ Church gate. / 1609.', the other, 'AT LONDON / . . . are / to be solde by *William Aspley*. / 1609.' Since neither state is a cancel, the change was made at some point in the press-run. Of the thirteen copies of Q that have survived (out of perhaps about a thousand printed[3]), four bear the Aspley imprint and seven the Wright imprint (the other two copies lack the title page; see Rollins, II, 1–2). Given the 'millioned accidents' that have threatened the survival of books, at least before the middle of the eighteenth century, such disproportion need not be taken to mean that the total number of copies was not divided more or less equally

---

[1] Variant versions of two sonnets (138 and 144) had escaped into print in *The Passionate Pilgrim* (1599), and manuscript versions of four sonnets (2, 8, 106, 128), though all were almost certainly transcribed after 1620, are now thought probably to preserve (like those in *The Passionate Pilgrim*) earlier, unrevised states of the Q text. See Appendix, p. 286 below, and Kerrigan, pp. 428–9.

[2] Only comparatively recently has Thorpe's reputation as a publisher been rescued from Sir Sidney Lee's biography in the *DNB* (1898), which describes Thorpe's publishing ventures as 'mainly confined, as in his initial venture [1600] of Marlowe's "Lucan," to the predatory work of procuring, no matter how, unpublished and neglected "copy"'. He is now thought of as a 'quality' publisher (Kerrigan, p. 427), who handled a number of works of unusual literary merit, including Jonson's *Sejanus* (1605) and *Volpone* (1607) and Chapman's *Byron* plays (1608). See Leona Rostenberg, 'Thomas Thorpe, publisher of "Shake-speares Sonnets"', *Papers of the Bibliographical Society of America*, 54 (1960), 16–37, and Duncan-Jones, pp. 151–71.

[3] About 1587 the Stationers' Company instituted a regulation that limited to between 1,250 and 1,500 the number of copies that a printer was permitted to run off from a single setting of type. Within these limits, the number printed would depend on the financial return anticipated. Randall McLeod ('A technique of headline analysis, with application to *Shakespeares Sonnets*, 1609', *SB* 32 (1979), 197–210) shows there was some slight resetting in the Q title page apart from the resetting in the imprint of the Wright and Aspley variant states (pp. 197–203); he also demonstrates that Q was probably set from cast-off copy (p. 209).

between Wright and Aspley, since Aspley was a much more prominent figure in the book-trade.

In assessing the authority of a printed text, two different, but related, points require special consideration: (1) the source of the printer's 'copy' (in the case of the Sonnets, manuscript copy) and (2) the degree of technical care with which the 'copy' was treated in the printing-house, the second an important consideration that received almost no attention before about 1930. Indeed, it was not until 1975 that Q was subjected to this kind of scrutiny in a seminal study by MacDonald P. Jackson,[1] a study that may be said to have revolutionised the whole textual approach to the Sonnets and rendered much earlier textual discussion obsolete. Since an adequate understanding of the kind of manuscript copy underlying Q depends on Jackson's analysis, it will be helpful to discuss the printing-house fortunes of Q first.

THE PRINTING OF Q

Jackson's statistically supported analysis shows, without question, that at least two compositors (hereafter referred to as A and B)[2] were responsible for setting up Q and possibly for the imposition[3] of the nine sheets (B–L, taking [A1] and [A2] as imposed along with L1 and L2) of which Q is made up.

On the evidence drawn from preferred compositorial spellings, punctuation, and typographical spacing practices, and using, as a control, the quarto text of *Troilus and Cressida* (1609), also printed by Eld and set by the same two compositors,[4] Jackson assigns twenty pages of the Sonnets to Compositor A (sigs. B1, B2 ^{V}, C2 (?), C3 ^{V}, C4 (?), C4 ^{V}, D1, D4, D4 ^{V} (?), E1, F3, F3 ^{V}, F4 ^{V}, G1, G1 ^{V}, G2, G4 ^{V}, 13, 14, 14 ^{V}) and the other forty-five pages to Compositor B (sigs. D2 ^{V}, E1 ^{V}, F4, G2 ^{V} being questionable). B, therefore, is the principal compositor, A's services being called upon only intermittently.

Compositor A always uses, or at least favours, such spellings as *shalbe, wilbe, ritch, Oh, dost, flowre, powre, hour, tongue, eie, tis*;[5] Compositor B, *shall be, will be, rich, O, doost,* etc., *flower, power, homer, toung,* etc., *eye, 'tis,* etc., *-les* or *-nes* (rather than *-lesse* or *-nesse*). In their use of punctuation, A and B differ most noticeably in their handling of the structural pause, usual in the English sonnet form, at the end of the first, second, and third quatrain. Setting aside the period (used with relatively the same frequency by

---

[1] 'Punctuation and the compositors of Shakespeare's *Sonnets,* 1609', *The Library,* fifth series, 30 (1975), 1–24.

[2] Jackson notes (p. 16) that he is unable to identify 'any third compositorial pattern which would clearly distinguish a hypothetical Compositor C from Compositors A and B'.

[3] i.e. arranging, in quarto format, the eight type-pages in their outer and inner formes, after which the outer and inner formes were locked in the chase for printing off.

[4] See Philip Williams, 'Shakespeare's *Troilus and Cressida*: the relationship of quarto and Folio', *SB* 3 (1950–1), 131–43, and Alice Walker (ed.), *Tro.,* 1957, pp. 122–31. Kenneth Palmer (ed.), *Tro.,* 1982, pp. 304–6, finds a third compositor responsible for setting sheet F (hitherto assigned to A), and W. C. Ferguson ('Compositor identification in *Romeo* Q1 and *Troilus* [Q]', *SB* 42 (1989), 214–18) also introduces a third compositor, who shares portions of work formerly attributed to A, including parts of sheet F.

[5] Jackson (privately) suggested to me that Q's use of '`tis', with or without an apostrophe, might be helpful in distinguishing the work of A and B. He was correct. Both A and B use 'Tis'; A uses only 'tis' (four times, without the apostrophe); B uses 'ti's', 'T'is' (once each), 'tis' (four times). The same distinction between A's and B's usage also occurs in Q *Troilus*.

both A and B), A employs 51 colons and only 6 commas; B, 47 colons and 67 commas. A thus shows a much stronger sense of the quatrain as a closed rhetorical unit than B. A, moreover, unlike B, seems to have felt that the third quatrain, followed as it is by the final, often summary, couplet, required a heavier stop than either the first or second quatrain (A, 10 colons, 1 comma; B, 12 colons, 29 commas). Finally, the evidence drawn from typographical spacing supports the division of work between A and B suggested by the spelling and punctuation criteria: A uses a noticeably higher percentage of spaced internal commas than B; B tends to set sonnet numbers and signature notations further to the right than A.

Jackson offers strong, statistically supported evidence for his page-by-page assignments to Compositor A or Compositor B for all but seven pages: 'the evidence for assigning C2, C4, and D4 $^{\rm V}$ to A and D2 $^{\rm V}$, E1 $^{\rm V}$, F4 and G2 $^{\rm V}$ to B is very slight' (p. 6). I have, therefore, concentrated my own compositor analysis on these seven pages in an effort to find possible additional evidence either for or against Jackson's tentative attributions. My findings support his assignments in all but one case. C2, which breaks a series of B pages, should I think be assigned to B rather than A, for the following reasons: (1) the only evidence cited (p. 18) for A is the spelling 'eies', the lack of commas at the end of a quatrain pause, and three quatrain-break colons. But comparable pointing can be found on B pages (H4, 11; B3, B4 $^{\rm V}$) and there are five 'eye/eyes' to one 'eies', 'eye' being (as Jackson notes, p. 16) 'strongly preferred' by B (65 times) to 'eie' (10 times). (2) The hyphenated form 'them-selues' occurs elsewhere only in B (B3 $^{\rm V}$, G3, H2, and *A Lover's Complaint* K3, a page which I would assign to B); A uses 'themselues' (D4, F4 $^{\rm V}$). The same distinction between B and A appears in Q *Troilus*, except at 3.3.189 where A uses the hyphenated form. (3) The use, perhaps retained from Q-copy, of the stressed *-ed* at the end of the line (not including *-ied* forms), which editors generally emend to the unstressed form (here 'beloued / remoued' (25.13–14)), is much more characteristic of B (12 other examples) than of A (twice); and the same is true of the use of stressed *-ed* forms within the line (here 'tottered' (26.11); compare A's 'totter'd' (2.4)): B (10 other examples); A (twice).[1] (4) The same slightly damaged initial capital L (25.1) occurs again on 12 $^{\rm V}$, a B page, and nowhere else in Q.

The last point (4) depends on the assumption, an assumption not contradicted by any evidence that I know of, that Compositors A and B each worked from different type cases. Jackson makes the same assumption when he notes (p. 17) that the appearance of the same damaged initial O three times in A's work (and never in B's) strengthens the assignment of these pages to A, and that a distinctive drop W, which is used twice elsewhere in B's work, helps to assign G3 to B (as does, I suggest, the hyphenated spelling 'them-selues' (107.7; see point (2) above). Moreover, the assumption that A and B worked from different type cases may explain, I believe, B's apparent carelessness in ending eight sonnets with a comma (one other example occurs on a page (C4) tentatively assigned to A), something that can scarcely have been intentional. If the period box in B's type case had accumulated a sizeable number of missorted commas (the comma box

---

[1] Only in B's pages do we find a final stressed form rhymed with an unstressed form (70.10, 12; 104.10, 12; 124.2, 4).

was adjacent to the period box), B could easily and inadvertently have set a comma when he thought he was setting a period. Such an explanation may also account, perhaps, for some of B's misleadingly light comma punctuation at quatrain-breaks within the sonnet.

Jackson's compositor analysis clears away a lot of dead wood in earlier discussions of the kind and quality of the Q text. It shows, for example, that what has been described as inconsistency in the use of spelling-forms in Q does not necessarily reflect a similar inconsistency in the Q-copy, but arises, in some part at least, from the different spelling preferences of the two compositors (A and B) and warns us that it is very dangerous to draw conclusions based on spelling evidence about the source of the Q-copy (see below). Even more important, however, is what this analysis tells us about the punctuation of the Q-copy. At this time, many authors (and some professional scribes) when transcribing verse (both stanzaic and blank verse) tended to omit end-line punctuation, even when they made sporadic use of internal pointing within the line.[1] As a result of this tendency, it often became the responsibility of the compositor (occasionally perhaps of an in-house editor) to supply punctuation, particularly end-line punctuation, as he was setting the text line by line. Indeed, and rather ironically, this kind of essentially unpunctuated verse copy may, I think, explain why, as in Q and in so many sixteenth- and early-seventeenth-century verse texts, lines which should be unpointed in terms of either rhetorical or logical pointing are end-stopped: that is, influenced by the implications of their manuscript copy, compositors developed a sense that a verse line was a self-contained unit and therefore called for some kind of closure. Since, as Jackson shows, Compositors A and B treated end-line punctuation in recognisably different ways, especially in their handling of the three quatrain-breaks, it is, I suggest, a fair inference that in the Q-copy end-line punctuation was most probably either very light and sporadic or in most cases lacking and that in large part end-line punctuation in Q (the compositors' stints cutting across the work of whatever person or persons had been responsible for preparing the Q-copy) may be attributed to the Q compositors. In effect, then, Jackson's analysis strongly supports the view that the dependability and authority of the punctuation in Q is neither much better nor much worse than that to be found in the average volume of verse published in the first decade of the seventeenth century. Such a conclusion, if accepted (as I believe there is good reason for doing), completely undercuts, as wishful thinking, all the extravagant praise that some critics[2] have lavished on what they consider the delicately sensitive rhetorical pointing of Q, which a few critics have even attributed to Shakespeare himself.

Q is a rather carelessly printed volume, if we compare it, for example, with the first quartos of *Venus and Adonis* (1593) and *The Rape of Lucrece* (1594), both of which had the

---

[1] See, for example, *The Arundel Harington Manuscript of Tudor Poetry*, 2 vols., ed. Ruth Hughey, 1960; the Todd MS. of Henry Constable's *Diana*, ed. Joan Grundy, 1960; the 147–line scene, generally accepted as being in Shakespeare's handwriting, in *Sir Thomas More*, without end-line punctuation except for one raised period where a question mark is called for (line 107); the Westminster MS. of Sonnet 2 (see Appendix, pp. 268–70 below).

[2] See, as extreme examples, George Wyndham's edition of the *Poems*, 1898, pp. 265–9, and Robert Graves and Laura Riding, 'A study in original punctuation and spelling', in Graves's *The Common Asphodel*, 1949, pp. 84–95.

good fortune to be printed by the unusually meticulous Richard Field, probably from Shakespeare's holograph and perhaps proofread by him as the individual sheets were being printed off. An exact estimate of the number of compositorial literal errors and substantive misreadings (not always easy to distinguish) in Q is difficult to determine, partly because editors differ over what should be considered an 'error' (see Rollins, II, 11–17) and partly because some of these 'errors', both literal and substantive, may be due not to the compositor but to Q-copy. The present text, which is generally representative of recent editorial practice, admits 57 emendations, of which 16 may be described as literals (e.g. 'wit' for 'with' (23.14), 'guil'st' for 'gild'st' (28.12), 'stainteh' for 'staineth' (33.14), 'mighst' for 'mightst' (41.9 and 96.11), 'perfects' for 'perfect'st' (51.10), 'preuenst' for 'preuent'st' (100.14),[1] etc.) and 41 as some form of compositorial misreading (e.g. 'or siluer'd ore' for 'all silvered o'er' (12.4) (see note), 'their' for 'thy' (26.12) (and 13 more times),[2] 'losse' for 'cross' (34.12), 'fel' for 'tell' (76.7), 'th'are' for 'y'are' (112.14), 'eye' for 'eyes' (153.14), etc.). Of the total 57, 18 occur in the work of Compositor A and 39 in the work of Compositor B. It is not surprising, then, considering the number of literal and substantive errors or misreadings noted above, that Q shows little evidence of careful proofreading: only six certain stop-press corrections, equally divided between the work of A and B, have been recorded (see Rollins, II, 5), of which only one ('proface' corrected to 'prophane' (89.11)) is of a significantly substantive nature.[3] The weight of such evidence, then, makes it next to impossible to suppose that Shakespeare himself had any in-house connection with the printing of Q.

If we consider their relative work stints (B setting more than twice as much text as A), A and B are about equally guilty of both literal misprints (A with 5; B with 10) and substantive misreadings (A with 12; B with 30). But the fact that 12 of the proposed 15 examples of the 'thy/their' misreading occur in B's work (the three in A's work in 35.8 (2) and 37.7, against one (26.12) in B's work, being challenged as misreadings by some editors), certainly suggests that B was less alive and attentive to the sense of what he was setting than A. Moreover, B's insensitive handling of punctuation (see above) points to a similar conclusion; it requires more frequent attention from an editor than A's work, and B may be responsible for four of the most serious pointing cruxes in Q (16.10, 29.10–12, 51.11, 148.8–9). On the other hand, A may be charged with having committed more seriously substantive misreadings than B: e.g. 'worth' for 'fight' (25.9), 'losse' for 'crosse' (34.12), 'lack' for 'latch' (113.6), word omitted (113.14), 'sight' for 'side' (144.6), two singular forms where the rhyme requires a plural (55.1, 153.14), and, most notoriously, the repetition in 146.2 of the last three words of line 1 as the opening three words of line 2. Even though several of these presumed 'memorial errors' may very well have resulted from A's following of his Q-copy, Jackson's summary comment on Compositors A and B seems justified: 'A was the more intelligent workman, but his

---

[1] The last three, all of which omit a *t* before *s*, may be inherited from Q-copy ('mighst' almost certainly is since it occurs twice, once in B's work and once in A's) and, though such forms occur nowhere else in Shakespeare, they may reflect forms adopted by Shakespeare for the sake of euphony. See 51.10 n. for non-Shakespearean uses of 'perfects' for 'perfect'st'.

[2] Here given as thirteen, instead of fourteen, because the present text accepts one 'their' in 35.8.

[3] If the formes underwent any earlier pre-press correction (i.e. by pulls taken before the forme was bedded in the press) it must have been of the most cursory kind. See D. F. McKenzie, 'Printers of the mind: some notes on bibliographical theories and printing-house practices', *SB* 22 (1969), 42–9.

susceptibility to memorial substitution may have caused more permanent damage to the text than B's dullness' (p. 10).

THE QUARTO-COPY

One must begin with a caveat. Much of the 'evidence' for the source of the Q-copy discussed below is speculative, ambiguous, and sometimes even conflicting. Some earlier editors and critics, as I noted above, have argued that Q was printed from a carefully prepared and sensitively punctuated manuscript, either holograph or at least overseen by Shakespeare. Recent editors, however, while admitting that the underlying manuscript was 'good' and 'authoritative', now believe, partly as a result of Jackson's compositor analysis, that Q was set up wholly, or for the most part, from some kind of non-authorial transcript, probably the work of more than one scribe, a transcript in which, I have suggested, the Q compositors were probably responsible for most, if not all, of the end-line punctuation (see above). Such a transcript may have been based directly on holograph copy, either in whole or in part; or it may have been a scribal copy of an earlier transcript, at one or more removes from Shakespeare's autograph. The fact that no distinctive Shakespearean spellings or compositorial misreadings associated with Shakespeare's handwriting occur in Q (as they sometimes do in play-texts set from holograph copy) is of little help in determining the direct or indirect origin of the postulated transcript, since non-authorial copy was subject to the spelling preferences of at least two intermediary agents – scribe and compositor.

One of the principal arguments against the use of holograph copy lies in the fifteen compositorial misreadings of 'thy' as 'their' (26.12, 27.10, 35.8 (twice), 37.7, 43.11, 45.12, 46.3, 8, 13, 14, 69.5, 70.6, 128.11, 14), all, except those in 26.12 (Sisson only), 35.8 and 37.7, universally accepted as misreadings since Capell and Malone first emended them. Malone suggested that this confusion arose from misreading a contracted form of 'thy' (i.e. 'y^i' or 'y^{ie}') for a contracted form of 'their' (i.e. 'y^r' or 'y^{er}'), in both of which 'y' represents a debased form of the Old English 'Þ' (= 'th'), as, for example, in 'y^e' (= 'the'), a commonly used contraction that survived in printed works well into the seventeenth century and in written documents into the eighteenth.[1] This particular misreading occurs nowhere else in the standard Shakespeare canon, most significantly in none of the plays or poems that are believed to have been set from Shakespeare's autograph (e.g. *Romeo and Juliet* Q2, *Hamlet* Q2, *Venus and Adonis* Q1); nor does the 'y^i' or 'y^{ie}' contraction appear in the 147–line scene in *Sir Thomas More* generally considered to be in Shakespeare's hand.[2] Thus, although the absence of this particular compositorial misreading elsewhere in Shakespeare does not prove that he

---

[1] I know of no examples of 'y^i' (or 'y^{ie}') (and 'y^r' was comparatively rare) in printed works of the period, but both contractions were still being used in written documents. See P. J. Seng's edition (1978) of British Library MS. Cotton Vespasian A-25 (c. 1575), in which both contractions occur, and Edward Doughtie's edition (1985) of *Liber Lilliati* (Bodleian Library MS. Rawlinson Poetry 148), dating from about 1585, where (p. 54), in a single six-line stanza, 'y^i', 'y^{ie}' and 'thy' are used indiscriminately.

[2] Two recent publications lend support to the view that this scene is in Shakespeare's handwriting: *Shakespeare and 'Sir Thomas More': Essays on the Play and Its Shakespearian Interest*, ed. T. H. Howard-Hill, 1989, p. 8, and G. E. Dawson, 'Shakespeare's handwriting', *S.Sur.* 42 (1989), 119–28. Even the common contraction 'y^e' (= the) does not appear in this scene, though 'the' is used 45 times.

never used this contraction, it tells strongly against holograph printer's copy.[1] There are, however, several examples (not hitherto noticed, I believe) of this very rare misreading in *Edward III* (published 1596, probably written between 1590 and 1592), two of 'their' for 'thy' (2.1.91, 404) and one of 'their' for 'your' (2.1.202) in the so-called 'Countess scenes' (2.1–2) generally accepted as by Shakespeare, and one example of 'their' for 'thy' in 3.1.105, a scene of more questionable Shakespearean authorship.[2] Perhaps the Shakespearean link suggested is nothing more than coincidence, but if not, depending on the source of the printer's copy for *Edward III*, it may have some bearing on the nature of the Sonnets copy: (1) if the printer's copy for *Edward III* was authorial, the link suggests that the Sonnets copy may also have been partly authorial; (2) if the printer's copy for *Edward III* was scribal, the link suggests the possibility that the same scribe, earlier associated with Shakespeare's work, may have been employed by him, when, as is now thought to be likely, he was revising and ordering the Sonnets and adding *A Lover's Complaint* some time after 1603/ 4,[3] to transcribe substantial portions (if not all) of the Sonnets copy directly from holograph copy. Lapides (pp. 60–3) argues that *Edward III* was set from authorial copy, but the kinds of evidence adduced (irregularity of speech headings, types of, or omission of, stage directions, and a general lack of the kind of consistency until quite recently felt to be properly characteristic of a scribal transcript) are inconclusive, and very few Shakespearean spellings survived the compositor(s) in the 'Countess scenes' or elsewhere in the play. Thus, although the suggested *Edward III* link raises once again the possibility of holograph Sonnet copy, the weight of other evidence (the lack of such misreadings elsewhere in the Shakespeare canon and the absence of any distinctive Shakespearean spelling-forms in Q) still favours, I believe, the use of basically scribal copy for Q.

If, then, we accept the probability that Q-copy was, at least for the most part, a scribal transcript, is there any evidence to suggest that more than one scribe was responsible? Again the 'their/thy' misreadings come into play. It has been noticed that thirteen (out of a possible fifteen) of these misreadings occur in Sonnets 26–70 (sigs. C1–E3 ^{v}) and then none until two in 128, thus leaving a group of some 56 sonnets (sigs. E4 ^{v}–H3) in which this particular error does not appear. Considering Compositor B's penchant for misreading 'y^{i}' or 'y^{ie}' as 'their' (B set eighteen of the twenty-five pages containing sonnets 71–128), it seems unlikely that this contraction was used in the manuscript copy behind this group of sonnets and suggests that a second hand, scribal or possibly authorial, is here involved. A somewhat different scribal division of Q-copy is suggested, as Jackson points out (p. 13), by the use of parentheses in Q, a use that cuts across compositorial stints: all but five out of a total of 43 occur in

[1] Excluding the Sonnets, there are some 4,138 other uses of 'thy' in the accepted canon (many of them in texts printed from holograph copy). If, indeed, Shakespeare himself used the 'y^{i}' or 'y^{ie}' contraction, it is surely highly unlikely, among so many possibilities, that some examples of the 'their' for 'thy' misreading would not have occurred elsewhere in his works.

[2] My references are to C. F. Tucker Brooke's edition in *The Shakespeare Apocrypha*, 1908. For the most recent views on the authorship of *Edward III*, see the edition by Fred Lapides (1980), and Eliot Slater, *The Problem of 'The Reign of King Edward the Third': A Statistical Approach*, 1988. Lapides and Slater (like Capell in his 1760 edition) would assign the whole play to Shakespeare. For a more cautious assessment, see Gary Taylor in *William Shakespeare: A Textual Companion* (1987), pp. 136–7.

[3] See Duncan-Jones, pp. 165–71, and Kerrigan, p. 429.

sonnets 26–98 (sigs. C2–G1), two of the other five occurring in 126 which is close to 128 with its two 'their/thy' errors.[1] But, as he wisely adds, 'Upon such matters we can only speculate.'

THE USE OF ITALICS IN Q

Aside from italicised proper nouns and proper adjectives (both commonly italicised in printed and manuscript works at this time), Q contains fourteen italicised words (all nouns) scattered, apparently at random, in sonnets 1–126. In the past, this occasional use of italics has usually been dismissed as nothing more than a compositorial whim. Now, however, since Jackson has established that two compositors are responsible for the setting of Q, the fact that these fourteen words are divided between the work of Compositors A and B makes such an assumption highly unlikely. Five appear in A's stints: 'Rose' (1.2), 'Statues' (55.5), 'Intrim' (56.9), 'Satire' (100.11), 'Alcumie' (114.4); nine, in B's: 'Audit' (4.12), 'Hews' (20.7), 'Alien' (78.3), 'Autumne' (104.5), 'Abisme' (112.9), 'Hereticke' (124.9), 'Informer' (125.13), 'Audite' (126.11), 'Quietus' (126.12). The division of these italicised words between A and B supports the view that they were in some way distinguished in the Q-copy and that both compositors were, in all these instances, simply following copy. A single whimsical compositor is a possibility; the idea that there were two like-minded compositors (all but four or five of the words italicised are of a 'learned' nature, etymologically Greek or Latin, and rarely used by Shakespeare) defies the laws of probability. Moreover, I suggest, there is some evidence that such use of occasional italics may be attributed to Shakespeare himself. Words of a similar nature are italicised in Eld's quarto (1609) of Troilus and Cressida, now thought to be set from Shakespeare's 'foul papers', in portions of the text set by the same two compositors (e.g. A: 'indexes', 'modicums', 'pia mater', 'Compters', 'Genius'; B: 'maxim', 'chaos', 'Moral Philosophie', 'Amen', 'chipochia'), and three of the italicised words in Q are also italicised in three of Shakespeare's plays: 'Satire' in A Midsummer Night's Dream 5.1.54 (the quarto (1600) text printed from Shakespeare's 'foul papers'); 'intrim' in Twelfth Night 5.1.95 (the Folio text printed from authorial 'fair copy' or scribal transcript); and 'Autumne' in Troilus and Cressida 1.2.138 (quarto text; see above). The example from Troilus and Cressida is particularly significant. 'Autumne' was italicised by A in Troilus and by B in Q. That two compositors should independently choose to italicise such a relatively common (and 'unlearned') word unless it was italicised in their copy is at best extremely improbable. Does the strong likelihood that Shakespeare is responsible for this sporadic use of italics bear on the authorial or scribal provenience of the Q-copy? Unfortunately, as usual, the evidence is ambiguous: a scribe, in this respect, would be as likely to follow copy as a compositor.

The second edition: Poems (1640)

A second edition of the Sonnets was included in a small octavo volume entitled 'POEMS: / WRITTEN / BY / Wil. Shake-speare. / Gent.' It was published by John Benson in 1640 and printed by the reputable and experienced Thomas Cotes,

---

[1] No parentheses are used in the 147-line scene in Sir Thomas More (see p. 261 above, n. 1).

who, in 1632, had printed the Second Folio of Shakespeare's plays.[1] 'Reputable', however, is not a word that can be applied to John Benson. He quite deliberately set out to deceive his readers. The title 'POEMS' is misleading, since neither *Venus and Adonis* nor *Lucrece* was included. Copyright on both poems had been carefully maintained by official transfers in the Stationers' Register, and new editions of each had appeared in the 1620s and 1630s, whereas copyright had been allowed to lapse on the Sonnets, and *The Passionate Pilgrim* had never been entered on the Stationers' Register; thus the right to reprint either one belonged legally to the Company of Stationers. And, in his address 'To the Reader', Benson appears to claim, in discreetly veiled terms, that the Sonnets and other poems included in his 'collection' were newly recovered and hitherto unpublished: 'I here presume (under favour) to present to your view, some excellent and sweetely composed Poems of Master *William Shakespeare*, Which in themselves appeare of the same purity, the Authour himselfe then living avouched [in acknowledging *Venus* and *Lucrece* as his]; they had not the fortune by reason of their Infancie in his death [i.e. they were written shortly before he died], to have the due accomodation of proportionable glory, with the rest of his everliving Workes . . .' In fact, the volume, aside from a few poems at the end admittedly by other hands (see below), is a reprint, substantially rearranged, of Thomas Thorpe's 1609 *Sonnets* (omitting the dedication to 'M^r. W. H.' and eight sonnets) and most of William Jaggard's 1612 edition of *The Passionate Pilgrim* (including the nine unattributed poems lifted from Thomas Heywood's *Troia Britanica* (1609)). To these Benson added 'The Phoenix and Turtle' from Robert Chester's *Love's Martyr* (1601), where it is attributed to Shakespeare, and concluded the volume with a small group of poems 'By other Gentlemen' (the last being the only part of this venture entered in the Stationers' Register, 4 November 1639). Benson's 1640 text, therefore, at least so far as Shakespeare's work is concerned, is entirely derivative and has no independent manuscript authority, and, though it corrected a number of Q's typographical errors, it also contributed more than twice as many new errors of its own.

Further to cover his tracks, Benson reordered the Sonnets (omitting eight and inserting poems from *The Passionate Pilgrim* into the mix), in the process manufacturing seventy-two 'poems' made up of either single sonnets or groups of two to five sonnets run tightly together, each with a not always happily contrived title. He begins the collection with a 'poem' combining Sonnets 67–9 (entitled '*The glory of beautie*') and follows it with a 'poem' made up of Sonnets 60 and 63–6 (entitled '*Injurious Time*'). This rearranging and topical grouping and labelling shows no discernible pattern and was clearly intended to give old ware a new look.

Benson also did a little gender meddling. Near the end of his reordering and grouping of Sonnets 1–125 (he omits 126), Benson seems to have become aware of their possible homoerotic implications, implications he had hitherto ignored, and made a belated attempt to suggest that some at least were addressed to a woman by substituting a

---

[1] See Rollins, II, 18–28, for a detailed treatment of Benson's 1640 edition, and J. W. Bennett, 'Benson's alleged piracy of *Shakespeares Sonnets* and some of Jonson's works', *SB* 21 (1968), 235–48 (a defence of Benson against literal piracy).

few feminine for masculine nouns and pronouns (see collation to 101.11, 14; 104.1; 108.5) and inventing three titles (for 113–15, 122, 125) that indicate a woman as the recipient. Considering the second-hand and misleading nature of Benson's edition, it is, indeed, one of the great ironies of literary history that it became the *textus receptus* for eight eighteenth-century editions (from Charles Gildon's in 1710 to Thomas Evans's in 1775), until, in 1780, Malone finally restored the Q text and order. Some years earlier (c. 1766), however, Edward Capell, in a copy of Lintott's 1711 reprint of Q, had prepared an edition, which he never published, but which, it has been suggested, Malone made use of, though without acknowledgement.

The present edition

Although basically a modern-spelling edition, the present text retains a few characteristic and recognised variant Elizabethan spellings that indicate a distinctive difference in pronunciation from other contemporary forms of the same word (e.g. 'bankrout'/'bankrupt', 'vild'/'vile', 'burthen'/'burden'), the second forms being those that have survived in modern English usage.

The regular Elizabethan orthographic distinction in verse between the past tense in -'d (non-syllabic) and -ed (syllabic) has been levelled to -ed, the stressed form being indicated by a grave accent (e.g. 'usèd', 'well-tunèd'). Metrically ambiguous cases in which Q uses syllabic -ed – usually reduced to unstressed -ed in conformity with modern editorial practice – are here, for the first time, recorded in the collations. The collations also record, again for the first time, the editorial source of personified forms (e.g. 'Nature', 'Time', 'Death') not already personified in Q.

Even though the Q punctuation (especially end-line punctuation) is now considered to be for the most part the work of Compositors A and B (see p. 261 above), it nevertheless represents, except when it is patently in error, a contemporary reader's (particularly A's) feeling for the sense, syntax, and rhetorical interrelation of the verse lines, a contemporaneous immediacy denied to later readers or editors. I have, therefore, made some attempt to preserve, whenever it seemed feasible, the often fluid rhetorical movement of the Q punctuation.

APPENDIX: MANUSCRIPT COPIES OF THE SONNETS

Comparatively few copies of the Sonnets found their way into seventeenth-century manuscript verse miscellanies or 'commonplace books'. Peter Beal (*Index of English Literary Manuscripts, 1450–1625*, 1980, Part ii, 452–4) records copies of twelve sonnets (Sonnets 1, 2 (13 copies), 8, 32, 33, 68, 71., 106 (2 copies), 107, 116, 128, 138), all of them transcribed almost certainly after 1620. In the case of most of these sonnets the manuscript copies are derived from printed texts (either the 1609 Q or the 1640 *Poems*) and their occasional variants are, therefore, without authority and may be dismissed as copyists' errors or intentional adaptation, but the manuscript texts of four sonnets (2, 8, 106, and 128) appear to derive from a manuscript source and thus may preserve authorial variants reflecting an earlier (or later) state of Shakespeare's text than that found in Q (see particularly the headnote and collation for Sonnet 2 below). A collation has been included for a manuscript text of Sonnet 116, not because it preserves possible authorial variants, but because it illustrates what could happen to a poem when it was adapted for a musical setting. For the arguably earlier states of Sonnets 138 and 144, as published in *The Passionate Pilgrim* (1599), see the headnotes and collations to those sonnets.

Sonnet 2

Thirteen manuscript texts of Sonnet 2 are listed by Beal, all almost certainly transcribed after 1620. Of these thirteen MSS., eleven bear witness to a text of 2 that is believed to represent an earlier state of Shakespeare's text, of which the Q text is generally considered to be a later revision (see Gary Taylor, pp. 210–46). Using Taylor's sigla, the eleven MSS. are as follows: BL (= British Library) Add. MS. 10309, fol. 143 (= B1); BL Add. MS. 21433, fol. 114^V (= B2); BL Add. MS. 25303, fol. 119^V (= B3); BL Add. MS. 30982, fol. 18 (= B4); BL Sloane MS. 1792, fol. 45 (= B5); Folger (Shakespeare Library) MS. V.a.170, pp. 163–4 (= F2); Folger MS. V.a.345, p. 145 (= F3); University of Nottingham, Portland MS. Pw V 37, p. 69 (= N); Rosenbach Museum and Library, MS. 1083/17, fols. 132^V–133 (= R); Westminster Abbey, MS. 41, fol. 49 (= W); Yale University, Osborn Collection, b. 205, fol. 54^V (= Y). Taylor considers W, the Westminster Abbey MS., as offering the best text. In the following collation (the lemma taken from Q and the MS. variants from Taylor's collation) w+ indicates that all the MSS. agree with W unless otherwise noted.

Title: 2]   Q; Spes Altera B1, B2, B3; Spes Altera A song F3; To one y^t would dye a Mayd
    B4, B5, F2, W, Y; A lover to his Mistres N; The Benefitt of Mariage R
1 fortie]   Q, w+ (*except* threscore B1)
1 Winters]   Q, w+ (*except* yeares R)

2 digge deep trenches]   Q; trench deepe furrowes w+ (*except* drench *for* trench R)

2 thy beauties field]   Q; y^t louely feild w+ (*except* cheeke *for* feild B2, B3)

3 youthes]   Q, w+ (*except* youth B5, F3)

3 proud]   Q; faire w+ (*except* fairer R)

3 liuery]   Q, w+ (*except for* feild R; *Taylor misreads* w *as* Liu'rie)

3 gaz'd on]   Q; accounted w+ (*except* accompted B3 *and* esteemed N)

4 Wil be a totter'd weed of smal]   Q; Shall bee like rotten weeds of no w+ (*except* cloaths *for* weeds F2)

5 being askt]   Q, w+ (*except* if we Ask B2, B3; askt R)

5 thy]   Q, w+ (*except* this B3)

5 lies]   Q, w+ (*the* s *is cropped in* w)

6 Where]   Q, w+ (*except* Where's B1, B2, B3, F3, N, R)

6 treasure of thy lusty]   Q; lustre of thy youthfull w+

7 thine owne deepe sunken]   Q; these hollow suncken w+ (*except* those *for* these Y *and* hollow-sunken B1)

8 all-eating shame, and thriftlesse]   Q; all-eaten truth, & worthlesse w+ (*except* beaten *for* eaten F2)

8 praise]   Q, w+ (*the* e *is cropped in* w; *except* prayes B4; pleasure B5)

9 How much more praise deseru'd]   Q; O how much better were w+ (*except* O *and* much *omitted* B5; far *for* much Y)

9 beauties]   Q, w+ (*except* bewtious Y)

10 answere this faire]   Q; say this pretty w+ (*except* little *for* pretty B2, B3)

11 Shall sum my count]   Q; Saues my account w+ (*except* Saud Y; mine N; accompt B3)

11 make my old]   Q; makes my old w+ (*except* makes me old B4; makes no old F2; yeilds mee an N; makes the old R; makes no old Y)

12 Proouing]   Q; Making w+

13 new made]   Q; new borne w+ (*except* made younge B2, B3)

14 feel'st]   Q, w+ (*except* felst B2, B3, B4)

As Taylor points out, these eleven MSS. fall into two groups: (1) a group (w, B4, B5, F2, Y, the last two MSS. derived from a postulated [x]) descended from w, itself at one or more removes from Shakespeare's autograph; and (2) a group (B1, B2, B3 (copied from B2), F3, N, R) descended from a postulated [z], also at one or more removes from Shakespeare's autograph. One of the other two extant MSS. (St John's College, Cambridge, MS. S. 23 (James 416), fol. 38^{r-v}, attributed to 'W. Shakspere') is excluded by Taylor in his collation because it reproduces the text of Q in all but four readings, three of which are either indifferent or wrong. Taylor notes, however, that the fourth variant ('say that this faire' (line 10)) combines Q ('answere this fair') with w+ ('say this pretty'). This combination suggests that this MS. may not be a mere transcript from Q but derives from some independent source that reflects perhaps a late stage in Shakespeare's revision.

Taylor (pp. 228–44) discusses the relative dating on linguistic evidence of the w and Q versions and the apparent difference in the portrait of the 'youth' that seems to emerge as a result of the Q revision. See the note on 2.9–14.

Sonnet 8

Variant readings in British Library Add. MS. 15226, fol. 4ᵛ (= B). MS. attributes the sonnet to 'W: Shakespeare.'; arranged in three stanzas of four, four, and six lines respectively, and numbered '1', '2', '3'.

Title: 8] Q; In laudem Musicae et opprobrium Contemptorii eiusdem. B
1 hear'st] Q; hearest B
2 Sweets] Q; Sweete B
3 lou'st] Q; louest B
3, 4 receaust . . . receau'st] Q; receauest . . . receauest B
6 thine] Q; thy B
8 the parts that] Q; a parte, Wᶜʰ. B
10 in] Q; on B
11 sier, and child,] Q; Childe, & Syer, B
12 Who] Q; wᶜʰ. B
12 one pleasing note do] Q; this single note dothe B
14 wilt] Q; shalt B

Sonnet 106

Variant readings in Rosenbach Museum and Library MS. 1083/16, p. 256 (= R), and Pierpont Morgan Library MA 1057 (Holgate Commonplace Book), p. 96 (= H).

Title: 106] Q; On his Mʳⁱˢ Beauty: R; On his Mistris Beauty H
1 Chronicle of wasted time] Q; Annales of all-wasting time R; Annalls of all wastinge Time H
2 discriptions] Q, R; discription H
3 rime] Q, R; mine (*underlined and* rime *written following it in another hand*) H
6 Of hand, of foot] Q; Of face, of hand R; of face of hand H (*Kerrigan, p. 451, mistakenly, reads* hands)
6 of eye, of brow] Q; or eye or brow R; of eye, or brow H
8 Euen] Q, R; Eu'n H
9 are] Q; were R, H
10 this our time] Q; these our dayes R; those our dayes H
11 look'd] Q; say R; saw H
11 deuining] Q, H; deceiuing R
12 still] Q; skill R, H
12 your] Q; thy R, H
13 we] Q, H; me R

13 present]   Q, H; pleasant R
14 lack toungs]   Q; noe tongue R; no tonges H

Sonnet 116

Variant readings in Drexel MS. 4257, No. 33 (New York Public Library, Music Division) (= D). This is the only sonnet for which we possess a near-contemporary musical setting (see illustration , p. 27 above); it was set by Henry Lawes, who composed the music for, and acted in, Milton's *Comus*. See Willa McClung Evans, 'Lawes' version of Shakespeare's sonnet CXVI', *PMLA* 51 (1936), 120–2 (contains a facsimile of words and music). The sonnet text is divided into three six-line stanzas, the last two numbered '2' and '3', each ending with a couplet (the first two not in Q).

1 Let me not . . . true]   Q; Selfe blinding error seazeth all those D
2 Admit impediments, . . . not]   Q; who with falce-Appellations call that D
4 Or bends . . . remoue.]   Q; or with the mouer hath a power to moue / not much
        vnlike ye hereticks p^{re}tence / that scites trew scripture but p^{re}vents the sence: D
5 it]   Q; Loue D
6 and]   Q; but D
8 higth be taken.]   Q; height be taken / Noe mowntebanke with eie-deludeing
        flashes / But flameing Martyr in his holly ashes D
10 bending sickles compasse come]   Q; hynding Circle compas rownd D
12 beares]   Q; holds D
13 vpon me proued]   Q; not truth approu'd D
14 I neuer . . . loued.]   Q; Cupids noe god nor Man nere lou'd D

Sonnet 128

Variant readings in Bodleian MS. Rawl. poet. 152, fol. 34 (= R).

1 my musike]   Q; deere, deer'st R (*Kerrigan reads* deeist)
1 playst]   Q; plaiest R
2 motion]   Q; mocions R
3 swayst]   Q; swaies R
4 confounds]   Q; consoundes R
5 Do]   Q; o how R
5 Iackes]   Q; kies R
5 leape]   Q; leapes R
7 reape]   Q; reped R
8 woods]   Q; wood R
9 tikled they]   Q; touched the faine R
11 Ore]   Q; ouer R
11 their]   Q (*misreading for* thy); youre R
13 sausie Iackes]   Q; then those keyes R
14 their fingers]   Q (their *misreading for* thy); youre fingers R
14 thy lips]   Q; youre lipes R

READING LIST

This list includes some of the works referred to in the Introduction or Commentary and may serve as a guide to anyone wishing to undertake further study of the Sonnets.

Akrigg, G. P. V. *Shakespeare and the Earl of Southampton*, 1968

Baldwin, T. W. *On the Literary Genetics of Shakspere's Poems*, 1950

Bate, Jonathan. 'Ovid and the Sonnets; or, did Shakespeare feel the anxiety of influence?', *S.Sur.* 42 (1989), 65–76

Booth, Stephen. *An Essay on Shakespeare's Sonnets*, 1969

Campbell, S. C. *Only Begotten Sonnets*, 1978

Crosman, Robert. 'Making love out of nothing at all: the issue of Story in Shakespeare's Procreation Sonnets', *SQ* 41 (1990), 470–88

Cruttwell, Patrick. *The Shakespearean Moment and Its Place in the Poetry of the Seventeenth Century*, 1955

Donow, H. S. *A Concordance to the Sonnet Sequences of Daniel, Drayton, Shakespeare, Sidney, and Spenser*, 1969
  The Sonnet in England and America: A Bibliography of Criticism, 1982 (contains an index to criticism on each of Shakespeare's Sonnets)

Dubrow, Heather. *Captive Victors: Shakespeare's Narrative Poems and Sonnets*, 1987
  Echoes of Desire: Petrarchism and Its Counterdiscourse, 1995

Duncan-Jones, Katherine. 'Was the 1609 *Shake-speares Sonnets* really unauthorized?', *RES*, ns, 34 (1983), 151–71

Ferry, Anne. *All in War with Time: Love Poetry of Shakespeare, Donne, Jonson, Marvell*, 1975
  The 'Inward' Language: Sonnets of Wyatt, Sidney, Shakespeare, Donne, 1983

Fineman, J. *Shakespeare's Perjured Eye: The Invention of Poetic Subjectivity in the Sonnets*, 1987

Fowler, Alastair. *Triumphal Forms: Structural Patterns in Elizabethan Poetry*, 1970

Garber, Marjorie. *Vice Versa: Bisexuality and the Eroticism of Everyday Life*, 1995 (see pp. 505–20)

Giroux, Robert. *The Book Known as Q*, 1982

Grazia, Margreta de. 'The scandal of Shakespeare's Sonnets', *S.Sur.* 46 (1993), 35–49

Hammond, Gerald. *The Reader and Shakespeare's Young Man Sonnets*, 1981

Hernstein, Barbara (ed.). *Discussions of Shakespeare's Sonnets*, 1964

Hotson, Leslie. *Mr W. H.*, 1964

Hubler, Edward. *The Sense of Shakespeare's Sonnets*, 1952

Hubler, Edward, Northrop Frye, L. A. Fiedler, Stephen Spender, and R. P. Blackmur. *The Riddle of Shakespeare's Sonnets*, 1962

Jackson, MacD. P. 'Punctuation and the compositors of Shakespeare's *Sonnets*, 1609', *The Library*, fifth ser., 30 (1975), 1–24

Jakobson, Roman, and Lawrence Jones. *Shakespeare's Verbal Art in 'Th'Expense of Spirit'*, 1970

John, L. C. *The Elizabethan Sonnet Sequences: Studies in Conventional Conceits*, 1938 (contains a useful 'Table of Conceits' that lists wherever such conventional conceits occur in all the English sonnet sequences)

Jones, Peter (ed.). *Shakespeare: The Sonnets. A Casebook*, 1977

Klause, John. 'Shakespeare's *Sonnets*: age in love and the goring of thoughts', *SP* 80 (1983), 300–24

Knight, G. W. *The Mutual Flame: On Shakespeare's Sonnets and 'The Phoenix and the Turtle'*, 1955

Krieger, Murray. *A Window to Criticism: Shakespeare's Sonnets and Modern Poetics*, 1964

Landry, Hilton. *Interpretations in Shakespeare's Sonnets*, 1963 (ed.). *New Essays on Shakespeare's Sonnets*, 1976

Leishman, J. B. *Themes and Variations in Shakespeare's Sonnets*, 1961

Lever, J. W. *The Elizabethan Love Sonnet*, 1956

Martin, Philip. *Shakespeare's Sonnets: Self, Love, and Art*, 1972

Melchiori, Giorgio. *Shakespeare's Dramatic Meditations: An Experiment in Criticism*, 1976

Pequigney, Joseph. *Such Is My Love: A Study of Shakespeare's Sonnets*, 1985

Ramsey, Paul. *The Fickle Glass: A Study of Shakespeare's Sonnets*, 1979

Roche, Thomas P. *Petrarch and the English Sonnet Sequences*, 1986

Schaar, Claes. *An Elizabethan Sonnet Problem: Shakespeare's 'Sonnets', Daniel's 'Dalia', and Their Literacy Background*, 1960

Schiffer, James (ed.). *Shakespeare's Sonnets: Critical Essays*, 1999

Shakespeare Survey 15, 1962 (devoted largely to Shakespeare's songs, sonnets, and other poems)

Shakespeare's Poems (A Facsimile of the Earliest Editions), ed. J. M. Osborn, L. L. Martz, and E. M. Waith, 1964

Smith, Hallett. *Elizabethan Poetry*, 1952

Stirling, Brents. *The Shakespeare Sonnet Order*, 1968

Vendler, Helen. 'Reading, stage by stage: Shakespeare's Sonnets', in *Shakespeare Reread*, ed. Russ McDonald, 1994, pp. 23–41
  The Art of Shakespeare's Sonnets, 1997

Wait, R. J. C. *The Background to Shakespeare's 'Sonnets'*, 1972

Warren, Roger. 'Why does it end well? Helena, Bertram, and the Sonnets', *S.Sur.* 22 (1969), 79–92

Weiser, David K. *Mind in Character: Shakespeare's Speaker in the Sonnets*, 1987

Wilson, J. Dover. *Shakespeare's Sonnets: An Introduction for Historians and Others*, 1963

Wilson, Katherine M. *Shakespeare's Sugared Sonnets*, 1974

Winny, James. *The Master-Mistress: A Study of Shakespeare's Sonnets*, 1968

Wright, Eugene Patrick. *The Structure of Shakespeare's Sonnets*, 1993

INDEX OF FIRST LINES